PAGES PACKED WITH ESSENTIAL INFORMATION

"Value-packed, unbeatable, accurate, and comprehensive."

—The Los Angeles Times

"The guides are aimed not only at young budget travelers but at the independent traveler; a sort of streetwise cookbook for traveling alone."

—The New York Times

"Unbeatable; good sight-seeing advice; up-to-date info on restaurants, hotels, and inns; a commitment to money-saving travel; and a wry style that brightens nearly every page."

—The Washington Post

THE BEST TRAVEL BARGAINS IN YOUR BUDGET

"All the dirt, dirt cheap."

—People

"Let's Go follows the creed that you don't have to toss your life's savings to the wind to travel—unless you want to."

—The Salt Lake Tribune

REAL ADVICE FOR REAL EXPERIENCES

"The writers seem to have experienced every rooster-packed bus and lunar-surfaced mattress about which they write."

—The New York Times

"[Let's Go's] devoted updaters really walk the walk (and thumb the ride, and trek the trail). Learn how to fish, haggle, find work—anywhere."

—Food & Wine

"A world-wise traveling companion—always ready with friendly advice and helpful hints, all sprinkled with a bit of wit."

—The Philadelphia Inquirer

A GUIDE WITH A SPIRIT AND A SOCIAL CONSCIENCE

"Lighthearted and sophisticated, informative and fun to read. [Let's Go] helps the novice traveler navigate like a knowledgeable old hand."

—Atlanta Journal-Constitution

"The serious mission at the book's core reveals itself in exhortations to respect the culture and the environment—and, if possible, to visit as a volunteer, a student, or a teacher rather than a tourist."

—San Francisco Chronicle

LET'S GO PUBLICATIONS

TRAVEL GUIDES

Australia
Austria & Switzerland
Brazil
Britain
California
Central America
Chile
China
Costa Rica
Costa Rica, Nicaragua & Panama
Eastern Europe
Ecuador
Egypt
Europe
France
Germany
Greece
Guatemala & Belize
Hawaii
India & Nepal
Ireland
Israel
Italy
Japan
Mexico
New Zealand
Peru
Puerto Rico
Southeast Asia
Spain & Portugal with Morocco
Thailand
USA
Vietnam
Western Europe
Yucatan Peninsula

ROADTRIP GUIDE

Roadtripping USA

ADVENTURE GUIDES

Alaska
Pacific Northwest
Southwest USA

CITY GUIDES

Amsterdam
Barcelona
Berlin, Prague & Budapest
Boston
Buenos Aires
Florence
London
London, Oxford, Cambridge & Edinburgh
New York City
Paris
Rome
San Francisco
Washington, DC

POCKET CITY GUIDES

Amsterdam
Berlin
Boston
Chicago
London
New York City
Paris
San Francisco
Venice
Washington, DC

LET'S GO

ISRAEL

RESEARCHERS
**TERESA COTSIRILOS RUTH PIMENTEL
MARK VAN MIDDLESWORTH**

IYA MEGRE MANAGING EDITOR
DAVID ANDERSSON RESEARCH MANAGER

EDITORS
**COURTNEY A. FISKE   SARA PLANA
RUSSELL FORD RENNIE   CHARLIE E. RIGGS
OLGA I. ZHULINA**

HOW TO USE THIS BOOK

COVERAGE LAYOUT. *Let's Go Israel* begins in **Jerusalem**, the heart of Israel and its most politically and religiously charged city. We then head over to **Tel Aviv**, Jerusalem's hip and modern coastal counterpart. From there, coverage extends up the gorgeous **Northern Mediterranean Coast,** after which it heads inland to history-rich **Galilee.** The coverage of northern Israel ends with the **Golan Heights**, home to many of Israel's most beautiful nature reserves. The next chapter, the **West Bank**, makes up the entirety of the Palestinian Territories. Due to recent political unrest, the **Gaza Strip** has not been included in the guide. We then head down to the southern half of Israel, beginning at the **Dead Sea**, where you can float your skin diseases away. We then head to the expansive and arid **Negev**, before finishing up at the southernmost point of Israel: the resort city of **Eilat**. The final chapter covers **Petra** and **Sinai**, two popular destinations in nearby Jordan and Egypt, respectively.

TRANSPORTATION INFO. For making connections between destinations, information is generally listed under both the arrival and departure cities. Parentheses usually provide the trip duration followed by its frequency and price, which is for one-way trips unless otherwise stated. For more general information on travel, consult **Essentials** (p. 8).

COVERING THE BASICS. Before departing, consult the **Discover Israel** chapter (p. 1) for recommendations on when to go and for country-wide suggested itineraries (p. 5). Logistical and practical questions are answered in the **Essentials** chapter (p. 8), and the **Life and Times** chapter (p. 37) gives an overview of Israeli and Palestinian history, culture, and customs. **Beyond Tourism** (p. 73) suggests volunteer, study abroad, and temporary work opportunities to enrich your travel experience. The **Appendix** (p. 412) lists Hebrew and Arabic phrases, pronunciations, and other quick and helpful resource info.

PRICE DIVERSITY. Our researchers list establishments in order of value from best to worst, with absolute favorites denoted by the Let's Go thumbpick (◪). Since the cheapest price does not always mean the best value, we have incorporated a system of price ranges for food and accommodations; see p. VIII.

PHONE CODES AND TELEPHONE NUMBERS. Area codes for each region appear opposite the name of the region and are denoted by the ☎ icon. Phone numbers in text are also preceded by the ☎ icon.

LANGUAGE AND OTHER QUIRKS. The Hebrew or Arabic name of each city and town is printed after its English name, and popular alternative transliterations are often included in the introduction to the city. For a guide to Hebrew and Arabic, see the **Appendix** (p. 412).

A NOTE TO OUR READERS. The information for this book was gathered by Let's Go researchers from May through August of 2009. Each listing is based on one researcher's opinion, formed during his or her visit at a particular time. Those traveling at other times may have different experiences since prices, dates, hours, and conditions are always subject to change. You are urged to check the facts presented in this book beforehand to avoid inconvenience and surprises.

CONTENTS

DISCOVER..............................1
When To Go 1
What To Do 2
Suggested Itineraries 5
ESSENTIALS.........................8
Planning Your Trip 8
Safety And Health 14
Getting to Israel 20
Getting Around Israel 23
Keeping in Touch 26
Accommodations 29
The Great Outdoors 31
Specific Concerns 33
LIFE AND TIMES...................37
Land 37
History 37
Today 50
Economy 53
People 55
Culture 65
The Arts 67
Holidays and Festivals 70
BEYOND TOURISM..................73
Volunteering 74
Studying 78
Working 81
JERUSALEM.........................85
Daytrips 155
TEL AVIV-JAFFA...................158
Tel Aviv 158
Jaffa (Yafo) 188
Ramla 192
Ashkelon 197
Rishon le-Tziyon 199
NORTHERN MEDITERRANEAN
COAST................................201
Haifa 201
Netanya 218
Caesarea 222
Akko (Acre) 227
Nahariya 234
GALILEE............................240
Nazareth 240
Tiberias 250

Sea of Galilee (Lake Kinneret) 260
Tzfat (Safed) 263
Kiryat Shmona 275
Tel Khai (Tel Hai) 278
Khula Valley (Hula Valley) 279
Metulla 281
GOLAN HEIGHTS...................283
Katzrin 285
WEST BANK.........................294
Essentials 294
Life and Times 297
Bethlehem 302
Jericho 312
Ramallah 319
Nablus (Sachem) 324
Hebron 327
THE DEAD SEA.....................330
Ein Gedi 333
Masada 336
Northern Dead Sea 340
Southern Dead Sea 343
THE NEGEV.........................346
Be'er Sheva 346
Arad 359
Sde Boker 361
Mitzpe Ramon 365
EILAT................................371
PETRA AND SINAI.................382
Petra 382
High Sinai 390
Mount Sinai 393
Saint Catherine's 395
Sinai Desert 398
Gulf of Aqaba (Gulf of Eilat) 399
Dahab 400
Nuweiba 404
Sharm al-Sheikh 407
APPENDIX..........................412
Climate 412
Measurements 412
Language 412
Phrasebook 414
INDEX................................418
MAP INDEX.........................421

RESEARCHERS

Teresa Cotsirilos
Jerusalem, Tel Aviv, and Northern Mediterranean Coast

Plucky, witty, and resourceful, this California native stood up to her foes—whether they were kind elderly guards at the Dome of the Rock, tipsy Tel Aviv bartenders, or friendly police officers who were just trying to keep her from harm. Teresa researched some of the most politically-charged places in the world (and did it well) while keeping a positive attitude and a quick wit.

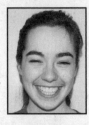

Ruth Pimentel
Northern Mediterranean Coast, Galilee, and Golan Heights

A true international citizen, this spunky, sociable, and eager-to-please freshman was a dream researcher. Ruth's personality attracts everyone from a vanload of nuns to a gang of friendly soldiers to the bearded leader of an unofficial micronation. She braved solo hikes and epic travel delays, but was always able to find her way out of sticky situations (e.g. by taking a ride on a tractor).

Mark van Middlesworth
West Bank, Dead Sea, Negev, Eilat, Petra, and Sinai

Chill and easygoing, Mark learned quickly that if you make the right friends, you can find all the best-hidden secrets in an unknown place. With his trusty Netbook in tow, he endured treacherous hikes and three different currencies. He always stuck to his convictions, and his discerning eye was invaluable to the thoroughness and political correctness of the guide.

STAFF WRITERS

Megan Lee Amram
Charles Fisher-Post
Alexandra Perloff-Giles
Jake Segal

R. Kyle Bean
Nadav Greenberg
Megan Popkin
Sara Joe Wolansky

Lauren Brown
Tamara Harel-Cohen
Harker Rhodes

CONTRIBUTING WRITERS

David Andersson graduated from Harvard University with a concentration in Social Studies, focusing on social movements and public space. He is currently traveling around the world using *Let's Go* as his trusty guide.

Hadas Reich graduated from Binghamton University where she majored in biology and minored in international studies. She lived in Israel as a child and spent a semester studying at Tel Aviv University.

ACKNOWLEDGMENTS

DAVID THANKS: Ruth, for her enormous smile. Mark, for keeping me on track politically. Teresa, for teaching me the many uses of a ballpoint pen. Iya, for peanut butter frosting. Nadav, for laying the groundwork. Hadas, for writing from Costa Rica. Laura, for beirut. Rotio, for the maps (oh, the maps). Andrew, for something, I forget what. Mamshit. Public apology to Sassley for the tiramisu incident. RMs+Eds=SummerUnfun09. RIP Creedence.

THE EDITORS THANK: First and foremost our lord (Jay-C) and savior (Starbucks, Terry's Chocolate Orange). We also owe gratitude to Barack Obama (peace be upon Him), the Oxford comma, the water cooler, bagel/payday Fridays, the HSA "SummerFun" team for being so inclusive, Rotio (wherefore art thou Rotio?), the real Robinson Crusoe, the Cambridge weather and defective umbrellas, Bolt-Bus, Henry Louis Gates, Jr. (sorry 'bout the phone call), the office blog, gratuitous nudity, the 20-20-20 rule and bananas (no more eye twitches), the Portuguese flag, trips to the beach (ha!), sunbathing recently-married Mormon final club alums, non-existent free food in the square, dog-star puns, and last but not least, America. The local time in Tehran is 1:21am.

But seriously, the MEs and RMs, our researchers (and all their wisdom on tablecloths and hipsters), LGHQ, HSA, our significant others (future, Canadian, and otherwise), and families (thanks Mom).

LET'S GO

Publishing Director
Laura M. Gordon
Editorial Director
Dwight Livingstone Curtis
Publicity and Marketing Director
Vanessa J. Dube
Production and Design Director
Rebecca Lieberman
Cartography Director
Anthony Rotio
Website Director
Lukáš Tóth
Managing Editors
Ashley Laporte, Iya Megre,
Mary Potter, Nathaniel Rakich
Technology Project Manager
C. Alexander Tremblay
Director of IT & E-Commerce
David Fulton-Howard
Financial Associates
Catherine Humphreville, Jun Li

Managing Editor
Iya Megre
Research Manager
David Andersson
Editors
Courtney A. Fiske, Sara Plana, Russell Ford Rennie,
Charlie E. Riggs, Olga I. Zhulina
Typesetter
C. Alexander Tremblay

President
Daniel Lee
General Manager
Jim McKellar

PRICE RANGES

ISRAEL

① **②** **③** **④** **⑤**

Our researchers list establishments in order of value from best to worst, honoring our favorites with the Let's Go thumbpick (▨). Because the best *value* is not always the cheapest *price*, we have incorporated a system of price ranges based on a rough expectation of what you will spend. For **accommodations**, we base our range on the cheapest price for which a single traveler can stay for one night. For **restaurants**, we estimate the average amount one traveler will spend in one sitting. The table below tells you what you'll *typically* find in Israel at the corresponding price range, but keep in mind that no system can allow for the quirks of individual establishments. Note: price diversities for Petra and Sinai are listed on p. 383 and p. 391, respectively.

ACCOMMODATIONS	RANGE	WHAT YOU'RE *LIKELY* TO FIND
①	under NIS75	Campgrounds, lower-end hostels, and basic dorms. In the summer, you may find converted student dorms. Expect bunk beds and a communal bath; you may need—or want—to bring your own towel and sheet.
②	NIS75-150	Upper-end (or sometimes HI) hostels or lower-end hotels. You may have a private bathroom, or you may have to share. Breakfast is sometimes included, or meals may be inexpensive for hostel guests.
③	NIS151-300	A small room with a private bath, probably in a budget hotel. Will likely have decent amenities. Breakfast may be included for your food-hoarding convenience.
④	NIS301-400	Similar to ③, but should have more amenities or be in a more highly touristed or conveniently located area. Breakfast is often included in the price of your room—yay!
⑤	over NIS400	Large hotels, upscale chains, or conveniently located B&B-style hotels. If it's a ⑤ and it doesn't have the perks or service you're looking for, you've probably paid too much.

FOOD	RANGE	WHAT YOU'RE *LIKELY* TO FIND
①	under NIS30	Probably a falafel or shawarma stand, a sandwich shop, or a bakery; essentially, an addiction waiting to happen.
②	NIS30-65	Sandwiches, salads, piles of unidentified meat on rice, and other entrees. Most likely sit-down, though perhaps without a server.
③	NIS66-100	Usually sit-down. Mid-priced entrees, pub fare, seafood, a wine list—and a little something extra for tip.
④	NIS101-135	Entrees are more expensive than ③, but you're paying for quality service, ambience, and decor. Few restaurants in this range have a dress code, but you'll want to clean yourself up after a day of travel.
⑤	over NIS135	Your meal might cost more than your hostel, but here's to hoping it's something fabulous, famous, or involving a lot of good wine.

ABOUT LET'S GO

THE STUDENT TRAVEL GUIDE

Let's Go publishes the world's favorite student travel guides, written entirely by Harvard students. Armed with pens, notebooks, and a few changes of clothes stuffed into their backpacks, our student researchers go across continents, through time zones, and above expectations to seek out invaluable travel experiences for our readers. Because we are a completely student-run company, we have a unique perspective on how students travel, where they want to go, and what they're looking to do when they get there. If your dream is to grab a machete and forge through the jungles of Costa Rica, we can take you there. If you'd rather bask in the Riviera sun at a beachside cafe, we'll set you a table. In short, we write for readers who know that there's more to travel than tour buses. To keep up, visit our website, www.letsgo.com, where you can sign up to blog, post photos from your trips, and connect with the Let's Go community.

TRAVELING BEYOND TOURISM

We're on a mission to provide our readers with sharp, fresh coverage packed with socially responsible opportunities to go beyond tourism. Each guide's Beyond Tourism chapter shares ideas about responsible travel, study abroad, and how to give back to the places you visit while on the road. To help you gain a deeper connection with the places you travel, our fearless researchers scour the globe to give you the heads-up on both world-renowned and off-the-beaten-track opportunities. We've also opened our pages to respected writers and scholars to hear their takes on the countries and regions we cover, and asked travelers who have worked, studied, or volunteered abroad to contribute first-person accounts of their experiences.

FIFTY YEARS OF WISDOM

Let's Go has been on the road for 50 years and counting. We've grown a lot since publishing our first 20-page pamphlet to Europe in 1960, but five decades and 54 titles later our witty, candid guides are still researched and written entirely by students on shoestring budgets who know that train strikes, stolen luggage, food poisoning, and marriage proposals are all part of a day's work. This year, for our 50th anniversary, we're publishing 26 titles—including 6 brand new guides—brimming with editorial honesty, a commitment to students, and our irreverent style. Here's to the next 50!

THE LET'S GO COMMUNITY

More than just a travel guide company, Let's Go is a community that reaches from our headquarters in Cambridge, MA all across the globe. Our small staff of dedicated student editors, writers, and tech nerds comes together because of our shared passion for travel and our desire to help other travelers get the most out of their experience. We love it when our readers become part of the Let's Go community as well—when you travel, drop us a postcard (67 Mt. Auburn St., Cambridge, MA 02138, USA), send us an e-mail (feedback@letsgo.com), or sign up on our website (www.letsgo.com) to tell us about your adventures and discoveries.

For more information, updated travel coverage, and news from our researcher team, visit us online at www.letsgo.com.

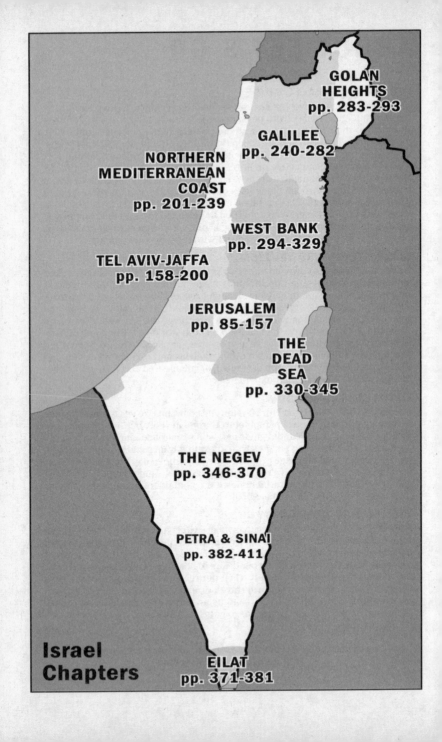

GOLAN
HEIGHTS
pp. 283-293

GALILEE
pp. 240-282

NORTHERN
MEDITERRANEAN
COAST
pp. 201-239

WEST BANK
pp. 294-329

TEL AVIV-JAFFA
pp. 158-200

JERUSALEM
pp. 85-157

THE
DEAD
SEA
pp. 330-345

THE NEGEV
pp. 346-370

PETRA & SINAI
pp. 382-411

EILAT
pp. 371-381

Israel
Chapters

DISCOVER ISRAEL

Halfway through its first century, Israel has yet to resolve a psychological struggle between secularism and reverence. A powerful sense of religion and history permeates its modern cities, where pensive philosophers and microchip millionaires sit on park benches with patriotic Zionists and dedicated discogoers. The nation's heterogeneity is most apparent on Friday evenings, when Tel Aviv clubs and Eilat pubs explode with revelry that can almost be heard in the reverent streets of Tzfat or in Jerusalem's Jewish Quarter. Israel has been controversial since its inception. As a result of persecution culminating in the Holocaust, Jews of all cultures came together to fashion a new state and to remake themselves, sometimes at the expense of the Palestinian arabs.

It is almost impossible to spend time in Israel and not encounter the effects of the Israeli-Palestinian conflict. The West Bank is currently under Israeli occupation, but is populated primarily by Palestinians. In response to several Palestinian terrorist attacks on Israel about a decade ago, the State of Israel began to construct an imposing wall between itself and the West Bank (see **Another Brick in the Wall**, p. 298). The conflict comes to a head within the city of Jerusalem, where there is a clear divide between the ethnicities.

With the country's identity and culture in constant flux, all Israelis and Palestinians have their own visions of what Israel and the territories could or should be. Ask them about their bewildering national situation and they will tell you at length how they see their country—there is no lack of impassioned political or apolitical opinions. But a fundamental optimism shines through; talk with them long enough, and they will eventually smile or shrug and say, *"Yihiyeh tov"* (It will be okay).

FACTS AND FIGURES

OFFICIAL NAME: Medinat Yisra'el

POPULATION: 7,233,700

AREA: 8,522 sq. mi., about the size of New Jersey

CAPITAL: Jerusalem

OFFICIAL LANGUAGES: Hebrew, Arabic

PRIME MINISTER: Binjamin Netanyahu

GDP PER CAPITA: US$28,200

AGE (AS ISRAEL): 51

AGE (AS A CIVILIZATION): 11,000+

RELIGIONS: 76% Jewish, 16% Muslim, 2% Christian, 2% Druze, 4% undeclared

THINGS WE OWE TO ISRAEL: The cell phone, the instant message, Itzhak Perlman, Natalie Portman, and much more

WHEN TO GO

Due to Israel's mild Mediterranean climate, seasonal factors need not play a huge role in deciding when to go, although spring (roughly March to May) is far and away the best time to go hiking and to explore the northern wilderness. Parts of Israel can get stiflingly hot between July and August, and Jerusalem can get chilly in January (see **Climate Chart**, p. 412). Your concern, however, should be holiday season, when the country becomes jam-packed with pilgrims, hotel prices skyrocket, businesses shut down, and transportation stops running. The holidays to watch out for are in September and October, when the country is mostly closed due to Rosh Hashanah, Yom Kippur, and Sukkot. March and April in Jerusalem and Bethlehem are also busy due to the Orthodox Easter, but buses still run. All festivals and holidays in Israel run from sundown the day before to nightfall the next day. For longer holidays, businesses are closed for the first day (and in the case of Passover, the last day) but remain open after that. For a comprehensive chart of all festivals in Israel, see **Holidays,** p. 70.

WHAT TO DO

Israel is a land of great historical and religious significance, and its ancient ruins and holy sites attract visitors from around the world. There's more to do here than just tour ancient marvels, though—Israel is a modern, thriving country with a little bit of everything, from world-class scuba-diving to Dadaist art colonies. Here are some of the best attractions and activities in Israel and the Palestinian territories.

OLDIES BUT GOODIES

Israel and the Palestinian territories have been the stomping ground of dozens of peoples over as many centuries—the layers of civilization date back to ancient **Jericho** (p. 312), which, at 10,000 years, is the oldest known city in the world. As the sun sets over **Jerusalem** (p. 85), the remnants of fallen civilizations and startling architectural achievements shine with the city's famous gold. The hilltop fortress of **Masada** (p. 336) served as a Jewish refuge, Herod's citadel, and the site of mass suicide in the face of Roman conquest. **Petra** (p. 382), carved into the red cliffs of Jordan, is the country's mystical treasure. On the Mediterranean Coast, **Caesarea** (p. 222), Herod's first-century city, is remarkably intact; to the south are the hidden caves and tombs of **Beit Guvrin** (p. 194). **Nimrod's Fortress** (p. 289), an impressive crusader castle in the Golan Heights, features a secret passageway, winding stone stairways, and a magnificent view. Other highlights include **Beit She'an** (p. 258), a mound with twenty archaeologically distinct layers, and **Tzippori** (p. 249), which boasts exquisite mosaics, a synagogue, and an amphitheater. Fortress walls surround the Crusader city of **Akko** (p. 227), while long, damp Templars' tunnels burrow beneath.

HOLY MOLY

If religious history is your thing, then you've come to the right place. Jerusalem is holy to three of the world's major religions: Jews pray at the **Western Wall** (p. 121), Muslims worship at the **Dome of the Rock** (p. 126), and Christians walk the **Via Dolorosa** (p. 127). Nevertheless, the spiritual richness and diversity of Israel and the Palestinian territories owe substantially to the region's many lesser-known religious and cultural centers as well. **Tzfat** (p. 263) inspired the birth of the Kabbalah, which, along with its beautiful synagogues, attracts seekers of spirituality (and mystic aspirants) to its narrow streets. The world headquarters of the Baha'i religion and the gold-domed Baha'i Shrine are in **Haifa** (p. 201), where lush surrounding gardens welcome visitors of all denominations. Traditionally nomadic people, many of Israel's Bedouin now live in villages;

the Joe Alon Bedouin Museum in **Be'er Sheva** (p. 346) lends insight into their unique past and uncertain present. In 1969, the first members of the Hebrew Israelite Community (or Black Hebrews) left Chicago for Liberia, en route to the Holy Land. Forty years later, their thriving community in **Dimona** (p. 356) runs a vegan restaurant and an annual music festival.

AIN'T NO MOUNTAIN HIGH ENOUGH

Northern Israel in the spring is a hiker's paradise, overflowing with animals, wildflowers, and snow-melt springs and waterfalls. Well-marked trails maintained by the Society for the Protection of Nature in Israel (SPNI) criss-cross nature reserves and national parks. The mountains—try **Mount Meron** (p. 271)—offer relatively gentle climbs to beautiful outlooks, many with views of neighboring countries. Head out to **Montfort** (p. 237) for the isolated ruins of a Crusader castle; "Danger of collapse," say signs, a threat that will be all too real if you don't remember to bring water. For the truly hardcore, a trail of epic proportions called **Shvil Isra'il** spans the country from north to south. Intricate maps and numerous trail guides with internet updates attempt to make the trip seem manageable. At the Dead Sea, escape the tourist traps by heading for the hills: **Mitzokei Dragot** (p. 340) has some serious hikes that will leave typical Dead Sea floaters in the dust. For a more relaxing escape, the nature reserve in **Ein Gedi** (p. 333) has freshwater pools fed by waterfalls and surrounded by lush green vegetation. The powdery white rock of **Mount Sodom** (p. 343) hides a few short hikes that are great for an afternoon. **Ein Avdat** (p. 364) has some of the driest, emptiest desert in Israel. The nearby crater and cliffs of **Mitzpe Ramon** (p. 365) have some of the most accessible and breathtaking climbs in the country, with a wide range of difficulties. But when it comes to rock, **Petra** (p. 382) can't be beat. The tourist-choked entrance quickly gives way to miles of serene canyons and sculpted pink stone.

SWIM FAN

Natives and tourists alike agree that the sunbathing along the Mediterranean is **Tel Aviv's** (p. 158) *raison d'etre;* the city's beaches are constantly crawling with beautiful—and sometimes not-so-beautiful—people playing ping-pong in bikinis. The beaches of **Netanya** (p. 218) have famously been considered a more relaxing, less congested alternative to Tel Aviv's urban bustle; they have consequently become packed with European tourists. For hard-won, beachy solitude, head north and hike 4km from the local bus stop for **Kibbutz Dor** (p. 216). Then spread out on gloriously serene sand just next to a *tel* full of Crusader ruins—and the occasional excavator. To go freshwater, try the expensive resort hotel beaches in **Tiberias** (p. 250) on the Sea of Galilee, or embrace the rustic and camp out on the rocky shores north of town. The beaches of **Eilat** (p. 371) draw tens of thousands of sun-lovers every year, but the coral reefs beneath the waves are at least as colorful as the board shorts above. The diving gets even better along the coast of the Sinai Peninsula—get your PADI cert in budget-friendly **Dahab** (p. 400), then head south for the world-famous reef and wreck dives **Sharm al-Shiekh** (p. 407). At the **Dead Sea** (p. 330), get your feet wet but keep your face above the surface of the painfully mineral-rich water.

DISCOVER

☙LET'S GO PICKS

BEST PLACE TO GET BAPTIZED: Wade with crowds of pilgrims into the Jordan River at **Yardenit** (p. 263), to be cleansed of your sins. Both the pure and impure are welcome in the gift shop.

BEST PLACE TO WATCH A BRAWL: Control of the **Church of the Holy Sepulchre** (p. 129) is divided between rival Christian orders, who enact Jesus's message of unconditional love by squabbling constantly over who controls the site of His crucifixion and burial.

BEST PLACE TO ELEVATE YOUR INNER SPARK: Mountaintop Tzfat is home to the **Ascent Institute** (p. 271). Come for lectures on Kabbalah and Talmud, stay to hang out with the jolly Khasidic rabbis.

BEST VIEW FROM A TOILET SEAT: You might need relief after the hike to Petra's **Nabatean Museum** (p. 390), and this is the place to do it. Take your time, and don't bother bringing reading material.

BEST USE OF 1980S SPECIAL EFFECTS TECHNOLOGY: The **Masada Sound and Light Show** (p. 361) packs a surprising amount of history into its decidedly low-tech presentation, driven by colored spotlights and red sparklers. And yes, that is an actual slide projector.

BEST POLITICAL COFFEE SHOPS: Conversations at Jerusalem's **T'mol Shilshom** (p. 98) range from gay rights to racial politics. Tel Aviv's **Tamar Cafe** (p. 172) is haphazardly decorated with framed political cartoons featuring the cafe's owner with a variety of political figures.

BEST POLITICAL GRAFFITI: The streets of **Bethlehem** (p. 302) are littered with political paint: see if you can spot the "no tank parking" stencils on Manger St. Tags by international graffiti artist Banksy can be found on the separation wall in **Dheisheh refugee camp** (p. 310) and on the road from Beit Jala to Manger Sq.

OLDEST PEOPLE: For elderly-Israeli sightings, no place beats **Nahariya** (p. 234), where hotels are being converted into nursing homes as fast as pedestrian speed is plummeting.

HIPPEST HIPPIES: In Mitzpe Ramon, the modern dance company **Adama** (p. 366) has every sign of hippiedom: vegan food, meditation, soap-making, African drum music, and a flower-power obsession with peace. The only thing that might be missing is political awareness.

CHOCOLATIEST MILK: Apparently, cows can survive in the desert. But chocolate cows? Nobody knows how **Kibbutz Yotvata** (p. 380) keeps theirs from melting, but you'll be happy they do.

PROUDEST UNOFFICIAL MICRONATION: Long-bearded dreamer Eli Avivi settled a gorgeous chunk of the Mediterranean Coast and declared independence from Israel in the 1950s. **Akhzivland** (p. 238), as its ruler proudly calls it, has stuck out decades of government disapproval and still offers a pristine beach and serene, open-air beds to visitors.

HIGHEST CONCENTRATION OF THINGS TO SEE UNDERGROUND: Jerusalem's **Old City** has been settled, burned down, and resettled so many times that some of its most incredible sights are underneath the current city. Visit ruins from the Second Temple Period 3m below street level at the **Burnt House** (p. 114). Get close to the Holy of Holies on the **Western Wall Tunnel Tours** (p. 121). Wade through icy water in the dark with screaming children—and adults—at **Hezekiah's Tunnel** (p. 136).

STATE OF THE ART

The **Tel Aviv Art Museum** (p. 180) boasts a small but impressive collection. The city is also peppered with hole-in-the-wall galleries, which are both difficult and exciting to find. In Jerusalem, watch the artists themselves at work in the Artists Colony (p. 145) and House of Quality (p. 145). Devotees will be happy to discover a Japanese art museum in **Haifa** of all places (p. 201). Renfair enthusiasts, too, can zero in on unexpected Israeli contributions to the scene with **Yekhi'am's** annual Renaissance Festival (p. 239). Israel's wildest art experience, of course, can be found wandering the unnamed streets of **Ein Hod** (p. 215), a Surrealist/Dadaist artists' colony where every building and public bench (and trash can) doubles as a gallery. Abandoned warehouses in the Negev have begun to attract artists whose work is deeply tied to their environment; **Mitzpe Ramon** (p. 365) and **Arad** (p. 359) are both worth a visit for their decidedly desert-oriented artist's colonies. Aerosol fans should check out the graffiti on the Palestinian side of the separation barrier, where artists (including Banksy) have left miles of politically-motivated stencils, slogans, and tags.

A LOT ON YOUR PLATE

Israeli fast food is restricted, without variation, to shawarma, falafel, and hummus. Expect to encounter more kinds of olives and pickled vegetables than you knew existed—pickled lemon slices aren't half bad. One of Israel's most enduring conflicts is over which single-room falafel joint has the best hummus in the country; Abu Taher's in the Muslim Quarter of **Jerusalem** (p. 85) and Abu Hassan in **Jaffa** (p. 188) are two of the front runners. In general, Tel Aviv and much of West Jerusalem offer diverse fare, from vegan oases to Asian fusion to some high-class hot chocolate. The **Sea of Galilee** (p. 260) specializes in what touristy restaurants like to call St. Peter's fish, more commonly known as tilapia. Land flowing with milk and honey? **Arab confectioneries** everywhere dish up *kunaifa* and baklava literally dripping in clear honey, and **kibbutzim** commonly open restaurants devoted to their homemade cheese, butter, and (yes) milk. This is not the place to go for skim. The concrete and barbed wire of **Be'er Sheva** (p. 346) hide a wealth of cheap sushi restaurants with a Middle Eastern twist. The **Dahab** (p. 400) shoreline is littered with restaurants serving heaping plates of fresh fish, fruits, and vegetables for the price of a Happy Meal. Some of the falafel stands in **Sinai** remove the falafel all together; the resulting french-fry and veggie pita sandwich is interesting in concept if not in execution.

SUGGESTED ITINERARIES

The following itineraries are designed to lead you to the highlights of Israel and the Palestinian Territories, from cosmopolitan hubs to sleepy villages. While these itineraries are intended for those who haven't traveled around Israel very much, even seasoned explorers can use them as a template for daytrips and excursions. Still, there are many ways to explore the country, not all of which we can cover. For more specific regional attractions, see the **Highlights of the Region** section at the beginning of each chapter.

DISCOVER

DOING WHAT COMES NATURALLY (2 WEEKS)

Banyas (1 day)
Hit this fabulous northern nature reserve to see transparent, icy water filtered through Mt. Khermon and thurdering through the dense forest (p. 288).

Khula Valley (1 day)
Expect stepping stones and bridges and watch for spotted salamanders at Tel Dan, the least touristy of this valley's nature reserves (p. 279).

Rosh ha-Nikra (1 day)
Scour chalk cliffs for fossils of sea anemones, then venture inside the mountain where stormy waves have carved grottoes out of the multi-colored stone (p. 237).

Ramat ha-Nadiv (1 day)
Go wild in a national park just outside Zikhron Ya-akov, tamed only by grazing goats (p. 218).

Mitzpe Ramon (1 day)
Rent a knobby-tire ride and take advantage of the fantastic mountain biking on cliffs overlooking layers of colored sand (p. 365).

Ein Avdat (1 day)
Find the trickling spring cutting into the stark desert landscape of Ein Avdat national park, providing welcome relief for humans and animals alike (p. 365).

START

Sea of Galilee (2 days)
Rent a bike in Tiberias and devote a day to following the shore (p. 259).

Golan Mountains (1 day)
A local joke says that someone trying to commit suicide will die of starvation before getting hit by a car—but the wild isolation of these rocky slopes makes exploration all the more dramatic (p. 283).

Mitzokei Dragot (1 day)
Lose your breath on the drive to this national park high above the Dead Sea (p. 340).

Netanya (1 day)
Take a horseback tour of the local beaches at sunset. It's nature minus the dirt, ants, and physical exertion (p. 218).

END

The Dead Sea (2 days)
Try the iconic Dead Sea float-and-coat—the healing properties of the Dead Sea water and mineral mud have been touted for centuries (p. 330).

Ein Gedi (1 day)
Take a break from the arid land and swarms of tourists at the Dead Sea by visiting the waterfall-fed pools (p. 333).

THINGS NOT TO MISS: OFF THE BEATEN TRACK EDITION

Ein Hod
Check out this surrealist artist's colony with exclusive residency rules but extremely inclusive visiting policies (p. 215).

Tel Dor
Take a break on gorgeously sandy beaces complete with Crusader ruins and sun umbrellas (p. 216).

Caesarea
Brave the busloads of tourists and inconvenient bus schedules to see arguably the best ruins in Israel, complete with stunning views of the sea (p. 222).

Tel Aviv-Jaffa
Wander in the constellation of tangled, arsty alleyways of Neve Tzedek, Tel Aviv's oldest Jewish neighborhood (p. 158).

Jerusalem
See souqs like no other at Jerusalem's Mahane Yehuda market and Old City souq (p. 92). The Ethiopian Monastery (p. 131) and St. James' Cathedral (p. 132) offer cool and quiet respites from the crush the crowds.

The Negev Craters
Hike it up at Maktesh Ramon, the biggest and most well-known of Israel's craters.

Akko
Stumble through the ruins, and then wait your turn at Hummus Said's (p. 227) to devour a cheap, creamy-hummus-fulled pita. All will be right with the world.

Nazareth
Meditate in the adorned courtyard of the Church of the Annunciation (p. 240).

Petra
Marvel at the engineering skills of the 2nd-century BCE Nabateans, who carved the facade of the treasury into the striking pink stone (p. 382).

Herodion
Journey inside this hollow, flat-topped mountain to find the magnificent palace built by King Herod (p. 309).

Ein Gedi
Relax at the freshwater pools after trekking along the craggy ridges and valleys of the Natural Park (p. 335).

Hebron
Brace yourself for a tour organized by a politically-oriented guide service; though it may not always be the calmest experience, you won't soon forget it (p. 327).

Dahab
Snorkel around coral at the spectacular Blue Hole dive site and Lighthouse Beach (p. 400).

ESSENTIALS

PLANNING YOUR TRIP

BEFORE YOU GO
Passport (see opposite page). Required for all non-citizens of Israel.
Visa (see opposite page). Not required for citizens of Australia, Canada, Ireland, New Zealand, South Africa, the UK, and the US. Visit www.israelemb.org/consular_Visa.html for more details.
Recommended Vaccinations (p. 18). Tetanus-diphtheria vaccine, measles vaccine and varicella (chicken pox) vaccine are all recommended.

EMBASSIES AND CONSULATES

ISRAEL'S CONSULAR SERVICES ABROAD

Australia: Embassy of Israel, 6 Turrana St., Yarralumla, Canberra, ACT 2600 (☎61 2 6215 4500; http://canberra.mfa.gov.il).

Canada: Embassy of Israel, 50 O'Connor St., #1005, Ottawa, Ont. K1P 6L2 (☎+1-613-567-6450; ottawa.mfa.gov.il). **Consulates** in Toronto (http://toronto.mfa.gov.il) and Westmount (http://montreal.mfa.gov.il).

Ireland: Embassy of Israel, Carrisbrook House, 122 Pembroke Road, Ballsbridge, Dublin 4 (☎+353 01 230 9400; dublin.mfa.gov.il).

New Zealand: Embassy of Israel, 13th fl., Equinox House, 111 The Terrace, P.O. Box 2171, Wellington (☎+64 04 472 2368 or 2362; www.israel.org.nz).

UK: Embassy of Israel, 2 Palace Green, London W8 4QB (☎+44 020 7957 9500; http://london.mfa.gov.il).

US: Embassy of Israel, 3514 International Dr. NW, Washington, D.C. 20008 (☎+1-202-364-5500; www.israelemb.org). **Consulates** in Atlanta (http://atlanta.mfa.gov.il), Boston (http://boston.mfa.gov.il), Chicago (http://chicago.mfa.gov.il), Houston (http://houston.mfa.gov.il), Los Angeles (www.israeliconsulatela.org), Miami (http://miami.mfa.gov.il), New York (www.israelfm.org), Philadelphia (http://philadelphia.mfa.gov.il), and San Francisco (www.israeliconsulate.org).

CONSULAR SERVICES IN ISRAEL

Australia: Australian Embassy, 23 Yehuda Halevi St., Tel Aviv 65136 (☎03 693 50 00; www.israel.embassy.gov.au).

Canada: Canadian Embassy, 3/5 Nirim St., 4th fl., Yad Eliyahu, Tel Aviv 67060 (☎03 636 33 00; www.canadainternational.gc.ca).

Egypt: Egyptian Embassy, 54 Basel St., Tel Aviv (☎+03 546 51 51 or 51 52). **Egyptian Consulate,** 68 Ephroni St., Bna Betkha, Eilat (☎02 637 68 82).

Ireland: Irish Embassy, 3 Daniel Frisch St., 17th fl., Tel Aviv 64731 (☎03 696 41 66; www.embassyofireland.co.il).

New Zealand: The **British Embassy** in Tel Aviv serves New Zealanders (see below).

UK: British Embassy, 192 Hayarkon St., Tel Aviv 63405 (☎03 725 12 22; http://ukinisrael.fco.gov.uk/en). **Consulates** in Eilat, Jerusalem, and Tel Aviv; see the UK Embassy website for more info.

US: Embassy of the United States, 71 Rehov Hayarkon, Tel Aviv 63903 (☎03 519 74 57 or 75 75; www.usembassy-israel.org.il). **Consulates** in East and West Jerusalem; see http://jerusalem.usconsulate.gov for more info.

TOURIST OFFICES

Israel's official tourist board operates an extensive website at www.tourism. gov.il/Tourism_Eng. The board also has offices abroad in Canada and the US.

Canada: Tourist Office of Israel, 180 Bloor St. W., Ste. 700 Toronto, ON M5S 2V6 (☎+1-416-964-3784; fax 416-964-2420; www.goisrael.ca).

US: Tourist Office of Israel, 800 2nd Avenue, New York, 10017 (☎+1-212-499-5650; fax 212-499-5655). Additional offices in Chicago, IL (☎+1-312-803-7080), Los Angeles, CA (☎+1-323-658-7463) and Atlanta, GA (☎+1-404-541-2770).

DOCUMENTS AND FORMALITIES

PASSPORTS

REQUIREMENTS

Citizens of Australia, Canada, Ireland, New Zealand, the UK, and the US need valid passports to enter Israel and to re-enter their home countries. Israel does not allow entrance if the holder's passport expires in under 6 months; returning home with an expired passport is illegal and may result in a fine. Your passport will prove your most convenient method of identification and, if the photo was taken long ago, a source of humorous conversation.

PASSPORT MAINTENANCE

Photocopy the page of your passport with your photo as well as your visas, traveler's check serial numbers, and any other important documents. Carry one set of copies in a safe place, apart from the originals, and leave another set at home. Consulates also recommend that you carry an expired passport or an official copy of your birth certificate in a part of your baggage separate from other documents.

If you lose your passport, immediately notify the local police and your home country's nearest embassy or consulate. To expedite its replacement, you must show ID and proof of citizenship; it also helps to know all information previously recorded in the passport. In some cases, a replacement may take weeks to process, and it may be valid only for a limited time. Any visas stamped in your old passport will be lost forever. In an emergency, ask for immediate temporary traveling papers that will permit you to re-enter your home country.

VISAS, INVITATIONS, AND WORK PERMITS

VISAS

Citizens of Australia, Canada, Ireland, New Zealand, the UK, and the US do not require a visa for entrance into Israel if the stay is under 3 months, but they must possess a valid passport. Tourist visas cost approximately $28 and can be purchased in person at one of the above mentioned embassies or consulates (p. 8). Double-check entrance requirements at the nearest embassy or consulate of Israel (listed on p. 8) for up-to-date info before departure. US citizens can also consult http://travel.state.gov.

Entering Israel to study requires a special visa. For more information, see the **Beyond Tourism** chapter (p. 73).

WORK PERMITS

Admittance to a country as a traveler does not include the right to work, which is authorized only by a work permit. For more information, see the **Beyond Tourism** chapter (p. 73).

IDENTIFICATION

When you travel, always carry at least two forms of identification on your person, including a photo ID. A passport and a driver's license will usually suffice. Never carry all of your IDs together; split them up in case of theft or loss and keep photocopies in your luggage and at home.

STUDENT AND YOUTH IDENTIFICATION

The **International Student Identity Card (ISIC),** the most widely accepted form of student ID, provides discounts on some sights, accommodations, food, and transportation, access to a 24hr. emergency help line, and insurance benefits for US cardholders. In Israel, for example, cardholders receive 10% savings on Israel Railways and Pizza Hut and 25% off entrance to the Tel Aviv Museum of Art. Applicants must be full-time secondary or post-secondary school students at least 12 years old. Because of the proliferation of fake ISICs, some services (particularly airlines) require additional proof of student identity. For travelers who are under 26 years old but are not students, the **International Youth Travel Card (IYTC)** also offers many of the same benefits as the ISIC.

Each of these identity cards costs US$22. ISICs and IYTCs are valid for one year from the date of issue. To learn more about ISICs and IYTCs, try www.myisic.com. Many student travel agencies (p. 21) issue the cards; for a list of issuing agencies or more information, see the **International Student Travel Confederation (ISTC)** website (www.istc.org).

CUSTOMS

Upon entering Israel, you must declare certain items from abroad and pay a duty on the value of those articles if they exceed the allowance established by Israel's customs service. Goods and gifts purchased at duty-free shops abroad are not exempt from duty or sales tax; "duty-free" means that you won't pay tax in the country of purchase. Upon returning home, you must likewise declare all articles acquired abroad and pay a duty on the value of articles in excess of your home country's allowance. Jot down a list of any valuables brought from home and register them with customs before traveling abroad. It's a good idea to keep receipts for all goods acquired abroad.

Tourists who pay for goods and services in foreign currency are exempt, in certain cases, from value added tax (VAT). (See **Taxes,** p. 13.)

MONEY

CURRENCY AND EXCHANGE

Israel's official currency is the **shekel (NIS)**. The currency chart below is based on August 2009 exchange rates between shekels and Australian dollars (AUS$), Canadian dollars (CDN$), European Union euro (EUR€), New Zealand dollars (NZ$), British pounds (UK£), and US dollars (US$). Check the currency converter on websites like www.xe.com or www.bloomberg.com for more info.

SHEKEL (NIS)		
AUS$1 = NIS3.2	NIS1 = AUS$0.31
CDN$1 = NIS3.5	NIS1 = CDN$0.29
EUR€1 = NIS5.4	NIS1 = EUR€0.18
NZ$1 = NIS2.6	NIS1 = NZ$0.39
UK£1 = NIS6.3	NIS1 = UK£0.16
US$1 = NIS3.8	NIS1 = US$0.26

As a general rule, it's cheaper to convert money in Israel than at home. While currency exchange will probably be available in your arrival airport, it's wise to bring enough foreign currency to last for at least 24-72hr.

When changing money abroad, try to go only to banks or currency exchange shops that have at most a **5% margin** between their buy and sell prices. Since you lose money with every transaction, it makes sense to convert large sums at one time (unless the currency is depreciating rapidly).

TRAVELER'S CHECKS

Traveler's checks are one of the safest and most convenient means of carrying funds. **American Express** and **Visa** are the best-recognized brands. Many banks and agencies sell them for a small commission. Check issuers provide refunds if the checks are lost or stolen, and many provide additional services, such as toll-free refund hotlines abroad, emergency message services, and assistance with lost and stolen credit cards or passports. Traveler's checks are readily accepted in unlimited amounts across Israel. Ask about toll-free refund hotlines and the location of refund centers when purchasing checks. Remember, too, always to carry emergency cash.

American Express: Checks available with commission at AmEx offices and select banks (www.americanexpress.com). AmEx cardholders can also purchase checks by phone (☎+1-800-528-4800). Cheques for Two can be signed by either of 2 people traveling together. For purchase locations or more information, contact AmEx's service centers: in Australia ☎+61 2 9271 8666, in Canada and the US +1-800-528-4800, in New Zealand +64 9 583 8300, in the UK +44 1273 571 600.

Visa: Checks available at banks worldwide. For the location of the nearest office, call the Visa Travelers Cheque Global Refund and Assistance Center: in the UK ☎+44 800 895 078, in the US +1-800-227-6811; elsewhere, call the UK collect at +44 2079 378 091. For more information on Visa travel services, see http://usa.visa.com/personal/using_visa/travel_with_visa.html.

CREDIT, DEBIT, AND ATM CARDS

Where they are accepted, credit cards often offer superior exchange rates—up to 5% better than the retail rate used by banks and other currency-exchange establishments. Credit cards may also offer services such as insurance or emergency help and are sometimes required to reserve hotel rooms or rental cars. **MasterCard** and **Visa** are the most frequently accepted; **American Express** cards work at some ATMs and at AmEx offices and major airports.

The use of ATM cards is widespread in Israel. Depending on the system that your bank at home uses, you can most likely access your personal bank account from abroad. ATMs get the same wholesale exchange rate as credit cards, but there is often a limit on the amount of money you can withdraw per day (usually around US$500). There is also typically a surcharge of US$1-5 per withdrawal, so it pays to be efficient.

Debit cards are as convenient as credit cards but withdraw money directly from the holder's checking account. A debit card can be used wherever its associated credit card company (usually MasterCard or Visa) is accepted. .

The two major international money networks are **MasterCard/Maestro/Cirrus** (for ATM locations ☎+1-800-424-7787; www.mastercard.com) and **Visa/PLUS** (for ATM locations visit http://visa.via.infonow.net/locator/global/). Most ATMs charge a transaction fee that is paid to the bank that owns the ATM. It is a good idea to contact your bank or credit card company before going abroad; frequent charges in a foreign country can sometimes prompt a fraud alert, which will freeze your account.

GETTING MONEY FROM HOME

If you run out of money while traveling, the easiest and cheapest solution is to have someone back home make a deposit to your bank account. Otherwise, consider one of the following options.

WIRING MONEY

It is possible to arrange a **bank money transfer,** which means asking a bank back home to wire money to a bank in Israel. This is the cheapest way to transfer cash, but it's also the slowest, usually taking several days or more. Note that some banks may only release your funds in local currency, potentially sticking you with a poor exchange rate; inquire about this in advance. Money transfer services like **Western Union** are faster and more convenient than bank transfers—but also much pricier. Western Union has many locations worldwide. To find one, visit www.westernunion.com or call in Australia ☎+64 1800 173 833, in Canada and the US +1-800-325-6000, in the UK +44 0800 735 1815, or in Israel +972 1 800 213 141. To wire money using a credit card, call in Canada and the US ☎+1-800-CALL-CASH, in the UK +44 0800 833 833.

US STATE DEPARTMENT (US CITIZENS ONLY)

In serious emergencies only, the US State Department will forward money within hours to the nearest consular office, which will then disburse it according to instructions for a US$30 fee. If you wish to use this service, you must contact the Overseas Citizens Services division of the US State Department (☎+1-202-501-4444, in US 888-407-4747).

COSTS

The cost of your trip will vary considerably, depending on where you visit, how you travel, and where you stay. The most significant expenses will probably be your round-trip (return) airfare to Israel (see **Getting to Israel: By Plane,** p. 20) and a bus pass.

STAYING ON A BUDGET

To give you a general idea, a bare-bones day in Israel (camping or sleeping in hostels/guesthouses, buying food at supermarkets) would cost about US$40 (NIS157); a slightly more comfortable day (sleeping in hostels/guesthouses and the occasional budget hotel, eating one meal per day at a restaurant, going out at night) would cost US$60-90 (NIS236-354); and, for a luxurious day, the sky's the limit. Don't forget to factor in emergency reserve funds (at least US$200).

TIPPING AND BARGAINING

THE ART OF THE DEAL. Bargaining in Israel is a given: no price is set in stone, and vendors and drivers will automatically quote you a price that is several times too high. It's up to you to get them down to a reasonable rate. With these tips and some finesse, you might impress even the most hardened hawkers:

1. **Bargaining needn't be a struggle laced with barbs.** Quite the opposite— good-natured wrangling with a cheerful face may prove your best weapon.
2. **Use your poker face.** The less your face betrays your interest in the item the better. If you touch an item to inspect it, the vendor will be sure to "encourage" you to name a price or make a purchase. Coming back again and again to admire a trinket is a good way of ensuring that you pay a ridiculously high price. Never get too enthusiastic about the object in question; point out flaws in workmanship and design. Be cool.
3. **Know when to bargain.** In most cases, it's quite clear when it's appropriate to bargain. Most private transportation fares and things for sale in outdoor markets are all fair game. Don't bargain on prepared or pre-packaged foods on the street or in restaurants. In some stores, signs will indicate whether "fixed prices" prevail. When in doubt, ask tactfully, "Is that your lowest price?" or whether discounts are given.
4. **Never underestimate the power of peer pressure.** Bargaining with more than one person at a time always leads to higher prices. Alternatively, try having a friend discourage you from your purchase—if you seem to be reluctant, the merchant will want to drop the price to interest you again.
5. **Know when to turn away.** Feel free to refuse any vendor or driver who bargains rudely and don't hesitate to move on to another vendor if one will not be reasonable about his final price. However, to start bargaining without an intention to buy is a major faux pas. Agreeing on a price and declining it is also poor form. Turn away slowly with a smile and "thank you" upon hearing a ridiculous price—it may plummet.
6. **Start low.** Never feel guilty offering a ludicrously low price. Your starting price should be no more than one-third to one-half the asking price.

A 10% tip will generally suffice in Israel. Bargaining—although discouraged in department stores supermarkets, drug stores, and restaurants with full-priced menus—is extremely common, especially at markets.

TAXES

Israel levies a **VAT (Value Added Tax)** of 15.5%, but it also offers a refund to tourists purchasing more than US$100 worth of goods at a shop approved by the Ministry of Tourism. To collect the refund, you must hold a foreign passport, be a non-Israeli citizen, and pay for your purchase in foreign currency (cash or international credit cards). Approved stores will be marked; look for the Ministry of Tourism insignia or a sign reading "VAT Refund." In order to collect your refund, you will need to present a VAT receipt at the point of departure from Israel (if you are leaving from **Ben-Gurion International Airport,** go to the refund counter of Change Place Ltd.). Be sure to ask for the invoice and fill it out in the shop. Both your purchase and the invoice must be sealed in a bag at the shop and must remain sealed until your departure. Pack the sealed bag in your hand luggage, as you will need to present it for inspection. The official will stamp the invoice and refund the VAT in US dollars; if the bank cannot scrape together enough, the refund will be mailed to your home address. **Eurocheques** may be written in shekels and counted as foreign currency for discounts. The bank does charge a commission: US$2 on refunds of up to US$30; US$5 on refunds ranging from US$30 to US$100; and US$8 for refunds greater than US$100. If you leave Israel from a departure point other than Ben-Gurion Airport, the refund will be mailed to your foreign address with no charge. Note that no VAT is charged on items purchased in Eilat, which is a free trade zone. There is no VAT refund for the following items: food, drinks, tobacco products, electrical appliances, cameras, film or other photography equipment. For information on large purchases, consult the Ministry of Tourism (p. 304).

PACKING

Pack lightly: lay out only what you think you absolutely need, then pack half of the clothes and twice the money. The **Travelite FAQ** (www.travelite.org) is a good resource for tips on traveling light. The online **Universal Packing List** (http://upl. codeq.info) will generate a customized list of suggested items based on your trip length, the expected climate, your planned activities, and other factors. If you plan to do a lot of hiking, also consult **The Great Outdoors,** p. 31.

LIQUIDS IN THE AIR. Travelers should note new EU and US travel restrictions on liquids—including drinks, toiletries, and gels—on airplanes. At the time of printing, liquids could be transported only in containers of 100mL (3 fl. oz. in the US) or less. Each passenger could carry only as many containers as fit in a 1L (1 quart in the US) clear plastic bag. To avoid hassles, put as many of your liquids as possible in your checked luggage. Contact the Israel Airport Agency or Ben-Gurion International Airport for the latest policy.

Converters and adapters: In Israel, electricity is 230 volts AC, enough to fry any 120V North American appliance. Americans and Canadians should buy an **adapter** (which changes the shape of the plug; US$5) and a **converter** (which changes the voltage; US$10-30). Electrical outlets in Israel consist of Type H and Type C. Don't make the mistake of using only an adapter (unless appliance instructions explicitly state otherwise). Australians, Brits, and New Zealanders (who use 230V at home) won't need a converter but will need a set of adapters to use anything electrical. For more on all things adaptable, check out http://kropla.com/electric.htm.

SAFETY AND HEALTH

GENERAL ADVICE

In any type of crisis, the most important thing to do is **stay calm.** Your country's embassy abroad (p. 8) is usually your best resource in an emergency;

registering with that embassy upon arrival is a good idea. The government offices listed in the **Travel Advisories** box (p. 17) can provide information on the services they offer their citizens in case of emergencies abroad.

LOCAL LAWS AND POLICE

Israel is a country with an array of passionately practiced religions and cultures. Visitors should be aware of this at all times. For example, it is not wise to go into very orthodox Jewish areas of Jerusalem on Shabbat (Saturday). Also, during the holy month of Ramadan, Muslims (except children under the age of eight) fast, refusing food, drink, or smokes between sunrise and sunset. As a courtesy, visitors may wish to avoid drinking, eating and smoking in public places during Ramadan, though it is not required.

Israel has a well-respected and competent police force whose task it is to ensure order throughout the country. Along these lines, during periods of unrest, the Israeli Government sometimes closes off access to the West Bank and Gaza, which may be placed under curfew.

DRUGS AND ALCOHOL

In Israel, a meek "I didn't know it was illegal" will not suffice. Remember that you are subject to the laws of the country in which you travel, not to those of your home country; it is your responsibility to familiarize yourself with these laws before leaving. If you carry **prescription drugs** while you travel, it is vital to have a copy of the prescriptions themselves when you cross borders.

Israeli drug laws are not lenient. Cannabis is widely smoked and widely prosecuted. Sentences range from heavy fines to imprisonment, though foreigners are most likely to get deported. Police periodically sweep the hostels, especially in Eilat and some areas of Tel Aviv. Carrying quantities of cannabis of more than 15g or smuggling drugs across Israeli borders will land you in prison. The thorough security searches are meant to prevent terrorism, but there isn't much that slips through.

The drinking age in Israel is 18 and bars and discotheques are beginning to enforce it. Eilat in particular has begun to card stringently; a foreign driver's license usually serves as adequate identification. Avoid public drunkenness—it can jeopardize your safety and earn the disdain of locals.

SPECIFIC CONCERNS

The situation in Israel and the Palestinian territories is extremely volatile. Ongoing violence has caused considerable civilian death and injury, and tourists have been affected as well. At press time, the US State Department warns all US citizens to avoid travel to the Gaza Strip. If you do choose to visit, you should stay on top of current events so that you know where and when the risks are highest. Several web pages have up-to-date information, including the pages of the US Embassy in Israel (http://usembassy-israel.org.il) and the US State Department (http://travel.state.gov/travel/cis_pa_tw/cis/cis_1064.html).

NATURAL DISASTERS

EARTHQUAKES. Israel experiences regular earthquakes, especially near the Jordan Rift Valley, most of which are too small to be felt. If a strong earthquake does occur, it will probably last only one or two minutes. Open a door to provide an escape route and move underneath a sturdy doorway, table, or desk.

SANDSTORMS. These phenomena of airborne dust and sand are fueled by gusts of wind and sometimes occur during the spring and summer in Israel's desert south. If you find yourself caught in a sandstorm, cover your face with any sturdy fabric and run for the nearest shelter.

FLASH FLOODS. In Israel, flash floods are unpredictable in timing and intensity. Safety measures during a flash flood include getting to higher ground immediately, keeping an eye on rising water, and staying away from drainage systems and particularly low terrain most susceptible to flooding.

POLITICAL DEMONSTRATIONS

In the West Bank and Gaza, demonstrations are frequent and can occur without warning, always with the potential of evolving into more violent altercations. If such disturbances occur, visitors should leave the area immediately; if in Jerusalem's Old City, where exits are limited, seek refuge inside a shop or restaurant until the incident is over. Demonstrations are particularly dangerous in checkpoint areas, settlements, military areas, and major thoroughfares where protesters are likely to encounter Israeli security forces.

BLENDING IN

Tourists are particularly vulnerable because they often carry large amounts of cash and are not as street savvy as locals. Luckily, Israel has a very large immigrant population and many foreign (predominantly English-speaking) students, so not speaking Hebrew doesn't automatically scream "tourist." To avoid unwanted attention, try to blend in as much as possible. Visitors to Jerusalem should be extra cautious at religious sites on holy days (Fridays, Saturdays, and Sundays) and **dress appropriately** when visiting the Old City and ultra-orthodox Jewish neighborhoods. Most roads into these neighborhoods are blocked off on Friday nights, Saturdays, and Jewish holidays. Assaults on secular visitors, often for being "immodestly dressed," have been known to occur in these areas.

Cities covered in this book fall into three major categories of dress code: modest and religious (Jerusalem, Tzfat, the West Bank); immodest, secular, and down-right sexy (Tel Aviv, Eilat), where baggy jeans and a t-shirt might attract more attention than a mini-skirt and mesh tank top; and somewhere in between (Haifa, Be'er Sheva, and the rest of the country).

TERRORISM

More than most everywhere else, terrorism is a threat in Israel. Since its founding, Israel has been a target for many Palestinian nationalists and Islamic radicals. Travelers need not feel like powerless bystanders, however. The chances of becoming a victim of terrorism are relatively low and can be lowered further by taking certain precautions; you should be aware of the possibility of danger without letting it paralyze you.

Avoid crowded areas and visiting the West Bank or the Gaza Strip, especially in the days following the announcement of a new building project or on the anniversary of previous attacks. Traveling in the Palestinian territories can be dangerous, especially in a car with the yellow license plates that identify the vehicle as Israeli. Jewish travelers should avoid identifying themselves as such in certain areas. Simply placing a baseball cap over a *kippah* can prevent stares and hostility. Be aware of potential unrest in the West Bank by staying up to date with the news and contacting the consular division of the US Consulate General (see p. 9). **Public transportation** has been the target of several terrorist bombings, particularly local buses in Jerusalem and Tel Aviv. Most bus bombings have occurred in the early morning rush hour; if your plans are flexible, avoid bus travel at this time.

Despite these problems, travelers in Israel are more likely to be affected by anti-terrorist measures than by terrorism itself. The Israeli soldiers on every corner are there for your protection, but the prevalence of gun-toting 20-year-olds can be a little shocking. Do not leave bags unattended in public places; they will be dealt with in a serious manner. In the past, bombs have been left in trash cans (which now have only small receptacles) or on street corners. They will generally be destroyed within minutes. Finally, expect stringent security measures, including bag searches or metal detectors, at museums, bus stations, shopping malls, and public events.

In times of emergency, the Israeli government has had the responsibility to supply the entire population with gas masks. The ministry of tourism has declared that there are enough masks for all tourists; those residing in hotels will receive them directly from these hotels, while others can obtain them from designated department stores.

The Gaza War was fought between Israeli and Palestinian forces (mostly Hamas) and lasted from late December 2008 to January 18, 2009. As of the time of printing, the cease-fire remains fragile between the two parties and tensions are still relatively high. Travel to Gaza, the West Bank, and nearby areas is highly discouraged due to the risk of a re-escalation of violence and the ever-present threat of kidnapping raids by terrorist groups.

The box below lists offices to contact and websites to visit for the most updated list of your government's advisories about travel.

TRAVEL ADVISORIES. The following government offices provide travel information and advisories by telephone, by fax, or via the web:

Australian Department of Foreign Affairs and Trade: ☎+61 2 6261 1111; www.dfat.gov.au.

Canadian Department of Foreign Affairs and International Trade (DFAIT): ☎+1-800-267-8376; www.dfait-maeci.gc.ca. Call or visit the webside for the free booklet *Bon Voyage... But.*

New Zealand Ministry of Foreign Affairs: ☎+64 4 439 8000; www.mfat.govt.nz.

United Kingdom Foreign and Commonwealth Office: ☎+44 20 7008 1500; www.fco.gov.uk.

US Department of State: ☎+1-888-407-4747, from abroad 202-501-4444; http://travel.state.gov.

PERSONAL SAFETY

EXPLORING AND TRAVELING

Familiarize yourself with your surroundings before setting out and carry yourself with confidence. Check maps in shops and restaurants rather than on the street. If you are traveling alone, be sure someone at home knows your itinerary and **never tell anyone you are by yourself.** When walking at night, stick to busy, well-lit streets and avoid dark alleyways. If you ever feel uncomfortable, leave the area as quickly and directly as you can. There is no sure-fire way to avoid all the threatening situations that you might encounter while traveling, but a good **self-defense course** will give you concrete ways to react to unwanted advances. **Impact, Prepare,** and **Model Mugging** (www.modelmugging.org) can refer you to local self-defense courses in Australia, Canada, Switzerland, and the US.

If you are using a car, learn local driving signals and wear a seat belt. Children under 40 lb. should ride only in specially designed car seats, available for a small fee from most car-rental agencies. Study route maps before you hit the road and, if you plan on spending a lot of time driving, consider bringing spare parts. For long drives in desolate areas, invest in a cell phone and a roadside assistance program (p. 25). Park your vehicle in a garage or well-traveled area and use a steering-wheel locking device in larger cities. Sleeping in your car is the most dangerous way to get your rest. For info on the perils of **hitchhiking,** see p. 26.

POSSESSIONS AND VALUABLES

Never leave your belongings unattended; crime can occur in even the most safe-looking hostel or hotel. Bring your own padlock for hostel lockers and don't ever store valuables in a locker. Be particularly careful on **buses** and **trains;** horror stories abound about determined thieves who wait for travelers to fall asleep. Carry your bag or purse in front of you where you can see it. When traveling with others, sleep in alternate shifts. When alone, be careful in selecting a train compartment: never stay in an empty one and always use a lock to secure your pack to the luggage rack. Use extra caution if traveling at night. Try to sleep on top bunks with your luggage stored above you (if not in bed with you) and keep important documents and other valuables on you at all times.

There are a few steps you can take to minimize the financial risk associated with traveling. First, **bring as little with you as possible.** Second, buy a few combination **padlocks** to secure your belongings either in your pack or in a hostel or train-station locker. Third, **carry as little cash as possible.** Keep your traveler's checks and ATM/credit cards in a **money belt**—not a "fanny pack"—along with your passport and ID cards. Fourth, **keep a small cash reserve separate from your primary stash.** This should be about US$50 (US dollars or euro are best) sewn into or stored in the depths of your pack, along with your traveler's check numbers and photocopies of your important documents.

In large cities like Tel Aviv, **con artists** often work in groups and may involve children. Beware of certain classics: sob stories that require money, rolls of bills "found" on the street, mustard spilled (or saliva spit) onto your shoulder to distract you while they snatch your bag. **Never let your passport or your bags out of your sight.** Hostel workers will sometimes stand at bus and train arrival points to recruit tired and disoriented travelers to their hostel; never believe strangers who tell you that theirs is the only hostel open. Beware of **pickpockets** in city crowds, especially on public transportation. Also, be alert in public telephone booths. If you must say your calling-card number, do so very quietly; if you punch it in, make sure no one can look over your shoulder.

If you will be traveling with electronic devices, such as a laptop computer or MP3 player, check whether your homeowner's insurance covers loss, theft, or damage when you travel. If not, you might consider purchasing a low-cost separate insurance policy. **Safeware** (☎+1-800-800-1492; www.safeware.com) specializes in covering computers and charges US$90 for 90-day comprehensive international travel coverage up to US$4000.

PRE-DEPARTURE HEALTH

In your passport, write the names of any people you wish to be contacted in case of a medical emergency and list any allergies or medical conditions. Matching a prescription to a foreign equivalent is not always easy, safe, or possible, so, if you take **prescription drugs,** carry up-to-date prescriptions or a statement from your doctor stating the medications' trade names, manufacturers, chemical names, and dosages. While traveling, be sure to keep all medication with you in your carry-on luggage.

IMMUNIZATIONS AND PRECAUTIONS

Travelers over two years old should make sure that the following vaccines are up to date: MMR (for measles, mumps, and rubella); DTaP or Td (for diphtheria, tetanus, and pertussis); IPV (for polio); Hib (for *Haemophilus influenzae* B); and HepB (for Hepatitis B). For recommendations on immunizations and prophylaxis, consult the Centers for Disease Control and Prevention (CDC; below) in the US or the equivalent in your home country and check with a doctor for guidance.

INSURANCE

Travel insurance covers four basic areas: medical/health problems, property loss, trip cancellation/interruption, and emergency evacuation. Though regular insurance policies may well extend to travel-related accidents, you may consider purchasing separate travel insurance if the cost of potential trip cancellation, interruption, or emergency medical evacuation is greater than you can absorb. Prices for travel insurance purchased separately generally run about US$50 per week for full coverage, while trip cancellation/interruption may be purchased separately at a rate of US$3-5 per day, depending on length of stay.

Medical insurance (especially university policies) often covers costs incurred abroad; check with your provider. **Homeowners' insurance** (or your family's coverage) often covers theft during travel and loss of travel documents (passport, plane ticket, railpass, etc.) up to US$500. **American Express** (☎+1-800-528-4800) grants most cardholders automatic collision and theft car-rental insurance on rentals made with the card.

STAYING HEALTHY

Common sense is the simplest prescription for good health while you travel. Drink lots of fluids to prevent dehydration and constipation and wear sturdy, broken-in shoes and clean socks.

ONCE IN ISRAEL

ENVIRONMENTAL HAZARDS

Heat exhaustion and dehydration: Heat exhaustion, characterized by dehydration and salt deficiency, can lead to fatigue, headaches, and wooziness. Drink plenty of fluids (when hiking drink a liter every hr.), eat salty foods (e.g. crackers), and avoid dehydrating beverages (e.g. alcohol, coffee, tea, and caffeinated soda). Wear a hat, sunglasses, and a lightweight long-sleeved shirt in hot sun. Continuous heat stress can eventually lead to **heatstroke,** characterized by a rising temperature, severe headache, and cessation of sweating. Victims should be cooled off with wet towels and taken to a doctor.

Sunburn: As a general rule, always wear sunscreen (SPF 30 or higher) when spending significant amounts of time outdoors. If you get sunburned, drink more fluids than usual and apply an aloe-based lotion. Severe sunburns can lead to sun poisoning, a condition that can cause fever, chills, nausea, and vomiting. Sun poisoning should always be treated by a doctor. Be mindful of particularly sunny areas of Israel such as the Jordan Rift Valley and Eilat. If you're heading toward the Negev or Golan, particularly hiking, buy sunscreen in the city and bring it with you.

INSECT-BORNE DISEASES

Many diseases are transmitted by insects—mainly mosquitoes, fleas, ticks, and lice—especially West Nile Virus in Israel. Be aware of insects in wet or forested areas, especially while hiking and camping. Wear long pants and long sleeves, tuck your pants into your socks, and use a mosquito net. Use insect repellents such as DEET and soak or spray your gear with permethrin (licensed in the US only for use on clothing). **Mosquitoes**—responsible for West Nile virus—can be particularly abundant in wet, swampy, or wooded areas.

> **West Nile virus (WNV):** Mostly spread through mosquito bites, West Nile is a viral infection that within 3-14 days causes symptoms such as nausea, headache, high fever, coma, convulsions, and vision loss, though approximately 80% of infected people will show no symptoms whatsoever. The young and the old are the most affected. Although the most severe cases took place in 2000, it is still best to be cautious and prevent WNV by using insect repellents and wearing light-weight long-sleeved shirts and pants.

OTHER HEALTH CONCERNS

MEDICAL CARE ON THE ROAD

Israel overall conforms to the standard of healthcare found in the West. For minor illnesses, go to a **pharmacy.** Israeli law requires that at least one pharmacy in a neighborhood be open or on call at all times. Pharmacists offer expert advice as well as medication and most speak English. In more serious situations, see a doctor. Almost all Israeli doctors speak nearly fluent English. Despite its socialized and universal healthcare, private practice is very expensive, and medical insurance is a must. Medical care in Israel is generally more available and of higher quality than in the Palestinian territories.

If you are concerned about obtaining medical assistance while traveling, you may wish to employ special support services. The **International Association for Medical Assistance to Travelers** (**IAMAT**; in the US ☎+1-716-754-4883, in Canada +1-416-652-0137; www.iamat.org) has free membership, lists English-speaking doctors worldwide, and offers details on immunization requirements and sanitation. For those whose insurance doesn't apply abroad, you can purchase additional coverage (see previous page).

GETTING TO ISRAEL

BY PLANE

When it comes to airfare, a little effort can save you a bundle. Courier fares are the cheapest for those whose plans are flexible enough to deal with the restrictions. For those with flexibility *and* patience, **standby flights** are one way to save; call major airline companies for details. Tickets sold by consolidators are also good deals, but last-minute specials and airfare wars often beat these fares. The key is to hunt around, be flexible, and ask about discounts. Students, seniors, and those under 26 should never pay full price for a ticket.

AIRFARES

Airfares to Israel peak between mid-June and mid-August; holidays are also expensive. The cheapest times to travel are spring and fall. Midweek

(M-Th morning) round-trip flights run cheaper than weekend flights, but they are generally more crowded and less likely to permit frequent-flier upgrades. Not fixing a return date ("open return") or arriving in and departing from different cities ("open-jaw") can be pricier than round-trip flights. Patching one-way flights together is the most expensive way to travel. Flights between Israel's capitals or regional hubs—Ben-Guiron International Airport near Tel Aviv and Ovda International Airport in Eilat are among the most frequented—will tend to be cheaper.

If Israel is only one stop on a more extensive globe-hop, consider a round-the-world (RTW) ticket. Tickets usually include at least five stops and are valid for about a year; prices range US$3000-8000. Try the airline consortiums **Oneworld** (www.oneworld.com), **Skyteam** (www.skyteam.com), and **Star Alliance** (www.staralliance.com).

Fares for round-trip flights to Tel Aviv from the US or Canadian east coast cost US$1000-2900 in the low season (Sept.-May.); from the US or Canadian west coast US$1100-2000/1400-2700; from the UK, UK£300-400/300-360.

BUDGET AND STUDENT TRAVEL AGENCIES

While knowledgeable agents specializing in flights to Israel can make your life easy, they may not spend the time to find you the lowest possible fare—they get paid on commission. Travelers holding ISICs and IYTCs (p. 10) qualify for big discounts from student travel agencies. Most flights from budget agencies are on major airlines, but in high season some may sell seats on less reliable chartered aircraft.

The Adventure Travel Company, 124 MacDougal St., New York City, NY 10021 (☎+1-212-674-2887; www.theadventuretravelcompany.com). Offices across Canada and the US including New York City, San Diego, San Francisco, and Seattle.

STA Travel, 2871 Broadway, New York City, NY 10025 (24hr. reservations and info ☎+1-800-781-4040; www.statravel.com). A student and youth travel organization with offices worldwide, including US offices in Los Angeles, New York City, Seattle, Washington, DC, and a number of other college towns. Ticket booking, travel insurance, railpasses, and more. Walk-in offices are located throughout Australia (☎+61 134 782), New Zealand (☎+64 0800 474 400), and the UK (☎+44 8712 230 0040).

FLIGHT PLANNING ON THE INTERNET. The internet may be the budget traveler's dream when it comes to finding and booking bargain fares, but the array of options can be overwhelming. Many airline sites offer special last-minute deals on the web.

STA (www.statravel.com) and **StudentUniverse** (www.studentuniverse.com) provide quotes on student tickets, while **Orbitz** (www.orbitz.com), **Expedia** (www.expedia.com), and **Travelocity** (www.travelocity.com) offer full travel services. **Priceline** (www.priceline.com) lets you specify a price and obligates you to buy any ticket that meets or beats it; **Hotwire** (www.hotwire.com) offers bargain fares but won't reveal the airline or flight times until you buy. Other sites that compile deals include www.bestfares.com, www.flights.com, www.lowestfare.com, www.onetravel.com, and www.travelzoo.com.

Cheapflights (www.cheapflights.co.uk) is a useful search engine for finding—you guessed it—cheap flights. **Booking Buddy** (www.bookingbuddy.com), **Kayak** (www.kayak.com), and **SideStep** (www.sidestep.com) are online tools that let you enter your trip information and search multiple sites at once. *Let's Go* does not endorse any of these websites. As always, be cautious and research companies before you hand over your credit card number.

TRAVELING FROM NORTH AMERICA

Standard commercial carriers like **American** (☎+1-800-433-7300; www.aa.com) and **United** (☎+1-800-538-2929; www.ual.com) generally offer the most convenient flights, but they may not be the cheapest, unless you snag a special promotion or airfare-war ticket. You will probably find a better deal from one of the following "discount" airlines, if any of their limited departure points is convenient for you.

Air France: ☎+1-800-237-2747; www.airfrance.us. Tickets available from New York, Boston, and Miami to Tel Aviv (US$1600).

British Airways: ☎+1-800-247-9297; www.britishairways.com. Tickets available from New York, Boston and other cities to Tel Aviv (US$1500).

TRAVELING FROM IRELAND AND THE UK

British Airways: ☎+44 0844 493 0 787; www.britishairways.com. Tickets available from London, Dublin among others to Tel Aviv (UK£262).

KLM: ☎+44 0871 222 7740; www.klmuk.com. Cheap tickets to from London, Dublin, and elsewhere to Tel Aviv (UK£307).

TRAVELING FROM AUSTRALIA AND NEW ZEALAND

From Australia and New Zealand, there are limited direct flights to Israel. The best bet to reach Israel is to connect through Europe through one of the discount airlines outlined above. Look for consolidator ads in the travel section of the Sydney Morning Herald and other papers for more information.

BY BOAT AND BY LAND

Ferries depart from Israel for Greece and Cyprus and from Sharm al-Sheikh for Hurghada in Egypt. For more information see **Tel Aviv** (p. 158), **Haifa** (p. 201), and **Sharm al-Sheikh** (p. 407). Visitors can also cross into Israel through its myriad borders with Egypt and Jordan, the two countries in the region with which it has peaceful relations. Given the recent upsurge in violence, border crossings are regularly fluctuating, so check with local police or military officials for of-the-moment accessibility.

BORDER CROSSINGS

Tourists can cross into Egypt from Eilat at the Taba border crossing. For Sinai stays of 14 days or less, get a Sinai-only visa stamp on the Egyptian side of the border. This visa limits travel to the Gulf of Aqaba coast as far south as Sharm al-Sheikh (but not the area around Sharm al-Sheikh, including Ras Muhammad) and to St. Catherine's monastery and Mt. Sinai (but not sites in the vicinity of St. Catherine's). Unlike ordinary one-month Egyptian visas, the Sinai-only visa has no grace period; you'll pay a hefty fine if you overextend your stay. For more border crossing information into **Egypt,** see p. 391.

There are three border crossings from Israel into Jordan (or vice versa): one in Jericho (p. 385) at the King Hussein/Allenby Bridge in the West Bank, one near Beit She'an (p. 258) in the North of Israel, and one close to Eilat (p. 383). Travelers to Petra usually cross at Eilat, which is only a few hours away.

GETTING AROUND ISRAEL

BY TRAIN

Trains in Israel are generally comfortable, convenient, and reasonably swift, but they stop during Shabbat. Second-class compartments are great places to meet fellow travelers. Trains, however, are not always safe; for safety tips, see (p. 17). For train schedules, check out the **Israel Railways** website at www.israrail.org.il.

BY BUS

In Israel, buses are the most popular and most convenient mode of transportation. Except for the **Dan Company** (☎03 639 44 44) in Tel Aviv and the **Arab buses** serving the West Bank, Galilee, and Gaza, the **Egged Bus Cooperative** (www.egged.co.il) has a monopoly on intercity and most intracity buses in Israel. The modern, air-conditioned buses are either direct (*yashir*), express, or local (*me'asef*). Students with ISICs receive a 10% discount on some fares; show your ID first to the ticket seller, then to the driver, then to the ticket inspector. Buses can get crowded, especially on Saturday nights after Shabbat and during morning and afternoon rush hours.

Most bus stations have printed schedules, often in English. Egged has an intercity information line at ☎03 694 88 88. Signs in stations direct you to buy your ticket at the ticket window. This is only really necessary for highly-traveled, long-distance routes; otherwise, buy the ticket from the driver. Most local bus rides cost NIS5. A season ticket (*kartisia*), available from any bus driver, gives you 10 local rides for the price of 7 (NIS45); a one month pass that includes unlimited local rides in Haifa, Jerusalem, and Tel Aviv costs NIS200. Buses between cities usually leave from the central bus station. Roundtrip (or two-trip) tickets may be 15% cheaper.

BY CAR

Generally, cars offer speed, freedom, access to the countryside, and an escape from the town-to-town mentality of trains. The US State Department advises caution while driving in Israel because of its notoriety for crowded roads.

DRIVING PERMITS AND CAR INSURANCE

INTERNATIONAL DRIVING PERMIT (IDP)

If you plan to drive a car while in Israel, you must be over 21 and have an International Driving Permit (IDP).

Your IDP, valid for one year, must be issued in your own country before you depart. An application for an IDP usually requires one or two photos, a current local license, an additional form of identification, and a fee. To apply, contact your home country's automobile association. Be vigilant when purchasing an IDP online or anywhere other than your home automobile association. Many vendors sell permits of questionable legitimacy for higher prices.

CAR INSURANCE

Most credit cards cover standard insurance. If you rent, lease, or borrow a car, you will need a **green card,** or **International Insurance Certificate,** to certify that you have liability insurance and that it applies abroad. Green cards can be obtained at car-rental agencies, car dealers (for those leasing cars), some travel agents, and some border crossings. Rental agencies may require you to purchase theft insurance in countries that they consider to have a high risk of auto theft.

RENTING

RENTAL AGENCIES

You can generally make reservations before you leave by calling major international offices in your home country. It's a good idea to cross-check this information with local agencies as well. The local desk numbers are included in town listings; for home-country numbers, call your toll-free directory. Most car rental services have offices in major cities and at the Ben-Gurion International Airport.

To rent a car from most establishments in Israel, you need to be at least 21 years old. Some agencies require renters to be 25, and most charge those aged 21-24 an additional insurance fee (around US$7 per day). Small local operations occasionally rent to people under 21, but be sure to ask about the insurance coverage and deductible and always check the fine print.

Car rental in Israel is available through the following agencies:

Avis (in Israel ☎+972 03 617 00 00; www.avis.com).

Budget (in Israel ☎+972 03 935 00 00; in the US ☎+1-800-527-0700, outside the US ☎+1-800-472-3325; www.budgetrentacar.com).

Eldan (in Israel ☎+972 06 565 45 45; www.eldan.co.il).

Hertz (in Israel ☎+972 03 684 10 56; in the US ☎+1-800-654-3131, outside the US ☎+1-800-654-3001; www.hertz.com).

Shlomo Sixt (in Israel ☎1 700 501 502; www.shlomo.co.il).

COSTS AND INSURANCE

Rental prices are usually US$100-300 per week, plus tax (15-25%), for a tiny car. Expect to pay more for larger cars and for four-wheel drive. Reserve ahead and pay in advance if at all possible. Always check if prices quoted include tax and collision insurance; some credit card companies provide insurance, allowing their customers to decline the collision damage waiver. However, cars rented on an **American Express** or **Visa/MasterCard Gold** or **Platinum** credit card in Israel might not carry the automatic insurance that they would in some other countries; check with your credit card company. Ask about discounts and check the terms of insurance, particularly the size of the deductible. The minimum rental age in Israel is usually 21; renters must possess an international credit card, a passport and a driver's license printed in English or an International Driving Permit with a non-English license. It is always significantly less expensive to reserve a car from the US than from Israel.

Remember that, if you are driving a conventional rental vehicle on an unpaved road in a rental car, you are almost never covered by insurance; ask about this before leaving the rental agency. Insurance plans from rental companies almost always come with an **excess** of around US$400-800 for conventional vehicles. This means that the insurance bought from the rental company only applies to damages over the excess; damages up to that amount must be covered by your existing insurance plan. Some rental companies in Israel require you to buy a **collision damage waiver (CDW),** which will waive the excess in the case of a collision. **Loss damage waivers (LDWs)** do the same in the case of theft or vandalism.

National chains often allow one-way rentals (picking up in one city and dropping off in another). There is usually a minimum hire period and sometimes an extra dropoff charge of several hundred dollars.

ON THE ROAD

In Israel, like in the United States and most other countries, cars drive on the right side of the road and the steering wheel is on the left side of the car. Israeli law dictates that all car passengers wear seat belts at all times and cell phone use is strictly prohibited while behind the wheel. Intercity drivers are also required to use headlights during daylight as well as nighttime hours during the winter, and carry a florescent vest with them at all times to be worn when replacing tires or making repairs. These vests may be purchased at most convenience stores or gas stations. Most traffic signs in Israel are tri-lingual, including English, Hebrew, and Arabic, though many are rendered in poor translations. Speed limits are normally around 30-40mph in the city and 60-70mph on highways. The only toll road in Israel is the north-south Road Number 6; due to its relative novelty, parts of it are still under construction. Gasoline (petrol) prices vary, but they average about US$1.30 per liter.

 TRANSLITERATION STATION. *Let's Go* does its best to include the names of towns in Hebrew and Arabic as well as their standard English transliterations; that said, many towns have numerous—and counterintuitive—transliteration variants. Try pronouncing things aloud—Tsfat and Sefad aren't so far off. For more details, see p. 57.

DANGERS

The roads and highways in Israel tend to be fairly crowded, especially near urban areas. The **Association for Safe International Road Travel** (www.asirt.org) advises drivers in Israel to keep a look out for and steer clear of aggressive and careless drivers. Drivers in the West Bank and Gaza should be extra careful; during heightened tensions, cars with Israeli license plates can be targeted.

 DRIVING PRECAUTIONS. When traveling in the summer or in the desert, bring substantial amounts of water (a suggested 5L of water per person per day) for drinking and for the radiator. You should always carry a spare tire and jack, jumper cables, extra oil, flares, a flashlight, and heavy blankets (in case your car breaks down at night or in the winter). If you don't know how to change a tire, learn before heading out, especially if you are planning on traveling in deserted areas. If your car breaks down, stay in your vehicle.

CAR ASSISTANCE

Information about Israel's primary auto assistance organization, **Memsi,** can be found at www.memsi.co.il, though the website is exclusively in Hebrew.

BY TAXI AND SHERUT

Israeli companies offer both private and less expensive **sherut** (shared) taxis. Regular private taxi rides are called *special* (pronounced "spatial"). City taxis operating as *special* must use a meter *(moneh);* make sure the driver turns it on. Offers of unspecified "discount" rates (translation: no meter and an exorbitant fare) should be adamantly refused. If you can estimate a decent price, you'll get a better rate by setting the price before you enter the taxi. Taxi drivers do not expect tips but accept them.

Sherut taxis hold up to seven people and operate like a bus service only with an added convenience of stopping wherever needed. Certain companies operate *sherut* taxis daily from offices in each city. Intercity *sherut* operate on loose schedules, departing when they fill up; on Saturdays, they often whiz along the streets in search of passengers. Intracity *sherut* never follow a schedule. Most routes have set fares comparable to bus prices; ask for quotes at tourist offices or from the nearest Israeli. Always settle on a price before you depart.

BY THUMB

 LET'S NOT GO. *Let's Go* urges you to consider the risks before you choose to hitch. We do not recommend hitching as a safe means of transportation, and none of the information presented here is intended to do so.

No one should hitchhike without careful consideration of the risks involved. Hitching means entrusting your life to a random person who happens to stop beside you on the road, and hitchers always risk theft, assault, sexual harassment, and unsafe driving. Hitchhiking at night can be particularly dangerous.

The incidence of sexual harassment and assault has increased dramatically in recent years. License plates carry meaning: yellow are Israeli, black with an "m" are army, red are police, blue or gray are from occupied territories, and white are diplomatic. Those who hitch in the **Negev** or **Golan** (where sometimes the only option is a military vehicle) run the risk of getting a ride that doesn't go all the way to their destination, in which case they are stranded. Keep in mind that it is considered especially dangerous to hitchhike in the West Bank. *Tremping*, as hitchhiking is called, is not what it used to be in Israel.

KEEPING IN TOUCH

BY EMAIL AND INTERNET

All in all, Israel is a highly networked and internet-savvy country, as illustrated by the Israeli Defense Force's YouTube channel and the New York Israeli Consulate General's Twitter. Although in some places it's possible to forge a remote link with your home server, in most cases this is a much slower (and thus more expensive) option than taking advantage of free **web-based email accounts** (e.g., ⬛**www.gmail.com**). **Internet cafes** and the occasional free internet terminal at a public library, university or hotel are listed in the **Practical Information** sections of major cities. For lists of additional cybercafes in Israel, check out www.cybercaptive.com.

Laptop users can occasionally find internet cafes that will allow them to connect their laptops to the internet. Travelers with wireless-enabled computers may be able to take advantage of an increasing number of internet "hot spots," where they can get online for free or for a small fee. Newer computers can detect these hot spots automatically; otherwise, websites like www.jiwire.com, www.wififreespot.com, and www.wi-fihotspotlist.com can help you find them. For information on insuring your laptop while traveling, see p. 18.

WARY WI-FI. Wireless hot spots make internet access possible in public and remote places. Unfortunately, they also pose **security risks.** Hot spots are public, open networks that use unencrypted, unsecured connections. They are susceptible to hacks and "packet sniffing"—the theft of passwords and other private information. To prevent problems, disable "ad hoc" mode, turn off file sharing and network discovery, encrypt your email, turn on your firewall, beware of phony networks, and watch for over-the-shoulder creeps.

BY TELEPHONE

CALLING HOME FROM ISRAEL

Prepaid phone cards are a common and relatively inexpensive means of calling abroad. Each one comes with a Personal Identification Number (PIN) and a toll-free access number. You call the access number and then follow the directions for dialing your PIN. To purchase prepaid phone cards, check online for the best rates; www.callingcards.com is a good place to start. Online providers generally send your access number and PIN via email, with no actual "card" involved. You can also call home with prepaid phone cards purchased in Israel (see **Calling Within Israel,** p. 27).

Another option is to purchase a **calling card,** linked to a major national telecommunications service in your home country. Calls are billed collect or to your account. Cards generally come with instructions for dialing both domestically and internationally.

Placing a collect call through an international operator can be expensive but may be necessary in case of an emergency. You can frequently call collect without even possessing a company's calling card just by calling its access number and following the instructions.

PLACING INTERNATIONAL CALLS. To call Israel from home or to call home from Israel, dial:
1. The **international dialing prefix.** From **Australia,** dial ☎0011; **Canada** or the **US,** ☎011; **Ireland, New Zealand,** or the **UK,** and **Israel,** ☎00.
2. The **country code** of the country you want to call. To call **Australia,** dial ☎61; **Canada** or the **US,** ☎1; **Ireland,** ☎353; **New Zealand,** ☎64; the **UK,** ☎44; **Israel,** ☎972.
3. The **city/area code.** Let's Go lists the city/area codes for cities and towns in Israel opposite the city or town name, next to a ☎, as well as in every phone number. If the first digit is a zero (e.g., ☎03 for Tel Aviv), omit it when calling from abroad (e.g., dial ☎3 from Canada to reach Tel Aviv).
4. The **local number.**

CALLING WITHIN ISRAEL

The simplest way to call within Israel is to use a coin-operated phone. Prepaid phone cards (available at newspaper kiosks, gas stations, and tobacco stores) can save time and money in the long run. Phone rates typically tend to be highest in the morning, lower in the evening, and lowest on Sundays and at night.

CELLULAR PHONES

The international standard for cell phones is **Global System for Mobile Communication (GSM).** To make and receive calls in Israel, you will need a GSM-compatible phone and a **SIM (Subscriber Identity Module) card,** a country-specific, thumbnail-size chip that gives you a local phone number and plugs you into the local network. Many SIM cards are prepaid, and incoming calls are frequently free. You can buy additional cards or vouchers (usually available at convenience stores) to "top up" your phone. For more information on GSM phones, check out www.telestial.com. Companies like **Cellular Abroad** (www.cellularabroad.com) rent cell phones that work in a variety of destinations around the world.

 GSM PHONES. Just having a GSM phone doesn't mean you're necessarily good to go when you travel abroad. The majority of GSM phones sold in the US operate on a different frequency (1900) than international phones (900/1800) and will not work abroad. Tri-band phones work on all three frequencies (900/1800/1900) and will operate through most of the world. Additionally, some GSM phones are SIM-locked and will only accept SIM cards from a single carrier. You'll need a SIM-unlocked phone to use a SIM card from a local carrier when you travel.

TIME DIFFERENCES

The entirety of Israel is 2hr. ahead of Greenwich Mean Time (GMT) and observes Daylight Saving Time.

BY MAIL

SENDING MAIL HOME FROM ISRAEL

Airmail is the best way to send mail home from Israel. **Aerogrammes,** printed sheets that fold into envelopes and travel via airmail, are available at post offices. Write "airmail" or *"par avion"* on the front. Most post offices will charge exorbitant fees or simply refuse to send aerogrammes with enclosures. Surface mail is by far the cheapest and slowest way to send mail. It takes one to two months to cross the Atlantic and one to three to cross the Pacific—good for heavy items you won't need for a while.

SENDING MAIL TO ISRAEL

To ensure timely delivery, mark envelopes "airmail" or *"par avion."* In addition to the standard postage system whose rates are listed below, **Federal Express** (☎+1-800-463-3339; www.fedex.com) handles express mail services from most countries to Israel. Sending a postcard within Israel costs NIS1.60, while sending letters (up to 20g) domestically requires NIS1.60.

There are several ways to arrange pickup of letters sent to you while you are abroad. Mail can be sent via **Poste Restante** (General Delivery) to almost any city or town in Israel with a post office, and it is very reliable. Address Poste Restante letters like so:

ESSENTIALS

Jesus CHRIST of Nazareth
Poste Restante
Jerusalem, Israel

The mail will go to a special desk in the central post office, unless you specify a post office by street address or postal code. It's best to use the largest post office, since mail may be sent there regardless. It is usually safer and quicker, though more expensive, to send mail express or registered. Bring your passport (or other photo ID) for pickup. If the clerks insist that there is nothing for you, ask them to check under your first name as well. *Let's Go* lists post offices in the **Practical Information** section for each city and most towns.

American Express has travel offices throughout the world that offer a free **Client Letter Service** (mail held up to 30 days and forwarded upon request) for cardholders who contact them in advance. Some offices provide these services to non-cardholders (especially AmEx Travelers Cheque holders), but call ahead to make sure. For a complete list of AmEx locations, call ☎+1-800-528-4800 or visit www.americanexpress.com/travel.

ESSENTIALS

ACCOMMODATIONS

HOSTELS

Many hostels are laid out dorm-style, often with large single-sex rooms and bunk beds, although private rooms that sleep from two to four are becoming more common. They sometimes have kitchens and utensils for your use, breakfast and other meals, storage areas, laundry facilities, internet, transportation to airports, and bike or moped rentals. However, there can be drawbacks: some hostels impose a maximum stay, close during certain daytime "lockout" hours, have a curfew, don't accept reservations, or, less frequently, require that you do chores. In Israel, a dorm bed in a hostel will average around US$10 (NIS40) and a private room around US$15-20 (NIS60-80).

 A HOSTELER'S BILL OF RIGHTS. There are certain standard features that we do not include in our hostel listings. Unless we state otherwise, you can expect that every hostel has no lockout, no curfew, free hot showers, air conditioning, some system of secure luggage storage, and no key deposit.

HOSTELLING INTERNATIONAL

Joining the youth hostel association in your own country (listed below) automatically grants you membership privileges in **Hostelling International (HI),** a federation of national hosteling associations. Non-HI members may be allowed to stay in some hostels, but they will have to pay extra to do so. HI hostels are scattered throughout Israel and are typically less expensive than private hostels. HI's umbrella organization's website (www.hihostels.com), which lists the web addresses and phone numbers of all national associations, can be a great place to begin researching hosteling in a specific region. Other hosteling websites include www.hostels.com and www.hostelplanet.com.

Most student travel agencies (p. 21) sell HI cards, as do all of the national hosteling organizations listed below.

Australian Youth Hostels Association (AYHA), 422 Kent St., Sydney, NSW 2000 (☎+61 2 9261 1111; www.yha.com.au). AUS$42, under 26 AUS$32.

Hostelling International-Canada (HI-C), 205 Catherine St., Ste. 400, Ottawa, ON K2P 1C3 (☎+1-613-237-7884; www.hihostels.ca). CDN$35, under 18 free.

Hostelling International Northern Ireland (HINI), 22-32 Donegall Rd., Belfast BT12 5JN (☎+44 28 9032 4733; www.hini.org.uk). UK£15, under 25 UK£10.

Youth Hostels Association (England and Wales), Trevelyan House, Dimple Rd., Matlock, Derbyshire DE4 3YH (☎+44 1629 592 600; www.yha.org.uk). UK£16, under 26 UK£10.

Youth Hostels Association of New Zealand Inc. (YHANZ), Level 1, 166 Moorhouse Ave., P.O. Box 436, Christchurch (☎+64 3 379 9970, in NZ 0800 278 299; www.yha.org.nz). NZ$40, under 18 free.

Hostelling International-USA, 8401 Colesville Rd., Ste. 600, Silver Spring, MD 20910 (☎+1-301-495-1240; www.hiayh.org). US$28, under 18 free.

OTHER TYPES OF ACCOMMODATIONS

YMCAS

Young Men's Christian Association (YMCA) lodgings are usually cheaper than a hotel but more expensive than a hostel. Not all locations offer lodging; those that do are often located in urban areas. Many YMCAs accept women and families; some will not lodge those under 18 without parental permission.

Jerusalem International YMCA, 26 King David Street, P. O. Box 294, Jerusalem, Israel 91002 (☎+972 02 569 26 92; www.jerusalemymca.org). Contains a few accommodation options within its bounds, including some hotels.

HOTELS, GUESTHOUSES, AND PENSIONS

Hotel singles in Israel cost about US$100-190 (NIS395-750) per night, doubles US$180-220 (NIS710-870). If you make **reservations** in writing, indicate your night of arrival and the number of nights you plan to stay. The hotel will send you a confirmation and may request payment for the first night.

BED AND BREAKFASTS (B&BS)

For a cozy alternative to impersonal hotel rooms, B&Bs (private homes with rooms available to travelers) range from acceptable to sublime. Rooms in B&Bs generally cost US$50-100 for a single and US$70-150 for a double in Israel. Many websites provide listings for B&Bs; check out **BedandBreakfast.com** (www. bedandbreakfast.com) and **Bed and Breakfast In Israel** (www.b-and-b.co.il).

UNIVERSITY DORMS

Many **colleges** and **universities** open their residence halls to travelers when school is not in session; some do so even during term time. Getting a room may take a couple of phone calls and require advanced planning, but rates tend to be low, and many offer free local calls and internet access.

Hebrew University of Jerusalem, The Maiersdorf Faculty Club, Mt. Scopus, Jerusalem 91905 (☎+972 02 581 92 66; www.bmfc.huji.ac.il/eng/default.asp).

University of Haifa, Mount Carmel, Haifa 31905 (+972 04 8240111; http://hudorms. haifa.ac.il/html/framesets_eng/english.htm).

LONG-TERM ACCOMMODATIONS

Travelers planning to stay in Israel for extended periods of time may find it most cost-effective to rent an **apartment**. A basic one-bedroom (or studio) apartment in Jerusalem will range US$800-1600 (NIS3500-6500) per month. Besides the rent itself, prospective tenants usually are also required to front a security deposit (frequently 1 month's rent). It is also wise to have a rental agreement reviewed by an attorney to ensure that you are not overlooking or are not caught unaware of any existing Israeli laws differing from your home country. Rentals are ideal for families with children or travelers with special dietary needs as you often get your own kitchen, maid service, TV, and telephones.

For detailed and frequently updated listings in Haifa, Jerusalem and Tel Aviv, pay a visit to the handy and miraculous **craigslist** at its Israel site (http://geo.craigslist.org/iso/il).

THE GREAT OUTDOORS

The **Great Outdoor Recreation Page** (www.gorp.com) provides excellent general information for travelers planning on camping or enjoying the outdoors.

CAMPING AND NATIONAL PARKS

Israel's campsites usually provide electricity, sanitary facilities, public telephones, first aid, a restaurant or store, a night guard, and on-site or nearby swimming areas. In July and August most sites charge NIS20-50 per night. The campgrounds of **Hurshat Tal National Park** in the northern part of the Khula Valley provide some wet fun through waterslides. The **Yehudiya Forest Nature Reserve** in the Golan is famous not only for its quirky shape; a valley is the palm and five rivers constitute the fingers of an outstretched hand prepared to pull you into the outdoorsy adventures unique to Israel. Be aware that at the mountainous **Mount Carmel National Park,** the campground recommends reservations and charges a fee for overnight stays. Another opportunity for spending some quality time with the outdoors appears in the unique **Massada National Park;** with its location in the Judean Desert, your experience is guaranteed to be on fire.

LEAVE NO TRACE. *Let's Go* encourages travelers to embrace the "leave no trace" ethic, minimizing their impact on natural environments and protecting them for future generations. Trekkers and wilderness enthusiasts should set up camp on durable surfaces, use cookstoves instead of campfires, bury human waste away from water supplies, bag trash and carry it out with them, and respect wildlife. For more detailed information, contact the **Leave No Trace Center for Outdoor Ethics,** P.O. Box 997, Boulder, CO 80306, USA (☎+1-800-332-4100 or 303-442-8222; www.lnt.org).

USEFUL RESOURCES

For further details about camping, hiking, and biking in Israel, write or call the organizations listed below.

Israeli National Parks Authority, 3 Am VeOlamo St., Givat Shaul, Jerusalem 95463 (☎+972 02 500 62 61; www.parks.org.il/ParksENG/). Info on parks and historic sites.

Society for the Protection of Nature in Israel (SPNI; ha-ªevra LeHaganat ha-Teva). ASPNI, 28 Arrandale Ave., Great Neck, NY 11024 (☎800-411-0966; www.aspni.org). Call ☎03 638 86 88 for accommodation reservations at field schools, though keep in mind the first menu is in Hebrew. Organizes hikes, sightseeing tours in English, and camping trips.

WILDERNESS SAFETY

Staying **warm, dry,** and **well hydrated** is key to a happy and safe wilderness experience. For any hike, prepare yourself for an emergency by packing a first-aid kit, a reflector, a whistle, high-energy food, extra water, rain gear, a hat, mittens, and extra socks. For warmth, wear wool or insulating synthetic materials designed for the outdoors. Check weather forecasts often and pay attention to the skies when hiking, as weather patterns can change suddenly. Always let someone—a friend, your hostel, a park ranger—know when and where you are going. See **Safety and Health,** p. 14, for info on outdoor medical concerns.

DANGEROUS WILDLIFE

Mosquitoes will be your main source of agony in Israel during the summer. Though these creatures start cropping up in spring, the peak season runs June-August before tapering off at the approach of fall. Mosquitoes can bite through thin fabric, so cover up as much as possible with thicker materials. 100% DEET is useful, but mosquitoes are so notoriously ravenous that nothing short of a mosquito hood and netting really stops every jab.

CAMPING AND HIKING EQUIPMENT

WHAT TO BUY

Good camping equipment is both sturdy and light. North American suppliers tend to offer the most competitive prices.

Sleeping bags: Temperature ratings can be misleading; err on the side of being too warm by choosing a bag for the highest altitude and the coldest night of your trip. Bags are made of **down** (durable, warm, and light, but expensive, and miserable when wet) or of **synthetic** material (heavy, durable, and warm when wet). Prices range from US$70-200 for a summer synthetic to US$200-400 for a good down winter bag. **Sleeping bag pads** include foam pads (US$30-80), air mattresses (US$30-90), and self-inflating mats (US$60-120). Bring a **stuff sack** to store your bag and keep it dry.

Tents: The best tents are freestanding (with their own frames and suspension systems), set up quickly, and only require staking in high winds. A-frame and dome tents are the best all around. Worthy 2-person tents start at US$150, 4-person tents at US$200. Make sure yours has a rain fly and seal its seams with waterproofer. Other useful accessories include a **battery-operated lantern,** a plastic **ground cloth,** and a nylon **tarp.**

Backpacks: Internal-frame packs mold well to your back, keep a lower center of gravity, and flex adequately to allow you to hike difficult trails, while **external-frame** packs are more comfortable for long hikes over even terrain, as they carry weight higher and distribute it more evenly. Make sure your pack has a strong, padded hip belt to transfer weight to your legs. There are models designed specifically for women. Any serious backpacking requires a pack of at least 4000 cu. in. (16,000cc), plus 500 cu. in. for sleeping bags in internal-frame packs. Sturdy backpacks cost anywhere from US$125 to US$420—your pack is an area where it doesn't pay to economize. On your hunt for the perfect pack, fill up prospective models with something heavy, strap it on correctly, and walk around the store to get a sense of how the model distributes weight. Either buy a rain cover (US$10-20) or store all of your belongings in plastic bags inside your pack.

Boots: Be sure to wear hiking boots with good **ankle support.** They should fit snugly and comfortably over 1-2 pairs of **wool socks** and a pair of thin **liner socks.** Break in boots over several weeks before you go to spare yourself blisters.

Other necessities: Synthetic layers, like those made of polypropylene or polyester, will keep you warm even when wet. A **space blanket** (US$5-15) will help you to retain body heat and doubles as a **ground cloth. Water bottles** are vital; look for metal ones that are shatter- and leak-resistant. Carry **water-purification tablets** for when you can't boil water. Although most campgrounds provide campfire sites, you may want to bring a small **metal grate** or **grill.** For those places that forbid fires, you'll need a **camp stove** (starts at US$50) and a propane-filled fuel bottle to operate it. Also bring a **first-aid kit, pocketknife, insect repellent,** and **waterproof matches** or a **lighter.**

ORGANIZED ADVENTURE TRIPS

Organized adventure tours offer another way of exploring the wild. Activities include archaeological digs, biking, canoeing, climbing, hiking, kayaking, photo safaris, rafting, and skiing. Tourism bureaus often can suggest parks, trails, and outfitters. Organizations that specialize in camping and outdoor equipment like REI and EMS (above) also are good sources for info.

Specialty Travel Index, P.O. Box 458, San Anselmo, CA 94979, USA (in the US ☎888-624-4030, elsewhere 415-455-1643; www.specialtytravel.com).

SPECIFIC CONCERNS

SUSTAINABLE TRAVEL

As the number of travelers on the road rises, the detrimental effect they can have on natural environments is an increasing concern. With this in mind, *Let's Go* promotes the philosophy of sustainable travel. Through a sensitivity to issues of ecology and sustainability, today's travelers can be a powerful force in preserving and restoring the places they visit.

Ecotourism, a rising trend in sustainable travel, focuses on the conservation of natural habitats—mainly, on how to use them to build up the economy without exploitation or overdevelopment. Travelers can make a difference by doing advance research, by supporting organizations and establishments that pay attention to their carbon "footprint," and by patronizing establishments that strive to be environmentally friendly. Useful resources include **Ecotourism Israel** (☎54 998 9922; www.ecotourism.org.il), which operates in most of Israel's national parks and reserves, and the Ecotourism page of Israel's Tourism website (www.goisrael.com). See the **Beyond Tourism** chapter, p. 73.

> **ECOTOURISM RESOURCES.** For more information on environmentally responsible tourism, contact one of the organizations below:
> **Conservation International,** 2011 Crystal Dr., Ste. 500, Arlington, VA 22202, USA (☎+1-800-429-5660 or 703-341-2400; www.conservation.org).
> **Green Globe 21,** Green Globe vof, Verbenalaan 1, 2111 ZL Aerdenhout, the Netherlands (☎+31 23 544 0306; www.greenglobe.com).
> **International Ecotourism Society,** 1301 Clifton St. NW, Ste. 200, Washington, DC 20009, USA (☎+1-202-506-5033; www.ecotourism.org).
> **United Nations Environment Program (UNEP;** www.unep.org).

WOMEN TRAVELERS

Women exploring on their own inevitably face some additional safety concerns. Single women can consider staying in hostels that offer single rooms that lock from the inside or in religious organizations with single-sex rooms. It's a good idea to stick to centrally located accommodations and to avoid solitary late-night treks or metro rides. Always carry extra cash for a phone call, bus, or taxi. **Hitchhiking** is never safe for lone women or even for two women traveling together. Look as if you know where you're going and approach older women or couples for directions if you're lost or feeling uncomfortable in your surroundings. Generally, the less you look like a tourist, the better off you'll be.

Israeli women generally dress in Western style, making it fairly easy to blend in. In the Palestinian territories, and in both the Orthodox Jewish and Arab sections of Israel, however, it is advisable to dress modestly (nothing sleeveless or tight and skirts and pants well below the knees) and adhere to local standards of behavior as much as possible. This is particularly important when visiting religious sites. Wearing a conspicuous **wedding band** sometimes helps to prevent unwanted advances.

Your best answer to verbal harassment is no answer at all; feigning deafness, sitting motionless, and staring straight ahead at nothing in particular will usually do the trick. The extremely persistent can sometimes be dissuaded by a firm, loud, and very public "Go away!" in English or in Hebrew. Don't hesitate to seek out a police officer or a passerby if you are being harassed. Memorize the emergency numbers in places you visit and consider carrying a whistle on your keychain. A self-defense course will both prepare you for a potential attack and raise your level of awareness of your surroundings (see **Personal Safety,** p. 17). Also, it might be a good idea to talk with your doctor about the health concerns that women face when traveling (see this page).

GLBT TRAVELERS

Israeli attitudes toward non-heterosexual persuasions are considered the most tolerant of the Middle East. In fact, Israel law recognizes same-sex marriages performed elsewhere, and the Israeli armed forces allow enlistment regardless of sexual orientation. Listed below are contact organizations, mail-order catalogs, and publishers that offer materials addressing some specific concerns. **Out and About** (www.planetout.com) offers a comprehensive website and a weekly newsletter addressing gay travel concerns.

Gay's the Word, 66 Marchmont St., London WC1N 1AB, UK (☎+44 20 7278 7654; http://freespace.virgin.net/gays.theword). The largest gay and lesbian bookshop in the UK, with both fiction and nonfiction titles. Mail-order service available.

Giovanni's Room, 345 S. 12th St., Philadelphia, PA 19107, USA (☎+1-215-923-2960; www.giovannisroom.com). An international lesbian and gay bookstore with mail-order.

International Lesbian and Gay Association (ILGA), 17 Rue de la Charité, 1210 Brussels, Belgium (☎+32 2 502 2471; www.ilga.org). Provides political information, such as homosexuality laws of individual countries.

TRAVELERS WITH DISABILITIES

Israel, much like the Western world, takes special care to provide accessibility to all of its citizens, as well as its visitors. Check **Israel's Tourism** website (www.goisrael.com) for more specific information. Travelers with disabilities should inform airlines and hotels of their disabilities when making reservations, as some time may be needed to prepare special accommodations. Call ahead to restaurants, museums, and other facilities to find out if they are wheelchair-accessible. **Guide-dog owners** should inquire as to the quarantine policies of each destination country.

For those who wish to rent cars, some major car-rental agencies (e.g., Hertz) offer hand-controlled vehicles.

Accessible Journeys, 35 W. Sellers Ave., Ridley Park, PA 19078, USA (☎+1-800-846-4537; www.disabilitytravel.com). Designs tours for wheelchair users and slow walkers. The site has tips and forums for all travelers.

Mobility International USA (MIUSA), 132 E. Broadway, Ste. 343, Eugene, OR 97401, USA (☎+1-541-343-1284; www.miusa.org). Sells *A World of Options: A Guide to International Educational Exchange, Community Service, and Travel for Persons with Disabilities* (US$35).

Society for Accessible Travel and Hospitality (SATH), 347 5th Ave., Ste. 605, New York City, NY 10016, USA (☎+1-212-447-7284; www.sath.org). An advocacy group that publishes free online travel information. Annual membership US$49, students and seniors US$29.

MINORITY TRAVELERS

The primary problem in this regard is for Palestinians; if you happen to be a Palestinian dual national and/or are entering the country for the purpose of working in the Occupied Palestinian Territories, you may be refused entry. Otherwise, immigration from Ethiopia as well as an influx of foreign workers from Southeast Asia has recently made minority travelers stand out a little less. Still, Israelis are known for their abrupt and direct method of questioning, and some comments could be interpreted as offensive. Aside from a slew of questions, minority travelers are unlikely to encounter harassment in Israel, particularly in large cities that see many tourists, such as Jerusalem and Tel Aviv. Smaller towns and less-populated regions may bring some unwanted attention, but it probably won't amount to more than staring. Jews traveling in Arab areas such as East Jerusalem, the West Bank, and Gaza should make their tourist status pronounced and avoid external signs of their religious affiliation (i.e. wear a hat instead of a *kippah*).

DIETARY CONCERNS

Vegetarians will have an easy time keeping themselves happily fed in Israel. Some of the most common and cheapest Middle Eastern food, such as the ubiquitous falafel, is vegetarian. In addition, many restaurants are vegetarian because of the kosher restriction on mixing milk and meat. The Hebrew Israelite Community has a chain of good vegan restaurants, which *Let's Go* lists under individual cities.

The travel section of **The Vegetarian Resource Group's** website, at www.vrg.org/travel, has a comprehensive list of organizations and websites that are geared toward helping vegetarians and vegans traveling abroad. They also provide an online restaurant guide. *Vegetarian Israel* is particularly handy for those travelers seeking a wide variety of veggie-oriented meals in this Middle Eastern region (US$10). Vegetarians will also find numerous resources on the web; try www.vegdining.com, www.happycow.net, and www.vegetariansabroad.com.

Israel is well-known for its elaborate options for those visitors following **kosher.** Travelers looking for **halal** places may find www.zabihah.com useful.

 LET'S GO ONLINE. Plan your next trip on our newly redesigned website, **www.letsgo.com.** It features the latest travel info on your favorite destinations as well as tons of interactive features: make your own itinerary, read blogs from our trusty Researchers, browse our photo library, watch exclusive videos, check out our newsletter, find travel deals, and buy new guides. We're always updating and adding new features, so check back often!

LIFE AND TIMES

LAND

Israel has a total land area of approximately 20,770 square kilometers. In addition to the West Bank and Gaza Strip, it borders Egypt, Jordan, Lebanon, and Syria. Its western boundary is the Mediterranean Sea. A small stretch of coastline in the south also meets the Red Sea.

LANDSCAPE & ENVIRONMENT

The Israeli landscape is dominated by the **Rift Valley,** an enormous fissure between two tectonic plates that extends from Mozambique through eastern Israel to Turkey. Located in this trough, the **Dead Sea** is the lowest point on the surface of the earth, at 412m below sea level. The center of the country is characterized by highlands, with **Mount Meron** (1208m) as its highest peak. Along the **Mediterranean** lies a fertile coastal plane. The **Negev Desert** in the south covers more than half of Israel's area.

Israel struggles with **limited arable land**—less than 20% of its territory can support agriculture. There is also a major shortage of fresh water. The **Jordan River,** the country's main waterway, has been overexploited, and the sea of Galilee and the coastal aquifer, Israel's main water reservoirs, have become polluted. The **Society for the Protection of Nature** in Israel has been a prominent force in environmentalism since its foundation in 1953. Check out its website (www.spni.org) for more information.

FLORA & FAUNA

Despite its small size, Israel is home to a rich variety of plants and animals. **Wildflowers** are abundant almost everywhere. In the more fertile regions, crops like oranges, dates, and tobacco flourish. Israel also plays host to many **migrant bird species.** Its terrestrial species include **ibexes** and **gazelles,** as well as wild boars and wild cats.

HISTORY

ANCIENT HISTORY

The first true empire in world history emerged in the 24th century BCE, when a dynasty of Semitic rulers conquered all of Upper Mesopotamia, including Asia Minor and southeastern Arabia, dubbing itself the **Akkadian Empire.** Substantial urban development led to the construction of several famed Biblical towns, and the predominantly **Canaanite** population spoke a language from which Biblical Hebrew evolved. Unsurprisingly, such a volume of early religious activity would set the stage for conflict across the ages.

An important trade route between Egypt and Mesopotamia spanned the territory that makes up modern-day Israel and was periodically conquered by both civilizations, as well as by the chariot-racing Hyksos and Hittite forerunners of the Iron Age. This area's recorded history begins in the same book as Christianity's, with the story of **Abraham,** the first of the Patriarchs. The Semitic-speaking people linked with him may have been the ancestors of the **Hebrews,** those who would eventually lay claim to the kingdom of Israel and Judah and rebrand themselves the **Israelites.**

Some scholarship suggests that the Hebrews are related in some way to the semi-nomadic **Apiru** people. Whether or not the Apiru became the Israelites remains a mystery, however. Some theorize that the Israelites were these highlanders who united, Braveheart-style, in opposition to the urban, valley-dwelling Canaanite traders. Others believe that the Israelites were forced from the coast by invading "sea peoples" (later known as the **Philistines,** perhaps a jab at all the arts scholarship they missed while at sea).

THE IRON AGE (1200-586 BCE)

The next two centuries are known as the **Period of the Judges.** Local leaders, Gideon and Samuel among them, united the Israelite tribes under a new god, Yahweh, to fight off the encroaching Egyptians, Canaanites, and Philistines. Despite their efforts, the Philistines triumphed in 1200 BCE, likely as a result of a monopoly on iron technology. The Philistines left behind two lasting contributions: expertise in iron work and an infiltration of Semitic language that led to a new name for the country—Palestine, derived from the root word Philistia. Possibly inspired by the arrival of Semitic brethren from Egypt (the Exodus), the Israelites founded their own kingdom under **Saul** at the end of the 11th century BCE, around the same time as his successor, **David,** asymmetrically felled Goliath.

The Israelite kingdom reached its peak during the reign of Saul's successor David, and that of David's son, **Solomon.** The construction of the **Temple of Jerusalem** is considered Solomon's most formidable feat (only more so considering it is the "footstool" of God's presence in the world). After Solomon's death in 922 BCE, social and political unrest split the empire into the **Kingdom of Israel** in the north and the **Kingdom of Judah** in the south.

The **Assyrians** conquered Israel in the late eighth century BCE. The ten tribes of northern Israel were taken into captivity and never returned, hence their moniker: the Ten Lost Tribes. Judah became a vassal state of the Assyrian empire until the Assyrians themselves were crushed by the Babylonians. The Babylonian king **Nebuchadnezzar II** conquered Judah, razed the Temple, burned Jerusalem, and deported many Jews to Mesopotamia (the Babylonian Captivity or Exile) in 587 BCE. When the Persians defeated Nebuchadnezzar II's successor some 50 years later, King Cyrus the Great permitted the Jews to return to Jerusalem and build the **Second Temple** (completed in 515 BCE). Though small, this new Jewish community was revived by the Jewish governor **Nehemiah** and by the Babylonian Jew **Ezra.**

GREEKS & NABATEANS (332-63 BCE)

The Israelites prospered intellectually and economically under the Persians, until **Alexander the Great** conquered the region in 332 BCE. The Syrian-based **Seleucids** displaced his heirs in 198 BCE and attempted to Hellenize the Jews. Judah Maccabee led a revolt of the Jewish lower classes, now commemorated by Hanukkah. Victorious, the **Maccabees** re-sanctified the Temple in 164 BCE and founded the **Hasmonean Dynasty,** emboldening a lasting spirit of Jewish nationalism.

The **Nabateans,** originally a nomadic Arab tribe, moved into the area south of the Dead Sea around the second century BCE. They emerged as an independent kingdom by about 169 BCE. They took control of at least a part of the Red Sea trade route, which became an important source of income. With **Petra** (in modern Jordan, p. 382) as its capital, the Nabatean kingdom continued to flourish. In 106 CE, the Roman emperor **Trajan** was finally able to conquer Petra. He abolished the kingdom and reorganized its territories into a Roman province named **Arabia.**

ROMANS (63 BCE-324 CE)

In 63 BCE, the Roman general **Pompey** swept in and secured much of modern-day Israel for Rome; it was ruled via the **Herodian Dynasty,** including, infamously, **Herod the Great** (not all that great, actually—he murdered his own family and a number of rabbis). In 70 CE, however, the Roman general **Titus** burned Herod's Temple with the rest of Jerusalem. The destruction led to dramatic upheaval among the Jewish people. Three years later, the Romans captured the last Jewish stronghold at **Masada,** ending the First Jewish-Roman War. The Romans exiled the majority of Jerusalem's population, dispersing the exiles throughout the empire.

Jewish hopes for liberation from Roman rule were raised again when an uprising, headed by Simon Bar Kokhba, broke out in 123 CE. Although the Jews made some headway, Roman troops pushed them back to their fortress in Judea, which fell in 135 CE. In the wake of the revolt, many towns and villages in Judea were razed. Perhaps to obliterate the land's connection with the Jews, **Emperor Hadrian** bestowed on the territory the name Syria/Palestine, after the name passed down by the Philistines.

BYZANTINES (330-637)

With the division of the empire into Latin West and Byzantine East in 395 CE, Palestine came under the supervision of **Constantinople.** Although little changed administratively, the earlier adoption of Christianity by **Emperor Constantine** in 325 CE generated new interest in what to many was the "Holy Land." Led by pilgrim St. Eleni (Constantine's mother), worshippers built churches and endowed monasteries and schools as opposed to razing temples as their predecessors had done.

EARLY ARABS (636-1095)

After the death of the **Prophet Muhammad** in 632 CE (see **Islam,** p. 60), Bedouin armies, inspired by Islam and the prospect of substantial booty, ventured outside their traditional strongholds in central Arabia. By 642, they had conquered Mesopotamia, Palestine, Syria, Persia, and Egypt.

Muhammad's death gave rise to political confusion, as he had designated no successor. Amid vigorous debate as to whether the successor had to be a blood relative, Abu Bakr was chosen as the first successor (*khalifa*, or caliph). The choice of his descendant Ali as the third successor incited a civil war and produced a lasting schism in Islam between the **Sunni** (the "orthodox," who believed that the caliph should be chosen by the community of believers), and the **Shi'a** (who supported Ali's claim and believed that the caliph should be a direct descendant of the prophet).

The advent of the **Umayyad Dynasty,** founded in 661, installed a Sunni hereditary caliphate (unrelated to the Prophet). Eighty years later, the Islamic world stretched from Narbonne to Samarkand. By 750, when the 'Abbasids overthrew the Umayyads, the majority of the peasantry had converted to Islam. A mammoth bureaucracy, composed of everything from tax officials to scribes to Islamic jurists *(ulama)*, helped run the empire.

The **Shi'a Fatimids,** attacking eastward from their domain in Tunisia, expelled the 'Abbasids from Egypt in 969. By 977, the Fatimids had captured most of Palestine and controlled Jerusalem. It was the Fatimid Caliph al-Hakim who broke the long-established trend of Muslim toleration of other faiths and destroyed the Church of the Holy Sepulchre.

THE CRUSADES (1095-1291)

Europe's internal violence and rumors of Seljuk Muslim policies regarding the treatment of Christian pilgrims prompted western Europeans to launch a series of **Crusades** to recapture the Holy Land, an attempt to glorify God not only by reclaiming Israel but also by sending many of their compatriots to meet him. Impelled by desires for land, power, and heavenly reward, the Crusaders wreaked havoc on Israel. Massacring the Muslim and Jewish inhabitants of Jerusalem in 1099, the Crusaders established a feudal kingdom under **Godfrey I** and then **Baldwin I.**

The success of the first Crusaders was short-lived, however. The members of the second and third Crusades were staved off by the leadership of **Salah al-Din** (a Kurd), founder of the short-lived **Ayyubid Dynasty** (1171-1250). Salah al-Din dethroned the Fatimids in 1192 with an army of Turkish slaves (Mamluks). One by one, the Crusader States eventually fell.

MAMLUKS & OTTOMANS (1291-1882)

Salah al-Din's slave armies became a problem for his successors. While their arms were under his authority, the **Mamluks** were technically the property of the sultan. In 1250, **Izz al-Din,** a Mamluk of the Bahri clan, resolved to rule the sultanate directly. By 1291, Mamluks controlled all of the former Crusader outposts. Slave had indeed become master.

When the **Ottoman Empire,** a formidable Turkish empire founded in 1299, gained formal sovereignty over Palestine and Egypt in the early part of the 16th century, the Mamluks still retained most of their political power as a vassal state. Through appointments, bribery, and assassination, however, the Ottoman sultans garnered real control. With military innovations, including Jannisary and Sipahi corps who were armed with gunpowder weapons, the Ottoman Empire thrived and expanded.

When the gates of Vienna stood firm against Ottoman armies in 1683, however, the Ottomans began to worry about the fate of their increasingly decrepit empire. The ports of Palestine, Syria, and Egypt had once provided the sole access to the East; now, sailors steered their way around the Horn of Africa. The Spanish discovery of the New World created opportunities for major economic expansion that left the Ottomans out. The once-formidable empire became "the sick man of Europe," and it became increasingly clear that another power would eventually fill the Ottoman vacuum.

EARLY ZIONISM AND THE FIRST ALIYOT (1882-1914)

Although small Jewish communities were present in Palestine over the 18 centuries following the Roman exile, the vast majority of the world's Jews existed in **diaspora** communities throughout Europe, the Middle East, North Africa, and, more recently, the Americas. Throughout this period, many Jews maintained the hope of someday returning to the ancient homeland. This ideal began gaining practical momentum in the late 19th century, when **Theodor Herzl,** a Jewish Austrian journalist, founded Zionism as an international political movement devoted to creating a Jewish state in Palestine. Herzl stated that the creation of such a homeland was a necessary response to the persecution Jews faced across the Diaspora. The movement began to act in earnest in 1897, when the First Zionist Congress was held in Basel, Switzerland. Herzl and the leaders of political Zionism first considered alternative sites for a Jewish state, such as Uganda and Argentina, but ultimately realized that only Palestine had the emotional and spiritual lure to unite Diaspora Jewry, and began to use their political leverage to bring about the founding of a Jewish state in Palestine.

Meanwhile, the first major waves of secular Jewish immigration to Palestine, each called an *aliyah* (literally "ascension" in Hebrew), began to arrive. In 1882 the **First Aliyah** began, bringing Jewish immigrants from Eastern Europe and Yemen. These immigrants founded the first modern Jewish agricultural settlements. The First Aliyah ended in 1903 and was quickly followed in 1904 by the **Second Aliyah,** which brought to Palestine around 40,000 Jews from Russia and Poland, most of them fleeing attacks and persecution. These new immigrants brought with them the ideals of socialism and founded the first Jewish communal agricultural settlements, or **kibbutzim,** in Palestine. The Second Aliyah lasted until the outbreak of WWI in 1914.

The new Jewish communities developed a complicated relationship with the local Arab population, with each side appealing to the Ottoman authorities to advance their goals. The Jews sought to gain land and security to accommodate additional immigrants, in anticipation of the founding of the Jewish state, while the Arabs preferred to maintain the status quo in which they had lived for centuries. It was at this time that tension began to develop between the two religious and ethnic groups, and in 1909 the first Jewish security organization in Palestine was founded, named HaShomer ("the Watchman").

WORLD WAR I AND THE END OF OTTOMAN RULE (1914-1920)

The outbreak of WWI in Europe brought a shift of power to the entire Middle East, and to Palestine in particular. During the War, the British government, seeking to topple the German-allied Ottomans, conducted secret and separate negotiations with both the Arabs and the Jews in Palestine to enlist their help. To obtain Arab support, Britain pledged to back "the independence of the Arabs" in exchange for an Arab declaration of war against the Ottomans. The **Arab Revolt** started in June 1916, facilitated by British emissary **T.E. Lawrence** ("Lawrence of Arabia"), who convinced and aided the Arab leader **Sherif Hussein** to lead attacks on Ottoman forces throughout the Middle East. The Revolt was instrumental in ending Ottoman dominance in the region.

At the same time, Britain sought political support from Jews by offering public support for the goals of the Zionist movement. The collaboration succeeded: Jewish military units under the flag of the Jewish Legion fought alongside British troops for the liberation of Palestine from Ottoman rule, and in November 1917 the British government issued the **Balfour Declaration,** which expressed British support for a Jewish homeland in Palestine while stipulating that it should not "prejudice the civil and religious rights of existing non-Jewish communities in Palestine." Many Arabs throughout the region were outraged, and felt that the British had violated their agreement.

To complicate matters further, the British and French had made a separate deal at the end of the War. The **Sykes-Picot Agreement** in 1916 divided the Middle East region, newly conquered from the crumbling Ottoman Empire, into zones of British and French influence. At the war's end, the various promises made by Britain to the Arabs, the Jews, and the French resulted in a muddled system of mandates: the newly created **League of Nations** awarded the Western European powers control over the territories from which the Ottomans had been expelled with the stated purpose of preparing these countries for independence. Great

Britain was thus given a mandate over Palestine (which included the areas of modern-day Israel, Jordan, the West Bank, and Gaza) and Iraq, while France was accorded Syria and Lebanon.

THE BRITISH MANDATE (1920-1948)

Throughout the inter-war years, rising Arab and Jewish nationalism and increasing instances of mutual violence constantly tested British mandatory rule in Palestine. On the Jewish side, the Third, Fourth, and Fifth Aliyot, prompted by continued persecution of Jews in Europe and by the rise of the Nazi Party in Germany, had swelled the Jewish population in Palestine to 450,000 by 1940. The intervening 30 years of British rule saw a considerable expansion of the Jewish demographic, as well as institutional and economic development, under the leadership of **David Ben-Gurion's** labor-oriented party, **Mapay.** During these years, the small security organization HaShomer was expanded and upgraded into the paramilitary HaHaganah ("the Defense"), whose main task was to repel Arab attacks on Jewish settlements. The top priority of the Jewish leadership in Palestine at this time was the continuation of Jewish immigration and the expansion of local Jewish land ownership, mostly by purchasing from Arab owners.

At the same time, the Arab population of Palestine grew anxious of losing its clear majority and influence in the region. Distinctly Palestinian Arab nationalist organizations, such as the Higher Arab Committee were established in an effort to combat Zionist activities and to exert organized influence on British policy. Muslim religious leaders, such as the Grand Mufti of Jerusalem, Haj Amin al-Husseini, sought support abroad for the termination of the British mandate and the cessation of Zionist activities toward the establishment of a Jewish state in Palestine.

The British tried various unsuccessful tactics to appease each side. To assuage Arab fears about mass Jewish immigration, they issued the **White Paper** of 1939, which strictly limited the number of legal Jewish immigrants per year. Jews argued that these quotas were particularly unacceptable given the dire state of the Jews in Nazi-dominated Europe, and continued to facilitate illegal immigration. Underground Jewish efforts to assist illegal immigration led to greater friction between the Zionists and the Mandatory Government, culminating in a 1946 bombing of the British headquarters in the King David Hotel in Jerusalem by the militant Zionist groups Irgun and Lechi. Meanwhile, growing Arab discontent with the developing situation led to the **Arab Revolt of 1936-39,** which the British were only able to put down with considerable military force. With the outbreak of WWII, mainstream Zionist leaders tried to patch up their relationship with the British to support the war effort against Germany. Elements of the Palestinian Arab leadership, discouraged by England's ambiguity, negotiated with the Germans for control of Palestine and continued to try to thwart the Zionist effort at establishing a Jewish state.

PARTITION AND WAR (1948-1970)

THE 1948 WAR. Shortly after the conclusion of WWII, Great Britain, weary of trying to mediate between the Jews and Arabs and rule a contested piece of land, submitted the question of Palestine to the newly formed **United Nations.** The UN General Assembly voted in 1947 to accept a partition plan for Palestine, splitting the territory into two states, Jewish and Arab, and putting the contested holy city of Jerusalem under international control. The Jewish leadership accepted the resolution with some reluctance, while Palestinian Arab leaders and the governments of neighboring Arab states rejected the plan completely, denying the UN's authority to divide and distribute territories they considered to be Arab patrimony. The Arabs also criticized the UN's decision to assign over half of the land of Mandatory Palestine to the Jewish State, even though the Jews at that time represented only a third of the area's population. As the British prepared to evacuate Palestine in accordance with the partition resolution, Jews and Arabs clashed in sporadic skirmishes, purchased arms overseas, and planned for war.

On May 14, 1948, the British mandate over Palestine ended and David Ben-Gurion declared the independence of the **State of Israel.** The new state was quickly recognized by the two major world powers—the United States and the Soviet Union—and by a host of additional countries. The next day, the combined armies of Syria, Iraq, Lebanon, Egypt, and Jordan, aided by troops from Saudi Arabia and Yemen, mobilized for war against Israel. In the war that ensued, called the **War of Independence** by Israelis and **al-Nakbah** ("the catastrophe") by Arabs, the newly established **Israeli Defense Forces** were able to conquer large swaths of land, some of which were not originally allotted to the Jewish state according to the UN partition plan. When the final armistice agreement was signed in late 1949, the vast majority of mandatory Palestine was under Israeli control, with the Gaza Strip being held by Egypt, and the West Bank and East Jerusalem (containing the Old City and its holy sites) in Jordanian hands. During the war, hundreds of thousands of Palestinian Arabs, who either fled from their homes or were banished by Israeli forces, became refugees. They crowded into massive temporary camps in the West Bank, Gaza, and bordering Arab states, expecting to soon return to their original homes, in accordance with UN Resolution 194. The Arabs that remained in areas conquered by Israeli forces were ultimately given full Israeli citizenship, but placed under martial law until the 1960s. Israel, in the meantime, had asserted itself as a legitimate independent state in the region, and began the process of building its national institutions and infrastructure.

MASS IMMIGRATION, AUSTERITY, AND THE SUEZ CRISIS. Israel's early years were focused on receiving the huge streams of Jewish refugees coming out of post-Holocaust Europe and escaping from oppressive regimes in Arab states. Between 1948 and 1960, the population of Israel skyrocketed from 800,000 to over to two million. The massive influx of poor, and in many cases uneducated, refugees created significant social and economic challenges for the young state. The government of Prime Minister David Ben-Gurion, following the socialist ideology upon which the state was founded, instituted a regime of **Austerity,** in which the distribution of crucial items like furniture and food was centralized and heavily rationed. At the same time, the government struggled to integrate its sizable and highly diverse immigrant communities, most of which lived in temporary camps, into Israeli society. Many of the social inequalities and tensions that still plague Jewish Israeli society today originated during this time.

On the Israeli-Arab front, things stayed fairly quiet throughout the decade, with occasional attacks on Israeli civilians carried out by Palestinian Arab infiltrators (called *Fedayeen* in Arabic), and Israeli military retaliation against the alleged bases of these infiltrators in Jordan, Egypt, and Lebanon. In 1956, Egyptian leader **Gamal Abd al-Nasser,** trying to rally the Arab world, engaged in a series of diplomatic standoffs with Western powers and Israel, which culminated in the closing of the **Suez Canal** to Israeli shipping. Acting under an agreement with France and the United Kingdom, Israeli troops conquered the Sinai Peninsula and Suez Canal in October 1956, but withdrew several months later due to American and Soviet pressure, with guarantees that the Canal would remain open to Israeli ships.

THE 1967 SIX-DAY WAR. During the mid-1960s there was an increase in raids on Israel backed by the newly formed **Palestinian Liberation Organization (PLO),** which served as an umbrella organization for the various Palestinian nationalist groups. In return, Israel intensified its retaliations against Palestinian refugee camps. In the meantime, tensions heightened between Israel and its Arab neighbors, with Nasser demanding a removal of UN buffer troops that had been stationed in Sinai since the 1956 Suez crisis, and Israeli Prime Minister **Levi Eshkol** warning that any blockade of the Straits of Tiran, which served as the sole gateway to one of Israel's main shipping routes, would be interpreted as an act of war. Nasser, under pressure from Syria and Saudi Arabia, initiated the blockade on May 22, 1967. Israel called up its reserve troops and Jordan, Iraq, and Syria deployed their troops along Israel's borders. A tense waiting period ensued, during which neither side admitted it was headed for war, but both made preparations.

On June 5, Israel launched a preemptive air strike, which obliterated most of the air forces of Egypt, Jordan, Syria, and Iraq. A massive ground battle ensued, with Syria, Jordan, and Egypt simultaneously attacking Israel. Backed by its unchallenged air force, the Israeli army was able to quickly defeat the Arab armies, and within six days had conquered the Sinai peninsula, the Gaza Strip, the West Bank (with East Jerusalem), and the Golan Heights, increasing its territory threefold. The capturing of the Old City of Jerusalem, and in particular the Jewish holy site of the Western Wall, was an emotional high point for Israelis, and represented a symbolic return to the site of the Temple after centuries of exile and rule by foreigners. Following the war, Israel annexed East Jerusalem and the Golan Heights, though this act was never recognized by the international community. Shortly after the war, the UN Security Council passed **Resolution 242,** which called for the withdrawal of Israeli forces from territories it had occupied during the war. Though the resolution was accepted by all parties, debates over ambiguous wording in its text persist even today.

For the Palestinians and the Arab countries, the war was a humiliating defeat. It created an additional 400,000 Palestinian refugees, the majority of which fled or were banished from the West Bank into Jordan, and placed those who remained in their homes under Israeli martial law. The situation on the Israeli-Egyptian border (the Suez Canal) gradually degenerated into the **War of Attrition** (see opposite page).

THE PLO AND JORDAN

Following the influx of Palestinians, the Jordanian government and the PLO were thrown together into a tense relationship: **King Hussein** of Jordan wanted to hold secret peace negotiations with the Israelis, while the PLO hoped to use Jordan as its headquarters and as a base for attacks on Israeli-held territory. Responding to PLO raids, the Israeli army attacked the Jordanian town of Karameh. Though the town's resident Palestinians were defeated, the image of Palestinian militants standing together with Jordanians against Israeli forces became a successful image for the PLO. Young recruits flocked to it, giving the PLO greater control over the refugee camps and threatening Hussein's sovereignty.

In September 1970, Hussein's and PLO leader **Yassir Arafat's** conflicting ambitions collided. Infuriated by a hard-line PLO faction's hijacking of a number of commercial airliners, Hussein declared war on the PLO. Martial law was imposed, and thousands of Palestinians were killed by the Jordanian army. September 1970 became known among Palestinians as **Black September.** After Arab League mediation and Nasser's personal intervention, an agreement was forged, requiring the PLO to move its headquarters to Lebanon.

In October 1974, the Arab League declared in Rabat, Morocco that the PLO, not Jordan, was "the sole legitimate representative of the Palestinian people." This incensed King Hussein, but when the other 20 Arab nations assented to PLO representation in the League, he was forced to agree. In November 1974, the UN General Assembly granted the PLO observer status in the UN.

WAR AND PEACE (1970-1982)

WAR OF ATTRITION. In 1969, with the help of Soviet military instruction and supplies, Egypt launched the **War of Attrition** against Israel, a drawn out series of tit-for-tat skirmishes along the Israeli-Egyptian border. The Egyptians and Soviets hoped to extract concessions from Israel by inflicting heavy material and human losses on the country. Within a few years, the war became too heavy a burden for Egypt to bear. In order to alleviate his country's financial crisis, Nasser's successor, **Anwar Sadat,** sought to reopen the lucrative Suez Canal and reclaim the desperately needed Sinai oil fields. In 1972, he expelled the Soviet military advisors in Egypt, and, seeing little hope in negotiations, began to prepare an attack on Israel.

THE 1973 WAR AND ITS CONSEQUENCES. On October 6, 1973, when most Israelis were in synagogues or at home for Yom Kippur (the Day of Atonement), the holiest day of the Jewish year, Egypt and Syria launched a coordinated surprise assault. In the first three days of the war, Egyptian forces crossed the Suez Canal, while Syrian troops swept through the Golan Heights and almost reached the Jordan River. Within a matter of days, Israel launched a series of fierce counter attacks, and relying heavily on emergency military supplies and equipment provided by the United States, was able to stop the Arab advance. The Arab states later initiated an oil embargo against the United States and Holland in retaliation for their support of Israel. The war ended when a UN-backed ceasefire went into effect on October 22.

The 1973 War had significant political ramifications for all countries in the region. In Israel, the political and military leadership faced fierce criticism for the country's lack of preparedness for the war, and for the atmosphere of arrogant confidence that had developed within the Israeli defense establishment since the Six-Day War. In 1974, Prime Minister **Golda Me'ir** and her cabinet were forced to resign. For the Arab states, the 1973 War was viewed as a victory after the humiliation of 1967, even though they had not reconquered any of the territory that they had lost.

Throughout the 1970s, an increasing number of Israelis began to settle in the West Bank and Gaza Strip. On November 11, 1976, the UN Security Council condemned this policy and demanded that Israel follow the Geneva Convention's rules regarding occupied territory. Although Prime Minister **Yitzhak Rabin** (of the left-leaning **Labor Party**) discouraged permanent West Bank settlement, the right-wing **Likud,** which first came to power in 1977, led by Prime Minister **Menahem Begin,** actively encouraged the development of the settlements.

PEACE WITH EGYPT. Eager to regain the Sinai and reestablish Egypt as a leader in the Arab world, Sadat decided to seek a peace agreement with Israel. In November 1977, he made a historic visit to Jerusalem and spoke before the Israeli Knesset (the parliament). By September 1978, Begin and Sadat had forged an agreement with the help of US President **Jimmy Carter** at **Camp David,** the presidential retreat in Maryland. This was the first official peace treaty between Israel and any Arab state. The most successful and lasting stipulation was Israel's agreement to relinquish the Sinai in exchange for peace and full diplomatic relations with Egypt. However, the stipulations concerning Israel's control of the West Bank and Gaza were more muddled. Sadat returned to Cairo content that Palestinians in the occupied territories would be granted full personal and territorial sovereignty within the next five years, whereas Begin maintained that nothing regarding the occupied territories had been agreed upon.

After the Camp David Accords, early hopes that other Arab states would negotiate with Israel evaporated. In October 1981, in a response to his government's crackdown on Islamic fundamentalists, Sadat was assassinated and **Hosni Mubarak,** Sadat's Vice President, was sworn in. Though sticking to the terms of the 1979 Camp David peace treaty, Mubarak kept the diplomatic air cool for most of the 1980s in an attempt to reintegrate Egypt with the rest of the Arab world. In 1984, Egypt restored relations with the Soviet Union and was readmitted to the Islamic Conference, and by 1988, the Arab League had invited Egypt to rejoin and dropped demands that it sever its ties with Israel.

THE 1982 LEBANON WAR. Throughout the late 1970s and early 1980s the PLO established a strong presence in the Palestinian refugee camps in southern Lebanon, and began to launch raids against Israeli civilians in northern Israel. In 1981 these violent exchanges escalated, with Israel launching air strikes against the PLO, and the PLO responding by shelling northern Israel. On June 6, 1982, Israeli ground troops invaded Lebanon. The offensive, dubbed "Operation Peace of the Galilee" by Defense Minister **Ariel Sharon,** was supposedly intended to create a protective buffer zone; many, however, believe that the attack aimed to wipe out the PLO forces that had been operating out of Lebanon and to install a Lebanese government that would have been sympathetic to Israel. The Israeli army surrounded the PLO in Beirut and began shelling the city at an enormous civilian cost, earning both domestic and international disapproval. The war quickly deteriorated from what was supposed to be a rapid operation into a messy and drawn out campaign against guerilla forces, in the midst of a civil war in Lebanon. As a result of the clashes, the PLO leadership was forced to relocate its headquarters to Tunis. Between September 16th and 18th, 1982, Lebanese Christian militias entered the Sabra and Shatila Palestinian refugee camps, which were under Israeli guard, and, as a retaliation for the assassination of Christian Lebanese President Bashir Jumayyil, massacred innocent Palestinian refugees. Israel's failure to prevent the massacre, despite its knowledge that it was occurring, was met with a huge public outcry within Israel and internationally.

Under an agreement negotiated by the United States, most fighting ended in 1983. Worried about the Syrian presence and active Shi'a militia in Lebanon, Israel withdrew in 1985, but maintained a strip of southern Lebanese territory as a security zone until May of 2000.

THE FIRST INTIFADA (1987-1990)

Throughout most of the 1970s and 1980s a tense quiet held in the West Bank and Gaza, with hundreds of thousands of Palestinians living under Israeli martial law. On December 8, 1987, an Israeli armored transport and several Arab cars collided in Gaza; four Palestinians were killed and several injured in the crash. The Palestinians' despair after 20 years of Israeli military occupation turned demonstrations at the victims' funerals into an upheaval that spread to the West Bank. Clashes between the Israeli military and rock or Molotov cocktail-wielding Palestinian civilians became commonplace, and the widespread unrest received the popular name *intifada* ("uprising" in Arabic). At first, Israeli authorities viewed the *intifada* as a short-lived affair that would dissolve as earlier agitations had. But after Palestinians in the territories began establishing networks to coordinate their hitherto sporadic civil disobedience, the *intifada* came alive, gaining its own leadership. In the midst of all the turmoil, the world began to reconsider Israel's Palestinian policies. In the summer of 1988, King Hussein of Jordan suddenly dropped his claims to the West Bank and ceased assisting in the administration of the territories, which Jordan had been doing since 1967. Arafat seized the opportunity to assert the PLO's international recognition as the official representative of the Palestinian people by renouncing terrorism and recognizing Israel's right to exist. Israeli Prime Minister **Yithzak Shamir** presented his own proposal promising elections in the territories but insisted that neither the PLO nor PLO-sponsored candidates take part.

THE GULF WAR (1990-1991)

The Gulf Crisis began when Iraqi troops marched into Kuwait on August 2, 1990. Early on, Iraqi President **Saddam Hussein** had slyly suggested he would withdraw from Kuwait when Israel withdrew from the West Bank, Gaza, and Golan, and when Syria withdrew from Lebanon. This gesture, along with promises to liberate Palestine, won Saddam the support of Palestinians. In fighting that lasted from January 16 to February 28, 1991, a coalition formed by the United States, various European countries, Egypt, Syria, Saudi Arabia, and the other Gulf states forced Iraq to withdraw from Kuwait. During the conflict, 39 Iraqi SCUD missiles fell on Tel Aviv and Haifa, cheered on by Arafat and the Palestinian population. Israel, under pressure from the US and fearful of a Palestinian-led conflagration in Jordan, did not retaliate.

THE PEACE PROCESS (1991-2000)

THE MADRID CONFERENCE. When the Gulf War cease-fire was announced, hope was high that parties like Israel and Syria—for the first time on the same side of a regional conflict—could be brought to the bargaining table. In July 1991, Syria surprised the world with the announcement that it would attend a regional peace conference. At a summit meeting in Moscow, US President George Bush and Soviet President Mikhail Gorbachev decided to host the conference jointly. A hesitant Israeli cabinet, led by the right-wing Shamir, and uneasy about jeopardizing US aid, voted to attend the proposed conference provided that the PLO and residents of East Jerusalem not take part. On October 30, 1991, the Madrid peace conference was convened, with Israel carrying on separate negotiations with Syria, Lebanon, Egypt, and a joint Jordanian-Palestinian delegation. While the act of convening the conference was significant in and of itself, the unprecedented gathering quickly became bogged down in discussions of Security Council Resolution 242, Palestinian autonomy and rights, Jerusalem, Israeli settlements, refugees, and the PLO's political scope, and did not produce any substantial results. Subsequent sessions held in Washington, DC did not get much further.

THE OSLO ACCORDS AND PEACE WITH JORDAN. On June 23, 1992, an Israeli election ousted Shamir's Likud and ushered in a left-wing government led by the Labor Party and Prime Minister **Yitzhak Rabin.** While Rabin's rhetoric had been harsh against the Palestinians in the days of the *intifada*, he curtailed settlement growth and promised Palestinian autonomy. Optimism accompanying the first round of talks under the new Israeli government, held in November 1992, was soon undermined. **Hamas,** a nationalist Islamic socio-political movement struggling for Arab control of all of historic Palestine, carried out several terrorist attacks in Israel which prevented any progress.

Almost a year later, Israel and the PLO surprised the world by announcing that a group of academics and non-political representatives meeting secretly in Oslo had successfully negotiated an agreement on the framework for solving the Israeli-Palestinian conflict peacefully. The Declaration of Principles on Interim Self-Government Arrangements (the DOP—also known as the **Oslo Accord**) was signed at the White House on September 13, 1993, with President Bill Clinton presiding over the ceremony. The DOP provided mutual recognition between Israel and the PLO and established the land-for-peace model as the basis for Israeli-Palestinian negotiations. It also included a plan for immediate implementation of Palestinian autonomy in the Gaza Strip and the Jericho area, with the autonomous areas to be expanded in stages over a five-year transitional period. The DOP was followed by the negotiation of several other Israeli-Palestinian agreements. The first was the **Gaza/Jericho Agreement,** which provided the details for Israeli withdrawal from these areas and the creation of a **Palestinian Authority (PA),** headed by Yassir Arafat and a 24-member council.

The signing of the Oslo Accords was met with widespread optimism both in Israel and in the West Bank and Gaza. As Israeli troops began to pull out of cities and territories in the West Bank and Gaza, ceding security and civil responsibilities to the Palestinian Authority, hopes began to set in that the long and bitter Israeli-Arab conflict was finally coming to an end. Arafat returned to a jubilant Gaza in 1994 after 27 years in exile, and with the Palestinian issue seemingly well on its way to being solved, the Arab world began to warm toward Israel. On October 26, 1994, Jordan and Israel signed a peace treaty, establishing full diplomatic relations between the two countries and opening their borders, allowing Israelis and Jordanians to visit each other's countries for the first time since 1948. In early 1995, bilateral negotiations with Syria began, focused on peace between the two countries in exchange for the withdrawal of Israeli troops from the strategic Golan Heights. Such a withdrawal would have been highly controversial within Israel, and the Israeli government stated that it would place any agreement negotiated with Syria on a national referendum to be decided upon by the Israeli public.

ASSASSINATION OF RABIN. While much of the Israeli public supported the peace agenda that Rabin's government had pursued, the land-for-peace policies that he advocated met with a fierce resistance from a growing right-wing opposition. On November 4, 1995, after attending a massive peace rally in Tel Aviv, Rabin was shot and killed by a 25 year-old right-wing Jewish university student named Yigal Amir. Over one million shocked Israelis, Jews, and Arabs alike filed by the slain leader's coffin in the days following the murder. Rabin's funeral drew over 50 world leaders to Jerusalem, including United States President Bill Clinton, Jordan's King Hussein, Egyptian President Hosni Mubarak, and representatives from four other Arab states.

THE LATE 90S. Following Rabin's assassination, the Labor Party's **Shimon Peres** became Prime Minister, but he was defeated in the May 1996 elections by **Benjamin Netanyahu,** leader of the conservative Likud party. Many attribute Peres's loss to a series of suicide bombings that Palestinian militant groups, like Hamas, carried out throughout Israel in the months before the elections. Netanyahu's term as Prime Minister marked a turn away from Rabin's peace-oriented politics, and his continued support of Israeli settlements in the West Bank and East Jerusalem prompted violent clashes. In September 1996, the Israeli government's decision to open a tunnel entrance adjacent to the Temple Mount and to Muslim holy sites in Jerusalem sparked protests that degenerated into deadly fighting. Thirty-seven Palestinians and 11 Israelis died in the conflict as the spectacle of gunfights between Israeli soldiers and the PA's police force seemed to announce the near-collapse of the peace process. Throughout the fall of 1996, US President **Bill Clinton** met with Arafat and Netanyahu to try to salvage relations between the two groups, and a 1997 agreement on an Israeli withdrawal from Hebron raised some hopes that the peace might still be possible. The persistence of suicide bombings and an Israeli reluctance to relinquish further territories, however, caused the peace process to stall until Netanyahu was defeated in the 1999 elections by the Labor Party's **Ehud Barak.**

Barak tried to resurrect hopes in Israeli-Arab peace, voicing a renewed commitment to the land-for-peace model, and to finally tackling the long-standing core issues of the Israeli-Palestinian conflict, particularly refugees, Jerusalem, the settlements, and borders. In September 2000, Barak announced that Israel would withdraw its troops from southern Lebanon, where they had been positioned since the 1982 campaign. Barak hoped the pullout would indicate Israeli goodwill and encourage peace-talks with neighboring Syria. Throughout the winter, however, escalating skirmishes prompted Barak to advance the pullout to June 1, 2000. When attacks by the militant Lebanese Islamist organization **Hezbollah** intensified, Barak realized that holding out an extra six days would only lead to increased conflict. On May 24th, when Israeli forces executed an expedited withdrawal from all of southern Lebanon, Israel's 20-year occupation of southern Lebanon came to a close.

Shortly after the Lebanon pullout, Barak's attention focused to solving the core issues of the Israeli-Palestinian conflict. On July 11, 2000, Barak and Arafat convened at US President Clinton's invitation in Camp David, with the stated purpose of working out a comprehensive framework for solving all of the core issues of the conflict. While the sides came closer than ever before on resolving the core issues, agreeing on border, land, and water arrangements, wide gaps still existed on the issues of Jerusalem and the right of Palestinian refugees to return to their homes. After two weeks of negotiations, on July 25th, the summit ended without the sides having reached a comprehensive agreement. The failure of Camp David created widespread frustration amongst the Palestinian population, and in late September 2000, when Israeli opposition leader **Ariel Sharon** made a controversial visit to the Temple Mount, violent protests broke out across the West Bank and Gaza.

THE SECOND INTIFADA, THE GAZA DISENGAGEMENT, AND THE RISE OF HAMAS (2000-PRESENT).

The violence that followed Sharon's visit quickly spread and intensified, and within a few weeks it became clear that a **second intifada** (sometimes called the **Al Aqsa Intifada** for the Al Aqsa mosque on the Temple Mount) was in full swing. Compared to the first *intifada*, this violence was more severe, with guns and roadside bombs replacing rocks and burning tires. The outbreak of the second *intifada* also caused a conflagration within the Israeli-Arab community, and in a stretch of several days in October 2000, 13 Israeli Arabs were killed by Israeli police. In the wake of mounting violence, Barak's left-wing government fell, and a right-wing government led by the hard line Sharon took power in February 2001.

The rise of Sharon's government marked an end to the Oslo Process of the 1990s and a move away from peace negotiations. Though the Bush Administration made several attempts to negotiate a ceasefire between the sides and return them to the negotiation table, the violence continued. Sharon's government, convinced that Arafat was actively promoting the Palestinian violence, declared that there was "no partner" on the Palestinian side, and confined Arafat to his Ramallah compound. This essentially meant the end of substantial peace talks. Meanwhile, Hamas and other militant groups continued to attack Israeli soldiers and civilians, both in Israel proper and in the West Bank and Gaza. Israel retaliated against these attacks by setting up a comprehensive system of checkpoints and beginning construction on a 436-mile security barrier (sometimes called the "separation fence" or simply the "wall") to separate Israel from the West Bank. Israel also carried out several extensive military operations in Palestinian cities aimed at crippling the militant organizations. The barrier has since become a major source of contention, with the Palestinians claiming that it cuts into Palestinian territory and attempts to unilaterally establish borders on the ground, and the Israeli government responding that the barrier is necessary for security purposes and not related to any political disagreement over borders.

In the summer of 2005, Sharon announced the **Disengagement Plan,** ordering the unilateral evacuation of all Israeli settlements and military personnel from the Gaza Strip, explaining that the continued presence of settlers in Gaza had become untenable for Israel. Despite fierce and sometimes violent protests by the settlers and large parts of Israel's right-wing population, the disengagement proceeded, removing all Israeli presence from the Gaza Strip within a matter of days.

Shortly thereafter, major changes shook up both Palestinian and Israeli leadership. Arafat became very ill and died in November 2004, leaving the largely unpopular **Mahmoud Abbas** (Abu Mazen) as the leader of his Fatah party and as President of the Palestinian Authority. While Israel and the United States were more willing to engage with Abbas, his lack of legitimacy among the mainstream Palestinian population prevented him from taking decisive action on many issues. In January 2006, Abbas's Fatah was decisively defeated by Hamas in general elections that took place throughout the West Bank and Gaza. The political leader and new Palestinian Prime Minister **Isma'il Haniya** quickly formed a unity government with Fatah, which both Israel and the United States refused to recognize. In Israel, Sharon, after calling for new elections and creating the new centrist **Kadima** party, suffered a massive stroke in early January and was left in a coma. His deputy **Ehud Olmert** subsequently led Kadima to a victory in the elections, based on a platform of further unilateral withdrawals of settlements from the West Bank, and established a unity government together with the Labor Party in March 2006.

TODAY

RECENT NEWS

In the summer of 2006, a 34-day war broke out between Lebanon and northern Israel, resulting in the deaths of over a thousand Lebanese people and a much smaller number of Israelis. The first attack consisted of several rockets fired at Israeli border towns by Hezbollah militants as a diversion for a subsequent anti-tank missile launch. The PLO has been engaging in attacks on Israel from southern Lebanon since 1968, so this conflict was not without historical precedent. Israel responded heavily to the Hezbollah attack with air strikes, an air and naval blockade, and a ground invasion. The hostilities were ended by a United Nations resolution that called for the withdrawal of Israel from Lebanon and the disarmament of Hezbollah. Israel and Lebanon remain in a tense, though relatively peaceful, ceasefire to this day.

The following summer, escalating tensions between the two Palestinian political parties Fatah and Hamas led Hamas to violently seize the Gaza Strip, and to begin governing it completely independently of Palestinian President Mahmoud

Abbas. As a result, Israel immediately closed off all access to the Gaza Strip and has since strictly limited the passage of goods, water, and electricity into Gaza in an attempt to pressure Hamas to relinquish power. Abbas, for his part, dissolved the Palestinian unity government, and has since run the West Bank through his Fatah party without the involvement of Hamas, essentially creating two separate Palestinian entities, one in the West Bank and the other in Gaza. In January 2009, Abbas' presidential term officially ended, though he independently declared an extension of his term for an extra year. Hamas does not currently recognize Abbas as the president of Palestine.

The Gaza Strip continues to be a major hub of unrest in the region. From 2001 until fairly recently, Hamas has used the Strip as a base from which to launch Qassam rockets—mostly smuggled in from Sinai through underground tunnels—against Israeli civilian targets in the south of Israel. With all border crossings in and out of Gaza closed by Israel and Egypt since Hamas's 2007 seizure of power, and with only about 100 trucks per day with food and medicinal supplies flowing in, the situation of the already impoverished local Palestinian population has worsened. In late December 2008, after the six-month truce between Israel and Hamas expired and an unusually large number of rockets hit southern Israel, the Israeli military launched a three-week campaign in the Strip intended to neutralize the Qassam threat and weaken Hamas. Hamas responded to the offensive by bombarding the south of Israel with hundreds of rockets and mortars. Over 1000 Palestinians and 13 Israelis died in this latest bout of violence. In the summer of 2009, Hamas suspended its use of rockets (only two rockets were fired in June, in comparison to the sometimes dozens a day of earlier years), claiming them ineffective. It has also transferred much of its energy from armed resistance to cultural resistance. Though the active battle has calmed down somewhat, the Gaza Strip is still extremely dangerous (and nearly impossible to enter) for travelers; as a result, the Gaza Strip has not been included in this edition of *Let's Go Israel*.

The West Bank has been somewhat quieter in recent years, as improving economic conditions and the steady withdrawal of Israeli military forces from major Palestinian population centers have led to a significant reduction in violence. There are still several major sources of tension, however. Since 2002, Israel has been building a "Separation Barrier" (or "Apartheid Wall," as many Palestinians call it) dividing the West Bank from the rest of Israel, and isolating numerous Palestinian communities from their resources (see **Another Brick in the Wall**, p. 298). The Israeli settlements in the West Bank (which the United Nations has deemed illegal) continue to expand despite Palestinian and American objections. The Israeli government has said that it plans to dismantle illegal outposts, but that it will continue to support building and expansion in the major settlement blocs. Other relevant sources of tension are Palestine's unwillingness to recognize Israel as a Jewish state and Israel's unwillingness to allow the more than four million Palestinian refugees—currently living in Jordan, the West Bank, Gaza, and several other countries—to return to their hometowns within Israel's borders. All in all, it is a prickly (though improved) situation.

The most recent Israeli parliamentary elections were held in February 2009, resulting in a right-wing government led by Likud's Benjamin Netanyahu, largely supported by hardliner Avigdor Lieberman's Yisrael Beitenu Party and Ehud Barak's Labor party. The opposition is led by Tzipi Livni, head of the centrist Kadima Party, which currently holds the most seats in the Israeli Knesset. Netanyahu has sought to shift Israel's foreign policy away from Israeli-Palestinian negotiations and from the idea of a two-state solution, focusing instead on building a regional and global coalition to oppose Iran and its nuclear ambitions.

LIFE AND TIMES

GOVERNMENT AND POLITICS

BASIC LAWS

The State of Israel was founded on May 14, 1948 as a parliamentary democracy. Although it was stated in the Proclamation of Independence that the first Constituent Assembly would draft a constitution for Israel, disagreements between the religious and secular parties precluded the ratification of a written constitution at that time. In its place, a series of **Basic Laws** were laid out as a framework for legislation. These laws were to be incorporated into a future constitution, but little progress has been made in the decades since. Several of the Basic Laws can only be amended by an absolute or special majority of the legislative body. There are 11 of these laws, which define the major ideological principles of Israel and lay out the basic rights and duties of the Israeli government and citizens.

KNESSET AND GOVERNMENT SYSTEM

The Basic Laws also provide the framework for the **Knesset,** the Israeli parliament. The Knesset contains 120 representatives, or Members of Knesset, who are elected in direct general elections. Israelis do not vote for a particular candidate; instead, they vote for political parties who are then allotted a particular number of seats in proportion to the percentage of the popular vote that they received, provided they receive more than 2% of the popular vote. The leader of the largest party, or of the party most likely to successfully build a coalition of at least 61 Members of Knesset, is then given authority by the **President of Israel** to build a coalition, appoint a government, and become **Prime Minister.** The President has a largely ceremonial role, and is elected every seven years by the Members of Knesset.

While parliamentary elections are officially supposed to take place only once every four years, the party-based system has led to many weak governments that were toppled before their terms were finished, leading to early elections. The past five elections have all occurred earlier than their official date. Because of this, the current government has stated that one of its priorities is reforming the system of government in Israel and turning it into a Presidential system.

Israel has a strong and independent **judiciary branch,** anchored by the **Supreme Court.** New Supreme Court Justices are nominated by a committee composed of three existing Justices, two government Ministers, two Members of Knesset, and two members of the Israeli Bar Association, and are officially appointed by the President of Israel. Justices serve on the court until they reach age 70, die, or decide to resign.

POLITICAL PARTIES AND MAJOR POLITICAL FIGURES

The current Knesset contains 12 parties, the largest being **Kadima** ("forwards"), led by opposition leader Tzipi Livni; **Likud,** led by Prime Minister Binyamin Netanyahu; **Yisrael Beiteinu** ("Israel is our home"), led by Foreign Minister Avigdor Lieberman; and **Labor,** led by Defense Minister Ehud Barak. Likud and Yisrael Beiteinu belong to the right wing bloc in the Knesset, while Kadima and Labor belong to the center-left camp. The current President of Israel is Shimon Peres. Traditionally, the critical issue separating right and left in Israeli politics is the question of territorial compromise in exchange for peace with the Palestinians.

MEDIA

Israelis tend to have something of an obsession with the news. Most read at least one newspaper daily, listen multiple times a day to news reports broadcasted on the radio, watch the news on television every night, and religiously post 'talkbacks' or responses to online articles and blog posts. The Israeli press is far livelier than the Western norm; politics are taken seriously and opinions expressed vociferously. Accordingly, Israelis tend to have pronounced political views and expound upon them freely. The liberal *Ha'Aretz*, published in both Hebrew and English editions, is the most respected daily. *Yediot Aharonot* and *Ma'ariv*, which lean right of center, are more widely read and more tabloid-esque in their coverage. The other English-language daily, *The Jerusalem Post*, is right-leaning, and also publishes the bi-weekly *Jerusalem Report*. The most popular television stations are the privately-owned **Channel 2** and **Channel 10,** offering a mix of reality TV, news programs, and other entertainment. The state-owned **Channel 1,** while less glitzy than the newer channels, still retains a loyal following.

ISRAELI DEFENSE FORCES (IDF)

The state of Israel requires army service for all Israeli men and women at the age of 18. Men serve for a minimum of three years, and women for two. The vast majority of new conscripts are put in combat support roles, such as logistics, planning, and intelligence, while a little less than a quarter are sent to actual combat units. The IDF has several elite combat units, including **Sayeret Matkal** and the **paratroopers,** and many high school graduates compete in rigorous tests and physical exercises to be accepted into the top units. After being discharged from mandatory service, Israeli men are still required to carry out **reserve duty** *("Milu'im")* for up to a month each year until the age of 45 or 50. The personal experience that most Israelis have had with the army make it one of the most popular Israeli institutions, and one of the few common denominators in a deeply divided society.

While mandatory conscription has traditionally maintained the stature of the army as the great social leveler, instrumental in integrating the various ethnically and economically diverse segments of the Israeli population, increasing exemptions have recently challenged this view. The most controversial of these is a full exemption from service for Ultra-Orthodox Jews who elect to study in a Yeshiva instead of serving. This arrangement has been in place since the establishment of the state, and was part of a compromise between the secular government and the religious authorities. Israeli-Arabs are also automatically exempt from service, though many of them, especially from the Bedouin community, volunteer to serve. Exemptions are also possible for women on religious grounds or for reasons of conscientious objection. They are often required to complete some national service *(sherut leumi)* in lieu of military service. All told, recent numbers released by the army suggest that more than 30% of eligible Israelis do not serve in the army.

ECONOMY

Poor in natural resources, stymied by socialist inefficiencies, and hamstrung by the burdens of large defense expenditures and Jewish refugee absorption, Israel for years relied upon substantial financial assistance from diaspora

Jewish communities and foreign governments, especially that of the US. In the last few years, however, the country has begun to reap the fruits of extensive privatization, free trade with the US and the European Community, and the development of a high-tech export-oriented economy of $205.7 billion.

Israel's growth rate is extremely high, averaging 3.1% from 2002-2006, and in May 2007 it was invited to join the OECD (Organization for Economic Co-Operation and Development, which includes the United Kingdom and the United States). Its per capita GDP (approximately $28,900) was the 27th highest in the world in 2007. Israel's trade deficit has been a persistent problem, and its reduction has been a primary goal of every Israeli government. The deficit now approaches $91.25 billion, though it is decreasing in relative terms: exports now finance around 85% of imports, as opposed to 14% in 1950. In total, Israel's industrial exports have grown over 1550 times since 1948 and now exceed $54.2 billion.

The country's main industries are chemicals, diamond cutting and polishing, textiles, high-tech (especially bio-medical and computer) products, and military hardware. Israel is also a leader in desert agriculture and plant genetics. Of particular note is the role of solar power in the economy. Since the 1950s, the use of solar energy to help solve energy shortages in Israel has produced a thriving eco-friendly industry boom of solar power companies, which provide energy in over 90% of Israeli homes.

Israel's economy has always suffered from high inflation. By the early 1980s, the annual inflation rate had reached the triple digits. In 1985, when inflation threatened to reach four digits, the government implemented an emergency stabilization program that has helped curb inflation substantially. The **new Israeli shekel (NIS)** has held relatively steady against the dollar, and inflation from 2002-2006 was roughly 1.9%.

The two greatest burdens on Israel's economy are defense and social spending. The former has declined markedly as a result of the peace process—expenditures on defense now make up 6% of the GDP, as opposed to 23% in 1980. Immigration, however, continues to exert pressure on the economy. Since it attained independence, Israel has absorbed more than 2.6 million immigrants, four times the number of Jews living in the country in 1948. In the early 1990s alone over 800,000 immigrants, primarily from the former Soviet Union, flooded the country, driving unemployment to 11.2% in 1992. Because Israel has always been committed to providing social services, the immigration boom has been a financial strain. Over 50% of public expenditure is spent on health care, unemployment assistance, and other social service programs.

At the same time, recent immigration has flooded Israel with highly educated workers and professionals. While it took time for the economy to accommodate so many skilled individuals (horror stories abound of scientists forced to sweep streets), the net result has been a tremendous economic boom. With incomes rising, Israel has begun importing tens of thousands of workers from Asia and Eastern Europe to work the menial jobs Israelis no longer want. The country's newfound prosperity and the current focus of the US government on domestic issues have led many to predict that the large American foreign aid traditionally received (US$3 billion per year plus loan guarantees) will be reduced in coming years.

KIBBUTZIM AND MOSHAVIM

Two percent of the Israeli population lives on about 270 kibbutzim (plural of kibbutz), somewhat socialist rural communities where resources are communally owned and production is controlled by the members. The kibbutzim of today hardly resemble the fiercely ideological pioneer agricultural settlements that began 80 years ago, which were based on strong egalitarian and communal values. These days, most kibbutzim rely more on industry than on agriculture, and most use immigrant workers in the fields. In addition, the passion for austerity is subsiding; kibbutzniks now demand the same luxuries enjoyed by other Israelis (like, for instance, larger living quarters, multiple televisions and computers, and trips to Disney World). Most kibbutz children now live with their parents in nuclear family homes, whereas just a decade or two ago nearly all children lived in separate dormitories and saw their parents only at designated times. Many of the communal dining rooms have also disappeared or become supplemental to private meals at home.

KIBBUTZ! If the idea of kibbutz life gives you the warm fuzzies, be aware that the application process is long, rigorous, and highly selective. As one *kibbutznik* explains, "we're one big family, and you don't want just anyone in your family." Applicants first go through a series of interviews and background checks to assess the contribution they would make, both professionally and socially. Hermits need not apply. They then have a two-year trial period, after which applicants must be accepted by a two-thirds majority vote of all members. Legacies aren't guaranteed a spot, either: kids who grew up on a *kibbutz* and spouses of members must go through the same process. Get cracking on those applications—most kibbutzim don't accept anyone over 45.

Today's kibbutzim face mounting problems. Labor shortages are becoming common as around two thirds of younger members leave the settlements to test their skills elsewhere. More non-member workers are being brought into the kibbutzim to fill in labor shortages. At the same time, more kibbutz members are finding outside employment and giving their salaries to the kibbutz, a practice which, though financially beneficial to the community, detracts from the communal feel. In addition, billions of dollars in kibbutz debt, accumulated over years of living beyond community means, pose a daunting obstacle.

Approximately 3.2% of the Israeli population live on 450 *moshavim*, another type of rural settlement where property is privately owned, and which provide roughly 40% of Israel's food. *Moshavniks* typically harvest their own piece of land, though marketing is often done collectively; some have a crop that all members help cultivate. Recently, many *moshavim* near big cities have gone suburban—their members commute to the city.

PEOPLE

DEMOGRAPHICS

Of the 7.2 million residents in Israel, 76% are Jewish and 16% are Muslim; of the remaining 5%, about half are Christians. Most of these Muslims and Christians are Arabs.

JEWS IN ISRAEL

Many Israeli Jews are first- or second-generation immigrants, and are often divided along ethnic lines. These differences lead to a society riddled with tensions, where social and religious alliances are frequently of painful importance. Disputes between these groups tend to play out in the public and political arenas, and stereotypes abound.

ASHKENAZIM AND SEPHARDIM

Sephardic Jews (many of pre-1492 Spanish origins) come from Arab or other Mediterranean countries; Ashkenazi Jews have northern or eastern European origins. The rift between these groups in Israeli society is deep, and goes back to the 1950s, when Sephardic Jews from Arab countries were brought to an already established, Ashkenazi-dominated state. Although Sephardim compose roughly half of the Jewish population in Israel, and developments in recent years have narrowed the gaps between the ethnic groups somewhat, Ashkenazim still fill most of the positions of power in government, the military, and academia, and Sephardim are much more likely to be poor.

RUSSIANS AND ETHIOPIANS

After the massive immigration from Russia and Ethiopia throughout most of the 1990s and early 2000s, the numbers of immigrants have begun to taper off in recent years. Currently, a few thousand Russian and Ethiopian Jews arrive in Israel every year. Significant portions of both groups have had difficulties integrating successfully into Israeli society, though Russians have found it easier to find employment and gain acceptance in Israel's institutes of higher education. Many Jewish Ethiopian communities remain impoverished and alienated, living on the fringes of Israeli society.

ISRAELI-ARABS AND PALESTINIANS

The vast majority of the non-Jewish population in Israel, the West Bank, and Gaza is Arab, whether Muslim or Christian. Israeli-Arabs and Palestinians are similar culturally and ethnically, and the only major differentiating feature between them is the possession of Israeli citizenship. Many Israeli-Arabs identify far more with Palestinians than they do with Jewish Israelis.

Israeli-Arabs live in Arab cities and towns scattered throughout the country, and in several mixed Jewish-Arab cities, such as Jerusalem, Haifa, and Jaffa. In general, Arab towns and cities in Israel tend to be poorer than Jewish ones, receiving less support from the government. Arab citizens of Israel tend to be less well paid and less educated than their Jewish counterparts. While recent Israeli governments have recognized the need to close the socioeconomic gap between Jews and Arabs in Israel, few steps have been taken.

The **Bedouin** are a distinctive subgroup within the Arab population in Israel, mostly concentrated in the Negev desert and the West Bank. Many of them still live in temporary, seasonal homes, or in makeshift villages that are unrecognized by the Israeli government. Over the past few decades, the Israeli government has tried to settle most of the Bedouin in more permanent towns and cities; this effort has faced various difficulties.

LANGUAGE

The **Hebrew** language contains 22 characters, written from right to left. Vowels are generally left unwritten, but may appear underneath regular characters as smaller markings. The contemporary Hebrew language was created from biblical Hebrew by **Eliezer Ben-Yehuda,** who compiled the first modern Hebrew dictionary in the 1920s. In a surprisingly short period of time, the revived biblical dialect matured into a full-fledged language, spanning from colloquial speech to poetry. While a Semitic language (like Arabic) in structure, modern Hebrew contains elements of European languages; many words for which no equivalent Biblical concept exists have been lifted almost as is. Modern spoken Hebrew contains a large number of Hebraicized versions of English words that may be understandable to careful English-speaking listeners. Most Israelis speak English, and signs are usually written in English as well as Hebrew and Arabic, the official languages of Israel.

ISRAEL PLACE NAMES are transliterated from Hebrew in many different ways. Here are some standardizing rules *Let's Go* employs:
1. **E.** Whenever there is an option between "eh" and "e" at the end of the word, we use "e." (E.g.: Sde Boker instead of Sdeh Boker)
2. **KH.** Whenever there is an option between "h" and "kh," we use "kh." (E.g.: Rekhovot instead of Rehovot; Khula Valley instead of Hula Valley.)
3. **TZ.** Whenever there is an option between "ts," "tz," and "z," we use "tz." (E.g.: Rishon le-Tziyon instead of Rishon le-Zion; Tzfat instead of Tsfat or Zefat; Tzippori instead of Zippori.)
4. **LE, EL, AL & HA.** When we use the prefix "le-," "el-," "al-," or "ha-," we do not capitalize it, but we do include a dash after it. (E.g.: Rishon le-Tziyon instead of Rishon LeTziyon; Rosh ha-Nikra instead of Rosh HaNikra; el-Azariya instead of El-Azariya.)
5. **K.** Whenever there is an option between "k" or "q" or "c," we use "k." (E.g.: Sorek Cave instead of Soreq Cave; Zikhron Ya'akov instead of Zikhron Ya'acov or Zikhron Ya'aqov; Kumran instead of Qumran.) One exception: Caesarea.
6. **Y.** Whenever there is an option between "y" and "yy" and "i," we use "y." (E.g.: Nahariya instead of Nahariyya; Banyas instead of Banias.)
Note: these do not apply to Sinai, Petra, and some places in the West Bank.

Several dialects of colloquial **Arabic** are spoken throughout Israel, the West Bank, and Gaza, though the most common are the Palestinian urban dialect and the Bedouin dialect. The official Arabic used in the media and in official documents is Modern Standard Arabic or *fusha*. The **appendix** (p. 412) of this book contains a list of useful Hebrew and Arabic words and phrases.

RELIGION

Each religious community in Israel has its own religious authorities, funded by the Ministry of Religion, and controls its own holy sites. Freedom of religion is safeguarded by the state under the 1948 **Declaration of Establishment.**

JUDAISM

Neither theologians nor historians can pinpoint a date for the founding of Judaism, but the Israelite religion is believed to have been evolving for perhaps the past four millennia. According to the Bible, **Abraham** was the first to establish a covenant with God through his self-circumcision at the ripe old age of 99. This act is symbolically repeated with each generation of Jewish males. Abraham's grandson Jacob (later renamed Israel) fathered twelve sons from whom descended twelve tribes, the nation of Israel. Abraham, his son Isaac, and his grandson Jacob are believed to be buried with their wives, Sarah, Rebecca, and Leah, in the Cave of the Patriarchs in Hebron (p. 329). Because Ishmael,

YIDDISH-ISH

Kvetch. Tchotchke. Mishpocheh.
No, these words weren't pulled from the coughing fit of a tuberculosis patient. A new tongue reached the Jews of the Israeli Parliament in 2009, and it wasn't between two slices of deli rye. Yiddish, that spell check-unfriendly language, was celebrated for the first time in 2009 with the creation of **Yiddish Culture Day.**

A German-based language written in the Hebrew alphabet, Yiddish is spoken by Eastern European Jews who have since emigrated to other parts of the world—Israel, Brooklyn, etc. For decades, Yiddish was frowned upon by Hebrew-speaking Jews in Israel, as it ostensibly symbolized the Jewish Diaspora. During the Holocaust, though, the majority of native Yiddish speakers were killed, and the ancient vernacular was left in danger of extinction.

The Israeli Parliament created Yiddish Culture Day in an attempt to preserve the history and usage of a language so enmeshed in Jewish culture and history. The Yiddish Culture Day of 2009 fell 150 years after the birth of Sholem Aleichem, a famous Russian-Jewish author who wrote in Yiddish.

During the first observation of the day, events included a concert in Yiddish. Yiddish handbooks, filled with traditional Yiddish phrases, were provided for Israeli legislators. Though Yiddish has hung in the balance for decades, it looks as though, with the help of the government, *mensches* will be *kibbitzing* for years to come.

Abraham's other son, is believed to be the ancestor of Islam, this resting place is holy to both faiths.

The Bible says that the founding period of the Israelite nation was the generation spent wandering in the Sinai desert en route from Egypt to the Holy Land, under the leadership of Moses. It was this generation that received the **Torah,** the central text of Judaism, at **Mount Sinai.** Historians theorize that the disparate tribes later known as the Israelites had gradually united under a common god by the third millennium BCE. This god, **Yahweh,** is thought to have been a young, warlike version of the older Canaanite deity, El (or Elyon; see Exodus 3:15). Some scholars believe Yahweh (God) was introduced to the highland Canaanites by Semitic tribes escaping from Egypt, and that he was worshipped as an alternative to the lowland storm-god, Ba'al. When the Israelites formed a kingdom, worship of God was centralized in the capital, Jerusalem. The religion became focused around the Temple, or *beit hamikdash,* where sacrifices were brought under the supervision of the priests, or *kohanim.* Judaism became decentralized, however, after the destruction of the first Temple. Prayer replaced sacrifice as a significant daily ritual, taking place three times each day on weekdays and four times each day on Shabbat and on holidays.

Historians estimate the present form of the Torah to be 2500 years old, although it has been continuously interpreted and re-interpreted over the centuries in an effort to maintain its vitality and applicability. The Written Torah (also known as the Pentateuch, or the Books of Moses), which consists of the first five books of the Bible, formed the template for the Oral Torah, a series of interpretations and teachings eventually codified in final form around 200 CE as the *Mishnah.* The *Gemara* then formed an additional layer of interpretation. The *Mishnah,* along with the *Gemara,* form the basis of the Babylonian and Jerusalem **Talmud,** finalized during the fifth century CE. The Talmud, organized as a transcribed series of discussions aimed at interpretation of the Mishnah, was the springboard for a new series of interpretations that continue to build upon each other. "Torah," which has come to refer to all Jewish thought and teachings, has been at the core of Jewish life throughout its history.

In Judaism, faith in God is central, but the energy of Jewish life is concentrated on observing the commandments. The Torah contains 613 **mitzvot** (commandments), including directives for ritual observances and instructions concerning moral behavior. Over the ages, rabbis have interpreted and expanded these *mitzvot.* The entire set of laws is called *halakha* ("the way"). These laws are codified in intricate detail and cover every aspect of life.

Much of modern Jewish life revolves around the **synagogue,** which plays a multifaceted role. The Hebrew word *(beit knesset)* means "house of assembly" and the Yiddish word *(shul)* means "school." The *aron ha-kodesh* (Holy Ark) houses the Torah scrolls and determines the orientation of the synagogue. Synagogues normally face toward Jerusalem; within Jerusalem, they face the Temple Mount. Above the *aron ha-kodesh* hangs a flickering *ner tamid* (eternal flame). The raised platform from which prayers are led is called the *bima*. Most synagogues in Israel are Orthodox and contain a *mechitza*, a partition between men's and women's sections. Usually, the two sections have separate entrances. Men should cover their heads when entering a synagogue, since head coverings symbolize a reverence for God. Often there is a box of **kippot,** or head coverings, by the entrance. Worshippers wear other items as reminders of their devotion. The *tallit*, or prayer shawl, has four *tzitzit*, sets of strings twisted and knotted to symbolize the commandments. On weekdays, worshippers wear *tefillin*, boxed scrolls wrapped around the arm and head with leather straps.

Visitors are welcome at most synagogues during prayer services. There are three prescribed prayer times every day: in the morning (the *shacharit* service), in the afternoon (the *mincha* service), and in the evening (the *ma'ariv* service). Smaller synagogues, however, do not meet for every service. On **Shabbat** (the Jewish Sabbath) and holidays there is an additional service during the day. The Kabbalat Shabbat service, on Friday nights, welcomes in Shabbat. Visitors to a synagogue should dress modestly, and nicer attire is in order on Shabbat or holidays. Photographs during the special days are highly inappropriate.

HEADS UP. Head coverings can provide a lot of information about their wearers. Black hats generally indicate affiliation with an ultra-Orthodox religious group, while Orthodox men with a more centrist or national-religious affiliation generally wear knit *kippot*. More spiritual or even hippie religious types often tend to wear large and colorful *kippot* or white knit caps. The intricacies of this code are subtle and complex, often revealing possible political and social affiliations.

JUDAISM IN ISRAEL

Although Judaism is the predominant religion in Israel, by no means is it unified. The diversity of Jewish ideology in Israel governs the codes of everyday interaction among its people. A little over half of Israeli Jews identify themselves as secular; 30% identify as **Orthodox,** and 18% of those as **Ultra-Orthodox.** Most of the remainder define themselves as traditional *("mesorti")*, meaning they celebrate Jewish holidays and respect certain Jewish traditions in their daily life, but do not adhere to the bulk of Jewish law *("halacha")*. Israel also has small **conservative** and **reform** Jewish communities. The religious-secular divide forms something of a fault line in Israeli society. The religious establishment is quite powerful and the electoral system has helped Jewish religious parties wield disproportionate power. Much to the aggravation of many non-Orthodox Israelis, rabbinical courts have a state monopoly on matrimonial issues among Jews. Jews wishing to get married have to fulfill the conditions of specific religious courts, and must use an officially recognized rabbi. Service in the Israeli army (mandatory for all Israelis at the age of 18) is not required for Ultra-Orthodox Jews, which leads to secular resentment. Recent alterations to the **Law of Return,** which guarantees citizenship to any Jew "who has expressed his desire to settle in Israel," have excluded Jews converted by non-Orthodox rabbis and further strained relations. Outbreaks between these groups range from minor protests and demonstrations to more violent clashes, and it is becoming rare for Ultra-Orthodox and even regular Orthodox and secular Jews to live in the same areas.

ISLAM

The Arabic word *islam* translates, in its general sense, as "submission." The basic tenet of Islam is submission to God's will. Islam has its roots in revelations received from 610 to 622 CE by **Muhammad,** who was informed by the Angel Gabriel of his prophetic calling. These revelations, codified in the **Qur'an** (recitation), form the core of Islam. Muslims believe the Arabic text to be perfect, immutable, and untranslatable. Consequently, the Qur'an appears throughout the Muslim world—the majority of which is non-Arabic speaking—in Arabic. Muhammad is seen as the "seal of the prophets," the last of a chain of God's messengers that includes Jewish and Christian figures such as Abraham, Moses, and Jesus. The Qur'an incorporates many of the Biblical traditions associated with these prophets.

Though Muhammad rapidly gained a following in his faith, staunchly monotheistic Islam was met with ample opposition in polytheist Arabia. Persecuted in his native city of Mecca, Muhammad and his followers fled in 622 to the nearby city of Medina, where he was welcomed as mediator of a long-standing blood feud. This *Hijra* (flight or emigration) marks the beginning of the Muslim community and of the Islamic calendar. For the next eight years, Muhammad and his community defended themselves against raids and later battled the Meccans and neighboring nomadic tribes. In 630, Mecca surrendered to the Muslims, and afterwards numerous Meccans converted to the new faith voluntarily. This established the pattern for **jihad** (struggle), referring first and foremost to the spiritual struggle against one's own desires, then to the struggle to make one's own Muslim community as righteous as possible, and lastly to the struggle against outsiders wishing to harm the Muslim community.

Muhammad is not believed to be divine, but rather a human messenger of God's word. His actions, however, are sanctified because God chose him to be the recipient of revelation; several verses of the Qur'an demand obedience to the Prophet. The stories and traditions surrounding the Prophet's life have been passed on as **sunna,** and those who follow the *sunna* in addition to the teachings of the Qur'an are considered especially devout. (In fact, the term **Sunni** is derived from *sunna.*) The primary source for sunna is the **Hadith,** a written collection of sayings attributed to Muhammad. Each hadith had to go through a rigorous verification process before it was accepted as truth; the tale had to be verified by several sources, preferably those who saw the action with their own eyes, and the greatest weight was given to testimony by Muhammad's close followers.

Islam continued to grow after the Prophet's death, flourishing in the "Age of Conquest." The four Rightly Guided Caliphs *(Rashidun)* who succeeded Muhammad led wars against apostate nomadic tribes. Faith in Islam was the strength of the Arab armies, which defeated the once-mighty Persian empire by the year 640. The fourth Caliph, Muhammad's nephew and son-in-law **Ali,** was the catalyst for the major split in the Muslim world. Ali slowly lost power and was murdered in 661. The Shi'at Ali (Partisans of Ali or **Shi'a**) believe Ali, as a blood relative of the Prophet, to have been the only legitimate successor to Muhammad, thus separating themselves from Sunni Muslims. Contrary to popular Western perception, Shi'ite Muslims are not fanatics, but rather Muslims with a sharp focus on divinely chosen leaders (or **Imams**) who are blood descendants of the Prophet through Ali.

In the 10th century, under the weight of tradition and consensus, Sunni Muslim scholars **(ulama)** proclaimed the gates of *ijtihad* (individual judgment) closed; new concepts and interpretations could no longer stand on their own but had to be legitimized by tradition. This proscription notwithstanding, *ijtihad* continues today, as within several generations the formal prohibition against forward thinking was removed. There have been numerous reform movements throughout the Islamic world, including the **Wahhabbi** movement in the Arabian peninsula, the movement of the thinker **Jamal al-Din al-Afghani** in the Middle East, and **Muhammad Iqbal** in South Asia. There are four main schools of thought in the Islamic legal system, and the applicability of **sharia**, or Islamic law, is a subject of much strife in a number of Muslim countries, which have seen challenges to entrenched governments by movements carrying the banner of Islam.

The **Sufis** are a mystical movement within Islam, stressing the goal of unity with God. They are organized in orders, with a clear hierarchy from master to disciple. Different orders prescribe different ways of life in order to reach Allah; some preach total asceticism and others seem almost hedonistic in their pursuit of pleasure. Sufi *sheikhs* (masters) and saints are reputed to perform miracles, and their tombs are popular pilgrimage destinations. **Jalal al-Din Rumi,** the great medieval intellectual, founded the famous order of the whirling dervishes. The term "whirling dervish" comes from the joyous spinning and dancing meant to produce a state of mind conducive to unity with Allah. Substances such as wine were often used for similar purposes, though the great poets like Rumi treat the effects of alcohol more as a metaphor for the individual's journey with God.

FIVE PILLARS OF ISLAM

Ash-hadu an la ilaha illa Allah. Ash-hadu anna Muhammadan rasul Allah. (I swear that there is no god but Allah. I swear that Muhammad is God's Messenger.) These words constitute the first lines of the Islamic call to prayer *(adhan)*, which emanates hauntingly five times a day from live or recorded *muezzins* perched atop their minarets. Any person who wishes to convert to Islam may do so by repeating these lines three times, thereby completing the **first pillar** of Islam and becoming a Muslim. Enemies of Islam often memorized the lines before battles, thus providing themselves with an emergency survival tactic.

The second pillar is **prayer** *(salat)*, performed five times per day, preferably following the call of the *muezzin*. Prayers, preceded by ablutions, begin with a declaration of intent and consist of a set cycle of prostrations. No group or leader is necessary for prayers—they constitute a personal communication with God. The person praying must face Mecca. The word for Friday in Arabic means "the day of gathering"; on that day, communal prayer is particularly encouraged.

The third pillar is **alms** *(zakat,* or purification). Because all belongs to God, wealth is only held in trust by people, and *zakat* represents the bond between members of the community. *Zakat* has been historically administered as a tax, and the level of giving is determined as a percentage of the surplus wealth and earnings of the individual.

It is believed that Muhammad received the Qur'an during the month of **Ramadan. Fasting** during this holy month is the fourth pillar of Islam. Between dawn and sunset, Muslims are not permitted to smoke, have sexual intercourse, or let any food or water pass their lips. Exceptions are made for women who are pregnant or menstruating, the sick, and people who are traveling—they must make up the fast at a later date. As soon as the evening *adhan* is heard, Muslims break the fast and begin a night of feasting, visiting friends and relatives, and revelry.

The last pillar, required only once in a lifetime, is pilgrimage **(hajj).** Only Muslims who are financially and physically able are required to fulfill this pillar by journeying to Mecca and Medina during the last month of the Muslim calendar. While *hajj* is essentially a recreation of the actions of the Prophet Muhammad, its effects are to unite Muslims and to stress the equal status of all people who submit to the will of Allah, regardless of gender, race, nationality, or degree of wealth. All pilgrims, from Gulf princes to Cairo street-sweepers, must wrap themselves in white cloth and remove all accessories (which might indicate wealth).

CHRISTIANITY

Christianity began in Judea among the Jewish followers of **Jesus.** The most significant sources on the life of Jesus are the **Gospels.** Scholars agree that the gospels of Mark, Matthew, and Luke were written in that order some time after 70 CE, drawing on an oral tradition which recorded the words of Jesus. The Gospel of John was written in about 100 CE, but it has roots as old as those of the others. These sources provide a history influenced by the experiences of the church fathers and the belief that Jesus was the **Messiah** ("anointed one").

Various historical events date the birth of Jesus, the man regarded by millions as their savior, between 4 BCE and 6 CE. According to Matthew, **Bethlehem** (p. 302) is the birthplace of Jesus, and Mary and Joseph moved to **Nazareth** to protect him; in Luke, Jesus' parents are only temporarily in Bethlehem, and in Mark and John, the birth is not even mentioned. The Bible says that Jesus was born through an **Immaculate Conception:** he was conceived and brought forth by Mary, a virgin, making him a product of God's creative power and free from humanity's original sin. Afterwards, Jesus preached in the **Galilee,** speaking for the poor and the righteous, most notably in the Sermon on the Mount (Matthew 5-7).

After about three years of preaching, Jesus went to Jerusalem, where he was condemned to death by Pontius Pilate and the Romans at the urging of the Pharisees. The events leading up to his death are known as the **Passion.** On Good Friday, he carried his cross down the Via Dolorosa in Jerusalem, stopping at what became known as the Stations of the Cross, until he reached the hill of Golgotha (or Calvary), now marked by the Church of the Holy Sepulchre, where he was crucified.

According to the Gospels, three days after Jesus's crucifixion, on what is now Easter, Mary and two other women went to Jesus's tomb to anoint his body and discovered the tomb empty. An angel announced that Jesus had been resurrected; Jesus subsequently appeared to the Apostles and performed miracles. The **Resurrection** is the point of departure for the Christian faith, the beginning of a new age that the faithful believe will culminate in Christ's *parousia*, or **second coming.**

At first, Christianity was a sect of Judaism that accepted the Hebrew Bible. But the sect's defining tenet that Jesus was the Messiah severed it from mainstream Judaism. **Saint Paul** (originally Saul of Tarsus) successfully adapted Christianity to meet the spiritual needs of the largest body of converts: former pagans. Paul abandoned standard Jewish practices like mandatory circumcision, further separating Christianity from Judaism. The **Book of Acts** documents the actions of the early Christians, and the **Letters of Paul,** which comprise most of the rest of the **New Testament,** give advice to the early Christian communities and explain the delay of the second coming. As Christianity developed, it absorbed earlier practices. The incorporation of ancient festivals such as the winter solstice helped draw the common people to the new religion, and the use of Platonic doctrines converted many intellectuals.

The Christian faith was officially legitimized by the **Edict of Milan,** issued by Emperor Licinius in 313 CE, which proclaimed the toleration of Christianity. In 325, the **Emperor Constantine** made Christianity the official religion of the struggling Roman Empire. Constantine also summoned the first of seven Ecumenical Councils, held in Nicaea, to elaborate and unify the content of the faith. The Council of Nicaea came up with an explicit creed, declaring that Jesus Christ was of the same essence as the Father, and that there were three equal parts to God. This crucial doctrine of the **Trinity,** which is only implicitly supported in the Gospels, maintains that the Father, Son, and Holy Spirit are distinct persons yet all one God.

The Church was called "the body of Christ" and believed to be integral and indivisible. Nonetheless, the Christian community suffered many schisms. The **Egyptian (Coptic) Church** broke off in the third century, when other eastern branches (including the Nestorians and Maronites) began to drift apart from western Christianity. In 1054, the **Great Schism,** caused primarily by the inflexible Cardinal Humbert, split Christendom into the western **Roman Catholic Church** and the **Eastern Orthodox Church.** Whereas Rome upheld the universal jurisdiction and infallibility of the Pope, Orthodoxy stressed the infallibility of the church as a whole. The Spirit, according to the Orthodox, proceeds through the Father, while Roman theology dictates that the Spirit proceeds from the Father and the Son. Orthodox Christians believe that God is highly personal, that each man can find God by looking within himself. In 1517, the German monk Martin Luther sparked the **Reformation,** which quickly split northern Europe from Roman Catholicism, and led to the development of **Protestantism.** Protestantism is composed of many sects, which generally believe in salvation through faith rather than good works. Eastern Orthodoxy, too, is divided into multiple nationalist traditions (Greek, Russian, and Armenian). Only in the 18th century did these diverse churches come to speaking terms, and only in the 20th has the ecumenical movement brought about extensive cooperation.

The central part of the service for Catholics is the mass, which is essentially a reenactment of the last supper: the priest blesses bread and wine and they are changed to Jesus's body and blood by the Holy Spirit. The congregation receives the host just as the apostles did. It is inappropriate for non-Catholics to partake in Catholic communion.

OTHER FAITHS

THE DRUZE

The faith of the Druze, a staunchly independent sect of Shi'ite Muslims, centers around a hierarchy of individuals who are the sole custodians of a religious doctrine hidden from the rest of the world. Many Druze consider themselves a separate ethnicity as well as a religious group, while others consider themselves Arabs. They do not allow conversions into or out of the religion. The Druze believe that the word of God is revealed only to a divinely chosen few, and that these blessed few must be followed to the ends of the earth. The Druze generally remain loyal to their host country. Israel has a Druze population of about 85,000.

The religion was founded in 1017 CE by an Egyptian chieftain, **al-Darazi,** who drew upon various beliefs in the Muslim world, especially **Shi'ism.** The Druze believe that God was incarnated in human forms, the final incarnation being the **Fatimid Caliph al-Hakim,** who lived from 996-1021 CE. The Druze have suffered a history of persecution and repression for their beliefs, which may partially explain the group's refusal to discuss its religion. The late 1600s was a period of prosperity, however, and under **Emir Fakhir al-Din** the Druze kingdom extended from Lebanon to Gaza to the Golan Heights. Sixteen villages were built from the Mediterranean Sea to the Jezreel Valley to guard the two major roads on which goods were transported. In 1830, a Druze revolt against the Egyptian *pasha* was crushed, along with all but two of the 14 Druze villages in the Carmel. In the 1860s, the Ottomans encouraged the Druze to return to the Carmel.

Because the Druze will not discuss their religion, most of what Westerners know about them comes from British "explorers" who fought their way into villages and stole holy books. Many of the Druze themselves are not completely informed. As far as outsiders know, **Jethro,** father-in-law of Moses, is their most revered prophet. The most important holiday falls in late April. In Israel, Druze gather in the holy village of Hittim, near Tiberias. Devout Druze are forbidden to smoke, drink alcohol, or eat pork, but many young Druze do not adhere strictly to these prohibitions. Some Druze believe in reincarnation and speak of their past lives. Gabriel Ben-Dor's *The Druze in Israel: A Political Study* details their ideology, lifestyle, and political situation.

When the State of Israel was established, the Druze living in Israel decided to align themselves with the new state, and declared their full loyalty as Israeli citizens. Most Druze men and women proudly serve in the Israeli army, and it is common to see Israeli flags prominently displayed throughout many of the Druze villages concentrated in the north of Israel. Because of this, Druze towns and villages tend to receive more government support than Arab towns, and Druze are generally more integrated than Arabs into Israeli society. One exception to this is the community of Druze living on the Golan Heights, many of whom bear allegiance to Syria and do not define themselves as Israeli.

THE BAHA'I

The Baha'i religion was born in Tehran in 1863, when Mirza Hussein Ali (a son of Persian nobility) turned 46, renamed himself **Baha'ullah** ("Glory of God"), and began preaching non-violence and the unity of all religions. Baha'u'llah's arrival had been foretold in 1844 by the Persian **Siyyid Ali Muhammad** (also known as **al- Bab,** or "Gateway to God"), the first prophet of the Baha'i religion, who heralded the coming of a new divine teacher and messenger. Baha'ullah was imprisoned and then exiled to Palestine, where he taught in Acre (Akko). He is buried near the city. Al-Bab is buried in Haifa, which is now home to a large Baha'i population.

Baha'ullah's teachings fill over 100 volumes, and his religion incorporates elements of major Eastern and Western religions. Baha'i believe in a Supreme Being, accepting Jesus, Buddha, Muhammad, and Baha'ullah as divine prophets. The scripture includes the Bible, the Qur'an, and the Bhagavad Gita. A central doctrine of the faith regards the Baha'i vision of the future. Instead of warning of a final Judgement Day or an end of the world (like many other religions), Baha'ullah prophesied a "flowering of humanity," an era of peace and enlightenment to come. Before this new age can arrive, however, the world must undergo dreadful events to give civilization the impetus to reform itself. The Baha'i espouse trans-racial unity, sexual equality, global disarmament, and the creation of a world community. The rapidly growing Baha'i faith currently boasts more than six million adherents, with two million conversions worldwide in the last decade.

THE KARAITES

The small sect of Jews known as the Karaites dwell principally in Ashdod, Be'er Sheva, and the Tel Aviv suburb of Ramla. The community of 15,000 traces its roots to the ninth century CE. Formed out of the political and religious turmoil following the Muslim invasion, Karaites adhere strictly to the five books of the Torah, but they reject all later Jewish traditions. They are generally cohesive, and have their own religious courts. To an outsider, however, their practices appear similar to those dictated by traditional Jewish observance.

THE SAMARITANS

Currently, the Samaritan community is a tiny one, with roughly 500 adherents divided between Nablus on the West Bank and holon, a suburb of Tel Aviv. Originally the residents of Samaria, Samaritans consider themselves the original Israelites, descended from the tribes of Joseph (Manasseh and Ephraim) from whom other Israelites learned monotheism. The religion is seen by non-members as an offshoot of Judaism marked by literal interpretation of the Samaritan version of the Old Testament and the exclusion of later Jewish interpretation (e.g. the *Mishnah*, the Talmud, and all books of the Hebrew Bible after Joshua) from its canon. A gradual, centuries-long separation between the two religions culminated with the destruction of the Samaritan temple on Mt. Gerizim by the Hasmonean king John Hyrcanus in 128 BCE. The mountain is still the most holy site of the Samaritan religion. Centuries of persecution by the various rulers of Palestine and thousands of deaths in a 529 CE uprising against Byzantine rule shrank the community to its present size. While the Rabbinate does not recognize Samaritans as Jews, the Israeli government applies the Law of Return (the granting of settlement rights) to them.

CULTURE

CUSTOMS AND ETIQUETTE

Among Israelis, the standard introduction on the first meeting is "Shalom" followed by a handshake. Orthodox Jewish men are not supposed to shake hands with women; it is often the best policy for women to allow men to initiate the gesture. Israelis tend to speak at a closer distance to each other than Westerners do. There is also typically more physical contact during conversations—again, women should not initiate such contact. Extreme gesturing is acceptable in Israeli society, but pointing is taboo.

The traditional Arab greeting involves each grasping the other's right hand, placing the left hand on the other's right shoulder, and placing kisses on each cheek. Nevertheless, Palestinians accustomed to foreign visitors will likely initiate a standard handshake. In the Arab world, the left hand is believed to be unclean. Eat only with the right hand. To show the bottom of the foot is considered gravely offensive. When entering mosques, be sure to remove your shoes.

For more information on proper conduct, see **Religion** (p. 57). In most religious settings, and in Muslim settlements in general, modest dress is required. Since religion is very important to many Israelis and Palestinians, travelers to the area should always be sensitive to religious practices and regulations.

FOOD & DRINK

Food is taken very seriously in Israel, where a mix of Eastern and Western cuisine provides a formidable list of culinary options. Some Jewish Israelis' diets are affected by the laws of *Kashrut*, the Jewish dietary laws, which require rabbinical approval for all food consumed. Observant Jews will not eat or shop in a place that carries non-kosher goods (e.g., meat that has not been prepared in a specific way); to respect kosher clientele, the big supermarket chains in Israel carry only kosher products, and many restaurants and most hotels serve only kosher food. Nevertheless, observance of *kashrut* is hardly the norm in Israel—many restaurants, particularly in Haifa and Tel Aviv, are avidly *non*-kosher.

The typical Israeli eats a large breakfast, a big mid-day lunch, and a light, late supper. Because of the poor quality and high cost of beef and lamb, Israelis rely largely on chicken, dairy, and vegetable products. Popular items in the Israeli diet include **hummus** (mashed chick-peas, garlic, lemon, and *tahina*, a sesame concoction); Middle Eastern salad, a finely chopped mix of tomatoes, cucumbers and onion, garnished with oil and vinegar; *gvina levana*, soft white cheese; *schnitzel*, breaded and fried chicken breast; chips (french fries); and a variety of sweet dairy snacks. Recently, a large number of modestly priced gourmet hamburger restaurants and fast food joints have popped up around the country.

 TIP

ISRAELI CRUNCH. Israel has two "indigenous" snack foods that generally inspire intense love-hate reactions from tourists. *Bamba* are crispy peanut buttery puffs eaten as a pseudo-protein by Israeli kids. *Bissli* is a more complex taste to acquire, as it comes in a variety of flavors, ranging from falafel to pizza, as well as a variety of pasta-esque shapes. Shun the *Bissli* imposter *Shosh* if a storekeeper tries to pan it off as the real thing, identifiable by the bee mascot on its package. Try eating these in front of a television to get an authentically Israeli couch potato experience.

The variety of ethnic cuisines in Israel is impressive: restaurants run the gamut from Chinese to French to Moroccan to American to Yemenite. Many restaurants serve typical Middle Eastern food, and in many cases this will be the freshest, tastiest option. Restaurants serving Eastern European Jewish food are rare and very expensive. **Falafel,** Israel's most popular street food, consists of deep-fried ground chick-pea balls served in pita bread with vegetables and *tahina* sauce. Other common pita-fillers are hummus and **shawarma** (chunks of roast turkey or lamb). Falafel, hummus, and shawarma stands always have a colorful selection of salads and toppings such as *harif*, a red-hot sauce. *Burekas* (filo dough folded over a cheese, potato, spinach, or meat filling) are available at pastry and some fast-food shops. The inside is edible, though the seeds may give some indigestion. (*Sabra* is also a term for a native Israeli; both the fruit and the people are said to be thorny on the outside, sweet on the inside.)

Preparing your own food is cheap, especially in summer, when fresh fruits and vegetables are available at every outdoor *shuk* (market). You can buy groceries inexpensively at local *shuks*, at a *makolet* (small grocery store), or in supermarkets.

Two Israeli **beers** are the excellent, deep-amber Goldstar and the lesser Maccabee lager. Goldstar is a common draft beer; Maccabee comes in bottles only. Other brews commonly available on tap are Carlsberg, Tuborg, and Heineken. Supermarkets carry a small selection of liquor; note that Nesher "black beer" is a sweet, non-alcoholic malt brew. The official drinking age is 18.

In Arab restaurants, if you ask for coffee with no specifications, you'll get a small cup of strong, sweet, Arabic coffee, sometimes referred to as *turki* (Turkish). If you want something standard, ask in Hebrew for *hafukh* (a latte) or filter (regular filtered coffee). Instant coffee *(nes)* is also popular. "Black" *(shahor)* or "mud" *(botz)* coffee is Turkish coffee brewed in a cup; watch out for the sediment at the bottom.

THE ARTS

LITERATURE

LIFE AND TIMES

ISRAELI LITERATURE

Israel has a rich literary culture, which draws both upon ancient biblical and post-biblical sources (such as the *Mishnah* and the Talmud) and modern themes. Modern Hebrew literature first started appearing in 19th-century Europe, with writers like **Josef Perl** in Vienna and **Abraham Mapu** in Lithuania writing the first novels in modern Hebrew. The subject matter for most of these early Hebrew works was the narrative of the Jewish people from ancient times to the present, some of them portraying modern Jewish social life in a fictional context for the first time. The generations that followed moved toward realism, often employing Yiddish.

Toward the turn of the 20th century, many prominent Jewish European writers who were writing in Hebrew began to take up the cause of Zionism in their works, and to focus their poetry and prose on the lives of the pioneers establishing the Jewish state. Their writing mixed historical Jewish themes with modern European literary trends. Major early Zionist writers and poets include **Hayyim Nahman Bialik,** later recognized as Israel's national poet, and Nobel laureate **Shmuel Yosef (Shai) Agnon,** who confronted the breakdown of cultural cohesion among modern Jews in *A Guest for the Night* and *The Bridal Canopy.*

Just before the creation of the State of Israel, a group of native Hebrew authors rose to prominence. Their style, characterized by concern for the landscape and the moment, and focused on the tension between the individual and society, is exemplified in **S. Yizhar's** *Efrayim Returns to Alfalfa.* Beginning in the late 1950s, writers like **Amos Oz** and **A. B. Yehoshua** began to experiment with psychological realism, allegory, and symbolism. In the 1960s, new skepticism surfaced in Israeli literature, driven to a great extent by Israel's new position in the West Bank and Gaza Strip after the Six Day War. **David Shahar** was hailed as the Proust of Hebrew literature for his *The Palace of Shattered Vessels,* set in Jerusalem in the 1930s and 40s. **Ya'akov Shabtai's** *Past Continuous,* about Tel Aviv in the 1970s, is one of the most well-known Israeli novels of the decade. A stunning, though initially confusing, must-read is *Arabesques* by **Anton Shamas,** an Arab Israeli writing in Hebrew. At the same time, modern Israeli poets and songwriters, such as **Yehudah Amichai** and **Naomi Shemer** captured the challenges facing the young state in their writing. Most major Israeli works have been translated into English, and many have received widespread critical renown.

An increasingly prominent genre of Israeli literature focuses on the Israeli-Palestinian conflict by way of fiction, nonfiction, or some combination thereof. Oz's *In the Land of Israel* is a series of interviews with native Israelis and West Bank Palestinians that documents the wide range of political sentiment. His *A Perfect Peace* is a semi-allegorical account of kibbutz life just before the Six-

Day War. **David Grossman's** *Yellow Wind* tells of one Israeli Jew's journey to the West Bank just prior to the *intifada*, while his *Sleeping on a Wire* explores the precarious predicament of Israeli Arabs. For a lighter note, pick up **Ze'ev Chafetz's** *Heroes and Hustlers, Hard Hats and Holy Men*, a hilarious satire of Israeli society and politics.

Contemporary Jewish Israeli literature is highly influenced by immigrants from vastly different cultures, tumultuous politics and violence, and conflicts between individualism and nationalism. A cadre of young writers, including **Etgar Keret, Orly Castel-Bloom,** and **Gafi Amir,** has highlighted the disaffected and cynical outlook characteristic of the post-Zionist era.

Israel's short but tumultuous history has inspired a number of historical works. They tend to idealize and dramatize a bit excessively, but offer an entertaining introduction to Israeli history. Consider trying **Chaim Potok's** *Wanderings,* **James Michener's** *The Source,* **Leon Uris's** *Exodus,* and **Sabri Jiryis's** *The Arabs in Israel.* For a more sober textbook history of the land, read **Barbara Tuchman's** *Bible and Sword,* which chronicles Palestine from the Bronze Age to the Balfour Declaration of 1917. The elegant works of **Solomon Grayzel** also give historical background.

PALESTINIAN LITERATURE

Alongside the development of Jewish Israeli literature, the founding of Israel in 1948 also brought with it a distinctly Palestinian branch of Arab literature, which mixed classic themes such as the desert, the city, and the Arab individual's response to colonialism with the new reality of Palestinians living in or alongside Israel. Major themes in Palestinian literature are the deep connection to land and territory, the related struggle to create a collective Palestinian identity, and the reality of life in exile. Given the difficult history of the region, the topics of loss and longing are common in this literature. Central Palestinian literary figures include **Ghassan Kanafani,** who was also a leading member for the Popular Front for the Liberation of Palestine, and the internationally acclaimed **Mahmoud Darwish,** regarded widely as the Palestinian national poet.

Another notable branch of Palestinian literature is that written by Israeli-Arabs, or Palestinians who are also Israeli citizens. Much of this work deals with the reality of Arab life under Jewish Israeli rule, and the struggle to define one's identity as both Palestinian and Israeli. **Emil Habibi's** *The Secret Life of Saeed the Pessoptimist* and, more recently, **Sayyid Kashua's** *Let it be Morning* are good examples of works in this genre.

MUSIC

After WWI, Jews in Palestine assembled chamber groups, a symphony orchestra, an opera company, and a choral society. During the 1930s, with the rise of Nazism in Europe, Jewish musicians fled to Israel. This influx spurred the formation of vibrant classical music culture. Today, musical performances and activities take place around the country year-round in settings as varied as the historic Crusader Castle in Akko and the modern, 3000-seat Mann Auditorium in Tel Aviv (see **Festivals,** p. 72).

Israeli popular music started emerging from its folk-chant origins (often echoing Russian folk melodies) in the early days of the Jewish immigration, in the decades before the founding of the state. In the 1950s, 60s, and 70s international music trends began to take hold in Israel, and popular rock bands like **Kaveret** (known as Poogy abroad) and **Gazoz** brought thousands out to Israel's parks and concert venues. Some of Israel's greatest popular musicians emerged during this time, with mainstays such as **Arik Einshtein, Yehuditz Ravitz,** and **Dani Sanderson** still drawing massive audiences today. Since the 1970s, Israel has been catching up with international music fashions; local bands have momentarily lingered on punk, reggae, funk, heavy metal, grunge, and even rap. The local army-run radio station **Galgalatz** keeps Israeli youths abreast of the goings-on in London and New York, and Israelis expect nothing less of their own local acts. Tel Aviv is the unequivocal hub of the cutting-edge music scene in Israel, though performances occur throughout the country.

Today Israel is home to a thriving local music scene, with multiple festivals, major concerts, and small-venue live music available most nights of the week in the major cities. The most popular performers in Israel play music that's somewhere in between rock and a more mellow sound, placing a strong emphasis on meaningful lyrics. Some native classics still on the performance circuit are **Shlomo Artzi, Yehudit Ravitz, Beri Saharof,** and **Gidi Gov. Achinoam Nini** (known abroad as **Noa**), who blends American rock with Middle Eastern sounds, while **David Broza** throws in Eastern and Latin American influences. **Zahava Ben,** a Sephardic Jew, is one of the more popular Israeli singers. She frequently tours in the Arab world and has achieved a great deal of success in Egypt singing the songs of the legendary Umm Kulthoum. Transsexual drag queen **Dana International** brought Israeli pop international fame in 1998 when she won the Eurovision Song Contest. Many of Israel's most popular singers today, such as **Ninet Tayeb,** gained their fame in the local version of American Idol—**Kochav Nolad.** Local funk and hip hop group **Hadag Nachash** keeps bodies grinding, and the home-grown electronica duo **Infected Mushroom** are welcome in major techno clubs worldwide. In many places in Israel Middle Eastern-style music, heavy on *oud* (a guitar-like instrument), synthesizers, and drum machines, blasts from car stereos: this is **muzika mizrahit** ("oriental music"), very popular with Sephardic Jews (a good example is **Sarit Hadad**). Israel also has a rapidly growing local jazz scene, with homegrown musicians like base player **Avishai Cohen** taking the international festival circuit by storm, and new venues popping up around the country, particularly in Tel Aviv, Jerusalem, and Haifa.

STUDIO ART AND ARCHITECTURE

Israel boasts a vibrant art scene, which incorporates both folk and modern art. Many works are inspired by Jewish themes. Check out *Israel Art Guide* (www.israelartguide.co.il) to find out about current exhibitions throughout the country. The urban landscape in Israel is dominated by Israeli architecture—not much construction took place in Palestine before the Zionists arrived. Many of the area's finest old Arab buildings are located in Jerusalem's Old City and in old Arab towns like Jaffa and Akko. When the Zionists came to Israel, they desired to begin life afresh; as a result, much Israeli architecture is characterized by design styles that were cutting-edge in the early 20th century, such as the Bauhaus style, common in central Tel Aviv.

THEATER AND DANCE

The Israeli national theater, the **Habimah,** is in Tel Aviv. The slightly less prestigious **Khan** theatre operates out of Jerusalem. The most famous Palestinian theater group is **al-Hakawati,** based in East Jerusalem. Israel's most famous and critically acclaimed dance company is the **Batsheva** group, and it often tours internationally. Group dances play an important part in ceremonies in both Israel and Palestine.

THE LOCAL STORY

MOVIE WITH ARI

As a 19 year-old soldier, Ari Folman fought in the Lebanon War of 1982. Like many soldiers, Folman found himself stuck between the duty he felt for his country and his hatred of war. The Sabra and Shatila Massacre—the killing of Palestinian and Lebanese civilians, that the Israeli Defense Force allowed to occur when they let Lebanese Phalangist militiamen in the refugee camps—had a deep impact on Folman. He realized later in life that he and his fellow soldiers had blocked the events of the war out of their memories. As the son of Holocaust survivors, Folman recognized the danger in forgetting his past and set about artistically exposing the Massacre.

In 2008, Folman released his film *Waltz with Bashir*, an animated documentary about the Lebanon war. He took his own experience and that of many Israeli soldiers and presented their dilemma and trauma—thus, Folman gave voice to the feelings of an entire generation.

Waltz with Bashir is a feature-length documentary that combines unique graphics with a thrilling and shocking story. As Folman's character in the film searches for his lost memories, he and the audience relive the past. The film successfully marries a strong political, anti-war message with the art of animation.

Waltz with Bashir, nominated for many awards—including an Oscar for Best foreign Language Film—won a Golden Globe.

FILM

Israel has a thriving film industry that has taken off over the last decade. Israeli films, both fictional and documentary, have become common at major international festivals such as Cannes and Sundance, and more Israelis than ever are watching local productions in Israel's cinemas. Every year, Israel holds its own local version of the Academy Awards, called the **Ofir Awards,** where the country's top productions are showcased. Recently, the Israeli films *Waltz with Bashir* and *Beaufort*, both dealing with Israel's wars in Lebanon, have been nominees for best foreign film in the American Academy Awards. Other recent success stories include *The Band's Visit*, telling the comical story of an Egyptian military band that goes astray in Israel, and *Jellyfish*, a surreal piece that tells the parallel stories of three modern Israeli women. Contemporary Israeli films often focus on the complexities of life in 21st-century Israel, in many cases portraying the way the Israeli-Arab conflict filters down into the lives of individuals. Several major film festivals take place in Israel annually. See **Festivals,** p. 72, for more info.

HOLIDAYS AND FESTIVALS

Arrange your itinerary with an awareness of holidays. Dates listed in this section are for 2010. In Israel, most businesses and public facilities close Friday afternoon for Shabbat, the Jewish Sabbath, and reopen at sundown on Saturday. They also close for Jewish holidays, which begin at sunset on the previous day. While many restaurants and bars remain open during these days, especially in Tel Aviv, for other commercial services you'll have to venture into Arab neighborhoods. **Pesach,** or Passover (March 29-April 5), celebrates the exodus of the Jews from Egypt. Observant Jews refrain from eating bread and pastries; products made with regular flour and leavening agents may be hard to come by in Jewish areas. **Shavuot** (May 18) celebrates the giving of the Torah, the Hebrew name for the first five books of the Old Testament, and involves the consumption of dairy products. **Rosh Hashanah** (September 8-10) is the Jewish New Year. On **Yom Kippur** (September 18), observant Jews fast in atonement for their sins and Israel shuts down entirely. In more observant towns, such as Jerusalem and Be'er Sheva, traffic stops completely and pedestrians take to the streets for the day. **Sukkot** (September 22-29), the festival of the harvest, commemorates the Israelites' voyage through the Sinai desert and culminates with **Simhat Torah** on September 30.

In Muslim areas, most businesses close on Friday, the day of prayer. On holidays, they may close during the afternoon, but are generally open in the morning. As with Jewish holidays, the dates of Muslim holidays are set according to the lunar calendar and vary from year to year. The most important event and the one most likely to complicate travel is **Ramadan** (August 11-September 9), the annual month-long fast during which Muslims abstain from food and drink from dawn to sunset. During this time, most restaurants close up shop until sundown. Shops may open for a few hours in the morning and a short time after *iftar*, the breaking of the fast; government services are either closed entirely or open only in the morning. It would be rude to smoke or eat in public at this time. The celebratory, three-day **Eid al-Fitr** (September 8-10) feast marks the end of Ramadan. **Eid al-Adha** (November 16) commemorates Abraham's intended sacrifice of his son Ishmael and coincides with the *hajj* (pilgrimage) to Mecca, the fifth pillar of Islam (see **Islam,** p. 60). The festivities generally last for three days and involve the sacrifice of sheep, cows, or goats, and the distribution of the meat among the poor. **Ras al-Sana** (December 18) is the Islamic New Year's Day, and **Mawlid al-Nabi** (February 26) celebrates Muhammad's birthday.

Christian holidays are also celebrated throughout Israel and the Palestinian territories; because the majority of the population in most towns is either Jewish or Muslim, services tend to affected less due to these holidays. One exception to this is **Christmas** and **New Year's** in Bethlehem.

Secular Israeli holidays in 2010 include **Yom ha-Sho'ah** (Holocaust Memorial Day, Apr. 11), **Yom ha-Zikaron** (Memorial Day, April 18), and **Yom ha-Atzma'ut** (Independence Day, April 19). On both Yom ha-Sho'ah and Yom ha-Zikaron, sirens signal moments of silence throughout Israel, and the entire country (traffic included) stops for their duration.

DATE	HOLIDAY	AFFILIATION
Feb. 26, 2010	Birth of Muhammad	Muslim
Feb. 28, 2010	Purim	Jewish
March 28, 2010	Palm Sunday	Christian
March 30-April 5, 2010	Passover (Pesach)	Jewish
April 2, 2010	Good Friday	Christian
April 4, 2010	Easter	Christian
April 10, 2010	Holocaust Memorial Day (Yom Hashoah)	Israeli
April 19, 2010	Memorial Day (Yom HaZikaron)	Israeli
April 20, 2010	Independence Day (Yom Ha'atzmaut)	Israeli
May 19, 2010	Shavuot	Jewish
May 23, 2010	Pentecost	Christian
July 20, 2010	9th of Av (Tisha Be'Av)	Jewish
August 11-September 9, 2010	Ramadan	Muslim
September 10, 2010	Eid al-Fitr	Muslim
September 9-10, 2010	Rosh HaShanah (Jewish New Year)	Jewish
September 18, 2010	Yom Kippur (Day of Atonement)	Jewish
September 23-30, 2010	Sukkot	Jewish
October 1, 2010	Simchat Torah	Jewish
November 15, 2010	Eid al-Adha (Holiday of the Sacrifice)	Muslim
December 2-10, 2010	Hanukkah	Jewish
December 7, 2010	Islamic New Year	Muslim
December 16, 2010	Ashura	Muslim-Shi'ite
December 25, 2010	Christmas	Christian

LIFE AND TIMES

FESTIVALS

Throughout the year, Israel hosts a variety of festivals and major cultural events, both secular and religious, that cater to audiences of all ages. The months of May to August tend to have the largest concentration of festivals, with plenty of free or cheap student-oriented concerts and outdoor events happening in the major cities. Some major festivals to look out for are the **Jerusalem International Film Festival** (www.jff.org.il), Israel's major cinematic event, held every July in Jerusalem; the **Red Sea Jazz Festival** (www.redseajazzeilat.com), a world-class four-day jazz extravaganza that takes place annually in the resort town of Eilat at the end of August; and **The Israel Festival** (www.israelfestival.com), held annually May-June, which brings together hundreds of local and international performers and artists for free and ticketed events around Jerusalem.

For those looking for a more laid back affair, Israel also plays host to several major back-to-nature hippie-style festivals throughout the year. These popular events usually draw thousands of young Israelis looking to leave their worries and most of their clothes behind and spend a few days dancing, relaxing, and grooving to a variety of live music styles. The main festivals are **Boombamela** (www.boombamela.co.il), held every spring on the Nitzanim beach, **Beresheet** (beresheet.co.il), held during the holiday of Sukkot on the Sea of Galilee, and the more family oriented **Jacob's Ladder** (www.jlfestival.com), a folk, bluegrass, and world music festival that is usually dominated by American and British expats.

BEYOND TOURISM

A PHILOSOPHY FOR TRAVELERS

HIGHLIGHTS OF BEYOND TOURISM

BUILD a sustainable ecological community in Kibbutz Lotan's **Green Apprenticeship Program** (p. 81).

WORK ON YOUR TAN while unearthing thousand-year-old cities on one of Israel's varied **archaeological digs** (p. 77).

GET TO KNOW Israeli communities by living and volunteering in their midst on one of the many programs offered by **Shatil** or **Otzma** (p. 75).

BRING HAPPINESS to Palestinian schoolchildren in Nablus by volunteering with **Project Hope** (p. 76).

FLIP to our "Giving Back" sidebar features for even more regional Beyond Tourism opportunities (p. 147 and p. 355).

As a tourist, you are always a foreigner. Sure, hostel-hopping and sightseeing can be great fun, but connecting with a foreign country through studying, volunteering, or working can extend your travels beyond tourist traps. We don't like to brag, but this is what's different about a Let's Go traveler. Instead of feeling like a stranger in a strange land, you can understand Israel and the Palestinian Territories like a local. Instead of being that tourist asking for directions, you can be the one who gives them (and correctly!). All the while, you get the satisfaction of leaving the region in better shape than you found it. It's not wishful thinking—it's Beyond Tourism.

As a **volunteer** in Israel or the West Bank, you can roll up your sleeves, cinch down your Captain Planet belt, and get your hands dirty doing anything from picking bananas on a kibbutz to working as an assistant medic on an ambulance. This chapter is chock-full of ideas to get involved, whether you're looking to pitch in for a day or run away from home for a whole new life in Israeli or Palestinian activism.

Ah, to **study** abroad! It's a student's dream, and when you find yourself crawling through thousand year-old tunnels and visiting some of the world's holiest sites for school-related assignments, it actually makes you feel sorry for those poor tourists who don't get to do any homework while they're here. Israel and the Palestinian Territories are packed with incredible history, the remains of which are still present throughout the country. With plenty of study abroad opportunities and short travel distances, there is no better place to get to know the history and culture of the Middle East.

Working abroad is one of the best ways to immerse yourself in a new culture, meet locals, and learn to appreciate a non-US currency. Yes, we know you're on vacation, but we're not talking about normal desk jobs—we're talking about entertaining visitors at a Red Sea resort and herding goats at an independently owned desert farm, in the name of funding another month of globe-trotting.

SHARE YOUR EXPERIENCE. Have you had a particularly enjoyable volunteer, study, or work experience that you'd like to share with other travelers? Post it to our website, www.letsgo.com!

VOLUNTEERING

Feel like saving the world this week? Volunteering can be a powerful and fulfilling experience, especially when combined with the thrill of traveling in a new place. After decades of conflict have taken their toll on the area and when most local resources have been diverted toward security needs, Israel and the Palestinian Territories provide plenty of opportunities to leave your mark on the region. Between helping impoverished families in Israel and the West Bank, cleaning up the region's limited water sources and beaches, and rebuilding homes destroyed by recent violence, there is always plenty to do.

Most people who volunteer in Israel and the Palestinian Territories do so on a short-term basis at organizations that make use of drop-in or once-a-week volunteers. The best way to find opportunities that match your interests and schedule may be to check with the **Jewish Agency,** which serves as a good clearinghouse for work and volunteer opportunities throughout the country. Their multilingual representatives specialize in the various programs and options available throughout the country, and they are trained to work both with long and short-term visitors. Check out their website at www.jewishagency. org or call their Information and Service Center (☎+1-866-835-0430 in the US, +44 0800 404 8984 in the UK, +972 1 800 228 55 in Israel). Most of the Jewish Agency's programs deal with getting to know Israel and assisting its Jewish population. If you are Jewish, you may be able to receive full or partial funding for your program. For those looking for programs more focused on Israel's minorities or on social justice, the **New Israel Fund** (www.nif.org) is a good place to start. Both of these offer a range of volunteer opportunities, dealing with social, political and environmental issues, among others. As always, read up before heading out.

I HAVE TO PAY TO VOLUNTEER? Many volunteers are surprised to learn that some organizations require large fees or "donations," but don't go calling them scams just yet. While such fees may seem ridiculous at first, they often keep the organization afloat, covering airfare, room, board, and administrative expenses for the volunteers. (Other organizations must rely on private donations and government subsidies.) If you're concerned about how a program spends its fees, request an annual report or finance account. A reputable organization won't refuse to inform you of how volunteer money is spent. Pay-to-volunteer programs might be a good idea for young travelers who are looking for more support and structure (such as pre-arranged transportation and housing) or anyone who would rather not deal with the uncertainty of creating a volunteer experience from scratch.

Those looking for longer, more intensive volunteer opportunities usually choose to go through a parent organization that takes care of logistical details and often provides a group environment and support system—for a fee. There are two main types of organizations—religious and secular—although there are rarely restrictions on participation for either. Websites like **www.volunteerabroad.**

com, **www.servenet.org**, and **www.idealist.org** allow you to search for volunteer openings both in your country and abroad.

SOCIAL ACTIVISM AND COMMUNITY SERVICE

Despite the major economic steps forward that Israel has taken over the past few decades, over 1.6 million Israelis live under the poverty line. In the West Bank, the numbers are even more dismal, with many suffering from a severe lack of the most basic necessities and services. The good news is that there are an increasing number of programs bringing volunteers to these poverty-stricken areas, and a variety of ways to help the region's poorer populations.

Amirim: YJ Impact (☎+1-202-303-4585; www.yjimpact.org). A summer volunteering program for college students and young professionals. Places volunteers at NGOs and Jewish community service organizations that deal with a range of social issues. Participants live in communal apartments in the Tel Aviv or Jerusalem areas, and also partake in additional group activities to get to know the country and Israeli society.

International Palestinian Youth League (IPYL), Al Isra'a Building, 5th fl., Jaffa St., Hebron, West Bank (☎02 222 9131; www.ipyl.org). A Palestinian non-profit organization based in Hebron. Focuses on outreach to Palestinian youth, involving participants in community building, urban development, social activism and human rights initiatives, among others. Founded in 1997 by Palestinian community activists, the IPYL has many connections with grassroots initiatives throughout the West Bank, and has both short and long term volunteering opportunities for foreigners. Residents of the European Union can receive funding from the European Commission for their volunteer work.

Kibbutz Volunteers (☎03 530 1440; www.kibbutzprogramcenter.org). Israel's United Kibbutz Movement coordinates the placement of volunteers at 1 of Israel's many communal kibbutzim. Volunteers participate in kibbutz life, working 6-8hr. per day in agriculture, industry, or services on the kibbutz. Programs usually last 2-6 months.

Magen David Adom (☎+1-866-835-0430 in the US, +44 0800 404 8984 in the UK, 1 800 228 055 in Israel; www.jewishagency.org). Provides the opportunity to volunteer for 2 months as an assistant medic on Israeli ambulances, following a 9-day first aid course. No previous medical experience is necessary, but some basic knowledge of conversational Hebrew is required.

Otzma, Suite 1700, 25 Broadway, New York, NY 10004, USA (☎+1-877-466-8962; www.otzma.org). Runs a variety of 10-month volunteer programs for young Jewish adults. Geared toward allowing participants to experience a more authentic side of Israel and have an opportunity to make an impact on the community they live in. Most of Otzma's community service programs focus on poor or neglected Jewish periphery towns.

Shatil, 6th fl., 1101 14th St. NW, Washington, D.C. 20005, USA (☎+1-202-842-0900) or PO Box 53395, Jerusalem 91533 (☎02 673 5149; www.shatil.org.il). A project of the New Israel Fund (www.nif.org). Places volunteers with organizations working in issues related to social change such as civil and human rights, Jewish-Arab coexistence, the status of women, and religious tolerance.

Volunteers for Peace, 1034 Tiffany Road, Belmont, VT 05730, USA (☎+1-802-259-2759; www.vfp.org). This American-based organization partners with local groups in Israel and the West Bank to coordinate volunteer work on Israeli and Palestinian political, social and environmental issues. Their extensive online database contains comprehensive up-to-date info on available projects, their costs, and the experience necessary.

EDUCATION

While almost every Israeli or Palestinian you meet will happily give you an extensive lecture on his or her view of the world, you may want to consider imparting some of your own knowledge while in the region. The Israeli and particularly the Palestinian school systems are chronically underfunded, and English teachers are always in demand. The following is a list of programs that last from a range of a few weeks to two years that involve volunteers from abroad in local education projects. For job opportunities in teaching English, see p. 83.

Project Hope, 29 An-Najah al-Qadim St., Nablus (☎09 233 7077; www.projecthope. ps). A non-profit organization working in the Palestinian city of Nablus. Provides local children with after-school programming and services. Activities encompass education, recreation and medical and humanitarian aid. International volunteers work side-by-side with local Palestinian staff teaching English and leading after-school activities. Accommodations in Nablus are provided for a nominal fee. Free Arabic classes included.

ENVIRONMENTAL ISSUES AND WILDLIFE CONSERVATION

With security concerns and politics getting the national spotlight and top priority in the public eye, environmental issues often fall between the cracks in Israel and the Palestinian Territories. That said, recent decades have seen an increase in environmental awareness, and multiple local organizations now work to preserve Israel's varied scenery and diverse wildlife. The following organizations have considerable experience in involving visitors and non-Hebrew speakers in these efforts. Flip to **Studying** (p. 78) for more long-term environmental programs in Israel.

Green Course: Students for the Environment, 3 Hashfela St., Tel Aviv (☎077 210 2003; www.green.org.il/eng/). As the only Israeli national student organization devoted to environmental preservation, Green Course is a fantastic way to get involved in grassroots environmental activism and education together with local volunteers. Works both on local and national levels, raises awareness on university campuses, and runs multiple initiatives around the country. Though slightly less structured than Israel's other environmental volunteer or education programs, Green Course provides more of an opportunity to get involved directly with local student activists.

Go Eco (☎03 647 4208; www.goeco.org). An Israeli-founded organization that coordinates environmentally oriented volunteering and ecotourism projects around the country and around the world. Options for volunteering include both environmental and cultural components. Available in both the Jewish and Arab sectors of Israel. Projects are 2-8 weeks and usually require payment of a small fee.

HUMAN RIGHTS

The complex reality of the Israeli-Arab conflict has created a good deal of challenges to human rights in the region. While these rights are recognized as universal, and the following organizations are non-partisan, the debate over human rights in Israel and the Palestinian Territories is often heavily politicized. If you're looking to get some hands-on human rights experience while plunging yourself into some of the stickier issues stemming from the Israeli-Arab conflict, get in touch with one of the following organizations.

B'Tselem, 8 HaTa'asiya St., Jerusalem 91531 (☎02 673 5599; www.btselem.org). The main Israeli information center for human rights abuses in the West Bank and Gaza Strip. Focuses on collecting information about human rights violations, both by Israelis and Palestinians, which take place in these territories and acts to publicize them and combat them with legal and political means. B'Tselem's staff is made up of both Jews and Arabs, Israelis and Palestinians, who live and work in Israel, the West Bank, and Gaza. International visitors with some knowledge of Hebrew or Arabic can apply to volunteer as interns at B'Tselem's main office in Jerusalem and sometimes become involved in the organizations fieldwork in the West Bank.

Physicians for Human Rights: Israel, 9 Dror St., Tel Aviv 68135 (☎03 687 3718; www.phr.org.il/phr/). A non-profit organization devoted to guaranteeing health-related human rights to all residents of Israel, the West Bank, and Gaza. The organization, which is not directly affiliated with the global Physicians for Human Rights, is involved both in legal advocacy and active fieldwork. The volunteering physicians who make up the bulk of the organization work together with other volunteers, staff, and interns to promote the organization's goals. International volunteers are welcomed by the organization and are involved in the various branches of its activity.

Rabbis for Human Rights, 9 Harekhavim St., Jerusalem 93462 (☎02 648 2757; rhr. israel.net). A unique Israeli organization comprised mainly of Israeli rabbis who seek to connect between Jewish and Zionistic ideals and human rights work throughout Israel, the West Bank, and Gaza. The organization actively campaigns for a wide variety of causes relating to social justice and human rights. While it has no official volunteer positions in its staff, Rabbis for Human Rights often welcomes international volunteers to help with various projects around the country on an ad hoc basis.

ARCHAEOLOGY

With 5000-year-old shards of pottery still strewn casually throughout the countryside and a rich history of settlement and civilization, Israel is a fantastic place to pick up a shovel and get in touch with the long lost past that everyone seems to be fighting about. Archaeological digs take place throughout the country, mostly during the summer months, and their organizers often welcome volunteers from abroad to assist in the digging or in the sorting and processing of artifacts that are found. The **Biblical Archaeology Review** maintains the local **Find a Dig** website (www.findadig.com), which contains an extensive and updated list of digs within Israel, accompanied by background information on the digs themselves and the archaeologists leading them. Logistical information regarding timing, cost and possible academic credit is also listed for each dig. The following agencies are good resources for getting in touch directly with the universities or the archaeologists leading the digs.

The Archaeological Institute of America, 6th Floor, 656 Beacon St., Boston, MA 02215, USA (☎+1-617-353-9361; www.archaeological.org). Provides a global database of digs that are accepting volunteers on the "Fieldwork" section of their website. Complete info on multiple digs taking place within Israel and its neighboring countries available.

The Israeli Ministry of Foreign Affairs, 9 Yitzhak Rabin Blvd., Kiryat Ben-Gurion, Jerusalem (☎02 530 3111; www.mfa.gov.il). Annually compiles a list of the various digs taking place around the country that accept volunteers. The Ministry's website provides information about the digs' location, dates and duration, cost and details about whom to contact. From the main website, search for "archaeological digs".

BEYOND TOURISM

STUDYING

> **VISA INFORMATION.** Foreigners wishing to study in Israel for a period of longer than three months must obtain a **one-year student visa.** Student visas are available through Israeli embassies or consulates (p. 8). The application requires a letter of acceptance from the educational institution, a valid passport, a roundtrip ticket, and a bank statement proving that the applicant can support him or herself financially for his or her period of study. The application cost is $25. For more information, check with your local Israeli embassy or consulate, or at the website of Israel's Ministry of Foreign Affairs, www.mfa.gov.il.

It's completely natural to want to play hooky on the first day of school when it's raining and first period Trigonometry is meeting in the old cafeteria, but when your campus overlooks the Old City of Jerusalem and your meal plan revolves around freshly-made hummus and kebab, what could be better than the student life? A growing number of students report that studying abroad is the highlight of their learning careers. If you've never studied abroad, you don't know what you're missing—and, if you have studied abroad, you do know what you're missing.

Study-abroad programs range from basic language and culture courses to university-level classes, often for college credit (sweet, right?). In order to choose a program that best fits your needs, research as much as you can before making your decision—determine costs and duration as well as what kinds of students participate in the program and what sorts of accommodations are provided. For those coming to Israel or the Palestinian Territories, you'll also want to decide if you're more interested in getting to know the Jewish parts of the region, or the Arab Muslim and Christian areas, as well as whether you want a more traditional urban university program or a unique local setting, such as a kibbutz.

In programs that have large groups of students who speak English, there is a trade-off. You may feel more comfortable in the community, but you will not have the same opportunity to practice a foreign language or to befriend other international students. For accommodations, dorm life provides a better opportunity to mingle with fellow students, but there is less of a chance to experience the local scene. If you live with a family, you could potentially build lifelong friendships with natives and experience day-to-day life in more depth, but you might also get stuck sharing a room with their pet iguana. Conditions can vary greatly from family to family.

UNIVERSITIES

Most university-level study-abroad programs in Israel and the West Bank are conducted in English, although those with decent Hebrew or Arabic skills can also enroll in regular courses with local students. Savvy linguists may find it cheaper to enroll directly in a university abroad, although getting college credit may be more difficult. You can search **www.studyabroad.com** for various semester-abroad programs that meet your criteria, including your desired location and focus of study. If you're a college student, your friendly neighborhood study-abroad office is often the best place to start.

AMERICAN PROGRAMS

The following American universities all run their own study abroad programs in Israel. The website **www.iiepassport.org** also maintains and updated list of study abroad programs for English speakers in Israel.

Boston University, BU Office of International Programs, 888 Commonwealth Ave., Boston, MA 02215, USA (☎+1-617-353-9888; www.bu.edu/abroad/programs/israel/). BU offers 2 semester- or year-long programs in Israel: an engineering program in Tel Aviv or a liberal arts program in Haifa. Both include excursions around the country and offer classes either in English or in Hebrew.

New York University in Tel Aviv, Lower Level, 110 E. 14th St., New York, NY 10003, USA (☎+1-212-998-4433; studyabroad.israel@nyu.edu). A semester-long program in Tel Aviv geared toward getting to know modern Israel. Particularly well suited for those interested in social sciences, media, politics and law. Includes both courses in a classroom setting and trips and tours around the country.

ISRAELI AND PALESTINIAN PROGRAMS

All of the major Israeli and Palestinian universities have well-established study abroad programs as well as departments or entire schools geared specifically toward international students. It's common to see hordes of foreign students strewn about the various Israeli campuses, eagerly soaking in the Middle Eastern sun. While Hebrew and Arabic lessons or classes in the local languages are usually available for those interested in them, the majority of these programs are run in English, and direct enrollment is a fairly straightforward process for students from English-speaking countries.

Ben-Gurion University of the Negev: The Overseas Student Program, 8th fl., 1430 Broadway, New York, NY 10018 (☎+1-800-962-2248; http://w3.bgu.ac.il/cisp/). Studying at BGU in Be'er Sheva will put you on the doorstep of the majestic Negev desert—and will bring you to a university campus with a national reputation for its diversity and vibrant social life. A variety of term-time and summer programs are available, nearly all of them including excursions into the Negev and extensive Hebrew classes.

Bir Zeit University: The Palestine and Arabic Studies (PAS) Program (☎02 298 2153; www.home.birzeit.edu/pas/). For those more interested in getting to know the culture of the West Bank and Palestinian life, this university near the major city of Ramallah is for you. The PAS program offered for international students combines Arabic language studies with courses about the history and culture of the Arab world in general and Palestinians in particular. The social science classes are all taught in English. Prospective students should note that the fees at Bir Zeit are considerably lower than those at any of the Israeli universities, though the programs and resources are also more basic. Students live in rented apartments in Ramallah or in the suburb of Bir Zeit.

Hebrew University of Jerusalem: Rothberg International School, Boyar Building, Mount Scopus, Jerusalem 91905 (☎02 588 2363; http://overseas.huji.ac.il). Israel's oldest and most established university offers an array of undergraduate and graduate-level programs on 4 campuses throughout the capital. Programs run throughout the year can be taken for 1 or 2 semesters, with language school and summer programs options available. On-campus housing is offered in the new student village adjacent to the Mount Scopus campus, though those wishing to live off-campus may do so.

The International School at the University of Haifa (☎04 824 0766; http://overseas.haifa.ac.il). As the only liberal arts program in Israel's mountainous north, Haifa University brings together thousands of Israeli and international students in an impressive setting overlooking the Galilee and the Mediterranean Sea. Haifa is also known as one of the few cities in Israel where Jews, Muslims, and Christians successfully live side by side. Standard undergraduate- and graduate-level programs are offered year-round and in the summer, as well as special honors-only programs in peace and conflict studies or psychology. Most foreign students live in the dorms on campus.

Tel Aviv University School for Overseas Students, Carter Building, Ramat Aviv 69978 (☎03 640 8639; www.tau.ac.il/overseas). For those more interested in beaches and nightlife than hills and history, the bustling urban campus of Tel Aviv University might be for you. The School for Overseas students runs a variety of semester, year and summer-term programs, with courses that are taught in English and a required amount of credits in Hebrew language studies. Both undergraduate and graduate programs are available.

LANGUAGE SCHOOLS

Old lady making snarky comments to you in the market? Impudent cashier at the falafel joint? Cute moped girl that is totally into you? To communicate is to be human, and without the local language in your toolbelt, you're up a creek without a *mashot*. Fear not! Language school here to help.

While language school courses rarely count for college credit, they do offer a unique way to get acquainted with the culture and language of Israel. Schools can be independently run or university affiliated, local or international, youth-oriented or full of old people—the opportunities are endless. And while you might manage to get by in Israel with English, your relationships with Israelis and Palestinians will be far more meaningful with some knowledge of the local languages. All of the major Israeli universities listed above maintain high quality term-time or summer language schools, though if you're looking for a less academic environment, you might also want to check out the following:

Kibbutz Ulpan, 114 W. 26th St., New York NY, 10001, USA (☎+1-212 462 2764) and 1 Hayasmin St., Ramat Efal 52960 (☎03 635 2961; www.kibbutzulpan.org). Many of Israel's communal kibbutzim offer visitors a chance to take intensive conversational Hebrew classes from certified teachers while working and living on a kibbutz. Both religious and secular kibbutzim are available. Participating kibbutzim are located around the country. A small fee is usually required, but basic housing and meals are provided. While kibbutz language programs are often reported to be the most socially engaging and rewarding type of language program, living and working mostly with foreigners means that it will not be a total-immersion Hebrew environment.

Language Immersion Institute, State University of New York at New Paltz, 1 Hawk Dr., New Paltz, NY 12561. USA (☎+1-845-257-3500; www.newpaltz.edu/lii). Short, intensive summer language courses and some overseas courses in Hebrew and Arabic. Program fees are around US$1000 for a 2-week course, not including accommodations.

Ulpan Akiva (☎09 835 2312; www.ulpan-akiva.org). For those who want a no-nonsense, full-immersion, results-guaranteed language education, Ulpan Akiva is the undisputed king of Israeli language schools. Over 1 month, students from around the world are put in intensive 30hr. per week language classes, learning conversational Hebrew as well as taking classes on Israeli culture, religion, and history. The program's complex is located in a pleasant beachside neighborhood in the coastal city of Netanya. Those looking for even more thorough language training can enroll in Ulpan Akiva's special 5-month "Maof" program, which includes language training for specialized professional and academic fields. Those fluent in Hebrew can also enroll in a full immersion Arabic program.

ENVIRONMENTAL SCHOOLS AND PROGRAMS

A fantastic way to get off the common tourist track and to see Israel from a unique perspective is to participate in one of the following environmental or ecotourism programs. In addition to learning about Israel's diverse geography and myriad environmental concerns, you will also be located smack in the middle of stunning, impossibly tranquil desert scenery.

The Arava Institute for Environmental Studies, Kibbutz Ketura, DN Hevel Eilot 88840 (☎08 635 6618; www.arava.org). The Arava Institute, affiliated with Be'er Sheva's Ben-Gurion University, is Israel's premiere environmental school. Located in Kibbutz Ketura near the southern trip of the country, the Institute's main goal is to allow Jews, Arabs, and foreigners to study and work together to solve Israel's environmental challenges. The Institute offers both graduate and undergraduate programs, for full academic credit, both during the year and in the summer. Classes are held on topics that range from water management in the Middle East to the history of human settlement in the south of Israel. Seminars on leadership, coexistence and peacemaking are also built into the curriculum. All courses for foreign students are conducted in English.

Kibbutz Lotan: Green Apprenticeship (☎08 635 6811; www.kibbutzlotan.com/creativeEcology/ga/index.htm). Located in the Arava desert valley in the south of Israel, Kibbutz Lotan is a national mecca for communal and sustainable living. As one of the few kibbutzim that still has managed to remain fully committed to its founding ideology, Lotan is a fascinating place to learn about Israel's social and environmental ideals. Participants in the 6-week Green Apprenticeship program gain extensive hands-on experience in designing, building and running sustainable communities. The program includes both theoretical and practical components. Housing and meals are provided in a sustainable environment on the kibbutz, and participants are integrated into kibbutz life during their stay. Kibbutz Lotan is also a major part of the international **Living Routes** program in Israel (www.livingroutes.org/programs/p_lotan.htm), which combines ecological studies with lessons on social justice and community building in Israel.

WORKING

We haven't yet found money growing on trees, but we do have a team of dedicated Researchers looking high and low. In the meantime, while it won't necessarily be easy to save up a great deal of money working in Israel, there are definitely plenty of great opportunities around the country to support yourself while on the road. As with volunteering, work opportunities tend to fall into two categories. Some travelers want long-term jobs that allow them to integrate into a community, while others seek out short-term jobs to finance the next leg of their travels. In Israel, visitors interested both in short- and long-term jobs will probably have the best luck looking for work in the hotel industry, particularly in the resort city of Eilat, or in agricultural work, such as picking fruit and working in the fields in kibbutzim. Those more focused on the short term should also check for available jobs before or during major festivals around the country. American or European companies with branches in Israel are good avenues to explore for those looking for more lucrative longer-term solutions. **Transitions Abroad** (www.transitionsabroad.com) also offers updated online listings for work over any time period.

Sababa

"Everything is *sababa*."

You'll undoubtedly hear this answer when asking Israelis about themselves, their family, their friends, their work, their dog, or anything else. If you spend any time in Israel you

"classes and [the] future—they're important, but not all-important"

will become familiar with the word *sababa*—loosely translating to good, great, or cool. The word, however, has deeper meaning; it summarizes a laidback attitude with which Israelis approach many aspects of their lives.

Israel is a place where polar opposites exist side by side and in close vicinity to each other: secular and religious, urban and rural, conservative and liberal, immigrant and native-born Sabra. This co-mingling is also seen in the attitudes of the local people. Israelis have a reputation for being brash and aggressive, a quality affectionately known as *chutzpah*. While this is certainly true, they simultaneously exhibit the *sababa* attitude, accepting things as they come and remaining chill whenever they can.

As the daughter of an Israeli immigrant to New York City, I was long familiar with both of these aspects of the Israeli culture from my frequent short visits to the country over summer breaks and talks with my Sabra cousins. However, it wasn't until I studied abroad at Tel Aviv University and lived in Israel for six months that I truly grasped the *sababa* attitude and learned to live it myself. True, I often had to be aggressive and bend the rules in order to get what I wanted. Getting aggressive in line for the last available bus to Eilat, for example, was the only way that my friends and I would get there that weekend—and besides, everyone else was doing it. But once I used my Israeli *chutzpah* to get myself there, I used my newfound *sababa* attitude to kick back and enjoy myself in Eilat; I breezed

through my time in a cramped hostel and was able to keep calm and help a friend with food poisoning.

When on the tight schedule of a short tourist stint, you often don't have the time to adopt the attitude of a country. But exploring a new place beyond a typical tourist experience allows you to reinvent yourself, if even for only a short time. For example, getting lost in Jerusalem's *souq* on Friday, right before it closed for Shabbat, might have freaked me out if I had only a tourist mentality. But as someone living in Israel, I learned how to keep this in perspective and enjoy my adventure; I even picked up a lot of fresh produce for the dirt-cheap prices (3 mangos for NIS5!) that vendors resort to as they try to get rid of anything that will go bad.

Studying abroad in Israel gave me a break from my stressful life in New York. I was still a student, but instead of being a student obsessed with classes and my future—they're important, but not all-important—I was a student who went to the beach several times a week, ate copious amounts of hummus, and kicked back with a nice, cold Goldstar at the quintessentially Israeli bar where my friends and I became regulars. There is no way that anything can not be *sababa* when you are on the shore playing *matkot* (a popular Israeli paddle game which is hard to master, but fun even when failing), enjoying a fresh passion-fruit shake, and watching a breathtaking sunset.

In short, to experience Israel as it should be experienced, sit back, relax, and learn how to keep your life truly *sababa*.

Hadas Reich graduated from Binghamton University where she majored in biology and minored in international studies. She lived in Israel as a child and spent a semester studying at Tel Aviv University.

A DIFFERENT PATH

MORE VISA INFORMATION. All non-citizens wishing to work in Israel have to obtain a **one-year work visa,** which is usually provided by the employer. High unemployment in the country means that foreigners may have a hard time lining up employment in advance, but some good places to start are the tech industries, ESL teaching, agriculture, and tourism, particularly in the resort town of Eilat. The easiest path might be finding work with an American or European company with a local branch. For more information on working in Israel, check out the migrant worker section on the Israeli government web portal at **http://www.gov.il/firstgov/english.**

LONG-TERM WORK

If you're planning on spending a substantial amount of time (more than 3 months) working in Israel, search for a job well in advance. International placement agencies are often the easiest way to find employment abroad, especially for those interested in teaching. Although they are often only available to college students, internships are a good way to ease into working abroad. Many students say the interning experience is well worth it, despite low pay (if you're lucky enough to get paid at all). Be wary of advertisements for companies offering to get you a job abroad for a fee—these same listings are often available online or in newspapers. Also, keep in mind that most legal long-term work options in Israel are actually volunteer programs that at best will provide you with room and board. It is quite difficult for travelers to make a lot of money while in Israel. Some reputable organizations include:

International Association for the Exchange of Students for Technical Experience (IAESTE), Technion Israel Institute of Technology, Technion City, Haifa 32000 (☎04 822 5915; www.iaeste.org). Chances are that your home country has a local office, too; contact it to apply for hands-on technical internships in Israel. You must be a college student studying science, technology, engineering, agriculture, or applied arts (check their website for a list of accepted fields of study). "Cost of living allowance" covers most non-travel expenses. Most programs last 8-12 weeks.

The Jewish Agency, 33 King George St., Tel Aviv (☎1 800 228 055; www.jewishagency. org). Coordinates many different work, volunteer, and studying opportunities in Israel. A good place to start for anyone looking for a long-term job.

TEACHING ENGLISH

Suffice it to say that teaching jobs abroad pay more in personal satisfaction and emotional fulfillment than in actual cash. Nevertheless, even volunteer teachers often receive some sort of a daily stipend to help with living expenses. In almost all cases, you must have at least a bachelor's degree to be a full-fledged teacher, although college undergraduates can often get summer positions teaching or tutoring. In order to teach English in Israel you must have a bachelor's degree, and while TEFL certification isn't required, it will be extremely helpful when trying to find a job, and might even get you the bigger bucks. The good news is that Israel's economic development and increasing integration with the world economy have raised the demand for English lessons considerably, so you should be able to find plenty of teaching opportunities. If you're having a hard time finding work in a classroom setting, you may want to consider posting notices on city bulletin boards offering private lessons.

The Hebrew or Arabic-impaired don't have to give up their dream of teaching, either. Private schools usually hire native English speakers for English-immersion classrooms where no Hebrew or Arabic is spoken. (Teachers in public schools will more likely work in both English and Hebrew or Arabic.) Placement agencies or university fellowship programs are the best resources for finding teaching jobs. The alternatives are to contact schools directly or try your luck once you arrive in Israel. In the latter case, the best time to look is several weeks before the start of the school year. For volunteer opportunities in education, see p. 76. The following organizations are helpful in placing teachers in Israel:

English Teachers Network in Israel (ETNI; www.etni.org.il). Maintains a website with useful information for anyone wishing to teach English in the country. The portal also contains bulletin boards for schools and individuals seeking English teachers.

International Schools Services (ISS), 15 Roszel Rd., Princeton, NJ 08543 (☎+1-609-452-0990; www.iss.edu). Hires teachers for more than 200 overseas schools, including in Israel. Candidates should have teaching experience and a bachelor's degree. 2-year commitment is the norm.

Tel Aviv Teach and Study Program (TASP; ☎09 899 5644; www.tasp.org.il). An extensive 2-year teach and study program that allows international university graduates to teach English in the Israeli public school system while studying for an MA in Teaching English as a Foreign Language (TEFL). Includes an extensive introduction to Israeli society and the country's education system, as well as a comprehensive Hebrew course (Ulpan).

SHORT-TERM WORK

If you're more of a dishwasher than an au pair, or if you'd just like to work an odd job for a few weeks to fund another month of traveling, short-term work might be right up your alley. While it is not legal for employers to pay non-residents who do not have a workers visa, some say that there are unofficial short-term jobs available. Catering work, private lessons in language or music, house and office cleaning, and odd agricultural jobs might be available with a little snooping around. Another popular option is to work several hours a day at a hostel in exchange for free or discounted room and/or board. Most often, these short-term jobs are found by word of mouth or by expressing interest to the owner of a hostel or restaurant; due to high turnover in the tourism industry, many places are eager for help, even if it is only temporary.

JERUSALEM

ירושלים الْقُدس

Maybe you were raised to revere this place, or maybe you weren't and it's always just been a troubled city in a newspaper to you. Either way, let's face it: the historical hometown of prophets and kings, several key stones in Jerusalem have touched all of our lives through the religions they inspired, and have galvanized two millennia of conflict that continue to shape the world we live in. Whether you are religious or not, Jerusalem is probably the reason you came here.

Falling in love with Jerusalem is a complicated process. If you're confident in your understanding of the city after your first day, you're either the next saint/prophet/Messiah/*bodhisattva*/scientology alien, or you're kidding yourself. This is not the most glamorous city in Israel; it is anything but relaxing. You may be struck by the profoundly unholy actions of some of the supposedly holy people here. You will begin to suspect that the taxi drivers, street vendors, and locals-turned-tour guides are trying to scam you. Sooner or later—perhaps through a taxi driver's offhand comment or a debate on the roof of your hostel—the Palestinian-Israeli conflict will come and find you. Unease and ambivalence comes with it. As Israeli poet Yehuda Amihai commented, the "air over Jerusalem is saturated with prayers and dreams, like the air over industrial cities. It's hard to breathe."

The trick is to give Jerusalem time. The city has been working its indefinable charm and spiritual power on its visitors for thousands of years, and it is nothing less than infectious. Jerusalem's bitter conflicts are rooted in its cultural diversity, and exploring the city's patchwork of neighborhoods can be as enriching as paying homage to its majestic religious sites. Jews, from ultra-Orthodox to secular, Christians of all denominations, Muslims, missionaries, pilgrims and tourists from every continent, mystics, and raving lunatics all come to Jerusalem with their spiritual baggage in tow. The time warp is most evident on a city bus, where black robes, habits, and *kefyehs* mingle with halter tops and baseball caps.

Three world religions agree that this is the Holy Land. But this is also the most *human* city—with its dueling capacities for greed and generosity, dogmatism and enlightenment—that you will ever see. After struggling to untangle Jerusalem, don't be surprised if you get depressed when you have to pack up and go sunbathe in Tel Aviv.

HIGHLIGHTS OF JERUSALEM

WATCH the bickering monks at the **Church of the Holy Sepulchre** (p. 129).

SPELUNK in the passageways beneath the **Western Wall** (p. 121).

DEVOUR cheap, delicious falafel in front of the **Damascus Gate** (p. 105).

✈ INTERCITY TRANSPORTATION

Flights: Ben-Gurion Airport (TLV; info for all airlines ☎03 972 3344. El Al English info tel 972 3388. Automated flight reconfirmation 972 2333; www.iaa.gov.il/Rashat/

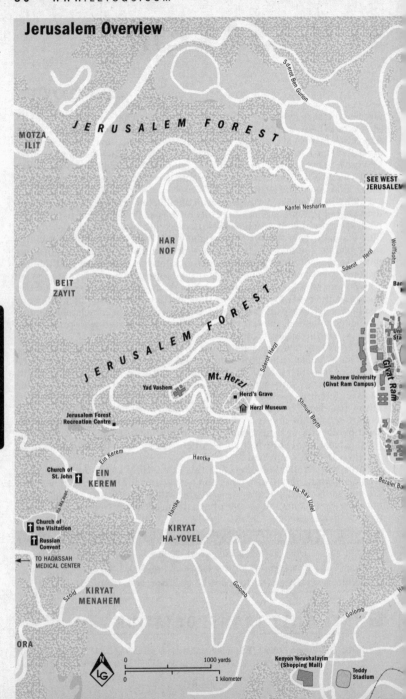

Jerusalem Overview

JERUSALEM

MOTZA ILIT

JERUSALEM FOREST

S.derot Ben Gurion

SEE WEST JERUSALEM

Kanfei Nesharim

HAR NOF

BEIT ZAYIT

Wolfsohn

Sderot Herzl

Bar

JERUSALEM FOREST

Uni Sta

Givat Ram

Yad Vashem

Mt. Herzl

Herzl's Grave

Herzl Museum

Hebrew University (Givat Ram Campus)

Sderot Herzl

Jerusalem Forest Recreation Centre

Shmuel Beyth

Ein Kerem

Hantke

Church of St. John

EIN KEREM

Ha-Ma-apil

Bezalel Ba

Church of the Visitation

Russian Convent

Hantke

KIRYAT HA-YOVEL

Ha-Rav Uziel

TO HADASSAH MEDICAL CENTER

Szold

KIRYAT MENAHEM

Golomb

ORA

Golomb

Ha

N

LG

0   1000 yards

0   1 kilometer

Kenyon Yerushalayim (Shopping Mall)

Teddy Stadium

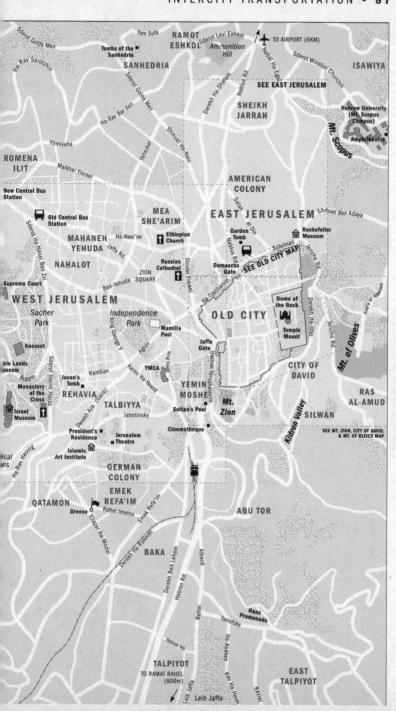

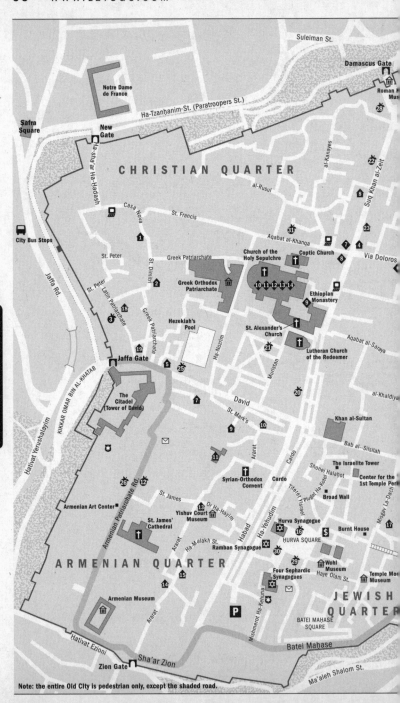

JERUSALEM

Note: the entire Old City is pedestrian only, except the shaded road.

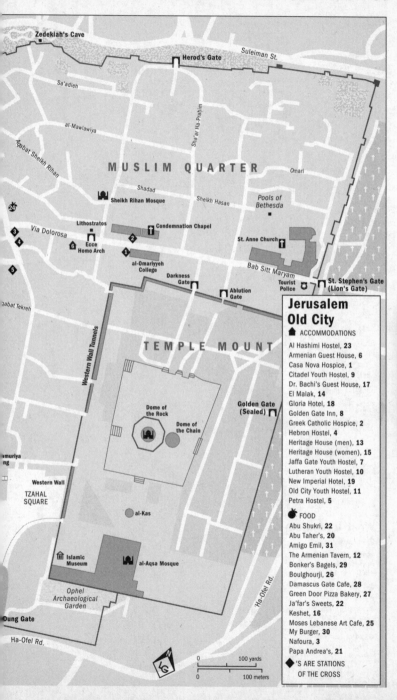

Zedekiah's Cave

Herod's Gate

Suleiman St.

Sa'adieh

al-Mawlawiya

Aqabat Sheikh Rihan

MUSLIM QUARTER

Omari

Shadad

Sheikh Rihan Mosque

Sheikh Hasan

Pools of Bethesda

Sha'ar Ha-Prahim

Lithostratos

Via Dolorosa

Condemnation Chapel

Ecce Homo Arch

St. Anne Church

al-Omariyyeh College

Bab Sitt Maryam

qabat Tekreh

Darkness Gate

Ablution Gate

Tourist Police

St. Stephen's Gate (Lion's Gate)

Western Wall Tunnels

TEMPLE MOUNT

Dome of the Rock

Dome of the Chain

Golden Gate (Sealed)

amuriya ng

Western Wall

TZAHAL SQUARE

al-Kas

JERUSALEM

Jerusalem Old City

ACCOMMODATIONS

Al Hashimi Hostel, **23**
Armenian Guest House, **6**
Casa Nova Hospice, **1**
Citadel Youth Hostel, **9**
Dr. Bachi's Guest House, **17**
El Malak, **14**
Gloria Hotel, **18**
Golden Gate Inn, **8**
Greek Catholic Hospice, **2**
Hebron Hostel, **4**
Heritage House (men), **13**
Heritage House (women), **15**
Jaffa Gate Youth Hostel, **7**
Lutheran Youth Hostel, **10**
New Imperial Hotel, **19**
Old City Youth Hostel, **11**
Petra Hostel, **5**

FOOD

Abu Shukri, **22**
Abu Taher's, **20**
Amigo Emil, **31**
The Armenian Tavern, **12**
Bonker's Bagels, **29**
Boulghourji, **26**
Damascus Gate Cafe, **28**
Green Door Pizza Bakery, **27**
Ja'far's Sweets, **22**
Keshet, **16**
Moses Lebanese Art Cafe, **25**
My Burger, **30**
Nafoura, **3**
Papa Andrea's, **21**

'S ARE STATIONS OF THE CROSS

Islamic Museum

al-Aqsa Mosque

Ophel Archaeological Garden

Dung Gate

Ha-Ofel Rd.

Ha-Ofel Rd.

0   100 yards
0   100 meters

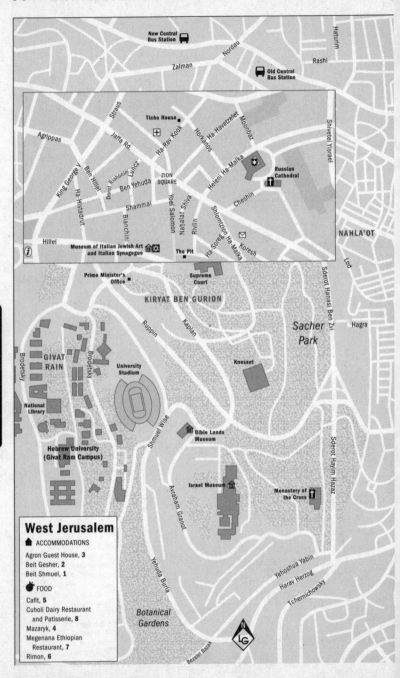

JERUSALEM

New Central
Bus Station
Old Central
Bus Station

Haturim
Nordau
Rashi
Zalman

Shivtei Yisrael

Straus
Ticho House
Ha-Havatzelet
Moohaz

Agrippas
Jaffa Rd.
Ha-Rav Kook
Horkanos
Heleni Ha-Malka

King George V.
Ben Hillel
Dorot Rishonim Lunciz
Ben Yehuda
ZION
SQUARE
Russian
Cathedral

Ha-Histadrut
Shammai
Bianchini
Yoel Salomon
Nahalat Shiva
Rivlin
Shlomtzion Ha-Malka
Cheshin

Hillel
Museum of Italian Jewish Art
and Italian Synagogue
The Pit
Ha-Soreg Ha-Malka
Koresh

NAHLA'OT
Lod

Prime Minister's
Office
Supreme
Court

KIRYAT BEN GURION
Sderot Hanasi Ben Zvi
Hagra

Ruppin
Kaplan
Sacher
Park

GIVAT
RAIN
Brodetsky
Brodetsky
University
Stadium
Knesset

Brodetsky
National
Library
Shmuel Wise
Bible Lands
Museum

Hebrew University
(Givat Ram Campus)
Israel Museum
Monastery of
the Cross

Avraham Granot
Sderot Hayim Hazaz

West Jerusalem

🏠 ACCOMMODATIONS

Agron Guest House, **3**
Beit Gesher, **2**
Beit Shmuel, **1**

🍴 FOOD

Cafit, **5**
Cuholi Dairy Restaurant
and Patisserie, **8**
Mazaryk, **4**
Megenana Ethiopian
Restaurant, **7**
Rimon, **6**

Yehuda Burla
Botanical
Gardens

Yehoshua Yabin
Harav Herzog
Tchernichowsky

Bezalei Bazak

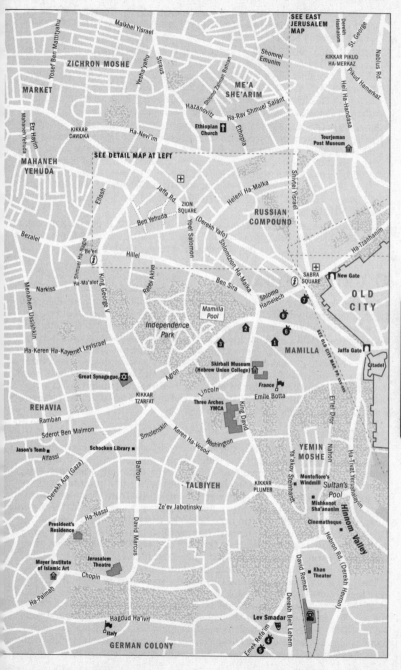

JERUSALEM

en-US/Airports/BenGurion), only 1hr. from Jerusalem. Easily accessible; you do not need to go to Tel Aviv first, no matter how early your flight, thanks to the 24hr. sherut service offered by **Nesher** (see below).

Sherut: Ha Bira (☎02 625 4545), at the corner of ha-Rav Kook St. and Jaffa Rd., near Zion Sq. To **Tel Aviv** (every 20min. 6am-2am; NIS22, after 11:30pm NIS27, Shabbat NIS30). Office open Su-Th 5:30am-11pm and F 5:30am-5:30pm. **Nesher,** 23 Ben-Yehuda St. (☎02 625 7227). 24hr. door-to-door service to the airport from anywhere in Tel Aviv. (NIS50, reserve at least 24hr. in advance). To **West Bank** towns, *service* taxies (the Arab equivalent of *sherut*) leave from outside Damascus Gate.

Buses: Egged Central Bus Station, Jaffa Rd. (☎*2800 or 03 694 8888; www.egged.co.il), west of city center just past the Mahane Yehuda district. Times, frequencies, and prices are very much subject to change, so be sure to check the website or the information desk at the station before planning your trip. To: **Eilat** (5hr.; Su-Th 4 times per day, F 3 times a day; NIS70); **Haifa** (2-2½hr.; Su-Th every 20-30min., F every 30min. until 11am, Sa every 15-20min. 8pm-midnight; NIS42); and **Tel Aviv** (55min.; Su-Th every 15-30min. 5:50am-midnight, F every 20-30min. 6am-3:45pm, Sa every 20-30min. 5:20pm-10:30pm; NIS19).

Car Rental: Budget (☎*2200; www.budget.co.il). Cars from US$45 per day; 3-day rentals US$40 per day, including unlimited mileage; 23+. **Eldan,** 24 King David St. (☎02 625 2151; www.eldan.co.il). Rentals from US$24 per day, US$119 per week.

✠ ORIENTATION

Jerusalem can be a difficult city to navigate. This is particularly true of the **Old City,** a compact labyrinth of crooked cobbled streets where you should expect to be lost most of the time. Haphazard alleyways and poorly labeled intersections make the Old City a navigational nightmare. The good news is that the City is so small it's usually easy to find your way again, and so dense that aimlessly wandering its streets leads to the discovery of silent historic treasures. By contrast, the rest of Jerusalem is a sprawling city, most of which was only developed in the last 50 years of the capital's three-millennium history. Distances are still relatively short, however, and make for reasonable, pleasant walks if you don't mind the hills or the heat.

OLD CITY

Jerusalem's most important historical and religious sites are concentrated within the walls of the Old City, which is still divided into the four quadrants laid out by the Romans in 135 CE. **Jaffa Gate** and **Damascus Gate,** the two main entrances to the Old City, tend to be good reference points for locating sights and hostels. To reach Jaffa Gate from West Jerusalem, walk down Jaffa Rd. to its end and continue straight across the intersection, or take bus #38; you can take buses #1 or #3 there from the Central Bus Station. To reach Damascus Gate, walk through the Old City from Jaffa Gate down **David Street,** then turn left on **Souq Khan al-Zeit Street** or al-**Wad Street.** From further up Jaffa St. (i.e., near Mahane Yehuda), walking straight down ha-Nevi'im St. provides a more direct route.

The two main roads in the Old City are the roof-covered David St., beginning inside Jaffa Gate and running west to east across the city, and Souq Khan al-Zeit St., which begins inside Damascus Gate and runs north to south across the city. To make matters more complicated, the names of David St. and Souq Khan al-Zeit change when they intersect. Coming from Jaffa Gate, David St.'s name changes to **Bab al-Silsilah Street** (Gate of the Chain) after intersecting with Souq Khan al-Zeit as it approaches the Temple Mount. Souq Khan al-Zeit St.

becomes **the Cardo** after intersecting with David St. as it enters the **Jewish Quarter.**

Damascus Gate is Arab East Jerusalem's entryway into the Old City, leading right to the heart of the **Muslim Quarter's** *souq*. Just inside Damascus Gate, the road culminates in a fork with al-Wad St. on the left and Souq Khan al-Zeit St. on the right. The Cardo leads into the Jewish Quarter; this quarter is also directly accessible through **Dung Gate.** The **Armenian Quarter** is to the right as you enter through Jaffa Gate and is directly accessible via **Zion Gate.** Inside Jaffa Gate to the left is the **Christian Quarter,** which can also be reached directly from the **New Gate.** Of the other three gates, **Saint Stephen's Gate** is closest to both the **Mount of Olives** (outside the Old City) and the start of the **Via Dolorosa. Herod's Gate** enters into a less-touristed section of the Muslim Quarter, and the entrance at the **Golden Gate** is blocked.

WEST JERUSALEM

This section includes the Jewish parts of Jerusalem, from **French Hill** in the northeast and **East Talpiyot** in the southeast, to **Kiryat Menahem** in the southwest and **Ramot** to the northwest. The main street is **Jaffa Road** (Derekh Yafo), running west to east from the central bus station to the Old City's Jaffa Gate. Roughly midway between the two, **Zion Square** (Kikkar Tzion) sits at the corner of Jerusalem's triangular *midrakhov* bounded by Jaffa Rd., **Ben-Yehuda Street,** and **King George Street.** Upscale eaters line **Yoel Salomon Street** and **Rivlin Street,** off Zion Sq.

North of the city center, the hip **Russian Compound** hugs the old-word **Mea She'arim** like spandex on a *yenta*. Northwest on Jaffa Rd. are the teeming outdoor markets of **Mahane Yehuda** and, farther down, the central bus station. Southwest of the triangle is the **Givat Ram** neighborhood, which houses the **Knesset** building and the hilltop Israel Museum complex. The beautiful **Independence Park** lies south of the city center, ringed by luxury hotels; farther south are the cafes of the **German Colony** and the discotheques of **Talpiyot.** The artists' district of **Yemin Moshe** huddles southeast of Zion Sq.

EAST JERUSALEM

The old, invisible **Green Line** separating Jordan from pre-1967 Israel runs along **Route 1** and remains a good general demarcation between the Palestinian and Jewish areas of Jerusalem. East Jerusalem is the name normally given to the Palestinian parts of Jerusalem just outside of the Old City to the north, east, and southeast; many Palestinians include the Old City's Muslim Quarter in their demarcation

LOCAL LEGEND

WALLED IN, WALLED OUT

Despite their ancient antecedents, the walls that stand today around Jerusalem's Old City were built as recently as the 16th century by Ottoman Sultan Suleiman after a particularly bad dream. According to legend, the Sultan was drifting off to sleep one night in 1538, pondering how best to punish the citizens of Jerusalem, when he was disturbed by a nightmare in which a pair of lions were about to shred him to pieces. When he told his dream interpreter of the experience, the wise man told him that God must have been displeased, and wanted to protect, rather than raze, the Old City.

At that time, the walls around Jerusalem had been lying in rubble for decades. Eager to appease God—and probably concerned that Emperor Charles V of Austria wanted to launch a new crusade against the city—Suleiman ordered architects from Istanbul to refurbish Jerusalem's defenses.

When the walls were finished in 1541, Suleiman had the two architects murdered. Some say he was so pleased with their magnificent job, he never wanted their talent exploited by another. Others say he was enraged by the fact that Mt. Zion and the Tomb of David, historically part of the city, had been left to the south of the city walls. Just inside the Jaffa Gates, on the left beyond the tourist office, are two graves, believed to be the final resting places of the two men who had dared undersell the city limits.

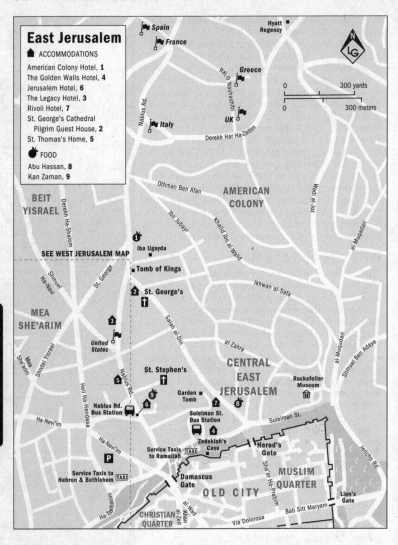

East Jerusalem

ACCOMMODATIONS

American Colony Hotel, **1**
The Golden Walls Hotel, **4**
Jerusalem Hotel, **6**
The Legacy Hotel, **3**
Rivoli Hotel, **7**
St. George's Cathedral
Pilgrim Guest House, **2**
St. Thomas's Home, **5**

FOOD

Abu Hassan, **8**
Kan Zaman, **9**

of East Jerusalem as well. The main thoroughfares are **Suleiman Street,** which runs in front of Damascus Gate; **Nablus Road,** which runs northeast into East Jerusalem from Damascus Gate; and **Salah al-Din Street,** which runs out from Herod's Gate. All three streets converge in a small but busy area that stretches from Damascus Gate to Herod's Gate; the intersection has many falafel and shawarma stands, fruit vendors, and dry goods stores, and often acts as an extension of the Muslim Quarter's *souq.* This area, or **Central East Jerusalem,** is the financial and cultural hub of the Arab community.

A small hub of decent restaurants has sprung up on **Shim'on Ha'tsadik Street,** catering to the vast number of workers from the United Nations, International

Committee of the Red Cross, and various NGOs who frequent the region. To get there, walk up Nablus Rd. or Salah al-Din St. to **Derech Shchem Street,** and walk up that street for an additional 10min. The street will bring you through the **American Colony** neighborhood and **Sheik Jarah,** a residential area that is generally safe for tourists but prone to political unrest; as of this writing, it has become an epicenter of the recent conflict over house demolitions in East Jerusalem, so to be on the safe side, research the situation before you go. After walking through Sheik Jarah and up a slight hill, you will reach Shim'on Ha'tsadik St; turn left to reach the restaurants.

▣ LOCAL TRANSPORTATION

Buses: Most distances in Jerusalem are walkable and all sections are easily reachable by bus from the **Central Bus Station,** 224 Jaffa Rd., west of the city center, just past the Mahane Yehuda district. There is sadly no city bus map, and the Egged website, while useful for people who already know the name of the stop they are traveling to, can be confusing. Common bus routes are listed below; they can be subject to change, so check with the local tourist office or hostel before hopping on. Taxis are also widely available, but are more expensive. Common bus routes include: **#3** to Dung Gate/Western Wall; **#9, #19, #27, #31** to the Zion Sq. area; the 19 begins at Mount Scopus, Hebrew University; **#12** to Hadassah Ein Kerem Medical Center; **#20** to Jaffa Gate; **#24** to Israel Museum; **#28** to Givat Ram; **#31** to Mahane Yehuda; **#32** to Rehavia.

▣ PRACTICAL INFORMATION

CITY-WIDE

Police: ☎100.

Ambulance: ☎101.

Fire: ☎102.

Tourist Police: ☎03 516 5382.

Hospital or Medical Services:

Terem Emergency Medical Centers: Branches in Jerusalem are located at Beit YaHav, Rehov Yirmeyahu 80 in Romema neighborhood; Yanovsky 6, East Talpiot in HaTayelet; Rehov Tilltan 8 in Modi'in (☎1 599 520 520). Recommended by Tourist Information Center. Insurance not necessary to be treated, though you may need to pay for services. Very tourist friendly; many doctors fluent in English and other languages available to help foreigners.

Hadassah University Hospital: Mt. Scopus branch (☎02 584 4111; emergencies: 12 155 121). Ein Kerem branch (☎02 677 7111; emergencies: 12 55 122). If you go to the branch in Ein Kerem, you can always swing by the Chagall Windows (p. 147).

Crisis Lines

Combat Violence Against Women: ☎1 800 353 300 or 09 950 5720; www.no2violence.co.il/index_eng.htm.

Crisis Center for Religious Women: ☎02 673 0002. Jerusalem-specific. Available 24hr.

Narcotics Anonymous Hotline: ☎052 477 0205.

MiLev Crisis Helpline: ☎050 594 7837. Specific to English speakers. Open daily 9am-9pm.

Consulates: For more information, see **Essentials,** p. 8.

Egged Bus Passenger Information: ☎*2800 or 03-694-8888. See **Intercity Transportation,** p. 85.

Taxi Information: For more info, see **Intercity Transportation,** p. p. 92.

Egged Taxi Information: ☎*5657.

Nesher: ☎02 625 7227

Ha Bira: ☎02 625 4545

Telephones: The easiest way to handle communications in Israel is to buy an Israeli SIM card for your phone, available for purchase at the Ben-Gurion Airport (US$26.50). For more info, see **Keeping in Touch**, p. 26. Phones can also be rented through the following agencies:

Rent-a-Phone Communications Ltd., 12 Tuval St., Ramat Gan (☎03 613 9899; www.rent-a-phone.co.il).

Global Cellular/Israel Phones, 19 Hamelech David St. (☎77 300 9341).

OLD CITY

TOURIST AND FINANCIAL SERVICES

Tourist Offices:

Tourist Information Center (☎02 628 0382), on the left just inside Jaffa Gate. Hands out free maps, information for free tours, and brochures with the location and phone numbers of main Old City sights. Busy but exceptionally helpful and knowledgeable staff. If you're new in the Old City, this is the 1st place you should go. Open Su-Th and Sa 8:30am-5pm, F 8:30am-1:30pm.

Christian Information Center (☎02 627 2692; http://198.62.75.1/www1/ofm/cic/CICmainin. htm), inside Jaffa Gate, opposite the Tower of David. Information on Jerusalem's pilgrimage sights and Christian accommodations. Open M-F 8:30am-5:30pm, Sa 8:30am-12:30pm.

Jewish Student Information Center, 5 Beit El St. (☎02 628 2634; http://www.jeffseidel.com/), in Hurva Sq. in the Jewish Quarter. Run by friendly and enthusiastic Jeff Seidal and his charming staff. The center sells comprehensive Jewish Student's Travel Guide with religious information for most countries around the world. Open Su-F 9am-3pm.

Guided Tours:

Sandeman's New Jerusalem Tours (☎+49 30 510 50030; www.newjerusalemtours.com). Holds free crash course tours (3½hr, 11am and 2:30pm) of the Old City in English. Also offers tours of Mount of Olives and a more in-depth Holy City tour for NIS75, students NIS70. Bike tour NIS200. Tours begin at Jaffa Gate, in front of Tourist Information Center.

Zion Walking Tours (☎02 627 7588; zionwt.dsites1.co.il), right inside Jaffa Gate, opposite the Tower of David. 12 guided routes on different days of the week in and around the Old City. Most popular tour is of the 4 quarters of the Old City (3hr., daily 10am and 2pm, NIS120).

Alternative Palestine Tours (☎054 693 4433; www.toursinenglish.com). Tours in the Old City, greater Jerusalem, and the West Bank. A decidedly different take on Israel's reality than the tour guides' at, for example, the City of David. Tour of Old City NIS145, Tour greater Jerusalem NIS170. Reserve in advance.

Currency Exchange: The best places to exchange money in Jerusalem are, oddly, the **post offices** (p. 97); their commission fees are the most reasonable. There are a variety of money changers clustered around Jaffa Gate who will also make small withdrawals for you with varying commission; know your exchange rate before handing over your money. The money-changer across the side-street next to the Tourist Information Center has an **ATM,** as do several of the money-changers on David St.

EMERGENCY, COMMUNICATIONS, AND SERVICES

Laundromat: Mike's Centre, 172 Souq Khan as-Zeit St (☎628 2486; www.mikescentre. co.il), on the 2nd fl. of Abu Assab Establishment on Souq Khan al-Zeit St, near the 9th Station of the Cross and Hebron Hostel. Wash and dry NIS30. Open daily 9am-11pm.

Police: (☎100 or 02 539 1360). Central station on Armenian Patriarchate Rd., behind the Tower of David, inside Jaffa Gate. There are also stations next to the Church of the Holy Sepulchre, at the corner of al-Wad and Iron Gate near the Western Wall, and o1 in front of Lion's Gate.

24hr. Pharmacy: Superpharm, 9 Shlomo Hamelech (☎02 636 6000). It's not 24hr., and it's not in the Old City; but at a 5min. walk down the Mamilla Promenade from Jaffa Gate, it's the most comprehensive pharmacy you'll find in the area (or any area), with a cadre of very helpful, English-speaking pharmacists. Su-Th 8:30am-11pm, F 8:30am-3:30pm, Sa from sundown to midnight.

Internet Access: Most hostels, hotels, and cafes have free Wi-Fi; most hostels also have computers that guests can use either for free or NIS10-NIS20 per hr. For internet outside of the hostels, try **Mike's Center,** 172 Souq Khan al-Zeit St. (☎02 628 2486), at the turn off for the 9th Station of the Cross. Boasts "the fastest line in Israel." NIS10 per hr.

Post Office: 23 Jaffa Road (☎02 629 0686). Open Su-Th 7:30am-2:30pm, F 8am-noon. There's also a post office on Habad St. For mailing substantial packages, most people leave the Old City and go to the **central post office** in East Jerusalem, a 2min. walk from Damascus Gate, on the corner of Suleiman St. and Salah al-Din St., next to the police station.

WEST JERUSALEM

TOURIST AND FINANCIAL SERVICES

Tourist Offices:

MTIO, 3 Safra Sq. (☎02 625 8844), in the City Hall complex off Jaffa Rd. From behind the large water fountain in the municipal plaza, the entrance is on the right. Excellent computerized info. Pamphlets and maps. Open 9am-4:30pm, F 9am-1pm.

Alternative Information Center, 4 Shlomzion HaMalka St, 2nd fl. (☎02 624 1159; www.alternativenews.org). Small but excellent info center with very helpful staff. Human rights focus, and far more radicalized perspective of the "facts on the ground" in Israel. Open Su-Th 9:30am-5:30pm, F from 9:30am to 1hr. before sundown.

Tours

Egged Tours, Jerusalem Central Bus Station, 224 Yafo Rd. (☎1 700 70 7577 or 02 530 4962; www.eggedtours.com), in Central Bus Station. This offshoot of Israel's public transit system offers popular and reasonably priced tours of both Jerusalem and sights throughout the country, including Masada, Caesarea, and more. Tour of Jerusalem Old and New City US$62; multiple-day tour of Jerusalem, Dead Sea, and adjoining spa US$265. Open Su-Th 8am-3pm.

United, King David Hotel Annex (☎02 625 2187; www.unitedtours.co.il), next to King David Hotel. Reasonably-priced bus tours of Jerusalem and throughout Israel, in multiple languages. Check the website for tours offered each week. 10% ISIC discount. Tours US$79-US$99.

Mazada Tours, Jerusalem Pearl Hotel, 15 Jaffa St. (☎02 623 5777; www.mazada.co.il). Popular company specializing in Middle Eastern tourism, particularly in Israel and its neighbors. Includes tours of both Old and New Jerusalem, as well as of Mazada, the Dead Sea and Ein Geidi. Tours US$42-99.

Currency Exchange and Banks: The **post office** (p. 97), is among the only places that exchanges currency without charging a commission. Banks and **ATMs** line Ben-Yehuda St. and the greater Zion Sq. **Bank ha-Poalim** (☎03 567 4999), at the corner of Ben-Yehuda and Jaffa Rd. in Zion Sq., is perhaps the most obvious. Open Su-Th 8am-midnight, F 8am-1pm. **Leumi** (☎03 514 9400). Open M and Th 8:30am-1pm, Tu-W 8:30am-2:30pm, F 8:30am-12:30pm. **Union Bank of Israel** (☎03 437 5100). Open Su and Tu-W 8:30am-2pm, M and Th 8:30am-1pm and 3:30pm-5pm, F 8:30am-noon. All right across the street. There are only Israeli banks in Jerusalem, so expect ATM machines to occasionally and spontaneously reject your foreign ATM card.

LOCAL SERVICES

Bookstores:

Steimatzky, 39 Jaffa St. (☎02 625 0155; www.steimatzky.co.il), other locations on 7 Ben-Yehuda and 9 King George St. Great place for books, maps, magazines and travel guides. Selection in Hebrew and English. Open Su-Th 8am-7pm, F 8am-2pm.

Sefer VeSefel, 2 Ya'vets St. (☎02 624 8237), in the city center off Jaffa St., just east of King George St. Jerusalem's best place for new and used books. Open Su-Th 9am-7pm, F 9am-2pm.

T'mol Shilshom Read an eccentric used book while drinking coffee in a creative, bohemian environment. Books available in English and Hebrew. See **Food,** p. 105.

GLBT Resources: Jerusalem Open House (JOH), 2 Hasoreg Street (☎02 625 0502; www. joh.org.il), in city center at the intersection of Jaffa St. and Queen Shlomtzion St. A community center with a small library, lounge, and bulletin boards. Organizes and advertises activities, concerts, discussion and support groups, poetry readings, folk dancing, and occasional excursions. Free, anonymous HIV testing Su 5-9pm. Open Su-Th 10am-5pm.

Laundromat: Laundry Place, 12 Shamai St. (☎02 625 77 14). From Ben-Yehuda St., turn left onto Lunz St., then left onto Shamai. NIS47 per load. Open Su and Th 8am-9pm, M-W and F-Sa 8am-8pm. Cash only.

EMERGENCY AND COMMUNICATIONS

Pharmacy: Superpharm, 3 ha-Histradrut (☎624 6244 or 624 6245), between Ben-Yehuda St. and King George St. Open Su-Th 8am-midnight, F from 8am to 1hr. before sundown, Sa from 1hr. after sundown to midnight.

Internet Access: Free Wi-Fi is available throughout West Jerusalem. Ben-Yehuda and its side streets, the Rivlin-Nachlat Shiva mall, Shlokzion Hamalka St. and Safra Square are all networked sites. Many local cafes have free Wi-Fi as well:

Cafe Net, Jerusalem Central Bus Station, 232 Yafo Rd. (☎02 537 9192; www.cafenet.co.il), on the 3rd fl. NIS10 per hr. Open daily 5:30am-midnight. Credit cards accepted.

Internet Cafe, 31 Jaffa Rd. (☎02 622 3377), in the city center at Yafo Rd.'s intersection with Rivlin St. NIS12 per hr. Open daily 9am-6am. Credit cards accepted.

Post Office: 23 Jaffa Rd. (☎02 624 4745). Open Su-Th 7am-7pm.

ACCOMMODATIONS

In terms of food, accommodations, shopping, and other dimensions of Jerusalem to explore, the very general guideline to follow is this: the Old City has the cheapest and funkiest, West Jerusalem is more refined with the prices to match, and East Jerusalem has fewer options but some of the best deals. Applying this logic to accommodations in Jerusalem, the cheapest and most idiosyncratic options are in the Old City; look out for roof mattresses for rent, religious establishments with curfews, and fantastic views of the Dome of the Rock. For a dramatically different cultural setting and experience, try the hostels of West Jerusalem, which are closer to the vibrant restaurant scene of the downtown and farther from the historical landmarks and cultural unrest. They are also a bit more expensive. If your parents or their credit cards are traveling with you, the most luxurious hotels are in West Jerusalem around **David Street** and **Central East Jerusalem;** while the hotels around David St. are more popular, the hotels in East Jerusalem are often better priced for the services they offer.

OLD CITY

Old City accommodations generally fall into two categories: quieter, cleaner establishments that sometimes have curfews and are often religiously affiliated, and the less clean, less comfortable, but more fun hostels populated by young backpackers. Some of the latter operate without government permits—nevertheless, many patrons swear by them as the only way to meet fellow travelers and get to know the Old City. Most of the hostels are clustered around

Jaffa Gate or close to **Damascus Gate** in the *souq*. Accommodations that are not in these locations are often on streets that are not accessible by car, so be prepared for a schlep. Use caution: even the most rambunctious of alleyways can become eerily empty after nightfall.

Petty theft can be a problem, so use private lockers where available; most hostels don't have them, so if you're concerned about theft you may want to bring your own luggage locks.

MUSLIM QUARTER

Al Hashimi Hostel and Hotel, 73 Souq Khan al-Zeit St. (☎02 628 4410; www.alhashimihotel.com), take the right fork from Damascus Gate. Al Hashimi may cost slightly more than its competitors in the Muslim Quarter, but given its beautiful rooftop seating and remarkably helpful staff, the prices are surprisingly reasonable. Saleh, one of the proprietors, regularly Facebook-friends customers and offers valuable advice about the area; several customers have even gone as far as suggest he run for president. A/C and TV in each room. Breakfast US$5. Free Wi-Fi. Check-in noon. Check-out 10:30am. Dorms NIS100; singles NIS250; doubles NIS400; triples NIS515; quads NIS675. Please be aware that this is a religious Muslim establishment; alcohol is not allowed, and unmarried couples are not allowed to share rooms. Cash only. ❷

Hebron Hostel, 8 Aqabat at-Takiya (☎02 628 1101). From Damascus Gate, walk down Souq Khan al-Zeit past Hashimi Hostel; signs for Hebron Hostel will appear to your left. Local tradition says that the low-ceilinged room that makes up the downstairs of Hebron Hostel is 1500 years old. Accordingly, the young backpacker crowd that stays here venerates the building's age by writing their impressions of Jerusalem on the ancient stones with Sharpie. Comments range from the politically eccentric ("F*ck Israel, New Castle is Promised Land!") to profound ("boose"). Breakfast is served in the tea room; dig your paws into some pancakes with chocolate and bananas (NIS15) or a hummus platter (NIS16). Hot water 7am-9pm only. Free Wi-Fi. Small computer lab in tea room (NIS10 per hr.). Check-out 11am. Curfew 1am-6am. Quiet hours after midnight. Dorms NIS40; singles NIS150; doubles NIS120, with bath NIS150; triples NIS180/250. Cash only. ❶

Armenian Guest House, 36 Via Dolorosa (☎02 626 0880; armenianguesthouse@hotmail.com). Across the street from the Sisters of Zion Convent, several blocks from the northern wall of the Temple Mount. An international array of nuns make up a sizeable percentage of the Armenian Guest House's boarders, contributing to its quiet atmosphere. Bright, sparse, and immaculate rooms, each furnished with a desk, TV, and fan. Breakfast included. Reservations recommended. Dorms NIS100; singles NIS300; doubles NIS400; triples NIS515. Cash only. ❷

Golden Gate Inn, Souq Khan al-Zeit St. (☎02 628 4317; goldengate442000@yahoo.com). From Damascus Gate, turn right down Souq Khan al-Zeit; on the street right after its intersection with Aqabet al-Batiq St. Clean if sparse, with a quiet tile patio overlooking the bustle of the *souq*. Great location. Breakfast included. Free Wi-Fi. Kitchen access. Dorms NIS50; singles NIS150; doubles NIS200. Cash only. ❶

DEAD ZONE. If you're a night owl staying in the Old City, be sure to eat dinner and stock up on your bottled water and snacks before 8pm, at the latest; the Old City closes down as soon as the shoppers leave, and the *souqs* become a series of empty and mildly creepy tunnels. If it's 11pm and you're desperate for something to eat, hostels with attached restaurants such as **Hebron Hostel** are a good bet; you can always beg for a midnight snack.

JERUSALEM

ARMENIAN QUARTER

⬛Lutheran Guest House, St. Mark's Rd (☎02 626 6888; www.luth-guesthouse-jeru-salem.com), the 1st alley to the right off David St. when coming from Jaffa Gate; a few doors down from Citadel Hostel, on the left side of the street. The garden with a large fountain and nearby dining hall is an oasis of calm punctuated by occasional church bells. A/C in all rooms. Breakfast included for private rooms. Free Wi-Fi and computer access. Singles NIS300; doubles NIS445; triples NIS575. AmEx/D/MC/V. ❸

Citadel Hostel, 20 St Mark's Rd (☎02 628 4494; reservation@citadelhostel.com), a few doors up from the Lutheran Guest House, on the right side of the street. For the dirt cheap, Citadel Hostel has achieved a comfortable balance between the dirt and the cheap. Overrun with backpackers, Citadel Hostel's cave-like staircases lead to dark, somewhat musty private rooms with vaulted ceilings. The best deal is renting a mattress on the roof, which provides a stunning panoramic view of the Old City. Bathrooms down the hall. Wi-Fi. Kitchen access with free tea and coffee. 1-week max. stay. Check-out 11am. Curfew midnight. Reserve in advance. Roof mattress NIS50; dorms NIS65; quads NIS320, with bath NIS340. Cash only. ❶

Jaffa Gate Hostel (☎02 627 6402; jaffa_gate_hostel@yahoo.com), in the Jaffa Gate area across from the Tower of David; a black and pink sign points down a short alley to the reception. The dorms are close quarters and smell a little like feet, but the hostel is clean with a good sitting area, a backpacker vibe, and a prime location. Dorms NIS70; doubles NIS120; triples NIS100. Reservations recommended. Cash only. ❶

JEWISH QUARTER

⬛Heritage House. Office: 90 Habad St. (☎02 627 1916); men's hostel: 2 Or ha-Hayim St (☎02 627 2224); women's hostel: 7 ha-Malakh St (☎02 628 1820). Both hostels are accessible off Habad St. In the spirit of promoting Jewish education and awareness, the Heritage House is free for all guests. While the men's building has a more traditional hostel set up, the women's hostel is situated in the home of a tremendously friendly Orthodox family, adding an intimate feel to the experience. Kosher dairy kitchen for guests. Bathroom down the hall. A/C and/or fans in all rooms. Dorms only; suggested NIS25 donation per night, NIS50 suggested donation on Shabbat. On Shabbat, guests can be placed with local families. ❶

El Malak, 18 el-Malak and 27 Ararat St. (☎02 628 5382). 3 doors down from the Heritage House on the right hand side. Ask for Claire Ghawi. Series of rooms in the renovated basement of a friendly Armenian grandmother. The house smells faintly of cigarette smoke, and some of the rooms do not have windows, but they stay cool during the day while the rest of the Old City roasts. Bathroom down the hall. Kitchen access. Dorms NIS70; private rooms NIS100 per bed. ❶

Dr. Bachi's Guest House, 11 Misgav Ladach St. (☎02 628 6668; www.geocities.com/rooms4rental). From Tferet Yisrael St. turn left onto Misgav Ladach, right before the stairs that lead to the Western Wall; building is on the righthand side, right after Treasures of the Temple Museum. The elderly Dr. Bachi rents out the homey, intimate guest bedrooms of her picturesque house, which is a 2min. walk from the Western Wall. Though you are technically sharing the facilities with Dr. Bachi, she usually lives elsewhere, giving guests free use of her home and its facilities. A great way to settle into the Old City. No A/C, but cool inside and fans are available. Kosher kitchen. Reservations recommended. Rooms NIS600. Cash or direct wire transfer only. ❺

CHRISTIAN QUARTER

⬛Gloria Hotel, 33 Latin Patriarchate Rd. (☎02 628 2431). Turn left up Latin Patriarch-ate Rd from Jaffa Gate area. From the lobby's polished floors to the crisply packaged soaps in each bathroom, Gloria Hotel exchanges the creeks and quirks of many Old City hotels for modern comfort. Its prices are also freakishly reasonable, given its prime location and amenities. A/C and TVs. Breakfast included. Wi-Fi. Reservations recommended. Singles NIS400; doubles NIS515; triples NIS600. AmEx/D/MC/V. ❹

New Imperial Hotel, Jaffa Gate (☎02 628 2261; www.newimperial.com), right inside the gate. The New Imperial Hotel was originally built to welcome Kaiser Wilhelm II of Germany to the Holy Land in 1898 in an effort to bolster Turkish-German relations. A historical landmark in and of itself, its steep stairs and dim hallways have become a bit idiosyncratic with age, but lend the New Imperial an air of distinction. Rooms are sparse but clean. Hotel Manager A. Walid Dajani may be the most courteous man in the Old City. Singles NIS220; doubles NIS340; triples NIS415. Cash only. ❸

Casa Nova Franciscan House for Pilgrims, Casa Nova St. (☎02 628 2791; www.custodia.org). From Jaffa Gate, take the 2nd left up Greek Patriarche Rd. Despite the scandalous image its name evokes, Casa Nova is the Italian-speaking Christian pilgrim's heaven, with pink marble pillars in the lobby and pictures of the pope above the desk. Rooms are spacious if simple, with uncommonly large bathrooms complete with bidets. Fans in all rooms. Breakfast included; additional meals $10 each. Curfew 11pm-5am. Pilgrims are given priority booking, so make reservations in advance. Singles NIS200; doubles NIS315; triples NIS400. Cash only. ❸

Greek Catholic Patriarch, Greek Patriarchate Rd. (☎02 627 1968). From Jaffa Gate, take the 2nd left; the elegant hospice is on the right, under a sign that reads "Patriarchat Grec-Catholique." Mostly patronized by pilgrims, the hospice has its own small Greek Catholic church; there is a mass Su in Arabic, and the resident Egyptian priest speaks (and presumably conduct prayers in) multiple languages. Beautiful rooftop view where French and German pilgrims often go to pray. Breakfast included. Singles NIS300; doubles NIS440; triples NIS540. Cash only. ❸

Petra Hotel, 1 David St. (☎02 628 6618). Just inside Jaffa Gate, on the left before the entrance to the market. Built more than 175 years ago, this is the oldest accommodation in the Old City. Mark Twain and Herman Melville stayed here; since then, the grand building has become progressively worn down, with peeling paint and the occasional trail of ants. Fantastic rooftop views, however, and a vast, sunny lounge alongside some of the cheapest prices in the city. Fans in all rooms. Kitchen access. Showers down the hall; 5min. showers only, with hot water from 5am-10am and 5pm-10pm. Rooftop mattresses NIS20; dorms NIS50; singles NIS170; doubles NIS200; triples NIS240. AmEx/D/MC/V. ❶

WEST JERUSALEM

Choosing to set up camp in West Jerusalem as opposed to, say, a mattress on the roof of a colorful Old City backpacker hostel, is like choosing to stay in another country. Old City hostel-goers can't get a falafel after 9 pm, and go to sleep to the muezzins' echoing calls to prayer; West Jerusalem hostel-goers may elect to not go to sleep and stay out clubbing all night instead. Most establishments here have no curfew, and some are located directly above the action. Accommodations in West Jerusalem are generally roomier than their Old City counterparts, though not always. They are always more expensive, however, and what they post in amenities they lack in rustic charm.

West Jerusalem Hostels are generally situated in the Zion Square area or around David St. in Talbieh. Privately-run small-scale bed-and-breakfasts are excellent alternatives to hostels. They are often more private and comfortable, and they provide some contact with an Israeli family. The **Home Accommodation Association** (http://www.bnb.co.il) is a group of independent apartment owners who offer rooms of all ranges. These all come with a telephone, TV, kitchenette, bathroom, and usually air-conditioning. Prices range widely based on the

B&B owner, and the actual office of the Association is rarely if ever staffed; be sure to contact each owner individually to negotiate rates. The upside is that the Association's website is simple but exceptionally clear, listing all of the B&B's present room availability and contact info with sample pictures of the rooms; there is an interactive map of the city and a list of links to helpful tourist sites included as well. For more detailed information about the arrangements, and about accommodations in West Jerusalem in general, visit the government tourist office in Safra Sq. (see **Tourist Information**, p. 96).

ZION SQUARE

Hotel Noga, 4 Bezalel St. (☎02 566 1888; kristalt@bezeqint.net). Several blocks from Zion Sq. Walk down King George, turn right on Be'eri, left onto Shmuel ha-Nagid, and right onto Bezalel. Comfortable walk to Mahane Yehuda or to the area of the Knesset and Israel Museum. The elderly married couple who runs the place have a collection of potted plants in the stairwell lobby, and are up there with the most courteous of Jerusalem hostel owners. Each floor has 1 full bath and kitchen. For longer stays, ask about the apartment down the block. Reception until 2pm. Be sure to reserve in advance; there are only 10 rooms, and they tend to fill up quickly. Singles US$40; doubles US$55. Ask about the tiny US$10 rooms. Cash only. ❷

The Jerusalem Hostel and Guest House, 44 Jaffa Rd. (☎02 623 6102; www.jerusalem-hostel.com). Right in the center of the Zion Sq. area. Best located hostel in West Jerusalem, hands down. Clean rooms and whitewashed hallways, with high ceilings, fading red Oriental carpeting, and soothing muzak. Don't let the woman at the front desk, who is about as helpful as your average DMV employee, deter you. All rooms have private bath, A/C, and free Wi-Fi. Breakfast included. Kitchen access available to guests. Safe available for valuables. Reception Su-Th 8am-10pm, F 8am-3pm, S from 10pm. Rooms divided into A rooms, B rooms, C rooms and dorms, in descending order of spaciousness; A and B rooms also have balconies and cable TV. Dorms NIS70; A/B/C singles NIS310/260/230; A/B/C doubles NIS340/290/250. AmEx/D/MC/V. ❶

Jerusalem Inn Hotel, 7 Horkanos St. (☎02 625 2757; info@jerusalem-inn.com). From Yafo Rd., turn right on Heleni Hamalka St., then left on Horkanos. Small, comfortable hotel right off the city center; a bit more expensive than its neighbors, but more comfortable too. Most of the rooms have small terraces over looking the bustling streets below. A/C, free Wi-Fi, TV, and small fridge in each room. Check-in 3pm. Check-out 11am. Singles US$99-119; doubles $125-145; triples $180; quads $200. Prices vary seasonally. Credit cards accepted. ❹

Davidka Hostel (HI), 67 ha-Nevi'im St. (☎02 538 4555). Between the Zion Sq. area and Mahane Yehuda. Take bus #27, 36, or 6 from the central bus station. From the city center, walk up Yafo until it crosses Hanevi'im. A lobby that smells pungently of cigarette smoke, a faded blue pool table apparently robbed of its balls and pool cues, a small pile of trash against the building on the walk from the lobby to the apartment complex—make no mistake, Davidka Hostel's not a looker. What it is, though, is one of the few places in town that offers rooms that border on studio apartments, with a fridge, extra sink, and extra set of cupboards in every room for long-term stays. Rooms are spartan with foggy glass doors that lead to balconies over looking the noisy street. A/C, TVs, and Wi-Fi free in every room. All rooms 2 beds. Rooms NIS180. Cash only. ❷

Hotel Kaplan, 1 Havazelet St. (☎02 625 4591; natrade@netvision.net.il). In the city center, right off Yafo St.; from Yafo turn right onto Havazelet, and it will be on your left. Small, ideally-located place up several flights of steps with festive day-glow yellow walls and bright blue metal railings. Rooms are sparse but clean, and the proprietor is friendly. All rooms have A/C, free Wi-Fi, and free kitchen access. Singles US$50; doubles US$75; triples US$85. Credit cards accepted. ❸

KING DAVID STREET (TALBIEH)

Beit Shmuel Guest House, 6 Shammai St. (☎02 620 3445; www.merkazshimshon. com). Right off of David St., around the corner and across the street from the massive David Citadel Hotel. Part of the Beit Shmuel Center for Progressive Judaism complex. Breezy central courtyard for sitting and eating. Beds are comfortable, and can be pushed together to form a queen-size for couples; bunk beds fold out of the wall for larger parties. Many of the rooms have balconies with lovely views of the Old City. A/C and free Wi-Fi available. Breakfast included. Singles US$84, doubles US$99; groups of 6 US$219. AmEx/D/MC/V. ❹

Beit Gesher Guest House, 10 King David St. (☎02 624 1015; gesher@gesher.com.il). Cross the street from the David Citadel Hotel, and then turn onto the short, unnamed side street directly behind it; you'll see the sign. Clean and airy 39-room hostel in a beautiful old building. Frequented by youth groups in the summer but quiet the rest of the year. A patio, dining room, series of seminar rooms, and synagogue are attached. All rooms with private bath and A/C. Singles US$50, with breakfast US$55; doubles US$55/65. Discounts available for large groups. Credit cards accepted. ❶

Agron Guest House, 6 Agron St. (☎02 6217555 ext. 3; http://www.iyha.org.il/eng/ Index.asp?CategoryID=72& ArticleID=56). From David Citadel Hotel, turn right onto Gershon Agron St.; Agron Guest House is several blocks up the hill, close to the intersection with Keren Heyesod St. Innocuous but comfortable; the elevator smells like cigarette smoke, but the blue-tiled hallways have large windows that offer views of the city. Rooms are small but clean with narrow bunks, A/C, and private baths. Breakfast included. Check-in 2pm. Check-out 10am. Singles NIS295; doubles NIS390. Extra person NIS115, extra child NIS90. Credit cards accepted. ❸

YMCA Three Arches Hotel (☎02 569 2692; www.YMCA3arch.com.il), across the street from the King David Hotel. This is not your local YMCA with cheap swim classes for kindergarteners and a locker room that smells like feet. The YMCA 3 Arches Hotel is one of the nicest places to stay in Jerusalem, period, and if you're a student with a backpacking backpack chances are you can't afford it. Designed by the same architect who brought us the Empire State Building, the lush gardens, marble hallways, and detailed painting on the lobby's blue arched ceiling rivals some of Jerusalem's local cathedrals; the hotel's tower offers a stunning panoramic view of the area. Rooms are meticulous. Hotel lobby houses both a very good restaurant and coffee shop. Indoor pool, fitness center, tennis and squash courts open to all customers. Singles US$120, doubles US$145, triples $160, suite $185. AmEx/D/MC/V. ❺

King David Hotel, 23 King David St. (☎02 620 8888; www.danhotels.com). Opened in 1931, this majestic accommodation is Israel's 5-star hotel. Regularly frequented by presidents and famous actors, it has a long history and an impressive list of former guests, all of whom have signed the famed white carpet that runs the length of the lobby. You cannot afford to stay here. You can, however, stroll around the gardens or order a drink while relaxing on the terrace overlooking the Old City. The rooms are impossibly comfortable and luxurious. If you must know, a standard double is US$490 per night; the grand suite costs US$3,900. ❻+

EAST JERUSALEM

East Jerusalem contains a beautiful and vibrant slice of Palestinian life, and represents a stark contrast to the western parts of the city. After over 40 years under Israeli governance, Jerusalem is still very much divided along its pre-1967 borders; don't be surprised if some of your Jewish Israeli friends in West Jerusalem have not only never set foot on Salah al-Din St., but are also surprised that you would even consider doing so. This area has been a hotbed for political tension in the past, so be sure to feel out the situation before deciding to stay here; visibly Jewish travelers (particularly men in *kippot*) should exercise caution, and you should remember that this area can be unsafe at night. But the majority of travelers don't have any problems here. Most of the time, East Jerusalem is a community bustling with women doing their daily shopping, street venders hawking cheap produce, and children running foot races or biking through the streets. Don't be surprised if locals who you only met and talked to once, in a coffee shop several weeks ago greet you on the street like an old friend.

In regards to accommodations, East Jerusalem has fewer options than the city's other neighborhoods. There are not many hostels; for a better ratio of cheapness to comfort in a similar neighborhood, try the hostels right inside Damascus Gate. All accommodations listed in this section are situated in the central East Jerusalem neighborhood.

Jerusalem Hotel (☎02 628 3282; www.jrshotel.com), across the street from the Nablus Rd. bus station, on a side street off Nablus Rd. Up there with the American Colony Hotel as one of the most comfortable places to stay, and its prices are much more reasonable. Rooms mix old stone ceilings and stately carved wardrobes with flatscreen TVs; the hallways are decorated with detailed wooden lattice work and other lovely local art pieces. The hotel's restaurant, the Han Zaman, is situated on a candlelit garden patio, and is among the best places to eat in East Jerusalem. Breakfast included. A/C, free Wi-Fi, and TV in each room. Computer use available. Singles US$130; doubles US$190; triples US$220. AmEx/D/MC/V. ❺

St. George's Cathedral Pilgrim Guest House, 20 Nablus Rd. (☎02 628 3302; sghostel@bezeqint.net). A 10-15 minute walk down Nablus Rd. from Damascus Gate. A peaceful and secluded place to stay adjacent to the historic St. George's Cathedral. Rooms have remarkable domed ceilings, TVs, bathrooms, phones, free Wi-Fi, fan and sumptuous bedding. Cafe and sitting area in an airy and green courtyard with roses. Check-out 10am. Singles US$80; doubles $120; triples $160. V. ❹

The Golden Walls Hotel, Sultan Suleiman St. (☎02 627 2416; www.goldenwalls.com). Next to Suileman St. Bus Station; take bus #1 or 3 from the Central Bus Station. Directly across the street from Zedekiah's Cave, to the right and across the street from Damascus Gate. Up 2 flights of gleaming stairs above a block of small and raucous East Jerusalem shops, the Golden Walls Hotel is a quiet, well air-conditioned hotel in an ideal location. Rooms are clean with green patterned curtains. A roof garden overlooks the intersection and dignified Damascus Gate below; the management is currently installing a hot tub up there. Breakfast included. Free Wi-Fi, TV corner, and bar in the lobby. High-season singles US$198; doubles US$242; triples US4270. Low-season singles US$120; doubles US$150; triples US$185. Contact them in advance to lower rates by up to 50% for groups of over 20. AmEx/D/MC/V. ❺

Legacy Hotel, 29 Nablus Rd. (☎02 627 0800; www.jerusalemlegacy.com). A 5min. walk up Nablus St. from Damascus Gate. Originally part of a large YMCA, the Legacy Hotel has undergone a serious make over; its aging facade now houses a sleek modern lobby, which vaguely resembles the architectural style seen in modern art museums. Rooms are comfortable with blond wooden floors, deep closets, and white bathrobes folded neatly on each bed; many of the rooms have terraces that are almost as big as the rooms themselves. The desk staff is very helpful, and good for tips on both East Jerusalem and Israel at large. Guests can use the extensive YMCA next door for free. Breakfast included. A/C, free Wi-Fi, TV, mini bar, and a safe in each room. Check-in 2pm. Check-out noon. Singles July-Oct. US$160, Sept.-July US$150; doubles $180/170; triples US$200. AmEx/D/MC/V. ❺

Rivoli Hotel, 3 Salah al-Din St. (☎02 628 4871; rivoli_hotel@yahoo.com). Take buses #1 or 3 from the Central Bus Station to Suleiman St. Bus Station. From there, walk straight on Suleiman St. and turn left on Salah al-Din St.; Rivoli Hotel will be on your right. The big 2nd floor dining room has dim white hallways, thin carpeting, and slightly saggy mattresses with armchairs that vaguely look like the business-class seating on airplanes. The rooms are clean, ideally located, and inordinately cheap for their location; if you can, try to get a room that looks into the lush gardens of the buildings next door. Fans and free Wi-Fi in each room. Check-out noon. Singles NIS200; doubles NIS300. Cash only. ❸

◘ FOOD

Food in Jerusalem somewhat complicates the guidelines for the city laid out in the Accommodations section (to recap: the Old City is cheap and funky, West Jerusalem has higher quality and higher prices, and East Jerusalem is full of hidden deals). The cheapest and strangest places to eat are still in the Old City, but you have to comb through the **Muslim Quarter** to find them; restaurants in the other three Quarters are more focused on tourists than the authenticity or artistry of their food, and price their dishes accordingly. West Jerusalem is home to a truly fantastic restaurant scene, but you will have to watch your budget in order to eat well; restaurants that are buried away in the Mahane Yehuda market like **Azura** are much more reasonably priced. East Jerusalem does not have as many options, and many of its best restaurants are attached to luxury hotels. The fresh falafels served at the local stands, however, are sold at rock bottom prices and appear to be big enough to feed a starving family for several years. To eat as cheaply as possible, the best thing to do is to skip the restaurants all together and shop in the *souq* and the *shuk*. The produce is fresh, the pita is hot, and the spices are sold from wooden bins in big pyramids of color; if your hostel has a kitchen, you're good to go.

OLD CITY

While tourist-priced places entice the mobs around Jaffa Gate and the Temple Mount, hole-in-the-wall Middle Eastern restaurants crowd the narrow alleyways of the Old City are often cheaper and much tastier. The Muslim Quarter's **souq** has the best food in the City, hands down. The chicken restaurants on **Suq Khan al-Zeit,** inside Damascus Gate, are popular with locals (look for huge rotisseries and follow the smell). Sit-down restaurants line **al-Wad Road** and **Bab al-Silsilah Street,** and some, like **Abu Taher** and **Abu Shukri,** are exceptionally good. Street vendors sell fresh, soft sesame *ka'ak* throughout the *souq;* ask for *za'tar* to go with it and dip away (NIS2-3). The market drips with honey-drenched Arab pastries; **Ja'far Sweets Company** makes the best. Beyond the Muslim Quarter, food gets more touristy and correspondingly more pricey, though some places, like **Keshet,** are definitely worth it. This is a religious town, so barflies might want to venture beyond the Old City walls for a good time; if you'd rather stay closer to home, try the **Armenian Tavern** or **Boulghourji** in the **Armenian Quarter,** which both have full bars.

> **⚡TIP** **FAST FALAFEL FIX.** If it comes down to a falafel at a stand in front of Jaffa Gate and a falafel at a stand in front of Damascus Gate, always, always, **always** go to Damascus. It will be cheaper and taste better, every time.

MUSLIM QUARTER

 Abu Taher, from David St. turn onto Souq al-La'h'hamin St., the street right before Souq Khan al-Zeit; Abu Taher's is about a 2min. walk down Souq al-La'h'hamin on the left hand side. There's no street number, but if you get lost, ask a local shopkeeper to direct you.

When you arrive at Abu Taher's, the owner will usher you into the closet-sized kitchen, point at each enormous pot of food sizzling on the stove and ask which dish you want. Somewhat hard to find with 4 tables, no menu, and odd hours, locals swear by this place; it is rumored that Abu Taher provides the best Palestinian homecooking in the Old City. Be prepared to share your table with local customers on their lunch breaks. Chicken and rice plate NIS25. Hummus and pita NIS15. Open daily 8am-3pm. Cash only. ❷

🖾 **Ja'far Sweets Company,** Souq Khan al-Zeit (☎02 628 3582). Walk down Souq Khan al-Zeit for 1min. past Hashimi Hostel, toward Damascus Gate; it will be on the left. Offers the cheapest, gooiest, most authentic pastries in the area. Munch on homemade baklava at gray tables with local families. Baklava with nuts NIS1. Sweet cheese NIS5 per slice. Open daily 7am-7:30pm. Cash only. ❶

Abu Shukri, 63 al-Wad St. (☎02 627 1538). Walk down al-Wad St. away from Damascus Gate; it is on the left-hand side of the street. Another local favorite with great hummus and no set menu. Sit back with the locals, listen to clink of dishes and the caged parrot in the corner, and watch the street traffic bustle by. Cash only. ❷

Damascus Gate Cafe (☎02 627 4282), on your immediate left inside Damascus Gate. Large shaded terrace grants a welcome respite from the daily bustle of the gate. Sit and "gate-watch" with a cadre of locals who come regularly to the cafe to smoke and occasionally talk politics. Tea NIS10. Armenian pizza NIS25. Open daily 7:30am-8pm. ❶

Green Door Pizza Bakery (☎02 627 6271), right off al-Wad St. Coming in Damascus Gate, make a sharp left when the road forks. Abu Ali has been serving his renowned Arabic-style pizza for over two decades. Don't let the peeling walls or bare wires deter you; this place is worth the stop. Filling personal pizzas (NIS15) are topped with cheese, egg, meat, and as many vegetables as the chef happens to have. He'll also do individual orders, including vegetarian. Open daily 6am-11pm. Cash only. ❶

ARMENIAN QUARTER

Moses' Lebanese Art Cafe, Jaffa Gate (☎02 628 0925), across the street from the Citadel. Walk toward Armenian Patriarchate Rd., past the intersection for David St.; it will be on your left. Established in 1917, Moses' Lebanese Art Cafe is much older than the country it resides in. Moses manages to make his cafe feel intimate and well-lived in despite the gunning motors of the taxis on Armenian Patriarchate Rd. or the kitsch souvenir shops next door. The customers seated at the 4pink tables are mostly older men who appear to have frequented the cafe for decades. Falafel NIS40. Stuffed Lebanese meal NIS110. Open daily 7:30am-11pm. Cash only. ❸

Armenian Tavern, 79 Armenian Orthodox Patriarchate Rd. (☎02 627 3854), take a right inside Jaffa Gate and follow traffic on the too-narrow street. Armenian Tavern is on the left and down the steps. Blissfully cool and warmly furnished, with tile-studded walls and indoor fountain. One of the few good places for Armenian food in town that is accessible to visitors. Armenian pizza NIS12. Kebab NIS50. Open M-Sa 12pm-10pm. Cash only. ❷

Boulghourji Bar and Gardens, Armenian Orthodox Patriarchate Rd. (☎02 628 2080), 3 storefronts down from the Armenian Tavern; the yellow door before the tunnel, on the right side. Classy restaurant with a full bar and huge, buttery servings. Armenian locals occasionally hold kids' birthday parties in the peaceful garden courtyard outside. Armenian kebab NIS75. Lamb cutlets NIS85. Open daily noon-11pm. AmEx/D/MC/V. ❸

JEWISH QUARTER

Keshet, 2 Tiferet Yisrael St. (☎02 628 7515), in Hurva Square. The only extensive outdoor seating in the square, so look for the tables. Delicious grub includes Jewish specialties like potato latkes with sour cream and applesauce (NIS46), or a fresh lox bagel and shmear (NIS52). When it's not oppressively hot, eat outside in the shade of the trees and umbrellas. Open Su-Th 8am-6pm, F 8am-3pm. AmEx/D/MC/V. ❷

Bonker's Bagels, 2 Tiferet Israel St. (☎02 627 2590), several blocks east from Western Wall, across the street from the Burnt House. Recognizable by its grinning and googly-eyed cartoon bagel logo, Bonker's Bagels is conveniently situated several blocks from the Temple Mount. While it's not exactly on par with the famed delis of New York or Los Angeles, the prices are great, the bagels taste wonderfully fresh, and the octagonal tables outside make for peaceful people-watching. Bagel NIS5, lox spread NIS17. Kosher. Open Su-Th 7am-10pm, F 8am-3:30pm. Cash only. ❶

My Burger, 128 Jewish Quarter Rd. (☎02 627 1332). Walk south down Jewish Quarter Rd. toward Jewish Quarter parking lot from Hurva Sq.; it will be immediately on the right. Though it's name mysteriously suggests otherwise, My Burger mostly sells goopy falafels wrapped in thin green paper through the shop window. The hummus doesn't compete with the likes of, for example, **Abu Taher** (p. 105), but it gets the job done. The little outdoor seating area is lovely too. Falafel NIS15. Hamburger NIS42. Kosher. Open daily 10am-6pm. ❷

CHRISTIAN QUARTER

Amigo Emil, al-Khanqa St. (☎02 628 8090). After exiting the Church of the Holy Sepulchre, turn right on Christian Quarter Rd., then left onto al-Khanqa; Amigo Emil is ½ a block down on the left. A peaceful and classy place to rest after a day of getting lost in the Old City, provided that you don't get lost trying to find it. Serves succulent kebabs at very reasonable prices, as well as Arabic coffee in little gold teapots that look like Disney genie lamps. Shish kebab NIS60. Hamburger NIS35. Open daily 11am-9:30pm. AmEx/D/MC/V. ❷

Papa Andrea's, 64 Afterneos St. (☎02 628 4433), 1 block away from the Church of the Holy Sepulchre; follow the signs to the roof. The waiters may have little patience for dumb questions ([Jetlagged] Let's Go Researcher: Do you speak English? Waiter: Sometimes. When I feel like it.), but Papa Andrea's is worth the stop, if only for its spectacular view. You can see the Dome of the Rock, the Church of the Holy Sepulchre, and the Mount of Olives from the 3rd fl. rooftop, as well as the jumble of satellite dishes sprinkling the fading terracotta roofs of the local houses. The view becomes extraordinarily vivid at sunset. Jerusalem plate NIS35. Kebab NIS55. Open daily 9am-9pm. Cash only. ❷

Nafoura, 18 Latin Patriarchate Rd. (☎02 626 0034). When entering Jaffa Gate, turn left, then left again on Latin Patriarchate Rd. (you'll see the street sign); Nafoura will be on your left. A regular stomping ground for tour groups, Nafoura is another respite from the chaos of Jerusalem. Listen to the sound of the fountain and the clinking dishes in the kitchen from the quiet, outdoor garden. Falafel platter NIS30. Lamb cutlets NIS60. All-you-can-eat lunch buffet NIS75. Open daily 11am-11pm. 10% discount for tour groups. Credit cards accepted. ❷

WEST JERUSALEM

West Jerusalem's restaurant scene reflects the international makeup of its growing population. Dining here spans a full spectrum of price ranges, from fried falafel to fancy French. Restaurants with outdoor tables line the Salomon, Rivlin, and Ben-Yehuda St. **midrakhovot,** all within a couple square blocks in the city center. Look for inexpensive "business lunch" specials at any city-center restaurants. Many establishments straddle the boundaries between restaurant, bar, and cafe. The Jerusalem specific website, www.go-out.com, is jam-packed with listings in town.

Most of the restaurants in West Jerusalem are in the Zion Sq. area. From greatest hot chocolate in the world (Babbette's) to vegan salads by the kilo

(Vegetable Green), these diverse restaurants are the most likely to be open late or on Shabbat. For the cheapest of the fresh and the freshest of the cheap, head for the raucous open-air **Mahane Yehuda market.** Supermarkets include **Supersol,** on the corner of Agron and King George St. (☎02 625 0657).

ZION SQUARE

🍴 **Alma,** 18 Rivlin St. (☎02 502 0069), at the end of Rivlin St., right where it intersects with Hillel St. Literally the new kid on the block among the rowdier bars of Rivlin St., Alma is inventive and classy with some of the best food in town. The white umbrellas and narrow window boxes of the outside seating area make for a wonderful respite on a hot day. Steak NIS85. Chocolate souffle NIS22. Open daily noon-midnight. Credit cards accepted. ❸

🍴 **Vegetable Green,** 33 Yafo St. (☎02 625 3065), between Rivlin St. and Nahalat Shiva. When the reasonably priced food of Jerusalem seems like an indistinguishable sea of greasy falafels and kebabs, head over to this popular joint. Even carnivores will marvel over the salad bar, which is priced by weight. Kosher, organic, vegan—you got it. Salads from NIS8.5. Everything else within NIS18-NIS29. Open Su-Th 9am-10pm and F 9am-3pm. Credit cards accepted. ❶

🍴 **Babbette's Party,** 16 Shammai St. (☎02 814 1182), near the corner of Yoel Salomon. Israelis flock here just to get a whiff of Babbett's 14 amazing Belgian waffle varieties (butter and cream, NIS14; Grand Marnier, NIS17). Also hands-down the best hot chocolate in Israel (some would say the world). Small hot chocolate NIS8. Waffles NIS21-25. Open Su-Th noon-2am, F 10am-5pm. Cash only. ❶

🍴 **T'mol Shilshom,** 5 Yoel Salomon St. (☎02 623 2758; www.tmol-shishlom.co.il). Down a small domed alleyway at the top of Yoel Salomon St., on the lefthand side. This bookstore-cafe, named after a Shai Agnon book, is frequented by writers and poets such as Yehuda Amihai; he and other local greats give occasional readings here (sometimes in English; call in advance or check the website for details). F renowned all-you-can-eat breakfast buffet. GLBT-friendly. Fettuccini in fresh tomato-basil cream sauce NIS48. Tuna fillet NIS75. Open Su-Th 9am-1am, F 9am-sundown. Credit cards accepted. ❸

🍴 **Humus Ben Sira,** 3 Ben Sira St. (☎054 754 2954), across the street from Cielo. Perhaps the best hummus joint in West Jerusalem. Helpings are enormous and the pita is served fresh from the oven. Sit at the blue-tiled counter under the wonderfully aggressive A/C unit and watch the chef prepare your food. Falafel platter NIS30. Hummus plate NIS21. Open Su-Th 11am-2am, F 11am-5pm. Cash only. ❶

Spaghettim, 8 Rabbi Akiva St. (☎02 623 5547), off Hillel St. Bear left at the sign, through the gates of an Italian-style villa. Snappy and elegant restaurant serves spaghetti prepared over 75 different ways from "gorgonzola spinachi" (NIS38) to "spaghetti napolitana" (NIS35). Beautifully-lit interior and refreshing outdoor seating. Open noon-midnight. Credit cards accepted. ❷

Zuni's, 15 Yoel Solomon St. (☎02 625 7776). Arrived in Jerusalem jet-lagged at 5am? Got the munchies at 2am? Look no further. A classy upstairs restaurant with dark wood banisters and Ella Fitzgerald playing in the background, Zuni's claim to fame is that it is the only restaurant in Jerusalem open 24hr. 7 days a week. Rotates breakfast, lunch, and dinner menus throughout the day. French toast NIS37. Grilled chicken breast NIS67. Reservations recommended, particularly on F nights, when locals flock to Zuni's after all other restaurants close for Shabbat. Credit cards accepted. ❸

Foccaccia Bar, 4 Rabbi Akiva (☎02 624 6428). Offers a variety of freshly-baked focaccia breads either with dips or as part of a pizza or sandwich, on a lovely outdoor patio. Check out the regular focaccia: apparently cooked like an Indian naan, served warm on a pizza pie pan and smelling of olive oil and fresh garlic (NIS26). Goat cheese pizza NIS48. Open daily 10am-2pm. Credit cards accepted. ❷

JERUSALEM

Cielo, 18 Ben Sira (☎02 625 1132), across the street from Humus Ben Sira. Cozy Italian restaurant with good service and a looped track of old-school Italian music. A great place to get your Italian homecooking fix if Spaghettim (p. 108) isn't authentic enough for you. *Gnocchi alla sorrentina* NIS49. *Pollo alla diavola* NIS78. Open Su-Th 1-4pm and 6:30-11:30pm, F 8:30-11:30pm. Credit cards accepted. ❸

Adom, 31 Yafo Rd. (☎02 624 6242). A haven for non-observant Jews and seafood lovers, Adom deliciously violates kosher laws: like Zuni's, it remains open through Shabbat. Choose from an array of red meat and seafood cuisine. Useful location within proximity to local bars; great place to crash after a night out. Adom hamburger NIS58. Purple calamari stuffed with polenta and goat cheese NIS48. Open daily 6:30am-3pm. Credit cards accepted. ❸

Melekh Ha'Falafel V'ha Shawarma (King of Falafel and Shawarma) (☎02 636 5372), on the corner of King George St. and Agrippas St. Acclaimed parlor dominates the midtown scene; the tiny store is always packed. It's also one of the cheapest options you'll find outside of the *souq* or the *shuk*. Savory falafel NIS10. Pita and hummus NIS10. Open Su-Th 8am-midnight, F 8am-1pm. Cash only. ❶

Magic Fruit Juice, at the corner of Ben-Yehuda and King George St. Fresh-squeezed juice stands are scattered on and near the *midrakhov*, but Magic is generally regarded as the best of the lot. Choices include mango, fig, carrot, peach, watermelon, and the rest of the juice rainbow. Small juice NIS12, medium NIS15, large NIS19. Open Su-Th 8am-9pm, F 8am-4pm. Cash only. ❶

MAHANE YEHUDA

▨ **Azura,** 8 Mahane Yehuda St., Iraqi Market (☎02 623 5204). From the bottom of Mahane Yehuda, take the first right and follow the winding street until it ends at a T-stop; Azura is on the right hand side. Excellent traditional Jewish food. The crowd of locals waiting for tables often clogs the market street outside. Regulars recommend the roasted eggplant and the soups, and emphasize the exceptionality of the meatballs. Entrees NIS35-NIS70. Open Su-Th 8am-8pm, F 8am-4pm. Cash only. ❷

▨ **Emile,** 8 ha-Tut St. (☎054 240 5654; www.2eat.co.il/eng/emile). Enter the market through Mahane Yehuda St.'s market, coming from Agrippas St.; ha-Tut is your first right. A cozy alcove in the chaotic market, with awe-inspiring coffee to boot. In the evenings, it becomes a hot spot for local youth and develops more of a bar feel. Check out the website for announcements on live summer music performances, theme nights, and small-time art exhibitions. Eggplant panini with feta cheese NIS31. *Shakshuka* NIS53. Open Su 8am-8pm, M-Th 8am-midnight, F 7am-10pm. Credit cards accepted. ❷

▨ **Topolino,** 62 Agrippas St. (☎02 622 3466; www.tapolino.biz), a 15-20min. walk along Agrippas St. from Zion Sq. Bright and friendly atmosphere. The homemade pastas may be the best Italian food in Jerusalem. Figs baked with goat cheese filling NIS41. Chestnut gnocchi in cream sauce NIS57. Kosher. Open Su-Th 8:30am-11:-30pm, F 8:30am-3pm. Credit cards accepted. ❷

Ichikidana, 4 Haeshkol St. (☎050 224 7070). From Yafo Rd., turn left on Mahane Yehuda St., then take your 3rd right onto Haeshkol St.; Ichikidana is on your right. This funky hole-in-the-wall will satisfy any craving for authentic Indian *thali* you may have. Tables are collaged with cut-outs of Bollywood stars and snapshots of the Taj Mahal. Entrees NIS77-155. Open daily 11am-midnight. Cash only. ❹

GERMAN COLONY

▨ **Lev Smadar,** 4 Lloyd George (☎02 561 7819). Lev is the movie theater with old pictures of Humphrey Bogart and Ingrid Bergman taped to the appropriate restroom doors; Smadar is the bright coffee shop in front of it, its walls decorated with old pictures of the German Colony and framed posters of classic movies. Locals come here to pre-

THE BIG SPLURGE

FILET MIGNON WITH A SIDE OF DIPLOMACY

"And how would you like your steak cooked, Mr. President?"

Don't be surprised if you find yourself seated across from dignitaries, ambassadors, and government officials at **Arabesque,** Jerusalem's gourmet 5-star restaurant located in the premier American Colony Hotel, known for hosting big-time international politicians. Arabesque's ambience recalls the simple elegance and romanticized exoticism of the British empire with a delicate combination of Western and Eastern styles to make both top dogs and tourists feel welcome.

Its legendary Saturday luncheon buffet features all-you-can-eat soup, salad, appetizers, entrees, and desserts, including quirky dishes such as curried banana soup and ostrich stew. On its outdoor terrace, Arabesque serves local Middle Eastern specialties, such as *shashlik* kebab and a variety of *mezze*, as well as international foods—dignitaries tend to be picky eaters. You are, after all, in Jerusalem, so try a dish with Israeli flavor such as the *mussachan*, a Bedouin mix of rice, marinated chicken, and fresh vegetables. Regardless of what you order, Arabesque's superior service is sure to make you feel like royalty (or the prime minister of Lithuania).

Arabesque, 17 Nablus Rd., American Colony Hotel, Jerusalem (☎02 627 9777).

game shows or just sit and chat at all hours. Drink coffee (NIS10) or draft beer (NIS19-NIS24) to top hits of the Beatles, and soak in the scene. Health sandwich NIS26. Tuna carpaccio NIS44. Open daily 8:30am-midnight. Credit cards accepted. ❷

Masaryk, 31 Emek Refaim (☎02 563 6418). Comfortable cafe with plush grey upholstered seats, dark wood paneling, and a glass veranda. Staff keeps the cafe open until the last customer leaves, regardless of the time. Goat cheese gnocchi NIS59. Vegetable and herb salad NIS52. Open Su-Th 8:30am-late, F 8:30am-4:30pm, Sa from sundown to late. Credit cards accepted. ❷

Cafit, 35 Emek Refaim (☎02 566 3062). Bustling, popular lunch place for locals and their families. In the afternoon, try to snag a table inside for the A/C; the lovely patio can heat up. Brick oven focaccia NIS22. Bagel sandwiches NIS38-NIS49. Open Su-Th 8am-midnight, F from 8am to 1hr. before sundown, Sa from 1hr. after sundown to midnight. Credit cards accepted. ❷

MAMILLA

▨ **Megenana Ethiopian Restaurant,** 17 Yafo Rd. (☎054 974 8694). 10min. walk from Jaffa Gate in the Old City, on the 1st block of Yafo Rd on the left hand side; 1 block before the municipality building. Excellent food from Jerusalem's most recent immigrant community. Take in the barrage of green, red, and yellow, listen to North African jazz, and get tips from the owner on how to best mop up his delicious curries with enjera. Be sure to try some of their coffee (NIS8); Megenana imports the beans from Ethiopia, then adds a pinch of roasted cinnamon to the mix. Entrees NIS35-NIS45. Open M-F noon-midnight, Sa 5:30pm-midnight. Cash only. ❷

Cuholi Dairy Restaurant and Patisserie, Mamilla Promenade (☎02 500 4006). About halfway down the Promenade, above the Candyland ice-cream and crepe shop on the righthand side. An oasis for tourists and mallrats, but don't hold that against it. The tables on the restaurant's bridge, which stretches over the promenade, are perfect for gazing at the Old City or watching the diverse crowds of people below. Make sure to check out the dessert: Cuholi brews its hot chocolate with pure Belgian chocolate (NIS15) and devotes an entire page of its menu to mousse. Ravioli with whipped sweet potato NIS57. Goat cheese salad NIS53. Open Su-Th 8am-11pm, F 8am-3pm, Sa 9am-11pm. Credit cards accepted. ❷

✗ **Rimon,** Mamilla Promenade (☎02 625 2772; www.caferimon.co.il). About a 5min. walk from Jaffa Gate down the Mamilla Promenade, past the Aroma Cafe on the left; look for the triangular, live-flame outdoor heaters. Classy place with a peaceful view of the Yemin Moshe neighborhood. The outdoor seating is particularly nice, with clusters of low black wicker chairs cordoned off from the bustle of the mall by planter boxes of white zinnias. There is a 2nd, red-meat-serving branch of the same restaurant on Ben-Yehuda Dairy. Fettuccini alfredo NIS59. Fillet of salmon NIS82. Su-Th 8:30am-1am, F from 8:30am to 1hr. before sundown, Sa 9am-1am. Credit cards accepted. ❸

EAST JERUSALEM

CENTRAL EAST JERUSALEM AND AMERICAN COLONY

🏛 **Abu Hassan,** 1st major alleyway on the right off Salah al-Din St.; look for the red awning on the left side of the alley. No street address; no phone number; no menu. But as far as podunk Jerusalem falafel stands go, Abu Hassan is in the running for the best. The falafel balls are still hot when they are packed into the homebaked pita. If you like hot sauce be sure to request some of the freshly chopped stuff here. Look for the crowds of locals. Falafel NIS17. Open daily 7:30am-12:30pm. Cash only. ❶

🏛 **Kan Zaman** (☎02 628 3282; www.jrshotel.com), on the patio of the Jerusalem Hotel, just behind the bus station on Nablus Rd. Glass-enclosed garden restaurant with delicate tables shaded by vines. A favorite hangout for tourists and Palestinian locals, both of whom appreciate the ornate *argileyahs.* Aleppo kebab NIS52. Mixed grill NIS69. Open Su and Sa noon-11:30pm, M-F 11:30am-11:30pm. Kitchen open Su and Sa noon-2:30pm and 5-11:30pm, M-F 11:30am-2:30pm and 5-11:30pm; cold food only after 10pm. MC/V. ❸

American Colony Hotel Restaurant (☎02 627 9777; www.theamericancolony.com), in the courtyard of the American Colony Hotel, a few blocks past the US Consulate on Nablus Rd. A 15min. walk up Nablus Rd. from Damascus Gate. The fountained courtyard of this historic and picturesque luxury hotel is the city's most romantic and idyllic refuge. Spectacular food, priced for special nights only, but worth it. Hummus with lamb NIS86. Season penne NIS78. Open daily 7am-10:30pm. Credit cards accepted. ❸

SHIM'ON HA'TSADIK STREET (SHEIKH JARRAH)

Borderline Restaurant Cafe, 13 Shim'on Ha'tsadik St. (☎02 532 8342), behind Pasha's restaurant. 15-20 min walk from central East Jerusalem. Expats and NGO workers converge beneath the hulking eucalyptus trees in the Borderline's courtyard to drink at the full bar and swap (politically-charged) stories from their day. Smoky chicken with mushrooms NIS60. *Spaghetti ala puttanesca* NIS45. Drinks at bar from NIS20. Open daily 5pm-midnight or until everyone leaves. Credit cards accepted. ❷

Blue Dolphin, 7 Shim'on Ha'tsadik St. (☎02 532 2001). 15-20min. walk from central East Jerusalem. Dig into an entire fresh fish—head, tail, and all—on a plate of fresh grilled vegetables while listening to elevator musak on the relaxing outdoor seating. *Argeilehs* (water pipes) are available upon request. Kebab halabi NIS58. Sea bass steak NIS80. Open daily noon-midnight. Credit cards accepted. ❸

Pasha's, 13 Shim'on Ha'tsadik St. (☎02 656 8514). A 15-20min. walk from central East Jerusalem. Authentic regional cuisine with crisp white table cloths and green backlighting on the ferns in the garden outside. Mixed grilled plate NIS65. Minced lamb meat in oven NIS55. Open daily noon-midnight. Credit cards accepted. ❸

◎ SIGHTS

The hands down main attraction in Jerusalem is, of course, the **Old City,** which houses three foundationary sites of Judaism, Christianity, and Islam respectively. For those of you who were not raised within any of these three religions, do not read newspapers, do not retain information from high school World Civ unit tests, and/or have spent their lives living under a large rock, those three sites are **The Western Wall, The Church of the Holy Sepulchre,** and the **Temple Mount.** Known to Muslims as the Haram al-Sharif, the Temple Mount includes the Western Wall along its perimeter; the **Dome of the Rock** and **al-Aqsa Mosque** are situated within its plaza. There are four Quarters, or neighborhoods, in the Old City. The **Christian Quarter** is situated in the City's northwest corner, and is home to the Church of the Holy Sepulchre, part of the **Via Dolorosa**, and a myriad of other churches. To its left, in the northeast corner of the City, is the **Muslim Quarter**, the City's largest and most bustling area; **Damascus Gate** connects its *souq* to **East Jerusalem**. Below the Muslim Quarter in the southeast corner of the city is the **Jewish Quarter,** which like the Muslim Quarter is very residential; the Temple Mount borders both the Jewish and Muslim Quarters along the southwest corner of the City walls. Last but not least is the **Armenian Quarter**, the smallest residential area, situated in the southeast corner of the city. **David's Citadel,Jaffa Gate** and the swarm of hostels and restaurants that surround them are situated along the city walls where the Armenian and Christian Quarters intersect.

The Old City is ringed by sights that are nearly as important as the City itself. **Mount Zion** is to the Southwest, right outside of Zion Gate, and is home to the revered **Tomb of David**and the site of **the Last Supper,** as well as **Oskar Schindler's grave.** To the southeast of the Old City, right outside of Dung Gate by the Temple Mount, is the **City of David,** the extensive archaeological excavations of King David's original fortress. Running along the Old City's eastern wall is the narrow **Kidron Valley,** the dusty home to several ancient tombs; rising above it is the famed **Mount of Olives,** which overlooks the Old City. It is home to a variety of massively important sights, including the **Tomb of the Virgin Mary.**

A minute's walk to the west outside of the Old City's Jaffa Gate will bring you to **West Jerusalem**, which strikes a sharp cultural contrast to the walled city, to say the very least.**Jaffa Road** is the main thoroughfare here; a 10-15 minute walk from Jaffa Gate down Jaffa Rd. through the **Mamilla** neighborhood will bring you to **Zion Square** and the surrounding area, the center of the new city. Further down Jaffa Rd. is the **Mahane Yehuda Market,** an extensive *shuk* with excellently priced produce, and one of the few places where Jews of every religious and political persuasion mingle seamlessly together. Northeast of Zion Square is **Mea She'arim;** entering this famously Orthodox neighborhood can feel like stumbling into the alleyways of the 19th century. Southwest of the city center is **Givat Ram,** a neighborhood which hosts the **Knesset (Supreme Court),** and a variety of **museums.** The upscale neighborhoods of **Rehavia** and **Talbeiha** are south of the city center; south of Talbieh is the lovely **German Colony.** The artsy and historic **Yemin Moshe** is south of Mamilla, before the city center.

West Jerusalem is divided from East Jerusalem by **Route 1**, which runs along the historic pre-1967 Green Line that separated Israel from Jordan before the Six Day War. East Jerusalem's residential neighborhoods envelop the Old City on its northern, western, and southern sides; the neighborhoods of most note to travelers are all to the north of the City, outside of Damascus Gate. **Central East Jerusalem**'s *souq* is both the financial and falafel hub of the area. The main thoroughfares are **Nablus Street** and **Salah al-Din Street,** which both roughly run north-south from the Damascus gate area. North of Central East Jerusalem is the lovely **American Colony** neighborhood; north of that is **Sheikh Jarrah,** an area that is more residential and slightly rougher. **Shimon ha Tzaddik Street** contains a small strip of restaurants largely frequented by UN, NGO, and ICRC worker stationed in the area. Eavesdropping on these people as they rehash the dramas of their day's work can be a wild experience.

TOUR HOPPING. Visitors to Jerusalem have noted that so many school groups and travel groups hire tour guides in the city that an opportunity for the young and cheap has been inadvertently created: crashing other people's paid tours. At the Holy Sepulchre and Temple Mount in particular, there is such a convergence of tour groups that the tour guides usually don't notice if an extra person joins in the fun; when they do, they are often flattered by the interest in their spiel that they may let the unexpected visitor stay anyway.

OLD CITY

Its winding streets smooth and now blackened with age, the Old City is one sq. km on a hot desert hill with a historically unreliable water source. Though home to the majestic Dome of the Rock, most of its skyline is defined by a tangle of naked wiring and crooked satellite dishes; the scope of its archaeological discoveries pale in comparison to Mexico's Chitzen Itza or Egypt's pyramids. But there is something about this tiny plot of land that makes it holy—not only for Jews, Christians, and Muslims, but for dozens of ancient religious groups as well. Excavations under the Old City have uncovered over 20 distinct layers of civilization. At the City of David, tour guides half-jokingly use Bibles as reference manuals, as archaeologists unearth pottery from the times of Abraham. If you are traveling to Israel, chances are that one of the Old City's stones is the reason you came here, be it the rock that the Dome of the Rock encompasses, the masonry of the Western Wall, or the stone in the Church of the Holy Sepulchre on which Jesus' cross was found.

Beyond the sheer historic density of the streets and sensory overload of the tourist shops, the Old City very much remains a residential area. In the Jewish Quarter, small boys weave their tricycles between the ancient pillars of the Cardo; in the Muslim Quarter, laundry is hung from the windows of Mamluk architectural masterpieces blithely converted into apartment complexes and schools. Getting lost in the City is inevitable, so be sure to get a free map at the **Jaffa Gate Tourist Office** as soon as you arrive. A trip to the top of the Citadel or a walking tour will help you get your bearings.

 THE DATING GAME. Especially if you're a young woman, local shopkeepers and strangers will ask you out to drinks or coffee at least three times a day. If you feel like extracting some amusement out of this, keep a tally with your friends to see who receives the most invites. Remember to be cautious, though; unless it appears to be an uncommonly non-threatening situation, do not accept any of them.

WALKING TOURS OF THE OLD CITY

The Old City is only about 1 sq. km; a walking tour is a great way to get to know it. The following suggested routes cover most of the Old City and nearby sites, with almost no overlap. If you only have a few days to spend in Jerusalem, take Tour 1 on the first day, Tour 2 on the second, then spend the remainder of your time checking out the individual sights in West Jerusalem. If you have more time, break up Tour 2 into two days, as suggested below, and consider Tour 3. All bolded locations have separate listings later in the text; look under the section indicated at the beginning of the paragraph. All routes are free, but many optional sights along the way require entrance fees; those are marked

JERUSALEM

with a ($). See individual sight listings for the exact prices. For guided tours, see **Tours,** p. 97. Though brave, disabled locals are occasionally seen freewheeling through the *souq* down the slippery steps from Damascus Gate, the Jewish Quarter is the only neighborhood in the Old City that is reliably wheelchair-accessible. For a wheelchair-accessible tour through the Old City, start in the parking lot in the Jewish Quarter (which can be reached through Zion Gate or Jaffa Gate) and follow the arrows with the wheelchair icon.

TOUR 1: HIGHLIGHTS

Starting and ending point: Jaffa Gate. Approximate walking time (without side trip to Mt. Zion): 1½-2hr. Including all sights: 4-5hr. Best time to go: M-Th any time, but many of the sights along the way (including the Ramparts walk at the end) close at 4:30 or 5pm. Entrance fees (without side trip): NIS138, students NIS79. Modest dress recommended.

Inside Jaffa Gate, turn to the right and enter the **Tower of David** ($; p. 132) for an introductory film about Jerusalem. Climb up to the Phasel Tower for an amazing view of the Old City. Leaving the Tower of David, continue to your right, following Armenian Patriarchate Rd. into the **Armenian Quarter** (p. 100). The streets are narrow and the sidewalk disappears fast, so watch out for taxis. Under the short tunnel, turn to your right and peek into the **Armenian Art Center** (p. 133) for shopping or browsing. Continue down the road away from **Jaffa Gate** (p. 133), stopping next at the **Armenian Museum** ($; p. 133) on your left. From there, the road curves to the left; **Zion Gate** (p. 133) will appear on your right.

Side trip: **Mount Zion** (p. 134). *(Approximate walking time: 15-20min. Including all sights: 1hr.)* Exit through Zion Gate, and follow the path as it veers slightly to the right (rather than going down into the parking lot). Follow the signs for the **Dormition Abbey** (p. 134); go into the basilica and down into the beautiful crypt. Leaving the abbey, backtrack a few steps, then turn right and come next to the **Cenacle** (site of the Last Supper) and **Tomb of David,** both entered through the door to the **Diaspora Yeshiva,** on your left. Exit through the back entrance of the yeshiva, which will put you almost right across the street from the small, but powerful, **Chamber of the Holocaust** (p. 135). Next, head downhill and across the main road to the **Christian Cemetery** and **Schindler's Grave** (p. 135). Head back up the main road and back through Zion Gate to continue with the tour.

Back inside the Old City walls, the road curves to the left and heads into the **Jewish Quarter** (p. 100). Walk through the parking lot on your right to the far corner, where you will find the **Four Sephardic Synagogues** ($; p. 123) on your right, at the beginning of Mishmerot Ha-Kehuna Rd. Mishmerot Ha-Kehuna Rd. continues past the complex and leads into **Hurva Square** (p. p. 123). The entrance to the **Herodian Quarter** (p. 122) and **Wohl Archaeological Museum** ($; get the combo ticket) is on your right; the exit is farther down, so you'll have to walk back uphill to return to Hurva Sq. At the northeastern corner of the square, turn right on Tiferet Yisrael St. **The Burnt House** ($; p. 122) is tucked away on your left, just before the entrance to the Quarter Cafe. Continue past Bonker's Bagels until you reach a wide flight of steps and, in all probability, flocks of Israeli soldiers and school groups. Go down the steps and through the security point to enter Tzahal Sq., the plaza in front of the **Western Wall** (p. 121). Keep in mind that women who don't have their shoulders covered will be given a shawl. If you've been holding it until now, there are public restrooms by the men's side of the wall (to the left when facing the wall). Leave the plaza through the tunnel on the northwestern side (near the restrooms). Past the security point, you will be entering the busy **Muslim Quarter** (p. 124). Turn left on al-Wad Rd. You can take al-Wad straight through to Damascus Gate, getting a taste of the busy *souq* along the way. Exit through **Damascus Gate** (p. 133). A detour up the stairs to the right and along the outside of the wall leads to **Zedekiah's Cave** ($; p. 127). If you decide to go here, buy the combo ticket; it will come in handy if you visit Hezekiah's Tunnel and the Ophel Archaeological Garden another day. Back at Damascus Gate, take the stairs on your left (when facing away from the gate) down to the entrance of the **Roman Square Museum** ($; p. 127) and the **Ramparts Promenade** ($), both included in the combo ticket. Take the ramparts back to **Jaffa Gate** (p. 133), overlooking the Christian Quarter. For a free alternative, return to Jaffa Gate along the outside of the walls, or go back into Damascus Gate, take the right fork (Khan al-Zeit Rd.) through the *souq*, and turn right when you reach David St.; continue uphill until you get back to Jaffa Gate.

TOUR 2: RELIGION

Starting point: Chapel of Christ's Ascension (Mount of Olives). Ending point: Dung Gate. Approximate walking time (not including Western Wall Tunnel tour or City of David side trip): 3hr. Including all sights: 5-6hr. Best time to go: early morning (not before 8:30am, when the Pater Noster opens), on a Tu or Th if possible. Do not go on F or Su, as many of the sites will be closed. Cost (not including Tunnel tour or side trip): NIS25 for taxi to the starting point. Modest dress required. If you have more time, definitely break this tour into two halves: the first day, visit the Mount of Olives and Via Dolorosa; the second day, visit the Temple Mount and City of David—arrange to take a tour of the Western Wall Tunnels either afternoon.

Take a taxi to the top of the **Mount of Olives** (p. 139), disembarking at the **Chapel of Christ's Ascension** ($; p. 139). If you decide to skip the chapel, start instead at the much more memorable **Church of the Pater Noster** (p. 140), just downhill from the chapel. Leaving the church, follow the road down and to the left. Walk past the top of the paved path to stop in front of the Seven Arches Hotel for a fabulous view of the Old City. Backtrack a few steps and head down the path, stopping along the way at each of the Mount of Olives sights: the **Tombs of the Prophets** (p. 140), **Sanctuary of Dominus Flevit** (p. 140), **Russian Church of Mary Magdalene** (p. 140), **Church of All Nations** (p. 140), and **Tomb of the Virgin Mary** (p. 141). At the bottom of the path, turn right onto Jericho Rd. Take the second left onto Ma'aleh Motta Gur Rd. up to **Saint Stephen's Gate** (a.k.a. Lion's Gate). Not far from the gate, find the **Church of Saint Anne** (p. 127) on the right. Continue up the road to the start of the **Via Dolorosa** (p. 127). Follow Jesus' last steps, stopping at each of the Stations of the Cross and ending up in the **Church of the Holy Sepulchre** (p. 129). Be sure to stop by the meditative **Ethiopian Monastery** before you leave the complex. Leaving the church, turn right onto the Muristan; climb the tower in the **Church of the Redeemer** (p. 131), on your left, for a spectacular view of the Old City, including the path down the Mt. of Olives you just climbed.

Now you're on your way to the **Temple Mount** (p. 124); try to get there as close to 1:30pm as possible to avoid the formidable line to get through security. To get to the entrance to the Temple Mount, continue to the end of the Muristan and turn left onto David St. On the way, stop in at the **Cardo** (p. 122), a wide street filled with ancient pillars, foreign tour groups and pricey Judaica shops. Backtrack to David St. which turns into Bab al-Silsilah St., which leads directly up to the Temple Mount. The sights in the complex include the **Dome of the Rock** (p. 126), **al-Aqsa Mosque**, and the small **Islamic Museum**. Exit down the ramp that leads toward **Dung Gate** (p. 133) and go through the security point to enter Tzachal Sq., the plaza in front of the Western Wall. Take a guided tour of the **Western Wall Tunnels** ($; must be arranged in advance; p. 121) or head up the steps into the **Jewish Quarter** (see below) to see more of the synagogues or sights not covered in Tour 1.

Side trip: City of David. If you're not totally exhausted yet, skip the rest of the Jewish Quarter sights and head over to the City of David (p. 135): exit Dung Gate, turn left on Ha-Ofel Rd., right on Ma'alot Ir David St., and enter the

finish

start

Jaffa Gate

TO MT. ZION

Zion Gate

Sha'ar Zion

Hatzvi Etzioni

ARMENIAN QUARTER

Armenian Patriarchate Rd.

St. James' Cathedral

St. James'

Habad

Mishmerot

Batei Mahase

JEWISH QUARTER

HURVA SQUARE

Ha-Yehudim

BATEI MAHASE SQUARE

Dung Gate

Ha-Ofel Rd.

TZAHAL SQUARE

Western Wall Tunnels

Try not to get swept away by the commotion and clamor of the **Muslim Quarter souq**, where raw meat, textiles, and chintz abound.

The glorious ceramics in the **Armenian Art Center** are sure to make you shell out every last shekel.

Make like a high priest and saunter around the ruins of a decadent second-temple era mansion in the **Herodian Quarter (Wohl Museum)**.

The Burnt House serves as a reminder that violence has necessitated the rebuilding of the city of gold a thousand times over.

Once a clandestine spiritual refuge, now an overt religious core, the half-a-millennium year-old **Sephardic Synagogues** still fill with song and prayer.

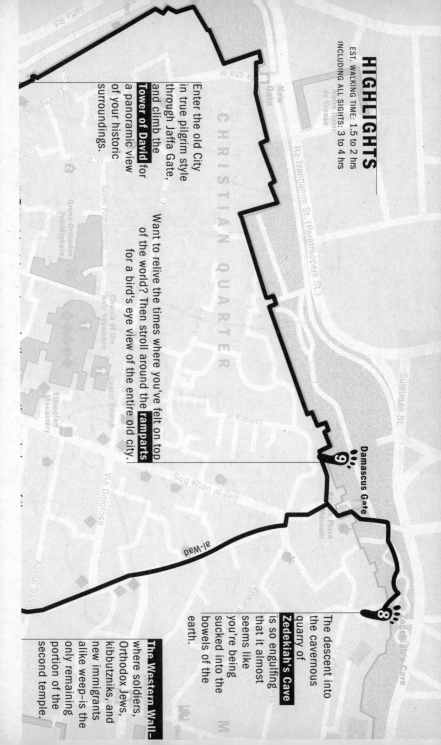

HIGHLIGHTS

EST. WALKING TIME: 1.5 to 2 hrs
INCLUDING ALL SIGHTS: 3 to 4 hrs

Enter the old City in true pilgrim style through Jaffa Gate, and climb the **Tower of David** for a panoramic view of your historic surroundings.

Want to relive the times where you've felt on top of the world? Then stroll around the **ramparts** for a bird's eye view of the entire old city.

The descent into the cavernous quarry of **Zedekiah's Cave** is so engulfing that it almost seems like you're being sucked into the bowels of the earth.

The Western Wall— where soldiers, Orthodox Jews, kibbutzniks, and new immigrants alike weep—is the only remaining portion of the second temple.

CHRISTIAN QUARTER

New Gate

Ha-Tzanhanim St. (Paratroopers St.)

Suleiman St.

Damascus Gate

Suq Khan al-Zeit

Via Dolorosa

al-Wad

al-Kanayes

Ethiopian Monastery

Coptic Church

Church of the Holy Sepulchre

Greek Orthodox Patriarchate

Jaffa Rd.

9

8

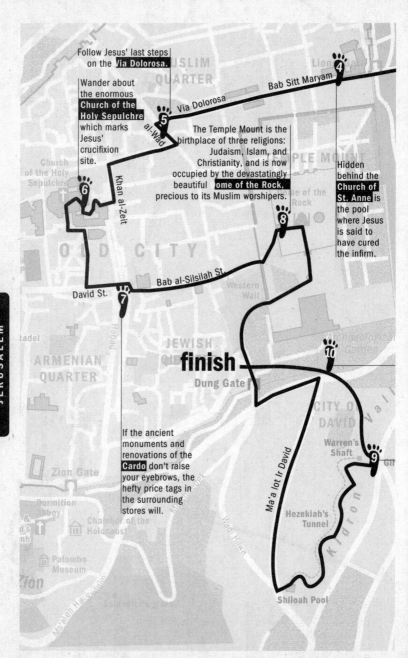

JERUSALEM

Follow Jesus' last steps on the Via Dolorosa.

Wander about the enormous Church of the Holy Sepulchre which marks Jesus' crucifixion site.

MUSLIM QUARTER

Bab Sitt Maryam

Via Dolorosa

al-Wad

The Temple Mount is the birthplace of three religions: Judaism, Islam, and Christianity, and is now occupied by the devastatingly beautiful Dome of the Rock, precious to its Muslim worshipers.

TEMPLE MOUNT

Dome of the Rock

Hidden behind the Church of St. Anne is the pool where Jesus is said to have cured the infirm.

Church of the Holy Sepulchre

Khan al-Zeit

OLD CITY

Bab al-Silsilah St.

Western Wall

David St.

Habad

ARMENIAN QUARTER

JEWISH QUARTER

finish

Dung Gate

Zion Gate

If the ancient monuments and renovations of the Cardo don't raise your eyebrows, the hefty price tags in the surrounding stores will.

Ma'a lot Ir David

Wad Hilwa

CITY OF DAVID

Warren's Shaft

Hezekiah's Tunnel

Kidron Valley

Dormition Abbey

Chamber of the Holocaust

Palombo Museum

Shiloah Pool

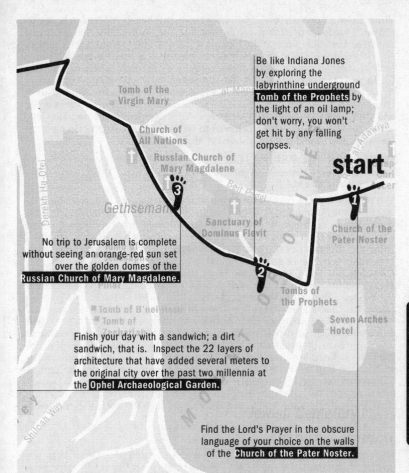

Be like Indiana Jones by exploring the labyrinthine underground **Tomb of the Prophets** by the light of an oil lamp; don't worry, you won't get hit by any falling corpses.

start

No trip to Jerusalem is complete without seeing an orange-red sun set over the golden domes of the **Russian Church of Mary Magdalene.**

Finish your day with a sandwich; a dirt sandwich, that is. Inspect the 22 layers of architecture that have added several meters to the original city over the past two millennia at the **Ophel Archaeological Garden.**

Find the Lord's Prayer in the obscure language of your choice on the walls of the **Church of the Pater Noster.**

Prepare to get soaked in the waist-deep waters of **Hezekiah's Tunnel,** designed by King Hezekiah to hide the city's water supply and deter invaders.

JERUSALEM

RELIGION

EST. WALKING TIME: 2 hrs
INCLUDING ALL SIGHTS: 5 to 6 hrs

Tomb of the Virgin Mary

Church of All Nations

Russian Church of Mary Magdalene

Gethsemane

Sanctuary of Dominus Flevit

Tombs of the Prophets

Church of the Pater Noster

Seven Arches Hotel

Tomb of B'nei Hezir

Tomb of Zechariah

SILWAN

AL-AMUD

Visitors Center on your left. If you have the extra shekels, it is much better to pay for a guided tour of the site. The ruins are so, well, ruined that it's sometimes hard to know what you're looking at; also, the highly informative movie, *Hezekiah's Tunnel*, and the newly discovered sites accessible through Hezekiah's Tunnel are only available to tour groups ($). If you're too claustrophobic for Hezekiah's Tunnel and don't like movies anyway, walk up the stone steps to the left, right before the City of David's Visitor's Center, to the Beit Hatsofeh Overlook to get your bearings. Walk back down the stairs to the Visitor's Center and then descend beneath its floorboards, down the metal staircase to the left, to see the remains of what is believed to be King David's Palace. Go back up the stairs and meander ahead toward your right to Area G.

TOUR 3: ON THE PERIMETER

Promenade open in summer Sa-Th 9am-5pm, in winter Sa-Th 9am-4pm. NIS16; students, children and seniors NIS8.)

The present walls of the Old City, with a circumference of 4km, were built by Suleiman the Magnificent in 1542. The city had gone without walls since 1219, when they were torn down to prevent the Crusaders from seizing a fortified city. There are eight gates to the Old City, some of which have names in three languages: Hebrew (Jewish), Latin (Christian), and Arabic (Muslim). The most commonly used names are listed below.

Topping the Old City walls, the Ramparts Promenade affords an amazing overview of the Old City. The most popular place to start is Jaffa Gate; climb the hidden steps immediately on the left. The 20min. stretch from here to Damascus Gate curves around the **Christian Quarter** (p. 127), offering views of Old City rooftops on one side and both West and East Jerusalem on the other. At Damascus Gate, it is possible to either descend into the market or continue on toward Saint Stephen's Gate, the beginning of the **Via Dolorosa**. Ascent to the ramparts is possible only at Jaffa and Damascus Gates, and it is not possible to walk all the way around the city's walls; the ramparts that border the Temple Mount are closed off for security reasons. To ascend the ramparts from Damascus Gate, face the gate from the plaza outside and go down the steps on the right, passing under the bridge and entering through the ancient carriageway to the left of the Roman Plaza.

JEWISH QUARTER

Known as "ha-Rovah" by Israelis, the picturesque Jewish Quarter is in the southeast quadrant of the Old City, the site of the posh Upper City during the Second Temple era. The quarter extends from ha-Shalshelet St. (Bab al-Silsilah) in the north to the city's southern wall, and from Ararat St. in the west to the Western Wall in the east. From Jaffa Gate, either head down David St. and turn right onto Souq Khan el-Zeit, the first large intersection just before David St. becomes Bab al-Silsilah.

After being exiled when the Second Temple was destroyed, Jews settled here again when they returned to Jerusalem in the 15th century. The Jewish community grew from 2000 in 1800 to 11,000 in 1865, when settlement began outside the walls. Today, about 650 families live in the Jewish Quarter. Much of the Jewish Quarter was damaged in the 1948 War, and after two decades of Jordanian rule the Quarter lay in ruins. After the Israelis annexed the Old City in 1967, they immediately began extensive restoration of the neighborhood. Today the Jewish Quarter is an upper-middle-class area, with an almost exclusively Orthodox Jewish (and largely American) population. City planners made archaeological discoveries with every lift of the shovel and have managed to gracefully integrate the remains into the new neighborhood. Pockets of ancient ruins are nestled between or beneath modern apartment buildings, forming a constellation of small museums; the **Cardo,** the **Burnt House,** and the **Herodian Quarter** are perhaps the best.

THE WESTERN WALL

(The Wall can be reached by foot from Dung Gate, the Jewish Quarter, Bab al-Silsilah St., or al-Wad Rd.)

Originally built by King Herod to support the Second Temple, this 2020-year-old retaining wall is 67m long, 18m tall wall and Judaism's holiest sight. *Ha-Kotel ha-Ma'aravi* in Hebrew, or just "The Kotel," the Western Wall is the largest section of the Temple area that remained standing after its destruction in 70 CE; a small part of the 488m long wall that originally encircled the Temple Mount, the rest of it is now part of Arab houses in the Muslim Quarter. The **Wailing Wall,** a dated moniker, refers to Jewish worshipers who visited in centuries past to mourn the destruction of the Temple. About 3m off the ground, a gray line indicates the surface level before 1967. Nearly 20m of Herodian wall still lies underground; Byzantines, Arabs, and Turks added the smaller stones above. Pre-1948 photos show Orthodox Jews praying at the wall in a crowded alley. After the 1967 War, the present plaza was built, and Israeli paratroopers are now sworn in here to recall the Wall's capture.

Today, the Wall is not only one of the most sacred sites in Jerusalem, but also often one of the most frenetic. Tourists and young Israeli school groups press toward the wall with crowds of Orthodox Jews from around the world; on Mondays and Thursdays, they are punctuated by families performing *b'nai mitzvah,* ceremonies which mark the coming of age of Jewish boys. Visitors, Jewish or otherwise, often see the Wall as a direct connection with God, and tuck written prayers into its cracks. Don't expect your scribbles to wait there for the Messiah; all notes are periodically removed from the overburdened wall and buried, in accordance with Jewish law. An innovative service from **Bezeq** (the telephone company) lets you fax messages to be deposited in the crevices, in case of emergencies.(☎ 02 561 2222.)The prayer areas for men and women are separated by a screen, with the Torah scrolls kept on the men's side. Look out for women with plates of baklava wrapped in cellophane or baskets of small candies, standing on white plastic lawn chairs and peering over the screen; they are participating in relatives' *b'nai mitzvah,* occurring on the other side of the boundary. Because Orthodox men are not allowed to hear women's voices singing, observers will notice that the men's side is much louder and more active than the women's side. Men must cover their heads (paper *kippot* are in a box by the entrance) and women must cover their legs (wraps can be borrowed from the Holy Sites Authority).

Friday evenings are the best time to visit the Wall, when Jews come from all over the city (and world) to usher in Shabbat. The festivities start before sundown and go until late. Photography is appropriate at these occasions, but not on Shabbat or holidays.

▨WESTERN WALL TUNNELS. One of the most popular tours in the city, the Western Wall Tunnels are a series of passageways that have been painstakingly carved out beneath the Old City's current neighborhoods at the Western Wall's original ground level. The colossal stones at the Wall's foundation truly convey the Second Temple's original magnitude. Ruins of the Herodian shops which once lined the Wall and the stones used by the Romans to destroy it are both part of the tour. (☎ 159 951 5888; www.thekotel.org. NIS25, students NIS15. Tours fill up very quickly, so be sure to book in advance.)

WILSON'S ARCH. Named for the English archaeologist who discovered it, **Wilson's Arch** is located inside an arched room to the left of the Wall, accessible from the men's side. It was once part of a bridge that spanned Cheesemakers' Valley, allowing Jewish priests to cross from their Upper City homes to the Temple. A peek down the two illuminated shafts in the floor of this room gives a sense of the Wall's original height. Women are not allowed to enter.

OTHER SIGHTS IN THE JEWISH QUARTER

HERODIAN QUARTER AND WOHL ARCHAEOLOGICAL MUSEUM. This museum consists of the huge excavation of three mansions, thought to belong to the family of a High Priest during the Second Temple period. Nine colorful mosaic floors were discovered in the ruins, five of which were probably in ancient bathrooms. After the Western Wall tunnels, this is perhaps the most interesting Old City excavation. *(Entrance is on ha-Kara'im St., right off Hurva Square; follow the signs. ☎ 02 626 5900. Sa-Th 9am-5pm, F 9am-1pm. NIS15, students NIS13, children NIS7. Free audio tours.)*

BURNT HOUSE. The Burnt House is the remains of a priest's dwelling from the Second Temple era. In 70 CE, the fourth year of the Jewish Revolt, the Romans destroyed the Second Temple and broke into Jerusalem's Upper City, burning its buildings and killing its inhabitants. The excavation of the house provided direct evidence of the destruction of the Upper City. Near a stairwell, the bones of a severed arm were found, but a few years ago the remains were taken and buried according to Jewish law. Sound and light shows are set inside the Burnt House, re-creating the events of its destruction—with virtual fire, of course. *(Down Tiferet Yisrael St. toward the Wall from Hurva Sq., across the street from Bonker's Bagels. Open Su-Th 9am-5pm, F 9am-2pm. NIS25, students NIS20, children NIS12.)*

OPHEL JERUSALEM ARCHAEOLOGICAL PARK. The extensive excavations at the southern wall of the Temple Mount are known as "Ophel," though the name technically refers to the hill just outside the southern wall, where the City of David is located. Scholars have uncovered 22 layers from 12 periods of the city's history. A tunnel leads out to the steps of the Temple Mount. *(From the Western Wall, head out past the security point toward Dung Gate; the entrance to the ruins is on the left just before the gate. ☎ 02 627 7550. Su-Th 8am-5pm, F 8am-2pm. NIS35, students and children NIS16. Virtual reality tours are available through advance booking with a local guide; call for details.)*

CARDO. A staircase descends to the remains of Jerusalem's main thoroughfare during Roman and Byzantine times. The enormous remaining pillars suggest its original monumental proportions. The uncovered section is built over a Byzantine extension of Emperor Hadrian's Cardo Maximus, which ran from Damascus Gate to about as far south as David St. Archaeologists suspect that Justinian constructed the addition so that the Cardo would extend as far as the Nea Church (beneath Yeshivat ha-Kotel). Sheltered by the Cardo's vaulted roof are the best Judaica shops in Jerusalem; most are fairly expensive, but the quality warrants the hefty price tags. Near the entrance to the Cardo, there is a climb down to an excavated section of the Hasmonean city walls and remains of buildings from the First Temple period. Farther along the Cardo is an enlarged mosaic reproduction of the Madaba map, the 6th-century plan of Jerusalem discovered in Jordan. *(Down Souq Khan ez Zeit St., between Habad St. and Jewish Quarter St. Cardo. Open and illuminated Su-Th until 11pm.)*

ALONE ON THE WALLS EXHIBIT. Also known as the **Last Battle for the Old City Museum,** the building displays the affecting photojournal of the British journalist John Phillips, who lived in the Old City during the Jordanian siege of 1947-1948. Dubbed the modern-day Josephus Flavius (historian who wrote on the Jewish Revolt against Rome in 66-70 CE), Phillips recounts life during the siege. After holding out against the Jordanians for ten days, the Jewish community in the Quarter finally started to negotiate a surrender when their ammunition was sufficient for only one more hour of combat; after the surrender was complete, the Jordanian army gave residents an hour to pack what they could carry and leave. The museum also contains a 5min. silent documentary film. *(In the first storefront on the right when entering the commercial center on the Cardo from Souq Khan al-Zeit. ☎ 02 626 5900. Open Su-Th 9am-5pm, F 9am-1pm. NIS15, students NIS10.)*

HURVA SYNAGOGUE. Built in 1700 by followers of Rabbi Yehuda, the synagogue was destroyed by local Arabs, thereby earning its ominous title (Hurva means "ruin"). In 1856, the building was restored as the National Ashkenazic Synagogue, only to be blown up during the 1948 War. In 1967, renovators opted to rebuild only the single arch as a reminder of the destruction; for the past several decades, a single stone arch has soared above the ruins of the synagogue in the square that is named for it, forming the center of the Jewish Quarter. Now, the state-run Company for the Reconstruction and Development of the Jewish Quarter is rebuilding it again. Let's hope the third time's the charm. *(Ha-Yehudim Rd., around the corner from Hurva Sq.)*

RAMBAN SYNAGOGUE. This synagogue was named for Rabbi Moshe Ben-Nachman, also known as Nachmanides ("Ramban" is an acronym for his name). Inside is a letter written by the rabbi describing Jerusalem's Jewish community in 1267, the year he arrived from Spain. During a period of nearly four centuries (1599-1967), Jews were forbidden to worship here and the building had stints as a store, butter factory, and mosque. Today it is open for morning and evening prayers. *(Ha-Yehudim Rd., next door to the Hurva Synagogue.)*

FOUR SEPHARDIC SYNAGOGUES. The **Synagogue of Rabbi Yochanan Ben-Zakkai, the Prophet Elijah Synagogue, the Middle Synagogue,** and the **Istanbuli Synagogue** were built by Mediterranean Jews starting in the 16th century. At the time, there were laws against building synagogues, so they were called study centers. The Middle Synagogue is the most recent; it was a courtyard until a roof was put over it in 1835. The four synagogues (with religious services held twice a day) remain the spiritual center of Jerusalem's Sephardic community. A Portuguese *minyan* (a religious service with at least 10 participants) gathers in the Istanbuli room on Shabbat. An exhibition features photographs of the synagogues before their destruction in the 1948 and 1967 wars. *(Down Mishmerot ha-Kehuna St., near the Jewish Quarter parking lot. Open Su-Th 9am-4pm. NIS7, children NIS5.)*

YISHUV COURT MUSEUM. This small museum exhibits 19th-century life in the Jewish Quarter. The rooms in this one-time home each depict a different element of life, from childbirth to haberdashery. One especially interesting attraction is the synagogue, built in the room where the famed mystic rabbi the Arizal was born. Rooms are furnished with period artifacts donated by the quarter's citizens, including a collection of ancient wooden Torah cases. *(6 Or Hachaim St., on the right when coming from St. James Rd. and Jaffa Gate. Open Su-Th 10am-5pm, F 10am-2pm.)*

BROAD WALL. This Israelite wall, which once encircled the City of David, the Temple Mount, and the Upper City, was built by King Hezekiah in the seventh century BCE and, along with his famous tunnel, formed part of the city's defenses. The chunk of wall is 7m thick—much broader than the current Ottoman fortifications. *(Plugat ha-Kotel Rd., off ha-Yehudim Rd.)*

CENTER FOR JERUSALEM IN THE FIRST TEMPLE PERIOD. This academic center has a small but fascinating museum and screens a 35min., partially 3D film presentation about Jerusalem in the First Temple period. The film and exhibit provide an excellent alternative for those who don't wish to tackle the City of David's many steps and Hezekiah's Tunnel's knee-deep waters. Visits must be coordinated in advance; a group of young women in their late teens/early twen-

ties work as enthusiastic and knowledgeable tour guides for all visitors. *(Around the corner to the right from the Broad Wall. ☎02 628 8593. Open Su-Th 9am-4pm. NIS18, NIS14 for children. Visits must be coordinated in advance.)*

MUSLIM QUARTER

The Muslim Quarter can be the most exciting of the four quarters. During the day, the main streets are crowded with tourists and merchants. At night, the quarter becomes dark and completely empty; though generally safe, it's best to avoid too much night travel. This is the largest and most heavily populated quarter in the Old City. The architecture dates mostly from the Ayyubid and Mamluk periods. Old City walking tours will pass through here; inquire with individual tour groups for more detailed excursions. Self-appointed tour guides of varying quality linger around Jaffa Gate; agree on a price before setting out. Don't pay more than NIS15 for a trip around the Quarter. Damascus Gate, the main entrance to the Quarter, is one of the finest examples of Islamic architecture around. The main thoroughfare and western border of the quarter is Khan al-Zeit Rd., leading from Damascus Gate to David St., with an infinite array of booths selling spices, candy, clothing, and souvenirs. Al-Wad Rd. connects the Western Wall area to Damascus Gate. A right off al-Wad Rd. onto the Via Dolorosa leads to an array of small ceramics shops. Women should dress modestly.

HARAM ASH-SHARIE (THE TEMPLE MOUNT)

The entrance to the Mount is up the ramp just right of the Western Wall. It is also accessible from the end of Bab al-Silsilah St. Visitors may enter the Temple Mount area in summer Sa-Th 7:30-11am and 1:30-2:30pm; in winter Sa-Th 7:30-10:30am and 12:30-1:30pm. Hours are subject to change during Ramadan and other Islamic holidays, usually open 7:30-10:30am. Non-Muslims are not permitted to enter the al-Aqsa Mosque or the Dome of the Rock. Free. The Mount is sometimes closed to visitors without notice.

The Temple Mount (*al-Haram al-Sharif* in Arabic; *Har ha-Bayit* in Hebrew), a 35-acre area in the southeastern corner of the Old City, is one of the most venerated religious sites in the world. A spiritual magnet, the hill is central to Judaism and Islam, and once served as a holy site for at least 10 ancient religions. The Temple Mount is traditionally identified with the biblical Mount Moriah, where God asked Abraham to sacrifice his son Isaac (Genesis 22:2). King Solomon built the First Temple here in the middle of the 10th century BCE (2 Chronicles 3:1), and Nebuchadnezzar destroyed it in 587 BCE, when the Jews were led into captivity (I Kings 5-8; II Kings 24-25). The Second Temple was built in 516 BCE, after the Jews' return from exile (Ezra 3-7). In 20 BCE, King Herod rebuilt the temple and enlarged the Mount, reinforcing it with four retaining walls. Parts of the southern, eastern, and western retaining walls still stand. Religious scholars believe that the Holy of Holies, the most sacred and important spot on the Temple, where only the High Priest was allowed to enter once a year, was closest to what is now the Western Wall, making this spot the holiest approachable site in Judaism. Some Jews won't ascend the Mount because of the chance that they will walk on the Holy of Holies, which is off-limits until the Messiah arrives.

Christians remember the Second Temple as the backdrop to the Passion of Christ. Like the First Temple, the Second Temple lasted only a few hundred years. In the fourth year of the Jewish Revolt (70 CE), Roman legions sacked Jerusalem and razed the Second Temple. Hadrian built a temple to Jupiter over the site, but the Byzantines destroyed it and used the platform as a municipal sewage facility. After Caliph Omar conquered Jerusalem in 638 CE (just six years after Muhammad's death), he ascended the Mount and began the clean-up himself, personally removing an armful of brown gook.

Today, this sacred ground and architectural triumph serves as a meditative space for pilgrims and locals alike removed from the tangled and bustling Jerusalem streets. Amongst the men performing ablution at **al-Kas** (p. 126) and the flocks of tourists milling through the hot white courtyard, look for families eating lunch in the Dome of the Rock's shadow and local children playing tag between the cyprus trees. Non-Muslims have not been allowed to enter the Dome of the Rock or al-Aqsa since Ariel Sharon and a cadre of soldiers visited the sight on September 28, 2000, an event which resulted in 4 deaths on the Mount during the ensuing protests, and sparked the second *intifada*.

Elderly Man: Your name is Teresa Maria?

Me: Yes. Well my mother's not Muslim. But my father is.

Elderly Man: And what is your father's name?

Me: *(pause)* George.

Elderly Man: *(smile widening)* And what is your father's father's name?

Me: *(longer pause)* George.

Elderly Man: *(looks at cohort, who looks away and tries not to laugh)* There is not a Muslim named George.

Me: Not, you know, any?

Elderly Man: No, madam.

Me: Oh. Well, it was worth a try.

Elderly Man: *(supportively)* It was. It was.

Me: I'm really not allowed in?

Cohort: Madam?

Me: Yeah?

Cohort: From the beginning, we saw you borrow your friend's scarf for hijab over there.

Me: *(pause)* Oh.

I walk away in humiliation. End scene.
    —Teresa Cotssirilos

SECURITY. Remember that the area is highly sensitive—incidents in the past have resulted in violence. While worshipers are accustomed to the tourists regularly visiting the sight, conspicuous actions, no matter how innocent, may result in ejection. Modest dress is required and wrap-around gowns are provided for those who need them. Non-Muslims are not allowed to enter al-Aqsa or the Dome of the Rock. Be aware that several additional sections considered off-limits by the police are not marked as such, including the Muslim cemetery. If you are Muslim, note that bags and packs are not permitted inside al-Aqsa or the Dome of the Rock and must be left outside along with your shoes; theft is not usually a problem, but you should refrain from bringing valuables when you visit. Photography is permitted on the Temple Mount, but not inside al-Aqsa or the Dome of the Rock.

DOME OF THE ROCK AND AL-AQSA MOSQUE. The Umayyad caliphs built the two Arab shrines that still dominate the Temple Mount: the silver-domed al-Aqsa Mosque (built in 715 and rebuilt several times after earthquakes) and the magnificent Dome of the Rock (built in 691). A stunning display of mosaics and metallic domes, the complex is the third-holiest Muslim site after the Ka'ba in Mecca and the Mosque of the Prophet in Medina. According to Muslim tradition, this is the point to which God took Muhammad on his mystical Night Journey *(miraj)* from the Holy Mosque at Mecca to the outer Mosque (*al-aqsa* means "the farthest") and then on to heaven. The Dome of the Rock surrounds what Muslims believe to have been Abraham's makeshift altar where he almost sacrificed Ishmael (not Isaac, as Christians and Jews believe), his son by Sarah's maid, Hagar.

The dome, once of solid gold, was eventually melted down to pay the caliphs' debts. The domes of the mosques and shrines were plated with lusterless lead until the structures received aluminum caps during the restoration work done from 1958 to 1964. The golden hue of the Dome of the Rock was previously achieved with an aluminum-bronze alloy, but in 1993, the dome was re-coated with new metal plates faced with a thin coating of 24-karat gold, leaving it more brilliant than ever. Many of the tiles covering the walls of the Dome of the Rock were affixed during the reign of Suleiman the Magnificent, who had the city walls built in the 16th century. Ceramic tiles were added in the 1950s and 60s through the private funds of the late Jordanian King Hussein. Between the al-Aqsa Mosque and the Dome of the Rock is **al-Kas,** a fountain, where Muslims perform ablutions (washing hands and feet) before prayer. Built in 709 CE, the fountain is connected to underground cisterns capable of holding 10 million gallons. The arches on the Temple Mount, according to Muslim legend, will be used to hang scales to weigh people's good and bad deeds. Next to the Dome of the Rock is the much smaller **Dome of the Chain,** the exact center of al-Haram al-Sharif, where Muslims believe a chain once hung from heaven that could be grasped only by the righteous.

OTHER SIGHTS IN THE MUSLIM QUARTER

THE SOUQ. The bustling *souq* is crammed at all hours; watch out for heavily laden wagons and tiny tractors, which charge gleefully through the crowds of shoppers. Palestinian crafts such as Hebron-style wine glasses, mother-of-pearl inlaid boxes, ceramic tiles, and spherical Jerusalem candles are beautiful; other items (cheap t-shirts and plastic Domes of the Rock) aren't. For those who cannot throw out enough t-shirts to fit an *argeileh* (waterpipe) into their packs, a short but powerful smoke (NIS1-2) at an *ahwa* (coffeeshop) provides adequate consolation. The apple tobacco is especially delicious. Several local haunts inside Damascus Gate rent *argeilehs* for NIS5 and they'll keep refilling the coals until your lungs say stop. Women should make sure the *ahwa* is not exclusively male. Much of the decorative masonry in the *souq* is characteristic of Mamluk architecture. Paintings of the Dome of the Rock and the Ka'ba shrine of Mecca adorn doorways; a painting of the latter signifies that a member of the family has been on the *hajj*, the Islamic pilgrimage to Mecca and Medina. The red and green painted dots on some whitewashed doors and walls are not graffiti; they too indicate the *hajj*.

SCOPE OUT THE GOODS. Do not buy from the first air-conditioned wonderland you enter. Often, the same wares are sold from closet-like alcoves for a lot less. There's a lot of supply in this market—remember the rules of economics and use them to your advantage. There's no backing off—you must be prepared to pay any price you offer.

CHURCH OF SAINT ANNE. Commemorating the birthplace of Jesus's mother Mary, the church is one of the best-preserved pieces of Crusader architecture in Israel. It survived the Islamic period intact because Salah al-Din used it as a Muslim theological school (hence the Arabic inscription on the tympanum above the doors). Extensive excavations behind the church clearly show the layers of history; the ruins of a fifth-century basilica cover those of a second- or third-century chapel. The church itself has fantastic acoustics. Its cool, beautiful crypt has a beaten-copper cross and inlaid stone floors. Within the grounds of the church is the **Pool of Bethesda,** straight ahead and down the stairs. Crowds of the infirm used to wait beside the pool for an angel to disturb the waters since the first person in after the angel would supposedly be cured. Jesus also healed a sick man here (John 5:2-9). *(Near St. Stephen's Gate, through the large wooden doors on the right. ☎02 628 3285. Church and grounds open in summer M-Sa 8am-12pm and 2-6pm; in winter M-Sa 8am-12pm and 2-5pm. NIS6, students NIS4.)*

ZEDEKIAH'S CAVE. Also known as King Solomon's Quarries, the cave extends far beneath the Muslim Quarter. According to tradition, stones from the quarry were used in the construction of the First Temple, but archaeological and geological evidence suggest that the cave was used no earlier than the Second Temple period. *(Entrance is about halfway between Damascus Gate and Herod Gate; exiting Damascus Gate, follow the wall to the right. Open Sa-Th in summer 9am-5pm; in winter 9am-4pm. NIS16, students NIS10.)*

ROMAN SQUARE MUSEUM. The Roman Square museum, one of the Muslim Quarter's oft-visited sights, is not actually within the Old City walls, but just outside and underneath them. The museum, at the Damascus Gate entrance to the Ramparts, is set among the excavations from Aoelia Capitolina (the name given to Jerusalem by Emperor Adrianus in 135 CE). Its centerpiece is a copy of the sixth-century Madaba map from Jordan, the earliest known blueprint of Jerusalem's layout. *(Exiting Damascus Gate, go down the stairs to your left. Open Sa-Th in summer 9am-5pm, in winter 9am-4pm. NIS10, students NIS6.)*

CHRISTIAN QUARTER AND VIA DOLOROSA

In the northwest corner of the Old City, the Christian Quarter surrounds the Church of the Holy Sepulchre, the site traditionally believed to be the place of Jesus's crucifixion, burial, and resurrection. The alleyways of the Quarter pass small churches and chapels of various denominations, and the streets bustle

JERUSALEM

with pilgrims, nuns, monks, and street vendors selling "My Grandma Went To Jerusalem And All I Got Was This Stupid T-Shirt" t-shirts.

The **Via Dolorosa** (Path of Sorrow) is the route that the cross-bearing Jesus followed from the site of his condemnation (the Praetorium) to the site of his crucifixion and grave. Each event on his walk has a chapel commemorating it; together these chapels comprise the 14 Stations of the Cross. The present route was mapped out during the Crusader period and passes through the Muslim and Christian Quarters. Modern New Testament scholars have suggested alternate routes based on recent archaeological and historical reconstructions. To begin the walk taken by Jesus and millions of tourists and pilgrims, you actually have to start at the far end of the Muslim Quarter at St. Stephen's Gate. When coming from Damascus or Jaffa Gates, it is necessary to walk along part of the Via Dolorosa to get to the starting point. While this may cause temptation to see the stations out of order, following the traditional sequence will provide a more rewarding experience. On Fridays at 4pm in the summer and at 3pm in the winter, a group of pilgrims led by Franciscan monks walk the Via Dolorosa starting at al-Omariyyeh College (the first station) and welcome guests.

THE STATIONS OF THE CROSS

I. One bone of contention between sects involves the starting point of Jesus's final walk as a mortal. It is generally agreed that Jesus was brought before Pontius Pilate, the Roman procurator, for judgment. Normally, Roman governors fulfilled their duties in the palace of Herod the Great, south of Jaffa Gate and the Citadel area. But on feast days such as Passover, the day of Jesus's condemnation, the governor and his soldiers presumably based themselves at the Antonia Fortress (also built by Herod) to be closer to the Temple Mount. Reflecting this holiday relocation, the Tower of Antonia, in the courtyard of **al-Omariyyeh College,** is considered to be the **First Station,** where Jesus was condemned. The station is not marked. For one of the best views of the Dome of the Rock plaza, walk into the courtyard of the school, turn left, and ascend the steps on the right. *(Just past an archway, 200m from St. Stephen's Gate, a ramp with a blue railing on the left returns to the courtyard.)*

II. Across the Via Dolorosa from the ramp is a Franciscan monastery; inside on the left is the Condemnation Chapel, complete with a three-dimensional relief above the altar. This is the **Second Station,** where Jesus was sentenced to crucifixion. On the right is the **Chapel of the Flagellation,** where he was first flogged by Roman soldiers. Inside the Chapel of the Flagellation, on the right, a crown of thorns adorns the dome. *(Open daily Apr.-Sept. 8-11:45am and 4-6pm; Oct.-Mar. 8-11:45am and 1-5pm.)*

Continuing along the Via Dolorosa, pass beneath the **Ecce Homo Arch,** built on the site of Pontius Pilate's mansion, where Pilate looked down upon Jesus and cried, "Behold the Man." The arch (identifiable by its two windows) is actually part of the triumphal arch that commemorated Emperor Hadrian's suppression of the Bar Kokhba Revolt in the second century. Half of the arch is inside the **Convent of the Sisters of Zion,** beneath which the **Lithostratos** excavations have cleared a large chamber thought by some to be a judgment hall, making it an alternative First Station. Within the excavations is evidence of a pagan game called the Game of King, which Roman soldiers played to torment prisoners. *(Open M-Sa 8:30am-5pm. NIS6, students NIS4.)*

III. Although the following stations—the destinations of countless pilgrims—are all marked, they are nonetheless difficult to spot. Immediately after the Via Dolorosa turns left onto al-Wad Rd., look left for the door to the Armenian Catholic Patriarchy. To the left of the door is the **Third Station,** where Jesus fell to his knees for the first time. A small Polish chapel inside a blue gate marks the spot; a relief above the entrance, marked "III Station," depicts Jesus kneeling beneath the cross. While you're there, look down and note the radical change in the street's cobblestones. The strip of smooth, massive stones in front of the Third and Fourth Station are a segment of the road from the Second Temple period, and were found by archaeologists three meters below the current street level. They were reinstated by the Jerusalem Municipality in 1980-1981.

IV. At the **Fourth Station,** a few meters farther on the left, just beyond the Armenian Orthodox Patriarchate, a small chapel commemorates the spot where Jesus saw his mother. Look for a metal plaque that simply says "IV" and a relief of Jesus and Mary above light blue iron doors, to the left of an arched alleyway.

V. Turn right on the Via Dolorosa to reach the **Fifth Station,** where Simon the Cyrene volunteered to carry Jesus's cross. Look for the brown door on the left, with the inscription "V St."

VI. Fifty meters farther, the remains of a small column designate the **Sixth Station** (marked with a "VI"), where Veronica wiped Jesus's face with her handkerchief. The mark of his face was purported left on the cloth, and is now on display at the Turin Cathedral in Turin, Italy. Look for a pair of doors on the left, one green and one dark brown; the column is set into the wall between the doors.

VII. The **Seventh Station,** straight ahead at the intersection with Khan al-Zeit, marks Jesus's second fall, precipitated by the sudden steepness of the road. In the first century, a gate to the countryside opened here, and tradition holds that the notices of Jesus's condemnation were posted on it.

VIII. Crossing Khan al-Zeit, ascend al-Khanqa St. and look left past the Greek Orthodox Convent for the stone Latin cross that marks the **Eighth Station.** Here Jesus turned to the women who mourned for him, saying, "Daughters of Jerusalem, do not weep for me, weep rather for yourselves and for your children" (Luke 23:28). The small stone is part of the wall and difficult to spot; a large red-and-white sign sticking out of the wall makes the task much easier.

IX. Backtrack to Khan al-Zeit, take a right, walk for about 50m through the market, ascend the wide stone stairway on the right (at Mike's Center), and continue through a winding passageway to the Coptic Church. The remains of a column to the left of the door mark the **Ninth Station,** where Jesus fell a third time. The Coptic complex there also contains three small churches, all of which are still in use.

X-XIV. The **Church of the Holy Sepulchre** marks **Golgotha,** also called **Calvary,** the site of the Crucifixion. The location was first determined by Eleni, mother of the Emperor Constantine, during her pilgrimage in 331 CE. Eleni thought that Hadrian had erected a pagan temple to Venus and Jupiter on the site in order to divert Christians from their faith. She sponsored excavations and uncovered the tomb of Joseph of Arimathea and three crosses, which she surmised had been hastily left there after the Crucifixion as the Sabbath approached. Constantine built a church over the site in 335, which was later destroyed by the Persians in 614, rebuilt, and destroyed again (this time by the Turks) in 1009. Part of the church's foundations buttress the present Crusader structure, built in 1149. When the present building was erected, its architects decided to unite all the oratories, chapels, and other sanctuaries that had cropped up around the site under one monumental cross. By 1852, tremendous religious conflicts had

MONKS GONE WILD

For nearly 2,000 years, the Christian faithful have examined the scriptures and diligently prayed, asking themselves again and again the same enigmatic question: what would Jesus do? If the behavior of the monks who control the Church of the Holy Sepulchre)—the site of crucifixion—is any indication, let it be known that Jesus would swat his rivals with a broom when they forgot to shut a door. Six distinct Christian sects control different parts of the Church of the Holy Sepulchre, and for hundreds of years have been locked in a power struggle for control of each part. Israeli riot police have repeatedly had to break up violent brawls in the cathedral. A few particularly classic controversies include:

The Ladder Fight: When entering the plaza in front of the Church of the Holy Sepulchre, look for the small wooden ladder that leads to a ledge over the entrance from a tall second story window on the right hand side. This ladder has been on the roof of the Church since the 19th century; the different sects have yet to decide who has the authority to move it.

The Door Fight: In September 2004, representatives of all six sects were celebrating the anniversary of Queen Helena's discovery of the True Cross in 327 when a Franciscan monk absentmindedly left the door to the Franciscan chapel open. Because this entrance is the point of separa-

developed within the Holy Sepulchre. The uninterested Ottoman rulers divided the church among the Franciscan, Greek Orthodox, Armenian Orthodox, Coptic, Syrian, and Ethiopian churches. The first three are the major shareholders, entitled to hold masses and processions and to burn incense in their shrines and chapels.

One of the most revered buildings on earth, the church is also somewhat decrepit. Bickering among the various denominations has kept it in a state of perpetual construction. Damage caused by major fires in 1808 and 1949 and an earthquake in 1927 demanded a level of cooperation and a pooling of resources that could not be mustered. Restoration work in any part of the basilica implies ownership, making each sect hesitant to assist and eager to hinder the others. The result is that little, if anything, is ever accomplished. In 1935, the church was in such a precarious state that the colonialists desperately propped it up with girders and wooden reinforcement. Since 1960, partial cooperation has allowed the supportive scaffolding to be gradually removed. To this day, however, the question of who gets to change a light bulb can develop into a month-long controversy.

The church's entrance faces the slab on which Jesus was supposedly anointed before he was buried. To continue along the stations, go up the stairs to the right just inside the entrance. The chapel at the top is divided into two naves: the right one belongs to the Franciscans, the left to the Greek Orthodox. At the entrance to the Franciscan Chapel is the **Tenth Station,** where Jesus was stripped of his clothes, and at the far end is the **Eleventh Station,** where he was nailed to the cross. The **Twelfth Station,** to the left inside the Greek chapel, is the unmistakable site of the Crucifixion: a life-size Jesus, clad in a metal loincloth, hangs among oil lamps, flowers, and enormous candles. Between the eleventh and twelfth stations is the **Thirteenth Station,** where Mary received Jesus's body. The station is marked by an odd statue of Mary adorned with jewels, a silver dagger stuck into her breast. Jesus's tomb on the ground floor is the **Fourteenth** (and final) **Station.** The Holy Sepulchre, in the center of the rotunda, is a large marble structure flanked by huge candles. The first chamber in the tomb, the **Chapel of the Angel,** is dedicated to the angel who announced Jesus's resurrection to Mary Magdalene. A tiny entrance leads from the chapel into the Sepulchre itself, an equally tiny chamber lit by scores of candles and guarded by priests. The raised marble slab in the Sepulchre covers the rock on which Jesus's body was laid. Nudging the back of the Holy Sepulchre is the even smaller **Coptic Chapel.** To the right of the Sepulchre, the **Chapel of Mary Magdalene** marks where Jesus appeared to her after his resurrection.

The rest of the church is a dark labyrinth of small chapels through which priests, pilgrims, and chatty tourists wander. Because the various denominations can't agree on an interior decorator, the building houses only religious paintings and oil lamps. Near the eastern end, steps lead down to two chapels commemorating the discovery of the true cross. In a small chapel on the ground floor just below Calvary, a fissure runs through the rock, supposedly caused by the earthquake following Jesus's death. According to legend, Adam (of Adam and Eve) was buried beneath Calvary, allowing Jesus's blood to drip through this cleft and anoint him. *(Church open daily in summer 5am-9pm, in winter 4am-8pm. Men and women must cover their knees.)*

OTHER SIGHTS IN THE CHRISTIAN QUARTER

◼**ETHIOPIAN MONASTERY.** The Ethiopians possess no part of the Holy Sepulchre itself, so they have become squatters on the roof. The modest compound houses a small but spiritual series of dark rooms, which are less crowded and more peaceful than the massive Church to which they are attached. *(Enter either through the roof and descend down the steep blackened staircase, or enter through the small open door in the right hand wall of the Church of the Holy Sepulchre's courtyard. Open daily dawn-dusk.)*

ALEXANDER'S CHURCH. Built over the Judgment Gate, the church marks the end of the Roman Cardo, through which Jesus exited the city on his way to Calvary. First-century stones line the floor, and a massive segment of wall from Jerusalem's Second Temple period has been painstakingly reconstructed in one of the galleries; after the Wall and the Cardo, it is probably the most complete ruin from that era in the Old City. Next to the gate is a small hole in the ancient wall—this is the famed Eye of the Needle, through which latecomers would sneak into the city when the gates were closed at night. The Russian Orthodox Palestine Society owns the church. *(☎02 627 4952. Open daily 9am-6pm. NIS5).*

LUTHERAN CHURCH OF THE REDEEMER. The church is off al-Wad St., across the street from St. Alexander's. Enter around the corner on Muristan St. and climb a seemingly endless

tion between Franciscan and Greek Orthodox territory within the Church, the Greek Orthodox monks thought that open door was a sign of disrespect, and said so. The brawl that ensued was diffused by the Israeli police, who arrested several monks in the process. The mug shots must have been priceless.

The Stairs Fight: This story is told by local tour guides and has yet to be verified, but is too good to pass up. The plaza in front of the church is under the control of the Greek Orthodox monks, which means they also have the rights to cleaning it. The Armenian Orthodox Church controls the Ethiopian Monastery's staircase, a steep flight of steps that goes up from the plaza to the right of the church's entrance. If you look closely, there's a small area at the bottom of the staircase that is about 1 ft. wide and 2-3 ft. long, sitting about 1 in. higher than the plaza. The Greek Orthodox and the Armenian Orthodox monks cannot decide whether or not this tiny space is part of the plaza or a tiny step in the staircase, and therefore are unable to conclude whose job it is to clean it. Everyday, as they clean their respective areas, they meet at this designated area. And a nasty, bickering fight ensues.

To keep the hostility to a minimum, the keys to the church were given to a local Muslim family. Representatives of the family still come to the church twice a day to lock and unlock the doors.

spiral staircase (actually 178 steps) to the bell tower for an amazing view. *(Open M-Sa 9am-noon and 1-3pm.)*

CHURCH OF SAINT JOHN THE BAPTIST. Obscure and usually closed to visitors, the Church of St. John the Baptist is the oldest church in the Old City, and the best (or worst) part about it is finding it. Its courtyard is only accessible through an uncommonly small doorway, and is hidden by the neighboring shops boasting overflowing leather bags and scarves; stepping through the doorway into the abrupt quiet of the hot courtyard is like ducking into another world. Originally built in the fifth century, the church was destroyed by the Persians in 614. It was rebuilt by the Crusaders centuries later. *(From Jaffa Gate, take David St. to Christian Quarter Rd. and turn left; door way is 7th storefront on the right-hand side, right after the shoes and leather bags shop.)*

ARMENIAN QUARTER

Cloistered in the southwestern corner of the Old City, Jerusalem's small Armenian Christian population lives in the shadow of tragedy. The Turkish massacre of one and a half million Armenians in 1915 remains one of the century's unacknowledged genocides and the persecution of those fleeing to Palestine has caused their numbers to dwindle even further. The 1200 Armenians remaining in the Quarter are haunted by this devastating past: posters mapping out the genocide line the streets. Although the **Armenian Compound,** their residential area, is not open to tourists unless they are friends of local residents, the few available glimpses of Armenian culture are fascinating. It's always worth asking the man at the front desk of St. James' Cathedral if he would be willing to make an exception for you.

⊠THE TOWER OF DAVID (CITADEL). The Tower of David gives an outstanding introduction to the Old City, and is definitely the place to start a tour if you're relatively uninformed about the area's dense history. The Citadel, also called the Tower of David (Migdal David in Hebrew), resembles a Lego caricature of overlapping Hasmonean, Herodian, Roman, Byzantine, Muslim, Mamluk, and Ottoman ruins, but nothing from David's era. (During his reign, this area was outside the city and unsettled.) The tower provides a superb vantage point for surveying the Holy City; illustrated placards of Jerusalem's skyline mounted on the tower's walls show you what's what. Winding through the rooms of the fortress, the high-tech, information-packed museum tells the story of the city in Hebrew, Arabic, and English. Begin with the excellent 14min. introductory movie. A complete tour of the site takes about 2hr. *(To the right inside Jaffa Gate. ☎02 626 5333; www.towerofdavid.org.il. Museum open Su-Th 9am-5pm, Sa 10am-2pm. NIS30, students and seniors NIS20, under 18 NIS15. Nighttime programs several nights of the week.)*

⊠SAINT JAMES' CATHEDRAL. The cathedral is only open to the public at odd times for services, but definitely arrange to make a trip: the spiritual center of the Quarter, its spindly, low-hanging lamps and Byzantine gold altar make it unique among the Old City's many places of worship. It was originally constructed during the fifth century CE, Armenia's golden age, to honor two St. Jameses. The first martyr, St. James the Greater, was beheaded in 44 CE by Herod Agrippas. His head, supposedly delivered to Mary on the wings of angels, rests under the altar. St. James the Lesser, entombed in a northern chapel, was the first bishop of Jerusalem, but he was run out of town by Jews who disliked his version of Judaism. Persians destroyed the cathedral in the seventh century, Armenians rebuilt it in the 11th, and Crusaders enlarged it in the 12th. Note: sitting cross-legged is forbidden. *(The massive cathedral is on Armenian Orthodox Patriarchate Rd., the main paved road leading right from Jaffa Gate. The entrance is on the* *left past the tunnel, under an arch reading "Couvent Arménien St. Jacques." Open for services M-F 6:30am-7:30am and 3-3:30pm, Sa 8:30am-10:30pm and 3-3:30pm. Free.)*

ARMENIAN MUSEUM. Chronicling the history of Armenia from pre-Christian times to the 1915 genocide, the small museum displays weapons and religious artifacts. *(Armenian Orthodox Patriarchate Rd., on the left from Jaffa Gate. Closed for renovations until 2010; check at the Jaffa Gate tourist office or the desk at St. James' Cathedral to see if it has re-opened.)*

ARMENIAN CERAMICS. While you're in the Quarter, be sure to stop in to one of Armenian Quarter Rd.'s worthwhile ceramics shops. Unlike the machine-produced plates and mirrors sold to tourists on David St. by insistent venders, these artists still paint tiles and pottery by hand; items may be more expensive, but you can see the individual brushstrokes. The **Armenian Art Center** has been an established vendor since 1983, and if you're lucky the proprietor will give you a lecture on the three periods of Armenian ceramics artistry. *(On the lefthand side of Armenian Patriarchate Rd. after walking through the tunnel, coming from Jaffa Gate. ☎ 02 628 3567; www.sandrouni. com. Tiles NIS68. Large plates NIS380. Open M-Sa 9am-7:30pm.)* At the **Studio for Armenian Ceramics and Pottery,** you can watch owner Hagop Antreassian hand-mix dyes and paint small plates and vases as you browse his shop. The best pieces are kept hidden from spying competitors; ask to see some of the work kept in the back of the store. *(Armenian Patriarchate Rd., 7th storefront down from Zion Gate. ☎ 02 626 3871; www.hagopceramics.com. Small jars NIS50. Tiles NIS100. Open M-Sa 8:30am-5pm.)*

SYRIAN ORTHODOX CONVENT. Also known as **Saint Mark's Church.** Aramaic, the ancient language of the Levant, is spoken here during services and in casual conversation. The Syrian Church believes the room in the basement to be St. Mark's house and the site of the Last Supper (most other Christians recognize the Cenacle on Mount Zion as that hallowed place). Decorated with beautiful gilded woodwork, the chapel contains a 150-year-old Bible in Old Aramaic and a painting of the Virgin Mary rumored to have been painted by St. Mark himself. *(Turn left from Armenian Orthodox Patriarchate Rd. onto St. James Rd. and left onto Ararat St. The convent, marked by a vivid mosaic, is on the right after a sharp turn in the road. Open daily 8am-5pm. Ring the bell if the door is closed.)*

OTHER OLD CITY SIGHTS

THE GATES. The sole entrance in the western Old City wall, **Jaffa Gate** is the traditional entrance for pilgrims and the gate used most often by people arriving via West Jerusalem. Consequently, it doubles as a congested knot of quirky hostels, highly persistent shopowners, and tour groups clad with matching fanny packs. There has been a gate on this site since 135 CE; the fortified right-angle tower has since been breached by the adjacent cobbled road. Opened in 1889 to facilitate access to the Christian Quarter, the **New Gate** sits just a few steps from Jaffa Gate, along the northern wall. Built over the Roman entrance to the Cardo, **Damascus Gate** faces East Jerusalem and provides direct access to the Muslim Quarter's chaotic *souq*, placing it in competition with Jaffa Gate for status as the city's most trafficked gate. Many of the Old City's cheaper hostels are in the vicinity. If you book a hostel here, your sherut driver from the airport will probably stop in front of the gate, throw your backpack out after you onto the side of the road, and drive away without giving you directions. The backpack will land somewhere between the woman selling parsley out of a burlap sack and the guy selling live baby chicks out of big metal cages. Just try to blend in. **Herod's Gate** stands to the east of Damascus Gate and reaches the deeper sections of the Muslim Quarter. Also known as Lion's Gate, **Saint Stephen's Gate** is located along the eastern wall. It faces the Mount of Olives and marks the beginning of the Via Dolorosa. Blocked by Muslim graves, **the Golden Gate** gate has been sealed since the 1600s. It is thought to lie over the Closed Gate of the First Temple, the entrance through which the Messiah will purportedly pass (Ezekiel 44:1-3). On the southern wall, **Dung Gate** opens onto the Western Wall plaza. First mentioned in 445 BCE by Nehemiah, it was given its name in medieval times because dumping dung here was considered an especially worthy act. On the opposite end of the ancient thoroughfare from Damascus Gate, **Zion Gate** appropriately connects the Armenian Quarter with Mount Zion.

NEAR THE OLD CITY

MOUNT ZION AND ENVIRONS

To reach the mount, exit the Old City through Zion Gate, near the Jewish Quarter parking lot off Armenian Orthodox Patriarchate Rd., and go straight along the short path opposite the gate, bearing right at the Franciscan convent. At the next fork, a left leads to the Cenacle and David's Tomb; a right leads to Dormition Abbey.

Rising outside the city walls opposite Zion Gate and the Armenian Quarter, Mount Zion *(Har Tzion)* has long been considered the site of the Tomb of David, the Last Supper, and the descent of the Holy Spirit at Pentecost. Despite the ancient events they commemorate, some of the sites here are quite new in comparison to the Old City, a reminder that Jerusalem is just as politically entangled now as it has always been. The name Zion, also applied to Israel as a whole, was first used by King David when he conquered the eastern territory. During the siege of the Jewish Quarter in 1948, the area around Zion Gate was the scene of some of the fiercest fighting in Jerusalem; bombshell pockmarks remain.

⟩COENACULUM (CENACLE). The humble appearance of this church, identified by most as the site of the Last Supper, is due in part to an attempt by the British Mandate to avoid sectarian disputes by forbidding any change to the building. The Cenacle was converted from a mosque into a church almost four centuries ago, but the mosque's *mihrab* (prayer niche) is still visible in the southern wall. *(Take the left fork after the Franciscan convent and ascend a stairway through the Diaspora Yeshiva door on the left. The church is on the 2nd floor. Open daily 8:15am-5:15pm. Free.)*

DAVID'S TOMB. Archaeologists are skeptical about the authenticity of this site; it is written that kings and only kings were buried within the city, and Mount Zion was never encompassed by David's walls. Neither the historical accuracy nor the idiosyncrasies of the sight, however, have ever reduced the fervor of worshippers at the tomb, many of whom whisper David's psalms in the room. Emerging from a dark recess in the wall, the tomb's dignified Torah case has blackened with sheer age. Like the Western Wall, men and women must pray in gender-specific areas separated by a screen. *(To enter, go through the Cenacle, descend the stairs, and turn right around the corner. Open in summer Su-Th 8am-6pm, F 8am-2pm; in winter Su-Th 8am-5pm, F 8am-1pm. Modest dress required; men should cover their heads with the available cardboard kippot. Free, although members of the yeshiva next door happily accept donations.)*

BASILICA OF THE DORMITION ABBEY. This monumental edifice was completed in 1910 and commemorates the death of the Virgin Mary. One of the most recently built basilicas in Jerusalem, its artists and architects clearly took pains to venerate both past and present traditions. A gold and Byzantine-inspired mosaic rises above the apse. Closer inspection reveals that the artist has used at least three different tile colors to texture the clothes of the figures depicted. Downstairs in the crypt, allegedly the site where Mary lived and died after the Resurrection, an ornately carved coffin of a resting Mary is encircled by religious interpretations of her from around the world, including a vividly rendered *Virgen de la Guadalupe* from Mexico. Parts of the precariously situated basilica were damaged during battles in 1948 and 1967 and never repaired. Head down to the bathrooms; by the entrance are the excavated ruins of a Byzantine church. *(Off the right fork of the road leading to the Cenacle. ☎02 565 5330; www.dormitio.net. Open M-W and F 8:30am-noon and 12:40-6pm; Th and Sa 8:30am-noon and 12:40-5:30pm; Su 10:30-11:45am and 12:40-5:30pm. Free. Call for info on occasional classical music concerts.)*

CHAMBER OF THE HOLOCAUST. Nowhere near the scale of the Yad Va-Shem museum in West Jerusalem, this small, simple memorial was not initially intended to be a museum. A year after Israel's independence, Rabbi Herzog traveled to the site of a European death camp, collected the ashes, and brought them to this site to bury them properly. Organizations of survivors, some of whom were the only Jewish survivors from entire towns in Europe, installed one gravestone per extinguished community along the walls in order to commemorate their dead, and the small series of rooms soon became a designated place to mourn. Now almost exclusively a museum, the rooms contain haunting photographs, memorabilia, and newspaper clippings from the Holocaust, as well as desecrated Torah scrolls which have been put to rest in accordance with Jewish law. *(Across the street from the back entrance of David's Tomb. Alternatively, bear left at the Franciscan convent. Open Su-Th 9am-3:45pm, F 9am-1:30pm. Free. Donations encouraged.)*

SCHINDLER'S GRAVE. Visitors pay homage to Oskar Schindler, the man credited with saving more than 1300 Jews from Nazi persecution, by placing stones on his grave. Though its hours are erratic and location hard to find, it's definitely worth the stop, if only to pay your respects. *(In the Christian Cemetery across the main road, downhill from the other Mount Zion sights. The gate is open at inconsistent hours. Once inside, go down 2 flights of stairs toward the cemetery's bottom.)*

CITY OF DAVID

☎02 626 8700; www.cityofdavid.org.il. Open Su-Th 8am-5pm, F 8am-1pm. NIS25, students NIS21 with valid ID. Tours NIS30. Because tourists have limited access to the site without a guide, it is strongly recommended that you shell out the extra shekels and take the tour. Book tour at least 1 day in advance.

Perhaps the only place in the world where archaeologists regularly consult the Bible to illuminate their findings, any exploration of Jerusalem's conception must begin outside its walls, right here in the most ancient part of the city. The City of David housed the throne of the biblical Kings of Israel and was included within the walls during the First Temple period, while today's walled city dates from the mostly Hellenic period of the Second Temple. The earliest origins of biblical Jerusalem are still shrouded in mystery, but archaeologists have confirmed that the Ophel ridge, just south of the Old City walls, is the site of **Jebus,** the original Canaanite city King David captured and made his capital.

Excavations of the site indicate that the Jebusites were confined to an area of about eight acres. The city's location above the Kidron Valley was selected for its proximity to the Gihon Spring and its defensibility on the ridge. In times of peace, townspeople passed through a "water gate" to bring water into the city. For continued supply during times of siege, an underground tunnel provided access to a large reservoir. David's strategy for taking Jebus relied on finding the water source; his soldier Joab succeeded when he found a natural shaft that led up to the tunnel and therefore into the city. Later, King Hezekiah devised a system to keep David's strategy from being turned against the Israelites by the encroaching Assyrians. He built a 500m long tunnel to bring the Gihon waters into the city walls and hid the entrance of the spring, preventing invaders from finding water when they camped outside the wall. In 1880, a few years after the tunnel was excavated, a local boy discovered an inscription carved by Hezekiah's engineers describing the jubilant moment when the north and south construction crews met underground. The original inscription is in Istanbul, but a copy is on display at the **Israel Museum** (p. 149).

Due to the religious significance of its excavations and their current geopolitical location, the City of David is hardly void of political strife today. Excavations have been stymied in the past by Orthodox Jewish demands for stricter adherence to Jewish Law. Excavations in the northern part of the Ophel, for example, were halted in 1981 when a group of Orthodox Jews protested that the area might be the Jewish cemetery mentioned in the diaries of several medieval pilgrims, instigating a considerable and occasionally violent political dispute which lasted until the excavations ceased in the late 90s due to a lack of funding. Additionally, while the City of David may have been the original Jewish capital historically, it is now situated in East Jerusalem's **Silwan,** a heavily Arab neighborhood that many Palestinians view to be occupied territory. Claiming the legacy of the ancient Jewish capital, Israeli nationalists have nevertheless established a Jewish presence in the area. The political situation has most recently been exacerbated by a wave of house demolitions in Silwan, which some Palestinian activists claim to be the government's attempt to "Judaize" the neighborhood. Despite the fact that, as of August 2009, Silwan is safe for tourists, the situation on the ground is very complicated; Let's Go advises caution.

▓HEZEKIAH'S TUNNEL. Provided that you don't have a phobia of tight spaces, the dark, dying in an avalanche, or drowning, Hezekiah's Tunnel is one of the craziest and coolest things to see in Jerusalem. Sloshing through King Hezekiah's 2700 year old tunnel takes approximately 40min., so be sure to bring a flashlight and water proof shoes. The water is cold but thankfully never higher than thigh deep. *(Available through guided tours only.)*

▓"THE LAST RESORT." This road may have been another section of the "Pilgrim's Way" road (p. 138), but the most incredible (and chilling) element of this site is not what it is, but what happened to it. The pavement of this otherwise excellently preserved street was found broken in a number of places; beneath the street archaeologists discovered cooking pots, completely intact, along with Roman coins from the Second Temple period. Experts have inferred that the last surviving Jewish rebels against the Romans fled to the sewer system that ran beneath the steps in 70 CE. When the rebellion famously went south, the Romans trapped them there, then methodically smashed open the street above them to ferret them out. *(Available through guided tour only.)*

BEIT HATSOFEH OVERLOOK. This is a great way to get yourself oriented at the site, not to mention a fabulous view of the surrounding area. The movie downstairs beneath the Overlook is only available to members of guided tours, but some try to sneak in anyway; it gives a good 15min. introduction to what you will be looking at, and you get to wear horn-rimmed 3D glasses. *(After entering the City of David, a small seating area with cafe tables and floppy umbrellas will be on your left, and the Visitor's Center will be on your right. Walk straight on the bath that runs between them and go up the steps in front of you, climbing the small tower.)*

Map: Mt. Zion, City of David, and Mt. of Olives

JERUSALEM

MOUNT OF OLIVES

Church of the Pater Noster

Tombs of the Prophets

Seven Arches Hotel

Jewish Cemetery

RAS AL-AMUD

al-Mansuiya

Sanctuary of Dominus Flevit

Bett Pagi

Russian Church of Mary Magdalene

Jericho Rd. (Derekh Yeriho)

Tomb of the Virgin Mary

Church of All Nations

Gethsemane

Tomb of Jehosaphat

Absalom's Pillar

Tomb of B'nei Hezir

Tomb of Zechariah

Kidron Valley

SILWAN

Derekh Ha-Ofel

Archaeological Garden

SEE OLD CITY MAP

Shiloah Way

Gihon Spring

Warren's Shaft

Hezekiah's Tunnel

Siloam Pool

Lions' Gate

Bab Sitt Maryam

TEMPLE MOUNT

Dome of the Rock

CITY OF DAVID

Ma'a lot Ir David

MUSLIM QUARTER

via Dolorosa

al-Wad

Western Wall

Dung Gate

JEWISH QUARTER

Wadi Hilwa

Malchizedek

Bab al-Silsilah St.

Habad

Khan al-Zeit

OLD CITY

Church of the Holy Sepulchre

David St.

Hezekiah's Pool

CHRISTIAN QUARTER

ARMENIAN QUARTER

Citadel

Zion Gate

Chamber of the Holocaust

Schindler's grave

'aleh Ha-Shalom

Dormition Abbey

Cenacle & David's Tomb

Mt. Zion

New Gate

Jaffa Gate

Jaffa Rd. (Derekh Yafo)

Hativat Yerushalayim

Sultan's Pool

Hebron Rd. (Derekh Hevron)

YEMIN MOSHE

Mishkenot Sha'ananim

SAFRA SQUARE

SEE WEST JERUSALEM

0   200 yards

0   200 meters

THE PALACE. Potentially the most momentous among the recent finds at the City of David, the palace and its underground remnants was discovered by archaeologist Dr. Eilat Mazar in 2005. Because of the building's age, size, and location within the ruins of the city, Mazar states that the ruins may well be of King David's original palace. The two *bullae*, or clay seals, found at the site bear the names of two men whom the Bible states were ordered to throw the prophet Jeremiah into a pit, preceding the Babylonian invasion. *(Facing the Visitor's Center, turn left and go down the wide metal staircase that descends beneath the Center itself.)*

ROYAL QUARTER (AREA G). The foundations of a house here date from the First Temple period; evidence of furniture made of imported wood and an ancient toilet have been found, indicating the considerable wealth of the people who lived or worked here. Archaeologists found 51 *bullae* in the house, representing 46 different names, leading some to speculate that this was possibly a post office or official archive building. *(Walk across the Visitor's Center plaza to the left to a flight of stairs. Go down the steps on the right-hand side and turn left at the junction of the paths.)*

ANCIENT TOMBS OBSERVATION POINT. View the ancient cemetery found at the foot of the Mount of Olives. The 50 or so burial monuments that have been found here date to the eighth and seventh centuries BCE; some may be even older. The Observation Point also provides a lovely view of the Mount of Olives and of Silwan, the Palestinian neighborhood which the City of David borders. *(Walk up the pottery path from Area G.)*

WARREN'S SHAFT. In 1867, the long, sleek shaft that Charles Warren discovered was thought to have been critically important. For many years, archaeologists believed that water was drawn up through this shaft by ancient Jebusites, but recent excavations found the continuation of the tunnel that led to the reservoir. The current theory is that the natural shaft was covered or ignored by the Jebusites and never used for drawing water. Despite the irrelevance of the shaft itself, Warren's discovery of it confirmed biblical accounts of the secret underground tunnels and fortifications, developed by Jebusites in the Middle Bronze II Age to protect their water source. David subsequently used their remarkably advanced system to gain access to the city and defeat them. *(Follow the steps down to the left from the Observation Point, then turn right.)*

FORTIFICATIONS OF THE SPRING HOUSE AND THE GIHON SPRING. The lifeblood of Jerusalem for several millennia, the Gihon Spring ensured survival for both city residents, who used it for drinking water, and local farmers, who diverted it outside the city walls for irrigation. The Fortifications of the Spring House demonstrate how precious, and consequently how protected, this spring was; after channeling the water into a collective pool, ancient Jerusalemites then fortified the pool with a system of towers. *(To see the fortifications, go down the spiral staircase through an ancient tunnel, then down another spiral staircase to the top of a large vertical shaft. The Gihon Spring itself is down the next spiral staircase ot the stone steps.)*

SHILOACH POOL. One of the most recently excavated areas of the City of David, this mammoth pool from the Second Temple Period apparently extended over the entire area of the adjacent orchard. Archaeologists believe that the water was used to prepare the "purification" waters used in the cleansing rites in the Temple. *(Available through guided tour only.)*

"PROMENADE" AND "PILGRIM'S WAY." These are two cobbled streets from the Second Temple era. The pillars that have been found near the Promenade indicate that the street was probably roofed, creating a pleasant place to stroll to and from the Pool. The "Pilgrim's Way" is believed to be a steep road leading directly from the Pool to the Temple; part of the street's extension may have been recently found by Robinson's Arch near the Western Wall. *(Available through guided tour only.)*

KIDRON VALLEY AND MOUNT OF OLIVES

The best way to visit the churches, tombs, gardens, and observation point is to start at the top and walk down the winding road that passes through the hill's sights. For the fit, the walk up to the top is strenuous but rewarding. In the morning, this route yields sparkling views of the Old City. Beware that in the early afternoon it can be stiflingly hot, particularly in the summer. Most churches are closed Su and M-Sa from about noon to 3pm. A taxi from Damascus Gate to the top should cost NIS25-30.

Christians revere the historic **Kidron Valley,** which runs between the Old City and the Mount of Olives, as the path of Jesus's last walk. To get there, turn left from Dung Gate and walk along Ruta Hoafel Rd., following the walls of the Old City. A new paved sidewalk leads to an observation point for the valley, the Mount of Olives in front of it, and the four tombs directly below; a dusty road leads down into the valley to the foot of the sites themselves. Running north-to-south are the **Tomb of Jehosaphat** and **Absalom's Pillar,** allegedly the tomb of David's favored but feisty son (II Samuel 15-18). A dirt path on the left leads to the impressive rock-hewn **Tomb of Zechariah.**

 ALL THE SINGLE LADIES. Though generally safe, Mt. of Olives can be unsafe for female travelers; it's wise for women to visit in a group.

The bone-dry slopes of the **Mount of Olives** (*Har ha-Zeitim* in Hebrew, *Jabal al-Zeitoun* in Arabic) to the east of the Old City are dotted with churches marking the sites of Jesus' triumphant entry into Jerusalem, his teaching, his agony and betrayal in **Gethsemane,** and his ascension to heaven. Jews believe that the Messiah will arrive in Jerusalem from the Mount of Olives. Tradition holds that the thousands of people buried here will be the first to be resurrected upon his arrival. Beyond its historical significance, the Mount of Olives also offers visitors terraced dirt paths that meander between silvery olive trees and glimmering views of Jerusalem. Bring your camera and a couple of extra shekels if you want a picture with the local camel.

For a monumental view of the Old City, check out the observation promenade outside the **Seven Arches Hotel.** From here look to the north: the bell tower of the **Augusta Victoria Hospital** on Mount Scopus marks the highest point in Jerusalem (903m above sea level). Unless you need a bathroom break or are dying of thirst, do not actually go inside and eat at the Seven Arches Hotel. Waiters at the restaurant sometimes need to be reminded of your order three times before they bring it, and they have been known to charge NIS42 for a bottled water.

CHAPEL OF CHRIST'S ASCENSION. Built in 392, this was the first church erected to commemorate Christ's ascension. It is the geographical (if not the aesthetic) apex of the area's noteworthy sights. Toward the end of the 11th century, the Crusaders adorned the tiny chapel with columns and arches, and in the late 12th century Salah al-Din fortified it and added a domed roof. The interior contains a candle-lighting stand and a sacred footprint, unidentifiable after generations of non-sacred treadings of relic-happy pilgrims. The chapel is small and quiet and echoes with the sounds of the pigeons that roost in its windows; it is most interesting on and near Ascension Day, when Christians from several denominations set up camp in the small courtyard during the celebration. *(To get to Chapel from the Mount of Olives observation point, walk slightly downhill and then straight uphill to the right, toward the Israeli flag; follow the curve of the street to the right.*

JERUSALEM

Turn left at the Pater Noster, which will appear on your right. It's easiest to find if you walk toward the minaret of the mosque next door to the Chapel. Open daily 8am-5:30pm; ask a guard in the mosque courtyard if closed. Free.)

CHURCH OF THE PATER NOSTER. When St. Eleni founded this church in the fourth century, she named it the **Church of the Disciples;** it is also referred to as the **Church of the Eleona** (Greek for "olive grove"). This was the site of the grotto where Jesus revealed the "inscrutable mysteries" to his disciples—foretelling the destruction of Jerusalem and his Second Coming. The church commemorates the first recitation of the Lord's Prayer *(pater noster)*. Polyglots can read the prayer in 161 languages and counting (including Quechua, Sotho, and Old Frisian) on the tiled walls. In the midst of the translations is the tomb of the Princesse de la Tour d'Auvergne, who worked here for 17 years (1857-74) and financed the excavations and renovations. The Lord's Prayer was her favorite prayer and she was determined to uncover the long-lost grotto where it was originally taught. The urn above the tomb holds the heart of her father, the Italian politician and poet Baron de Bossi. *(Below the Chapel of Christ's Ascension. Open daily 8:30am-noon and 2:30-5pm. Recommended contribution NIS7.)*

TOMBS OF THE PROPHETS. This site is the supposed resting place of the prophets Malachi and Haggai. Archaeological evidence, however, suggests that the graves are far too recent—probably dating back to the fourth century CE. Like an abnormal percentage of famed sites in Jerusalem, the Tombs of the Prophets involves going down an old flight of steps into a cave. The glass-enclosed home on the premises is the residence of the caretaker, who will show visitors around downstairs with a kerosene lamp if asked. *(To get to this site from the Mount of Olives observation point, turn right and walk downhill until you reach a staircase. Go down one flight of stairs and look to your left for a slightly battered blue sign reading "Tombs of the Prophets" in white letters. Open M-Th 9am-3pm. Free.)*

SANCTUARY OF DOMINUS FLEVIT. The sanctuary was erected in 1955 to mark the spot where Jesus wept for Jerusalem (Luke 19:41); hence the Latin name meaning "The Lord wept." Built in the shape of a teardrop, the chapel incorporates a Byzantine mosaic and altar with a large and modern window, offering a dazzling view of the Dome of the Rock. The glass shards of broken liquor bottles cemented to the top of the walls serve to protect the desert garden from trespassers. *(Downhill from the Tombs of the Prophets, on the right. Open daily 8am-11:45am and 2:30-5pm. Free.)*

RUSSIAN CHURCH OF MARY MAGDALENE. Czar Alexander III built the church in 1885 in the lavish 17th-century Muscovite style and dedicated it to his mother, the Empress Maria Alexandrovna. It is adorned with seven golden onion domes. The crypt houses the body of a Russian grand duchess, smuggled to Jerusalem via Beijing after her death in the Russian Revolution. Now a convent, the church claims a part of the Garden of Gethsemane. *(Past the Sanctuary of Dominus Flevit. Usually open Tu and Th 10am-noon.)*

CHURCH OF ALL NATIONS AND THE GARDEN OF GETHSEMANE. A site that has been continuously venerated and repeatedly destroyed since the 4th century, the current stately basilica, designed by Barluzzi, was built after WWI with contributions from many European countries, and is rich with the false optimism of its time. Among its highlights is a magnificent gold and red facade portraying Jesus bringing peace to all nations. When inside, focus on the deep blue ceiling, tiled to resemble a midnight sky, and see if you can spot the US State Department's logo amid the detail. Mosaics and sculptures depict Jesus's last days, including the proverbial kiss of death, but the real highlight is the Rock of the

Agony, where Jesus was so impassioned that he sweat blood (Luke 22:44). The garden outside is where Jesus spent his last night in prayer and was betrayed by Judas (Mark 14:32-43). *(The church is on the left near the bottom of the main path; the entrance is on the side. Open daily 8am-noon and 2-6pm. Free.)*

TOMB OF THE VIRGIN MARY AND GROTTO OF GETHSEMANE. The steep stairs down to Mary's tomb were built to prevent pagans from riding horses into the sacred space. Inside, the cavernous church, decorated with tarnished lamps hanging low from the black ceiling, smells of musk and incense. To the right of the building, the natural grotto is another candidate for the place of Jesus's betrayal and arrest. *(At the bottom of the main path on the right; across the street from the Church of All Nations. At the exit onto the main road are telephone booths and taxis. Damascus and St. Stephen's Gates are within walking distance. A taxi to the city center should cost NIS25-30. Open daily 6am-7pm.)*

WEST JERUSALEM

West Jerusalem is best known for the eateries, dance clubs, and sandal stores of the pedestrian *midrakhov*. The ever-popular city center *(merkaz ha-ir)* provides welcome entertainment for tourists, but explorations of West Jerusalem's subtler side—its elegant neighborhoods, well-kept parks, and impressive museums—are often more rewarding. Jerusalem has been dubbed "a city of neighborhoods" for good reason; each of its 20-something neighborhoods has a distinct flavor. A sampling of the subtleties: in **Yemin Moshe,** you can wander aimlessly between eccentric artist's studios in the Artist's Colony or House of Quality; the Ultra-Orthodox **Mea She'arim** area is one of the last strongholds of the Yiddish language; the **German Colony,** sometimes jokingly referred to as the "Sixth Borough," is replete with New Yorkers who have made *aliya* (immigrated to Israel).

Since 1860, when a few Jews moved outside the walls of the Old City, West Jerusalem has flourished. By municipal law, all new buildings must be cased with off-white Jerusalem stone, creating a harmony between the uninspired developments of the 50s, ritzy displays of the 90s, and the ancient buildings of the Old City.

ZION SQUARE ✻

Intersecting Jaffa Rd. just northwest of Zion Sq. and forming another boundary of the *midrakhov* is **King George Street,** a bustling extension of the city center. At the corner of King George St. and Ben-Yehuda St., uphill from Jaffa Rd., is one of the area's largest malls, **ha-Mashbir.** Across from Zion Sq. on the other side of Jaffa Rd., ha-Rav Kook St. eventually crosses ha-Nevi'im St. and turns into the quiet, stone-wall-lined **Ethiopia Street.**

ZION SQUARE (KIKKAR TZION). The center of West Jerusalem and one of the few places in the city that is lively at all hours. Less than 1km from the Old City along Jaffa Rd., it is the epicenter of the pedestrian malls of Ben-Yehuda, Yoel Salomon, Nahalat Shiva, and Rivlin St.—and a good reference point.

GREAT SYNAGOGUE OF JERUSALEM. The enormous and ornate synagogue is an inspiring architectural compromise between modernity and religion. Services here on holidays and Jewish new months feature an excellent men's choir meant to recall the Levites' choir in the ancient Temple. *(58 King George St. 3 blocks away from Jaffa Rd. ☎02 624 71 12. Open Su-Th 9am-1pm, F 9am-noon.)*

ETHIOPIAN CHURCH. This handsome church was built between 1874 and 1901. Inscriptions in Ge'ez, the ancient language of Ethiopia, adorn the gate and doors. Black-robed monks and nuns live in the surrounding compound and care for the distinctive, blue-domed church, which feels oddly like a cross between a church, mosque, and synagogue. Directly across from the entrance to the church, at #11, is the one-time home of the founder of the modern Hebrew language, **Eliezer Ben-Yehuda.** (☎02 628 28 40. *At the end of Ethiopia St. on the right. Open daily 9am-1pm and 2-6pm. Remove your shoes before entering.*)

MAHANE YEHUDA ✕

When in doubt, hit the *souq* or the *shuk.* In the Old City, the **Muslim souq** is the epicenter of cheap food and people-watching; West Jerusalem's less idiosyncratic, more organized equivalent is the **Mahane Yehuda shuk,** an open air market between Yafo Rd. and Agrippas St. west of the city center. Elbow past bag-laden fellow shoppers to the stands, pita bakeries, and sumptuous displays of pastries that line the alleys. There's a small grocery store (*makolet*) with rock-bottom prices at almost every corner. Ten pitas go for NIS3 or less; 1 kg grapefruit, tomatoes, or zucchini goes for the same price. The stands along **Etz ha-Hayim Street** sell the best *halva* (a dessert-like sesame marzipan) at NIS14-16 per kg. The best time to visit the *shuk* is close to closing (Su-Th 7-8pm, F 1-2hr. before Shabbat), when venders lower their prices shekel by shekel to sell off the day's goods. On Friday afternoons, families from Mea She'arim crowd the crooked alleyways along with New City citizens, curious tourists, and the occasional street musician, as shoppers scramble to get their kitchens in order for Shabbat; the market smells intermittently of fresh bread and produce. The worst day for the market is Sunday, when things are still slow after the weekend.

Buried behind the hollering shop venders are occasional cheap restaurants and coffee shops, including a couple of the best homecooking and funky hangouts in the city. Like the Muslim Quarter's *souq*, the best thing to do here is people-watch.

MEA SHE'ARIM ✕

Mea She'arim ("Hundredfold," an invocation of plenty), lies just north of Ethiopia St., on the other side of ha-Nevi'im St., and in another cultural universe from Zion Sq. To get there from Zion Sq., take Jaffa Rd. and turn right onto King George St., which quickly turns into Nathan Strauss St.; continue until it intersects with ha-Nevi'im. You will see a sign marking the entrance into the neighborhood. This intersection is known as Kikkar Shabbat; walk through on a Friday night to find out why.

SECURITY WARNING. The most conservative neighborhood in Jerusalem is by far Mea She'arim. Signs in the area caution, "Do not enter our neighborhood unless you dress and conform to the standards described below." Women wear skirts (not pants) at least knee-length, elbow-length sleeves, and nothing tight-fitting. Men must wear below-the-knee pants. Visitors are also advised not to enter in groups. Other signs remind outsiders that this is a residential area, not a "touristic site." Be warned that extremists have been known to stone tourists whom they deem improperly dressed. Whether you're Jewish or not, take these warnings seriously to avoid offending local Hasidim and being asked to leave the area.

The neighborhood, one of Jerusalem's oldest, is among the few remaining Jewish **shtetl** communities like those that once flourished in pre-Holocaust Eastern Europe. Several thousand Ultra-Orthodox Jews live here and in the neighboring **Geula** (Hebrew for "redemption") neighborhood, preserving traditional habits, dress, customs, and beliefs with painstaking diligence. Admire the pain threshold of local Hasidic men as they walk through the oppressive summer heat in coats and circular fur hats; the meticulous hair of the woman you just passed may well be a wig, as some ultra-Orthodox women shave their heads and then cover it to ensure modesty. If your newfound grasp of Hebrew lets you down, it may be because you're hearing Yiddish, spoken by residents who consider Hebrew too holy for daily use. The neighborhood, just like the Orthodox suburbs to the north and northwest of the city, is largely conservative, but Mea She'arim's relatively few extremists receive a good deal of publicity for opinions and actions that do not necessarily reflect those of the entire community. The **Neturei Karta** ("City Keepers"), the most extreme sect of the Satmar Hasidim, oppose the Israeli state, arguing that Jewish law prohibits the legitimate existence of a Jewish country until the coming of the Messiah. While other Ultra-Orthodox Jews hold similar views, the Neturei Karta once went so far as to ask Yasser Arafat to accept them as a minority in the future Palestinian State.

Like most Jerusalem neighborhoods, the best way to see Mea She'arim is (dress code permitting) to wander through it. The neighborhood features an eclectic mix of Judaic shops that sell CDs and modern women's clothes so long as they adhere to the strict religious codes. The residential sidestreets are occasionally dilapidated—weathered preservations of another time. Weary stone apartments with disheveled shingled roofs are slung with drying laundry and iron balconies are stuffed with plastic children's toys. Orthodox couples traditionally have large families, contributing to the increasing piety of Jerusalem's electorate. Mea She'arim is also probably the cheapest place in the world for Jewish books and religious items. Although the quality is not as high as in the Jewish Quarter of the Old City, the stores along Mea She'arim have vast affordable selections. **Meker Hasefer** and **Jerusalem Yarmulka** are good places to start for Judaic books and clothes respectively; Meker Hasefer even sells puzzle sets for children which depict the Western Wall and Jewish activities (see **Judaica,** p. 152). The neighborhood also has some of the city's best **bakeries;** walk into the nearest one for fresh challah and other treats.

GIVAT RAM

ISRAELI SUPREME COURT. This impressive neighborhood is the seat of the Israeli Supreme Court, completed in late 1992. The designers combined Modernist flair with themes from ancient Jerusalem's architectural traditions. This structural masterpiece is worth visiting for the aesthetic experience as well as for an understanding of the complex, constantly changing Israeli justice system; keep in mind that Israel has no constitution. Anyone may sit in on a trial—it's like Court TV, only live and in Hebrew. The best time to catch a court session is in the morning, just after the work day begins. (☎ 02 675 9612; http://elyon1.court.gov.il/eng/home/index.html. Open Su-Th 8:30am-2:30pm. English tour Su-Th noon; call for summer schedule. With advance notice, can accommodate most special needs, including touch tours for the blind.)

WOHL ROSE GARDEN. The Wohl Rose Garden, which forms a walking path between the Supreme Court and the Knesset, is a sublime picnic spot with beautifully manicured lawns and flowers. Near the back of the Supreme Court, part of the garden has been converted into a Garden of All Nations; a path winds past several dozen small plots growing native shrubs from countries around the world. (Take the path on the right when exiting the Supreme Court building, or climb up to it from anywhere on the main street; leaving the Knesset compound, the path is also on your right.)

KNESSET. Discover why Israeli schoolteachers compare excessively rowdy pupils to Parliament members. Free tours include an explanation of the structure of the Israeli government, a look at the magnificent Marc Chagall mosaics and tapestries—yes, they are woven, not painted—that adorn the building, and a peek into the room where some of the nation's most important decisions have been made—the cafeteria. *(On Eliezer Kaplan St. directly across from the Israel Museum. From the central bus station or Jaffa Rd., take bus #9 and ask the driver where to get off. Passports are required for entrance as part of a detailed search. ☎ 02 675 3416; http://www.knesset.gov.il/tour/eng/evisit.html. Tours last 30min., Su and Th. English tours offered at 8:30am, noon, and 1:45pm; arrive at least 15min. early. Open sessions M-Tu 4pm, W 11am; call to make sure that the Knesset is in session.)*

ARDON WINDOW. The Ardon Window in the **Jewish National and University Library** is another Givat Ram sight worth looking into—or, better still, out of. One of the largest stained-glass windows in the world, it depicts Jewish mystical symbols in rich, dark colors. The library, which boasts the world's largest collection of Judaica and Hebraica materials, also features temporary exhibits displaying different aspects of their collection. *(Take bus #9, 24, or 28 from the city-center. ☎ 02 658 5027; http://www.jnul.huji.ac.il/eng/index.html. Open Su, T, Th 9am-7pm; M and W 9am-9pm, F 9am-2pm. Free.)*

REHAVIA

South of Independence Park are some of Jerusalem's most elegant and affluent residential areas. Rehavia, the area trisected by Azza Rd. and Ramban St., was founded in the 1920s and became the refuge for the many German Jews fleeing Nazi persecution in the 1930s. For years, it was famous as a German high-culture enclave, where dark wood library shelves were lined with Goethe and Schiller while Mozart grooved on the gramophone. Today, the legacy lives on in the many International Style houses, designed in the German Modernism tradition. Flowery hedges fill the spaces between the well-kept stone buildings, making a walk around the neighborhood's lush streets a verdant pleasure.

JASON'S TOMB. In the middle of Rehavia on Alfassi St. is **Jason's Tomb** (near 12 Alfassi St., the sign says "Rock Cut Tomb"), built around 100 BCE as the burial site of a wealthy Hasmonean-era Jewish family. Pottery found at the site indicates that three generations were buried there. Charcoal drawings on the plastered porch wall depict ships, suggesting that one of the deceased was involved in naval excursions. The pyramid topping the tomb is a reconstruction.

PRIME MINISTER'S OFFICIAL RESIDENCE. Farther east past Azza Rd. is the **Prime Minister's official residence** in the heavily guarded house at the corner of Balfour St. and Smolenskin St.

SCHOCKEN LIBRARY. Next door on Balfour St. is the **Schocken Library**, designed by renowned architect Erich Mendelssohn, who resided in Jerusalem in the late 1930s. He lived in the windmill on Ramban St. near Kikkar Tzarfat, now a ritzy shopping complex.

TALBIEHA

Farther south is the neighborhood of Talbieha, which is still known by its pre-1948 Arabic names. The ornate villas, one of which was the home of renowned cultural theorist Edward Said, have become favorites of Hebrew University faculty and, more recently, well-to-do professionals. The **official residence of the Israeli President** is on ha-Nassi (President) St., and the plush **Jerusalem Theater** is on the other side of the block, on the corner of Chopin St. and Marcus Rd.

On the other end of Jabotinsky St. from the President's House is **King David Street,** running northward to the base of Shlomtzion ha-Malka St. and Shlomo ha-Melekh St., which runs uphill to Safra Sq. and the Old City. The street is a hotspot for accommodations of all price ranges, from hostels run by religious groups to the most luxurious hotels in Israel.

KING DAVID HOTEL. Be sure to pay a visit to this hotel, if anything to see its famous carpet; you know a hotel's posh when it has had the likes of Barack Obama, Bill Clinton, Kofi Annan, and others sign their autographs—on the floor. (☎ 02 620 8888; www.danhotels.com.)

THREE ARCHES YMCA. Built in 1933, the YMCA has an imposing bell tower with impressive views of the whole city. (Across the street from the King David. ☎ 02 569 2692. NIS5. 2-person min. in the tower at a time.)

LIBERTY BELL PARK. Just south of the intersection with Jabotinsky St. is the sprawling, green park, Gan ha-Pa'amon. An amphitheater, basketball courts, climbable sculptures, and a Liberty Bell replica grace the lawns. On Saturday nights, the park hops with folk-dancing festivities. (Take bus #14, 18, or 21 from the center.)

YEMIN MOSHE AND MISHKENOT SHA'ANANIM

In the valley between King David St. and the Old City lies the restored neighborhood of Yemin Moshe. It was here that Sir Moses Montefiore, a British Jew, first managed to convince a handful of residents from the Old City's overcrowded Jewish Quarter to spend occasional nights outside the city walls, thus founding West Jerusalem. To strengthen the settlers' confidence, Montefiore built **Mishkenot Sha'ananim** (Tranquil Habitations), a small, picturesque compound with crenellated walls resembling those of the Old City. The original buildings, located at the bottom of the hill, now house an exclusive municipal guest house and a pricey French restaurant. Montefiore also erected his famous stone windmill, now containing a tiny free museum. (Open Su-Th 9am-4pm, F 9am-1pm.) Yemin Moshe is crammed with artists' studios and galleries; a plaza with a fountain beneath the exclusive King David Apartments makes this a lovely spot to wander.

HUTZOT HAYOTZER ARTISTS' COLONY. Aspiring artists and collectors (with money) visit this small, stepped street lined with whimsical iron street lamps and local artist's workshops. (24 Hutzot Hayotzer, off Jaffa Rd. ☎ 02 622 1163; www.jerusalem-art.org.)

JERUSALEM HOUSE OF QUALITY. This house is a 100-year-old dignified former hospital with a prominent artist's studio in every room. A tunnel that runs under the building was stocked with explosives during the 1948 war. (12 Hebron Rd.; from the artists' colony, walk straight and then follow the street right, around the Sultan's Pool park uphill, past the pedestrian bridge that arches over the highway. ☎ 02 671 7968; www.art-jerusalem.com.)

SULTAN'S POOL. Now dry, this pool sits in the valley below the artists' colony. Named after Suleiman the Magnificent, who renovated this Second Temple reservoir in the 16th century, the pool figures prominently in Palestinian novelist Jabra Ibrahim Jabra's *The Ship.* Today, the Sultan's Pool is most famous for its open-air concerts and annual **art fair** in July or early August.

GERMAN COLONY

The German Colony, a neighborhood of somber European houses and spacious Arab villas, surrounds Emek Refa'im St., a beautiful upscale avenue with a lively cafe scene. Buses #4 and 21 run here from the city center. To the southeast, the **Haas Promenade** is a hillside park that commands unbelievable views of the Old City and the Dead Sea. The dusk experience alone is worth the trip. On foot, walk south on Hebron Rd., bear left onto Albeck St., and turn left onto Yanofsky St.

MAMILLA

Mamilla demonstrates just how much the contrast between Jerusalem's many neighborhoods can border on multiple personality disorder. A 30-second walk from Jaffa Gate, the **Mamilla Promenade** is a pristine outdoor mall that looks like a suburban sheesh and kitsch fest in the United States. Check out the vague imitations of Mamluk architecture, not a 2min. walk from one of the most historic centers of real Mamluk in the world. Consisting almost exclusively of overpriced national and international business chains, going to Mamilla from the Old City can be a nauseating exercise in superficiality; it can also be a much needed relief, and many locals feel this way too. Watch reform Jews and tourists mingle with religious Muslim women and nuns in local shoe stores and coffee shops, enjoying the area's air conditioning and cleanliness. Mamilla cafes also often have wireless, which occasionally beckons "commuters" from the Old City looking for a comfortable place to work. The best 24hr. pharmacy near the Old City is also located here (see **Practical Information,** p. 98).

NORTHERN OUTSKIRTS

TOMBS OF SANHEDRIN. A park carpeted with pebbles and pine needles houses the Tombs of Sanhedrin. Composed of 70 esteemed male sages and leaders, the Sanhedrin was the ancient high court of the Jews; it ruled on legal matters and even reviewed Jesus' case. Separate burial areas were designated for the members. The tombs are located in the ultra-Orthodox Sanhedria neighborhood, so be sure to dress modestly. *(Take bus #2 to ha-Sanhedrin St., off Yam Suf St. Open Su-F 9am-sunset. Free.)*

AMMUNITION HILL. Before the Six-Day War, Ammunition Hill (Givat ha-Tahmoshet) was Hordan's most fortified position in the city, and it commanded much of northern Jerusalem. Taken by Israeli troops in a bloody battle, the hill now serves as a memorial to the Israeli soldiers who died in the Six-Day War. The somber, architecturally striking museum is housed in a reconstructed bunker with a detailed account of the 1967 battle and a simple but lovely memorial with an eternal flame. *(5 Shragai St., near Shderot Eshkol. Take bus #8, 19, 25, 26 or 28 from Central Bus Station; they will stop at the bottom of the hill, and the museum is at the top. ☎02 582 8442; http://givathatachmoshet.org.il. Open in summer Su-Th 9am-6pm, F 9am-1pm; in winter Su-Th 9am-5pm, F 9am-1pm. NIS15, students NIS12. Credit cards accepted.)*

HEBREW UNIVERISTY OF JERUSALEM. After 1948, the Hebrew University of Jerusalem had to relocate from **Mount Scopus** (Har ha-Tzofim), where it was founded in 1925, to its new campus in Givat Ram. From 1948 to 1967, Mount Scopus was a garrisoned Israeli enclave in Jordanian territory. Every week for 19 years, UN supplies were flown in to relieve the community; every week, seven Israeli soldiers were let in and seven were let out. After 1967, all but the natural and physical sciences departments moved back to the original campus. Massive reconstruction was funded largely by international donors, whose names emblazon the libraries, promenades, and pebbles that compose modern Mount Scopus. Pick up a map from the Reception Center for an unguided stroll around Israel's top university and browse through the bookstore, library, computer labs, and botanical gardens. For a fabulous view of Jerusalem, head to the lookout point outside the university gates along the south side of the campus. The **Hecht Synagogue,** in the Humanities building, overlooks the Old City and is reputed to have the most magnificent view of Jerusalem in the entire city. Enter the synagogue via the Sherman Building. The university's gorgeous **amphitheater** faces the Palestinian Territories. *(Take bus #4a or 9 from the city center.)*

EIN KEREM AND WESTERN OUTSKIRTS

⧉CHAGALL WINDOWS. The synagogue at the **Hadassah Medical Center,** near Ein Kerem (not to be confused with Hadassah Hospital on Mount Scopus), houses the magnificent Chagall Windows, Marc Chagall's fantastical stained-glass depictions of scenes from Genesis 49 and Deuteronomy 33. Chagall donated the windows to the hospital in 1962. When four of the windows were damaged in the 1967 War, Chagall was sent an urgent cable. He replied, "You worry about the war, I'll worry about my windows." Two years later he installed replacements. Three of the windows still contain bullet holes. *(Hassadah Medical Center. ☎ 02 641 6333; http://www.md.huji.ac.il/chagall. Open Su-Th 8am-1:15pm and 2-3:30pm. Visitors are allowed inside in limited numbers as part of a tour; tours are every 15min., and last 20min. Language of tour is determined based on the language spoken by the majority of visitors present at that time. NIS10, students NIS5. Credit cards accepted.)*

MOUNT HERZL AND THE HERZL MUSEUM. This park was named after Theodor Herzl, a newspaper correspondent who made the most prominent modern articulations of Zionism and lobbied for the creation of a Jewish state (see **Zionism,** p. 40). Herzl was buried here in 1904; since then, the site has become the final resting place for many other of the nation's great leaders, including **Ze'ev Jabotinsky, Levi Eshkol, Golda Meir,** and **Yitzhak Rabin.** A small museum encapsulating the energy of Theodor Herzl is near the entrance, but it has been closed for over a year with no projected re-opening date. Nearby is the Israeli Military Cemetery, the resting place of fallen soldiers. Be aware that visitors are allowed into the Park by reservation only. *(Take bus #13. Heading out of the city center along Herzl Blvd. eventually leads to Mount Herzl Park. Open Su-Th 8:30am-4:30pm, F 8:30am-1:30pm. NIS25, students NIS20.)*

JERUSALEM FOREST AND EIN KEREM. The scenic Jerusalem Forest and the pastoral village of Ein Kerem, just west of Mount Herzl, are perfect for picnics and short hikes. Formerly an Arab village, tiny Ein Kerem (Fountain of Vines) is the tradition-

ally recognized birthplace of John the Baptist. The tranquil streets of this thriving artists' colony are now lined with charming studios and craft shops. *(To get to the village, take city bus #17 west from the central bus station or Zion Sq.)*

CHURCH OF SAINT JOHN. With its soaring clocktower, this church marks the spot where John was born. The church displays several paintings, including the Decapitation of Saint John. In the church's **Grotto of the Nativity,** there is a lovely Byzantine mosaic of pheasants—the symbol of the Eucharist. Ask the guard for a key. *(☎ 02 641 3639. Open M-F 8am-noon and 2:30-5pm, Su 9am-noon and 2:30-5pm. Free.)*

CHURCH OF THE VISITATION. Across the valley, down Ma'ayan St. from St. John's gate, the Church of the Visitation recalls Mary's visit to Elizabeth and contains a rock behind which the infant St. John hid when the Romans came to kill babies. *(☎ 02 641 7291. Open daily 11am-6pm. Free.)*

EAST JERUSALEM

GARDEN TOMB. The skull-shaped rock formations here, first noticed in 1860 by Otto Thenius, have led some to believe that this quarry hillside is Golgotha (the "place of the skull"), the site of Christ's crucifixion. A nearby rock-cut tomb is that of Joseph of Arimathea, who placed Jesus's body in his own tomb after the Crucifixion. A group of Christians not affiliated with any one church maintains the lovely garden that surrounds Sull Hill and the empty tomb. *(A short distance up Nablus Rd., on the right when coming from Damascus Gate; follow the signs. ☎ 02 627 2745; www.gardentomb.com. Open M-Sa 9am-noon and 2-5:30pm. Free.)*

ROCKEFELLER ARCHAEOLOGICAL MUSEUM. This museum records the region's history—beginning with the 250,000-350,000 year old remains of the "Galilee Man" (the oldest remains from the Levant)—and implicitly chronicles the cultural impact of imperialism on the region through its impressive collection of Greek-, Roman-, Umayaad-, and Muslim-inspired artwork. Check out the impressive, intricately carved wooden panels from the original ninth-century al-Aqsa mosque, as well as the original lintel from the Church of the Holy Sepulchre. The museum was designed in the 1920s by British Architect Austen S. B. Harrison in his inimitable Orientalist-Gothic style. *(Suleiman St., at the northeastern corner of the Old City walls. ☎ 02 628 2251. Open Su-M and W-Th 10am-3pm, Sa 10am-2pm. Free.)*

SAINT GEORGE'S CATHEDRAL. This cathedral, which features a gothic-style nave and one of Jerusalem's most impressive organs, is the church of the Anglican Episcopal Diocese of Jerusalem and the Middle East. The 100-year old cathedral is now home to both Arabic and English speaking congregations, both of which welcome visitors at their services. *(20 Nablus St. On the right, past the intersection and the gas stations along Nablus Rd. ☎ 02 628 3261. Open daily 6am-7pm. Free.)*

BASILICA OF SAINT STEPHEN. This stately but seldom-visited basilica was consecrated in 439. Impressive paintings of the 14 stations of the cross line the interior. The church runs an elementary school within its high protective walls. *(6 Nablus Rd., just past the Garden Tomb. ☎ 02 582 8149. No regular visiting hours, just ring the bell.)*

TOMBEAU DES ROIS (TOMB OF THE KINGS). Judean kings were once thought to be buried here, but evidence shows that the tomb was in fact built in 45 CE by the Mesopotamian Queen Helena for her family. The deep tombs are dimly lit and practically require crawling to enter. *(Salah al-Din St., at the intersection with Nablus Rd. Open M-Sa 8am-1pm and 3-5pm. NIS3.)*

🏛 MUSEUMS

ISRAEL MUSEUM. The Israel Museum is the largest and most comprehensive museum in Israel. With extensive collections of antiquities, sculptures, ancient and modern art, books, the legendary Dead Sea Scrolls, and even a children's section with hands-on exhibits, the museum has nearly as may facets as the country itself. As of this writing, the museum is also undergoing extensive renovation, which are due to be completed at the end of 2010; consequentially some of the exhibits have been periodically closed. Check with the tourist office or the museum's information desk to determine what's open and what's not. The Shrine of the Book, luckily, will remain open to the public.

Rock and rust enthusiasts should go straight to the **archaeology section** (pick up a map upon entering), where an extensive collection of tools and weapons records 30,000 years of human habitation in the Fertile Crescent. Straight ahead from the bottom of the stairs is the **ethnography** exhibit, tracing the important events of the Jewish life cycle. The museum boasts a fabulous collection of **art,** including the largest display of Israeli art in the world. There is a fairly large Impressionist and Post-Impressionist collection and even a few period rooms—including a spectacular **French Rococo salon** donated by the Rothchilds. The **Weisbord Pavilion,** directly across from the ticket building, houses a few Rodin sculptures, early modern paintings, and temporary exhibitions. The **Billy Rose Sculpture Garden** displays some incredible masterpieces by Henry Moore, Auguste Rodin, and Pablo Picasso. Pick up a schedule of evening outdoor concerts at the museum, and try to visit on a Tuesday night when the garden is illuminated.

The museum's biggest atteaction the **Shrine of the Book,** which displaces the Dead Sea Scrolls. Hidden for 2000 years in the Caves of Kumran (see Kumran, p. 341) near the Dead Sea, the scrolls date from the 2nd century BCE to 70 CE and were written by an apocolyptic, monastic Jewish sect called the Essenes. The scrolls contain fragments of every biblical text except the Book of Esther. These texts are nearly identical to their modern versions, supporting claims for the historical dating of the Hebrew Bible. The building's white dome and black walls symbolize the struggle between the Sons of Light and Dark, an important theme of the Qumran sect, and was designed to resemble the covers of the pots in which the scrolls lay hidden (though when the fountains are on it looks more like a Hershey Kiss taking a shower). *(Take bus 9 or 17 from King George St. On foot, walk up King George St., turn onto Ramban, cross Hazaz, and walk up Ruppin St. ☎02 670 8811; www.english.imjnet.org.il. Open Su-M and W-Th 10am-5pm, Tu 4pm-9pm, F 10am-2pm, Sa 10am-5pm. English guided tours of Shrine of the Book Su-M and W-Th 1pm, T 4:30pm, F-Sa 11am. 36NIS, students 26NIS, Aug T and S ages 5-17 free. Audio guides included.)*

YAD VA-SHEM. Meaning "a memorial and a name," Yad Va-Shem is the largest of Israel's Holocaust museums. Memorializing an event as broad-sweeping and traumatic as the Holocaust cannot be accomplished with any single medium; the juxtaposition of Nazi records, the testimony of victims, and documentation of resistance creates a powerful and disturbing experience. It's best to start at the **Historical Museum,** which traces the origins of the Holocaust through photographs, documents, and relics. The exhibit ends with a simple, powerful memorial: symbolic tombs showing the number of Jews were killed in each country and a tiny shoe that belonged to one of the Holocaust's 1.5 million younger victims. **The Hall of Names** contains an achingly low row of archive shelves with lists of all known Holocaust victims. Visitors may fill out a Page of Testimony recording the name and circumstances of death of family members killed by the Nazis. The **Hall of Remembrance** houses a *ner tamid* (eternal fire) to memorialize the Holocaust's victims, with the names of many concentration camps engraved into the floor. The nearby **art museum** displays drawings and paintings composed by Jews in the ghettos and concentration camps, while below it in the small **Children's Hall** is a display of toys and dolls which outlived their young owners. In the same room are visitors' books in which to share your impressions; reading through the thoughts and reflections left by others is at least as powerful as the formal exhibits. By far the most haunting part of Yad Va-Shem is the stirring **Children's Memorial,** where mirrors are positioned to create the illusion of an infinite sea of candles, while a recorded voice recites the names and ages of young victims. **The Avenue of Righteous Gentiles** honors non-Jewish Europeans who risked their own safety to aid Jews fleeing Europe. **The Valley of the Communities** is an enormous labyrinthine memorial dedicated to the destroyed villages of Europe. Carved in stone are the names of *shtetls* that are no more; surviving family members wander around in search of their former towns. Don't plan to do too much right after a visit; the museum's several buildings deserve some time and take an emotional toll. (*Take bus #13, 18 or 20 and get off at the huge, red arch just past Mt. Herzl. Turn around and take a left on Ein Kerem St., then follow the signs down ha-Zikaron St. for about 10min. Information ☎02 644 3802; www. yadvashem.org. Open Su-W 9am-5pm, Th 9am-8pm, F 9am-2pm. Free. Tours in English or Hebrew daily 11am, 30NIS. Audio guide 20NIS.*)

BIBLE LANDS MUSEUM. This museum records the ancient history of every geographic locale mentioned in the Bible. Ancient pottery, jewelry, seals, and figurines comprise the private collection of Dr. Elie Borowski, a Canadian antiquities collector. For an educational interlude, check out the interactive computer program on cylindrical stamps and seals. (*Across the street from the Israel Museum. Take bus #9 or 17 from King George St. ☎02 561 1066; wwwblmj.org. Open Su-M, T, Th 9:30am-5:30pm; W 9:30am-9:30pm; F 9:30am-2pm. English guided tours Su-Tu and Th-Sa 10:30am, W 10:30am and 5:30pm. 32NIS, students 20NIS.*)

TICHO HOUSE. On display are watercolors and drawings by artist Anna Ticho, who lived here with her prominent oculist husband, Dr. Avraham Albert Ticho, who opened Jerusalem's first eye clinic in 1912. His collection of menorahs is also on display, as are a series of traveling exhibits. The elegant building and well-groomed gardens are a relaxing city respite; the attached restaurant serves a classy all-you-can-eat wine, cheese and salad bar on Tu nights to a live jazz ensemble (95NIS; reservations recommended). (*9 ha-Rav Kook St. About 2 blocks up the hill from Zion Sq. ☎02 624 5068 or 624 4186. A small library shows a videotape of Anna Ticho's life and work upon request. Open Su-M and W-Th 10am-5pm, Tu 10am-10pm, F 10am-2pm. Free.*)

WOLFSON MUSEUM. This museum houses a wonderful collection of Jewish religious and ceremonial objects. Note the texts painted on eggshells and the Samaritan Torah. the museum also has a room of detailed dioramas depicting scenes from Jewish History. (*King George St., next to the Great Synagoge, on the 3rd floor of the Hehal Shlomo building. ☎02 624 7908; http://ilmuseums.com/museum _eng.asp?id=42. Open Su-Th 9am-3pm. NIS15.*)

MAYER INSTITUTE FOR ISLAMIC ART. The institute displays a significant collection of miniatures, paintings, and carpets from the Islamic world. Visitors may also take advantage of the comprehensive research library covering subjects in Islamic art and archaeology. (*2 ha-Palmah St., around the corner from ha-Nassi St. Take bus #15 from the center of town. ☎02 566 1291; www.islamicart.co.il. Open Su-Th 10am-3pm, F-Sa 10am-2pm. NIS20, students NIS13.*)

THE U. NAHON MUSEUM OF ITALIAN JEWISH ART. The small but impressive collection includes silverwork, tapestries, and gilded Torah arks, including 18th-century pieces from the Conegliano Veneto Synagogue. Services in the restored, old world synagogue are open to the public Friday nights and Saturday mornings. *(27 Hillel St., in city center near the midrakhov. ☎02 624 1610; www.jija.org. Open Su, T, W 9am-5pm; M 9am-2pm; Th-F 9am-1pm. NIS15, students NIS10.)*

THE UNDERGROUND PRISONER'S MUSEUM This museum commemorates the work of Israel's underground movement in pre-1948 struggles against British rule. Originally erected by Russian pilgrims, the hall was converted during the British Mandate into Jerusalem's main prison and is now a small but powerful exhibit. *(Behind the municipal tourist office in Safra Sq., off Shivtei Yisrael St. ☎02 623 3166. Open Su-Th 8:30am-4pm. Free.)*

BLOOMFIELD SCIENCE MUSEUM Kids will leap at the chance to interact with scientific phenomena in fun, hands-on exhibits covering topics such as gravity, waves, electricity (be prepared for a few shocks) and lasers. *(Take bus #9, 24, or 28 to Hebrew University, Givat Ram; the museum is a 5min. walk from there, opposite the stadium. ☎02 654 4888. Open M-Th 10am-6pm, F 10am-2pm, Sa 10am-4pm. NIS30, students NIS25.)*

🔘 SHOPPING

Budget shopping in the *souq* and *shuk* can be fun for those who keep their wits about them. Often the deal of the century can be found after relentless comparison shopping or by bargaining until blue in the face (for tips, see **Tipping and Bargaining**, p. 13). For arts and crafts that are a little pricey but very worth it, stroll down **Armenian Orthodox Patriarchate Road** in the Old City's Armenian Quarter; **Yoel Salomon Street** in the City Center is also home to a variety of ceramic and tile shops, albeit a very different style. Yemin Moshe's **Artists' Colony** and **House of Quality** are expensive but the real thing, with work sold out of artists' studios. If you're feeling homesick for large shopping malls, stroll down the oddly pristine **Mamilla Promenade** right by Jaffa Gate, or take bus #6 to the **Malcha Mall,** a three-story monstrosity with everything from a supermarket and post office to a movie theater and countless trendy clothing stores.

JEWELRY

Jewelry can be bought in many places in Jerusalem—in Arab *shuks*, on the Ben-Yehuda *midrakhov*, or from the fine shops on King David St. **Eilat stone,** a green or turquoise semi-precious stone from the hills around Eilat (p. 371), is a common element in rings, necklaces, earrings, and pendants. Booths of cheap rings and trinkets about at **The Pit,** also known as "The Cat Market" *(shuk ha-hatulim)*, an open-air market near the base of Rivlin and Yoel Salomon St. Merchants set up shop every afternoon and evening. On Friday, they start at 10am and end before Shabbat. On Saturday, they hawk from nightfall until past midnight.

CRAFTS

Israel is home to many accomplished artisans. Pieces are often made from olive-wood, Jerusalem stone, and other native materials. The city's most signature type of artistry is the Armenian communities' elegantly painted ceramics. While knock-offs and poor quality dishes are sold in abundance in the Old City *souq*, try the **Armenian Art Center** or **Studio for Armenian Ceramics and Pottery** in the Armenian Quarter for some of the most beautiful pieces (see **Old City Sights,** p. 132).

Most of the best deals are found in the Old City. In West Jerusalem, art stores with higher quality (and higher prices) line the *midrakhov*. A stroll down **Yoel Salomon Street** in the City Center or the **Artists' Colony** in Yemin Moshe will reveal artists of exceptional quality and creativity.

JUDAICA

If you are looking for *menorot, mezuzot, kippot,* or other ritual items, this is the right city. The Talmud says that it is not enough to fulfill the Commandments; one must beautify the ritual with pieces of art. As a result, making ceremonial objects is a practical outlet for talented Jewish artists. Rows of inexpensive Judaica shops crowd the streets of Mea She'arim. **Meker Hasefer,** 3 Malehelsa St., has a good selection of prayer books, many so beautifully done that Gentiles will be tempted to buy them too. (☎02 384 956. Open Su-Th 9am-9pm. Credit cards accepted.) **Jerusalem Yarmulka,** 21 Mea She'arim, sells *kippot, halah* covers, *tallit* bags, and baseball caps with snarky Yiddish slogans on them. (☎02 538 4048. Open Su-Th 10am-7:30pm, F 9:30am-2pm.) For truly high-quality merchandise, head to the **Jewish Quarter Cardo,** where the craftsmanship, individuality, and price of Judaica skyrockets. Dig deep enough, however, and there are deals to be had here too.

MUSIC

The cheapest place to buy CDs and tapes in Jerusalem is in the *shuk* of the Old City's Muslim Quarter. Unfortunately, most merchandise is pirated; there have been reports of tourists being fined for such purchases, although this is very rare. **Picadelly Music,** 4 Shatz St., right off Ben-Yehuda St. on the *midrakhov*, has a good selection of Israeli and international CDs, often at discount prices. (☎02 624 7983. Open Su-Th 8:30am-8pm, F 8:30am-3pm.)

❖ ENTERTAINMENT

If observing the daily awkward interactions between Orthodox Jews who believe God told them to come here, Palestinian Arabs who believe they are under military occupation, and American tourists who believe their neon fanny packs match their tivas in is not your idea of quality entertainment, you'd better keep reading this section. Jerusalem is not Tel Aviv, but there are several more than decent options for fun and games here. Jerusalem's **Cinemathique** shows a popular and unique mix of new releases, old classics, and indie films, with a great vegetarian restaurant attached to it; check their website to see what's playing. **Yellow Submarine** mixes a diverse series of both experienced and upcoming music artists with lessons and community outreach. Shopping is a perfect diversion in the Old City and West Jerusalem, with everything from the perfect cheap deal in the *souq* to chic arts and crafts in Yemin Moshe and the city center.

THEATER AND FILM

🎬 **Jerusalem Cinematheque,** 11 Derekh Kevron St. (☎02 672 4131; www.jer.cine.org.il/ defaulte.htm), right outside of Mt. Zion. Walk downhill from Jaffa Gate, or take bus #7 or 8. 2 screens show different films every evening. Mix of new releases, old classics, and independent film. Tickets NIS36. Credit cards accepted.

Gil Movie Theater (☎02 678 8448), in the Malcha shopping mall. Shows the latest Hollywood flicks on 8 screens. Most films are in English with Hebrew subtitles. Call or check newspaper listings for times.

JEST Theater (Jerusalem English-Speaking Theater) (☎02 642 0908; www.geocities. com/Jest-theatre). Amateur group performs 3 or 4 English plays per year. Community theater attracts a large expat crowd.

Khan Theater (☎02 671 8281; www.khan.co.il), across from the railway station in Remez Sq. Egged buses #4, 8, 18, 21, 48, 7 stop by the station. Built by Ottoman Turks in the 1880s as a caravan stop. Contains an intimate theater, restaurant, art gallery, and cafe featuring Hebrew stand-up comedy and classical music concerts. Rarely frequented by tourists, but the concerts and plays—mostly in Hebrew—are critically acclaimed.

MUSIC

Ein Kerem Music Center (☎02 641 1498; www.geocities.com/targ_center/), on ha-Ma'ayan St., opposite Mary's Well in Ein Kerem. Take bus #17 from the central bus station or Zion Sq. Features weekly classical music and operatic performances, usually on a F or Sa night. Call for a schedule of events.

Jerusalem Symphony Orchestra (☎02 566 0211; www.jso.co.il). Performs frequently at the **Jerusalem Theater** on David Marcus St. and the **Henry Crown Sympohony Hall,** 5 Chopin St. A schedule of events is available on the website.

Pargod Theater, 94 Bezalel St. (☎02 625 8819; www.pargod.org), in the Mahane Yehuda area. Hip, young crowd for jazz and special performances. Billboard in front announces special events.

Sultan's Pool (☎02 629 6841), in Yemin Moshe, downhill from Jaffa Gate. Open in summer only.

Yellow Submarine, 13 Erkavim St. (☎02 679 4040; www.yellowsubmarine.org.il). This theater-cafe features a different kind of performance 3-4 nights a week. Frequent musical guests from unknown locals to Israeli superstars. Check the website for upcoming shows.

▮ NIGHTLIFE

If you ask a Jerusalem native where the best clubs are, they'll make a face and tell you that there aren't any clubs, urge you with a "Dear God" not go to them, or insist that everyone goes to Tel Aviv for that instead. But, though Tel-Avivians hate to admit it, Jerusalem's nightlife is no longer a joke. Once the city's conservative majority is safely tucked into bed, the bar and club scene comes to life, peaking Thursday to Saturday nights. Cultural events, from lunchtime chamber music to the early summer **Israel Festival,** add to Jerusalem's arts scene. Buy Friday's *Jerusalem Post* for the "In Jerusalem" insert, the best weekly info in English. In June, look out for **Student Day** at Hebrew University, which features trips during the day and fireworks at night (see http://aguda.org.il/english for more info). Sadly, the gay community is not well represented in the city's nightlife; there are no gay bars in the city anymore, and while many of the bars are accepting of gay customers, few have a vibrant or regular gay clientele. The **JOH** (see **Practical Information,** p. 98) can help you find some good GBLT hotspots.

BARS

Most of the bars worth going to (and all the bars listed here) are located in the Zion Sq. area, down various side streets. Each nook and cranny has a different character. If you like cheap *argeilehs* (water pipes), tipsy tourists, and American teenagers on Birthright aggressively strutting their stuff, walk into any of the bars that line **Rivlin Street.** Israelis usually avoid Rivlin altogether and go to **Feingold Square,** the narrow and somewhat-hidden alleyway that runs parallel to it. To get there, walk to the end of Rivlin St. toward its intersection with Hillel, make a sharp right, and then take your first left through a stone archway up the narrow stepped street. **Yoel Salomon** is leftist, artsy, and can be pricey; it is not only home to the great T'mol Shilshom (p. 108), but also home to **Sira,** one of the most eccentrically fun places to drink in the city. For everything from stoned street musicians dancing to bonga drums to bemused Orthodox families going out for a little ice cream, walk down **Ben-Yehuda** and soak up the vibes.

Sira, 4 Ben Sira (☎02 623 4366). Walk down Hillel St. away from King George St. until it turns into Ben Sira; Sira is right by the turn off for Shlomtsion Hamalka St. Stories about Sira among Jerusalem's liberals border on Chuck Norris-style mythology. According to one T'mol manager, "Everyone goes there: Arabs, lesbians, left-wingers, lunatics." Apparently, if there are any Arab-lesbian-left-wing lunatics to be found in Israel, Sira would be the 1st place to look. Make no mistake, Sira takes anybody and everybody, and remains one of the few places in the city where Arabs and Jews actively socialize. Keep an eye out for the "Oo-Oo Man," a man who holds entire conversations with Sira regulars using a single, monosyllabic sound. Beer from NIS14. Mixed drinks NIS40. DJs rock the music every night. Open Su-Th 5pm-4am, F-Sa 6pm-7am. Credit cards accepted.

Uganda, 4 Aristobolus St. (☎02 623 6087; www.uganda.co.il). From Yafo Rd., turn right on Heleni HaMalka St., then left on Aristobolus. Geeks, freaks, and art students unite over drinks and impressive collections of old records and comic books, which line the walls of the bar. Most people opt to hang out on the eclectic assortment of seat cushions outside; if the woman playing with her puppy on the cushion next to you has dreadlocks and smells mildly of hippy grunge and pot, you have caught Uganda on a normal evening. Beer NIS18-22. Vodka NIS19-25. Open daily noon-late. Credit cards accepted.

Joshua, 18 Ben Sira (☎02 624 6076). Walk down Hillel St. away from King George St. until it turns into Ben Sira; Joshua is on the right-hand side, just past the restaurant Cielo. A classy and jazzy atmosphere with a definite youth focus; flocks of students dressed to impress cast long shadows against the dimly lit, orange walls and the dark wood tables. Beer NIS20-NIS28. Vodka NIS30-NIS40. Discount menu until 10:30pm. 23+. Open Su-Th and Sa 8:30pm-3:30am, F 9:30pm-3:30am. Credit cards accepted.

Constantine, 3 Hahistadrut (☎02 622 1155). In the city center; walk up Ben-Yehuda toward King George St., then turn right on the last cross street before you reach King George; Constantine is on the righthand side at the end of the block. The closest thing to a worthwhile club in Jerusalem, Constantine pulses with energy that only increases as the night wears on. The young, sleek crowd drinks to techno music in rooms with black walls and flashing blue neon lights; the less suave among us sway to the music awkwardly in corners and try to blend in. Beer from NIS23. Vodka from NIS46. M student night. Cover after 12:30am. NIS25. Open daily 10:30am-5:30am. Credit cards accepted.

Gullah (☎02 623 4333), in Feingold Square. Walk to the end of Rivlin St. toward its intersection with Hillel, make a sharp right, then take your first left through a stone archway up the narrow stepped street; it is on the right, after the restaurant Adom. A favorite local spot for drinking and catching up with friends. The music is not overbearing enough to drown out all conversation, and the dense collection of square tables on the veranda outside make for comfortable seating. Beer NIS19-25. Vodka NIS22-34. Open daily 7pm-6am. Credit cards accepted.

Hataklit, 7 Heleni HaMalka St. (☎02 624 4073; www.myspace.com/hataklit). From Yafo Rd., turn right on Heleni HaMalka St., and walk about 1 block uphill past Aristobolus St.; the bar will be on your left. Pounding rock and heavy metal. Mostly groups of young Israeli men letting loose after a long day, and getting progressively drunker as the night wears on. Try to see if you can catch the monthly DJ face-off, or the occasional live music show. Bottled beer NIS17-24. Whiskey NIS24-44. Mixed drinks NIS35-40. Open Su-Th and Sa 4:30pm-late, F 12:30pm-late. Credit cards accepted.

Barood, 31 Jaffa Rd. (☎02 625 9081). In Feingold Sq., across the street from Gullah. Walk to the end of Rivlin St. toward its intersection with Hillel, make a sharp right, then take your 1st left through a stone archway up the narrow stepped street. Sephardic restaurant and bar with a collection of old "My Goodness Guinness!" ads framed on the walls. Traditional, Mediterranean Sephardic food, and the best Guinness in Israel. Call ahead to see what live music is playing; Barood hosts jazz musicians frequently. Beer NIS22-26. Open M-Sa 12:30pm-1:30am. Credit cards accepted.

Stardust, 6 Rivlin St. (☎02 622 2196; stardust.com), toward the top of Rivlin St. near its intersection with Jaffa Rd. A lingering neighborhood hangout on Rivlin St. A smaller and more intimate alternative to the pounding music and raucous tourists of its neighbors. Beer NIS16-24. Whiskey NIS22-42. Open Su-Th and Sa 4:30pm-5am, F noon-5am. Credit cards accepted.

▶ DAYTRIPS FROM JERUSALEM

ABU GHOSH

אבו גוש   أبو غوش

Bus 185 (20min., NIS8.10) from the International Convention Center. To get to the International Convention Center, go to the Central Bus Station and cross the street. Walk past the orange and blue circular building selling lottery tickets and walk straight down the side street with a fence running along both sides. Turn left when the side street ends.

Overlooking the Judean hills west of Jerusalem, the Arab village of Abu Ghosh is revered by Christians and Jews alike as an early site of the Ark of the Covenant, which David later moved to Jerusalem (I Chronicles 13:5-8). In caravan days, the town was the last stop on the way to Jerusalem; its 18-century namesake, Sheikh Abu Ghosh, required pilgrims to pay a toll as they traveled to the Holy City. Historically, the Arabs of the village have always had good relations with neighboring Jewish settlements and the State of Israel, even during the 1948 War.

Translated as "Our Lady of the Ark of the Covenant," **Notre Dame de l'Arche d'Alliance** at the top of the hill was built on the site of the Ark's ancient holding place. To get there from the bus stop, turn right and walk straight until you see a brown road sign reading Crusader Church of the Resurrection. Turn left on the street and follow it down the hill, turning right when you get to the bottom. Take your first left up a small road to the side of a Muslim cemetery, and proceed all the way to the top of the hill. Turn left at the top the hill at the derelict former police station, then follow the signs. The current church was built in the 1920s on the ruins of its demolished Byzantine predecessor; beautiful fragments of the original mosaics are integrated into the marble floor. (Open M-Sa 8:30-11:30am and 2:30-5pm.) In the beautiful garden below the sacred hill stands **Crusader Church of the Resurrection.** To reach the church, go to the bottom of the aforementioned hill and follow the road straight ahead toward the minaret of the nearby mosque. You will quickly come to a building with a large gate, and a green metal door beside it. This magnificently-preserved church was built in 1142 and acquired by the French government in 1873. Excavations beneath the church have uncovered remains dating back to Neolithic times; the crypt contains evidence of Roman fortification. Today, nine monks and twelve nuns reside in the monastery and make their living from the ceramics handcrafted in their small pottery studio. (Open M-Sa 8:30-11am and 2:30-5:30pm.)

While you're in town, there are several enjoyable restaurants to curb your midday hunger as you hike between the sites. The verdant **Caravan Inn Restaurant ❷** serves slightly pricey main dishes on a breezy terrace, overlooking Abu Ghosh and the hills of Jerusalem. It is ideally located between the two churches on the hike to the Notre Dame de l'Arche d'Alliance. (☎02 534 2744. Entrees NIS30-NIS80. Open daily 11am-11pm. AmEx/D/MC/V.) In the opposite direction, about a 15min. walk along the main road to the left from the bus stop, is **Lebanese Food Restaurant ❸**, a regional favorite. Jerusalem families have been known to schlep into Abu Ghosh to eat here during Shabbat, when everything in their own city is closed. The many electric fans on the veranda make for a comfortable refuge from the midday heat. The food comes in generous helpings and is exceptionally good. (☎02 570 2393. Sinieh NIS30. Kebab NIS40. Open daily 9am-11pm. AmEx/D/MC/V.)

SOREK CAVE (ME'ARAT HA-NENETIFIM) ✖

The cave is 19km southwest of Jerusalem. It is most easily accessible from Jerusalem by taxi (about 40min., NIS60-70). Open Apr.–Sept. Su-Th 8am-5pm, F 8am-4pm; Oct.-Mar. Su-Th 8am-4pm, F 8am-3pm. NIS25, students NIS21. Visit comes with a guided tour of the site, except on Sa and holidays, when tours stop after 11am due to the sheer number of people. Tours are mostly given in Hebrew; English tours generally stop by 10am. Wheelchair-accessible. Animals and strollers not admitted to the caves.

The stalagmite and stalactite cave in the Avshalom Reserve (a.k.a. Me'arat ha-Netifim or Sorek Cave) contains spectacular speleological splendors. Discovered less than 30 years ago when a routine blast at a nearby quarry exposed a view into the cave, this site has been transformed into a major domestic tourist attraction. The otherworldly rock formations that have formed here been given a myriad of pop culture names derived from their whimsical shapes. Be sure to look out for: the Elephant Ears, a massive rock column that looks as if it has been draped and folded like slippery bags of skin; Romeo and Juliet, a stalactite and stalagmite whose points are within inches of touching each other, but which scientists predict may never meet; and Snow White and the Seven Dwarves, a series of small stalagmites which from the shadows look sureally similar to their Disney counterparts. The artificial lighting and paved pathways may disappoint adventurous spelunkers but do not detract from the cave's natural majesty.

LATRUN ✖

לטרון اللطرون

Bus #404, 433, or 435 (every 30min., NIS16) from Jerusalem's Central Bus Station. Ask at the Information Desk which of the 3 buses is going to Latrun at that time. Ask the driver in advance to stop in Latrun and remind him. Be prepared to be abruptly dropped off in what appears to be the middle of nowhere. Never fear; from the bus stop, the monastery is visibly to your left, and the filling station that leads to the Armored Corps Museum is visibly to your right.

A stern hilltop sentinel on the highway between Tel Aviv and Jerusalem, Latrun blends monasticism with an ancient tradition of militarism. The Bible says that Joshua fought the Canaanites here, and Latrun later served as base camp for the Romans, Richard the Lionhearted, and Salah al-Din. In 1917, the British took Latrun from the Turks and build a giant police fortress. Israeli forces tried unsuccessfully to capture Latrun in 1948 in order to divert supplies to the besieged city of Jerusalem. Only by carving out a new road (dubbed the **Burma Road**) almost overnight to circumvent Latrun were Israeli forces able to defend

Jerusalem. In 1967, the Israelis captured Latrun from the Jordanians and were able to build a more direct highway between Tel Aviv and Jerusalem.

Above the Alon filling station, the **Armored Corps Museum** contains 120 armored battle vehicles from Israel and surrounding countries. Highlights include an exhibit of stamps featuring armed forces from all over the world and a model of the tank planned by Leonardo da Vinci over 500 years ago. There is also a memorial to the 4864 armored corps soldiers killed in battle. (☎08 925 5268. Call ahead to arrange a tour with an English guide at no extra charge. Open Su-Th 8:30am-4:30pm, F 8:30am-12:30pm, Sa 9am-4pm. NIS30, children NIS20.) Famous for its wine, the hillside **Latrun Monastery** offers beautiful views of the surrounding area's nearby biblical sites, including Emmaus, Agalon, and Bathoron. A church and peaceful gardens sit beside the monastery. On Saturdays, a short film describing the life of a monk is screened. The French Trappist Order, part of the great monastic family of St. Benedict, founded the monastery as a center for silent contemplation and reflection. The shop near the main gate offers a wide selection of wines and spirits. To reach the monastery, whose orange rooftops are visible across the Tel Aviv-Jerusalem highway, go straight and uphill from the museum, following the curve of the road up the hill to the left; signs will direct you into the monastery gardens and to the entrance. (☎08 925 5180. Church and gardens open daily in summer 8:30am-noon and 3:30-6pm, in winter 8:30-11am and 2:30-4pm.) After his resurrection, Jesus was said to have appeared to two of his disciples on the site of the **Emmaus (Nicopolis) Church** (Mark 16:12-13, Luke 24:13-31), now the French Prehistorical Research Center. To reach the church, turn left out of the gas station and walk along the Tel Aviv-Jerusalem highway for about 500m, passing under an overpass. Another 100m along the road is the entrance to the **Canada Park,** a beautifully forested area with water holes and the remains of an amphitheatre.

TEL AVIV-JAFFA

TEL AVIV ☎ 03

טל אביב تل أبيب

Proudly secular and downright sexy, Tel Aviv pulses with cutting-edge energy. The people are beautiful, the bars close at 7am, and a thick strip of Mediterranean is visible from every street corner. Exuberant youth spend their time shopping for navel rings in trendy boutiques and bronzing at the beach on Shabbat. They have forged their city into a mecca of youth culture; as college students bounce between political cafes and fusion sushi restaurants, Tel Aviv's only underrepresented group may be adults.

Tel Aviv sprouted from Jaffa (Yafo, or "beautiful," in Hebrew; Yafa in Arabic), its neighboring city, at the end of the 19th century, when Jewish settlers founded the first two exclusively Jewish neighborhoods in 1887 and 1891. In 1909, a new, third suburb was named Tel Aviv (Spring Hill) after the town Theodore Herzl had envisioned in his turn-of-the-century utopian novel, *Altneuland* (Old-New-Land). The Jewish state that Herzl portrays in his novel is a beacon of art and political liberalism. Perhaps in an echo of that ideal, Tel Aviv is now the ultimate middle-class city, and it is defined by the culture of idiosyncrasy and exploration that develops from the leisure time that the upper classes can afford. Tel Avivians scribble in notebooks, shop at art fairs, cruise through skyscraper shopping malls, and debate the state of the world in eclectic cafes. ?he city is a bastion of the literati, most Israeli bands rocket to stardom from ?al clubs, and dozens of theater groups perform everything from Broadway ?rts to avant-garde Israeli plays.

?from forgotten, Jaffa is still an integral part of Tel Aviv and one of the ?unctioning harbors in the world. Though once the busiest port in the ?ffa has primarily harbored small fishing boats since the rise of modern ?nters in Haifa and Ashdod. Restaurants and galleries cater mostly to ?he city is still home to a vibrant group of Arab Israelis. Next to Tel ?ing hotels and glossy storefronts, the winding cobble-stone alleys ? vistas of Old Jaffa provide a breath of salty Mediterranean air.

? TEL AVIV-JAFFA

?odels at **Galina Hangar** club (p. 186).
?s at the **Carmel Market** (p. 178).
?political cartoons that line the **Tamar Cafe** (p. 172).

? TRANSPORTATION

?rt **(TLV;** ☎03 972 3344; in English 972 3388; automated ?2 2333; www.iaa.gov.il/Rashat/en-US/Airports/BenGurion), ?y in Lod. Egged **bus** #475 to the airport leaves from the

New Central Bus Station about every 20min., though like all Egged services the buses stop running on Shabbat (Su-Th 5:20am-11:40pm, F 5:30am-4:40pm, Sa 8:40pm-midnight; NIS12.60). **Shuttle bus #222** does a round-trip between the airport and Tel Aviv, passing most major hostels on the way, but as of this writing had been temporarily discontinued; check at the airport to see if it's up and running again. **Taxis** from the airport to Tel Aviv vary due to gas prices, but should never be more than NIS150.

Trains: Tel Aviv Savidor Central Railway Station, Arlozorov St. (☎03 577 4000; www.rail.co.il), across from Namir Rd. Take bus #68, 501, or 531 from New Central Bus Station. Open Su-Th 24hr., F until 4:45pm, Sa from 8:30pm. To: **Ashdod** (50min., every hr., NIS17); **Haifa** (1hr., every 20min., NIS26.50); **Jerusalem** (1hr. 40min., every 2hr., NIS20); **Netanya** (20min., every hr., NIS13.50).

Buses: New Central Bus Station, 108 Levinsky St. (☎03 638 4040). Services operated by Egged (☎2800 or 03 694 8888; www.egged.co.il). To: **Be'er Sheva** (#370, 1½hr., every 1½hr., NIS15); **Eilat** (#390, 5hr., every 1½hr., NIS70); **Ein Gedi** (#405 to Jerusalem, buses #421, 486, or 487 to Ein Gedi; 2hr. 20min.; every 20min.; NIS53.50); **Haifa** (#910, 1½hr., every hr., NIS25); **Jerusalem** (#405, 1hr., every 20min., NIS19); **Netanya** (#641, 1¾hr., every 30min., NIS16); **Tiberias** (#835 and 841, 2¾hr., every 20min., NIS45).

Car Rental: Avis, 113 Hayarkon St. (☎03 527 1752; www.carrentalisrael.com). Open Su-Th 8am-6pm, F 8am-2pm. Both manuals and automatics from US$42 per day for 2-6 days, US$38 for 7-24 days; prices liable to change. 21+ manuals, 23+ automatics. **Budget Israel Car Rental,** 99 Hayarkon St. (☎03 524 5233 or 523 1551; www.budget.co.il). Open 24hr. Manuals start from US$53 a day, automatics US$67. Drivers aged 21-23 can drive manual transmissions with prior approval; 23+ for all automatics.

▓ ORIENTATION

Located in the center of Israel's Mediterranean coastline, Tel Aviv is 63km northwest of Jerusalem and 95km south of Haifa. The two main points of entry into Tel Aviv are **Ben-Gurion Airport** and the **New Central Bus Station.** Frequent bus

Tel Aviv & the South Coast

Netanya
Poleg Nature Reserve
Kibbutz Ga'ash
0   10 miles
Herzliya
0   10 kilometers
Petaḥ Tikva
Tel Aviv-Jaffa (Yafo)
Ben-Gurion Int'l Airport
Bat Yam
Rishon Le Zion
Ramla
Reḥovot
Ashdod
Tel Ashdod
Ashkelon
Beit Guvrin
Kiryat Gat
Yad Mordekhai
Tel Maresha
GAZA STRIP
ISRAEL
Tel Lakhish
Gaza

and *sherut* (minibus) service from the airport is supplemented by the vans that warring hostels send to lure potential customers.

Tel Aviv is rather easy to navigate once you learn the few main roads that run parallel to the coastline and the thoroughfares that intersect them. The **tayelet** (promenade) extends from Jaffa up to Gordon beach (about two-thirds of the way to **the Port**). Parallel and one block inland is **Hayarkon Street**, followed by **Ben-Yehuda Street** another block inland. All three streets are lined with hotels, cafes, and restaurants—prices generally go down as you go further from the shore—and run through the most important sections of the city. Intersecting these streets are **Arlozorov Street** and **Bograshov Street**, which run east-to-west. Tel Aviv's neighborhoods' tend to be nebulous and blend seamlessly into each other, but Arlozorov St. and Bograshov St. more or less divide the city into three sections. The first section, **north Tel Aviv** is everything above Arlozorov St. Some of the most popular clubs in town are in the **Tel Aviv Port** in the city's northern corner; east of the port is the quiet **Little Tel Aviv. Ramat Aviv,** which is home to **Tel Aviv University** and many of Tel Aviv's best museums, is north of both of these neighborhoods on the opposite bank of the river. The train station, which has service to all major cities, is at the intersection of Namir Rd. and Arlozorov St.

The second section, Tel Aviv's large **city center,** is situated in between Arlozorov St. and Bograshov St. The main thoroughfare here is **Dizengoff Street,** home to some of Tel Aviv's trendy cafes and bars. It runs parallel to Ben-Yehuda St. before swerving away from the coast toward **Dizengoff Square,** an elevated plaza surrounded by shops and a cineplex. After intersecting with **Hamelekh George Street** at the sprawling shopping mall at **Dizengoff Center,** Dizengoff St. then continues to intersect the next big coastal parallel, **Ibn Gvirol Street,** with its arcades and cafes. A few blocks above this intersection is **Kikkar Yitzak Rabin,** in front of City Hall, at Ibn Gvirol's intersection with Ben-Gurion St.

Home to some of Tel Aviv's most historic and intriguing neighborhoods, the third section of the city, **south Tel Aviv,** is everything south of Bograshov St. but north of Jaffa. The area's funky, bustling epicenter is **David Magen Square** in the **Yemenite Quarter;** six major streets converge into a single point here, earning the square its name (*magen* means star in Hebrew). After its intersection with Dizengoff St. in the city center, Hamelekh George St. runs south at an angle until it intersects with Ben-Yehuda St. here; after hitting David Magen Sq., both streets' names change. Hamelekh George St. narrows and branches into the raucous, pedestrian only **Carmel Market** and **Nahalat Benyamin Street,** both of which are Yemenite Quarter landmarks. Ben-Yehuda St. turns into **Allenby Street,** which continues most of the way to the **New Central Bus Station.** The sixth street that converges at David Magen Sq. is **Sheinkin Street,** a street of hip cafes and shops that runs east-to-west. The triangle formed by Sheinkin St., Allenby St., and **Rothschild Boulevard's** intersections with each other marks a distinct Tel Aviv neighborhood of historic Bauhaus and exceptional restaurants.

After crossing **Hertzl Street,** Rothschild Blvd. dead-ends in the **Neve Tzedek** neighborhood, which is situated to the south of the Yemenite Quarter. South of that, below **Eilat Road,** is the bohemian **Florentine** neighborhood. **Jaffa** and its waterfront lie farther south, outside the downtown area. The entrance to **Old Jaffa,** marked by a famous clocktower, lies at the intersection of **Eilat Street** and **Goldman Street.**

▣ LOCAL TRANSPORTATION

Tel Aviv is mostly manageable by foot. On a hot August afternoon, though, a NIS5.50 bus ride may seem like the deal of the century. Buses in Tel Aviv are frequent, air-conditioned, and comfortable; they make trips to sights north of the Yarkon possible, as the ha-Tikva area, Ramat Aviv, and the south of Jaffa are all an easy walking distance from the city center.

Buses: New Central Bus Station, 108 Levinsky St. (☎03 638 4040). Can be scary and overwhelming the 1st time you experience it, not to mention a tad sketchy at night. Most local buses as well as local and intercity *sheruts* leave from the 4th fl., and most Egged intercity buses leave from the 6th fl.; both have information kiosks. Buses within Tel Aviv are operated by **Dan** (☎03 639 3333 or 639 4444; www.dan. co.il; open Su-F; NIS5.50). For extended stays, consider investing in Dan's *kartisiyot ha-noar* (youth subscription tickets), which will get you 20 bus rides for NIS53—less than you would otherwise pay. Unlike intercity buses, local buses travel both ways, so you must be conscious of the direction. The most frequent and important routes are listed below. Routes are prone to change, so make sure to check with hostel owners and locals for the best routes as well.

#4: From the New Central Bus Station, runs parallel to the coastline up Allenby and Ben-Yehuda St. and back.

#5: From the New Central Bus Station, runs up Rothschild Blvd. and Dizengoff St. through Dizengoff Center and Dizengoff Square, then turns right on Nordau Av. In North Tel Aviv, runs down Weizmann St. through Hamedina Sq., and ends at Tel Aviv Savidor Central Railway Station.

#10: Runs along the coast from Jaffa up Hayarkon St., then turns east on Ben-Gurion St., and takes Arlozorov to the Tel Aviv Savidor Central Railway Station.

#18: Runs from Jaffa up Allenby St. to David Magen Sq., then up Hamelekh George St. through Dizengoff Center to Rabin Sq., then in a loop to the Tel Aviv Art Museum and back down to Jaffa.

#25: Runs from Jaffa up Yerushalayim St. to David Magen Sq., then up Hamelekh George St. through Dizengoff Center to Ibn Gvirol St., which it takes up to Ramat Aviv.

#46: Runs from Jaffa Rd. in Jaffa to the New Central Bus Station, then up to the Tel Aviv Port.

Sherut: An alternative option to the bus system in Tel Aviv. NIS5 per person. Have routes that are loosely similar to those of the popular bus lines.

⛛ PRACTICAL INFORMATION

TOURIST AND FINANCIAL SERVICES

Tourist Office: Tourist Information Center, 46 Herbert Samuel Promenade (☎03 516 6188), on the *tayelet* at the corner of 2 Geula St. Small but incredibly helpful. Free maps and brochures in a variety of languages with tips on the best restaurants, clubs, tours, and more in town. In July and Aug., it is also one of the only tourist offices in the country that is open on Sa. Open July-Aug. Su-Th 9:30am-5pm, F 9:30-1pm, Sa 10am-4pm; open Sept.-June Su-Th 9:30am-5pm, F 9:30am-1pm.

Tours: Visit Tel Aviv Tourism, run in conjunction with the Tourist office. The tours are informative and, even better, free:

Tel Aviv University Art and Architecture, M 11am. Dyonon bookstore, campus entrance at intersection of Haim Levanon and Einstein St.

Tel Aviv by Night, Tu 8pm. Rothschild Blvd. and Hertzel St.

Old Jaffa, W 9:30am. Clock Tower on Yefet St.

Bauhaus "The White City," Sa 11am. 46 Rothschild Blvd.

Embassies: UK, 192 Hayarkon St. (☎03 725 1222; ukinisrael.fco.gov.uk/en/our-offices-in-israel/our-embassy-in-tel-aviv/). **US,** 71 Hayarkon St. (☎03 519 7575; israel.usembassy.gov). For more information, see **Essentials,** p. 8.

Bank: Bank ha-Poalim, 104 Hayarkon St. (☎03 520 0612). **Bank Leumi,** 130 Ben-Yehuda St. (☎03 520 3737). Nearly every other street corner in Tel Aviv has an **ATM.**

TEL AVIV-JAFFA

LOCAL SERVICES

English-Language Bookstore: Halper's, 87 Allenby St. (☎03 629 9710). 1 block after Allenby's intersection with Montefiore St. Good used book selection. Open Su-Th 9am-7pm, F 9am-3pm. Credit cards accepted. **Steimatzky,** 103 Allenby St. (☎03 522 1513). Branches of this chain are also located in the Opera Tower, and at Dizengoff Center.

GLBT Resources: Agudah (Association of Gay Men, Lesbians, Bisexuals and Transgenders), 28 Nachmani St. (☎03 629 3681; www.geocities.com/westhollywood/ stonewall/2295/). Turn left on Nachmani off Rothschild Blvd.; the intersection is right after Rothschild's intersection with Bezalel St. Offers support services, info on the latest gay hotspots in town, and the *Pink Times.*

Laundromat: KvisKal, 103 Ben-Yehuda St. (☎03 523 6411). Open Su-Th 7:30am-7pm, F 7:30am-2pm. **Laundry Cafe,** 110 Sheffer St. (☎03 516 4271), right by its intersection with Nahalat Benyamin St. Open Su-Th 9am-midnight, F 9am-5pm, Sa 5pm-2am.

EMERGENCY AND COMMUNICATIONS

Police: ☎100. **Tourist Police,** ☎03 516 5382.

Ambulance: ☎101.

Pharmacy: Superpharm, 50 Dizengoff St. (☎03 620 0975), in Dizengoff Center. Open Su-Th 9am-11pm, F 8:30am-5:30pm. Branches: 14 Weizman St. (☎03 609 0995; open Su-Th 8:30am-10pm, F 8:30am-4pm) and 4 Saul Hamelech Ave. (☎03 696 0106; open Su-Th 8am-midnight, F 8am-5pm). **New-Pharm,** 75 Ben-Yehuda St. (☎03 529 0037). Open Su-Th 9am-2am, F 9am-3pm. Branch: 71 Ibn Gavirol St. (☎03 527 9318; open Su-Th 8:30am-9pm, F 8:30am-3pm).

Medical Services: Ichilov Hospital, 6 Weitzman St. (☎03 697 4444). **Assuta Hospital,** 20 Habarzel (☎03 764 4000; http://en.assuta.co.il/).

Internet Access: IMAC Cafe, 12 Kaufman St. (☎03 795 1111), on the *tayelet* right before the Dolphinarium. US$8 (NIS31) per hr., US$10 (NIS40) with coffee and cake. Open daily 9am-midnight. **InterFun,** 20 Allenby St. (☎03 517 1448), on the block before Allenby's intersection with HaYarkon St. Open daily 10am-midnight or later.

Post Office: Central Post Office, 132 Allenby Rd. Open Su-Th 8am-12:30pm and 3:30-6:30pm. Other branches throughout the city, including 286 Dizengoff St., 61 HaYarkon St., and 138 Yeffet St. in Jaffa. Check with your hostel to find the closest one.

ACCOMMODATIONS

Tel Aviv does not have as many hostels as Jerusalem does, but the hostels here really have their act together. There's a bed for every budget, and most places come with all the fixings travelers crave. Even better, the vast majority of hostels are pretty much beachfront property, particularly those in south Tel Aviv. Most cluster on **Ben-Yehuda** and **Hayarkon Street,** with some just off **Allenby Road** or **Dizengoff Street.** When choosing, keep in mind that drunken revelry and honking horns downtown may continue into the wee hours. Also, consider the hostels in **Jaffa** (p. 190) for a change in cultural flavor but similarly rocking youth atmosphere. Hostels fill up very quickly in the summer, especially the private rooms, so make reservations in advance. Almost all have 24hr. reception, kitchen, and internet. A huge influx of long-term travelers lends a lived-in feel to some places. Sleeping on the beach is illegal and dangerous; theft and sexual harassment are not uncommon, so just don't do it.

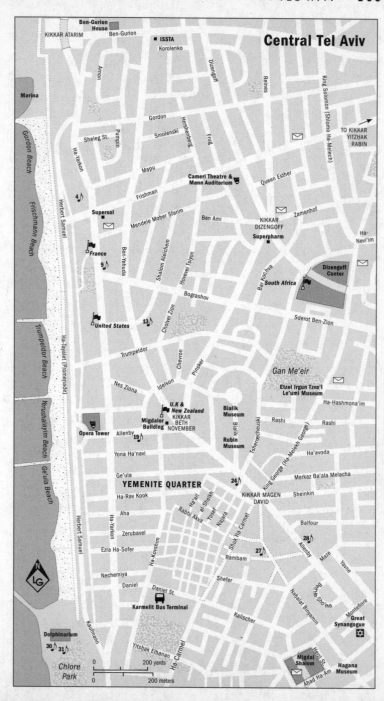

Central Tel Aviv

KIKKAR ATARIM
Ben-Gurion
House
Ben-Gurion
ISSTA
Korolenko
Marina
Arnon
Dizengoff
Reines
King Solomon (Shlomo Ha-Melech)
TO KIKKAR
YITZHAK
RABIN
Gordon
Sheleg St.
Pumpin
Smolenski
Hershenberg
Frug
Ha-Yarkon
Gordon Beach
Mapu
Frishman
Queen Esther
Cameri Theatre &
Mann Auditorium
Supersol
Mendele Moher Sfarim
Ben Ami
Zamenhof
KIKKAR
DIZENGOFF
Superpharm
Ha-
Nevi'im
Frishmann Beach
Herbert Samuel
Ben-Yehuda
France
Shalom Aleichem
Hovevey Tsiyon
Bar Kochva
South Africa
Dizengoff
Center
United States
Chovel Zion
Bograshov
Sderot Ben-Zion
Trumpeldor Beach
Ha-Tayelet (Promenade)
Trumpeldor
Chevron
Pinsker
Gan Me'eir
Etzel Irgun Tzva'l
Le'umi Museum
Ha-Hashmona'im
Nes Ziona
Idelson
Yerushalayim Beach
U.K &
New Zealand
KIKKAR
BETH
NOVEMBER
Bialik
Museum
Bialik
Rashi
Rashi
Tshernecheuski
Migdalor
Building
King George (Ha-Melekh George)
Ha'avoda
Opera Tower
Allenby
Rubin
Museum
Ge'ula Beach
Yona Ha'navi
Ge'ula
YEMENITE QUARTER
Ha-Rav Kook
Merkaz Ba'ala Melacha
Sheinkin
KIKKAR MAGEN
DAVID
Aha
Rabbi Akva
Ha'ari
al-Sheikh
Yoset
Najara
Balfour
Herbert Samuel
Ha-Yarkon
Zerubavel
Ezra Ha-Sofer
Ha-Kovshim
Shuk Ha-Carmel
Rambam
Allenby
Maze
Yavne
Nechemiya
Daniel
Shefer
Nahaat Binyamin
Beit Ha-Sho'eva
N
LG
Daniel St.
Karmelit Bus Terminal
Kalischer
Montefiore
Great
Synangogue
Dolphinarium
30
31
Chlore
Park
Yitzhak Elbanan
Ha-Carmel
Migdal
Shalom
Herzl St.
Ahad Ha-Am
Hagana
Museum
0   200 yards
0   200 meters

TEL AVIV-JAFFA

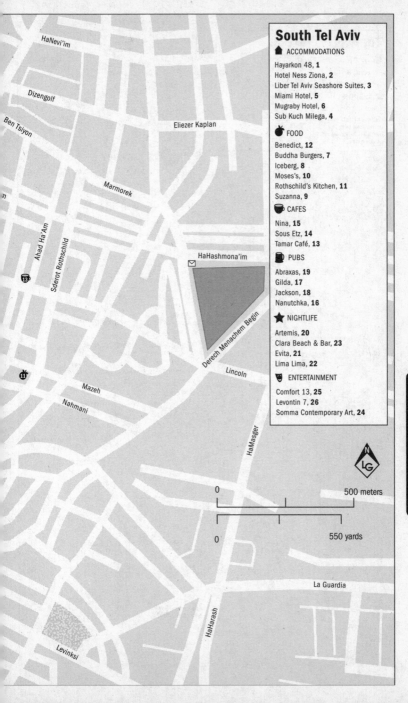

South Tel Aviv

🏠 ACCOMMODATIONS

Hayarkon 48, **1**
Hotel Ness Ziona, **2**
Liber Tel Aviv Seashore Suites, **3**
Miami Hotel, **5**
Mugraby Hotel, **6**
Sub Kuch Milega, **4**

🍅 FOOD

Benedict, **12**
Buddha Burgers, **7**
Iceberg, **8**
Moses's, **10**
Rothschild's Kitchen, **11**
Suzanna, **9**

☕ CAFES

Nina, **15**
Sous Etz, **14**
Tamar Café, **13**

🍺 PUBS

Abraxas, **19**
Gilda, **17**
Jackson, **18**
Nanutchka, **16**

⭐ NIGHTLIFE

Artemis, **20**
Clara Beach & Bar, **23**
Evita, **21**
Lima Lima, **22**

🎭 ENTERTAINMENT

Comfort 13, **25**
Levontin 7, **26**
Somma Contemporary Art, **24**

HaNevi'im

Dizengolf

Ben Tsiyon

Eliezer Kaplan

Marmorek

Ahad Ha'Am

Sderot Rothschild

HaHashmona'im

Derech Menachem Begin

Lincoln

Mazeh

Nahmani

HaMasger

0   500 meters

0   550 yards

La Guardia

HaHarash

Levinksi

TEL AVIV-JAFFA

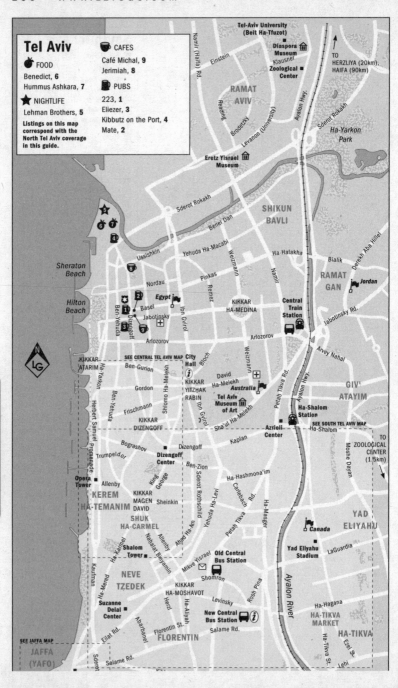

Tel Aviv

🍎 **FOOD**

Benedict, **6**
Hummus Ashkara, **7**

⭐ **NIGHTLIFE**

Lehman Brothers, **5**

Listings on this map
correspond with the
North Tel Aviv coverage
in this guide.

☕ **CAFES**

Café Michal, **9**
Jerimiah, **8**

🍺 **PUBS**

223, **1**
Eliezer, **3**
Kibbutz on the Port, **4**
Mate, **2**

Tel-Aviv University
(Beit Ha-Tfuzot)

Diaspora
Museum
Klausner
Zoological
Center

TO
HERZLIYA (20km),
HAIFA (90km)

RAMAT
AVIV

Ha-Yarkon
Park

Eretz Yisrael
Museum

SHIKUN
BAVLI

Sheraton
Beach

Hilton
Beach

Sderot Rokakh

Benei Dan

Yehuda Ha-Macabi

Ha-Halakha

Bialik

RAMAT
GAN

Jordan

Ussishkin

Nordau

Pinkas

Egypt

Basel

Jabotinsky

Dizengoff

Arlozorov

KIKKAR
ATARIM

KIKKAR
HA-MEDINA

Central
Train
Station

Jabotinsky Rd.

SEE CENTRAL TEL AVIV MAP

City
Hall

Ben-Gurion

Gordon

Frischmann

KIKKAR
DIZENGOFF

KIKKAR
YITZHAK
RABIN

David
Ha-Melekh

Australia

Tel Aviv
Museum
of Art

Ha-Shalom
Station

SEE SOUTH TEL AVIV MAP

GIV'
ATAYIM

Azrieli
Center

TO
ZOOLOGICAL
CENTER
(1.5km)

Bograshov

Trumpeldor

Dizengoff
Center

Dizengoff

Ben-Zion

Kaplan

Ha-Hashmona'im

Opera
Tower

Allenby

KEREM
HA-TEMANIM

KIKKAR
MAGEN
DAVID

SHUK
HA-CARMEL

Sheinkin

Canada

YAD
ELIYAHU

Shalom
Tower

NEVE
TZEDEK

Suzanne
Delai
Center

Shalom
Tower

Old Central
Bus Station

Shomron

KIKKAR
HA-MOSHAVOT

Levinsky

New Central
Bus Station

Salame Rd.

Yad Eliyahu
Stadium

LaGuardia

HA-TIKVA
MARKET

HA-TIKVA

FLORENTIN

JAFFA
(YAFO)

SEE JAFFA MAP

TEL AVIV-JAFFA

CITY CENTER

If you plan to spend your time in Tel Aviv staggering home in a Goldstar-generated haze at 6am in someone else's T-shirt, city center hostels have the best location for you. Accommodations here make up for what they lack in character and beach views with their proximity to many of the museums, restaurants, and party hotspots of the city; if you're not one for the nightlife, all hostels listed here preserve a sense of calm, cleanliness, and quiet despite their youthful clientele. Check out **Dizengoff Luxury Apartments** (below) for longer stays.

▨ **Gordon Inn Guest House,** 17 Gordon St. (☎03 523 8239), at the Ben-Yehuda St. More polished and proper than most in the price range, the Guest House resides conveniently between Dizengoff Center and the beach, but remains quiet and intimate despite its location. Rooms are bright with uncommonly thick mattresses, and the dense window boxes baking in the heat outside add a homey touch. Lovely bar-cafe with pool table open until 3am. A/C, TVs, and fridges included in rooms. Breakfast included. Free Wi-Fi. Dorms NIS90; singles NIS230; doubles NIS250; triples NIS290; quads NIS328. Credit cards accepted. ❷

Sky Hostel, 34 Ben-Yehuda St. (☎03 620 0044). Take bus #230 from New Central Station. Centrally located option with a dim lobby and bright, somewhat noisy rooms. Rooms are sparse with translucent, red curtains drawn over large windows, some of which open onto narrow balconies overlooking a tangle of telephone wires and traffic below. Friendly tattooed manager at the desk. Light breakfast of coffee and cake included. TV and fans in each room; A/C in NIS300 rooms. Free Wi-Fi. Dorms NIS78; singles NIS135-180; doubles NIS230-300. Credit cards accepted. ❷

Momo's, 28 Ben-Yehuda St. (☎03 528 7471; www.momoshostel.com). Take bus #230 from New Central Station. Owned by the same people who run Sky Hostel, Momo's is centrally located with refreshingly aggressive A/C and a hostel (not hostile) cat lounging on the counter of the front desk. It is also one of the only hostels which has a small bar; there are only 2 kinds of whiskey and 1 vodka, but it has a friendly and relaxed atmosphere. Light breakfast of coffee and cake included. Fans and free Wi-Fi in every room. Dorms NIS80; singles NIS135-150, doubles NIS180. Credit cards accepted. ❷

Dizengoff Luxury Apartments, 89 Dizengoff St. (☎03 524 1151; www.inisrael.com/hotel-apt), ½ a block up Dizengoff St. from Dizengoff Sq. Luxury might be a stretch, but Dizengoff Luxury Apartments are nevertheless comfortable, ideally located, and well-priced options for both short-term and long-term stays. Rooms come with generous kitchen equipment, including a microwave and several hot plates; the dusty narrow balconies overlook the noisy, graffitied square, though the rooms themselves are rather quiet. A/C, TV, and Wi-Fi in every room. High season singles US$150/NIS585; doubles US$150/NIS585. Low season singles US$100/NIS390, doubles US$110/NIS430. Credit cards accepted. ❺

SOUTH TEL AVIV

South Tel Aviv's hostels are among the best (see Hayarkon 48), the funkiest (see Sub Kuch Milega), and closest to the sea in the city. The beach views and exciting mix of international young travelers can be infectious. Take care to present yourself politely and professionally if you want to upgrade from hostels to any of the nearby beachfront hotels, though; the youthful reputation of South Tel Aviv's hostels is a double-edged sword, and some hotel staff can be reluctant to give rooms to students out of fear that they will bring their outdoor voices and cheap vodka bottles with them.

▨ **Hayarkon 48 Hostel,** 48 Hayarkon St. (☎03 516 8989; www.hayarkon48.com), right after Hayarkon's intersection with Allenby St. Take bus #4, 16, or 31 from New Central Bus Station; get off at the first stop on Ben-Yehuda St. and walk west 1 block to Hayarkon. The bright rooms and showers win popularity contests, but everyone spends their time in the TV lounge playing pool, drinking beer at the reception or on the rooftop bar. The staff is impressively helpful, and it's always easy to find cool people with whom to go out clubbing, sunbathing, or exploring throughout the day. Breakfast included. Dorm with ceiling fan US$21 (approx. NIS82), with A/C US$25 (approx. NIS97); singles US$87 (approx. NIS340); doubles with shared bath and fan US$87 (approx. NIS340), with bath and A/C US$99 (approx. NIS386). Credit cards accepted. ❷

Hotel Ness Ziona, 10 Ness Ziona (☎03 510 6084; www.hotelnessziona.com), just off Ben-Yehuda near its intersection with Allenby St. and Pinkser St. Simple rooms with translucent rose-gold curtains and watercolors of soothing scenes decorating the light yellow walls. The hotel can be a bit idiosyncratic (a bathroom sink in the shower?) but provides a peaceful escape from the grunge of the backpacking world. All rooms have TVs, A/C, and Wi-Fi. Check-out noon. Singles NIS200, with bath NIS250; doubles NIS200/350. D/MC/V. ❸

Liber Tel Aviv Seashore Suites, 6 Allenby St. (☎03 510 2310; www.inisrael.com/liber), across the street from the Opera Tower, right on the ocean. Take bus #4, 16, or 31 from New Central Bus Station, and get off at the 1st stop on Ben-Yehuda St. Walk toward the sea on Allenby St. for several blocks, past Mugraby Hostel, until you reach the ocean; Liber will be on your left. Community atmosphere created by friendly staff and traveling business men and families. Try to get a studio-style rooms with wide and comfortable balconies overlooking the sea. A/C. Reception 24hr. Rooms US$140/NIS545, with sea view US$165/NIS643. Credit cards accepted. ❺

Sub Kuch Milega, 22 Hamashbir St. (☎03 681 3412; www.subkuchmilega.com), in the Florentine neighborhood. Hamashbir branches off Yafo Rd. between its intersections with Allenby St. and Herzl St., right before its intersection with Herzl. Take bus #201 or 163 from New Central Bus Station. A small, hot cluster of rooms above a creaky Indian restaurant with a massive mural in the stairwell of a man ecstatically smoking a deliberately ambiguous object (hookah? bong? a live animal of some kind?). The #1 reason to stay at Sub Kuch Milega is to be able to brag that you stayed there. The co-ed dorms are clean and have balconies; the bathrooms are down the hall and a bit cramped, with no curtain or other separation between the toilet and the showerheads. Everything smells a little bit like curry and hippies. Access to laundry and kitchen, with a rooftop bar and cinema to boot. Fans and free Wi-Fi in all rooms. Dorms NIS70; doubles with shared bath NIS160, with private bath and A/C NIS280. Credit cards accepted. ❶

Miami Hotel, 8 Allenby St. (☎03 510 3868), next door to Liber Tel Aviv Seashore Suites. Narrow hotel with a large green fish tank and hilarious assortment of brusque, portly, middle-aged men slouched in the lobby. Rooms have thick red bedspreads and are periodically decorated with bouquets of fake flowers. Ideally located. A/C and TVs in all rooms. Singles and doubles US$50; bigger single $85. Credit cards accepted. ❸

Mugraby Hostel, 30 Allenby St. (☎03 510 2440; www.mugraby-hostel.com). Take bus #4, 16, or 31 from New Central Bus Station, and get off at the first stop on Ben-Yehuda St. Walk toward the sea on Allenby St. for several storefronts; Mugraby Hostel will be on your left. Centrally located hostel with dorms and funky paintings of dragons and gothic princesses on the walls in the stairwell. Breakfast included. Free Wi-Fi. Check-in and check-out 11am. Dorms NIS68; singles NIS220, with bath NIS250; doubles NIS250/NIS280. Credit cards accepted. ❶

◩ FOOD

Come mealtime, Tel Aviv rises above and beyond the call of duty. Restaurants range from Asian fusion to French *haute cuisine* to hummus and pita effectively sold by the pound. Most actual restaurants here are relatively expensive (generally NIS40 and up for entrees), but you don't have to go far out of your way to eat economically. For quick, cheap belly-fillers, head to the **self-service eateries** on Ben-Yehuda or Allenby, where stuff-your-own falafels go for NIS10 each. For the late-night crowd, many of the **bakeries** along Allenby between Shuk ha-Carmel and Hayarkon St. sell bagel toasts 24hr. (NIS5-10). Bakeries, falafel stands, and fast-food joints line the **Dizengoff Square** area. For those with a hostel kitchen who are willing to forage for goodies in local bazaars, the **Carmel Market shuk** in the Yemenite Quarter is crowded with cheap produce venders, and the Dizengoff Center hosts a weekly **Friday food fair** where people sell their homemade goodies—everything from Greek baklava (NIS103) to Chinese dumplings (NIS12 for 6)—from 10am to 4pm. **AM-PM,** the local supermarket/drugstore chain, sells basic produce and cooking materials as well. There is practically one on every corner; walk for 5min. in any direction and you will most likely find one. As their name suggests, they are open 24hr., including all holidays except Yom Kippur and Rosh Hashanah.

For those willing to spend a little extra, there are several Tel Aviv institutions whose addresses you should simply stick in your back pocket or memorize, just in case you fumble drunkenly into a cab at 4am and need somewhere to eat an early breakfast pronto. **Benedict** and **The Streets** are both open 24hr., seven days a week, and are incredibly popular with Tel Aviv's clubbing crowd. The same goes for the burger joint **Moses' Modern American Kitchen,** which doesn't close until 4am. A massive burger and side order goes for NIS36 here after midnight, and consequentially, Moses' may be one of the few restaurants around that recommends you call ahead if you want a table after 1am. **Iceberg** is a delicious local chain of homemade ice creams, which is based in the Port but, like Benedict and Moses, has branches throughout the city. It doesn't close until 4am.

Crowd-gazing is an art in Tel Aviv; chairs on the sidewalk and cafe au lait can be found just about anywhere in the city. **Sheinkin Street,** one of the hippest streets in town, has a long tradition of artsy liberalism and just seems to keep getting cooler. **Neve Tzedek** is another hotspot, as local artists energize themselves in the corner cafes that pepper the old winding streets. When it comes to coffee and conversation in Tel Aviv, though, you really have an excess of places to choose from in every neighborhood. Walk two to three blocks in any direction, and you're guaranteed to find a cluster of small outdoor tables with white cups of toothpicks and pink paper sugar packets, crowded with Israelis talking politics and eating lunch in the afternoon heat.

CITY CENTER

▨ **Carpaccio Bar,** 8 Ibn Gvirol St. (☎03 609 8118), between Eli'ezer Kaplan St. and Marmorek St. Take bus #89 from New Central Bus Station. Take Dizengoff St. to Ibn Gavirol St. and turn right; restaurant is on the left side of street. Serves *carpaccios* (dishes of raw beef, venison or tuna that have been thinly sliced and spiced) with fresh green salads and steaming hot bread rolls, and has broadened its horizons to other raw delicacies from tataki to tartar. One of the few restaurants with a Braille menu, replete with festive illustrations that the young waiters claim the blind very much enjoy. House roll NIS39. Israeli *carpaccio* NIS38. Sunday is *aperitivo* night, with a pseudo-tapas bar, cheap alcohol, and a laid back atmosphere; free glass of wine after 8pm. Buy 1 get 1 free drink every night until 9pm. Open Su-Th noon-1:30am, noon-3am on weekends. Credit cards accepted. ❷

▨ **The Streets,** 70 King George St. (☎077 351 1513; www.thestreets.co.il), at the corner of King George and ha-Nevi'im St. A cafe named after the favorite rock band of the

TEL AVIV-JAFFA

THE HIDDEN DEAL

CICI'S

In the heart of the Yemenite Quarter, this authentic local spot serves up homemade Yemenite food three times a day. While tourists flock to eat at oversized and overpriced eateries, Israelis are a few doors down eating better food for bargain prices.

Take a seat in Cici's homey interior or outside on one of Tel Aviv's oldest streets. Outdoor tables are shaded from the sun by a cheerful, red-sheet awning hanging between buildings. Occasionally, cars force their way down the street that was built for a horse and cart, but this *hutzpah* just adds to the authentic Israeli experience that is Cici's.

Everything that Cici cooks, from hummus to kebabs, is kosher, fresh, and delicious. Salads cost only NIS15, and a kebab complete with a healthy portion of rice and beans will only put you out NIS25. Other dishes include chicken skewers, *shishliks*, and the traditional Arab brown bean delicacy, *ful*. Ask if they have any homemade Iranian or lahuh pitas left from the fresh batches prepared every morning.

Be sure to wander through the market down the street to buy fresh food or to simply get a feel for one of Tel Aviv's most unique and charming neighborhoods.

Kihiah Kapach 31, Yemenite Quarter. Open M-Th and Su 9:30am-10pm, F 9:30am-3pm.

friends who founded the place. Friends lounge and chat on the wide porch swing located on the street outside, and play with the cafe dog. Party-goers and insomniacs can buy a sandwich and beer for an unmatched NIS37 from 11:30pm-7am. Working students enjoy the free Wi-Fi at the collection of tables outside, or climb the elegant old wooden staircase to the quiet study area on the 2nd floor. Homemade roast beef sandwich NIS40. Balsamic portobello salad NIS40. Hot drinks NIS8-19. Beer NIS21-28. Open 24hr. Accept credit cards. ❷

Giraffe Noodle Bar, 49 Ibn Gvirol St. (☎03 691 6294), between Netsach Israel and ha-Shoftim St. Take bus #89 from New Central Bus Station. From Dizengoff Sq., walk up Reines St. to Frishman and turn right. Walk east on Frishman and turn right on Ibn Gavirol St., then walk south several blocks. Bustling local favorite with an undercurrent of techno, floor-to-ceiling windows, and a young hip crowd. Asian fusion dishes are excellent, with large helpings and attractive layout: but where are the giraffes? Sushi combo NIS52. Fried rice NIS47. Open daily noon-1am. Credit cards accepted. ❷

Goocha, 171 Dizengoff St. (☎03 522 2886), at the corner with Ben-Gurion St. Eat fresh and excellent seafood to Bob Marley in a fishbowl of a restaurant, with full-length windows and a large bouquet of white lilies in the center of the blond wood bar. The seasoning of the mixed seafood platters is particularly divine, and definitely not kosher. Butter and garlic shrimp NIS52. Mixed seafood in cream and garlic NIS59. Open daily noon-1am or last customer. ❷

Atza, 128 Ben-Yehuda St. (☎03 527 0017), at the corner with Ben-Gurion St. Take bus #230 from New Central Station. An Israeli sushi bar with a Mary J. Blige soundtrack, Ukrainian waitresses, and a friendly Burmese kitchen staff, Atza epitomizes Tel Aviv's growing status as a globalized city. Small with bright geometric patterns printed on the white walls and a counter made of chopsticks. Sushi is remarkably well priced and creatively assembled; check out the use of sweet potato. Avocado maki NIS13. Sweet potato tempura with avocado and chives NIS19. Open Su-W 9am-1am, Th 9am-3am, F 11am-3am, Sa 3pm-1am. Credit cards accepted. ❶

Toto, 4 Berkovitch St. (☎03 693 5151), off Weizmann St., near the Tel Aviv Art Museum. Unfortunately most accessible by taxi; the upside is that the taxi will be the least expensive part of your evening. Toto's is a splurge: the food is some of the most delicious in town, the guests are refined, and the prices astronomical. Save up, don your most casual chic outfit, and pull out the stops (and your credit card) for birthdays or anniversaries. Soft polenta with crispy sweetbread in wild mushroom broth NIS78. Risotto with sweet corn sant Jacques and black velvet NIS96. Open daily noon-3pm and 7pm-midnight. Credit cards accepted. ❹

Hashdera 34, 34 Ben-Gurion St. (☎072 270 2600), between Dizengoff St. and Emile Zola St. Popular seafood restaurant with a young crowd, excellent prices, and christmas lights roped above the bar. The transparent plastic curtains that substitute for walls and windows are drawn up in the evenings when it's not too hot and not too cool, providing lovely terraced seating. Seafood plate NIS50. *Schnitzel* NIS35. Open daily noon-1am. Credit cards accepted. ❷

Thai House, 8 Bograshov St. (☎03 517 8568), at the corner with Ben-Yehuda St. Take bus #230 from New Central Station. While not as heavily spiced as the pad thai in the United States or, perhaps, Thailand, the Thai House is the real thing. The restaurant is run by a Thai woman and her Israeli husband and the kitchen is outfitted exclusively with Thai chefs. Brings a refreshing dose of the Far East to the Middle East, including a large collection of wooden Buddhas seated at the bamboo-thatch bar—no better drinking companion. Coconut milk delicacies NIS64-NIS69. Wok sautees NIS56-69. Reservations recommended. Credit cards accepted. ❸

NORTH TEL AVIV

▧ **Benedict,** 171 Ben-Yehuda St. (☎03 544 0345; www.benedict.co.il), on the corner with Jabotinsky St. Take bus #230 from New Central Station. Another branch is located at the corner of Rothschild Blvd. and Allenby St. in south Tel Aviv. Whether you stumble into their restaurant at 10am for breakfast, 10pm for dinner, or 3am after a night of partying, the waiters of Benedict will always greet you with a hearty "Good morning!" An immensely popular Tel Aviv institution, Benedict serves fresh eggs, pancakes, French toast, and other breakfast foods in a variety of styles at all hours. The midnight breakfast (NIS39) served midnight-8am is a particularly good deal for insomniacs. Israeli breakfast NIS46. Healthy morning breakfast NIS41. Open 24hr. Credit cards accepted. ❷

▧ **Hummus Ashkara,** 45 Yermiyahu St. (☎03 546 4547), 1 block up from Yermiyahu's intersection with Dizengoff St. Take bus #174 from New Central Bus Station to Dizengoff St. Widely acknowledged as 1 of the best hummus joints in Tel Aviv, Hummus Ashkara is open 23hr. a day (they have the audacity to stop between 2am and 3am to clean) and serves deep bowls of fresh, thick hummus for NIS20. Great value, especially for ritzy north Tel Aviv. Hummus NIS20, with egg NIS23. Open Su-Th 3am-2am, F 3am-5pm, Sa 8pm-2am. Cash only. ❶

▧ **Jeremiah,** 306 Dizengoff St. (☎077 793 1840), at the corner with Yermiyahu St. Take bus #174 from New Central Station. Hip and artsy coffee shop with modern art paintings in odd corners. The bar is part of a 12 ft. bookshelf stacked with both an excellent selection of liquor and an assortment of deliberately random objects, from birdhouses to typewriters to model cars and ships. Black coffee NIS10. Market salad NIS39. Schnitzel NIS44. Open Su-F 7:30am-2am, Sa 9am-2am. Credit cards accepted. ❷

Ha-Suka ha-Levana, 1 Yordei Hasira St (☎03 682 6558; hasukahalevana.rest-e. co.il), right on the Port at the southern end of the main boardwalk. Kosher seafood restaurant serves massive fresh, filleted fish. Dinner NIS60-NIS120. Open daily noon-2am. Credit cards accepted. ❸

Cafe Michal, 230 Dizengoff St. (☎03 523 0236), on the corner with Jabotinsky St. Peaceful, quaint cafe with rows of white teacups and 2 bundt cakes in round glass cases on the scuffed, dark wood counter; a dignified old Victorian love is seated in the corner by the windows. The outdoor seating is sequestered from the street by a white iron gate and a flourishing green row of planter boxes. Black coffee NIS9. Potato gnocchi NIS42. Mozzarella sandwich NIS28. Open daily 8am-midnight. Credit cards accepted. ❷

SOUTH TEL AVIV

▨ **Buddha Burgers,** 21 Yehuda ha-Levy St. (☎03 510 1222; www.buddhaburgers. co.il), off Herzl St. before the intersection with Rothschild Blvd., at the border of Neve Tzedek. Rumored to be the best vegan restaurant in Israel, Buddha Burgers serves burgers to die for (tell that to the cow). It also hosts a famous, remarkably well-priced salad bar with all organic ingredients. Provides numerous opportunities for its patrons to promote or donate to animal rights groups. Anticipate a line out the door, and sometimes winding around the block. Salads NIS18-NIS30. Burgers NIS22-NIS30. Open Su-W 11am-midnight, Th 11am-1am, F 11am-5pm, Sa from the end of Shabbat to midnight. Credit cards accepted. ❶

▨ **Iceberg** (☎03 522 5025), at the corner of Rothschild Blvd. and Allenby St. Another location at 108 Ben-Yehuda St. in the city center. Like Moses' or Benedict, Iceberg is one of those Tel Aviv places that the young and the beautiful are required to know about in case they get the munchies for the all-natural, creative, and delicious ice cream sold here. Apricot walnut. Pecan butter. Pears and wine. Just the names of Iceberg's many flavors make the mouth water. Mixes its ice cream somewhere in the Port and prides itself in being "100% low-tech," and the result is somehow an intensification of flavor. Small cup NIS18, large NIS24. Open daily 11am-4am. Credit cards accepted. ❶

▨ **Tamar Cafe,** 57 Shienkin St. (☎03 685 2376), 1 block up from the intersection with Rothschild Blvd. on the righthand side of the st. A vibrant and quintessentially Tel Aviv-ian cafe that has been immortalized by a series of indie artists. The Israeli pop trio Mango incorporated it into one of their songs. The cafe's walls are haphazardly decorated with original, framed political cartoons, each of which features Sarah, the cafe's owner, either conversing with, laughing at, or bitch-slapping a variety of political symbols or figures. The renowned cartoonist was apparently a beloved regular. Open daily 7am-8pm. Credit cards accepted. ❷

Suzanna, 9 Shabazi St. (☎03 517 7580), across the street from the Suzanne Dellal center. Airy restaurant with yellow and blue tile floors and a wide terrace overlooking the Center across the street. Creative interpretations of Iraqi cuisine. Try the prize puff pastries, monster egg rolls of creative combinations of food and seasonings wrapped in filo dough. The chicken, prune juice, and raisin pastry is particularly divine. Plate of varied stuffed dishes NIS66. Shrimp in olive oil, lemon, and garlic NIS74. Open Su-Th 10am-1am, F 9:30am-1am, Sa 10am-1am. Credit cards accepted. ❸

Moses' Modern American Kitchen, 35 Rothschild Blvd. (☎*9449; www.mosesrest. co.il), at the corner of Rothschild Blvd. and Yavne St.; look for the egg-yolk yellow, floppy awning. Simply put, Moses' is an institution. Chow down on dense fresh hamburgers and generous portions of hot french fries on a veranda crowded with beautiful young people at all hours of morning and night. The business menu starts at midnight; a burger and side order goes for a bargain NIS36. Classic Moses beef burger (100% prime cut) NIS42. Mania ribs NIS88. Open Su-W and Sa 10:30am-4am, Th and F 10:30am-4:30am. Reservations recommended after midnight on F and Sa. Credit cards accepted. ❷

Sous Etz, 20 Sheinkin St. (☎03 528 7955), 1 block from Sheinkin's intersection with Magen David Sq. Bustling with highly-fashionable young people, Sous Etz is the ideal place to sit and people-watch as throngs of eccentrics from Magen David Sq. and Shei-nkin St. converge. 2 men carefully placing a mannequin wrapped in tinfoil and missing several limbs into the trunk of their car, a cheerful Orthodox couple carrying yoga mats and medicine balls as they stroll toward the market—it's all here. Goat cheese sandwich NIS37. Fettuccini NIS43. Open daily 7:30am-midnight. Credit cards accepted. ❷

Nina, 29 Shabazi St. (☎02 508 4141), at the intersection with Ativa St. Located in the heart of Neve Tzedek, Nina Cafe is one of the best known haunts for students, artists, and people who want to look like artists. The intimate seating area has an old brown piano in 1 corner and a dignified, wall-length bookshelf in another, which hosts an eclectic mix of Hebrew, English, and Italian fiction. Open Su-Th 7:30am-midnight, F 7:30am-7pm, Sa 5pm-midnight. Credit cards accepted. ❷

Rothchild's Kitchen, 73 Rothschild Blvd. (☎03 525 7177). Creative and diverse bistro with Frank Sinatra-style covers of Nirvana songs playing in the background and an oddly soothing collection of plates decorating the walls. Located in the heart of the neighborhood. Lovely outdoor tables with crisp white tablecloths, overlooking the local International Style architecture and the leisurely promenade. Pasta primavera NIS51. Chicken schnitzel NIS54. Open Su-Th 11am-2am, F-Sa 9am-3am. Credit cards accepted. ❷

Sub Kuch Milega, 22 Hamashbir St. (☎03 681 3412; www.subkuchmilega.com), in the Florentine neighborhood. Hamashbir branches off Yafo Rd. between its intersections with Allenby St. and Herzl St., right before its intersection with Herzl. Take buses #201 or 163 from Central bus station. You've seen the hostel (see **Accommodations,** p. 168); now meet the equally hilarious restaurant below it. A long narrow room with a blue-tinted tropical fish tank, exposed wiring on the faded ceiling, and a black feather boa hanging with an old map of Tel Aviv's neighborhoods on the orange walls. The mix of South Asian and Israeli cuisine on the menu first comes across as suspicious (muesli and *lassi* together?), but the cheap food is surprisingly tasty. Try the Nepalese momos: 2 freshly fried dumplings for NIS18, with the added bonus of bonding with the restaurant's 2 dogs, is a bargain. Vegetarian. *Malai kofta* NIS35. *Alu goby* NIS33. Open Su-F 11am-4am, Sa noon-4am. Credit cards accepted. ❷

◉ SIGHTS

While Tel Aviv may not boast a laundry list of ancient synagogues and castles, its youthful and quintessentially cool neighborhoods supplement the short list of highlights. **Neve Tzedek,** just west of the intersection of Herzl St. and Akhad ha-Am St., is Tel Aviv's oldest Jewish neighborhood outside of Jaffa and one of the few with a 100-year-old history. The area is being gradually renovated to accommodate local artists and yuppies attracted to the Mediterranean-village charm of its narrow streets and stone architecture. Happily unrenovated is the **Yemenite Quarter** (the Yemenite Quarter), northwest of Allenby St. and King George St., near the **Carmel Market.** This area firmly maintains its village feel despite relentless skyscraper construction all around it.

Those who wish to soak in the newness of Tel Aviv's culture congregate at the waterfront **promenade,** where pre-teens neck, vendors hawk, and folk dancers strut their stuff all night long. The wide sidewalks of **Dizengoff Street** are still among the more crowded catwalks in town, though they are no longer at the peak of their glory due to the mutant-growth of shopping arenas in the area. The young and the restless generally roam here and on **Sheinkin Street,** while the bold and the beautiful head uptown to the northern parts of **Dizengoff Street, Ibn Gvirol Street,** and **Basel Street.** The drunk and short-skirted habitually prowl **Tel Aviv Port** at night.

CITY CENTER

Extending from **Bograshov Street** to the south to **Arlozorov Street** in the north, from **Ibn Gvirol Street** to the east to the Mediterranean to the west, the city center is largest and most bustling part of Tel Aviv. More evidently urban (read: grungy) than most of Tel Aviv, it lacks the idiosyncratic charm of the south or the ritz and kitsch of the north, but makes up for it with its high concentration of things people need: restaurants, movie theaters, and basic shopping opportunities, not to mention some very good bars. The main hubs here are **Dizengoff Square** and, to its south, **Dizengoff Center,** where **Dizengoff Street** and **Hamelekh George Street** intersect at a colossal urban mall with a Superpharm,

Steimatzky's, McDonald's, and every other chain you hate but will inevitably need to buy something from during your stay. Look out for street fairs, sweet graffiti art (amid the not-so-cool random tags), and the occasional impromptu bacchanalia hosted by bars celebrating important birthdays, anniversaries, or just looking for an excuse to start a party on a Wednesday afternoon.

KIKKAR YITZHAK RABIN. Formerly Kikkar Malkhei Yisrael (Kings of Israel Sq.), the square was renamed in 1995 in memory of Prime Minister Yitzhak Rabin. On November 4, 1995, Rabin was assassinated by Yigal Amir, a Jewish student, during a crowded peace rally. The square has since drawn mourners who once placed large painted portraits of Rabin and left candles, flowers, and poetry at the sight. Today, a lush oasis of greenery surrounding a massive, iron sculpture is a peaceful respite from the bustle of the city, and much more attractive than the rundown City Hall that sits opposite on the plaza. The official memorial is next to the City Hall. *(Just off Ibn Gvirol St., between Arlozorov St. and Ben-Gurion St.)*

DIZENGOFF SQUARE. The capital of the maze that is Dizengoff St. hosts an ever-changing scene, from retirees feeding pigeons in the midday sun to late-night punks cluttering the overpass stairs. The revolving, multicolored, slightly fading fountain, designed by illustrious Israeli artist Agam, crowns the square in an unsurpassed celebration of municipal kitsch. The tunes come from the fountain itself, which orchestrates its own hourly multimedia show to music ranging from Ravel's *Bolero* to Israeli folk songs. *(At the intersection of Dizengoff St., Ben-Ami St., and Pinsker St.)*

NORTH TEL AVIV

TEL AVIV PORT. The port itself may be inactive, but Tel Aviv Port most definitely is not; a recently renovated strip of (overpriced) seafood restaurants and swanky clubs hugging the water and docks, the Port is one of the most popular hangouts in Tel Aviv, with enough free-flowing liquor per square inch to fill several Olympic swimming pools. The neighborhood may only be 1km long, but it is so densely packed with entertainment opportunities that it even has its own website (www.namal.co.il) to provide a calendar for different upcoming events. **Nemal Tel Aviv Street** is the main drag.

LITTLE TEL AVIV. East of the Port is Little Tel Aviv, where cute cafes and Israeli designer clothing stores cluster around **Dizengoff Street** as soon as it crosses **Jabotinsky Street.** If you've got an invite to the Oscars or just want to look like a runway model regardless of the credit card debt incurred, this neighborhood is made for you. Dizengoff St. also becomes less grungy once it escapes the city center, and it transforms into a lovely place to simply meander through on a hot afternoon.

TEL AVIV UNIVERSITY. Home to the superb **Beit ha-Tfutzot** (see **Museums,** p. 180), the university remains Ramat Aviv's star attraction. The vast central lawn is flanked by palm trees, well-kept memorial gardens, and Modernist sculptures. When facing the fountains, the first building on the rights is the **Sourasky Central Library.** From here, the gently sloping path leads directly to the glitzy new main gate complex on Levanon St. The **Genia Schreiber University Art Gallery,** in the pink pavilion right next to the gate, keeps its modern art collection on the cutting edge by changing it every two months. Students give a free **Tel Aviv University Architectural and Art Tour** every Monday at 11am; it departs from the Dyonon bookstore next to the art gallery, and highlights the campus' unique Bauhaus and neo-postmodern architecture. *(Take bus #74 from the center of town to get to the Uni-*

versity gate. Library phone ☎ 03 640 8423. Gallery ☎ 03 640 8860. Library open Su-Th 9am-8pm, F 9am-12:30pm. Gallery open Su-Th 11am-7pm. Library NIS27 for non-students. Gallery free.)

ZOOLOGICAL CENTER. This combination drive-through safari park, circus, and zoo features 250 acres of African game in a natural habitat. Stare over the *wadi* at impossible cute gorillas and Syrian bears, or let an ostrich poke its head into your car for a bite of candy. People without picnics can have lunch at the moderately-priced restaurant, and those without a car can ride through the habitat in the park's own vehicles. Pedestrian tours offered as well. *(Take bus #501 from New Central Bus Station. From the bus stop, go 500m down ha-Tzvi Blvd; the park entrance is on the right. ☎ 1 800 382 829. NIS49, students NIS42.)*

SOUTH TEL AVIV

ROTHSCHILD BOULEVARD, ALLENBY STREET, AND SHIENKIN STREET

A network of historic promenades and lovely side streets defined by the triangle formed by **Rothschild Boulevard, Allenby Street,** and **Shienkin Street's** intersections with each other, this neighborhood's relaxing, shaded walkways and high concentration of restaurants make it one of the most leisurely places in the city to explore. Many of Tel Aviv's historic sites and architectural wonders are concentrated here, particularly around Rothschild Blvd., a street named after the tremendously influential Rothschild family. Ben-Gurion declared Israel's independence from 16 Rothschild Blvd., and the original headquarters Haganah, the paramilitary predecessor to the IDF, is located only a few doors down. Tel Aviv's haggard "White City" is concentrated here, and most of the buildings are named after the original, founding families who once lived there.

Perhaps more immediately relevant to your stay here, this area is also home to several Tel Aviv food institutions to which young people flock with almost rabid devotion for hangover cures at the wee hours of the morning; consequentially, the neighborhood is rapidly becoming the height of cool. The Port might have the beach and sweaty discoteques, but **Shienkin Street** has the indie cafes and the hip cheap shops that sell everything from designer sunglasses to flimsy party tank tops.

▧**THE WHITE CITY.** UNESCO named Tel Aviv's White City a World Heritage Site in 2003, and to the uninformed eye the reasoning behind their decision is initially elusive. Even now that these International Style buildings are internationally renowned, few of them have been properly renovated, and the result is that much of the White City is scuffed gray with peeling paint. Unless you know where to look, even the renovated buildings tend to innocuously disappear between the flashier modern buildings that now surround them; International Style, after all, prided itself in its simplicity and lack of unnecessary decoration. Built in the 1920s and 1930s by followers of the German Bauhaus School for Art and Design, International Style is characterized by its thin rounded balconies, crisp angles, and (yes) white walls. Bauhaus was one of the first modernist movements in architecture, and you might recognize its influence on the more recent modernist buildings of today. The International Style was brought to Israel by young Zionist architects who had been educated in the style and the modernist ideals of the Bauhaus School. Its concentration in Tel Aviv reflects a convergence of several accelerating ideologies from the 1920s, which would eventually define the course of the 20th century: modernism, socialism, and political Zionism. Some of the buildings themselves might not look like much, but they sure represent a powderkeg of ideas.

Hunting for International Style architecture in Tel Aviv is also an excuse to meander down Rothschild Blvd., Allenby St., and the surrounding area, whose green shaded promenades and corner cafes make it one of the most picturesque areas in Tel Aviv. This walking tour hits some of the more prominent buildings of the White City, as well as some of the neighborhood's museums, political history, favorite restaurants, and other sites. It should take no longer than 1½hr. Visit the **Bauhaus Center** for guided tours of Tel Aviv's architectural sites. *(99 Dizengoff St., 1 block up from Dizengoff Sq. ☎ 03 522 0249; www.bauhaus-center.com. Open Su-Th 10am-7:30pm, F 10am-2:30pm. Tours F 10am; US$15.)*

GUTMAN FOUNTAIN. Begin your walk at the very bottom of Rothschild St., where it dead ends. Theoretically, you will see this impressive and dreamlike fountain; the masterpiece has recently been moved there from its original home on Bialik St., though as of this writing, construction has yet to be finished. Nachum Gutman was a famous Israeli painter, engraver, and children's book writer who bore witness to Israel's growth from a few scattered Zionist enclaves under the Ottoman Empire to a powerful nation state. He also played a key role in forging a distinctly Israeli artistic style throughout the 1920s, 1930s, and 1940s. The fountain, which Gutman produced toward the end of his life in the 1970s, is not an example of International Style, but is something you have to see all the same. Incredibly intricate, it traces Jaffa and Tel Aviv's 4000 years of history. Check out Gutman's vivid and surreal depictions of everything from Jonah being swallowed by the fish to the early 20th-century settlements of his youth. *(1 Rothschild Blvd.)*

DIZENGOFF HOUSE AND THE FOUNDER'S MONUMENT. From the fountain, walk up Rothschild Blvd to the Dizengoff House and the Founder's Monument. The monument was installed on March 23, 1951 to memorialize the site of Tel Aviv's first town hall. A white, tombstone-shaped block facing a low fountain with green water, the western side of the monument neatly lists the names of 66 founding families who made the initial move from Neve Tzedek, the first neighborhood build by Jewish settlers in the region, to settle what is now the greater Tel Aviv area. On the opposite side of the monument is a **bronze tableau** by Aharon Priver, which depicts the history of Tel Aviv's development. Next to the monument is a bronze statue of **Meir Dizengoff,** the first mayor of Tel Aviv, riding a horse. His old home, aptly called **Dizengoff House,** is on the south side of the street; also known as **Independence Hall,** David Ben-Gurion declared the founding of the state of Israel here on May 14, 1948. *(On the promenade that runs down the center of the Blvd., across from 16 Rothschild Boulevard.)*

GOLOMB HOUSE. During the British Mandate, this building was the headquarters of the Haganah, the paramilitary organization that later morphed into the modern-day IDF. The building was (somewhat understandably) slated for demolition until Haganah veterans intervened, purchasing and renovating it. It now houses the **Haganah Museum** (see **Museums,** p. 176). *(23 Rothschild Blvd., down the street from Dizengoff House.)*

LEDERBERG HOUSE. The intersection on which the house is found displays the walk's first real examples of International Style architecture. Lederberg House is recognizable by Abraham Eisenberg's colorful ceramic designs embedded in the building's facade, which depict landscapes of Eretz-Israel and Biblical tales. The building is now home to South Tel Aviv's branch of **Benedict** (see **Food,** p. 171). The graying, domed building on the south side of the street is another good example of the 1920s architectural style. Across the street from Benedict on the eastern side of the street is **Iceberg** (see **Food,** p. 172), another immensely popular place that young people flock to after barhopping all night. *(At the corner of Rothschild Blvd. and Allenby St. Lederberg House is on the north side of the street.)*

GREAT SYNAGOGUE. The fading and water-damaged facade of the Great Synagogue is on the left, at 110 Allenby St. Completed in 1926 and renovated in 1970, this huge domed building showcases arched and stained-glass windows that are replicas of those from European synagogues that were later destroyed in the Holocaust. *(110 Allenby St. Turn left up Allenby St. and walk up the street for a little over a block, past Shabazi St. ☎ 03 560 4905 or 560 4066. Open Su-Th 10am-5pm, Sa 7:30am-11:30am. Sa prayer open to the public; head coverings and modest dress required.)*

LEVIN HOUSE. Perhaps the best renovated example of Bauhaus architecture in the city, Levin House will give you an idea of what much of Tel Aviv's White City area would look like if it were patched up and repainted. Originally built in 1924 as the Levin family's dream house, it was referred to as the Castle, probably because of its prominent turret. After becoming the Embassy of the Soviet Union, the building was bombed in 1953 by an activist who was passionate about the plight of Soviet Jewry and evidently apathetic toward architectural history. It was restored in the 1990s. *(On the corner of Rothschild Blvd and Shadai St.)*

KING ALBERT SQUARE. There is a shaded bench on the traffic island in the center of the quiet intersection, and you can sit there to take in the architectural eccentricity surrounding you. As far as 1920s architecture is concerned, look for the **Pagoda House** at the intersection of Nahmani and Montefiore streets. The eclectic **Shafran House** is built at the northern corner of Melchett St. *(To get to the square, turn left on Bezalel Yafe St., and walk 2 blocks to its intersection with Melcett St. and Nahmani St. For Shafran House, take Nahmani St. back down to Rothschild Blvd. and continue walking, stopping again within a block at Rothschild's intersection with Mazeh St.)*

ENGEL HOUSE AND BERLIN HOUSE. Roughly across the street from each other, both houses represent a remarkable before-and-after study in stylistic contrasts. The Engel House is quintessential International Style, and one of the best known buildings in the White City; make sure to note the elongated, rounded balconies and the long horizontal windows. Unfortunately, as of this writing, the building is also ugly as sin, gray, crumbling, and haphazardly patched with unpainted stucco. The tourist office assures tourists that the building is slated for renovation. Far better preserved is the Berlin House across the street. Once the personal residence of architect Joseph Berlin, it epitomizes his art deco tastes. *(Engel House at 84 Rothschild Blvd., at its intersection with Mazeh St. Berlin House is at 83 Rothschild Blvd., at its intersection with Balfour St; a few storefronts up from the Engel House, despite the numbering.)*

RUBINSKY HOUSE AND CASTLE HOUSE. The last stop in this walking tour, the Rubinsky House is crisp, bright, and airy. It is another paragon of the International Style, and one of the most impressively preserved. While a bit more cleaned up than its counterpart next door, the Castle House is equally impressive and gives off a distinct air of mystery, emerging from the local overgrown, jungle-like gardens. It is more ornate than its neighbor, and together they embody International Style's range in appearance, both in original artistic choice and current upkeep. *(For the Rubinsky House, walk up Rothschild St. to Shienkin St. and turn right. The house is several buildings in on the left hand side at 65 Shienkin, at its corner with residential Gilboa St. Castle House is at 3 Gilboa St.)*

YEMENITE QUARTER

Six-year-old twin girls in matching lavender Hello Kitty nightgowns offer tourists a red plastic bucket with two sleeping ducklings inside. An elderly woman with fire-engine-red lipstick sing covers of Israeli pop songs with a heavy vibrato to an amused audience. Welcome to **David Magen Square,** the epicenter of south Tel Aviv and arguably the city as a whole, as well as the main stop in the historic Yemenite Quarter. Characterized by the hunched water-damaged buildings with wrought iron balconies that line its windings streets, David Magen Square marks the convergence of **Allenby Street, Hemelekh George Street, Nahalat Benyamin Street, ha-Carmel Street,** and **Shienkin Street** into a thoroughly trafficked, star-shaped point. Like all Tel Aviv neighborhoods, don't forget to explore the forgotten alleyways.

CARMEL MARKET. Crowded to the point of fire hazard on and around ha-Carmel St. extending from David Magen Sq., the Carmel Market is Tel Aviv's vibrant and belovedly funky *shuk*. Like the entrepreneurs of the ever self-respecting *shuk*, the market's street venders shout aggressively at pedestrians to buy everything they do and do not need, from pyramids of spices in reed baskets to bootleg Middle Eastern music to knock-offs of brand-name bras and sneakers. Relinquish all concepts of elbow room and personal space, get ready to bargain, and enjoy.

NAHALAT BINYAMIN STREET. Animated by lovely architecture and an eccentric arts and crafts market, Nahalat Binyamin St. also extends into the Yemenite Quarter from David Magen Sq., and represents what much of the quarter would look like with a few renovations. The arts and crafts market features everything from surprisingly professional street musicians to ceramic menorahs to hairclips made of popcorn. Stop by for a slightly less frenetic experience after braving the Carmel Market.

BIALIK STREET. While not technically part of the Yemenite Quarter, Bialik St. is nearby, stemming off Allenby St. right after Magen David Sq.'s intersection with Hamelekh George St. This small, lovely street carries inordinate weight in the history of Israeli art; it was once the home of both renowned artist Reuven Rubin and national poet Chaim Nachman Bialik, after whom the street is now named. The **Rubin Museum** and **Beit Bialik,** both on this street, memorialize these artists' respective works (see **Museums,** p. 180).

MORE OF THE WHITE CITY. If you're not tired of International Style buildings after walking up Rothschild St., some of the best preserved examples of Tel Aviv's White City are also on Nahalat Binyamin St. The **Palm House,** at 8 Nahalat Binyamin St., both embodies the Style and creatively expands upon it, making it a must see for anyone interested in Bauhaus. A minute's walk down the street is the lovely **Rambam Square,** the intersection of Nahalat Binyamin St. and Rambam St. The building on the eastern side of the street, at 16-22 Rambam St., is the **House of Pillars;** the house on the western side of the street, across from Nahalat Binyamin, is called the **House of Jars.** The **Nordau Hotel** is situated at 27 Nahalat Binyamin St. at the street's intersection with Gruzenberg St. An art-deco gem from the 1920s, the lovely hotel has since been renovated and painted the color of raspberry sherbet. Look for its gray, gleaming dome.

NEVE TZEDEK

A horse drawn cart of coat racks and old wire baskets, followed by two chic and beautiful people on a puttering green Vespa, followed by a paunchy, sweating man pushing a shopping cart with an ornate bathtub. This could only happen in Neve Tzedek, Tel Aviv's oldest Jewish neighborhood and a constellation of tangled, artsy alleyways. Wander between the cafes and galleries along the shaded streets. Be sure to stop in at the **Suzanne Dellal Center** along the way; the complex of airy buildings and courtyards used to be an all-girls' school, and now houses a number of theaters, exhibiting music groups, dance troupes, and other performances year-round (see **Entertainment,** p. 182).

FLORENTINE

A rundown network of creaky historical buildings obscured by peeling paint and clumps of bare wiring, the Florentine, as its residents like to say, will be what Neve Tzedek is now in several years, as Neve Tzedek becomes too cool for school and the rent slowly becomes too high for the artists that live there. As it stands now, the Florentine is fast becoming a study in transition. Because renovations often fall to shop owners rather than building managers, look out for patchwork Bauhaus buildings exhibiting an almost comical identity crisis; it is not uncommon for a grayed neighborhood convenience store on a building's first floor to abruptly give way to a cherry red, gleaming office or studio on the second, only to be followed by the peeling blue shutters and overgrown window boxes of the apartment on the third.

🏛 MUSEUMS

🗐BEIT HA-TFUTZOT (THE DIASPORA MUSEUM). This museum chronicles the history of Jewish life outside of the land Israel, from the Babylonian exile (596 BCE) to the present day. A display of synagogue models show how Jews incorporated local architectural ideas in building their houses of worship; they resemble Italian villas, American ranches, and Chinese pagodas; there's even a model of a synagogue designed by architect Frank Lloyd Wright. Short films and multimedia displays throughout the museum highlight everything from the culture of the Yemenite Jewish community to the evolution of Yiddish theater. The museum also has a Genealogy Department that can trace the family trees of Jews whose relatives have registered. Check out the website to register for themed guided tours. *(On the Tel Aviv Unitersity Campus in Ramat Aviv. Take bus #74 from center of town to University gate. ☎03 745 7800; www.bh.org.il. Open M, T, Th 10am-4pm; W 10am-6pm; F 10am-1pm. NIS35, students NIS25. Credit cards accepted.)*

THE ERETZ YISRAEL MUSEUM. A veritable eight-ring circus, the Eretz Yisrael museum consists of eight pavilions covering vastly different topics spread over an archaeological site that is still being excavated. The most famous attraction in the complex is the **Glass Pavilion,** with one of the finest collections of glassware in the world. The **Nehushtan Pavilion,** with its cave-lake entryway, holds the discoveries of the excavations at the ancient copper mines if Timna, better known as **King Solomon's Mines,** located just north of Eilat. Across the patio, the **Kadman Numismatic Museum** traces the history of the region through ancient coins. The **Ceramics Pavilion** contains ancient Canaanite pottery, exhibits explaining its production, and artist Moshe Shek's ceramic sculptures. Across the entrance area, past the grassy crafts and techniques. Follow the road to the right and go up the stairs to reach the **Tel Qasile Excavations,** which have revealed a 12th-century BCE Philistine port city and ruins dating from around 1000 BCE. The area at the top of the hill contains the remains of three separate Philistine temples built on top of each other. Down the hill to the south are scattered remnants of the residential and industrial quarter of the city. Past the Philistine town is the **Folklore Pavilion,** with Jewish religious art, ceremonial objects, and ethnic clothing. The Eretz Yisrael complex also houses a library of over 30,000 books and periodicals (some in English) and the Lasky Planetarium. *(2 Levanon St., in Ramat Aviv, the northernmost part of the city. Take bus #501 from New Central Bus station. ☎03 641 5820; www.eretzmuseum.org.il. Open Su-W 10am-4pm, Th 10am-8pm, F and Sa 10am-2pm. NIS38, students NIS25.)*

TEL AVIV-JAFFA

TEL AVIV MUSEUM OF ART. The museum holds a sizeable collection of Israeli and international art. The handsome lobby boasts a Lichtenstein, and the museum itself runs the gamut from Impressionism (Renoir, Monet, Corot, and Pissarro) to Surrealism (including de Chirico and Magritte) to cutting-edge multimedia installations by more recent artists. Rotating thematic exhibits are exceptionally well-curated and range from "Music in Art" to "Stage Design"; local Israeli artists are prominently featured along with the curators' in-depth analyses of their work. An English program listing special exhibits and events is available in the ticket booth or the *This Week in Tel Aviv* insert in Friday's Jerusalem Post. *(27 Sha'ul ha-Melekh Blvd. Buses # 9, 18, 28, 70, 90, and 111 all stop nearby. ☎ 03 696 7361; tamuseum.co.il. Open M, W, Sa 10am-4pm; Tu and Th 10am-10pm; F 10am-2pm. NIS42, students NIS34.)*

HELENA RUBINSTEIN PAVILION OF CONTEMPORARY ART. This lovely museum houses mostly traveling exhibits of contemporary art. Many prominent Israeli artists got their start in the galleries here. The exhibits change frequently. The bad news is that as a result, the museum sporadically closes in order to install them; the good news is that the Pavilion never gets old. *(6 Tarsat Blvd., at its intersection with Dizengoff St., between Dizengoff's intersection with Ibn Gvirol St. and Hamelekh George St. Bus #5 stops nearby. ☎ 03 528 7196. Open M, W, Sa 10am-4pm; Tu and Th 10am-10pm; F 10am-2pm. Free, though admission to exhibits varies based on the artist.)*

RUBIN MUSEUM. Located in the former residence of Reuvin Rubin, this collection of his oil paintings represents the formative years of Israeli art. *(14 Bialik St., which branches off Allenby St. right after David Magen Sq. Buses #4, 16, 18, 24, and 25 all stop nearby. ☎ 03 525 5961; www.rubinmuseum.org.il. Open M, W-Th, and F 10am-3pm; Tu 10am-8pm; Sa 11am-2pm. NIS20, students NIS10.)*

HA-GANAH MUSEUM. This museum relates the history of the Israeli Defense Force (IDF). Two movies (in Hebrew and English) tell the stories of the Exodus, the first ship to make *aliya*, and the Palmah. *(23 Rothschild St., right before the street's intersection with Allenby St. Buses #4 and 5 stop nearby. ☎ 03 560 8624. Open Su-Th 8am-4pm. Free.)*

BEIT BIALIK MUSEUM. The former house of Hayim Nahman Bialik, one of Israel's greatest poets, now houses his manuscripts, photographs, articles, letters, and 94 books (with translations in 28 languages). The building is maintained almost exactly as it was when he died. *(22 Bialik St., which branches off Allenby St., right after David Magen Sq. Buses #4, 16, 18, 24, and 25 all stop nearby. ☎ 03 525 4530. Open Su-Th 9am-4:30pm, Sa 11am-2pm. Free.)*

DAVID BEN-GURION HOUSE. Peruse books, pictures, and mementos—including letters from Ben-Gurion to John F. Kennedy, Winston Churchill, and Charles de Gaulle—of Israel's first prime minister. In the Hillel Cohen Lecture Hall next door, invade Ben-Gurion's privacy even further as you examine his passports and one of his salary slips. *(17 Ben-Gurion Ave. ☎ 03 522 1010. Open Su and Tu-Th 8am-3pm, M 8am-5pm, F 8am-1pm, Sa 11am-2pm. Free.)*

🛍 SHOPPING

MALLS

If there's one thing Israelis love more than 80s music, it's huge shopping malls. Plan your dream wedding or the debutante ball you never had in the ritzy shops in Little Tel Aviv around **Dizengoff Street** and **Sderot Nordau.** Trendy clothing and jewelry boutiques line **Sheinken Street.** While many Tel Avivians fill their clubbing closets here, the price tags can be rather steep.

Azrieli Center, 132 Petah Tikvah Rd. (☎03 608 1198). Tallest mall in Israel—at least for now. Has a huge movie theater with the latest American fare.

Dizengoff Center (☎03 621 2416), close to the center of town. Overflows with stores, fast-food, video arcades, and 2 cineplexes.

Opera Tower, 1 Allenby St. (☎03 510 7496), at its intersection with the *tayelet.* Smaller selection of stores but sports a beautiful view of the Mediterranean.

Schwartz's Furs (☎03 517 6867), on the corner of Rambam and Nahalat Binyamin. Specializes in feather boas, Carnaval-style headdresses, and a growing collection of Venetian-inspired masks. Open Su-Th 9am-6pm, F 9am-2:30pm.

MARKETS

As rich with chic designers as the city may be, Tel Aviv is secretly the best friend of the down-and-dirty shopper: it pulses with street fairs almost every day. A full schedule of the markets are listed below, though keep in mind that the schedule is prone to change. The **Nahalat Benyamin Arts and Crafts Market** is particularly well known. The famed **Carmel Market,** at the intersection of Allenby Rd. and King George St., is open daily, with aggressive venders waving everything from Hello Kitty backpacks to bags of figs at passersby. **Bezalel Market,** a clothes market in Bezalel Street, is open daily, as is **Old Jaffa's flea market,** which features everything from antique rugs to cardboard boxes of ornate door knobs. Listed below are some of the most popular fairs in Tel Aviv.

Creative Artist's Fair, Dizengoff St., between Frishman St. and Dizengoff Sq. Exhibits original work by local artists. Open M noon-8pm, F 9am-4pm.

Antiques and Secondhand Fair, just off of Dizengoff Sq. Small, eclectic mix of everything from homemade barrettes to old tarnished lockets. Open Tu noon-10pm, F 8am-5pm.

Nahalat Benyamin Pedestrian Mall Crafts Market, crowded with the colorful stalls of local artists. Open W and F 10am-5pm.

Food Market, in Dizengoff Center. Internationally array of cheap ethnic food from the Tel Aviv community. Open Th 4-10pm and F 10:30am-4pm.

Shishpishim, Old Jaffa flea market. Funky exhibition of local arts and crafts, spiced by beer and high school musicians. Open July-Aug. 8pm-midnight.

THE HIDDEN DEAL

THE FINE ART OF HAGGLING

In any of Israel's numerous flea markets and *souqs*, all budget travelers must participate in one fundamental struggle: defending the honor of Anglophones everywhere by not getting ripped off (too much). Many describe bargaining as a dance, so to avoid stepping on anyone's toes or revealing that you have two left feet, keep the following tips in mind:

1. Learn the Hebrew for the numbers 1 through 10 and basic phrases (*"lo!" "kama zeh?"*—for more, see the **Appendix,** p. 414). If you can get through the experience without having to resort to English, more shekels to you.
2. Be prepared to walk away empty-handed and don't show too much interest in an item—every vendor from Akko to Jerusalem probably has 30 of them. If they discover you've become attached to an item, the battle is lost.
3. A counter-offer for half the offered price is generally appropriate, but use lower fractions for prices that seem unduly high.
4. At some point in the bargaining process, you are expected to start walking away; the salesmen generally reserve the biggest price drop for that point in the "dance."
5. Finally, if you really want something but the vendor just won't go down another shekel, keep in mind how much a shekel is actually worth (about a quarter) and just the chintzy little thing.

⚑ ENTERTAINMENT

LIVE MUSIC

Young Israeli rock bands have appointed Tel Aviv their headquarters and play at the clubs nightly. In addition, two amphitheaters at Hayarkon Park hold concerts. *Ha-Ir* (The Cirt), a weekly Hebrew magazine, has a section called Akhbar ha-Ir, with comprehensive listings. For listings in English, check the brochure *This Week in Tel Aviv*, produced by *Jerusalem Post*.

Comfort 13, 13 Comfort St. (☎54 773 7237; www.comfort13.co.il), in the Florentine. Take bus #40 to Eilat St. Comfort St. 2nd major intersection to the right on Eilat St., after Eilat's intersection with Elifelet. The name says it all. 2 dance floors and huge bar, with a variety of DJs and live shows. Trance night F. Prices vary based on the show and can be as much as NIS40; call in advance. Open Th-Sa 10pm-last customer.

Levontine 7, 7 Levontine St. (☎03 560 5084; www.myspace.com/levontine7), in the Florentine off Allenby St., before its intersection with Derech Jaffa Rd. One of the trendiest live music joints in the Florentine. Features everything from live jazz to some of Israel's most popular musicians. Shows NIS30-NIS60. Open F-Su 7:30pm-2am.

The Barby, 40 Salame Rd. (☎03 518 8123; www.barby.co.il), halfway between Herzl St. and Marzuk Veezar. Only accessibly by taxi. Look for a gray-striped awning or a big crowd. Some of the best rock bands in Israel and prominent bands from around the world frequent this garage-like space. Cover up to NIS100 for local acts, depending on band's fame. International bands NIS150-200. Open daily 9pm-late.

PERFORMING ARTS

THEATER

Habima Theater, 6 Tarsat Blvd. (☎03 526 6666; www.habima.co.il), on Tarsat Blvd. between Dizengoff St. and Bograshov St. Habima is Israel's national theater and its most respected. Its productions range from incendiary and groundbreaking new works from Israeli playwrights to much more traditional productions.

Beit Lessin, 101 Dizengoff St. (☎03 725 5333; www.lessin.co.il), after Dizengoff Sq. right before Dizengoff's intersection with Frishman St. Immensely popular both nationally and locally, which has helped foster a growing community of Israeli playwrights. Box office open Su-Th 9am-8pm, F 9am-1pm.

Tel Aviv Cameri Theater, 19 Shaul Hamelech Blvd. (☎03 606 0960 or 606 0900; www.cameri.co.il), several blocks east along Ha Nevi'im St. (which turns into Shaul Hamelech) from its intersection with Ibn Gvirol St.. The nation's biggest theater also offers simultaneous English translation at some performances.

MUSIC AND DANCE

Israeli Philharmonic Orchestra, Mann Auditorium, 1 Huberman St. (box office ☎03 621 1766; www.ipo.co.il), between Dizengoff St. and Sderot Ben Tsiyon St. Modern Israeli works as well as more internationally-known pieces.

Suzanne Delal Center, 5 Yehaiely St. (☎03 510 5656; www.suzannedellal.org.il), in Neve Tzedek. Take bus #8, 10, 25, or 61 from downtown or #40 or 46 from the New Central Bus Station. Specializes in indoor and outdoor dance, theater, and musical performances. The center houses a variety of different dance troupes, and is best known as the home of the **Bat Sheva Dance Company** (☎03 510 4037; www.batsheva.co.il), Israel's national dance company. Box office open daily 9am-7pm.

CINEMA

Tel Aviv Cinemathèque, 2 Sprinzak St. (☎03 691 7181; www.cinema.co.il), at the intersection with Carlebach St. Artsy favorite among local students, which specializes in both recent indie releases and re-releases of old classics.

Chen Cinema (☎03 528 2288), in Dizengoff Sq. Intimidatingly large cineplex that shows mostly mainstream releases.

VISUAL ARTS

Art galleries line **Gordon Street,** between Dizengoff St. and Ben-Yehuda St., and are scattered elsewhere throughout the city.

The Stern Gallery, 30 Gordon St. (☎03 524 6303; www.sternart.com). Showcases artwork by both classsic and up-and-coming Israeli and Jewish artists. Exhibits by Menashe Kadishman, Yigal Tumerkin, Anna Ticho, and other historic Israeli artists.

Sommer Contemporary Art, 13 Rothschild Blvd. (☎03 516 6400; www.sommergallery.com). Among the more prominent galleries in the city. Seen as a stepping stone for young local artists.

LIVE MUSIC

Young Israeli rock bands have appointed Tel Aviv their headquarters and play at the clubs nightly. In addition, two amphitheaters at Hayarkon Park hold concerts. *Ha-Ir* (The Cirt), a weekly Hebrew magazine, has a section called Akhbar ha-Ir, with comprehensive listings. For listings in English, check the brochure *This Week in Tel Aviv,* produced by Jerusalem Post.

Comfort 13, 13 Comfort St. (☎54 773 7237; www.comfort13.co.il), in the Florentine. Take bus #40 to Eilat St. Comfort St. 2nd major intersection to the right on Eilat St., after Eilat's intersection with Elifelet. The name says it all. 2 dance floors and huge bar, with a variety of DJs and live shows. Trance night F. Prices vary based on the show and can be as much as NIS40; call in advance. Open Th-Sa 10pm-last customer.

Levontine 7, 7 Levontine St. (☎03 560 5084; www.myspace.com/levontine7), in the Florentine off Allenby St., before its intersection with Derech Jaffa Rd. One of the trendiest live music joints in the Florentine. Features everything from live jazz to some of Israel's most popular musicians. Shows NIS30-NIS60. Open F-Su 7:30pm-2am.

The Barby, 40 Salame Rd. (☎03 518 8123; www.barby.co.il), halfway between Herzl St. and Marzuk Veezar. Only accessibly by taxi. Look for a gray-striped awning or a big crowd. Some of the best rock bands in Israel and prominent bands from around the world frequent this garage-like space. Cover up to NIS100 for local acts, depending on band's fame. International bands NIS150-200. Open daily 9pm-late.

▣ NIGHTLIFE

It's not clear what grown ups do in Tel Aviv—based on empirical observation, there might not actually be any. At night, Tel Aviv is ruled by the young, and the city's thriving nightlife has made it a kaleidoscope of cool and sexy for young people everywhere. Short-skirted women dance on the tables here, while young and fit men ask for their numbers within a minute of meeting them. From the grungiest of European backpackers to the most eager of American teens, students flock to the city to happily damage their ears, lungs, and livers, immersing themselves in the pounding music, smoky air, and drinks of the many local bars. Tel Aviv's party culture requires a hot outfit, cash for taxis, and a good deal of stamina. Most clubs and bars do not get hopping until at least 1am and don't close until 7am. The number of prominent restaurants that are open 24hr. or until 5am is a testament to how remarkably late most Tel Aviv party sessions run. The club and bar scene changes constantly, so consult publications such as *Time Out*, websites such as **www.telaviv4fun.com** or **www.telavivguide.net,** or local Tel Avivians for current hotspots. As of this writing, the clubs and bars here tend to follow a north-south gradation. The Port in the north is the ritziest, while the Florentine in the south keeps it the most "real." The farther North in the city you get, the less indie the nightlife will be. The city center is currently the least reliable of Tel Aviv's areas, with fewer establishments, but a handful of remarkable places can still be found. Thursday and Friday are the biggest party nights.

BARS

To get to a bar in Tel Aviv, walk for 10-15 seconds in any direction. Drinking—and looking uncommonly cool while doing it—is what this city does best. Each neighborhood's bars have a slightly different flavor. North Tel Aviv bars are more glamorous and expensive; they are also ideally located for pre-gaming a night of clubbing in the Port. South Tel Aviv is much more eclectic and alternative. Teenagers and college students opt out of the official bar scene altogether at the Rothschild Blvd. intersection with Hertzl St., camping out on the promenade with beer and wine from the nearby convenience stores to enjoy the fantastic evening weather. Bars gets artsier as you go South, particularly when you hit the Florentine, while the city center has fewer options.

CITY CENTER

▣ **70 Pilim,** 70 Bograshov (☎03 629 1777). From Dizengoff Sq., take Pinsker St. down to Bograshov and turn left. One of those innately cool places where everything just works. Warm and chic, the smoky bar is packed to capacity and beyond with hip and beautiful young people at all hours. Parties Aug.-June every F afternoon from 4pm. Beer NIS23-26. Vodka from NIS28. Open 9pm-last customer. Credit cards accepted.

▣ **Sex Boutique,** 122 Dizengoff St. (☎03 544 4555). From Dizengoff Sq., walk up Dizengoff past Frishman St.; on left-hand side before Gordon St. Let's just say that Sex Boutique is one of a kind. The sex shop in the basement sells a remarkable selection of festively colored and creatively sized vibrators, with posters that would even impress a San Francisco or Amsterdam native. The bar at street level is attractively backlit and sports large erotic pictures on the walls. Perhaps a little forward for parents, first dates, and impressionable high schoolers on Birthright. Gay friendly. Vibrators NIS50-1500. Beer NIS21-NIS28. Sex shop open 11am-1am. Bar open 11am-last customer. Credit cards accepted.

NORTH TEL AVIV

▣ **223,** 223 Dizengoff St. (☎03 544 6537), at the intersection with Jabotinsky St. Bus #35. Founded by local bartenders, 223 is a popular place for Tel Aviv's bartenders to go drink once they get off shift. Serves the best and most original mixed drinks in town. A crush of hipsters with horn-rimmed glasses and women in sundresses with exceptional tattoos pack into 223 at all hours to hangout at the gleaming counter. The atmosphere is both warm and the epitome of cool. The bright retro style, from the ornate gold picture frames to the suspenders the barmen wear, meshes eccentrically with the 80s soundtrack. Beer NIS22-26. Vodka NIS28-76, depending on the mixer. Open daily 7pm-last customer. Credit cards accepted.

▣ **Mate,** 222 Dizengoff St. (☎03 524 1615), near the intersection with Jabotinsky St. Take the #35 bus. Smoky English pub with a wide red pool table in the back room and a floor-to-ceiling bookshelf filled with aging liquor bottles. Among the few places in town where the patrons regularly wear jeans. The relaxed, all-ages crowd fosters a warm atmosphere. Beer NIS22-28. Happy hour 4-8pm. Open daily 4pm-the last customer. Credit cards accepted.

Eliezer, 186 Ben-Yehuda St. (☎050 322 3596), between the intersections of Ben-Yehuda St. with Arlozorov St. and Jabotinsky St. Sleek and friendly neighborhood bar with an exceptionally good selection of pounding pop music and a young, hip crowd. Even for Tel Aviv's bars, Eliezer is open late, frequently closing at 7am. Beer NIS24-26. 25+. Open daily 9pm-last customer. Credit cards accepted.

Kibbutz, Ha Ta'arucha St. (☎050 765 0089), on the Port 3. On your right when walking up Nemal Tel Aviv St, a block before Galina; look for the large curtains of white lights. The perfect place to pre-game. The Bob Dylan soundtrack, assortment of picnic tables, and mismatched armchairs make for a bustling but relaxing place to sit back and smoke a *nargileh* (NIS15). Beer NIS12-18. Cover NIS30. Open 7pm-last customer. Credit cards accepted.

SOUTH TEL AVIV

Nanutchka, 30 Lilenblum St. (☎03 516 2254), to the left of Lilenblum's intersection with Hertzl, when walking down Hertzl from Rothschild Blvd. Can be hard to find; look for the windows with the thick red curtains. This popular ▧**Georgian** restaurant and bar has something for everyone. The small outside courtyard's off-white umbrellas and thin barstools provide a quieter place to smoke and relax with friends. Most people come here for the wide and crowded bar, which is packed at all hours and known for its impromptu dance parties. Though there is no age limit, the crowd here tends to be a little older (i.e. late 20's-early 30's). *Chalapaly* NIS94. Kebabs NIS64. Mixed drinks NIS32-42. Open daily noon-late. Credit cards accepted.

Gilda, 64 Achad Ha'am St. (☎03 560 3588), at intersection of Achad Ha'am and Bezalel St. Can be a little hard to find; take Rothschild Blvd. past its intersections with Allenby St and Yavne St to Bezalel St., then turn left, walk a block, and turn right. Gilda's is on the left-hand corner; the door is on Achad Ha'am. Intimate and hip environment with a mix of Coldplay, Nirvana, and Israeli music, and the only spinning purple disco ball in Tel Aviv. Beer NIS22. Mixed drinks from NIS40. Make sure to hit their Su "Refuel": beer, wine, and champagne served all day, and the 2nd and 3rd drinks are only NIS10. Tu retro night. W Hebrew night. Gay friendly. Ages 27+. Open daily 8pm-last customer. Credit cards accepted.

Jackson, 4 Vital St., off Florentine St. Bus #18 stops on Derech Shlomo St, several blocks away. From Derech Shlomo, turn left onto Hertzl St., and left onto Florentine St. Walk 5 short blocks to Vital St. and turn right. Founded by a local Israeli musician, Jackson is a new neighborhood watering hole for the local artists. Charcoal sketches, bold murals, and posters for indie music performances showcase the work of the bar's patrons. Goldstar beer NIS23. Shots NIS17. W jazz night; frequented by guest DJs. Open daily 8pm-last customer. Credit cards accepted.

Abraxas, 40 Lilenblum St. (☎03 510 4435). The people are cool and they know it. Occasional exhibition of local art. Can get loud and sweaty, so it is more of a watering hole to pre-grame a long night of clubbing rather than a place to sit back and hang out. Goldstar beer NIS23. Shots NIS17. Open daily 8pm-last customer. Credit cards accepted.

CLUBS

Clubbing in Tel Aviv is a sweaty, claustrophobic, and altogether exhilarating affair that requires plenty of endurance and an ear to the ground. Hotspots change constantly and can be difficult to get into, with bouncers and glamorous, judgmental hostesses selecting their patrons at the door; if you are a guy, heighten your chances of getting in by going with an attractive woman. Many popular clubs also host events with varying age limits, hours, and entrance costs, so it's advisable to call before you go. Be aware that most clubs are 21+ and many are technically 25+, though some say they card irregularly. Tel Aviv Port's large former warehouses have been converted into some of the most trafficked clubs in the city, and the drunk and impeccably-dressed spend hours bouncing between them on weekends. The more alternative crowd prefers to hit the clubs in South Tel Aviv.

CITY CENTER

Ecopak, 2 Reines St. (☎03 523 7719), right by Dizengoff Sq. Take bus #174 from the New Central Bus Station. Ecopak is a hard place to pin down; each night is organized by a different guest group of people, who are charged with coming up with an exciting and eccentric new way to party. For the bar's 1 year anniversary, the booze started flowing at 4pm at a beach themed party with bean bags, inflatable swimming pools, and colossal speakers spilling into the streets of Dizengoff Sq. A recent theme in the works was to require all patrons to wear sandals... according to a friend of the manager's, just sandals. Be prepared for anything. Beer NIS21-27. Vodka NIS30-40. Open daily 10pm-last customer. Credit cards accepted.

TEL AVIV PORT

◪ Galina Hangar (☎03 544 5553). Walk up Nemal Tel Aviv St.; it's on the right after about 5min. Girls dressed like short-skirted supermodels dancing on the bar with the bartenders to **◪Michael Jackson.** Strobe lights, a fog of cigarette smoke, and thin vials of champagne create the ambience in what is currently considered the coolest place to dance in Tel Aviv. For those who would rather not dance like lunatics, there is a quieter outside seating area that overlooks the sea. Expect a ridiculously large crowd. Beer NIS27. Open daily 9pm-last customer. Credit cards accepted.

Whisky Gogo, 3 Ha Ta'arucha St. (☎03 544 0633). About a block before Galina on the main drag. Packed and sweaty dance club with a burlesque theme. The hexagonal mirrors that cover the walls floor-to-ceiling occasionally make the club look like a kaleidoscopic beehive. The light bulbs of the chandeliers are decorated with red mini-lampshades and blink in sync with the music beat. Beer NIS21-29. Open daily 9:30pm-last customer. Credit cards accepted.

Lehman Brothers (☎052 255 3333). Walk down Nemal Tel Aviv St. until you reach Beta Pizza, on the righthand side of the street. Take a left at the next sidestreet; Lehman Brothers is the 5th door down on the left. The aspiring rich and depressed, laid-off investment bankers converge to dance on bar counters or in conga lines to pounding dance tunes. Beer NIS24-26. Mixed drinks NIS32-62. Open daily 9:30pm-last customer. Credit cards accepted.

SOUTH TEL AVIV

◪ Artemis, 52 Nahalat Binyamin (☎03 510 663), a few doors down on the left from Nahalat Binyamin's intersection with Rothschild Blvd. Like 70 Pilim (p. 184), Artemis is one of those places that is simply the epitome of cool. Dance in the dimmed red light around the large, circular bar to pounding pop. It may be hard to get past the bouncers, but the vibe inside still manages to be exceptionally welcoming despite of the exclusivity. Look out for shows Th and F. Drinks from NIS24. Open daily 10pm-last customer. Credit cards accepted.

◪ Evita 3, Yavne St. (☎03 566 9559). Turn right on Yavne St. from Rothschild Blvd; the intersection is 1 block past the intersection of Rothschild and Allenby. Tel Aviv's most prominent gay bar and club. A high concentration of hot gay men cram themselves into

Evita's to dance beneath the classy hanging lights. While there only tend to be about 3 women in Evita at any given time, the bar is very friendly to members of all genders and sexualities; the manager is a veteran of the local LGBT community and will give pointers to any LGBT youth looking for hangouts. Beer NIS21. Vodka and redbull mixed drink (most popular) NIS43. Su Eurovision music. Tu drag night. W mature night (age 29+). Open daily 9pm-last customer. Credit cards accepted.

Lima Lima, 42 Lilenblum St. (☎03 560 0924). To the left of Lilenblum's intersection with Hertzl, when walking down Hertzl from Rothschild Blvd., about 1 block past Ninotchka. An immensely popular hangout, featuring regular concerts and guest DJs. Alternative and attractive people flock here to dance debaucherously or just lounge and drink on plush red sofas. Beer from NIS23. M Gay Night. Su and W concerts, with entrance tickets NIS10-15. Su and W-Th 21+, M-Th and F-Sa ages 25+. Open daily 9:30pm-last customer. Credit cards accepted.

Clara Beach and Bar (☎03 510 2060; table reservation 052 255 3333), near the Dolphinarium. At the Dolphinarium beach, follow the crowds of women in short skirts and high heels to this deserted looking, graffitied warehouse. You know that clique of gorgeous, exclusive, kind of bitchy girls you went to high school with? Yeah, they all go to Clara's. If the aloof young women at the door deem you suitable to enter, enjoy an attractively lit, sprawling outdoor bar and club on the edge of the Mediterranean, where beautiful people strike poses on the verandas, drink with friends at the tables, and pick up other beautiful people. Beer from NIS25. Whiskey from NIS530. Dress to impress. Cover F-Sa NIS20. Open daily 9pm-last customer. Credit cards accepted.

🚹 OUTDOOR ACTIVITIES

WALKS. Tel Aviv is easy to navigate (see **Orientation,** p. 159), but with few prominent historical landmarks or must-see-sights to use as reference points it can be a difficult city to actually get to know. The best way to acquaint yourself with it is to brave the formidable heat and take a very, very long walk. A stroll down the lovely **tayelet** along the Mediterranean takes about 1½hr., and skirts the edges of most of Tel Aviv's major areas, from **Old Jaffa** in the south to **Tel Aviv Port** in the north.

For a longer route that is less monotonous and more informative, trek uptown along Tel Aviv's main thoroughfares. To walk the full length of the city, start at Jaffa's famed **clock tower** and walk northeast along **Eilat Road,** which turns into **Yafo Road** as it enters the **Florentine.** Turn left on **Hertzel Street** and walk along the outskirts of **Neve Tzedek** to **Rothschild Boulevard.** Turn right on Rothschild Blvd. and then left on **Allenby Street,** and then take Allenby St. all the way up to the chaotic **David Magen Square.** At the Sq., turn onto **Hamelekh George Street** to go to the **Dizengoff Center.** From the center, turn left onto **Dizengoff Street** and take it all all the way up, through **Dizengoff Square,** the rest of the **city center,** and **Little Tel Aviv** to the Yarkon. Wear good walking shoes for this one: it should take a good 3hr., if not more. If you have extra time between bar-hopping and sunbathing, arrange to get lost in **Neve Tzedek** (p. 178) or the **Yemenite Quarter** (p. 177); both of these historic neighborhoods are pulsing with character.

BEACHES. Tel Aviv may party night after night, but somehow it manages to fit a busy day of sun and surf in between. All beaches have lifeguards on duty. (May-June and Sept.-Oct. 7am-5pm, July-Aug. 7am-7pm, and Nov.-Apr. 7am-2:30pm.) Theft can be a problem, so be sure to use the free safes at most hostels for any valuables you bring. From north to south, the most prominent beaches are **Metzizim, Hilton, Gordon, Frischmann** (at the ends of those streets), and the **Jerusalem Beach** at the end of Allenby Rd.; the last three are almost one continuous beach. Farther south are the **Banana Beach, the Dolphinarium, Alma Beach,** and **Jaffa Beach.** The southern coastline, with fewer amenities and luxury hotels, tends to be slightly less crowded and a little bit funkier; look out for the drugged-out Friday drum circle at the Dolphinarium Beach, for example. The **Sheraton beach** is also quite peaceful. **Gordon Beach** overflows with foreign tourists and people trying to pick them up, while the **Hilton beach** swarms with native surfers and people trying to pick them up. Avoid that whole scene altogether at **Nordau Beach,** a religious beach. (Open to men M, W, and Sa; to women Su, Tu, and Th.)

The **Octopus Diving and Sport Center,** at the marina, provides scuba diving courses and equipment. (☎03 527 3554. 5-day course NIS1100 but expect to pay at least NIS410 more for a certificate, mask, and log book.) **Surfboards** (☎03 524 2139) can be rented near the marina at Kikkar Atarim for NIS80 per hour.

OTHER ACTIVITIES. Beyond urban hiking and exploration, Tel Aviv has a number of options for the athletically-inclined. East of Namir Rd. (bus #25) is the **Sportek,** a collection of sports fields, a jogging track, and a miniature-golf course. (☎03 699 0307. Open 4-10pm. Free.) Tel Avivians crowd **Hayarkon Park,** just across the river from Sportek, home to a little train, water park, and bird safari. Nearby is **Ganei Yehoshua;** barbecue some kebab and play some *matkot* (paddleball), and you'll fit right in.

JAFFA (YAFO)

يَافا יפו

An Israeli folk song describes Jaffa as possessing a "mysterious and unknown" element that allows its atmosphere to "seep like wine into the blood." Indeed, the city has hosted a litany of mythical and religious occurrences throughout history. Greek mythology claims that Perseus and his trusty Pegasus rescued the princess Andromeda here, after she had been chained to a rock in the sea to appease an irksome local sea monster. According to the Bible, the recalcitrant prophet Jonah shirked his divine calling and fled to Jaffa to catch that fated boat to Tarshish (Jonah 1:3). Jaffa makes an appearance in the New Testament as well; here Peter had a vision telling him that the Gospel extended outside the confines of Judaism and that the dietary laws no longer applied.

The standard repertoire of conquerors also stomped through Jaffa. In 1468 BCE, the Egyptians captured Jaffa by hiding soldiers in human-sized clay jars brought into the city market. King David conquered the city around 1000 BCE, and under Solomon it became the main port of Judea until King Herod's Caesarea usurped that title. In the 12th century CE, the Crusaders, Salah al-Din, Richard the Lionheart, the Muslims, and Louis IX all had a go at the city. Finally, in 1267 the Mamluks captured Jaffa, and, apart from a brief stay by Napoleon around 1800, Jaffa remained an Arab stronghold.

The first Jewish settlers, who were mostly merchants and artisans from North Africa, arrived in 1820 and built the "Jewish House," a temporary hostel. The increased settlement of the area encountered protest, and in 1929, 1936, and 1939, Jaffa was the scene of anti-Zionist riots. When Jewish fighters captured the Arab section of Jaffa in 1948, much of Jaffa's Arab population fled the city. Jaffa was officially incorporated into the Tel Aviv municipality in 1950, but much of the city was left in ruins, and the areas around it filled with prostitution, drugs, and crime. In the late 1960s, the Tel Aviv Municipality decided to turn Jaffa into an artists' colony in an effort to clean it up. Under the auspices

Jaffa (Yafo)

🏠 ACCOMMODATIONS
Mishkenot Ruth Daniel Hostel, 1
Old Yafo Hostel, 2
🍴 FOOD
Abu Hassan, 5
Bernhardt Shaw Restaurant, 7
Dr. Shakshuka, 4
Said Abou Elafia & Sons, 3
Yafo Café, 6

of the Old Jaffa Development Company, whose name is still on many signs today, each artist bought a section of the ruins, eventually transforming them into today's galleries. The City's former and current development of Jaffa can be controversial, however. Critics assert that a combination of gentrification and governmental building policies is forcing Jaffa's remaining Arab citizens out of their original neighborhoods, and that the development of Jaffa is ideologically motivated. Keep an ear out for debates on the situation.

🔆 ORIENTATION

The **Jaffa Clocktower,** completed in 1906, stands by the entrance to Jaffa from Tel Aviv on **Yefet Street** and is a useful landmark. For those trying to orient themselves, Yefet St. turns into **Raziel Street,** then **Eilat Street** as you travel up the road northeast from Jaffa, ultimately becoming the Florentine thoroughfare **Yafo Road** in Tel Aviv. A free 2hr. **tour** of Old Jaffa by the Tourism Association begins here Wednesday at 9:30am, though many people line up at 9am; bus #46 from the New Central Bus Station also lets off in front of the clocktower. Running roughly parallel to Yefet St., a few blocks to the east is **Yerushalayim Boulevard,** a gentrified thoroughfare that has most of the practical stores you will need to visit if you stay here. Buses #18 and #25 stop here from the city center.

Branching off from the convergence of streets at the clocktower is **ha-Aliya Ha Sheniya Street,** the promenade that runs along the sea to Jaffa Port and provides stunning views of Tel Aviv's action-packed cost and skyline. A left from Yefet St. onto **Olei Tzion Street** will lead you into the **Flea Market,** and ultimately to Yerushalayim Blvd.

🏠 ACCOMMODATIONS

If all the beds in Tel Aviv are full, or if you just want something that feels a little less like a college dorm, the two hostels in Jaffa provide a unique, more communal cultural experience.

🏨 **Old Jaffa Hostel,** 8 Olei Tzion St. (☎03 682 2370; www.inisrael.com/oldjaffahostel). Walk 1 block past the clocktower on Yefet St. and turn left onto Olei Tzion St. True, there are occasionally mice in the common area, but Old Jaffa Hostel's historic building is so whimsically elegant that local fashion magazines regularly do photo shoots here. A large rooftop garden with a view of the sea makes for a delightful finishing touch. Fans and free Wi-Fi in every room. Free kitchen use. Breakfast (coffee, tea, and cookies) included. Dorms US$17 (NIS65); singles classes A/B/C US$70/55/48 (NIS267/210/183), doubles classes A/B/C US$83/63/55 (NIS317/241/210); triples classes A/C US$100/72 (NIS384/275); quads classes A/C US$117/89 (NIS447/340). Credit cards accepted. ❶

Mishkenot Ruth Daniel Hostel (HI) 47 Yerushalayim Blvd. (☎03 682 7700), at the corner of Yerushalayim Blvd. and Ben Zvi St. Directly across the street from bus stop; take #25 or #18 from city center. The latest branch in a local chain of Reform Jewish hostels. Pristine rooms have mint-green bedspreads, TVs, fridges, and A/C. Largely a Jewish-Israeli crowd. F Shabbat services. Breakfast included. Dorms NIS136; singles NIS298; doubles NIS394; triples NIS510; quads NIS626. Credit cards accepted. ❷

🍴 FOOD

Home to what are rumored to be the best bakery **(Aboulafia)** and best hummus restaurant **(Abu Hassan)** in Israel, the number one reason to visit Jaffa is arguably the food. The maze of narrow streets surrounding the Jaffa **clock tower** is full with cheap falafel stands (NIS7-10) and sweets vendors, some of which are open 24hr. Once you get into the **Old City** and port area, the cafes and restaurants of Jaffa tend to become generic and more expensive, but the surrounding gardens and views of the Mediterranean make them some of the loveliest tourist traps imaginable. For a touch of romance and a big hit to the wallet, head to **Jaffa Port,** off Pasteur St. on the far side of the artists' colony, where picturesque waterfront restaurants offer fresh seafood (daily catch entrees from NIS45). Jaffa is also one of the best places to get a great meal on Shabbat.

🍴 **Said Abou Elafia and Sons,** 7 Yefet St. (☎03 681 2340). ½ block up from the Clocktower; look for the crowds. Popularly known as "Aboulafia," this bakery is so famous that its name is used by Israelis to denote all stuffed-pita toasts. Try the zatar-spiced toasts, hot chocolate croissants, or honey-trenched baklava (all NIS3-6). Takeout only. Open 24hr. Cash only. ❶

🍴 **Abu Hassan,** 14 Shivtai Israel St. (☎03 682 0387). To get there from the clock tower, walk up Yefet St. to its intersection with Yehuda Hayamit St. Turn right, then turn left on Shivtai Israel St. Packed with disciples from throughout Israel, Abu Hassan serves the food of the gods, and is rumored to be a frontrunner in the eternal Best Humus in Israel competition. Be ready for chaotic lines and crowds. Hummus plates NIS15. Open daily 7am-3pm. Cash only. ❶

Dr. Shakshuka, 3 Beit Eshel (☎03 682 2842), a few doors down from the corner of Beit Eshel and Yefet St. Eponymous dish is the *shakshuka*—a mouth-watering tomato and egg concoction served in a hot skillet directly from the stove (NIS30). Relax with both tourists and locals beneath the canopy of tarnished pots and pans from the flea market. Open Su-Th 8am-midnight, F 8am-6pm, Sa 8:30pm-midnight. Cash only. ❷

Yafa Cafe, 33 Yehuda Meragusa (☎03 681 5746; www.yafabook.co.il), at the inter-section of Yefet St. and Yehuda Meragusa; about a 10min. walk up Yefet from the clock tower. Bright Arabic and Hebrew bookstore-cafe that regularly hosts political film screenings, poetry readings, and meetings between liberal Israeli and Palestinian activ-ists. The aggressive A/C, free Wi-Fi, and good Palestinian food makes it an ideal place to engage in political debates, get some work done, or just seek refuge from the heat. *Yafa majadara* NIS26. Mozzarella sandwich NIS30. Coffee NIS7-17. Open Su-Th 8am-11pm, F 8am-6pm, Sa 10:30am-11pm. Credit cards accepted. ❶

Bernhardt Show Restaurant, 10 Kikkar Kedamin (☎03 681 3898), to the right of the Church of St. Peter. Expensive but exceptionally good fish restaurant with wide table-cloths and 1 of the best sunset views of the sea in Jaffa. Come for a small splurge. Egg-plant stuffed with goat cheese, tomato, and cream cheese NIS42. Bouillabaisse NIS72. Open daily 11:30am-midnight. Credit cards accepted. ❸

🄢 SIGHTS

CLOCK TOWER AND ENVIRONS. Built in 1906 to celebrate the 25th anniversary of Sultan Abdul Hamid II's ascension to power, the clock tower marks the entrance to Jaffa from Tel Aviv. Originally, the clock tower's four faces were split between Israeli and European time for the convenience of European sail-ors. On the right of the clock tower is the **al-Mahmudiyya Mosque,** an enormous structure erected in 1812 that only Muslims may enter. The **Saraya,** an old Turk-ish government building dating to 1897, is nearby at the corner of Yefet St. and Ratzif Ha Aliya Ha'Shniya St. Head to the right and up the hill along Roslan St. to the **Museum of Antiquities of Tel Aviv-Jaffa,** which contains artifacts from Neo-lithic to Roman times and a collection of coins. It is currently closed for reno-vations; check to see if it is open during your stay.

KIKKAR KEDUMIM AND ENVIRONS. Prominently located at the head of Kikkar Kedumim Sq. is the red-brick facade of the **Church of Saint Peter.** Originally built in 1654 by the Franciscans, the church was subsequently destroyed twice and rebuilt in the 1890. It served as a hostel for pilgrims before its 19th-century renovation and counted Napoleon among its distinguished guests. Today, the church offers a number of Catholic services in a variety of languages throughout the week. *(☎03 682 2871. Open daily 8am-11:45am and 3-5pm. English services Sa 8pm, Su 9am. Italian services weekdays 6:30am. Polish services Su 6pm. Spanish services Sa 6:30pm.)*

The old city's **visitor's center** is also in Kikkar Kedumim. Follow the signs and head down the steps underground, beneath the plaza and to the ongoing exca-vations from 2300-year-old Tel Yafo. Watch the 16min. video for a short history lesson, and pick up the free maps. Portable audio tours for the city are also available (NIS42). *(☎03 518 4015. NIS8, students NIS6. Open Su-Th and Sa 10am-6pm.)*

HA-PIGSA GARDENS. The wooden footbridge from Kikkar Kedumim leading to the pristine green hills of the ha-Pigsa Gardens is locally known as the **Bridge of Dreams.** Legend has it that wishes will be granted to anyone who stands on it, touches his astrological sign along the railing, and faces the sea. Naturally, it is an immensely popular spot among both the Jewish and Arab communities for wedding pictures. The gardens contain a small, modern amphitheater for summer concerts, a brief excavation of Egyptian, Greek, and Roman remains, and a lookout point. The point offers Jaffa's best view of the coast, Tel Aviv, and **Andromeda's Rock.** According to Ancient Greek mythology, Andromeda was chained to the rock to appease a sea monster sent by Poseidon to terrorize Ethiopia after Andromeda's mother, Ethiopian queen Cassiopeia, boasted that her daughter was more beautiful than Poseidon's nymphs. Andromeda was rescued by Greek hero Perseus just in time thanks to his trusty Pegasus and his clever utilization of Medusa's head. Sadly, Cassiopeia was turned into stone along with the monster.

GALLERIES. Past the tourist center, a large ramp leads to the museums, restaurants, and galleries that constitute Jaffa's artists' colony. You can also get there by winding through the gardens, away from the sea. The galleries are often overpriced and occasionally kitsch. In general you are better off perusing the cheaper and more original work sold on Nahalat Benyamin St. (see **Tel Aviv Sights,** p. 178). Dwarfing the other galleries in the vicinity in both quality and fame is the lovely **Ilana Goor Museum,** which houses both Goor's artwork and her personal collection. Fun and funky jewelry, sculptures, and furniture (including a piano painted in psychedelic colors) are spread throughout the artist's home; the bookshelf in Goor's sitting room is also worth a browse. *(4 Mazal Dagim St., in Kikkar Kedumim Sq. to the left when exiting the Gardens. Follow the signs. ☎ 03 683 7676; www.ilanagoor.com. Open Su-F 10am-4pm, Sa 10am-6pm. NIS28, NIS24 students.)*

JAFFA PORT. The port, past the bottom of the artist's colony to the right along Pasteur St. was the perfect depth for King Solomon when he imported rafts of cedars from Lebanon to build his temple. It was too shallow, however, for larger ships. The infamous port caused Dutch sailors to term the impossible as "entering Jaffa." Today, the port is more accessible and is an active fisherman's wharf.

SHUK HA-PISHPESHIM. Back in town, Jaffa's large Shuk ha-Pishpeshim (Flea Market) is one of the livelier markets in Israel, with roofed rows of overflowing stalls that offer Middle Eastern knick-knacks, hand-dyed clothing, Persian carpets, leather goods, and brassware. A vast selection of enormous *nargilah* (waterpipes) is also available. It is busiest on Fridays when special permits are not required and is closed on Saturdays. An arts and crafts **festival** with local high school jazz musicians takes place every Thursday 8pm-midnight in July and August. *(Between Olei Tzion and Beit Eshel St; walk 1 block up Yefet and turn left.)*

NEAR TEL AVIV

RAMLA
☎08

رملة الرملة

Founded in 716 by the formidable Umayyad Caliph Suleiman ibn Abd al-Malik, Ramla is the only town in Israel established and developed by Arabs. Until the arrival of the Crusaders in the 11th century, Ramla was the capital of Palestine and was known for its magnificent palaces and mosques. After the 1948 War, much of the original Arab population was forced to flee. Today, Ramla is a dusty, occasionally rundown town with one of the most international communities you will find in Israel or anywhere else. Jewish immigrants from Russia, Ethiopia, and parts of South America mingle in the *souq* with Muslim and

Christian Arabs, as well as immigrants from Africa, Southeast Asia, and East Asia. Shopkeepers and *sherut* drivers automatically resort to hand signals and pantomime when they speak to customers, to pre-empt the anticipated language barriers. The diversity of Ramla's history and present population, as characterized by its crumbling grandeur and particularly vibrant Wednesday *souq*, make the town well worth the trip. Ramla's sights are primarily religious and historical; their authenticity compensates for their disarray.

TRANSPORTATION AND ORIENTATION. There are no direct **bus** routes to Ramla from Tel Aviv; the fastest way to get there is to take bus #201 to Rishon le-Tsiyon and then take bus #433 to Ramla's Central Bus Station (45min., every 15min., NIS17.20). You can also take #201 and transfer to #433 from Rekhovot (1¼hr., every 15min., NIS12.70). Once in Ramla, the best way to get around town is by **sherut** (NIS4.50). Most mosques and churches in Ramla are located in the center of town off of Herzl St.; all are within easy walking distance of another. If you have the time, start out at the Ramla Museum; the friendly staff will give you free brochures and help you get oriented.

FOOD. Food in Ramla is almost exclusively dedicated to standard falafel and shawarma fare. The *souq*, which is on Jabotinsky St. off Herzl St., offers a range of fresh fruits, veggies, sweets, and cheap plastic gadgets at rock bottom prices; falafels on **Herzl Street** near the *souq* and **Central Bus Station** go for NIS10. Located directly across the street from the *souq*, **Maharaja Indian Sweets** is a hole-in-the-wall Indian grocery store, which sells everything from fresh hot samosas (NIS3.50) to sticky traditional sweets (NIS1.50). There is a small, air-conditioned place to sit and eat behind the store, which is usually packed with local Indian families (open Su-Th 11am-3:30pm and 7-9:30pm, F 11am-3:30pm). For a less eccentric experience, **Nectar Cafe ❷**, Ramla's only coffee house and a local institution, is situated in the Government Complex mall, right next to the bus terminals. The young staff speaks fluent English and is exceptionally helpful, even by the standards of Ramla's friendly community; the cafe serves its breakfast special (NIS42) throughout the day (open Su-Th 7am-10pm, F 7am-5pm, Sa 8pm-midnight).

SIGHTS. The small, six-room **Ramla Museum** documents Ramla's 1300 years of history and also serves as an unofficial tourist office for visitors looking for directions or tips. The respectable collection of ancient artifacts includes ancient gold coins from the era of Suleiman, a segment of Byzantine mosaic floor, and clay spouts from early *argiliehs* (water pipes); it is supported by a series of dioramas of what the town looked like in its heyday. (112 Herzl St., across from Government Complex and Central Bus Station; enter on the right side of the building from President's Park next door. ☎08 929 2650. Open Su-Th 10am-4pm, F 10am-1pm. NIS6, students NIS5.) The **Crusader Cathedral of Saint John** became the **Great Mosque** when Ramla's Muslims recaptured the town from the Crusaders. Although the mosque consequentially retains little of Muslim architecture, the well-preserved minaret is breathtaking, and the peaceful, medieval vaulted arches are impressive. (From the bus station, walk right on Herzl St. and into President's Park, the lovely park with the rows of palm trees next to the Ramla Museum; walk through the park and cross the street behind it, then follow the minaret through the *souq* parking lot. ☎08 922 5081. Open daily 8am-4pm. Be sure to dress modestly; women should cover their legs.) Ramla is supposed to be the biblical Arimathea, where one of Jesus's earliest disciples, Joseph, is said to have lived. Together with St. Nicodemus, St. Joseph Arimathea made the preparations for Jesus's burial. The large stone **Catholic**

TEL AVIV-JAFFA

complex was built in his honor in 1296, with money donated by European Catholics. Renovated in 1902, it now serves as a school as well. The monks in the 18th-century **monastery** next door claim that Napoleon Bonaparte stayed in the upstairs chambers during his unsuccessful campaign against the Turks. (The complex is past the mosque at the corner of Herzl St. and Bialik St. The main gate of the church is on Bialik St.) This majestic **Tower of Forty Martyrs** was a 14th-century addition to an eighth century mosque, which is said to be the burial site of Mohammad's companions. A few stone arches and this tower are all that remain of the mosque. Napoleon allegedly coordinated his attack on Jaffa from the top of the tower. Climb the steps to the top for a birds-eye **view** of Ramla and the surrounding area. The noises inside are not the screams of the martyrs but the sounds of the many birds who now use it as a nesting spot. Next to the mosque is a crumbling Muslim cemetery. (To reach the tower, follow Herzl to Danny Mass St. and take a left on Danny Mass St.; the rectangular tower is visible. Open Su-Th 8am-2:30am, F 8am-2pm, Sa 8am-4pm. NIS5, NIS4.)

BEIT GUVRIN NATIONAL PARK ☎08

בית גוברין

Beit Guvrin National Park, encompassing the ruins of Maresha and Beit Guvrin, is one of Israel's secret treasures. The complex caves and magnificent views make this site unforgettable. The biblical city of Maresha was one of the cities fortified by Rehoboam (Joshua 16:44). Edomites and Sidonians both settled in the area, and Greeks eventually converted it into a bustling economic center. Before the turn of the first century BCE, the Hasmonean king John Hyrcanus I conquered the city and forced Judaism upon its inhabitants. The Parthian army destroyed the city in 40 BCE. Beit Guvrin became a flourishing Jewish settlement in the years between the destruction of the Second Temple and the Bar Kokhba Revolt (73 CE-135 CE). During the Byzantine period, the Christians made Beit Guvrin their home.

More recently, it was the site of an Arab village until the 1948 Arab-Israeli War. Upon entering through the main gate, turn left and follow the road to the Bell Caves. There is an information office behind the baths on the left, which can spontaneously close. Follow the signs to the large-domed, magnificent **Bell Caves** carved by the Greeks, Byzantines, and others as they quarried for limestone. Once dug, the caves were used for storage and later became sanctuaries for hermits and monks. St. John and others came here seeking solitude, and they often carved crosses into the walls. More recently, Sylvester Stallone made his own mark in the caves with the filming of *Rambo III*. The rest of the park is only accessible by car and a 2km. **hiking** trail, which leads from the Bell Caves toward the **Sidonian Burial Caves** and the ancient city of **Maresha.** The trail is marked with white stone markers, and if you are lucky you may see mountain goats along the way. The trail passes the ruins of the church of St. Anne, originally built during the Byzantine era. Be careful not to wander from the trail as there are many hidden caves in the area. Sidonians living in Maresha during the second and third centuries BCE buried their dead in decorated caves. Inside the caves you will see many burial niches and paintings of animals and mythological creatures. From these caves continue up the hill to see Maresha's other caves. Especially impressive are the dwelling houses and underground cisterns that connect to form a vast underground network of storage, work, and living rooms. Some of the caves were used for making olive oil, and the olive crushing apparatus is on display. The **Columbarium Cave** is an enormous room full of niches in which Mareshans raised pigeons for food, manure, and sacrificial purposes. Even those who yawn at the sight of ruins will appreciate the unbelievable view from atop **tel Maresha.** On a clear day, Tel Aviv may be visible in the west and the Hebron mountains in the east. (☎08 681 2957. Open daily Apr.-Sept. 8am-5pm, Oct.-Mar. 8am-4pm. NIS25.)

It is definitely best to visit Beit Guvrin with a rental car. The park is far from any prominent towns, and it can be quite a hike between the different sights; due to bus #11's erratic schedule and the general lack of human life in the area, let alone taxis, it can also be difficult to leave the park for civilization again. To reach Beit Guvrin by **bus,** travel to Kiryat Gat, accessible from Tel Aviv (#376, 1hr. 20min., daily 2:30pm, NIS22.20), Jerusalem (#446; 1½hr., every hr., NIS31.20), and Ashkelon (#25, 1hr., every 30min., NIS18.20). **Bus** #11 travels from Kiryat Gat to Beit Guvrin park daily 8:10am and 2:30pm; return buses do not have a written schedule and are a bit irregular for most travelers' tastes. **Taxis** from both Kiryat Gat (NIS60) and Ashkelon (NIS150) will take you to Beit Guvrin. With a little bargaining, a round-trip taxi from Ashkelon costs NIS280-300. The park is just off Rte. 35, near Kibbutz Beit Guvrin. Bring plenty of portable shade (a hat or scarf, sunglasses, and sunscreen) and at least 1.5L of water; there are water spigots but nowhere to buy water or food once you get there.

HERZLIYA

☎08

הרצליה

Named after Theodore Herzl by the seven Zionist pioneers who settled the area, Herzliya is known for the affluent tourists and Israeli vacationers who flock to its beautiful shores. In the never-ending battle for the Best Beach in Israel title, Herzliya is a prime contender. Only 15km. outside of Tel Aviv, Herzliya makes a great daytrip from the city; it's a good thing too because there are no budget accommodations.

The **beaches** in Herzliya Pituah, Herzliya's scenic suburb, range from the soft-sanded to the small and rocky type. The **Dabesh Beach** and **Arcadia Beach,** near the marina at the end of the bus line, belong to the former category and charge admission. While the size and sand of **Sidna Ali** beach pales in comparison, admission is free, and it is the only beach without umbrella-to-umbrella lounge chairs. People walking 1km. from Sidna Ali to the pay beaches (to your left as you face the sea) or those staying at one of the fancy hotels are often not required to pay. From the bus stop in Sidna Ali, the beach is up the hill through the gate. Herzliya's most worthwhile attraction is an inhabited sand castle known as the **Hermit's House.** This fantastical residence, built in the side of a cliff, by hermit **Nissim Kakhalon** is a must-see. Kakhalon claims, "I make it from my love. I make it good." In other words, he spent 29 years turning other people's garbage—tires, toys, tiles, and other old things—into this hallucinogenic maze of winding tunnels and lush gardens. Even more impressive, everything in the artful interior is absolutely functional, from the bathroom ceiling made entirely of Maccabee beer bottles to the loveseat with a mirrored mosaic on one side and a huge sculpted face on the other. Nothing goes to waste here; Kakhalon even uses the manure from his goats to grow fragrant basil. Kakhalon's tours depend on the extent to which his guests are appreciative. This hermit is quite friendly and more of a showman than a recluse. (Open Su-F 9am-sundown; hours erratic.) The other sites in Herzliya are more historically oriented. An additional reason to visit Sidna Ali beach is the **Sidna Ali Mosque.** Women must cover their heads and shorts are forbidden. After the Mamluks destroyed the area during the Third Crusade, the mosque was named after one of Salah al-Din's soldiers who died in a battle on the hill on which the mosque stands. Zionist history buffs may enjoy the

Beit Rishonim (Founder's Museum) at 8-10 ha-Nadiv St. The museum narrates the history of Herzliya, beginning with its days as a colony in 1924, through digital presentations. (☎09 950 4270. Open M 4-6:30pm, Tu-Sa 9am-12:30pm. Free.) Also of interest is the **Herzliya Museum of Contemporary Art.** (4 Ha'banim St. ☎09 950 0762; www.herzliyamuseum.co.il. Open M 10am-2pm, Tu 4-8pm, W 10am-2pm, Th 4-8pm, F-Sa 10am-2pm. 10NIS).

Buses # 501, 525, and 531 from Tel Aviv's Central Bus Station stop frequently at Herzliya's Central Bus Station (1hr., every 10min., NIS9.10). Buses stop running F 5:30pm and do not start running again until after 8pm on Sa.

REKHOVOT ☎08
רחובות

Rekhovot, a renowned center of technological and agricultural research, is home to three research institutions: the prestigious Weizmann Institute of Science, the research facilities of the Faculty of Agriculture of Hebrew University, and the Development Study Center, specializing in rural development. Due to the large number of recent immigrants from the former Soviet Union, Yemen, and Ethiopia, the crowded city boasts an interesting culture; the streets are populated by both falafel vendors and wealthy scientists. The world-famous **Weizmann Institute of Science** is named for Israel's first president, Dr. Haim Weizmann, the chemist who discovered an innovative way to produce acetone. This fluid proved essential to England's WWI military effort as well as to manicurists everywhere. Weizmann's discovery gave him the political clout necessary to persuade Lord Balfour to issue the 1917 Balfour Declaration, a statement of British support favoring the establishment of a Jewish national homeland. In 1934, Weizmann founded a chemistry research center in Rekhovot to carry out his mandate that Jews in Palestine stay on the cutting-edge of scientific research and development. Over the years this research facility has expanded to encompass all major fields of science and is responsible for Israel's first computer and particle accelerator. The campus's manicured lawns and winding shaded streets make for a relaxing stroll; look out for students and local families picnicking beneath the trees.

Tourists can visit the **Weizmann House,** where Dr. Weizmann lived as President of Israel. Walk to the back of the house to see his grave. A nearby building holds the **Weizmann Archives,** a collection of the statesman's papers. At the northern end of the campus, next to the solar tower, is the **Garden of Science,** which houses a collection of interactive science exhibits. Tickets, maps, 30min. free tours, and an introductory film are available at the **Visitors' Center.** (☎08 934 4500. Weizmann House open Su-Th 9am-4pm. Garden of Science open Su-Th 10am-4pm. Call in advance to schedule a tour of Weizmann House and view the film in English. Weizmann House NIS30, students NIS20. Combined ticket with Garden of Science NIS40, students NIS30.) Located about a mile from the Weizmann Institute is the **Ayalon Institute,** a kibbutz where Jewish freedom fighters in Palestine secretly manufactured over two million bullets between 1945 and 1948. Call to schedule an English tour of the underground factory and a screening of a historical video. (From the Weizmann Institute gate turn right and walk about 20min. to ha-Damah St. or take a bus toward Tel Aviv and ask the driver to stop at Kiryat Hadamah. Walk down Hadamah and turn left on Haaim Holtzman; the museum is up the hill to the right. ☎08 930 0585. Open Su-Th 8:30am-4pm, F 8:30am-2pm, Sa 9am-2pm. Free.)

The cheapest **falafel stands** (NIS6) are on Herzl St. south of the turnoff to the main bus station. Another alternative is to stop by the lively **souq** on Levkovitz St., between the bus station and Herzl St.

The Weizmann Institute is a 30min. walk back along Herzl St. from the central bus station. The **bus** from Tel Aviv (45min., NIS12.60) makes a stop directly across the street from the Institute, so watch for its large gates on the left. Return buses and *sherut* to Tel Aviv stop at the bus stop to the right when exiting the Institute.

ASHKELON

☎ 08

אשקלון

Ashkelon was first settled in the third millennium BCE. Strategically located on Mediterranean transport routes, it was a spoil of war for nearly every empire of the ancient era, including Philistines, Assyrians, Phoenicians, Greeks, Romans, Muslims, and Crusaders. First rising to prominence as one of the Philistines' five great cities, Ashkelon reached its zenith as an independent city state during the Roman period. Today Ashkelon's main attractions are its seaside national park and well-known archaeological sites. The city itself sprawls out to the sea and is largely untouristed, with several lovely beaches and a picturesque marina, but few attractions or helpful resources for visitors. Only 12km. from the Gazan border, Ashkelon recently endured a litany of rocket fire during the Gaza War; the area is safe now.

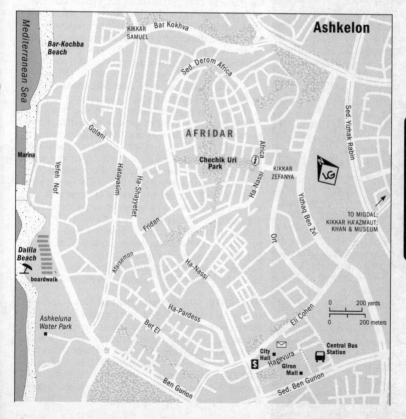

TEL AVIV-JAFFA

ISRAELI STUDENTS' DAY OFF

For one day a year, Israeli university campuses lock up their classrooms and libraries and host a day of celebration for their students. In mid-May, each university hosts its own **Yom ha-Student** (Student Day). Stages, food stalls, and bars pop up all over the campus lawns. From the early afternoon through to the early morning thousands of students gather for a stress-free day at their universities.

Yom ha-Student is a chance to get a taste of the Israeli university scene. Because of the compulsory army service, Israelis begin to study at 22 or later, giving their campuses a cool, relaxed vibe.

Each campus competes to have the best performing acts for their celebration, and DJs play throughout the day. Many of Israel's most famous musicians perform at Student Days across the country, and there is no better way to experience Israeli music than with thousands of lively students.

The Hebrew University in Jerusalem began the Yom Ha-Student tradition and continues to have one of the biggest celebrations. In 2009, the celebration attracted over 20,000 students, and Macy Gray performed alongside some of Israel's own talent.

Entry to Yom ha-Student NIS30-NIS60, depending on the campus. Each campus celebrates on a different day; for individual dates, visit the university websites.

TRANSPORTATION. Buses #300 and 301 run from Tel Aviv to Ashkelon's Central Bus Station (1½hr., every 15min.; about NIS20). Once in Ashkelon, buses #5 or #6 will bring you from the Statio to the *midrakhov*. A **taxi** from the Bus Station to Ashkelon National Park should not cost more than NIS20.

ACCOMMODATIONS AND FOOD. For people with an insatiable love of crumbling pillars and cheap accommodations on picturesque Mediterranean coastlines, **Ashkelon National Park ❶**, offers reasonably-priced camping opportunities in the Park for only NIS10 per person per night. The park gate closes at 8pm and the exit at 10pm, however, and they do not open again until 8am the next morning. Be sure to be in the park with enough food and water to last the night. (☎08 673 9660. M-F by reservation. Open Apr.-Oct. Check-out 5pm.) The **Herzl Street midrakhov** in the Migdal neighborhood has the highest concentration of affordable eateries, with an abundance of hole-in-the-wall places selling falafels (NIS13). Cheap produce is also always available in the nearby *souq*. Both the *souq* and the *midrakhov* are a bit of a hike from the Central Bus Station, in the opposite direction of the park; it's best to take the #5 or 6 bus or *sherut* (NIS5.50), or to take a taxi (no more than NIS20). Two well-priced, thoroughly obscure restaurants on the *midrakhov* are particularly worth the bus fare. Frequented by a clique of local Romanian families, **Restaurant Nitsaka ❶**, serves steaming flatbread, hot *tcharba* (NIS15), and other excellent traditional Romanian foods from a small establishment with lace curtains, at the beginning of the *midrakhov* on the right hand side. (☎08 672 7182. Open Su-Th 10am-10pm.) Across the street is **Roger's ❷**, an eccentric celebration of egocentrism with comfortable outdoor seating; every inch of wall space in the creaky, concave building is covered with framed pictures of the owner, Roger, posing with different celebrities he has met over the course of the decades that his restaurant has been open. (☎08 935 7408. Pizza NIS53. Sandwiches NIS20-25.)

SIGHTS. The **Ashkelon National Park** was built on the site of 40,000-year-old Canaanite remains, buried beneath ruins of Philistine, Greek, Roman, Byzantine, Crusader, and Muslim cities. Traces of the once-thriving Philistine city surround the picnic tables and snack bars of this well-used park. The **Bouleuterion**, a series of Hellenistic and Roman columns and capitals, graces the park's center. It served as the Council House Square when Ashkelon was an autonomous city-state under Severius in the third century CE. The courtyard next to the Bouleuterion is actually the inside of a Herodian assembly hall; it contains two statues of Nike, the winged goddess of victory, and an Italian marble statue of the goddess Isis with her child Horus, sculpted between 200 BCE and 100 CE. Behind the Bouleuterion lies an **amphitheater.** Along the southern edge of the park are segments of a wall from the 12th century **Crusader City.** A short **hike** past the amphitheater affords a close-up view of the walls and a glimpse of Ashkelon's Rothenberg Power Station. Most peculiar is the assembly of Roman **columns** jutting out of the ancient Byzantine sea wall on the beach. These massive marble columns were used to support the walls, which were destroyed in 1191 by Salah ad-Din. Richard Lionheart partly restored them in 1192, as did Cornwall in 1240, only to have them demolished by Sultain Baybars in 1270. (Bus #6 stops at the path leading to the park's entrance. The walk from the Central Bus Station to the park is about 30min. and the bus has a highly irregular schedule, so if you're in a hurry it's best to take a cab. If you do plan to walk, turn right onto Ben-Gurion Blvd. from the Central Bus Station and follow it to the T-junction at the coast, before the Arkeluna water park. Turn left onto the road to the park; a small orange sign points the way. ☎08 673 6444. Open Su-Th 8am-10pm. NIS25, children NIS13.) **Ashkelon Khan,** a seventh century tower and courtyard, houses the **Ashkelon Museum,** which traces the history of Ashkelon from Roman times to the present and has a small collection of modern paintings and sculpture. (Past the *midrakhov* at the very end of Herzl St; look for the tower on the left and enter through the courtyard; the museum door is on the left. ☎08 672 7002. Open Su-Th 9am-1pm, 4-7pm, F 9am-1pm, Sa 10am-1pm. Free.) A few blocks past the *midrakhov* on Herzl St., **Independence Square** (Kikkar Hatzmaut) was the site of the first reading of Israel's Declaration of Independence in 1948.

◪ **BEACHES.** Eashkelon's coast has four beaches where swimming is permitted with **Delilah Beach** being the most popular. Note the flag system: white flags signal safe bathing and black flags signal dangerously rough water. At Delilah Beach, breakwaters lessen the chance of black-flagging, and shady canopies and snack bars provide relief to sun-scorched bathers. Once the nighttime revelry begins, the crowd of sun bathers starts dancing to blaring Israeli pop music. For sand-free water fun, try the **Ashkeluna Water Park** (☎08 673 9970). Crowds of Israeli teenagers and youngsters from Be'er Sheva to Yavneh flock to Ashkeluna's extensive complex of water slides and games, set to the tune of Israeli pop. (Near Delilah Beach and the T-junction that branches off toward the national park. Open Su-F 9am-4pm. NIS60).

RISHON LE-TZIYON ☎03

ראשון לציון

Rishon le-Tziyon (First to Zion), founded in 1882 by 17 Russian immigrant families with the financial help of Baron de Rothschild, was the first modern Jewish settlement in Palestine. Since its founding, Rishon has been the site of several important firsts for Israel. In Rishon, the Jewish National Fund was created, the Israeli flag was first flown, and the world's first national Hebrew School opened its doors. Once a hotbed of Zionist resistance, Rishon has more recently become another extension in the ever-expanding Tel Aviv, and has acquired a suburban vibe. Young backpackers are about as common on the *midrakhov* as flying monkeys. The town's old industrial zone is the most welcoming, with a youthful subculture and what is rumored to be one of the best sushi restaurants in the region.

▣ TRANSPORTATION. Buses #201, 174, and 301 from Tel Aviv stop at Rishon le-Tziyon's old bus station in the historical district (30min., every 20min., NIS9.10) on their way to the new bus station in a mall on the other side of town. Buses back to Tel Aviv can be caught on the main highway and from the city's stations.

▣ FOOD. The *midrakhov* in the historic district is lined with falafel stands. In the old industrial section of Rishon, outside the town's historic area, hip restaurants attract an eclectic clientele. To get to the old industrial section, take bus #85 from the bus station or catch a pink, orange, and white *sherut* #85 at the stand on Herzl St., across from the bus station, and ask to be let off at Barshovsky St. in front of Nafis Restaurant (NIS5.50). Both will stop at the T-stop intersection with Moshe Beker St.; meander down either street to explore the city's best eats. The place for 20-somethings to be seen on Friday and Saturday nights is the Yemenite restaurant **Nafis ❷**, 10 Moshe Beker St., a local chain which serves everything from hummus plates (NIS14.80-21.90) to a variety of steak deals (NIS48.90), and specializes in Yemenite pastries. (☎03 966 7677. Open 24hr.) Across the street from Nafis is **Casa Do Brasil ❸**, 12 Moshe Becker St., whose festive atmosphere and wide selection of meat dishes entices carnivores despite the steep prices. A hamburger goes for NIS78; for NIS138 you can get a giant platter with 11 different kinds of meat of your choice. (☎03 950 4000. Open Su-Th noon-midnight, F noon-4pm, Sa noon-6pm.) Even Tel Avivians claim that **Soho Sushi Bar ❷**, 15 Moshe Beker, is one of the best sushi restaurants in the area, and for good reason. The kitchen keeps things interesting by introducing a constant stream of creative new, fusion dishes. The place crowds with young people at night. (☎03 965 8395. Tamaki NIS19-29. Combo platters from NIS69. Open daily 9am-2am.)

◪ SIGHTS. A yellow line painted along Rishon's pavement marks **Pioneer's Way**, which leads to 18 of the town's historic sites, each marked with a descriptive plaque in both Hebrew and English. The path starts and ends at the museum's gate. Most of Rishon's sights lie along the *midrakhov*. The **Village Well** and other sights are along the first section, and the museum is a bit farther up on the right, beyond where the *midrakhov* changes into a regular street with traffic and a sidewalk. **Rishon le-Tziyon Museum** traces the story of Israel's first Aliyah as it documents the history of the town from its pioneer days to the present. A tour of the museum includes a look at the first iron plow in Israel and a replica of the first Hebrew school room. Following the museum tour is a 10min. **sound and light show** in the old Village Well, detailing the town's initial struggle to find a water source of its own. (2-4 Ehad Haam street. On the right just above the *midrakhov* and across from the Great Synagogue. ☎03 968 2435. Open Su 9am-2pm, M 9am-1pm and 3-7pm, Tu-Th 9am-2pm. Free.) Across the street from the museum is Rishon le-Tsiyon's **Great Synagogue**. Built in 1885, it was used as a warehouse under Ottoman rule. Other nearby sights include the oldest Hebrew school and a military base from the beginning of the century. Built by Baron Edmond de Rothschild in 1887, Rishon le-Tsiyon's famous **Carmel Winery** was once used as a secret firing range by Zionist resistance fighters in the early 20th century. It currently produces the regionally well-known *Carmel Mizrahi* wine. The winery has been known in the past to provide tours of their facilities for those who schedule visits in advance, complete with a tasting and souvenir bottle. (25 ha-Carmel St. 03 948 8802; www.carmelwines.co.il.)

NORTHERN MEDITERRANEAN COAST

The stretch of coastline north of Tel Aviv is home to much of Israel's population and most of its agricultural output. Zionists and refugees poured onto the beaches for the first half of the 20th century and drained the swamps of the coastal plain, clearing the path for a modern, industrial state. Still, safely removed from the country's two largest cities, the region maintains an old-world character. Life here moves at a more luxurious pace; the ways of the West haven't completely taken over yet and many old villages remain remarkably well preserved.

Picturesque beach towns, friendly kibbutzim, and significant archaeological ruins dot the shore between Tel Aviv and the Lebanese border. Indeed, the coast and its attractions are incredibly idiosyncratic and travelers sun-worshiping one day may find themselves in a Druze village the next, and in a Crusader fortress the day after that. Almost every day, however, is bound to be followed by a glorious Mediterranean sunset and a night of relaxed strolling along a promenade.

HIGHLIGHTS OF THE NORTHERN MEDITERRANEAN COAST

JOIN the pilgrims in prayer at the **Baha'i Shrine** (p. 209).

PONDER the past at the ruins of **Caesarea** (p. 222).

CHEW THE FAT with colorful artists in the colony **Ein Hod** (p. 215).

HAIFA

☎04

היפה حَيْفَا

Since the prophet Elijah fled the wrath of King Ahab to the caves of Mt. Carmel (I Kings 18-19), Haifa has harbored religious minorities. Crusaders built the first of several monasteries above **Elijah's Cave,** which eventually gave shelter to the wandering Carmelite Order of Monks. **German Templars** established Haifa's German colony, and the **Baha'i** built their world headquarters here. In the 1930s, waves of European Jews seeking refuge from Nazism poured onto Haifa's beaches.

As a result, Haifa developed the philosophy, "live and let live." When the British decided to construct a port in the city, Arabs and Jews flocked to the economic opportunities and worked side-by-side in factories. Today, Haifa's population of a quarter million includes a sizeable Arab minority and a small Orthodox Jewish community, who live together with little tension. Haifa University has the largest Arab population of any university in Israel and a joint community center promotes relations at the local level, especially among children. Not surprisingly, supporters of the Israeli-Palestinian peace accords often cite Haifa as the paradigm for peaceful Jewish-Arab co-existence.

Now caught somewhere between poverty and luxury, Haifa exhibits an exotic mix of residents and lifestyles. Buildings still gouged with bullet

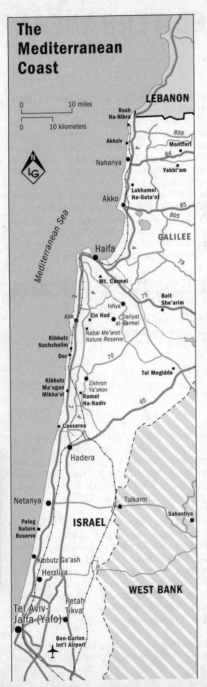

The Mediterranean Coast

0   10 miles
0   10 kilometers

LEBANON

Mediterranean Sea

Rosh Ha-Nikra
Akhziv
Nahariya
Akko
Lokhamei Ha-Geta'of
Montfort
Yekhi'am
899
84
85
805
GALILEE
Haifa
Mt. Carmel
Isfiya
Ein Hod
Atlit
Daliyat al-Karmel
Beit She'arim
75
79
Nahal Me'arot Nature Reserve
Kibbutz Nachsholim
Dor
70
Kibbutz Ma'agan Mikha'el
Zikhron Ya'akov
Ramat Ha-Nadiv
Tel Megiddo
65
Caesarea
Hadera
Netanya
Tulkarm
Sabastiya
Poleg Nature Reserve
ISRAEL
Kibbutz Ga'ash
Herzliya
Petah Tikva
Tel Aviv-Jaffa (Yafo)
Ben-Gurion Int'l Airport
WEST BANK

NORTHERN MEDITERRANEAN COAST

holes in Wadi Nisnas seem half a world away from the resort-like polish of the Baha'i gardens, and bronzed girls in bikinis share the sand of Hof Dado with Orthodox boys in earlocks. Haifa profits from its diversity, from both the long-existing cultural differences between Jews and Arabs, and the newer changes brought by immigrants, travelers, foreign businesses, and pilgrims. It has become a city that's difficult to surprise and that achieves its stability not from some central commonality, but from the strength of each separate origin. As such, travelers can relish its distinct cultural neighborhoods and practices, and watch for the surreal spaces of intersection.

INTERCITY TRANSPORTATION

No print schedules or maps are available for trains and buses in Haifa. Luckily, Egged bus company and Israel Railways have route-finders and price calculators on their websites (see **Essentials**, p. 23), and friendly locals are often more than willing to help out. Bus tickets are bought on the bus, and train tickets can be bought from ticket machines in the station.

Trains: Stations at **Hof ha-Carmel, Bat Galim,** and **Merkaz,** right next to the Dagon grain silos, off of ha-Atzma'ut St. (☎04 03 6117000; www.rail.co.il/). To: **Akko** (30min., NIS13.50); **Hadera** (50min., NIS20.50); **Nahariya** (40min., NIS17); **Tel Aviv** (1hr., NIS26.50). Students discounts available.

Buses: **Merkazit Hof ha-Carmel,** at Haifa South Interchange, next to the train station, and **Merkazit ha-Mifratz,** at Kishon Junction. Intercity buses generally run Su-Th 5:30am-10:30pm. To: **Ben-Gurion Airport** (#947, 1¾hr., every 20min., NIS34.50); **Jerusalem**

(2hr., NIS42); **Tel Aviv** (1½hr., NIS25); **Akko** (1½hr., NIS18.50); **Tiberias** (1½hr., NIS30).

Car Rental: Budget, 46 ha-Histadrut Blvd. (☎04 935 00 19). **Avis,** 39 ha-Histadrut Blvd. (☎04 861 04 44). **Eldan,** 84 ha-Histadrut Blvd. (☎04 841 09 10).

✦ ORIENTATION

Occupying a small, rounded peninsula that juts from the north of Israel into the Mediterranean Sea, Haifa slopes up Mt. Carmel from the coast on every side. Looping around the city's edges, along with the beaches and train tracks, is **ha-Haganna Avenue.** Within, the southwestern half of the city is less built-up, incorporating both forest and neighborhoods like the Muslim **Kababir** and French **Carmel.** The northeastern half, however, rising from **Haifa Port,** is the heart of Haifa's business and tourist activity. Spidering out from the port area in northwest Haifa, known as **Old City,** is **Allenby Road,** an artery that extends northwest to the Carmelite monastery and Elijah's cave. Just west of Old City and the start of Allenby is the **German Colony,** centered on **Ben-Gurion Street,** which holds the tourist office and cuts a straight line roughly from the port to the base of the **Baha'i gardens and shrine,** whose golden dome is Haifa's most prominent landmark. East of the dome are **Hadar** and finally **Carmel Center,** each a new level in the hierarchy of increasingly wealthy neighborhoods with accordingly expansive views. Running right across the highest (in both real-estate value and altitude) ridge of Carmel is **ha-Nassi Boulevard,** home of several large hotels and more than one expensive restaurant. In Hadar, **Balfour Street** runs uphill almost parallel to the Carmelit subway system, bridging the distance between the lower ground of Old City and Arab neighborhood **Wadi Nisnas** and the heights of Carmel Center.

NUMBERS OF THE WEEK. Hebrew abbreviations for days of the week don't work the same way English abbreviations do: since day names are ordinal numbers in Hebrew, and since each letter of the Hebrew alphabet has a numerical value, Sunday ("first day") can be abbreviated with the Hebrew letter alef, which is "worth" 1.

▛ LOCAL TRANSPORTATION

Buses: Egged (www.egged.co.il). NIS6. If you take another bus within 1hr., show your ticket to the driver to get it hole-punched instead of buying another. Bus lines running between the 2 central stations—Merkazit Hof ha-Carmel and Merkazit ha-Mifratz—need to be caught going in the correct direction but others will eventually end up where you need to go (read the yellow sign at each stop, one side in Hebrew, the other in English, to figure out destinations. Egged also runs intercity buses that usually leave from Merkazit Hof ha-Carmel. These tickets cost more, but can also be bought directly from a bus driver.

Subway: By far the easiest form of Haifa's transport to understand, the Carmelit subway system cuts a straight, steep line up Mt. Carmel from the old city to Carmel Center. Since the cars are always on a slope and never lie flat, they slant forward and stop at platforms made out of large steps. Invaluable for quickly covering what would be a circuitous and hilly walk, the Carmelit is also simple. From the bottom up, the stops are: Kikkar Paris, Solel Boneh, ha-Nevi'im, Massada, Golomb, and Gan ha-Em. NIS6. Buy tickets from the machines just inside each station. AmEx/MC/V.

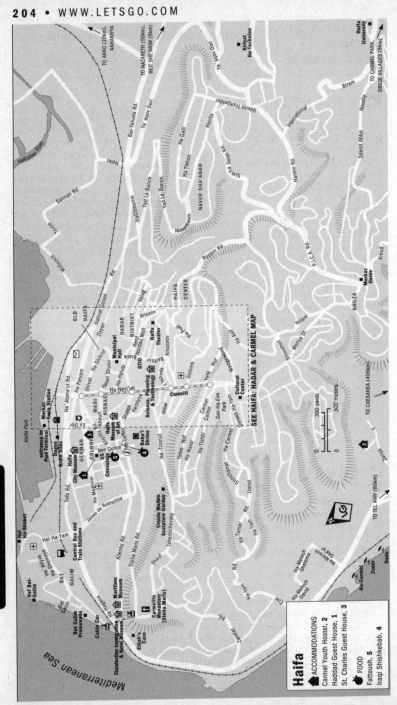

Haifa

ACCOMMODATIONS
Carmel Youth Hostel, 2
Haddad Guest House, 1
St. Charles Guest House, 3

FOOD
Fattoush, 5
Iraqi Shishkebab, 4

Cable Cars: (☎04 833 5870). These egg-shaped aerial cars start from the end of Bat Galim Promenade, on the water's edge, and climb Mt. Carmel to the **Stella Maris monastery** at its peak. NIS19; round-trip NIS28. Open 10am-6pm.

Taxis: Bros. Taxi (☎04 050 822 5200 or 04 050 834 2024). **Matam High Tech Center** (☎04 850 0550). **Ahuza Carmel** (04 838 2626). **Mercaz Horev** (☎04 888 8888). **Merkaz Metzpeh (The Central Observation Point Ltd.)** (☎04 866 2525). **Neve Shaanan** (☎04 866 2324). **Canyon Haifa (Haifa Shopping Mall)** (☎04 850 0886). **The Nitzahon** (☎04 866 3555). **Ha Ir (The City)** (☎04 852 5280). **Tax Rakevet (The Station Taxis)** (☎04 866 4422). **Yafo Taxis** (☎04 852 4442). **Kababir** (☎04 836 3622).

⑦ PRACTICAL INFORMATION

TOURIST AND FINANCIAL SERVICES

Tourist Office: 48 Ben-Gurion St. (☎04 853 5606; www.tour-haifa.co.il/eng). Walk west for 10min. from the Merkaz train station, then turn left onto Ben-Gurion. Free city maps, access to the Haifa Tourists Board website, and lots of brochures. Open Su-Th 9am-5pm, F 9am-1pm, Sa 10am-3pm.

Tours: Haifa "Regular" Tour, administered through the tourist office, departing from 48 Ben-Gurion St. and several local hotels. Bus-based day trips from and around Haifa on a weekly basis: W to Carmel, Th to Akko, F in Haifa, and Sa to Nazareth and the Sea of Galilee. Call the tourist office for more information.

Budget Travel: ISSTA, 20 Herzl St. (☎04 868 2222; www.issta.co.il/hfa). Carmelit.: Massada. Student tickets for planes, ferries, and organized tours. Open Su-M and Th 8:30am-6pm, Tu 8am-6pm, F 8:30am-1pm.

United States Consulate: 26 Ben-Gurion St. (☎04 853 1470; consage@netvision.net. il). Call before visiting Su-Th, preferably in the morning.

Currency Exchange: Any post office will exchange money without charging a commission. No-commission services also cluster around Merkaz train station, by the port.

LOCAL SERVICES

English-Language Bookstore: Steimatzky, a chain of stores all around town, including 16 Herzl St. **Lia's Books,** 5 Kiryat Safer St. (☎04 825 5467). Buses #12, 28, 37, 131, 133. Open Su, M, and Th 9am-1pm and 4-7pm; Tu and F 9am-1pm; W 9am-1pm and 2:30-5:30pm.

Laundry: Wash and Dry, 5 ha-Yam Rd. (☎04 810 78 50). Coming out of the Gan ha-Em Carmelit stop and facing the park, walk left along ha-Nassi Blvd. and turn right onto ha-Yam; on the left side of the road. NIS50 for up to 5kg, or self-service for NIS15. Dry NIS0.50 per min. Dry cleaning available. Open Su-M and W-Th 8:30am-7pm, Tu 8:30am-5pm, F 8:30am-2pm.

Public Toilets, Showers, and Baths: Maccabi, 19 Bikurim St. Swimming pool. NIS50, ages 6-18 NIS450, 3-6 NIS3, under 3 free. Open Su-Th 6am-10pm, F 6am-5pm, Sa 7am-5pm. Public toilets and showers are available to beachgoers on the promenade at Hof Dado and Hof Bat-Galim.

EMERGENCY AND COMMUNICATIONS

Police: 82 ha-Atzma'ut Ave. (☎100).

Pharmacy: Merkaz, 130 ha-Nassi Blvd. (☎04 838 1979). Open Su-Th 8am-7pm, F 8am-2pm.

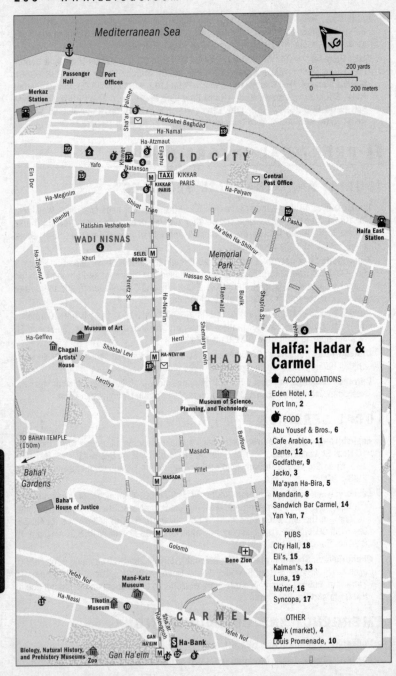

Mediterranean Sea

Passenger Hall

Port Offices

Merkaz Station

Sha'ar Palmer

Kedoshei Baghdad

Ha-Namal

Ha-Atzmaut

OLD CITY

Eliyahu

Yafo

Natanson

Khayat

Ein Dor

Ha-Meginim

TAXI KIKKAR PARIS

KIKKAR PARIS

Central Post Office

Ha-Palyam

Allenby

Hatishim Veshalosh

Shivat Tzion

Ma'aleh Ha-Shihrur

Al Pasha

Haifa East Station

WADI NISNAS

Khuri

Ha-Tziyonut

SELEL BONEH

Memorial Park

Peretz St.

Hassan Shukri

Baerwald

Bialik

Shapira St.

Ha-Nevi'im

Yehiel

Museum of Art

Ha-Geffen

Chagall Artists' House

Shabtai Levi

Herzl

Shemaryu Lewin

HADAR

Herzliya

HA-NEVI'IM

Museum of Science, Planning, and Technology

Balfour

TO BAHA'I TEMPLE (150m)

Baha'i Gardens

Masada

Hillet

MASADA

Baha'i House of Justice

GOLOMB

Golomb

Bene Zion

Yefeh Nof

Mané-Katz Museum

Ha-Nassi

Tikotin Museum

GAN HA'EIM

Sha'ar Halevanon

CARMEL

Yefeh Nof

Biology, Natural History, and Prehistory Museums

Zoo

Gan Ha'eim

Ha-Bank

Haifa: Hadar & Carmel

ACCOMMODATIONS

Eden Hotel, **1**
Port Inn, **2**

FOOD

Abu Yousef & Bros., **6**
Cafe Arabica, **11**
Dante, **12**
Godfather, **9**
Jacko, **3**
Ma'ayan Ha-Bira, **5**
Mandarin, **8**
Sandwich Bar Carmel, **14**
Yan Yan, **7**

PUBS

City Hall, **18**
Eli's, **15**
Kalman's, **13**
Luna, **19**
Martef, **16**
Syncopa, **17**

OTHER

Shuk (market), **4**
Louis Promenade, **10**

Hospital: Rambam, Bat Galim (☎04 854 2222). **Bnai Zion,** 47 Golomb St. (☎04 835 9359). **Carmel,** 7 Michal St. (☎04 825 0211).

Internet Access: Internet Cafe, 122 ha-Nassi Blvd. (☎04 838 4692). NIS15 per 30min., NIS25 per hr. Open Su-Th 9am-11pm. See **Food** (p. 208) and **Accommodations** (p. 207) for other establishments with internet.

Post Office: Branches at 19 ha-Palyam Blvd. (☎04 830 4193), 22 ha-Nevi'im St. (☎04 830 4354), 152 Yafo Rd. (☎04 852 2069), and elsewhere. Most open Su-Th 8am-5pm, with a midday break, and F 8am-noon.

TIP

SICK ON SHABBAT? At least one pharmacy in town is required to stay open on Saturdays in case of emergency. To limit the imposition on devout pharmacy owners, Haifa has a rotating schedule for which pharmacy will be open on the day of worship. The schedule is posted at every pharmacy in town, along with an emergency phone number.

ACCOMMODATIONS

The flow of Baha'i pilgrims into Haifa determines the availability of hostels—so make sure to call ahead, especially when planning to visit around a Baha'i holy day. The tourist office keeps a list on their website of B&Bs available in private homes. These openings are less predictable, but may offer more opportunity to interact with locals.

 Port Inn, 34 Yafo St. (☎04 852 4401; port_inn@yahoo.com), near Merkaz Train Station. From the intersection of Yafo St. and Ben-Gurion St., facing the Baha'i Shrine, turn left onto Yafo St. and walk about 10min. This busy hostel has high-ceilinged, air-conditioned, multi-bunk dorms, each with bath and shower. Tables in the back garden offer a sunny relaxation spot, and the owners (who know virtually everyone in downtown Haifa) are generous with maps and advice. Breakfast NIS30. Kitchen. Laundry NIS50. Wi-Fi NIS5 per 15min. Key deposit NIS20. Reception 24hr. Quiet hours from 10pm. Dorms NIS75. ❷

Haddad Guest House, 26 Ben-Gurion St. (☎04 077 201 0618; www.haddadguesthouse.com), near Merkaz train station. Facing the station, walk left along ha-Atzma'ut St. and turn left onto Ben-Gurion St. Extremely popular with Baha'i pilgrims and boasting a "Baha'i Gift Shop" in its front lobby, this hostel is home to the welcoming Haddad family. Free Wi-Fi; the owner will lend you his laptop if you don't have one. Dorms NIS80; singles with TV and bath NIS250; doubles NIS300. Reservations recommended. ❷

Eden Hotel, 8 Shmariyahu Levin St. (☎04 866 48 16). Carmelit: ha-Nevi'im. Walk down Herzl St. away from the Baha'i Shrine, turn left on Shmariyahu Levin, and watch for a sign on the left. Reception with retro art prints and bedrooms with low double beds, bright windows, and TV. Free Wi-Fi. Singles NIS120, with shower and A/C NIS150; doubles NIS250/300. MC/V. ❸

Saint Charles Guest House (the German Hostel), 105 Yafo St. (☎04 855 3705; stcharls@netvision.net.il), near Merkaz train station. Facing the station, walk left along ha-Atzam'ut Ave. until the intersection with Ben-Gurion. Turn left and then left again onto Yafo St.; follow Yafo a few blocks until you hit the sign on the right. Run by Catholic nuns, this guest house offers private rooms with A/C and bath. The beauty of the old stone building and the tranquil garden make up for the spare but clean furnishings. Breakfast included. Wi-Fi NIS10 per hr. Curfew 10pm. Singles NIS180; doubles NIS320. Reservations recommended. Cash only. ❸

Carmel Youth Hostel, Kfar Zamir, Hof ha-Carmel (☎04 853 1944; www.iyha.org.il/eng). Buses #3A, 43, 44, 114. A basic, campground-like collection of buildings, tucked away in the wooded hills south of Haifa. A long way from the city and not too close to the beach either. Breathtaking natural surroundings. Each dorm well-equipped with sturdy bunk beds, bedside lights, TV, bath and shower, and almost always a balcony with an ocean view. Breakfast NIS32.50. Reception Su-Th 8am-8pm. 5-bunk dorm NIS110; singles NIS222; doubles NIS286. ❷

🗋 FOOD

Like most places in Israel, Haifa culinary highlights include falafel, sha-warma, bureka, kebab, and hummus. Downtown, toward **Hof ha-Carmel,** the shawarma places crop up thick and fast, and they stay open late. The **port** and the **Wadi Nisnas** area are imbued with Arab influences and full of tiny, cheap falafel places. Lineups of casual restaurants that grill meat and mix delicious fruit shakes grace the beach. As a general rule, prices rise with altitude—food in Carmel Center costs more than it does farther down in the city. For groceries, visit **ha-Khi Zol** ("The Cheapest") in Kikkar Paris (open Su-F 24hr.), or drop into one of Wadi Nisnas' many corner stores.

DOWNTOWN

Abu Yousef, 1 ha-Meginim St. (☎04 866 3723). Carmelit stop: Kikkar Paris. Don't be put off by the tile surfaces and cafeteria-like ambience—this Arab eatery is a household name, rumored to serve some of Haifa's best hummus. Soup NIS13. 1st course of hum-mus or *fuul* (beans) NIS17-22. 2nd course with meat NIS27-50. Be sure to check out the baklava and burma behind the cash register for NIS3 a piece. Open Su-Th and Sa 9am-9pm, F 9am-5pm. AmEx/MC/V. ❷

Ma'ayan ha-Bira, 4 Natanson St. (☎04 862 3193). Carmelit: Kikkar Paris. Home to jazz, smoked meat, and beer, this rough-and-ready bar/restaurant is graced by a giant mural of King Arthur and his knights downing steins of Carlsberg. No English menu available, but the staff is happy to offer suggestions. Soup NIS25-30. Kebab, spare ribs, and other meat NIS40-60. Selection of cold salads, pickles, and fish, including *ikra* (caviar for the general) to order with bread. Tu live jazz from 8pm, but make reservations and be ready to spend at least NIS50. Open Su-M and W-F 10am-5pm, Tu 10am-midnight. AmEx/MC/V. ❷

Jacko Seafood, 12 Kehliat Saloniki (☎04 855 8813 or 862 6639). Carmelit: Kikkar Paris. Walk down Natanson St. toward the Dagon grain silos and turn right onto Kehliat Saloniki; restaurant is on the left. With its reputation as one of the best seafood restau-rants in town, this back-street, 2-room fish place draws crowds of happy locals. Shrimp, salmon, St. Peter's fish (a.k.a. tilapia), and other entrees NIS67-85. Lunch specials (Su-Th), written up on a chalkboard in Hebrew, knock NIS5-10 off many dishes and include a free salad and hot drink. Open daily noon-5pm. ❸

Iraqi Shishkebab, 59 Ben-Gurion St. (☎04 852 7576). Facing the Baha'i shrine, walk up Ben-Gurion past the intersection with Allenby; watch for the sign on the left. Popular with locals, this unassuming restaurant serves food quickly. Choose your meat raw from a deli-style counter or order from the menu. Two kebabs NIS42-44, depending on the meat ("spicy spleen" is cheapest, for the adventurous). Open Su-Th noon-6pm. MC/V. ❷

Fattoush, 38 Ben-Gurion St. (☎04 852 4930). Facing the shrine, Fattoush is on the right. Romantic outdoor dining cocooned by trees with hanging lanterns and a dainty fountain. Popular with both locals and tourists (usually headed to or coming from the Baha'i shrine), this sidewalk restaurant is people-watching heaven. Appetizers NIS22-70. Entrees NIS44-80. Desserts NIS16-30. Breakfast served 9am-1pm. Open daily 9am-2am. AmEx/MC/V. ❸

Yan Yan, 28 Yafo St. (☎04 866 0022). Carmelit: Kikkar Paris. A bright red exterior makes for easy recognition, but yields to a calmer pale yellow interior, where an exotic fish tank and painted scrolls mentally nudge patrons away from the Middle East. Great for a quick fix of late-night Chinese food. Entrees NIS24-79. Open daily noon-11pm. AmEx/MC/V. ❸

CARMEL CENTER

Mandarin, 129 ha-Nassi St. (☎04 838 0691; mcoffee@actcom.net.il). Carmelit: Gan Ha'em. Facing the park, walk left several blocks; Mandarin's sign is on the left. A pleasant retreat of wicker armchairs and leafy shades hidden from the street. Free Wi-Fi. Sandwiches NIS24-49. Desserts NIS6-31. Breakfast served 9am-1pm. AmEx/MC/V. ❷

Sandwich Bar, 128 ha-Nassi St. (☎04 838 0444). Carmelit: Gan ha-Em. Walk away from the park along ha-Nassi St. and look for a sign on the right. Displays cheeses, pastrami, and other sliced meats in its glass counter and invites you to pick your own toppings. Perch on a stool, stand inside, or settle at one of the few sidewalk tables. Sandwiches NIS25-30. Open 24hr. ❶

Ha-Bank, 119 ha-Nassi Blvd. (☎04 838 9623). Carmelit: Gan ha-Em. Next to Dante and McDonald's. A breezy, basic cafe with weathered wooden tables indoors; a sophisticated menu and attentive waiters compensate for the humble decor. Fills up with affable coffee drinkers in the morning and relaxing shoppers from the Panorama Center later in the day. Roast beef sandwiches and huge salads are popular here. Meat dishes NIS60-71. Seafood NIS72-76. Open daily 9am-1am. ❸

Cafe Arabica, 96 ha-Nassi Blvd.(☎04 810 7761; www.rol.co.il/sites/coffee-arabika). Carmelit: Gan ha-Em. Facing the park, walk left along ha-Nassi and look for a sidewalk sign on the left. This chill coffee place channels exoticism with a pink ceiling inside and Middle Eastern textiles and embroidered cushions outside. Unfortunately, the wrought-iron fence does little to block the sound of ha-Nassi traffic. Quiches NIS45-50. Salads NIS39-56. Also serves coffee. Open Su-Th 10am-1am, F 9am-3am, Sa 5pm-midnight. AmEx/MC/V. ❷

Greg, 3 Hayyam St. (☎04 837 1670). Carmelit: Gan ha-Em. Facing the park, walk right along ha-Nassi until the intersection with Hayyam, then turn left. Billing itself as "the only real espresso bar in town," this cafe boasts an elegant patio with white shade umbrellas and a sophisticated, high-ceilinged interior. Coffee from an immense selection (by Haifa's standards) NIS8-23. Entrees NIS30-57. Desserts NIS4-35. Breakfast served all day. Open 24hr. AmEx/MC/V. ❷

Dante, 119 ha-Nassi Blvd. (☎04 837 1173), next door to McDonald's. Carmelit: Gan ha-Em. High-backed chairs and a crystal chandelier inside contrast with casual outdoor seating at this traditional Italian restaurant. Pasta NIS53. Pizza NIS39 plus toppings. Entrees NIS68-93. Open daily noon-11pm. AmEx/MC/V. ❸

◎ SIGHTS

BAHA'I SHRINE. The golden-domed Baha'i Shrine that dominates the Haifa skyline commemorates the Persian Sayyid Ali Muhammad (the Bab), the first Baha'i prophet. In 1890, Baha'ullah, the founder of the Baha'i faith, chose this spot on Mt. Carmel, near where he pitched his tent following his exile from Persia to Akko, and instructed his son, Abdu'l-Baha, to bury the Bab there and build a great temple in his honor. Later, Baha'i leader Shoghi Effendi expanded the structure, which is now under renovation to strengthen its foundations.

LOUIS PROMENADE. This breezy pathway commands stunning views of the port as well as the Upper Galilee, Lebanon, and even snowy Mt. Khermon on clear days. If the Promenade proves difficult to find, face the Tikotin

PILGRIM'S PROGRESS

My hostel is full of pilgrims. Baha'i pilgrims, to be specific. They come to Israel to visit holy sights, neatly dressed and sporting plastic nametags. Their near-comical diversity is striking: I have yet to meet more than a handful who speak the same language. In Haifa, they climb the city's steep white steps, scaling Mt. Carmel to worship in the golden-domed Baha'i Shrine.

One sunny afternoon in the dorm, my bunkmate recounted how she had watched Baha'i missionaries talk to customers in her tea shop until they finally approached her, too. Baha'is embrace most other religions' teachings, and my mild-mannered friend, incapable of rejecting anyone, fully embraced the principle of unity amidst diversity. She straightened her bedsheets and explained gravely that the world is like a diamond; it needs many facets to sparkle. She confessed her hope the world would eventually become one happy family, able to communicate beyond differences.

It's the most unlikely collection of cliches and mixed metaphors I've ever heard, but here I am, sitting on a bunkbed with this gentle, foreign woman, sharing strawberries from the market, talking about faith. It's a start.

—Ruth Pimentel

Museum of Japanese Art and take the narrow path along its left side. *(Between Yefe Nof St. and ha-Nassi Blvd. Carmelit: Gan ha-Em. Free.)*

ELIJAH'S CAVE. Judaism, Christianity, and Islam all revere these grounds as sacred and even magical. According to the Bible, the caves at the base of Mt. Carmel sheltered Elijah from the wrath of the evil King Ahab and Queen Jezebel. They were more than a bit peeved at the prophet's drastic attempt to win the hearts of northern Israelites from Ba'al in the 9th century BC when he brought down a heavenly fire to consume his sacrifices and then slaughtered the 450 priests of Ba'al. Muslims dub Elijah al-Khadar the "green prophet" of the similarly-colored mountains; Jews believe he will return as the harbinger of the Messiah; while Christians hold that the caves protected the Holy Family upon their return from Egypt. Divided into two parts—one for women and the other for men—the main cave offers worshipers a tranquil, dimly-lit place to meditate and pray. Near the women's side, a smaller cave is found where the ceiling drips in scarves, tied up by faithful women to represent their prayers and the promises they have made if their wishes are granted. There is no eating or drinking inside the cave, but picnic tables populate the surrounding areas outside. *(230 Allenby St. Bus #114, or take the cable cars and walk down. Standing with your back to the National Maritime Museum, cross Allenby St. and take the staircase up to a narrow path that winds through some trees before ending at the cave. Open May-Aug. Su-Th 8am-6pm, F 8am-1pm; Sept.-Apr. Su-Th 8am-5pm, F 8am-1pm. Modest dress required. Free.)*

STELLA MARIS. The Carmelite order of the Catholic Church grew out of a community of hermits on Mt. Carmel in the 12th century, but the original monastery, built by the monks who were not allowed to live in Elijah's Cave, has been destroyed several times. The present monastery, which stands on a promontory over Haifa's bay, seems a more than reasonable replacement for the damp, dark cave. The church and monastery complex, called Stella Maris (Latin for Star of the Sea) after one of the Virgin Mary's many honorifics, was built in 1836 on the ruins of an ancient Byzantine chapel and a medieval Greek church. The unexpectedly luxurious interior of the chapel is crafted from imported marble, and its dome is crowned with paintings of Elijah in his chariot of fire; King David plucking a harp; the prophets Isaiah, Ezekiel, and Daniel; and scenes of the Holy Family. Beneath the altar is an opening to a small cave, where, as the legend has it, Elijah's midsummer prayer for rain was answered. The monastery's minuscule museum houses dusty, archaeological finds from the Byzantine and Crusader settlements on Mt. Carmel, including giant toes from a large statue of Jupiter that once stood on an altar on the mount. *(Stella Maris Rd. (Inside the entrance to the church, on the right. ☎04 833 7758. Bus #31 or the cable cars. Get off at the Gordon Institute and, facing the water, walk right as the road curves to the entrance of the monastery. Open daily 6am-1:30pm and 3-6pm. Modest dress required. Free.)*

ESHKOL TOWER. Few panoramas are more sweeping than the ones from the observatory on the 30th floor of Haifa University's tallest building. Though the university's use of the word "observatory" may be generous, there are plenty of windows looking out from the narrow hallways wrapping around the top story, providing 360-degree views of Haifa and its surroundings. *(☎04 824 0360. Buses #24, 31, 36, and 37 run to the university, a 30min. trip from Carmel Center. A set of ramps lead from the street with bus stops up to a parking lot and the entrance to Eshkol Tower. Once inside, the information desk is straight ahead, and elevators are to the left. Take the elevator to the 29th floor and then climb one flight of stairs to the top. Wheelchair-accessible. Parking available for a fee in Haifa University lots. Open Su-Th 8am-8pm, F 8am-1pm. Free.)*

URSULA MALBIN SCULPTURE GARDEN. This refuge from the bustle of Haifa is sealed in by tall trees and peopled by bronze statues, with stunning views of the city and sea. And if that isn't enough art, walk through Wadi Nisnas, the Arab-influenced neighborhood between Haifa Port and Hadar. Every year during the Holiday of Holidays festival (a mass celebration of Ramadan, Hanukkah, and Christmas), this unpretentious part of town brings in local artists to adorn its streets, and the collection it has already amassed is striking if you know where to look for it. Take notice of the buildings, murals, and long-term installations (some with small plaques naming the creator). *(Haziyyonut Ave.)*

🏛 MUSEUMS

HAIFA MUSEUM

☎04 159 950 2211. *The "museum" actually consists of 4 separate museums, each in a different part of the city. Individual tickets are available for each, but a combined ticket allows visitors into all 4. NIS45, students and ages 5-18 NIS33, seniors NIS22.50, families NIS120.*

HAIFA MUSEUM OF ART. Edgy exhibitions and a strong preference for modern work endow this avant-garde museum with more attitude than might be expected from its sleepy stone facade. Three floors all housing contemporary work include regularly changing exhibits and a permanent collection. The first floor contains a futuristic cafe with a black and red plastic decor and a gift shop selling design oddities and art books in both English and Hebrew. *(26 Shabtai Levi St. ☎04 911 5991; www.hma.org.il. Take bus #1, 2, 12, 23, 25, 26, 28, 37, 41, or 115. At the convergence of ha-Geffen St., Shabtai Levi St., and Haziyyonut St. Open Su-W 10am-4pm, Th 4-7pm, F 10am-1pm, Sa 10am-3pm. NIS29, students NIS22.)*

TIKOTIN MUSEUM OF JAPANESE ART. This minimalist museum embraces the Japanese tradition of displaying beautiful objects in harmony with the change of seasons. *Shoji*, sliding partitions made of wood and paper, soften the sunlight and make for delightful browsing. On the second story is an auditorium and a small cafe, both of which open for lectures and performances. *(89 ha-Nassi Blvd. ☎04 911 5955 or 04 838 3554; www.tmja.org.il. Carmelit: Gan ha-Em. Facing the park, walk right along ha-Nassi. Open Su-Th 10am-4pm, F 10am-1pm, Sa 10am-3pm. Guided tour Sa 11am, call ahead to find out if English will be available. NIS29, students and ages 5-18 NIS22.)*

THE NATIONAL MARITIME MUSEUM. The lowest branch of the Haifa Museum (in altitude, not quality) chronicles 5000 years of maritime history. Highlights include the obsessively detailed ship reconstructions and the exhibit on pirates with a furnished, life-size ship's cabin. All plaques include English, and an English map is also available. *(198 Allenby St. ☎04 853 6622 or 04 911 5746; www.nmm. org.il. Bus #114. Between the Allenby Interchange and Naftali Vidra Sq. Open Su-Th 10am-4pm, F 10am-1pm, Sa 10am-3pm. NIS29, students and ages 5-18 NIS22.)*

HAIFA CITY MUSEUM. Housed in the old Templar school of the German Colony, this part of the Haifa Museum focuses on Haifa itself, rotating exhibitions of photographs of the city, work by local artists that comments on Haifa's past and present, and other tributes to the city. It also occasionally shows exhibitions that link Haifa and one of its sister cities—as in 2008's "Masks and Magic," visiting from the Museum of Marseilles. *(111 Ben-Gurion St. ☎04 911 5888; www.hcm. org.il. Near Merkaz train station. Facing the station, walk left along ha-Atzma'ut St. until the intersection with Ben-Gurion. Turn left, and the museum is on the left at the intersection with Yafo St. Open M-Th 10am-4pm, F 10am-1pm, Sa 10am-3pm. NIS20, students and ages 5-18 NIS10.)*

OTHER MUSEUMS

CLANDESTINE IMMIGRATION AND NAVAL MUSEUM. Devoted to *ha-Apala*, the story of European Jewish immigrants smuggled into Palestine during the British mandate, the museum showcases impressive displays on Jewish underground movements and a recreation of a Cyprus deportation camp. Perched atop the museum is the *Af-al-Pi-Khen* ("In spite of everything"), a ship that once ran the British blockade in the 1940s. The missile boat, submarine, and other real naval vessels outside are open to visitors, so brace yourself against seasickness and climb in to explore. *(204 Allenby St. ☎04 853 6622. Bus #114. Climb a staircase down from the Allenby Interchange. Open Su-Th 8:30am-4pm. NIS15, ages 5-18 NIS10, soldiers of all kinds free.)*

CHAGALL ARTISTS' HOUSE. This bare-bones gallery feels a bit like a dentist's office with its pristine white, tile floors and walls, but nowhere else in Haifa is the work of local, contemporary artists presented with such raw immediacy. The blank walls reveal mediocre paintings for what they are and dramatize the beauty of the truly skilled pieces. Occasionally, the gallery hosts festive openings for new shows—check with the English-speaking staff. *(24 Haziyyonut Ave. ☎04 852 2355. Buses #1, 2, 12, 23, 25, 26, 28, 37, 41, 115. Walk down Shabtai Levi St., away from the Haifa Museum of Art and toward the Baha'i Shrine, turning right onto Haziyyonut Ave. Chagall Artists' House is the white house on the left, with sculptures in the front yard. Open Su-Th 10am-1pm and 4-7pm. Free.)*

MANE-KATZ ART MUSEUM. Set up in Jewish painter Mane-Katz's historic home, this small-scale museum keeps most of its permanent collection in storage and showcases exhibits instead, particularly work by Jewish painters of the School of Paris. Some Judaica unrelated to the exhibits is also on display, including carved wood furniture and religious metalwork. *(89 Yefe Nof St. ☎04 838 3482. Carmelit: Gan ha-Em. Facing the park, walk right along ha-Nassi Blvd. and right through a small park onto almost-parallel Yefe Nof St.; museum is on the right, down a flight of stairs. Open Su-M and W-Th 10am-4pm, Tu 2-6pm, F 10am-1pm, Sa 10am-2pm. NIS12.)*

NATIONAL MUSEUM OF SCIENCE, PLANNING, AND TECHNOLOGY. Packed with an overwhelming number of interactive displays and overactive kids, the historic home of the Technion Institute has been reinvented as the most exciting museum in town. No English maps are available, but there are excellent English captions and instructions to guide visitors through everything from noisy experiments with sound waves to a walk-in DNA nucleus and a room full of do-it-yourself magic tricks. There's no better place in Haifa to try lying on a bed of nails. *(Historic Technion Building, 25 Shmariyahu Levin St./12 Balfour St. ☎04 862 8111. Carmelit: Massada. Walk up ha-Nevi'im St., in the direction of the next Carmelit stop, turn left on Yona St., and turn right onto Shmariyahu Levin St. Open Su-W 10am-6pm, Th-Sa 10am-10pm. Gift shop open Su-W 11am-6pm, Th-Sa 11am-9pm. Wheelchair-accessible. NIS50, students NIS25.)*

🎵 ENTERTAINMENT

Cinematheque, 142 ha-Nassi Blvd. (☎04 835 3530; www.ethos.co.il/cinema). Carmelit.: Gan ha-Em. Shows hundreds of alternative films and documentaries in Hebrew, English, and other languages. A schedule of showings in English or with English subtitles is available on the website. Open 45min. before each day's first screening begins. Memberships available. NIS33, students with ID NIS27.

Haifa Municipal Theater, 50 Pevsner St. (☎04 860 05 00; www.ht1.co.il), by Binyamin Garden, in Hadar. Partner in the International Child and Youth Theater Festival, which has a competition and puts on children's plays during Pesach. See website (in Hebrew) for current productions and showtimes.

Haifa Symphony Orchestra (☎04 859 9499; www.haifasymphony.co.il). The city symphony offers several concert series (including Jazz, ClassiKids, and Friday Classic) in Haifa Auditorium, 138 ha-Nassi Blvd. (☎04 835 3555); the Krieger Center for Performing Arts, 6 Elihayu Hakim St. (☎04 833 4741); and other performance spaces around town. Detailed listings are available on the website along with subscription prices and other fees.

🍸 NIGHTLIFE

Haifa nightlife largely depends on its soldiers, the 18- to 22-year olds just old enough to drink but not yet old enough to be back in school after their mandatory military duty. They congregate in downtown bars starting at 10 or 11pm. Clubs are few and far between (although some host private events), and they generally don't open until midnight. Thursday, Friday, and Saturday nights are likely to be the most popular, particularly at newer places and ones that market to a younger crowd. Older pubs, like the ones at the port, are open more consistently, but their crowds tend to be quieter.

BARS

🍺 **Eli's,** 35 Yafo St. (☎04 852 5550). Carmelit: Kikkar Paris. Walk down Natanson St. toward the port and look for the sign on the left once Natanson becomes Yafo. This popular music bar inhabits an old Ottoman building and radiates chaotic fun, with a drum kit hung on the wall and kegs jumbled beneath the stairs. The clientele is a healthy mix of internationals and locals, with a wide range in age. Beer NIS23-26. Some food (salads, toasts, etc) available. M open mic. Tu and W live performances. Wheelchair-accessible. 18+. Open daily 8:30pm-late. AmEx/MC/V.

Syncopa, 5 Khayat St. (☎04 670 5865 or 04 918 8899; syncopabar@gmail.com). Carmelit: Kikkar Paris. Walk 1 block down Natanson St. toward the port, then turn left on Khayat St. A gay-friendly hangout (the co-owners are lesbian partners) that feels comfy and soft, with tapestry-like wallpaper, vinyl records on the walls, and classic rock downstairs. Upstairs is a filmy-curtained room that plays blues, with a small stage and lots of seating that gets shoved aside for weekly Th parties. Beer NIS20. M free movie screening. Sa live concerts. 21+. Open daily from 9pm until the drinking's done. AmEx/MC/V.

Godfather, 30 Qedoshe Baghdad St. (☎04 867 1888). At entrance to Haifa Port, near Merkaz train station. Bus to ha-Atzma'ut Ave. Facing the train station, turn right and walk down ha-Atzma'ut until the intersection with Khayat St., then turn left. This low-slung pub right next to the train tracks peddles late-night seafood (most entrees NIS85) and beer. Furnished with rough, dim lamps and stills from *The Godfather*. Press the red button at the door to get in. Open daily 2pm-2am. AmEx/MC/V.

Martef (Basement), 2 ha-Bankiim St. (☎04 853 2367; www.martef.co.il). Near the Merkaz train station; facing the station, turn right onto ha-Atzma'ut and follow it until turning right at the intersection with ha-Bankiim. Find the white awning that says "Finlandia," and take the stairs underground. Caters to a young crowd. Free use of a pool table and a video game console. Serves burgers, wings, and schnitzel to complement the drinks (beer NIS 22-26). Su open mic. 18+. Open daily 9pm-late. AmEx/MC/V.

Kalman's, 3 ha-Namal St. (☎04 862 0525), at Haifa Port, close to Merkaz train station. From the entrance to the port, follow ha-Namal St. to its end, walking away from the Dagon grain silos. A quiet place with better-than-average bar snacks and food (think thin-sliced deli meats). Attracts patrons older than the eager young soldier crowd. A personal favorite of the owner (who has opened a few bars), the establishment profits from his mean cooking skills. Beer NIS22-27. 18+. Happy hour daily 6-8pm. Open Su-Th 6pm-2am, F-Sa 8pm-2am. AmEx/MC/V.

CLUBS

City Hall, 7 Shabtai Levi St. (☎04 867 7772). Carmelit: ha-Nevi'im. Walk up Shabtai Levi St. toward the Baha'i shrine. Haifa's largest club, City Hall attracts multiple crowds to its 3 distinct halls, blasting alternative rock in the 1st, and 80s, new wave, and synth pop in the 2nd. The 3rd and largest includes a stage for live shows. Beer NIS8-14. Watch out for City Hall posters around town advertising specific parties (Sa is devoted to just-graduated high schoolers). Th 19+, F 18+. Cover Th NIS35, F NIS30-60, Sa NIS45, depending on the show. Open in summer Th-Sa midnight-late, in winter Th-F midnight-late.

◪ ◪ BEACHES AND OUTDOOR ACTIVITIES

The Society for the Protection of Nature in Israel (SPNI) has an office on the second floor at 90 Yafo St. (☎04 855 3860; open Su-Th 9am-4pm) and provides visitors with the resources to walk Israel's trails themselves. To that end, they offer information and maps (NIS85) that mark out walking trails and detail their difficulty and steepness—good news for serious hikers. Similarly adventurous walkers may want to contact the national park service (www.parks. org.il) about visiting nearby **Mount Carmel National Park** or **Hai Bar Carmel Nature Reserve** (where Biblical animals are bred for reintroduction into the wild). For smaller-scale nature walks within Haifa itself, pick up a free map in the tourist office and look for the blue dotted lines that traverse most of the city's forested areas. Some of these trails lead to springs in local parks, including **Gan ha-Em Park** in Carmel Center.

Haifa's free beaches are a testament to the city's multifaceted personality: each draws its own sector of the populace and cultivates a unique identity, from no-frills freedom to orthodox modesty to easy luxury. Choose carefully, or, better yet, explore several. These beaches may not be as large as Tel Aviv's or as beautiful as Netanya's, but they're still a great place to sun-worship or take a see-and-be-seen stroll.

HOF DADO. Named by the locals "the student beach," this sandy expanse has absolutely no facilities other than a massive gravel parking lot. Here, visitors' summery fun goes ungoverned by policemen or lifeguards, winning youthful crowds who play beach sports, tan, and swim. Just north of the student beach, the promenade begins. Still part of Hof Dado, this stretch of beach flirts with modern Western standards, providing bathrooms and showers free to the public, along with grassy patches for picnics and a children's wading pool guarded by a policeman. Populated by families and older visitors who enjoy casual restaurants and the protection of a first aid center and lifeguards, this part of the beach is inundated with crowds every weekend. *(Lifeguards on duty until 6pm.)*

HOF HA-CARMEL. Similar in atmosphere to the promenade portion of Hof Dado, Hof ha-Carmel is home to The Meridien Hotel, which offers public access to its pool (for a fee) in the summer.

HOF BAT-GALIM. Here, the luxury of the promenade fades, and more families with younger children take advantage of the playground and the scruffier but still functional and free facilities. This former separate-sex beach now has a dividing barrier stocked with benches and excellent seafood eateries.

HOF HA-SHEKET (QUIET BEACH). Tucked between Rambam Hospital and Haifa Porwhich, this modern separate-sex beach is just close enough to downtown for orthodox Jews to walk there while keeping Shabbat.*(Open 8am-6pm or women Su, Tu, Th; for men M, W, F; for both Sa.)*

▓ FESTIVALS

Haifa International Film Festival (www.haifaff.co.il). Organized by Cinematheque and the Haifa Auditorium and held annually during Sukkoth since 1983. As the festival approaches, more information will become available online, including films to be screened, ticket prices and reservations, and viewing spaces around the city.

▶ DAYTRIPS FROM HAIFA

▓ EIN HOD

עין הוד

Take bus #921 or 202 from Haifa, heading south along the road to Hadera (20min., every 30min., NIS14.60). From the junction where the bus stops, the town is a 2km walk uphill. To get to the center of town, turn right at the colorful wood sign and inventive gate, then right again when the road forks.

A colorful, messy commune in which everything seems handmade and nothing quite matches, Ein Hod is a natural home for artists and dreamers. Tin soldiers stand guard along nameless streets, funky mobiles swing between trees, and bronze nudes recline lazily against fences, transforming this artists' colony into an open-air museum. The village was established in 1953 by Dadaist Marcel Janco and other artists. Today, potential new residents must apply for membership, showing their artwork to a jury and undergoing multiple interviews, after which the entire community votes on the decision.

The air-conditioned **Main Gallery** displays the diverse work of residents, running the gamut from *mezuzahs* to giant multimedia paintings. (Open Su-Th 10am-4pm, F 10am-2pm, Sa 11am-4pm. Free.) Right across the street is the **Janco-Dada Museum.** The largest building in town, this museum shows work by contemporary Israeli Dadaists. In the center of town, a small **amphitheater** occasionally hosts summer concerts. For music of an entirely different kind, try the **Nisco Museum of Music Boxes and Mechanical Music,** a one-room museum of what is undoubtedly Israel's greatest antique music box collection. Elaborate gems from 1850-1900 and mechanical instruments like a player piano are lovingly explained to visitors by their devoted owner on a 40min. tour, included in the price of admission. (☎04 052 475 5313. Open M-Th and Sa 9:30am-4:30pm, F 9:30am-4pm. Groups of 15 or more can make reservations for 2hr. concert, with coffee and cake at intermission.) Though nearly every house in Ein Hod houses a workshop and gallery that are open to visitors, only one has extensive—even aggressive—ceramic signage all over town. **Naomi and Ze'ev's Pottery Studio** is on the outskirts of the village, but the signs make it easy to find. The cups, jars, and dishes for sale are attractive but are easily overshadowed by the incredible selection of secondhand books in English and Hebrew. Keep an eye out for Kaya, the studio dog, who weaves her perilous way through the displays without breaking a single mug. (☎04 984 1107. Open 24hr. Workshops Sa or any day if you call ahead. NIS55, children NIS25. The information office (☎04 984 2029) provides free maps and answers questions: it's in the village center, upstairs from the main gallery.)

Abu Yaakov ❷, a Middle Eastern food restaurant, sits at the top of the amphitheater's stairs. It has no menu, but the owner makes salads, hummus, falafel (NIS20), and kebabs (NIS40). (Open M-Sa 7am-3pm. Cash only.) A more reliable bet than the amphitheater for live music is **Cafe Ein Hod ❷,** Like everything in Ein Hod, the cafe doubles as a gallery, displaying photographs and other small works between its high, dusty windows, and has live music on Fridays from 9pm. A tiny menu lists salads and sandwiches (NIS35-40) that change daily, and there's Indian food on Thursdays. (Restaurant open daily 8:30am-7pm. Pub open Th-Sa. AmEx/MC/V.) Shack-like though it may appear, the village center's **ArtBar ❷** is absolutely not to be missed. Proprietor Danny brews what he proudly bills as "the best beer in the world" in giant, bubbling pots outside, and bakes up hot, thin-crusted pizzas (NIS25) inside. There's also a tiny gallery, and the outdoor tables (partially-finished slabs of wood) serve as concert seats for live music performances.\

DOR

דור

Take bus #921 or #202 from Haifa (30min., NIS12.60). After getting off at the Kibbutz Dor intersection, it's a flat 4km walk on the access road out to the beach and museum.

The pristine **Tel Dor** has smooth sand and water so clear that the ocean floor is visible beneath it. The paths there are rocky—don't go barefoot—and lead to unlabeled excavation sites, where the foundations of ancient buildings are visible in the frothy waves. The ruined city is thought to have been ruled by Canaanites, Israelites, Romans, and Greeks; scholars from institutions like the Hebrew University in Jerusalem continue excavations in the summer. (☎04 69 0265. Lifeguards on duty daily 8am-6pm. NIS10.) Hidden past the gates of the Nahsholim Kibbutz Hotel, **Hamizgaga Museum**—Baron Edmond de Rothschild's former glass factory—now houses archaeological finds. Exhibits include Byzantine jars, ships' anchors from the third millennium BCE, and muskets thrown overboard by Napoleon's soldiers in retreat from Akko. (☎06 639 0950. Open Su-Th 8:30am-2pm, F 8:30am-1pm, Sa 10:30am-3pm. NIS18, children NIS12.) A few kilometers north, next to Kibbutz Ein Karmel, the **Nahal Me'arot Nature Reserve** offers hiking trails and prehistoric caves from as far back as 200,000 years ago. The biggest cave is 70m deep and includes, at the push of a button, an audiovisual presentation on the life of the cave's former inhabitants; available in English. (Open Su-Th 8am-4pm, F 8am-3pm. NIS20, ages 5-18 NIS9. Tours NIS200.)

BEIT SHE-ARIM

בית שערים

The Nazarene Bus Company runs buses #331 and 332 from Haifa to Nazareth, stopping at the access road to Beit She-arim along the way. Get off at the stop right after passing through Qiryat Tiv'on; you should be able to see signs for Beit She-arim with "archaeological site" symbols on them on the right side of the road. Don't get off at the stop called Beit She-arim—it's a moshav (agricultural cooperative) of the same name. Once off the bus, cross the grassy traffic circle on the right and follow Yizre'el St. for 10-15min. Follow the Beit She-arim sign here, directing you to angle right out of the circle. This road leads to an intersection with Shikun Ella St., where another Beit She-arim sign directs you right. This road takes you past the ruins of the city gate and makes a giant U-turn, leading you directly to the park entrance. Just before it hooks, there's a steep pedestrian path on the left; climb this for a statue of site's discoverer, Alexander Zaid.

Beit She-arim may be hard to get to, but it's worth the effort, particularly for history buffs and explorer wannabes. Rediscovered accidentally in the 19th century, it comprises the remains of an entire ancient city, which according to the national park authority covers some 13 hectares. Finds include the foundations of the city gate, an olive oil press, and an extensive necropolis, with inscriptions in Hebrew, Aramaic, and Greek. Perhaps most significantly, Rabbi Yehuda ha-Nassi, ancient head of the Sanhedrin and recorder of the Mishnah (the Jewish oral scripture), is buried here. English maps are available at the entrance with a suggested walking route and explanations for each cave in the necropolis. (There is a helpful visitor's center (☎ 04 983 1643). Free tours led by Hebrew-speaking volunteer guides start at 10, 11am, noon, and 1pm. Open Sa-Th 8am-5pm, F 8am-4pm, entry 1hr. before close. NIS20, ages 5-18 NIS9.)

ZIKHRON YA'AKOV

זיכרון יעקב

Take Bus 202 from Haifa's Hof ha-Carmel station to any stop in downtown Zikhron Ya'akov.

Settled by Jewish Romanian immigrants in the 1800s, Zikhron Ya'akov's former swampland was generously drained by benefactor Baron Edmond de Rothschild to yield today's forested hills. Now Zikhron Ya'akov is a small, suburban faux-village, proud of its cobblestones and red roofs (all freshly recreated in the last few years—not the real McCoy). Town activity centers on ha-Meyasdim St., a central road lined with most of the sights and wine and gift shops.

The First Aliyah Museum, on the corner of ha-Nadiv St. and Herzl St., attempts to recreate the experience of the first Zionist settlers in the area in a walk-through exhibition accompanied by melodramatic film segments. (☎04 629 4777; oramuseumzy@bezeqint.net. Open M and W-F 9am-2pm, Tu 9am-3pm. NIS15, ages 6-12 NIS10, students and 12-18 NIS12, families NIS50.) Continuing down ha-Nadiv St. away from the First Aliyah Museum, the road ends at **Carmel Winery,** which offers tours to serious wine connoisseurs. (☎04 629 0977. NIS480; NIS48 for every person added to a group of 10.) Turning left from ha-Nadiv St. onto ha-Meyasdim St. leads to the **N.I.L.I. Museum** in the historic Aaronsohn family house. This small but gripping museum tells the story of the Jewish spy ring named *Netzah Israel Lo Ieshaker,* or, "the Eternity of Israel will not lie," formed by members of the Aaronsohn family to undermine Ottoman rule. A visit to the museum includes a very brief and slightly morbid tour (available in English) of the still-furnished home, including the bathtub in which Sara Aaronsohn shot herself to escape interrogation by the Turkish authorities. (☎04 639 0120. Open Su-M and W-Th 8:30am-3pm, Tu 8:30am-4pm, F 8:30am-1pm. NIS15, students NIS12. Calling ahead is recommended.)

Finally, Zikhron Ya'akov serves as the perfect base for a visit to **Ramat ha-Nadiv,** which comprises the Rothschild family tomb and memorial gardens, plus acres of surrounding wilderness and nature trails. The park is huge and gorgeous, begging for more exploring time than visitors could possibly have, and the memorial gardens are fascinating, including one devoted to palm trees and another—for the blind—specializing in scented plants. (Follow ha-Meyasdim St. south out of town, through four traffic circles, and turn right at the Ramat ha-Nadiv sign onto the park's access road. Walking takes 45min., but a sherut from Zikhron Ya'akov can drop you off at the access road. Open Su-Th and Sa 8:30am-4pm, F 8:30am-2pm, last entry 15min. before close. Free. The tourist office is on the same block of ha-Meyasdim St. as the Founders' Memorial, across from the cemetery and immediately south of the central bus station. ☎04 639 8811; www.zy1882.co.il. Open Su-Th 8:30am-1pm.)

NETANYA

☎09

נתניה

Netanya residents celebrate laziness in all its glorious forms—be it baking on the beach, strolling aimlessly along the Promenade, or sipping coffee and people-watching in ha-Atzma'ut Sq. In the 1920s, the town was established with a citrus farm and a few diamond factories, but the tantalizing call of idyllic beaches and its prime location between Tel Aviv and Haifa soon made Netanya one of the most popular hotspots in Israel. In both location and ethos, Netanya leans closer to Tel Aviv. A significant minority of the tourists hail from landlocked parts of Israel, but there is a decidedly European presence in Netanya, with so many French families chatting in the *midrakhov* restaurants that locals sometimes joke their city is part of France. Because of the large Russian immigrant population, signs and menus are more often in French and Russian than in English. The city is very touristy—with the prices to match—and the crowd is mostly affluent retirees and families (increasingly more of the latter); students and lone travelers can cobble together a cheaper trip to the area by eating at hole-in-the-wall falafel joints outside of the *midrakhov* or staying at Orit Hotel (p. 220). The blue Mediterranean and stunning purple sunsets make the prices worth the trip.

▐ TRANSPORTATION

Buses: Central Bus Station, 3 Binyamin St. (☎09 860 6202 or 860 6222), on the corner of Binyamin Blvd. and ha-Alutzim St. To: **Tel Aviv** (#641, 1hr., every 20min., NIS16), **Haifa** (#947, 40min., every 30min., NIS21.50), and **Jerusalem** (#947, 1hr. 40min., every 25min., NIS27).

Taxis: Hashabar (☎09 861 4444). **Chen** (☎09 833 3333). **Poleg** (☎09 882 6666).

Car Rental: Country, 6 Gad Machnes St. (☎09 862 0989). **Hertz,** 8 ha-Atzma'ut Sq. (☎09 882 8890). **Tamir,** 8 ha-Atzma'ut Sq. (09-861-6470).

✈ ? ORIENTATION AND PRACTICAL INFORMATION

Tourist Office: ha-Atzma'ut Sq. (☎09 882 7286), behind Batza Yarok restaurant, in the same building as the tourist police. Free maps and brochures of city's attractions. Staff can be remarkably curt and unhelpful, however; for more in depth advice on where to go in town, try chatting with the friendly tourist police in the office next door to the tourist office, in the same building. Open Su-Th 8am-4pm, F 9am-noon.

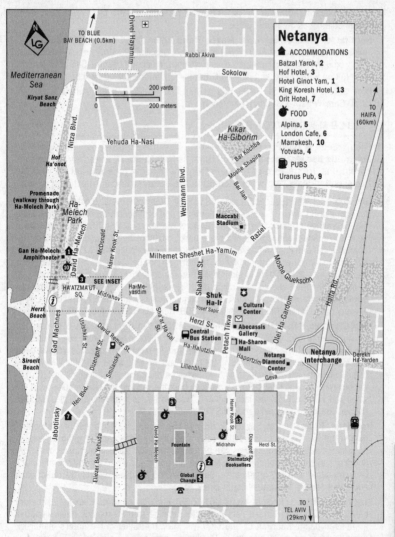

Netanya

ACCOMMODATIONS
Batzal Yarok, **2**
Hof Hotel, **3**
Hotel Ginot Yam, **1**
King Koresh Hotel, **13**
Orit Hotel, **7**

FOOD
Alpina, **5**
London Cafe, **6**
Marrakesh, **10**
Yotvata, **4**

PUBS
Uranus Pub, **9**

Currency Exchange/Bank: Banks and currency exchanges line the *midrakhov* and ha-Azma'ut Sq. **Global Change** (☎09 872 4756), on the let of ha-Atzma'ut Sq. Open Su-Th 8am-7pm, F8am-1pm. **Bank Leumi** (☎09 860 7333), on the corner of the *midrakhov* and Ussiskin St. Open Su and Tu-W 8:30am-1pm, M and Th 8:30am-1pm and 4:30pm-7pm, F 8:30am-noon.

Bookstore: Steimatzky Booksellers, 4 Herzl St. (☎09 891 7154), on the left of the *midrakhov*. Sells books and magazines in Hebrew, English and a variety of other languages. Open Su-Th 8am-8pm, F from 8am to 1hr. before sundown.

Tourist Police: ha-Atzma'ut Sq. (☎09 860 4444), behind Batza Yarok restaurant, in the same building as the tourist office.

Hospital or Medical Services: Magen David Adom (First Aid) (☎09 862 3333). **Laniado Hospital** (☎09 860 4666) is the main hospital. From the central bus station, head on Binyamin Blvd. several blocks past Herzl, which will become Sderot Weizmann. Turn left on Rabbi Akiva and right on Divrai ha-Yamim. The hospital will be on your right.

Post Office: 57 Herzl St. (☎09 862 1577). Open Su-Tu and Th 8am-12:30pm and 3:30-6pm, W 8am-1:30pm, F 8am-noon.

ACCOMMODATIONS

A cheap sleep is hard to find in Netanya. The hotels, most of which line the beach along **Gad Machnes Street** and **David ha-Melekh Street,** are fairly expensive. Reservations are necessary to secure one of the few pleasant and affordable options; call at least two weeks ahead in the summer and a month in August.

Orit Hotel, 21 Hen Blvd. (☎09 861 6818), off Dizengoff several blocks ot the left of ha-Atzma'ut Sq. When it comes to comfortable and economical travel in Netanya, looking for a place to crash can be reduced to 3 words: go to Orit. This hotel provides a peaceful, intimate atmosphere and many perks, including beach towels and a library of Scandinavian and English books, for a considerably lower price than its competitors. The Swedish management is uncommonly friendly; do not be surprised if someone gently knocks on your door at 9am to remind you that the breakfast service is ending soon and to ask whether they should save some food for you for later. Scrupulously clean rooms, private baths, fans, and balconies. No smoking. Breakfast included. A/C and free Wi-Fi in every room. Dorms NIS125; singles NIS200; doubles NIS280. MC/V. ❷

Hotel Ginot Yam, 9 David Hamelech St. (☎09 834 1007). Turn right at the end of ha-Atzma'ut Sq., right before the sea. Among the indistinguishable high rise hotels at the edge of the sea, this hotel has both the most reasonable prices and the most homey touches, with yellowed lace tablecloths on the small tables in the lobby and the occasional delightful idiosyncrasy (a pink converse sneaker painted with oil paints on the frame of a mirror, for instance) in the otherwise generic rooms. Rooms overlook both the sea and the children playing in the small park outside. Breakfast included. A/C, TVs, and fridges in all rooms. Singles NIS298; doubles NIS338. Additional person NIS119. AmEx/MC/V. ❸

Hof Hotel, 9 ha-Atzma'ut Sq. (☎09 862 1315). Among the cheapest of the central hotels, Hof is as close to the action (and the noise) as one can get without sleeping on a bench in the square. Rooms can be worn down, with occasional broken bathroom doors or strategic uses of duct tape, but they are immaculate and decently comfortable. TV, fridge, Wi-Fi, and A/C in all rooms. Singles 220NIS, doubles 250NIS; 50NIS for each additional person. Accepts all credit cards. ❸

King Koresh, 6 Harav Kook St. (☎09 861 3555). Turn right on Harav Kook St. just before ha-Atzma'ut Sq. King Koresh gets kudos for kookiness; the eccentric decor includes a life-sized painted portrait of "the big boss" (i.e., the father of the hotel's manager), which is wreathed in flashing green Christmas lights and surrounded by 5 ft. tall tarnished, genie-lamp style teapots. The princely sum is about as low as hotels in the area. Breakfast included. A/C, fridges, and TVs in all rooms. Check-in 2pm. Check-out noon. Singles NIS180, doubles NIS250, triples NIS350. Accepts all credit cards. ❸

FOOD

Cheap food is available in Netanya. During the day, the **Shuk ha-Ir** (the City Market), one block north of Herzl St., overflows with cheap produce and fresh pastries; pita and hummus go for NIS15 on the beach but prices go down and quality goes up closer to the central bus station. **Herzl Street** is lined with cheap self service falafel joints, and provides a welcome opportunity to eat with locals away from the French and/or geriatric who frequent the *midrakhov*. If you're willing to suck it up and pay the tourist prices, the restaurants on **ha-tAzma'ut Square** are generally delicious with generous portions, relaxing outdoor seating, and romantic views of the sea. A few favorites are listed here.

Batza Yarok, 12 Herzl St. (☎09 862 8883), on ha-Atzma'ut Sq. near the fountain, on the lefthand side when facing the sea. Great food with the prices to match. Plush white booths and electric pink and magenta walls. Make sure to try the house recommended cheesecake (NIS29). Salmon fettuccini NIS49. Trout in almond cream sauce NIS79. Kosher. Open Su-Th 7am-1am, F from 7am to 1hr. before sundown. Credit cards accepted. ❷

Yotvata, 3 ha-Atzma'ut Sq. (☎09 862 7576), at its corner with David Hamelech St. A neighborhood favorite, Yotvata is one of the few sit -down restaurants in the area where there are as many local Israeli families as tourists. Watch local kids in kippots chase their new French playmates past the restaurant's long tile counter onto the creaky wooden deck outside, then weave through Yotvata's collection of relaxing tables on the square. Greek salad NIS48, fettuccini in mushroom or tomato sauce NIS47. Open Su-Th 8am-midnight, F from 8am to 1hr. before sundown, Sa from after sundown to midnight. Credit cards accepted. ❷

Alpina, 2 Gad Machnes St. (☎09 82 9391), across the street from ha-Atzma'ut Sq. on the left. Classy restaurant with heavy gold drapes, pale lava lamps on the outdoor patio, and a stunning view of the sea. Considered one of the better restaurants in town, and accordingly costs an arm and 2 legs. Shrimp in garlic butter NIS89. Duck a l'orange NIS84. Open daily 11:30am-last customer. Credit cards accepted. ❸

London Cafe, 1 Herzl St. (☎09 833 8276). In the middle of the *midrakhov* on the righthand side; look for the neon blue London sign. Vaguely Italian food with hardy salads the size of small children. The outdoor seating is lovely even by *midrakhov* standards, with the collection of tables ringed by large lamps with colossal lampshades. Chicken schnitzel NIS29, St. Peter's Fish NIS39. Open daily 8am-1am. Credit cards accepted. ❷

Marakesh, 5 David Hamelech St. (☎09 833 4797). Turn right up the hill at the end of ha-Atzma'ut Sq. Decent Moroccan restaurant designed to resemble a massive Bedouin tent, with a fake cave wall surrounding the kitchen and an artificial waterfall outside. Kosher. Fish cooked in chili sauce NIS60. Moroccan mix NIS75. Open Su-Th noon-11pm, F from noon to 1hr. before sundown. Credit cards accepted. ❸

👁 🎭 SIGHTS AND ENTERTAINMENT

BEACHES. Netanya's beaches are certainly its *raison d'être*. The stunning Mediterranean coast in Netanya is clean, free, and stretches on for 11km. **Herzl Beach,**the most crowded one, just below ha-Atzma'ut Sq., has waterslides, playing courts, and surfboards for rent. **Sironit Beach,** just to the left of Herzl as you face the sea, is the only one open year-round; the others are open from May to October. Spend as much time here as humanly possible; Netanya's teleological purpose is sunbathing.

FREE ENTERTAINMENT. The Netanya municipality organizes various forms of free entertainment almost every night during the summer and often during the winter. Stop by the tourist office for a complete list of concerts, movies, and other activities. During the summer, you can watch the sun set over the Mediterranean while listening to classical music in the Amphitheater on the Promenade (check the tourist office for times). On Saturdays in summer, **folk dance** performers in ha-Atzma'ut Sq. passionately incite the crowd to come join their revelry. Every Monday at noon, talented Russian musicians give classical **concerts** at 11 ha-Atzma'ut Sq. *(☎09 884 0534.)*

ABECASSIS STUDIO. The art scene in Netanya is limited, but the small Abe-cassis Studio displays the work of Raphael Abecassis, an internationally acclaimed artist who works in the studio, using brilliant colors and modern design to portray ancient Sephardic themes. *(4 Razi'el St., next to the post office; from the midrakhov, walk 1km along Herzl St. and turn left on Razi'el St. ☎09 862 3528. Open Su-Th 10am-1pm and 4-8pm, F 10am-1pm.)*

THE RANCH. The ranch offers horseback riding along Netanya's beaches all day and by moonlight and is perfect for families with children. The rides last about an hour and cost NIS100. Call ahead. *(For a small group, a taxi will cost NIS35. Open daily 8am-7pm. Closing time varies, depending on business.)*

◈ NIGHTLIFE

A hotspot for the elderly and families with large children, Netanya is gener-ally a G-rated city; the result is that its nightlife is, shall we say, lacking. The *midrakhov* is generally dead by 1am, and the few bars and clubs that were in the downtown area have gone under in recent years. If you are dying for more variety, you can always take a taxi or sherut from the Central Bus Station to the **Industrial neighborhood,** where hangouts come and go quickly and attract many more locals than tourists. It's a bit of a schlep from the *midrakhov*, however, and at that point you may as well return to the party mecca that is Tel Aviv.

> **Uranus Pub,** 12 ha-Atzma'ut Sq. *(☎09 882 9919).* The lone place worth going to in downtown. Fashioned after traditional English pubs, Uranus skips the frou-frou and gets back to basics with a wide selection of beer (NIS18-26), straight-up liquor (from NIS26), and a laidback 20-something crowd. Expect the bar to be absolutely hopping by 1am, when the rest of Netanya has gone to sleep. Open daily 8pm-5am.

CAESAREA   ☎04

קיסריה, قيسارية

At the end of the first century BCE, Herod the Great, vassal king of Judaea, established Caesarea Maritima (Caesarea of the Sea; Kay-SAHR-ya in Hebrew). In only twelve years, he constructed a resplendent city of innovative architec-ture, huge entertainment complexes, and a harbor designed to bring his king-dom to the top of the pecking order of eastern Mediterranean ports. The multi-layered ruins—astonishingly resilient despite riots and rebellions, pillage and plunder, and a partial sinking of the coastline—now constitute one of Israel's finest archaeological sites and most popular tourist attractions. Caesarea can feel rather like a tour-bus unloading zone, and doing the area on the cheap can be quite difficult. Stocking up on groceries before you go to save on food costs, taking the daily bus there from Khadera, and then spending the night at the Caesarea Sports Center will save you shekels, but is not exactly efficient. The extent of the excavations and the diversity of previous inhabitants and cul-tures, however, makes the ruins more than worth the effort, and is remarkable enough to intrigue even the most devout of off-the-beaten-path types.

Right next to the ruins, but miles away from the Kodak-mentality, is Kib-butz Sdot Yam. They haven't ignored the occasional opportunity to profit off their prime location with tourist activities and several small but engag-ing museums. However, a peaceful stroll along shaded and landscaped paths followed by a peek in the small museums and a chat with the delightful curators provides a nice yang to Caesarea's ying.

TRANSPORTATION

Getting to Caesarea can be difficult. The only practical way is via **Khadera**, the nearest town. Buses to Khadera are plentiful: from **Tel Aviv** (#921, 823, 8230 and 851; 1 hr.; NIS19) and **Haifa** (#921, 45min, NIS19).

Buses: From Khadera, the only way to get to the ruins is to take bus #921 or 922, then transfer onto bus #43; the bus only travels to the ruins once a day in the morning, at about 9:15am (30min., fare varies). The bus stops at the 3 entrances to the archaeological park: next to the Roman theater, near the eastern gate of the Crusader wall, and just south of the Crusader city wall upon request only.

Taxis: The most convenient way to get to the city is by taxi from Khadera, but the ride is pricy (NIS50), and you will have to call a taxi to get back, which inevitably costs more.

ACCOMMODATIONS

The bad news is that there is a grand total of one budget accommodation around Caesarea. The good news is that has a prime location, uncommonly helpful staff, and stunning views of the sea.

Caesarea Sports Center (☎04 636 4394), to the left of Kibbutz Sdot Yam, a 20min. walk from Caesarea's ruins, and a stone's throw from the Mediterranean. Walk parallel to the coastline, past the Hannah Senesh House; after passing through the parking lot, the Center is just behind the big brown building. Sports plain but clean rooms with a log-cabin feel to them. Rooms have A/C and TVs. Wi-Fi available in the lobby. Singles NIS250; doubles NIS350; triples NIS430. Credit cards accepted. ❸

FOOD

Restaurant prices in Caesarea can be as high as the Crusader walls. Establishments within the ruins right at the harbor such as **Hametzuda Sushi Bar ❷** (☎04 636 0887) and **Aresto ❸** (☎04 636 3456) offer great views and comfortable seating, but their prices range from barely reasonable to borderline outrageous (Aresto foccaccia NIS29; Hemtzuda chicken breast sandwich NIS44). If you're staying near the Caesarea Sport's Center, a better bet are the small **falafel stands** that pepper the beach near the hotel, slightly removed from the tourist sights.

Aldo Cafe and Ice Cream Shop. The 1 good deal close to the ruins. Homemade ice cream in bulk, in a range of eccentric flavors (i.e. sweet potato). 100g of ice cream NIS10. Open daily 9am-last customer. Credit cards accepted. ❶

SIGHTS

THE ANCIENT CITY

Caesarea's main sights are in the Roman city, ancient port, and large Crusader fortress. A small map is given out for free at the three entrances of the **Caesarea National Park**, which provides a brief history of the city and explanations for the sites. A free, 25min, and very informative movie gives a more extensive overview of the area, and is offered directly inside the Crusader fortress entrance to the park (Park open Apr.-Sept. Su-Th 8am-6pm and F 8am-5pm, Oct.-Mar. Su-Th 8am-4pm and F 8am-3pm. NIS36. Hold onto your ticket stub for the movie.)

The numbers below that follow the sight names correspond to the numbers on the Caesarea map. These are the most important sites in Caesarea, but not

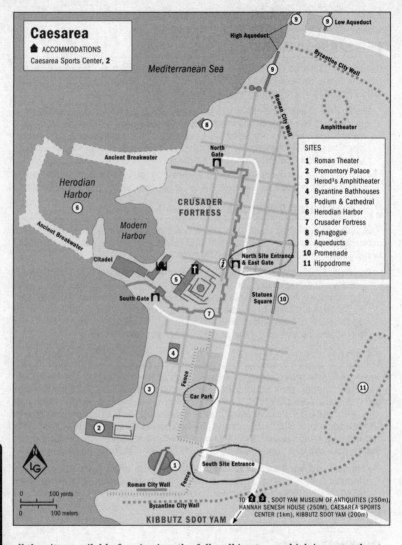

Caesarea

🏠 ACCOMMODATIONS
Caesarea Sports Center, 2

Mediterranean Sea

High Aqueduct

Low Aqueduct

Byzantine City Wall

Amphitheater

Ancient Breakwater

Roman City Wall

North Gate

SITES

1 Roman Theater
2 Promontory Palace
3 Herod¹s Amphitheater
4 Byzantine Bathhouses
5 Podium & Cathedral
6 Herodian Harbor
7 Crusader Fortress
8 Synagogue
9 Aqueducts
10 Promenade
11 Hippodrome

Herodian Harbor

CRUSADER FORTRESS

Modern Harbor

Ancient Breakwater

North Site Entrance & East Gate

Citadel

Statues Square

South Gate

Fence

Car Park

Roman City Wall

South Site Entrance

N
LG

0   100 yards
0   100 meters

Byzantine City Wall

KIBBUTZ SDOT YAM

TO 2 3, SDOT YAM MUSEUM OF ANTIQUITIES (250m), HANNAH SENESH HOUSE (250m), CAESAREA SPORTS CENTER (1km), KIBBUTZ SDOT YAM (200m)

all the sites available for viewing; the full walking tour, which is mapped out by the National Park's free brochures, takes about 5-6hr., and includes more minor sites. As they are ordered, the sights listed here form a large, rough look around the park that should take roughly three hours. Visitors seeking an even more abridged version might want to skip the aqueducts, promenade, and hippodrome. For this walking tour, it is best to start at the park's far entrance, by the Roman Theater.

ROMAN THEATER (1). Constructed by Herod, the theater was designed to bring Hellenistic culture to the city. Though reconstructed numerous times in the first few centuries, remains from Herod's period are still evident, such as the drainage system, the spectators' seats, and the multi-storied wall behind the stage floor designed to look like marble. In the 3rd and 4th centuries CE, Caesarea's elite flooded the orchestra with water using and intricate series of canales and aqueducts for mock battles and games; but by the 6th century CE, the tomfoolery got out of hand and the town's religious rulers turned the theater into a fortress. Restored and reopened in 1961, this 4000-seat structure has hosted Eric Clapton, the Bolshoi Ballet, Joan Baez, and Julio Iglesias. The **Caesarea Jazz Festival** also takes place here every summer *(Concert schedule ☎ 04 636 1358. Festival schedule and tickets *6550; http://jazz.caesarea.com.)*

PROMONTORY PALACE (2). Jutting into the sea, just west of the theater, are the excavated remains of an impressive palace with a pool in its western section. The palace dates back to the Roman and Byzantine periods, and there has been much debate over what this mysterious structure once was. Excavations of four more rooms once decorated with mosaic floors and Herodian-era pottery indicate it may have been the palace of Herod, where he and the town's governors lived. Archaeologists now believe that the ancient pool once served as the city's fish market, so the debate is clearly still alive and well.

HEROD'S AMPHITHEATER (3). Adjacent to the Promontory Palace lie the remains of Herod's Amphitheater. Herod originally built this 15,000 sq. meter, 15,000-seat complex as a hippodrome for chariot races and sporting events. According to Josephus, this is where Pontius Pilate announced that images of Caesar be placed on the Temple Mount. He ordered his soldiers to slaughter any Jews who refused his command. When the Jews submitted to impending execution instead of rioting in defense, Pilate, overcome by their self-sacrifice, sanctioned the removal of the images.

BYZANTINE BATHHOUSES (4). Fed by the city's main aqueduct, Caesarea's bathhouses offered a freshwater change from the salty sea. The baths included a cold water pool and a hot water pool, which was heated with outdoor furnaces.

CRUSADER FORTRESS (5). The walls of this fortress were built by Louis IX during his brief reign. The moat never held any water but its height and slanted bottom provided defenders a double advantage. Remnants of Christian churches, Arab granaries, and residences are scattered about the area. Don't be surprised to find pieces of marble columns used as street pavement—medieval contractors frequently re-used Roman remains when erecting cities.

SEBASTOS-HERODIAN HARBOR (6). Now partially submerged, Herod's port extended along the ancient city to welcome distinguished visitors and merchants. Herod originally had high hopes of grand international renown for this port, but remains found on the breakwaters indicate that it was already in decline by the tsunami waves and earthquake of 115 CE. A constant stream of international archaeologists and volunteers continue to excavate not only Caesarea's dry ground, but also its buried subterranean treasures.

PODIUM (7). The site of Caesarea's first temple served as a place of worship over the full course of the city's history. Herod built the large podium as a platform for the Temple of Augustus. In the 5th century CE, Christians converted the temple into a martyrium, which may have been a destination for Christian pilgrimages. Under Arab rule, the podium provided the base of a mosque. In 1101, the Crusaders reconverted the podium into a church.

THE STATUES SQUARE (8). Although most of the Roman ruins stand within the Crusader walls, several interesting relics lie outside the site proper. Across from the entrance to the Crusader city is an excavated Byzantine street and Caesarea's most famous find: colossal Roman **statues** from the 2nd century CE. Kibbutzniks plowing fields accidentally discovered the two headless figures, one of red porphyry, the other of white marble.

SYNAGOGUE (9). The synagogue was in use from the Herodian period until the 8th century CE, providing the first evidence of the Jewish community in Caesarea during the Talmudic era. Several important archaeological finds were uncovered in the 1920s, including a Corinthian capital and synagogue oil lamps, both decorated with menorahs, mosaic floors, and a hidden cache of 3700 copper coins.

AQUEDUCTS (10). So far, three of the aqueducts that provided Caesarea's water have been uncovered; two channeled water into the city from the north (the "high" aqueducts) and one from the south (the "low" aqueduct). The first high aqueduct was fed by the Shuni Springs by a 400m sandstone ridge. The second aqueduct was built under Emperor Hadrian, and drew on springs east of Shuni. *(The aqueducts are a 1km walk north along the water. Alternatively, the road that runs along the Crusader walls also leads to the Roman aqueducts, but unless you've got great hiking shoes, not much on your back, and a love of pain, take the road instead of the rocky beach path.)*

HIPPODROME (11). About 1km along the main road east of the theater stands an archway leading to the ruins of the Roman Hippodrome ("Circus"; from the Greek for horse and track), now overgrown with banana and orange groves cultivated by nearby Kibbutz Sdot Yam. Constructed in the mid-2nd century CE, the hippodrome replaced Herod's Amphitheater, which could no longer accommodate the huge population. In its heyday, the 450m by 90m racetrack could hold 30,000 spectators.

OTHER SIGHTS

KIBBUTZ SDOT YAM. A stroll through the peaceful kibbutz provides a good antidote to the feel of the ruins. Shaded paths wind lazily through the well-manicured landscape, past kibbutzniks' cottages and a playground constructed from an **airplane** donated by the Air Force in gratitude for seven kibbutzniks who served about 25 years ago. The two museums in the kibbutz (follow the signs) are small but staffed by knowledgeable and amiable curators.

OTHER SIGHTS. More of the relics unearthed at Caesarea are on display at the **Sdot Yam Antiquity Museum.** The archaeological garden and the museum's three rooms contain Jewish, Christian, Samaritan, and Muslim artifacts, Canaanite pottery, 3500-year-old Egyptian urns, and Roman coins and statues. Shield the eyes of any small children from the erotic oil lamps. *(☎04 636 4367. Open Su-Th 10am-4pm, F 10am-2pm. Free.)* Next to the museum is the **Hana Senesh House,** built in honor of a Sdot Yam parachutist who was captured, tortured, and executed by firing squad while trying to save Jews from the Nazis during World War II. Admission includes a short film about Senesh's life, offered in six different languages. *(☎04 636 4366. Open Su-Th 10am-4pm, F 10am-2pm. Free.)*

🎵 🎭 ENTERTAINMENT AND OUTDOOR ACTIVITIES

While the intensely blue water is cool and inviting, **swimming** within the walls of the city is not very economical (NIS25). Tickets can be bought at the office inside the Crusader fortress walls, but unless you wish to snorkel in the ancient harbor, the free public beach behind the aqueduct is a better place to swim. Diving in the harbor is an expensive but rewarding experience. In a concerted effort to make the town even more touristy, the city of Caesarea has put together an almost aggressively welcoming website (www.caesarea.com) that catalogs the different activities they offer. It's definitely worth checking out; listings include a variety of **hiking trails** through the ruins and beaches, and most importantly offers a detailed schedule of the variety of **music performances** that take place in the Roman Theatre. Highlights include the city's yearly **summer jazz festival.**

Underwater Archeological Park (☎04 626 5898). Provides both amateur and experienced divers with subterranean tours of Herod's remarkable feats of engineering, in addition to the motley remnants of ancient and modern shipwrecks. 1 of the park's 4r diving facilities is dedicated exclusively to **snorkeling** for those who do not have proper scuba diving training.

Beach Bar (☎050 636 0505). For those who prefer a more relaxing beach experiences, the Beach Bar offers free yoga and tai chi classes on the beaches at sunset (July-Aug. Tu and Th 7pm-8pm).

AKKO (ACRE) ⊁   ☎04

עכו عـکـّا

Dominated by the emerald-domed, 18th-century Mosque of al-Jazzar, the Old City of Akko (*Akka* in Arabic, historically written "Acre" in English) is surrounded on three sides by the Mediterranean Sea. It gazes across the bay at Haifa's crowded skyline, but the city's stone fortresses and underground Crusader City lend it a character far removed from that of its modern coastal neighbor. Visitors can stroll through the colorful, chaotic maze of the *souq* (or *shuk* in Arabic) or escape to the city's South Promenade and watch the waves crash against the city's white walls.

The Canaanite city-state of Akko is first mentioned in the *Book of Curses*, which records the curses of pharaohs on their enemies in the 19th century BCE. After this happy entry onto the international stage, Akko was conquered by the usual suspects: Egyptians, Persians, Greeks, Hasmoneans, Romans, and Umayyads. Crusaders came to the city in 1104 on their campaign to recapture the Holy Land for Christianity. In 1187, with the battle of the Horns of Hattim, Salah al-Din defeated the Crusader forces in Akko; three years later, Richard the Lionheart arrived from England and recaptured the city. During the next century, Crusader kings transformed Akko into the greatest port of their empire and a world-class showpiece of culture and architecture. The Mamluks ended Crusader rule in 1291, and Akko remained impoverished until the Druze prince Fakhr al-Din rebuilt it almost 500 years later. The Muslims built their city directly over the Crusader network of tunnels and basements and left the subterranean labyrinth for wide-eyed tourists. After his unsuccessful siege of the city in 1799, Napoleon claimed that had Akko fallen, "the world would have been mine." After a stint under the Egyptian Ibrahim Pasha, Akko returned to Ottoman control. When the British captured the port in 1918, it held a predominantly Arab population of about 8000; it retains a distinctly Arab flavor today.

Women traveling alone are strongly advised to be cautious with many of these would-be guides, and all solo travelers are advised to avoid the alleys of Old Akko after dark; stick to the well-lit promenade by the port for a safer stroll. That said, Akkan locals are eager to share thoughts on their home and their lives while offering much-needed guidance around the dizzying network of Old City streets, food stalls, and minarets.

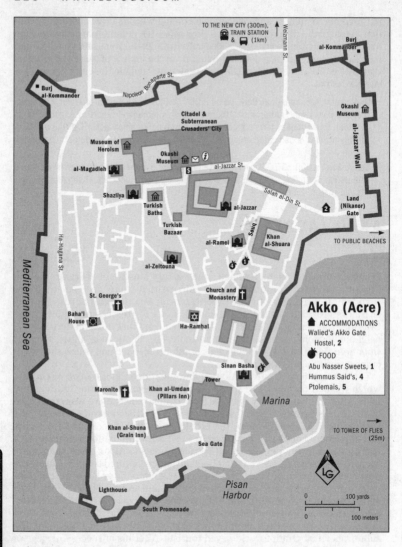

TO THE NEW CITY (300m),
TRAIN STATION
& (1km)

Weizmann St.

Burj al-Kommander

Napoleon Bonaparte St.

Burj al-Kommander

Okashi Museum

al-Jazzar Wall

Citadel & Subterranean Crusaders' City

Museum of Heroism

Okashi Museum

al-Magadleh

al-Jazzar St.

Shazliya

Salah al-Din St.

Turkish Baths

al-Jazzar

Land (Nikanor) Gate

Turkish Bazaar

Souq

al-Ramel

Khan al-Shuara

Ha-Hagana St.

al-Zeitouna

TO PUBLIC BEACHES

Mediterranean Sea

Church and Monastery

St. George's

Baha'i House

Ha-Ramhal

Akko (Acre)

🏠 ACCOMMODATIONS
Walied's Akko Gate Hostel, **2**

🍎 FOOD
Abu Nasser Sweets, **1**
Hummus Said's, **4**
Ptolemais, **5**

Sinan Basha

Maronite

Tower

Khan al-Umdan (Pillars Inn)

Marina

Khan al-Shuna (Grain Inn)

TO TOWER OF FLIES (25m)

Sea Gate

N

Lighthouse

0   100 yards

0   100 meters

Pisan Harbor

South Promenade

▣ TRANSPORTATION

Old Akko is easily navigable by foot, and the parts of New Akko that travelers might want to explore are also within reach. Most visitors will probably only need transportation to get to or from the city or to the more distant **Baha'i Shrine** and gardens.

Trains: David Remez St. (☎04 854 4444), 1 street behind the central bus station. Open Su-Th 24hr., F 12:01am-3pm, Sa 6:40pm-midnight. Trains are the best way to get to and from Haifa, especially during rush hour. To **Haifa** (30min., NIS13.50), **Nahariya** (10min., NIS7.50), and **Tel Aviv** (1½ hr., NIS35). All trains run regularly Su-Th 4am-10pm.

Buses: ha-Arba'a St. (☎04 854 95 55), in the New City. To **Haifa** (#271, 361, and 500; 45min.; every 10min.; NIS12.60), **Nahariya** (#271, 272; 35min.; every 15min.; NIS8.10), and **Old Akko** (#61, 62, 64, 68, 69, 343; 3min.; NIS4.90).

Taxis: ha-Arba'a St., near the bus station.

Sherut: ha-Arba'a St., either across from the bus station or farther toward the beach. The best way of getting to the Baha'i gardens (NIS6).

◄❚ ❷ ORIENTATION AND PRACTICAL INFORMATION

In **New Akko,** the central bus station is on ha-Arba'a St., and the train station is one block behind it on Remez St. To get to the **Old City,** walk down Herzl St. toward the sea (facing away from the train station) until just past **Recklinghausen Garden,** then turn left onto Weizmann St. and follow it until it ends at the entrance to Old Akko. Those arriving by bus should go left on ha-Arba'a St. (facing away from the bus station), left again on Ben-Ami St., and left once more onto Weizmann St. Once in Old Akko, visitors will likely be dismayed by the dearth of street signs—the best navigational tools are the small brown signs in some alleys pointing to major monuments, and there are always locals around to ask. **Al-Jazzar Street** and **Salah al-Din Street** extend in opposite directions from slightly different points near the main entrance on Weizmann St. Most sights are on al-Jazzar St., and the **souq** begins just past al-Jazzar Mosque. When entering on Weizmann St. ha-Hagana St. runs along the far side of the peninsula to the **Pisan Harbor,** which is lined with touristy seafood restaurants, a pleasant promenade, and sitting areas with great bay views.

Tourist Office: 1 Weizmann St. (☎04 991 2171, ext. 5; www.akko.org.il). Immediately inside Old Akko gates; follow signs on the right to the Visitors' Center. A lovely garden courtyard facing the citadel also leads to entrances to the information center, a reservation booth (maps available in English; NIS3), and the distribution point for city audio guides. Open in summer Su-Th and Sa 8:30am-6pm, F 8:30am-3pm; in winter Su-Th and Sa 8:30am-5pm, F 8:30am-2pm). **American Corner Akko,** Old Akko Center (☎04 955 8277; aca.usac.gov), around the corner from al-Jazzar Mosque. Information and resources on the US, with a small English library. Open Su and Tu-Th 2-6pm, M 8am-1pm.

Banks: Mercantile Discount Bank, on the corner between al-Jazzar St. and Weizmann St. Open M and Th 8:30am-1pm and 4-6:15pm, Tu and W 8:30am-3pm, F 8:30am-12-:30pm. **Bank Leumi,** Ben-Ami St., near Weizmann St. Open Su, Tu, and W 8:30am-2pm; M and Th 8:30am-1pm and 4-6:15pm. Both banks have **ATMs.**

Public Toilets: Scattered around Old Akko (1 near Land Gate, at the end of Salah al-Din St.). Public showers available at **Purple Beach,** east of the old city.

Police: 16 ha-Hagana St. (☎04 987 6808).

Pharmacy: Merkaz (☎04 991 0527), at the corner of Ben-Ami and Weizmann St. Open Su-Th 8am-8pm, F 8am-3pm.

Internet Access: See **Walied's Akko Gate Hostel** in **Accommodations** (p. 230). Also at the **city library,** NIS7 per 30min.

Post Office: 11 ha-Atzma'ut St. (☎04 991 3347 or 991 0023). Open Su and Th 8am-6pm, M and Tu 8am-12:30pm and 3:30-6pm, W 8am-1:30pm, F 8am-noon. Branches at 51 Ben-Ami St. and on al-Jazzar St. **Currency exchange** at all branches.

ACCOMMODATIONS

Budget accommodations are nearly impossible to find in Akko. A few expensive hotels are available, but those looking for a cheap bed may be better off staying in another town and taking the train.

Walied's Akko Gate Hostel, Salah al-Din St. (☎04 991 1982), close to the eastern Land Gate. A 15min. walk from the central train station. Follow Weizmann St. into the Old City, then go left at both forks in the road. Turn right when it ends; the hostel is on the right. The dorms are under renovation in this only hostel in Old Akko. Until they're done, the owners put up travelers who don't need private rooms on their co-ed back patio, with 1 section roofed and the other under the open sky. Don't count on electricity or a nice paint job, and beware clouds of mosquitoes. Small shared bathroom. A quick trip into the nicer part of the hostel wins you a hot shower. Breakfast NIS50. Internet NIS20 per hr. Reception 24hr. Check-in 11am. Check-out 10:30am. Patio NIS40; private rooms NIS250. MC/V. ❶

FOOD

Lovers of street food eat well in Akko, where cheap (NIS5-15) shawarma, falafel, and hummus joints cluster near **al-Jazzar Mosque,** at the beginning of the **souq,** and in the New City along **Weizmann Street** or across **ha-Arba'a Street.** Higher-end, touristy seafood restaurants can be found along the Pisan harbor. Although the Old City's *souq* is certainly the most interesting and likely the cheapest place for groceries, more standard supermarkets can be found in New Akko—try the intersection of Yehoshafat St. with Herzl St. or with Mordekhai Anilevitz St.

Hummus Said's (☎04 991 3945). In the middle of the *shuk* on your right when coming from the plaza off Salah al-Din St. Watch for windows and doors with green signs rather than an open stall. This legendary favorite is so packed with locals that getting up 1 step toward the entrance through the silent, anticipatory crowd feels like a life accomplishment. A synchronized swarm of waiters and chefs keeps everything cycling at top speed. Grab a pita stuffed with hot hummus and pickles to go for NIS5 or try to get a seat and a full spread with chickpeas or *fuul* (Egyptian beans). Open daily 6am-2:30pm. Cash only. ❶

Abu Nasser Sweets (☎04 685 26 21), in the *souq,* directly across from Said's. Stop here to try small pieces of baklava, *burma* (sweet, dried noodle rounds with pistachios in the middle), and *kunafa* (a creamy base with sweet, dried noodle topping). Servings NIS5-10. Sweets NIS35 per kg. Open daily Su and Tu-Sa 6am-6pm. Cash only. ❶

Tsunami (☎04 991 39 53). At the right on Salah al-Din St., before the plaza at the *souq* entrance, when coming from Weizmann St. Though similar to many of Old Akko's shawarma places, this one puts plastic wrap over the meat in its display case and has tasteful tile mosaics, which may inspire a little extra confidence in reluctant eaters. Hummus NIS15. Meat (such as kebab, schnitzel, and sausage) NIS19-33. Open daily Su and Tu-Sa noon-10pm. Cash only. ❷

Ptolemais (☎04 991 61 12), on the left side of the marina when facing the sea. A prime spot on the harbor gives patrons of this otherwise standard fish and meat restaurant enviable views of boats rocking in the water and fishing nets bundled out to dry. Hummus NIS18. Kebab NIS40. Lamb chops NIS70. Fresh orange juice NIS8. Open daily 10am-midnight. MC/V. ❷

👁 ◐ SIGHTS AND BEACHES

Sealed in by hulking stone walls, expansion was never an option for Old Akko. Instead, the city has been updating and adding new layers on top and secret tunnels underneath for centuries. The result is an unplanned, labyrinthine snarl of unlabeled streets. To grease the wheels of tourism in such a confusing setting, the **Old Akko Development Company** has concentrated all visitors' information and resources in one place, just outside the entrance to the Citadel, on the right when entering Old Akko from Weizmann St. Here, in a shady garden, is a universal box office where you can buy tickets to individual sights, a combined ticket that lets you into all of them (audio tour included), or one that also includes a tour to Rosh ha-Nikra. For more information, call ☎1 700 708 020.

HOSPITALLER FORTRESS. The most extensively excavated part of Akko's Crusader City, these soaring 12th-century halls were probably part of a medical complex where the military and religious Hospitaller Order treated pilgrims. From the courtyard beyond the entrance hall, fortifications built by Fakhr al-Din and Tahir al-Omar are visible. Halfway down the stairs on the left and along the wooden path are the rooms of the Hospitaller Castle, called the **Knights' Halls,** built on top of third-century BC Hellenistic foundations. Farther into the fortress is the refectory, once a large dining room where the Hospitallers held large feasts. Until excavations uncovered the *fleur-de-lis* in honor of Louis VII, archaeologists had mistakenly assumed the hall to be a large crypt. The Gothic vaulted ceilings resemble the architecture of many European cathedrals at the time. Make sure not to miss the staircase outside the refectory, connecting to a long, underground passageway dug by the Romans for drainage and used by the Crusaders as an escape tunnel during the Mamluk siege. The complex of arched rooms at the other end of the tunnel was used as a hospital for wounded knights, and a Crusader tombstone is displayed there. *(In the same complex as the visitors' center, on al-Jazzar St., on the right as you enter the Old City. Open in summer Su-Th and Sa 8:30am-6pm, F 8:30am-3pm; in winter Su-Th and Sa 8:30am-5pm, F 8:30am-2pm. Last entry 1hr. before closing. NIS27, children NIS24.)*

HAMMAM AL-BASHA (TURKISH BATHS). Built by Ahmed al-Jazzar in the 18th century, the baths include a progression of richly-tiled rooms that once gradually acclimatized patrons to greater and greater heat. The first has a central fountain, and the final, hexagonal one has a high domed ceiling with tiny glass windows scattered across it. The tour now includes an audiovisual presentation with the talkative "son of the last bath attendant." Private headsets available in English. *(Walk through the small square faced by al-Jazzar Mosque, the Okashi Museum, and the post office, with the mosque on your left, and turn left at its end. Open in summer Su-Th and Sa 8:30am-6pm, F 8:30am-3pm; in winter Su-Th and Sa 8:30am-5pm, F 8:30am-2pm. Last entry 1hr. before closing. Multimedia presentation at regular hours; ask at Visitor Information. NIS25, children NIS21.)*

OKASHI MUSEUM. This gallery displays many of the late Akko resident and acclaimed Israeli artist Avshalom Okashi's large, thickly-painted canvases, a demonstration that he did his work "relying mainly on the secrets of the color black," as the panels declare. Also on view are many of Okashi's rainbow-colored, abstract depictions of Old Akko. *(al-Jazzar St., opposite the mosque and just past the post office. Open in summer Su-Th and Sa 9:30am-6pm, F 9:30am-3pm; in winter Su-Th and Sa 8:30am-5pm, F 8:30am-2pm. Last entry 1hr. before closing. Wheelchair-accessible. NIS10, children NIS7.)*

MOSQUE OF AL-JAZZAR. The third-largest mosque in Israel, it dominates the city with its green dome and towering minaret. Ahmed al-Jazzar ordered its construction in 1781 on what is believed to have been the site of San Croce, the original Christian cathedral of Akko. Legend has it that al-Jazzar buried a large treasure underneath the mosque to ensure that there would be plenty of money to rebuild the place if it were ever destroyed. Through the gates is a graceful courtyard with Roman columns, and inside the mosque itself (though not visible to the public) is a green cage containing a hair from the beard of the prophet Muhammad. A digital clock displays the day's five prayer times, and blue and white Arabic script wraps around the inner face of the dome. Returning to the courtyard, to the right of the mosque is a small outbuilding containing the **sarcophagi** of al-Jazzar and his son, marble boxes visible only by peeking through the barred windows. *(al-Jazzar St., across from the post office. Walking toward the post office, climb a set of stone stairs on the left to an arched entryway. If prayers are in progress, visitors may be asked to wait. Modest dress required, although scarves are provided for those not already covered. NIS4. Cash only.)*

AKKO UNDERGROUND PRISONERS' MUSEUM (MUSEUM OF HEROISM). This citadel, built by the Ottomans on Crusader foundations, functioned as everything from a ruler's palace to a prison for important detainees. Under the Ottoman rule, it held Baha'ullah, founder of the Baha'i faith, and during the British Mandate, it housed significant members of violent, anti-British groups including Etzel, ha-Gana, and Lehi. Displays (partially in English) on the first floor explain the different resistance groups, and an exhibit on the second floor (also in English) presents the life of key dissident Ze'ev Jabotinsky. Visitors may also examine a memorial to those who died in a major Etzel-staged prison break. The cells are huge, echoing, and white-washed. A small archive, near the entrance, keeps records related to the former prison occupants. *(The citadel adjoins the Crusader City on ha-Hagana St., opposite the sea wall. To reach the museum from the Old City, go through the visitors' center garden and toward the Hospitaller Fortress entrance, then turn right just before the wall and climb the stairs to the upper level of the complex. At the top of the stairs, turn left and keep going until the entrance to the museum appears on the left. ☎04 991 1375 or 04 981 1020. Open Su-Th 8:30am-4:30pm, F 8:30am-1:30pm. Last entry 1hr. before closing. NIS15.)*

ETHNOGRAPHIC MUSEUM. A fairly new addition to Akko's tourist industry, this friendly place tackles history far more recent than the Crusaders and the Ottomans. Inside is a reconstructed Galilean village, complete with well-stocked shops, including those of a potter, a weaver, a cobbler, a carpenter, and a tinsmith. Most display tools and miscellanea that would have been used in the 40s. The other half of the museum is devoted to collectors' items like bank notes, old matchboxes, and exquisitely inlaid furniture. English labels are rare. *(On the eastern walls of the Old City. Turn left at the entrance from Weizmann St. and climb the first staircase, then follow the fortifications to the museum door. Open Sa-Th 10am-4pm, F 10am-2pm. NIS15, children NIS12.)*

TEMPLARS' TUNNEL. Built by the Knights Templar to connect the Hospitaller fortress to the port, this underground passageway was rediscovered in 1994 and is now open to curious tourists who wander along its dark path. Its wooden walkway is just high enough to elevate visitors from the streams of water rushing underfoot. The arc of the stone ceiling is extremely low at the non-port end of the tunnel: warning signs and white cushions on the stone give fair notice. *(One entrance is near the end of ha-Hagana St., a little behind Uri Buri fish restaurant, walking away from the city walls. The other entrance is in Khan al-Shuna, slightly southwest of Khan al-Umdan. Open in summer Su-Th 9:30am-6:30pm, F 9:30am-3:30pm; in winter Su-Th 9am-5:30pm, F 9am-2:30pm. Last entery 1hr. before closing. Elevators are provided for those in wheelchairs, but one end of the tunnel may not be high enough to allow passage. NIS10, children NIS7.)*

BAHA'I SHRINE AND GARDENS. Though less extravagant than the one in Haifa, this Baha'i holy place is actually more sacred, as the final resting place of the Baha'ullah himself. The gardens here are more limited—all on one level, rather than multiple terraces—but are easier to explore. Look for gardeners barbering bushes into perfectly rounded nubs. *(Catch a sherut on its way from Akko to Nahariya—the gardens are about 4km north of the New City. Ask the driver to let you off at the Baha'i shrine access road, then walk up it no more than 5min. to the main entrance. Open daily 9am-4pm. Shrine open 9am-noon. Free.)*

BEACHES. Decent beaches for swimming are located just east of Akko's Old City. Exit through the eastern Land Gate at the end of Salah al-Din St. by the Akko Gate hostel. Follow the road for 15min. in a loop around the gated naval academy and a straight stretch past the Muslim graveyard to sandy **Purple Beach,** which takes on the air of a crowded city festival every weekend complete with music, dancing, and concessions. Much farther along the shore (continuing in the same direction) is the **Palm Beach Hotel,** which boasts seafront property with swimming. *(Purple Beach open daily 8am-6pm. NIS10, children NIS5.)*

 FESTIVALS

Israel Fringe Theater Festival (www.accofestival.co.il/english). 4-day dramatic extravaganza during the Jewish festival of Sukkot. Excellent acoustics in the Knights' Halls make them the perfect location for this acclaimed festival each fall. Attracts small theater troupes and street performers from all over Israel and the rest of the world. Only a few of the productions are in English.

 DAYTRIPS FROM AKKO

LOKHAMEI HA-GETA'OT ✗

לוחמי הגיט אות

Take bus #271 north from Akko or south from Nahariya. Get off at the Lokhamei ha-Geta'ot stop, then walk to the kibbutz turnoff and follow signposts to get to the museum entrance. ☎04 995 8080; www.gfh.org.il/eng. Open Su-Th 9am-4pm. Wheelchair-accessible. Contact Simcha Molch (☎04 995 8035; smolcho@gfh.org.il) to schedule guided tours.

This kibbutz was founded in 1949 by young resistance fighters who had survived concentration camps and the Warsaw Ghetto uprising. It houses the **Ghetto Fighters' House Museum,** which examines Jewish life in Eastern Europe during the years leading up to WWII and during the Holocaust. The exhibits on Jewish Youth resistance movements during the war and ghetto uprisings are particularly heart-rending, as is a moving tribute to the "Righteous Among Nations," non-Jews who risked their lives in resistance or rescue efforts. In the lower-level **Hall of Remembrance,** the huge black walls double as eerie display cases. Visitors can activate individual lights to examine victims' personal belongings inside by laying a palm against the darkened glass. The emotionally intense displays of the museum eventually give way to a calming roof observatory, with gentle breezes and a view of the kibbutz's **Roman aqueduct** and surrounding mountains. The museum complex also features a quiet, air-conditioned library where any visitor can research Jewish history; some Holocaust reference books are in English. *(☎04 994 80 24. Open Su-Th 8:30am-3pm. NIS25. Books may be borrowed with a deposit of NIS100.)*

Entrance to the Ghetto Fighters' House Museum also includes entrance to adjacent **Yad Layeled,** a memorial to the child victims of the Holocaust. The experience is aimed at local children, so the English captioning for its collection

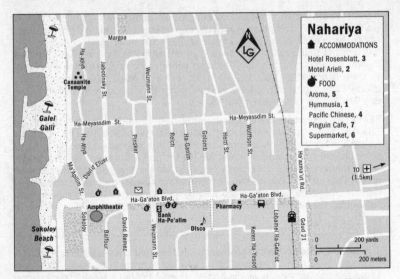

Nahariya

🏠 ACCOMMODATIONS

Hotel Rosenblatt, 3
Motel Arieli, 2

🍎 FOOD

Aroma, 5
Hummusia, 1
Pacific Chinese, 4
Pinguin Cafe, 7
Supermarket, 6

of childrens' diaries, letters, and interviews is minimal. But even non-Hebrew speakers will understand the memorial's message of grief. Children's names cover a stone tower and the highly visual displays curve along a downward-spiraling path from the top of the building to the bottom.

NAHARIYA   ☎ 04

נהריה نهاريّا

Nahariya, once northern Israel's honeymoon hotspot, saw a major drop in tourism after it was pummeled by rockets launched from Lebanon. Though vestiges of a once-thriving tourist industry remain (including a giant sign reading, in somewhat questionable English, "Nahariya: The Resort For Fun Lovers"), the visitor information office is closed, and many of the hotels have been converted to nursing homes. One advantage to the walker-dependent population of senior citizens, however, is a fairly quiet beach scene, particularly during the week. Sleepy Nahariya also makes an expensive but convenient base for travel to surrounding sites.

⊏ TRANSPORTATION

Trains: 1 ha-Ga'aton Blvd. Ticket desk open Su-Th 5am-9:15pm, F 6am-2:30pm, Sa 8:30pm-10:30pm. To **Akko** (10min., every hr., NIS7.50), **Haifa** (40min., every hr., NIS17), and **Tel Aviv** (1hr. 40min., every hr., NIS39).

Buses: 3 ha-Ga'aton Blvd. Served by both Egged and Nateev Express lines. To **Haifa** (1½hr., 30min., every 10min., NIS16) and **Akko** (20min., every 30min., NIS8.10).

Sherut: On the right of the central bus station when facing the street. Runs to **Akko** (NIS8.50) or to **Haifa** (NIS14).

Taxis: (☎04 951 2222, 04 951 3333, or 04 992 5555).

Car Rental: Or-Tour Rent a Car, 31 ha-Ga'aton Blvd. (☎04 992 5005), beside Pinguin Cafe. Roughly NIS200 per day for 3+ days, although the rates vary by season. Open Su-Th 8am-5pm, F 8am-2pm.

⬥🛈 ORIENTATION AND PRACTICAL INFORMATION

It's hard to get lost in Nahariya. The town centers on **ha-Ga'aton Boulevard,** a multi-block affair with a eucalyptus-lined **canal** down the center. Most visitors arrive at the bus or train station at one end of the street and walk to the sea at the other end. Major cross-roads include **Jabotinsky Street** (near the sea) and **Weizmann Street** (closer to the stations), although progressing too far down either of these quickly sends visitors into suburbia.

Currency Exchange: Change Spot, 36 ha-Ga'aton Blvd. (☎04 951 2760). Open Su-Th 9am-7pm, F 9am-2pm.

Banks: All of Israel's major banks are represented on ha-Ga'aton Blvd. **Bank ha-Po'alim,** on the corner with Weizmann St. Open M and W 8:30am-1pm and 4-6:30pm, T and Th 8:30am-1:15pm, F 8:15am-12:30pm.

Bookstore: Steimatzky, 23 ha-Ga'aton Blvd. (☎04 992 8688). Carries some English books and magazines with its larger Hebrew stock. Open Su-Th 9am-8pm, F 9am-2pm.

Public Toilets and Showers: Along the promenade and at the free Sokolov beach.

Emergency: First Aid ☎04 991 23 33. **Fire** ☎04 982 2222.

Police: 5 Ben-Zvi St. (☎04 951 8444).

Pharmacy: Szabo Pharmacy, 3 ha-Ga'aton Blvd. (☎04 992 1197), in the same complex as the bus station. Open Su-Th 8am-1:30pm and 4-8pm, F 8am-2pm.

Hospital: Western Galilee Hospital, Ben-Zvi St. (☎04 910 7107).

Post Office: 40 ha-Ga'aton Blvd. **Currency exchange.** Open Su and Th 8am-6pm, M and Tu 8am-12:30pm and 3:30-6pm, W 8am-1:30pm, F 8am-noon.

🏠 ACCOMMODATIONS

Nahariya's days of tourist crowds are long gone: accommodations here are increasingly difficult to find and cheap ones are oppressively rare. Try looking for "Rooms to Rent" signs, or consider staying elsewhere—Haifa is only a 30min. train ride away, and there's camping in nearby Akhziv National Park (see **Daytrips,** p. 237).

Rosenblatt Hotel, 59 Weizmann St. (☎04 808 1942 or 492 0070). Walking down ha-Ga'aton Blvd. toward the sea, turn right onto Weizmann. Entrance on the right, at the end of a store complex. Rooms with private showers and TVs. Guests may need to speak Spanish or Hebrew to communicate with the proprietor. Reception 11am-11pm. Check-in before 11pm. Reservations recommended. Singles NIS200. MC/V. ❸

Motel Arielli, 1 Jabotinsky St. (☎04 992 1076). At the intersection with ha-Ga'aton Blvd. Follow red and white signs to the office door for reception. Leafy paths off a tiny patio lead to miniature bungalows with private showers. Singles NIS300. Cash only. ❸

🍴 FOOD

In keeping with Nahariya's current role as Senior Citizen Central, most of the cafes along ha-Ga'aton Blvd. attract flocks of the elderly. They offer overpriced food to hapless, hungry tourists. Hole-in-the-wall places around the bus and train station fry up falafel or shawarma at much lower rates. For groceries, visit **Supersol,** on the corner of ha-Ga'aton Blvd. and Herzl St. (☎04 9927 21 011. Open Su-Th 7am-8pm, F 7am-4pm.)

NORTHERN MEDITERRANEAN COAST

☒ **Hummusia,** 33 ha-Ga'aton Blvd. Next to Pinguin Cafe, on the right when facing away from the street, tucked behind the gelateria. This 1-room hideaway has a chalkboard for a menu (ask the English-speaking waitress to explain). Thick and spongy pita and little bowls of spicy sauces enliven traditional hummus. Hummus NIS19, with mushrooms NIS25. For falafel or french fries, add another NIS5. Open Su and Th 10:30am-7:30pm, Tu and F 10:30am-4pm. Cash only. ❶

Pacific Chinese Restaurant, 28 ha-Ga'aton Blvd. (☎04 951 0877). Toward the end of ha-Ga'aton Blvd. closest to the beach; on the right when facing the sea. This 1-room, air-conditioned restaurant charms with its friendly staff, Chinese lanterns, and thick table-cloths. Most meat with rice dishes NIS51; shrimp dishes NIS65 or NIS87. Business lunch NIS49 or take-away NIS39. Open daily noon-3pm and 6:30-11pm. MC/V over NIS50. ❸

Aroma, 39 ha-Ga'aton Blvd. (☎04 900 0230; www.aroma.co.il/en). At left when walking down ha-Ga'aton toward the sea. Chain cafes don't get much more stylish: the trendy decor and the baristas' T-shirts are color-coordinated, and out-of-town beach-goers in sunglasses cluster at the tiny tables. While the mostly-Euro food (muesli, croissants, pesto mozzarella sandwiches) doesn't come at street prices, it's quick and tasty. Free Wi-Fi. Sandwiches NIS15-48. Israeli breakfast NIS39. Open 24hr. MC/V. ❶

Pinguin Cafe, 31 ha-Ga'aton Blvd. (☎04 992 0027). At left when facing the sea, with larger-than-life penguin statues at the entrance. Established in Nahariya's early days, this institution has outlasted everything from boom to bust to nearby rocket explosions. The food is pricy but beautifully presented. Sandwiches NIS32-41. Salads NIS41-51. English and kids' menus available. Open daily 8am-midnight. MC/V. ❷

👁 SIGHTS AND NIGHTLIFE

At night, Nahariya's elderly residents go to bed early, and so, apparently, does everyone else. Though the cafes on ha-Ga'aton Blvd. stay open, the only place where anything much happens is on the **Promenade.** Generally deserted during sweltering weekdays, this stretch of ice-cream vendors, tiny pubs, and playgrounds offers strolls with stunning sunset views over the water. There's also folk dancing W and S at 7:30pm and 9pm. Depending on how many guests are in town, the **Carlton Hotel** (in the middle of ha-Ga'aton Blvd., on left when facing the sea) has a disco on F at 10pm. (NIS60, no dress code.) The **Hekhal ha-Tarbout,** 7 ha-Atzma'ut Rd., sometimes screens movies in English (☎04 982 99 33).

BEACHES. The beach is easily the highlight of Nahariya. Follow ha-Ga'aton Blvd. until it hits the promenade, then turn left and walk a few minutes to the public **Sokolov Beach.** It's nothing elaborate, but there are lifeguards, changing rooms, and showers, and the sea is invitingly cool. Beware old women tanning topless! For more frills, turn right at the end of ha-Ga'aton Blvd. and look for the entrance to **Galei Galil,** a private, fenced beach with a breakwater that also includes a large pool and a small water park to entertain kids. (☎04 987 9872. Open June-Aug. 8am-5pm. NIS13. MC/V.)

BEITH LIEBERMAN. This municipal history museum hides at the far south of town, between the train tracks and a hulking mall. (Gdud 21 St. Facing away from the sea, turn right onto Gdud 21 and walk along the shoulder of the road for about 30min. ☎04 982 1516. Open Su, Tu, and Th 9am-1pm; M and W 9am-1pm and 4-7pm; Sa 10am-2pm.)

WATER TOWER AND CANAANITE TEMPLE. This tower once supplied irrigation to farms north of Nahariya and served as a WWII observation post to watch for enemy planes. No longer connected to the reservoir, it now functions as a gallery and arts event space. In the same neighborhood, the archaeologically important remains of a 4000-year-old **Canaanite Temple** dedicated to Asherah, the goddess of fertility, stands on a hill next to the shore. *(Jabotinsky St. ☎ 04 951 1214. Open Su-M and W 9am-1pm, Tu and Th 9am-1pm and 4-7pm, F 9am-noon, Sa 10am-2pm.)*

▶ DAYTRIPS FROM NAHARIYA

▨ MONTFORT AND NAKHAL KEZIV

Frequent buses leave Nahariya for the village of Mi'ilya (20min., NIS8.60). From the stop, turn left and climb up the steep road toward Mi'ilya for about 30min. Smaller roads branch off into residential neighborhoods, but stay on the main road as it weaves until the wooden sign for Montfort. Here the road veers right to Hilla. Don't go toward Hilla but continue straight. Follow red and white markers through a dirt parking lot and onto the rocky path to the castle (another 30min.). Once you arrive, the set of stone steps on the right is an alternate path to the ruins. Explore and take photographs, but watch for park signs that warn of insecure areas in danger of collapse. The same red and white route is also marked in reverse for the return hike.

The Crusader castle of Montfort rewards a challenging hike: the windswept ruins overlook the western Galilee's Keziv Valley. The Knights Templar built the main structure early in the 12th century CE, and Salah al-Din partially destroyed it in 1187. The Hospitaller Knights enlarged the fortress in 1230 and called it Starkenburg or Montfort ("strong mountain" in German and French, respectively). The complex's impressive 18m tall tower and 20m tall main hall stand among its remains.

Those who enjoy more strenuous pleasures should consider visiting by way of a longer hike, saving the castle for last. The four-hour loop beginning at the lookout point on the road to Hilla has spectacular views. To begin, coming from Mi'ilya, turn right where the road splits toward Hilla. The trail descends into the Nakhal Keziv Valley and then circles back up to Montfort. Follow black or blue and white markers down into the valley, green and white while along the river, and red and white up to the castle and back to the Mi'ilya road.

Several other trails branch off the loop. Following the river away from Montfort, green and white markers lead to the **Ein Tamir** and **Ein Ziv** springs. Hikers visiting in the hot months may want to bring along a swimsuit. Ascending the slope opposite Montfort leads to **Goren Park,** a perfect vantage point for the castle.

▨ ROSH HA-NIKRA ✂

ראש הנקרה

Buses #20, 32, and 33 depart from Nahariya (20min., NIS6.90). ☎ 07 32 710 1100; www.rosh-hanikra.com. Open in summer Su-Th and Sa 9am-6pm, F 9am-6pm; in winter Su-F 9am-4pm, Sa 9am-6pm. NIS42, students and ages 3-18 NIS34. Special rates available in combination ticket with Akko sights.

The spectacular white chalk cliffs and grottoes of Rosh ha-Nikra occupy the northernmost point on Israel's coastline. Rosh ha-Nikra's stunning caves, sculpted by millennia of lashing waves and colored by mineral deposits, nearly make one forget the mountain of barbed wire and the Uzi-toting soldiers who guard the tense Lebanese border only a few steps from the parking lot. The British enlarged the natural chalk grottoes when they drilled a tunnel through the cliffs during WWII in order to complete a railway line linking Turkey with Egypt. The nearby kibbutz, smelling the chance for a new tourist destination, blasted additional tunnels through the rock to improve access to the sea caves, topped the cliffs with an observation point and cafeteria, and connected the highway to the caves with a cable car billed as the steepest in the world (though the two-minute ride is hardly frightening). There's no arduous spelunking here: a slippery stroll through the grottoes is at most a 30min. affair.

The worse the weather, the better the show at Rosh ha-Nikra—waves pound the gaping caverns, forming powerful whirlpools and echoing thunderously through the grottoes. A free audiovisual show (available in English with cheesy special effects like sprinkling water on the audience) teaches visitors to keep an ear open for the moaning cries of "The Bride." Legend says she jumped out of a boat right near the cliffs to avoid an arranged marriage. Brown turtles visit to lay their eggs in the grottoes and rock pigeons nest in the cliffside cracks. Don't expect to have the wind and water to yourself; arrive early to avoid the noisy afternoon throngs of school and tour groups.

AKHZIV

אכזיב

All buses from platform #5 in Nahariaya (buses #22-25, 28 and 32) stop at the Akhziv National Park (10min., every hr., NIS7). Sherut NIS6. ☎04 982 3263. NIS30, students NIS16. Parking available. Open daily July-Aug. 8am-7pm, Sept.-June 8am-4pm; closes early on F. Camping allowed. NIS55, ages 3-15 NIS40.

The first historical records of Akhziv are 15th century BCE Egyptian letters found in Tel Amarna, which describe it as a fortified Canaanite port ciy. The city was juggled between different powers during every major conquest. Eventually the Crusaders built the large **L'Ambert Castle** to defend the coastal road. It fell to the sultan Baybars, and now Israeli brides have the weddings of their dreams amidst its gorgeous ruins.

Built on the site of an eighth century BCE Phoenician port town, the sprawling lawns and sheltered beach of **Akhziv National Park** are perfect for a lazy summer day. Facilities include changing rooms, a playground, and outdoor showers. The nearby micronation, **Akhzivland,** was founded in 1952 by the eccentric Eli Avivi. As the story goes, Eli was walking along the beach and saw the remnants of a village that the Israeli government had destroyed. Hopelessly in love, he claimed the land. The unamused Israeli government knocked down Eli's first house and arrested him on charges of "establishing a country without permission." Seeing himself as a savior of this area that he compares to Paradise, Avivi has tenaciously stayed put through a combination of stubborness and massive popular support in legal cases against the government. Making frequent trips into Nahariya for groceries and to see friends, Avivi is an unforgettable, eye-catching figure with long, white hair and flowing robes. Something of a local celebrity, he seems to know everyone for miles around, maintaining relationships with soft-spoken words of greeting and slow afternoons of sitting outside city cafes.

At home in Akhzivland, the gentle ruler wanders around with his dogs and sleeps in one of several tiny wood buildings on a hill above the beach. His wife, Rina, also putters about, watering the grass and keeping an eye on the tiny country. While there isn't strictly much to see in this dilapidated kingdom, curious explorers will find an inexplicably huge number of functioning refrigerators, retrieved cannonballs, and scattered archaeological finds. The most important of the latter fill **Eli's Museum,** housed in a deteriorating but striking Arab mansion. The benevolent dictator's extensive collection of mostly Phoenician implements and statue fragments pack the open-air and gracefully derelict rooms in no particular order, and with only a handful of labels. Eli will undo the padlock on the bone door handle at a polite request from a visitor and doesn't charge admission.

Beds in one of Eli's breezy guest rooms or cabins cost NIS100, and sleeping in the rugged camping area costs NIS80 per person. An outbuilding near the exquisite, sandy beach houses basic showers and toilets, and there are picnic tables and camping-style kitchen areas everywhere. Prices are negotiable, and though nothing is particularly clean or well-kept, the atmosphere is one of rustic comfort. (Next to Akhziv National Park, and served by the same bus stop. ☎054 498 23 25. Call ahead, but either Eli or Rina is almost always home. Free parking.)

YEKHI'AM (JUDIN) FORTRESS

מבצר יחיעם

Buses #39 and 42 to and from Nahariya stop at the kibbutz, but they run extremely infrequently, so plan as far ahead as possible. ☎04 985 6004. Open Su-F 8am-5pm; closes earlier on F. NIS30. MC/V.

In 1208, the Teutonic Knights inherited the Judin Fortress, built by the Templars in the 12th century CE. The Mamluk Sultan Baybars destroyed the fortress in 1265. What can be seen today is the result of Bedouin governor Dahr al-Omar's 18th-century restoration efforts. In 1946, Jewish settlers moved back into the deserted castle and founded Kibbutz Yekhi'am. Two years later, during the War of Independence, they became the most recent group to use it for protection. Though only half the relief convoy reached the site, the kibbutz held out until Israeli forces took control of Western Galilee in May of 1948. The fortress still stands within the kibbutz grounds and fills with dancers, musicians, and artisans during Sukkot for the **Days of Renaissance Festival** every year.

PEKI'IN

פקיעין البقيعة

Bus #44 on the Nateev Express line makes a round trip from Nahariya to Peki'in. Ask the driver to let you off near the cave and be sure to get off in Peki'in ha-Atika (Old Peki'in), not Peki'in ha-Khadasha (New Peki'in). Locals will direct you to the cave if asked. Watch for a beige and black sign in Hebrew and English near the top of the hill; it has a map on it, and the adjacent staircase leads down to the cave.

Rabbi Shimon Bar-Yokhai and his son Eliezer fled to Peki'in when a Roman decree during the Bar Kokhba revolt banned the study of Torah. For 12 years, this erudite duo hid in a small hillside cave and, sustained by a nearby spring and generous carob tree, delved into their illicit book. It is during this period that Bar-Yokhai is said to have composed the *Zohar*, the central text of Kabbalah (Jewish mysticism), though most evidence suggests it was composed about a millennium later. According to popular legend, Bar-Yokhai's gaze started angry fires in the fields of those less worthy; when God saw this, he sent Bar-Yokhai back into his cave for another year. In its present state, the smoke-stained, trash-strewn cave does not live up to the legend surrounding it.

Peki'in is the only city in Israel claiming continuous Jewish occupation since the Second Temple period. Though now predominantly Druze, its Jewish presence endures in one remaining Jewish family (the Zeynatis) and a 19th century CE synagogue with Temple-era stones built into the wall. To visit the synagogue, continue down the staircase near the cave to Kikkar ha-Ma'ayan. A beige and black map posted here highlights some other possible sights of interest, including a Druze cemetery and an old flour mill. Follow the street at the far right of the square, turn left at the first intersection, and take the curving road down to the synagogue's white gate on the right. If the gate is closed, knock on the Zeynatis' door.

For those planning on spending the night, **Peki'in Youth Hostel (HI)** has air-conditioned rooms, private showers, and free breakfast. Space in a dorm costs NIS90-100 for a night, though it varies from season to season. (Take Bus #44 from Nahariya to the first stop in Kfar Peki'in and follow the standard hostel sign with a green tree and red house for 2km. Alternatively, a taxi from Nahariya should cost about NIS80. ☎04 957 4111. Reception 24hr. MC/V.)

GALILEE

הגליל الجليل

When the ancient Israelites described their country as flowing with milk and honey, they must have been talking about the Galilee. This lush and fertile region—bordering the West Bank to the south, the Golan to the east, Lebanon to the north, and the Mediterranean coast to the west—is laced by cool, refreshing rivers and carpeted with rolling, green hills. The Galilee was originally a province of the ancient Israelite kingdom, ha-Galil (the district) in Hebrew, whose inhabitants prospered by fishing and farming. As communities in the Galilee grew, religious leaders flocked to the area. Jesus grew up in Nazareth, performed many of his first miracles near the Sea of Galilee, and gave his famous sermon atop the Mount of Beatitudes. His apostles lived and taught in nearby Capernaum. Fifty years later, when Romans destroyed the second Temple in Jerusalem, the Sanhedrin relocated to the Galilee and resided there for the next 250 years. Dozens of armies swept through the region during the following millennium. Despite a history of almost continuous war, today Galilee is one of the most peaceful areas in Israel. Since Israel captured the strategic Golan Heights in 1967 (p. 44), putting the Galilee out of range of Syrian rockets, the region has blossomed into a tourist mecca. Busloads of pilgrims descend into the Jordan River where John is believed to have baptized Jesus; wind surfers and cruise boats skim over the Sea's blue waters, watched by shoppers on the bustling Tiberias promenade; and hikers crowd the trails of the Upper Galilee where Crusader fortresses keep watch over forested valleys. Meanwhile, the ancient synagogues of Tzfat and the churches of Nazareth continue to attract the faithful.

HIGHLIGHTS OF GALILEE

TREK alongside the Dan River in the luscious **Khula Valley** (p. 280).

BIKE the perimeter of the peaceful, beach-filled **Sea of Galilee** (p. 260).

RELAX under the hand-painted ceilings of **Nazareth's** Fauzi Azar Inn (p. 243).

NAZARETH ☎04

נצרת الناصرة

A vibrant center of Arab life in the Galilee, Nazareth (al-Nassra in Arabic, Natzrat in Hebrew) is a far cry from Christmas-card pictures of pastoral churches, quiet convents, and grazing sheep. Nazareth is indeed dear to Christian pilgrims as the setting of Jesus's younger years and the traditional home of Mary and Joseph, but it is also a gritty, commercial hotspot. While devotees throng to a handful of neo-Gothic churches, drivers charge through dusty construction sites on the main road and crowds drift through the winding alleys of the hillside market. Nazareth's population is roughly 30% Christian and 70% Muslim, while neighboring Nazareth Illit has a mostly Jewish population. Life here is worlds away from the beaches of Haifa and Tel Aviv. Visitors—especially

GALILEE

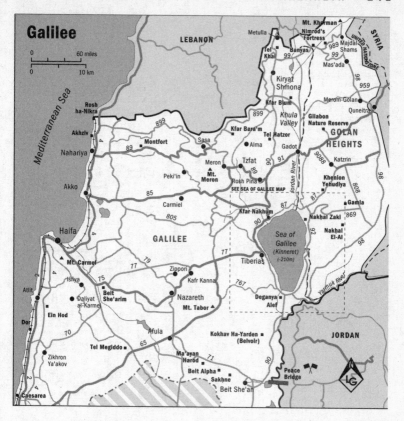

Galilee

women—should dress modestly to avoid harassment on the streets and difficulty entering churches.

TRANSPORTATION

Nazareth's heart, soul, hustle, and bustle are all grouped along Paul VI St. and in the *souq* area just uphill of the Basilica of the Annunciation. Though Paul VI St. streams thickly with buses, cars, and pretzel vendors, most of the interesting parts of town are much more easily accessible on foot.

Buses: The "bus station" consists of several stops on both sides of Paul VI St., near Casa Nova St. When taking a bus to Nazareth, make sure it goes to **Natzeret ha-Atika** (Old Nazareth), not **Natzeret Illit** (Upper Nazareth, another town). Buses leaving town head west on Paul VI St. to **Afula** (#355 and 823, 30min., 11 per day, NIS10.60), **Akko** (#343, 1½hr., 8 per day, NIS27), and **Jerusalem** (#955, 2¼hr., 5:45am and 8:45am, NIS45). Buses to Tiberias and Jerusalem connect through Afula.

Public Transportation: Buses with 1 and 2-digit route numbers stay in the area, mostly for making the steep trip uphill toward Salesian St. and Natzeret Illit.

Taxis: Ma'ayan (☎04 655 5105), **Abu al-Assal** (☎04 655 4745), **Galil** (☎04 655 5536), and **04 Saiegh** (☎04 646 3511) wait along the length of Paul VI St.

Nazareth

ACCOMMODATIONS
Al Mutran Guest House, **6**
Casa Nova Hospice, **5**
Casa Palestina, **1**
Fauzi Azar Inn, **3**
Sisters of Nazareth, **4**

FOOD
Abu Hani Baguette, **8**
La Fontana di Maria, **2**
Mahroum Sweets, **7**

Sherut: At the small side street just off Paul VI St., across from the central bus stop and right before a collection of sweet stores. They run only to **Tel Aviv** (NIS32), leaving in the mornings.

Car Rental: Goodluck Car Rental and Leasing (☎04 657 5313 or 050 527 1119), on Paul VI St., on the right after a 10min. walk from the central square, heading away from Mary's Well.

ORIENTATION AND PRACTICAL INFORMATION

Nazareth is a combination of two towns: Christian and Arab downhill **Natzeret ha-Atika (Old Nazareth),** and Jewish uphill **Natzeret Illit (Upper Nazareth).** All the sights are in Natzeret ha-Antika; Natzeret Illit is of little interest to travelers. The Arab town's main drag, **Paul VI Street,** lies to the east of the sights. Its intersection, at a circle, with **Casa Nova Street,** just below the basilica, is the busiest part of town. Uphill from Casa Nova St., among churches, is the **market** area. Higher quality accommodations and panoramic views are farther up the hill toward **Salesian Street** and **Mary's Well.** Obtain a map of the city from the tourist office, as most of the streets have four-digit numbers beginning with 6 rather than names, and very few have signs. Nazareth's Christian community shuts down on Sundays, but most establishments are open on Shabbat. Although

GALILEE

Arabic is the most widely spoken language, everybody speaks Hebrew and the proprietors of most tourist sights also speak Enlglish.

 LET'S NOT GO. Parts of Nazareth may be unsafe at night, especially for those traveling alone. As always, use caution after dark.

Tourist Office: Casa Nova St. (☎04 657 3003), near the intersection with Paul VI St., next door to Israel Discount Bank. Open M-F 8:30am-5pm, Sa 9am-1pm.

Tours: Fauzi Azar Inn (below) gives guests an English-language walking tour of the Old City at 10am. NIS15.

Currency Exchange: Arslan Exchange (☎054 538 5210), down Paul VI St. from the Basilica of the Annunciation, away from Mary's Well and on the left. No commission. Open M-Tu 9:30am-5pm, W-Th 9:30am-3pm, F 9:30am-5pm, Sa 9:30am-3pm.

Banks: Israel Discount Bank, Casa Nova St. (☎03 943 9111), by the tourist office. Open M 8:30am-1pm, Tu-W 8:30am-2pm, Th 8:30am-1pm, F 8:30am-12:30pm. **Bank ha-Poalim** and **Arab Israel Bank,** across Paul VI St. from the central bus stop. All have **ATMs.**

Police: ☎04 602 84 44.

Pharmacy: SuperPharm, Paul VI St. (☎04 601 0666), down Paul VI St. past the Basilica and away from Mary's Well. Open daily 9am-11pm.

Hospitals: Nazareth Hospital (☎04 657 1501), **Holy Family Hospital** (☎04 650 8900), and **French Hospital** (☎04 650 9000).

Internet Access: al-Mutran Guest House (☎052 722 9090), uphill from Mary's Well, above the Muslim cemetery. Facing Mary's Well, go up the street directly behind you, turning right when it forks at Tishreen Restaurant. Follow small signs; the guest house is on the right. Internet cafe on the 1st fl. NIS20 per hr.; includes 1 drink. Open 8:30am-2pm.

Post Office: Tawfiq Ziyad St. (☎04 646 3010), a left turn off Paul VI St. after the intersection with Casa Nova St. when traveling away from Mary's Well. Open M 8am-6pm, Tu 8am-12:30pm, W 8am-1pm, Th 8am-6pm, F-Sa 8am-12:30pm. Exchanges currency without commission.

ACCOMMODATIONS

Nazareth has surprisingly limited accommodations considering its high tourist volume. Several religious orders in town rent rooms, and, though often crowded with tour groups, they sometimes have a few beds to spare. Call ahead, particularly around Christian holidays.

Fauzi Azar Inn (☎04 602 0469 or 054 432 2328; www.fauziazarinn.com). Walk up Casa Nova St. and into the *souq*, following its fork to the right. Then follow small beige or green signs through the alleys to the large green door; it's on the right. While the dorms in this beautiful Arab mansion may not be luxurious, the convivial atmosphere is magical. Hang out in the upstairs salon, with its hand-painted ceiling and views over the Old City, and you'll get into engaging conversations with the staff and guests. Big breakfast NIS35, for dorm-dwellers NIS30. Free linens. Free internet and Wi-Fi. Key deposit NIS20. Reception 8:30am-10pm. Check-out noon. Dorms NIS70; singles NIS200, with bath NIS250; doubles NIS300/400. MC/V. ❶

Casa Nova Hospice, Casa Nova St. (☎04 645 6660), opposite the Basilica of the Annunciation. Walk up Casa Nova St. from the intersection with Paul VI St. and look for the gate on the left. Solemn and quiet, each private room comes with bath, phone, and A/C. Expect priests and religious tour groups as fellow guests. Breakfast included. Lunch and dinner US$8/NIS32 each. Wheelchair-accessible. Check-out 8:30am. Lockout 11pm. Singles US$44/NIS172; doubles US$29/NIS114. Cash only. ❸

Al-Mutran Guest House (☎04 645 7947 or 052 722 9090; www.al-mutran.com), next door to a cultural center near Mary's Well. It's on the right after taking the uphill fork in the road in front of Tishreen. 3 large private suites with kitchenettes and baths provide enough space for groups of 4 or more. Breakfast NIS35. Internet access NIS20 per hr.; includes 1 drink. Key deposit NIS20. Free parking. Reception 8:30am-2pm. Check-out noon. Suites NIS800-1400. MC/V. ❺

Sisters of Nazareth, P.O. Box 50274 (☎04 655 4304). From Paul VI St., walk uphill on Casa Nova St. and turn left at the Basilica's entrance. This convent, built in 1885, has an inviting courtyard garden, but the sisters can be distracted and reluctant to help. Breakfast NIS25. Lunch and dinner NIS50 each. Reception 6:30am-10:30pm. Curfew 10:30pm. Reservations recommended. Dorms NIS55; singles NIS75; doubles NIS200. Cash only. ❶

🍴 FOOD

Nazareth has an odd daily rhythm: the *souq* doesn't get going until 8 or 9 in the morning, while the city, bars, and the shawarma-falafel joints on **Paul VI Street** shut down by about 9pm. Eat early dinners and count on getting a lot of sleep while in town. For groceries, visit **Akhwaan Bishr,** across Paul VI St. from Mahroum Sweets (☎04 655 5638; open M-Sa 8:30am-9:15pm), or any of the other similar shops along Paul VI St. between the basilica and Mary's Well.

▧ **Tishreen** (☎04 608 4666; www.rest.co.il/tishreen), near Mary's Well. Facing the well, walk up the street behind, forking to the left and watching for the sign on the left. Warm and solicitous service is the rule at this popular, relaxing restaurant. Order creamy pasta or a huge salad. Stir-fry NIS37-49. Pasta NIS38-43. Salads NIS29-42. Entrees NIS35-95. Open daily noon-midnight. Credit cards accepted. ❷

▧ **El Babour,** Barclay's Bank St. (☎04 645 5596). Take a right off Paul VI St. when traveling away from Mary's Well and look carefully for the unmarked, open door on the left. This spice mill has been run by the same family for 3 generations and 280 years. Over the years, their machinery has modernized, but they still sell spices, grains, nuts, and dried fruit of all kinds out of bulging sacks lined up along the floor. Grab a plastic bag and make the best trail mix of your life. Options include hazelnuts, pine nuts, dried kiwi, and crystallized ginger. Nuts NIS30-40 per kg. Dried fruit NIS50 per kg. Open M-Sa 9am-7:30pm. Credit cards accepted. ❶

▧ **Casa Palestina** (☎04 602 1001), just uphill from Terra Santa Monastery and downhill from al-Abiad Mosque. Look for the mural to the right of the stone doorway. This Middle Eastern restaurant makes good grilled meat and tasty oven-baked dishes. What makes it stand out, though, is its gorgeous courtyard seating with drip grapes and pomegranates. If you're not too sick of history by the end of the day, get the owner to tell you about the neighborhood's past. Look for the unusually long *arak* list. Salads NIS35-45. Grilled dishes NIS60-90. Open M-Sa 1pm-midnight. Cash only. ❷

Diwan al-Saraya, St. 6133 (☎04 657 8697), in the *souq* and immediately uphill from al-Abiad Mosque. This 1-room market restaurant is a local favorite for tiny, deep-fried pancake pockets stuffed with cinnamon and nuts or soft sheep's cheese. They may be small, but the sweets pack a punch: 2 will be plenty. Paternal proprietor Abu Ashraf speaks good English and will tell you the history of his establishment, close to the city's old *saraya* (palace). 2 pancakes and coffee NIS15. Open 8am-7pm, although pancakes aren't ready until about 10am. ❶

Mahroum Sweets, Paul VI St. (☎04 656 0214; www.mahroum-baklawa.com), at the intersection with Casa Nova St. Locals' go-to place for baklava, the glitter-ceilinged shop also stocks a huge range of treats from neon gummies (for the perpetual 4th-graders among us) to soft cookies. Baklava NIS75 per kg. Cookies NIS50 per kg. Coffee NIS10. Open daily 8am-11pm. ❶

Abu Hani Baguette, Paul VI St. (☎04 608 4678), just past the intersection with Casa Nova St., on the right when traveling away from Mary's Well. Look for the large yellow signs advertising shawarma deals. This shawarma-only hole in the wall claims the title of "number 1 in Nazareth." Perhaps the only place in town where you can get a meal after midnight. Shawarma in pita NIS20, in bread NIS23; soft drink included. Open M-Sa 9am-3am. ❶

La Fontana di Maria, Paul VI St. (☎04 646 0435; www.la_fontana.co.il), to the right of Mary's Well. Inside a Turkish *khan* with high vaulted ceilings and lots of mirrors, this is Nazareth's oldest classy sit-down restaurant. Entrees NIS60-120. Fish NIS60-150. Desserts NIS20-40. Lunch *menù* NIS50. Open daily 10am-10pm. AmEx/V. ❸

⚙ SIGHTS

Nazareth received a much-needed 60 million dollar face-lift for the millennium that included repaving many of the old city streets (look for a very distinct line outside Fauzi Azar Inn where the funding ran out), constructing new promenades with scenic vistas and putting up prominent signs to help pilgrims find their way to the numerous religious sights in town. The majority of sights are clustered around **Paul VI Street** and the **souq,** but **Nazareth Village** also draws tourists up the hill to experience life as it was in ancient times. Nazareth's churches are all free to visitors, but they happily accept donations.

BASILICA OF THE ANNUNCIATION. Nazareth is synonymous with churches and none is more noticeable than the enormous basilica that dominates downtown with its lantern dome. Consecrated in 1969, the basilica is built on the site believed to be Mary's home, where the archangel Gabriel heralded the birth of Jesus. Inside the bronze doors depicting the life of Jesus is the **Grotto of the Annunciation,** supposedly Mary's house. The soaring, light-filled upper church, upstairs from the grotto, is lined with a series of large-scale artistic interpretations of the Annunciation. Outside, *Madonna and Child* mosaics from nearly every country in the world grace the courtyard walls. Churches have marked this spot since 356 CE; excavations of churches and ancient Nazareth lie in a garden underneath the plaza, accessible from the upper floor of the basilica. *(Walk up Casa Nova St. from Paul VI St.; the entrance is on the right. ☎04 657 2501. Grotto open 5:45am-9pm. Upper Basilica open 8am-6pm. Italian Mass in the grotto daily 6:30am. Arabic Mass in the grotto Su 7am, 5, and 6pm. Arabic Mass in the Upper Basilica Su 10am. Silent prayer daily 6-9pm. Modest dress required.)*

SAINT JOSEPH'S CHURCH. This church was built in 1914, on top of the cave thought to have been Joseph's house. The present structure incorporates remnants of a Byzantine church. Inside, stairs descend to caves that once stored grain and oil, as well as an early baptismal bath, with still-visible mosaic floors. *(Next to the Basilica of the Annunciation, in the same plaza on Casa Nova St. Open 7am-6pm. Arabic Mass M-Sa 7:15am and Su 8:30am.)*

GREEK-CATHOLIC SYNAGOGUE CHURCH. Under the care of the Melkite Greek Catholics, the church is built on the site of the synagogue where Jesus is believed to have preached at the beginning of his ministry (Luke 4:16-30). Next door is the beautiful 18th-century Greek-Catholic Church of the Annunciation. Two hundred meters up from the church on St. 6126, on the left in a small chapel, is the **Mensa Christi** stone where Jesus supposedly ate with his disciples after his resurrection, though the gate is almost always locked. *(In the center of the Arab market. Enter the souq from Casa Nova St., turn left when possible, and follow the street to the left. Open M-Sa 8am-5pm, Su 8am-noon.)*

GALILEE

WORMS, SNAILS, AND PUPPY-DOG TAILS. Immodestly dressed travelers in strongly religious parts of town should expect a little hassling. The unexpected bullies, though, are likely to be little boys. Don't act like a victim: a few sufficiently stern words should do the job.

NAZARETH BATHHOUSE. When a local couple began renovations to the space they intended for a perfume shop, they started turning up curious architectural elements that the national department of antiquities declared were part of a 19th-century Turkish *hammam* (bath). Since such a bath wouldn't have been old enough to qualify as an antiquity, the construction work continued. But as more and more visitors came to see the old clay pipes and furnace, foreign archaeologists insisted that the remains were actually of a Roman bathhouse. Certain decorative carvings suggest that the bathhouse really dates from about 100 BCE. A tour includes going underground into the maze-like hypocaust, which once channeled hot air beneath the stone floors. *(In the Cactus gift shop, just downhill from the Greek Orthodox Church of St. Gabriel, next to Mary's Well on Paul VI St. ☎04 657 8539 or 050 538 4343; www.nazarethbathhouse.com. Open M-Sa 9:30am-7pm. 1-4 person tour NIS120, bigger groups NIS28 per person. Tour lasts 30-45min. and includes refreshments.)*

SALESIAN CHURCH OF JESUS THE ADOLESCENT. This magnificent 80-year-old Gothic church is perched on a hilltop overlooking the old city of Nazareth. Climb the steep, winding 250 stairs past the Maronite Church through Nazareth's stone alleyways, or take bus #13 from the city center away from Mary's Well. The church is built into a huge school; enter through the main entrance to the school and walk straight past the classrooms to the sanctuary at the end of the main hall. *(Open by appointment only; call ☎04 646 8954 to arrange a visit.)*

NAZARETH VILLAGE. This (relatively) recent addition to the Nazareth tourist market is a recreation of the town of Nazareth as it was during the life of Jesus 2000 years ago. The stone houses, synagogue, furniture, and tools were built using the same materials and techniques of the time period. Costumed villagers engage in activities such as weaving, carpentry, grain-threshing, and posing for photographs. *(Up the hill toward Nazareth Hospital on al-Wadi al-Jawani St., on the left next to the YMCA. Enter the YMCA building and go upstairs to find the reception desk. ☎04 645 6042; www.nazarethvillage.com. Open M-Sa 9am-5pm. Last tour 3pm. Parking available. NIS50, students NIS32, volunteers NIS25, ages 7-18 NIS22. Credit cards accepted over NIS150.)*

 GO GREEN. If you're planning on visiting lots of national parks and reserves, do yourself a favor and plan ahead. The National Parks Authority sells a cleverly-named "Green Card" combination ticket at most major sites and at the main office in Jerusalem. NIS130 gives you 14 days and access to 65 sites, while NIS90 limits you to 6 parks of your choice.

GREEK ORTHODOX CHURCH OF SAINT GABRIEL. The Church of St. Gabriel stands over the town's ancient water source. The original church was built there on the logic that the Annunciation story in the Bible mentions Mary filling a pitcher with water, and this was Nazareth's only water source at the time. Hence, the Orthodox believe that this was the spot where Gabriel appeared. The present structure, built in 1750, has elaborate icons and a gold chandelier in the center. At night, look for the rooftop crosses in red neon. *(Northeast of the bus station on Paul VI St., left and uphill of Mary's Well. Open 7am-noon and 1-6pm.)*

GALILEE

🔲 DAYTRIPS FROM NAZARETH

TEL MEGIDDO (ARMAGEDDON—NO JOKE)

תל מגידו

Bus #823 runs from Nazareth to Tel Aviv, stopping at Megiddo (45min., 4 per day, NIS16). When the bus leaves Afula, remind the driver to stop at Megiddo Junction. From there, walk about 20min. north toward Yoqneam and Haifa, then turn left at the brown sign. ☎04 659 0316. Open M-Th 8am-5pm, F 8am-4pm, Sa 8am-5pm. NIS25, ages 5-18 NIS13.

Bible fans and heavy metal gurus have heard of Armageddon, but few realize that the demonic battleground for the End of Days (Revelations 16:16) is actually "Khar Megiddo" (Mt. Megiddo), an ancient *tel* and UNESCO World Heritage site located just southeast of Haifa. Excavations of the site have uncovered 20 layers of ruins, ranging in time from the pre-ceramic Neolithic Period (8000 BCE) to the end of the Persian Period (332 BCE). The vision of Megiddo as an apocalyptic gathering place derives from the city's central location. Commanding the crossroads between several ancient trading routes that linked Egypt to Syria and Mesopotamia, the fortress town was the site of many fierce battles. Megiddo was razed and rebuilt by numerous civilizations, including Canaanites, Hyksos, Egyptians, Assyrians, and Israelites.

The most impressive remains include a **Canaanite temple** (20th century BCE), **chariot stables** and a **palace** from Solomon's time (10th century BCE), a public **grain silo** built during the reign of the Israelite king Jeroboam II (eighth century BCE), and a **man-made tunnel** engineered by King Ahab (ninth century BCE) to allow access to water during a siege. Only a few of the ruins have been reconstructed, but so much stone is visible that it's easy to imagine how everything was once laid out. Before navigating the *tel*, check out the **museum** at the site's entrance. It explains some of Megiddo's layers, displays an interactive model of Solomon's chariot city, and shows a video in Hebrew and English. Multiple gift shops around the site wage their own capitalistic battle daily, although the only novel items in them are DVDs about the end of time, identifiable by the mushroom clouds on their packaging. There is also an overpriced buffet next to the museum. From the observation point atop the *tel*, you can look out over the **Jezreel Valley** (Emek Yizre'el), mostly swamp until 1920, when it was drained by Jewish immigrants. The lone mountain in the distance is Mt. Tabor; also visible are the Gilboa range and the hills of Nazareth.

TZIPPORI

צפורי

Bus #343 to Akko will stop at the junction, about 3km south of the site (8 per day, NIS5.90). ☎04 656 8272. Open daily Apr.-Sept. 8am-5pm; Oct.-Mar. 8am-4pm. NIS25, children NIS13.

About 6.5km northwest of Nazareth, excavations at Tzippori (Sepphoris) are uncovering a rich legacy from the Judeo-Christian, Roman, and Byzantine periods. The town was the seat of the Sanhedrin in the third century CE, as well as one of the places where Rabbi Yehuda ha-Nassi gathered the most learned rabbinic scholars to compile the Mishnah. Extensive finds include the remains of a 4500-seat Roman amphitheater, exquisite mosaics, a Crusader fortress, and a synagogue. Archaeologists have found over 40 ancient mosaics here; the most famous is the enigmatic, gently smiling woman, now dubbed the "Mona Lisa of the Galilee." Within the crusader citadel are a variety of multimedia programs on the history of the city and an exhibit of archaeological finds. One kilometer

GALILEE

east of the main excavations is an ancient reservoir carved into the bedrock; it was once part of the area's intricate system of aqueducts. The Crusaders believed Tzippori was the town where Mary's parents Ann and Joachim lived and built a church over the site of their house.

MOUNT TABOR (KHAR TAVOR)

הר תבור

From Afula, take bus #830 or 841 to the base of the mountain. Ask the driver to stop at Khar Tavor. From there, walk 2km through a Bedouin town to the spot where taxis shuttle pilgrims up to the top (round-trip NIS20). Or take bus #350 directly to the beginning of the winding uphill road. However, it is well worth the money to avoid the climb up the road. Church open Su-F 8-11:45am and 2-5pm, Sa 8-11:30am and 2-5pm. No visitors during services. Modest dress required.

Mt. Tabor, the traditional site of Christ's Transfiguration, has become a standard stop on pilgrimage tours. The 588m hilltop is shared by Franciscan and Greek Orthodox monks. The **Catholic Basilica of the Transfiguration,** built in 1924, sits atop a sixth-century CE Byzantine church, which marks the spot where Jesus spoke with Elias and Moses and was transfigured in the presence of apostles Peter, James, and John (Luke 9:28-36). Inside, minutely-pieced, realist mosaics soar to the high ceiling and separate shrines to Moses and Elias occupy the back corners. The peaceful **gardens** around the site provide views and space for contemplation. Mount Tabor is also the site where the prophetess Deborah led the Israelites to victory over Sisera's army (Judges 4-5). At the foot of the mountain is the Bedouin village of **Shibli;** roughly 1km downhill to the left from the turnoff of the climbing road (when facing up the mountain) is a small parking lot and gift shop as well as several restaurants advertising authentic Bedouin meat and rice.

TIBERIAS

☎04

טבריה طبرية

To accommodate its diverse group of visitors—vacationing Israeli families, party-seeking youths, weary backpackers, and Christian pilgrims from Hong Kong, Alabama, and everywhere in between—Tiberias has become a bizarre mix of flash and trash. Stores hawking Virgin Mary night lights and baby Jesus key-chains shut down just when the disco ball starts to twirl in the bar next door, and cafe waiters and shopkeepers stand ready to pounce on any potential customers. Worldly and commercialized, the city's wind-whipped streets don't get nearly as quiet for Shabbat as its neighbors to the north.

Herod Antipas, puppet king of Judea, built the city in 18 CE and named it for the Roman Emperor Tiberius. Despite the Romans' attempt to bring in settlers, most Jews, including Jesus, refused to enter the town because it was built on the site of older Jewish graves. Later, in the second century CE, Rabbi Shimon Bar-Yokhai declared the town pure, and it soon became the religious center of the Jews. Later conquests by Persians (614 CE), Arabs (636 CE), and Mamluks (1247 CE) emptied the Jews from the city. In the 16th century CE, during Ottoman rule, Sultan Suleiman the Magnificent handed the town over to a Jewish refugee from Spain, who reestablished a Jewish state. The city's 1940 population of 12,000 was evenly divided between Jews and Arabs but, since the 1948 War, the population has remained almost entirely Jewish.

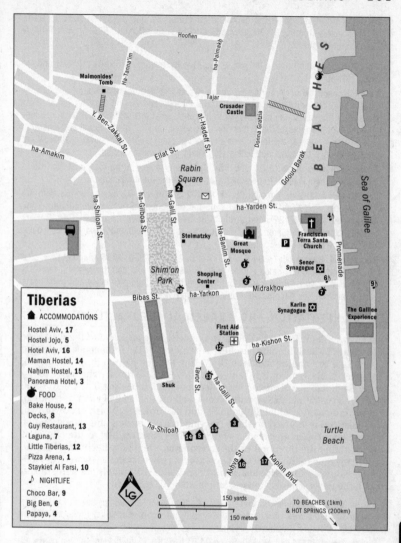

Tiberias

🏠 ACCOMMODATIONS

Hostel Aviv, 17
Hostel Jojo, 5
Hotel Aviv, 16
Maman Hostel, 14
Naḥum Hostel, 15
Panorama Hotel, 3

🍎 FOOD

Bake House, 2
Decks, 8
Guy Restaurant, 13
Laguna, 7
Little Tiberias, 12
Pizza Arena, 1
Staykiet Al Farsi, 10

♪ NIGHTLIFE

Choco Bar, 9
Big Ben, 6
Papaya, 4

Though its central location and cheap beds make it an ideal touring base for the Galilee and the Golan, its position 200m below sea level guarantees a hot, humid, and mosquito-ridden July and August. Of course, the action in Tiberias is also hottest during those months, with increased transportation, the best parties, street fairs, and everybody's favorite, price gouging.

🚌 TRANSPORTATION

Buses are usually the easiest way to get into Tiberias, and feet and bikes are far and away the best means for exploring downtown and the beaches.

Buses: Central station at the corner of ha-Yarden St. and ha-Shiloakh St. To **Haifa** (1¼hr., every 30min., NIS30), **Jerusalem** (3hr., every 30min., NIS45), and **Tel Aviv** (3hr., several per hr., NIS45).

Sherut: Wait in the parking lot just outside the bus station, to **Haifa** (NIS23) and **Tel Aviv** (NIS40)

Public Transportation: A few Egged **buses** (typically 3-digit route numbers) and Connex buses (mostly 1-digit route numbers) travel through and around the city. Though most places in Tiberias are an easy walk, the buses make jaunts to the upper-level, residential parts of town easier. Catch them on ha-Galil St., in front of the falafel and smoothie stands, or in the parking lot outside the central bus station. Schedules in Hebrew are posted in each bus stop, and locals are usually helpful when asked.

Taxis: Moniot ha-Biriya (☎04 655 55 50), at intersection of ha-Yarden St. and Gdud Barak St. Others line up in the parking lot outside the main bus station.

Car Rental: Avis, 2 ha-Amakim St. (☎04 672 27 66, ext. 4), directly across from the bus station. 21+. Ages 21-23 US$7 extra per day. Open Su-Th 8am-5pm, F 8am-2pm. **Eldan** (☎04 670 18 22), on ha-Banim St. near the Golden Tulip Hotel. 24+, 2 years driving experience required. 10% discount for tourists, unlimited mileage after 3 days. Su-Th 8am-5pm, F 8am-1pm.

Bike Rental: Hostel Aviv (☎04 672 3510 or 672 0007). Bikes NIS60 per day. Each bike comes with a bicycle, helmet, lock, and full insurance. Just call the hostel if there's a problem, and they'll drive a truck out to fix it for free. Children's bikes and baby seats also available. See **Accommodations,** opposite page.

✦ 🔢 ORIENTATION AND PRACTICAL INFORMATION

Downtown Tiberias forms a small, walkable square attached to the west side of the **Sea of Galilee.** Running parallel to the shore are the promenade, ha-Banim St., ha-Galil St., and ha-Shiloakh St. Meanwhile, ha-Kishon St. to the south, Hayarkon St. above it, and ha-Yarden St. above that all run at right angles to the shore. Each has a *midrakhov,* or pedestrian mall, in its last block before the water. The **central bus station,** within easy walking distance of all of downtown, is at the intersection of ha-Shiloakh St. and ha-Yarden St. North of downtown, **Gdud Barak Street** follows the shore, serving lots of beaches and campgrounds. South, **Eliezer Kaplan Avenue** also clings to the coast, leading to the city's hot springs and in the direction of the **Jordan River,** eventually becoming Rte. 90. Uphill, traveling to the right out of downtown (when facing the water), is Tiberias's less-interesting **residential area.** A handful of ritzy hotels are here, mixed in with the city's schools, houses, and municipal buildings.

Tourist Office: ha-Banim St. (☎04 672 56 66), in the archaeological park. Free city maps and brochures, and hostile advice—questions only occasionally tolerated. Open Su-Th 8am-4pm, F 8:30am-12:30pm.

Budget Travel: ISSTA, 34 ha-Galil St. (☎04 671 3000). Plane tickets, student cards, all the globetrotting basics. Open Su-Th 9am-7pm, F 8:30am-1pm.

Bookstore: Steimatzky, 19 ha-Galil St. (☎04 679 1288), on the right when walking toward ha-Yarden St. Carries some books and magazines in English along with its Hebrew selection. Open Su-Th 8:30am-7:30pm, F 8am-2pm.

Laundromat: American Express Laundry (☎04 672 2186), on Kikkar Rabin, near the post office. Facing into the square, it's on the left side of the wall straight ahead. As speedy as its name (get your clean clothes back in 3hr.), but don't over-interpret: payment is cash only. Open Su-Th 7:30am-6:30pm, F 7:30am-2pm.

Police: ☎04 632 74 44.

Pharmacy: Pharmacy Schwartz, 7 ha-Galil St. (☎04 672 0994). Open Su-M and W-Th 8am-8pm, Tu 8am-7pm, F 8am-2pm.

First Aid: Magen David Adom (Mada), (☎04 679 0111), on the corner of ha-Banim St. and ha-Kishon St. Open 24hr.

Internet Access: Solan Communication, 3 Midrakhov ha-Banim St. (☎04 672 6470; www.solantel.co.il), across from Big Ben. Sells cameras, phones, and SIM cards, as well as providing internet access, pay phones, and commission-free **currency exchange.** Internet NIS10 per 30min. Open Su-Th 9am-10pm, F 9am-3pm, Sa 5pm-10pm. AmEx/D/MC/V.

Post Office: 1 Kikkar Rabin (☎04 672 2266), in the parking lot off ha-Yarden St. Open Su and Th 8am-6pm, M-Tu 8am-12:30pm and 3:30pm-6pm, W 8am-1:30pm, F 8am-noon.

⚑⚑ ACCOMMODATIONS AND CAMPING

Tiberias has a skyline dominated by expensive resort hotels in familiar brand names. Happily, however, it also has a good crop of low-lying, inexpensive options. Cheap beds are often deservedly so: look before paying and pay for only one night in advance.

▨ **Hostel Aviv,** 66 ha-Galil St. (☎04 672 3510 or 672 0007; www.aviv-hotel.co.il), at the south end of downtown Tiberias, where ha-Banim St. and ha-Galil St. merge. Most of the budget travelers who go through town stay here, and with good reason. Friendly service, dorms converted from hotel rooms (with the associated comfortable beds and pristine bathrooms), and low prices make an irresistible place of this Tiberias classic. Breakfast NIS30, in next-door Hotel Aviv. Linens included. Deal with nearby Panorama Laundry gives guests a discount and delivery directly to the hostel. Free internet and Wi-Fi. Free parking available. Bike rental NIS60 per day, with full insurance. Wheelchair-accessible. Reception 24hr. Check-in noon. Check-out 10am. Dorms NIS70; private rooms NIS180-250. Prices vary significantly by season. AmEx/D/MC/V. ❶

Tiberias Hostel, in Kikkar Rabin (☎04 679 2611; m11111@012.net.il), across the square from the post office, up the inside stairs. This cramped establishment has similar rooms and prices to Hostel Aviv, but is lacking in its crowds of guests and its tons of amenities. The bonuses: a little more peace and quiet, and that rare find in the world of hostels, carpeted floors. Linens included. Internet NIS10 per 30min. Dorms NIS75; singles NIS250; doubles 350. Cash only. ❶

Panorama Hotel, ha-Galil St. (☎04 672 4811 or 672 0963), in the block before Hostel Aviv; on the right when the water is at left. Inexpensive rooms offer the privacy dorm-dwellers lack, but the quality is less than impressive. Every concrete-walled room has a TV, A/C, small fridge, and private bathroom. The promised panorama depends on the side of the building: either the Sea of Galilee or the cluttered out-skirts of commercial Tiberias. Linens included. Check-in noon. Check-out 11am. Singles NIS90; doubles NIS130. D/V. ❷

Aviv Holiday Flats, 66 ha-Galil St. (☎04 671 2272, 671 2273, or 617 2274; www.aviv-hotel.co.il). Just behind Hostel Aviv; the tall white building with a "Hotel Aviv" sign. Under the same management as Hostel Aviv, this well-run place will blow both mind and budget. Beautiful rooms with kitchenettes, some with balconies, views of the Sea of Galilee, and jacuzzis. Breakfast NIS30. Linens provided. Free internet and Wi-Fi. Free parking available. Bike rental NIS60 per day. Reception 24hr. Check-in from noon. Check-out 10am. No curfew. Doubles NIS250-NIS450, depending on season. AmEx/D/MC/V. ❸

Maman Hotel, Atzmon St. (☎04 679 2986). From the central bus station, walk right on ha-Shiloakh St. This former hostel converted all its dorms to private rooms, and has since gone silent. Attractive, well-appointed rooms provide a little luxury at less than top dollar, but don't expect anyone else around for conversation. Linens included. No reception—just call and someone will come. Check-in 2pm. Check-out 10am. NIS200 per person. V. ❸

Nakhum Hostel (☎04 672 1505, 671 7437, or 671 1505). Head right as you face the sea on either ha-Shiloakh St. or ha-Galil St. and turn onto Tavor St. A decrepit exterior houses surprisingly livable rooms. Bare lightbulbs dangle from the ceilings, stained grout decorates the bathrooms, and the owner swears there's hot water from the solar heating shed he built out of corrugated tin. Linens included. Parking available. No reliable reception hours—just call. Check-out 10am. Dorms NIS35-40; doubles NIS100-120. Prices vary by season. Cash only. ❶

Hostel Jojo, 8 Atzmon St. (☎04 679 1042), just before Maman Hotel near the corner with Tavor St. For the bravest (and stingiest) backpackers, this hostel occupies the bottom floor of what appears to be an abandoned building: prepare to share space with hungry kittens and a roving rooster. Shared bathrooms and open-air kitchen facilities, complete with greasy black stove. Parking available. Walk in past the patio table and knock on the door on the right for reception. Dorms NIS40. Cash only. ❶

🍴 FOOD

Tiberias can easily meet all your beach and hiking picnic needs. The *shuk,* in a square block starting at Hayarkon St. across from Shimron Park, sells cheap produce and baked goods every day except Shabbat. There is a **Supersol** supermarket on ha-Banim St. (☎04 679 2588. Open Su-W 8:30am-8pm, Th 8am-8:30pm, F 7:30am-3:30pm.) The restaurant scene, plagued by too many tourists, is not nearly so ideal. Grilleries on **ha-Banim Street** near the *midrakhov* serve *shishlik* with salad and pita, while waterfront seafood restaurants offer idyllic settings complete with jet skiers and plastic bottle flotillas. A dinner of **Saint Peter's fish,** a sea of Galilee specialty, costs NIS50-60.

Guy Restaurant, ha-Galil St. (☎04 672 3036), past ha-Kishon St. and on the right when coming from the center of town. No frills and no big bills will be found at this delicious Moroccan place. The menu is full of small, cheap, and tasty dishes, so forgo the steak platters (NIS65) and order several things to try. Stuffed vegetables NIS10-27. St. Peter's fish NIS52. Fried offerings and meatballs NIS7-15. Open Su-Th noon-10pm, F noon-4pm. Cash or check only. ❷

Staykiet al-Farsi, on the corner of Bilas St. and ha-Galil St., on the right when walking away from ha-Yarden St. This glorified kiosk doesn't bother with the superfluous; devoted locals pick their meat and wait while it sizzles on the gaping, blackened grill. No English menu. Entrees NIS20-40. Open Su-Th 9am-8pm, F 9am-4pm. Cash only. ❶

Pizza Arena, ha-Banim St. (☎04 672 6115) next to the grocery store. Good, hot fast food that isn't falafel can be hard to come by in Israel, and this little pizza joint delivers (both literally and metaphorically). Order pizza for 1 or larger to share, or try the Yemenite pastry at its windy outdoor tables. Individual pizzas NIS27-36. Open Su-Th 9am-midnight, F 10am-4pm, Sa nightfall-midnight. AmEx/MC/V. ❶

Decks (☎04 672 1538), at Lido Beach, across from Pagoda. A giant pavilion extending out over the water, this bustling restaurant has a short menu and massive crowds. Specializing in "ancient grilling techniques," the kitchen serves up almost exclusively meat and fish, along with a popular fried onion loaf. Those looking for a little glamor can get filet mignon served over hot coals (NIS75). Fresh fish NIS59-80; lamb chops NIS39. Occasional in-restaurant 🎆**fireworks** shows on busy nights. Open Su-Th noon-11pm, F noon-4pm. Reservations recommended. AmEx/D/MC/V. ❹

Pagoda (☎04 672 5513; pagoda@lido-galilee.com), at Lido Beach. Turn left at the end of the promenade and continue down Gdud Barak St. until the white gate on the right. Encompassing multiple Asian cuisines in 1 restaurant is not an easy task, but

Pagoda gamely attempts it with Chinese and Thai dishes, plus a sushi bar. A stone dining patio out back gives customers views of the water and returning Lido cruises, while the large but quiet space inside is decorated with small bamboo plants and carved wood. Noodles NIS43-56. Fish NIS80-82. Sushi rolls NIS32-49. Set meal for 2 NIS134. Open Su-Th noon-11pm, F noon-4pm, Sa 9:30pm-11pm. Reservations recommended. AmEx/D/MC/V. ❹

Little Tiberias, (☎04 679 2148 or 679 2806), on the ha-Kishon St. *midrakhov.* This well-loved retreat from the tacky and touristy *midrakhov* serves beautiful plates in a faintly rustic setting, with low ceilings, dark wood, and plain tables. Its entrees are pricy, but a devoted following still signs the guest book and pages through the handmade-paper menu. Get dessert or drinks to enjoy the vibe without breaking the bank. Fish NIS85-89. Lamb chops NIS119. Steak NIS135. Open daily noon-11pm. Reservations recommended. AmEx/D/MC/V. ❺

👁 SIGHTS

Tiberias' city-sanctioned tourist attractions tend to be dull; the real sights are its beach beauties, traveling families, and ragtag tour groups. Watch them hit the Hayarkon St. *midrakhov* to shop for souvenirs and strut their stuff after the sun goes down.

GALILEE EXPERIENCE. The T-shaped wharf along the promenade was once home to a multimedia production of epic proportions, covering 4000 years of Galilean history. At press time, a new and improved film was in the works. Meanwhile, visitors can still explore the extensive, religious-themed gift shop for all their *shofar* and wood-covered Bible needs. *(Follow the ha-Kishon midrakhov to its end and climb the stairs. ☎04 672 3620; www.thegalileeexperience.com.)*

MAIMONIDES'S TOMB. The best-known of the scholars laid to rest in Tiberias is Moses Maimonides, the hugely influential 12th-century physician and philosopher whose works synthesized neo-Aristotelian-Arab philosophy with Judaism. According to legend, an unguided camel carried his coffin to Tiberias. The white half-cylinder is the actual tomb; inscribed on it in Hebrew is the Jewish saying, "From Moses [the original] to Moses [Maimonides] there was no one like Moses [Maimonides]." Locals come to pray and chat in plastic chairs around the grave. To get there, look for the signs pointing to the tomb of "Rambam," the Hebrew acronym for Rabbi Moshe Ben-Maimon, his full name. *(Walk up Yokhanan Ben-Zakkai St. from ha-Yarden St.; the tomb is 2 blocks up on the right, up a wide stairway. Look for the giant red metal sculpture above the tomb. Modest dress required; kippot and scarves available to borrow at the entrance. Free.)*

BEN-ZAKKAI'S TOMB. Rabbi Yokhanan Ben-Zakkai sneaked out of besieged Jerusalem in a coffin, popped out of the casket in front of the Roman general Vespasian, and prophetically addressed him as "Caesar." When news of the old Caesar's death arrived, Vespasian graciously granted Rabbi Yokhanan one wish. The rabbi chose to found a house of study with his students. The tomb has no signs in English. *(Right next to Maimonides's tomb, on Ben-Zakkai St.)*

RABBI AKIVA'S TOMB. Rabbi Akiva, a woodcutter who began to study only after age 40, is one of the more frequently quoted rabbis in the Talmud and was one of the students who helped carry Rabbi Yokhanan out of Jerusalem. The lack of English signs makes visiting his grave unenlightening to non-Hebrew speakers, but its prominent location gives a mildly interesting view of downtown Tiberias and the lake. *(On the hillside directly above the city. Take bus #2 from the central station and ask for a point in the right direction; the tomb is close to the bus stop. Modest dress required.)*

GALILEE

FROM THE ROAD

DON'T MIND IF I DO

Considering Tiberias' sizeable population of mini-skirted babes walking chihuahuas and chewing gum, the resort city seemed particularly ill-suited to an Orthodox, all-women's beach. But even as I expected something odd, I was surprised when I found a faded, flowery retreat; the hand-painted signs and the scattered outdoor mattresses channeled Haight-Ashbury peace and love more than they evoked a sense of devout modesty. A tree loaded with white blossoms and dangling glass globes took up one corner of the property, and what seems to have been a tire lay abandoned on the rocky, littered water access.

A two-minute discussion with one of the women at the beach mysteriously won me an invitation to that night's wedding, held right on the water's edge. It was an Orthodox Jewish wedding, so the beach was split by gender, and I made a tentative wedding crasher in the women's half, giftless and camera-shy. Identifying the bride proved nearly impossible; instead, I submitted to the cries of, "It's a wedding! You are welcome! Eat! Eat!" and joined in the dancing. The musical highlight: a remix of Romanian pop with Hebrew lyrics praising a long-dead rabbi. All thoughts of chihuahuas and miniskirts long gone, the white-swathed, middle-aged matrons and I rocked out.

—Ruth Pimentel

KHAMEI T'VERYA NATIONAL PARK. Tiberias' hot springs were famous for their healing power long before Tiberias even existed. Ancient ruins of the bathhouses were discovered in the early 1920s during the building of a road from Tiberias to Tzermakh. Now the park shows the remains of several small synagogues that once stood on the site, some with extraordinary mosaics depicting the zodiac and a candelabrum. *(Just past Tiberias Hot Springs, on the right when traveling south out of Tiberias. ☎04 672 5287. Open Apr.-Sept. 8am-5pm; Oct.-Mar. 8am-4pm. NIS13, children NIS7.)*

FRANCISCAN TERRA SANTA CHURCH (CHURCH OF SAINT PETER). Built in the 12th century by Crusaders, the Terra Santa Church has diverging side walls and a pointed apse to resemble a fishing boat abandoned at the lake shore. It acts as a symbol of the fishing boat abandoned by Peter when he chose to follow Jesus of Nazareth, and is similarly water-tight: floodwater in 1934 filled the church with standing water above its altar and refused to escape out the doors. *(On the promenade in front of the Caesar Hotel; entrance next to Papaya. The entrance to the church is past a nondescript brown gate facing directly onto the water. Open for prayer only by special request, and for the Holy Mass M-F 6pm, Su 8:30am. Modest dress required. Free.)*

OUTDOOR ACTIVITIES

BEACHES. For many beaches on the Galilee, you'll have to bring your own sand—otherwise, bring sandals for walking over the sizzling rocks. Beaches in the city and the immediate vicinity are owned by hotels that charge hefty fees in exchange for changing rooms, showers, boat rentals, and food. The beaches just north of town are located along Gdud Barak St., off ha-Yarden St.; those to the south lie off the main coastal road (Rte. 90, with which ha-Galil merges). **Lido Kinneret,** the first thing on Gdud Barak St. past ha-Yarden St., has no swimming, but gives 30min. boat rides to individuals or small groups on the lake for NIS25. It also runs large boat rides for groups of at least 40—ask the guard at the gate to join one (NIS25 per person). These so-called "disco cruises" happen daily, complete with colored lights and music. *(☎04 672 1538. Boat rides 11am-late.)* Just north of Lido, **Khof ha-Sheket** (Quiet Beach), with a splash-happy kids' pool, is anything but quiet. *(☎04 670 0800. Open daily 9:30am-5:30pm. NIS40, children NIS25. Pay inside the Sheraton Moriah Hotel.)* Next in line to the north, **Khof Hatkhelet** (Blue Beach) boasts beautiful gardens, the largest swimming area, and the best view on the lake. *(☎04 672 0105. Open daily 9am-5pm. NIS40.)* A 15min. walk south from the city center leads to **Khof Ganim.** (☎ *050 333 0135. Open daily 9am-5pm. Swimming NIS15, ages 3-12 NIS10. Camping, with swimming included, NIS45, ages 3-12 NIS35.)* Next to it is **Holiday Inn Beach.** Look for the bridge connecting hotel and lakefront. *(☎ 04 672 8536.)* There are two religious beaches on Gdud Barak St.: **Khof Mehadrin,** between Lido Kinneret and Khof ha-Sheket, is men-only. *(☎ 050 655 5291. NIS20; includes both swimming and camping.)* Hand-painted signs next door indicate **Be'er Miriam,** for women only. *(NIS20 to swim; NIS35 to both swim and sleep, with outdoor mattresses provided.)* To avoid the hefty admission prices of most beaches, head to the north end of the promenade and take the stairs down to a small, **free beach** close to the Lido dock.

HOT SPRINGS. Those seeking a hotter and slimier time are in luck: Tiberias is home to the world's earliest-known hot mineral spring, **Khamei T'verya.** One legend maintains that the springs were formed in the Great Flood when the earth's insides boiled. Another holds that demons heat the water under standing orders from King Solomon. Cleanse both body and wallet. *(The springs are 2km south of town on the coastal road; bus #5 runs from the central bus station and ha-Galil St. NIS67, ages 3-12 NIS40, after 4pm NIS35.)* The older building, **Tiberias Hot Springs,** has single-sex baths. *(☎ 04 672 8500. Open Su-Th 8am-3pm, F 8am-2pm.)* The newer, co-ed building across the street, on the lake side, **Tiberias Hot Springs Spa,** contains a fitness room and jacuzzis. *(☎ 04 672 85 00. Open Su 8am-5pm, M and W 8am-8pm, Tu and Th 8am-10pm; F 8am-4pm; Sa 8:30am-5pm. Massage NIS145. Private mineral bath NIS110.)*

WATERSLIDES A tangle of waterslides swishes 1km south of Tiberias at **Gai Beach.** *(Walk or take bus #5 from the central bus station or ha-Galil St. ☎ 04 670 0713. Open daily 9:30am-5pm. NIS70.)* The mother of all water parks is **Luna Gal,** operated by Moshav Ramot on the eastern shore. This aquatic extravaganza has bumper boats, slides, pools, waterfalls, an inner tube ride, and an excellent beach. *(☎ 04 667 8000, 08, 09; www.dugal.co.il. Open Su, Tu, F-Sa 10am-6pm; M and Th 10am-9pm. NIS80, ages 2-10 NIS60. Prices drop slightly in Oct. Call ahead to make sure the park isn't closed for a group.)*

🎵 🎭 ENTERTAINMENT AND NIGHTLIFE

Nightlife in Tiberias centers on the *midrakhov* and promenade area. In summer, street musicians, popcorn vendors, and temporary-tattoo artists set up shop. Party where Jesus of Nazareth walked—on the water—on one of Lido Kinneret's 30min. **disco cruises** (see **Beaches,** previous page), and check with the municipality or the Tiberias Hotel Association to find out about on-again, off-again city festivals.

Turtle Beach (☎ 050 737 6136), at the south end of the old city walls. Walk through the parking lot past the boat storage area and through the gate with signs. This outdoor bar is right on the lake, with a stage-like frame for colored lights and disco balls above, astroturf beneath. An overwhelmingly young crowd dances the night away while the good-looking staff lounge around looking glamorous. Beer NIS25. Technically 24+. Open daily 7pm-late. Credit cards accepted.

Unique (☎ 04 679 0358), at the intersection of Gdud Barak St. and ha-Yarden St., at left when facing the water. Nestled between trees on a calm path out to the water, this beach hut-style bar offers pleasant, terraced tables on its outdoor decks. Popular with UN troops taking their R&R, the place is a low-key, friendly hang-out. Beer NIS17-22. Mixed drinks NIS35-45. Th Karaoke. F dancing. Open daily 7pm-late. Credit cards accepted.

Papaya (☎ 052 524 1205 or 524 1210). Turn left onto the promenade from the *midrakhov;* look for the Murphy's Irish Stout sign. This chic, black-and-white courtyard bills itself as a dance bar, but early on it's mellow and quiet, dotted with chatting tourists. Bottled beer NIS19-27. Open M-Sa 10:30pm-2:30am. Credit cards accepted.

Big Ben, ha-Kishon St. (☎04 672 22 48), in the *midrakhov* on the left when facing past all the souvenir stalls to the sea. Part of Tiberias nightlife for 25 years, this faux-English pub attracts excitable Taglit Birthright groups several times a week, when the tables are pushed aside for disco and karaoke. F and Sa are the busiest—other nights are for quiet drinks at the outside tables. Beer NIS20. Open Su-Th 8am-2am, F-Sa until later. AmEx/D/MC/V.

Choco Bar (☎050 488 18 11 or 303 02 34), on the T-shaped Galilee Experience wharf at the end of ha-Kishon St. Look for the sign with the giant neon cigarette. High tables and stools with reed umbrellas surround a central palm tree in this bar dangling over the marina. Late at night, it gets packed and pumps the volume of its hip-hop so that everyone on the *midrakhov* can hear it. Draft beer (NIS15-20) and a long whiskey list. Open daily 8pm-3am. AmEx/D/MC/V.

◪ DAYTRIPS FROM TIBERIAS

BEIT SHE'AN AND BORDER CROSSING

בית שאן بيسان

From Tiberias, take bus #961 to the Beit She'an bus stop. Follow signs in town to the site.
☎04 658 7189. Open in summer Su-Th and Sa 8am-5pm, F 8am-4pm; in winter Su-Th and Sa 8am-4pm, F 8am-3pm. NIS25, children NIS13.

One of the finest archaeological sites in the country, Beit She'an is a Sephardic development town containing a vast complex of mostly Roman and Byzantine ruins. Excavations on and around **Tel al-Husn,** the oldest archaeological mound, have revealed 20 layers of settlements dating back as far as the fifth millennium BCE (Neolithic period). Of particular interest is the **Roman theater,** one of the largest extant Roman constructions in Israel. Built in 200 CE by Emperor Septimius Severus, the theater accommodated 7000 riotous spectators in its three tiers of semi-circular seating. Newly renovated, it is now occasionally used for plays and dance performances. The remains of other grand structures branching off from the theater include a Byzantine bathhouse and a Roman temple to Dionysus, god of wine and the principal god of the city. Long before it became a Philistine, Jewish, Greek, Roman, and eventually Turkish city, the region was occupied by the Egyptians; the 14th-century BCE ruins of the **Ashtaroth Temple,** built on the *tel* by Ramses III for his Canaanite allies, is a remainder of that period. North of the *tel* is the **Monastery of the Noble Lady Maria,** founded in 567 CE and abandoned after the Persian invasion of 614. The best time to visit the site is in the early morning, before the sun makes climbing the *tel* unbearable.

The **Peace Bridge Border Crossing,** also known as the Jordan River or Sheikh Hussein crossing (not to be confused with the King Hussein crossing farther south), is one of Israel's busiest border crossings into Jordan; allow lots of extra time. From Beit She'an, take bus #16 (NIS5.80) or a taxi (☎04 658 8455; NIS50) to the border. Updated exit fees (currently NIS90) and possible exemptions are listed on www.iaa.gov.il, where paying online is also possible and may save time. Coming from the Jordanian side, the exit fee is JD5. Visas on the Jordanian side currently cost JD10 for foreign tourists, and shuttle tickets from the Israeli terminal to the Jordanian one cost NIS4.50, while the other direction costs NIS6. (☎04 609 3400 for the terminal operator, 648 0018 for customs, 648 1103 for the border police. Open Su-Th 6:30am-9pm, F-Sa 8am-8pm; closed on Yom Kippur and the Muslim new year, Eid al-Hijara.

BELVOIR (KOKHAV HA-YARDEN)

כוכב הירדן

About 25min. north of Beit She'an. Buses traveling between Beit She'an and Tiberias will stop at the bottom of the road to let you off, but the site is still 6km uphill—a long, tiring hike. Some say hitchhiking is an option, but Let's Go does not recommend it; it is best reached by car. ☎04 658 1766. Open daily Apr.-Sept. 8am-5pm; Oct.-Mar. 8am-4pm. Last entry 1hr. before closing. NIS20, children NIS9.

In the middle of the 12th century CE, a Tiberias Frenchman established a farm atop a small mountain overlooking the Jordan River valley, near the site of the ancient Jewish city Kokhav (Star). Only 20 years later, he sold the land to the Knights of the Hospitaller Order, who were interested in the hilltop location for tactical rather than aesthetic reasons, turning the peaceful farm into a fortress. But even the knights couldn't ignore the scenery, naming their compound Belvoir (beautiful view). The strong fortress withstood multiple attacks by Muslim forces in 1182-1184, but finally fell to Salah al-Din's forces in 1189, after a year-and-a-half-long siege. The soldiers ravaged the fortress, which was later demolished even further by Salah al-Din's nephew to prevent the Crusaders from returning. The ruins remained unoccupied until the early 19th century, when local Bedouin families established a small village there, which they called Kawkab al-Hawa (Star of the Winds). The site was abandoned as its population fled during the 1948 war; preservation and reconstruction work was carried out from 1966 to 1968. The ruins are not as ancient or extensive as those at nearby Beit She'an, but here you have the leisure to wander around the old rooms. Next to the fortress is a small **sculpture park** featuring the works of Israeli sculptor **Yigael Tumarkin.** A critic of Zionism and pioneer in environmental sculpture, Tumarkin uses stone and metal to "paraphrase" history and mourn the death of ideals.

THE ROAD TO AFULA

Buses #411 and 412 (40min., every 20min. 9am-11am) travelling between Beit She'an and Afula will stop at any of the sites upon request. On Sa, only bus #412 runs, and only in the evening. Buses from Afula and Beit She'an stop at the entrance to the kibbutz. Don't be misled by the sign for Kibbutz Beit Alpha (1km closer to Beit She'an). Gan ha-Shlosha ☎06 658 6219. Open Apr.-Sept. Su-Th and Sa 8am-5pm, F 8am-4pm; Oct.-Mar. Su-Th and Sa 8am-4pm, F 8am-3pm. NIS36, children NIS22. Museum ☎04 658 6352. Open Su-Th and Sa 10am-2pm. Park admission required to see the museum. Kibbutz Heftziba ☎04 653 2004. Open Su-Th and Sa 8am-5pm, F 8am-3pm. NIS20, children NIS9.

Along the beautiful valley road from Beit She'an to Afula are several sights of natural and historical interest. **Gan ha-Shlosha,** also known as **Sakhne,** is about a 15min. drive west of Beit She'an. Worth an afternoon excursion, its waterfalls and crystal-clear swimming holes are refreshing in both summer and winter (at a constant 28°C). The springs have been popular since Roman times; the waterslides haven't. The park includes the **Museum of Regional and Mediterranean Archaeology** with a collection of Hellenistic and Islamic art and pottery gathered from a local Canaanite temple, an Israelite community, and a Roman colony.

Within **Kibbutz Heftziba,** another few minutes' drive down the road toward Afula, is the beautiful sixth-century CE **Beit Alpha Synagogue,** whose highlight is a magnificently preserved mosaic of a zodiac wheel surrounding the sun god Helios, identified with the prophet Elijah.

**Sea of Galilee
(Lake Kinneret)**

SEA OF GALILEE (LAKE KINNERET) ☎06

ים כנרחבحيرة طبريا

Pleasant beaches, scenic trails, and historically and religiously significant sites grace the area that surrounds the Sea of Galilee.

▊ TRANSPORTATION

All the sights on the Sea of Galilee are in some way accessible by bus from Tiberias, but renting a mountain bike is the more convenient and scenic way to go. A complete circuit of the lake (55km) takes 5-6hr. Watch out for two tricky creatures: the furry little hyrax (a close relative of the elephant) and the screeching, careening Israeli driver (a close relative of the lemming). Leave as early as possible and bike clockwise around the lake to get the hilly part between Tiberias and Capernaum finished while your energy is high and the sun is low. Spring is the best time for biking; in July and August, the hills reach hellish temperatures. Bring more water than you think you'll need, and expect some strong headwinds off the water.

🏠 🏕 ACCOMMODATIONS AND CAMPING

While Tiberias is convenient to most attractions around the lake and provides plenty of hotel and hostel options, escaping its sweaty confusion can be a tantalizing idea. Plentiful **campgrounds** and **beaches** circling the Sea of Galilee offer cheap accommodations to travelers with tents and/or hardy constitutions.

> 🏨 **Karei Deshe (HI),** near Hukkok Beach. Follow signs indicating a right turn off of Rte. 90 (when traveling north from Tiberias). An uncharacteristically beautiful hostel built around a spacious courtyard garden, with welcoming dorms. Comforters, shampoo, and coffee-making supplies provided. Serene private beach. A/C. Breakfast included. Free linens. Internet available in the lobby: buy a prepaid card from reception. Parking available. Reception 24hr. Check-out 10am. Reservations recommended. Dorms NIS150, youth NIS110; doubles NIS480; suites NIS540. AmEx/MC/V. ❷

👁 📷 SIGHTS AND HIKES

ON THE SHORE

YIGAL ALLON CENTER. The low water level of the Galilee had one serendipitous effect in 1985-86—the discovery of an **ancient boat** under a segment of a newly exposed lake bed off the beach of Kibbutz Ginosar. Authorities filled and encased its wooden frame with hardening polyurethane foam and hauled it to shore. The boat, dating from between 100 BCE and 100 CE, has been restored to near-pristine condition, and experts are still coming back to study it. Noting its age, some Christians have dubbed it "the Jesus boat." While it is a fishing boat, even of the sort the apostles might have used, archaeologists suspect it sunk in a great sea battle between the Romans and Jews in 66 CE. It rests in a special wing of the Yigal Allon Center in a carefully climate-controlled room with a video presentation on its excavation and preservation. Tickets also include entrance to a **museum** with exhibits on the history of the Galilee, a Yigal Allon remembrance room, and an observation tower. *(Take bus #963 or 841 from Tiberias; several every hr. ☎06 672 7700; betalon@netvision.net.il. Open M-Th and Sa 8am-5pm, F 8am-4pm. Free parking available. NIS20.)*

KHAMAT GADER. These hot baths, known as al-Himmeh in Arabic, lie in former Syrian territory. In Roman times, the town, combined with its other (Jordanian) half on the western side of the Yarmouk River, formed part of the Decapolis. While the more interesting remains lie in Jordan, the Roman ruins here have been partially reconstructed. At the southwest corner of the complex sits the hottest spring in the area—so hot (51°C) that the Jews call it *Ma'ayan ha-Gehinom* (Hell's Pool) and the Arabs call it *'Ain Maqla* (Frying Pool). In another area, bathers slather on black mud that purportedly cures skin ailments. Khamat Gader also boasts an **alligator park,** where hundreds of large, sleepy gators from as far away as South America and Africa sun themselves and slog through murky water. Awed visitors watch safely from a bridge. Other attractions include rainbow-colored parrots and a couple of huge pythons. *(From Tzermakh Junction, at the south end of the Sea of Galilee, take Rte. 92 to Ma'agan Junction, then turn right onto Rte. 98, which leads straight to the baths. ☎06 665 9965 or 665 9999; www.hamat-gader.co.il. Open M-W and Sa 9:30am-5:30pm, Th-F 9:30am-10:30pm. Alligator park open daily. M-Th NIS69, F-Sa NIS79.)*

MOUNT ARBEL. Among the best **hikes** in the area, the Mt. Arbel National Park and Nature Reserve is northwest of the Sea of Galilee. It boasts a lookout cliff of roughly 400m, and two marked trails (in red and black) with

GALILEE

handholds in the rock where climbing is necessary. *(Egged buses from Tiberias run only to Kfar Khitim Junction—driving will be easiest. Follow Rte. 77 northwest out of town to Kfar Khitim Junction, then turn right onto road 7717. Turn right toward Moshav Arbel, but don't enter the compound; instead, go left for 3.5km to the park entrance. ☎ 06 673 2904. Open in summer 8am-5pm, in winter 8am-4pm. NIS20, children NIS9.)*

NAKHAL AMUD The Nakhal Amud stream flows from Mt. Meron all the way to Hukkok Beach on the lake. Along the banks are beautiful flowers and a natural pillar (*amud*, from which the stream gets its name) of rock. The whole length of the river is technically a nature reserve and has a great trail for **hiking,** especially in the flowery spring months.

NEW TESTAMENT SIGHTS

CHURCH OF THE MULTIPLICATION OF THE LOAVES AND THE FISHES (HEPTAPEGON). This is where Jesus is said to have fed 5000 followers with five loaves and two small fish (Matthew 14:13-21). The church is built around the rock upon which Jesus placed the bread, and a section of the mosaic has been removed to reveal part of the rock and the original fourth-century CE foundations. Luckily-timed visits may coincide with those of reverently-singing tour groups in the naturally-lit chapel, with windows open to the breeze off the sea. *(Take bus #841 or 963 from Tiberias to Kfar Nakhum Junction (15-30min., at least every hr., NIS14.60) and walk toward the sea, following signs to Tabgha and Capernaum. The Benedictine monks at the next-door monastery don't spend a lot of time in their offices, so try calling 8:30am-noon. ☎ 06 667 8100. Open M-Sa 8am-6pm, Su only for the Holy Mass. Free parking available. Modest dress required. Free.)*

CHURCH OF THE PRIMACY OF SAINT PETER. This church commemorates the spot where Jesus of Nazareth called Peter to be an apostle. According to the Book of John, Peter led the apostles on a fishing expedition 100m offshore from Tabgha. A man on shore called to them to cast their nets and assured them a catch. When the nets hit the water, a swarm of fish swam in. Peter jumped off the boat and swam to shore, where he found the man, whom he recognized as Jesus, preparing a meal for the twelve Apostles. The Church of the Primacy is built around a rock said to be the table of this feast. A Persian invasion in 614 CE destroyed the fourth-century church at this spot. Franciscans rebuilt it with black basalt in 1933. On the seaward side of the church are the steps where Jesus is said to have called out his instructions. The church itself is small and hot: one lazy dog sleeps by the back door. *(In Tabgha, about 200m past the Church of the Loaves and Fishes, through a gate on the right. ☎ 06 672 4767. Open daily 8am-4:50pm. Free.)*

MOUNT OF BEATITUDES. Jesus is supposed to have delivered his Sermon on the Mount (Matthew 5) and chosen his disciples at this site. On the way up the narrow, steep path, a small cave on the right has split log benches for resting. At a lookout point over the Sea of Galilee, an olive tree provides a little shade. A circle of stones includes one carved with a cross, another with an image of Jesus, and a third listing the groups that Jesus' sermon called "blessed." The unspoiled area with its wind and quiet allows for introspection—visitors may encounter a pilgrim or two reading the Bible. *(In Tabgha, about 100m past the Church of the Primacy: climb the steps to the dirt path on the left.)*

CAPERNAUM. In Capernaum (Kfar Nakhum in Hebrew, Tel Num in Arabic), Peter's birthplace, Jesus healed Simon's mother-in-law and the Roman centurion's servant (Luke 4:31-37 and 7:1-10). A modern church squats, suspended over the ruins of a fifth-century octagonal church, marking the site traditionally believed to have held Peter's house. The still-standing ruins of a nearby synagogue, perched in the middle of the old town, contain Corinthian columns and friezes dating from the fourth century CE. The synagogue, discernible by the black, basalt foundation, is built on top of an older, first-century CE synagogue in which Jesus may have preached. Visitors are asked to keep the entire village, as a holy site, free from the sinful influence of dogs, guns, cigarettes, and shorts. *(From Tabgha, about 2km farther along the lake shore, marked by a sign on the right. Open daily 8am-5pm. Last entry 30min. before closing. Free parking available. Modest dress required. NIS3. Cash only.)*

MIGDAL. Also called "Magdala," the possible birthplace of Mary Magdalene lies north of Tiberias. An agricultural community founded in 1910 now accompanies the tiny, white-domed shrine and largely unexcavated ruins. *(Take bus #56, 841, or 963 from Tiberias to Migdal Junction (several times every hr., NIS8.10). When biking from Tiberias, wait until the second Migdal sign to turn left off the road.)*

KURSI. The ruins of this Christian settlement, also known as Gergessa or Gerasa, date from early Byzantine times (fifth to sixth centuries CE). According to the New Testament, at Kursi Jesus supposedly exorcised several demons from a man's body and caused the demons to posses a grazing herd of pigs; the pigs raced into the sea and drowned. Jesus' feat came to be known as the "Miracle of the Swine" (Luke 8:26-36, Matthew 8:28-34). The sight, popular with Christian pilgrims, harbors impressive remains of a large, Byzantine monastery and a small chapel—both reconstructed and with richly-decorated mosaic floors. Some consider the so-called "magic bench" in the park capable of granting wishes made while sitting on it. *(Take bus #15, 18, 19, or 22 from Tiberias to Kursi junction, then follow the signs. ☎06 673 1983. Open Apr.-Sept. M-Th and Sa 8am-5pm, F 8am-4pm; Oct.-Mar. daily 8am-4pm. Last entry 1hr. before closing. NIS13, children NIS7.)*

YARDENIT. About 12km south of Tiberias, a cool, wooded area marks the exit of the Jordan River from the Sea of Galilee. Christian pilgrims congregate here to commemorate Jesus of Nazareth's baptism, and to be dipped or sprinkled with holy water. Although there's no clear evidence that Yardenit is the site of that particular baptism, a well-stocked gift shop, outdoor amphitheater for worship services, and ramps descending into the water provide a convenient framework for believing so. Walk on the paths around the site to enjoy the plants, and keep your ears open for occasional groups of singing and strumming worshipers. Fishing is not allowed. *(Easily accessed by bike from Tiberias: just follow Rte. 90 down the shore in a counter-clockwise direction. ☎06 675 9111; www.yardenit.com.)*

TZFAT (SAFED)   ☎04

צפת صفد

Situated on Mt. Canaan, the third highest peak in Israel, Tzfat (also known as Safed, Zefat, and every possible transliteration in between) is a town of mesmerizing tranquility. Streets wind through this city on a hill, and stone buildings with aging stained glass tumble over each other. Tzfat's beauty reflects not only its physical setting, overlooking the cool greenery of the Galilean hills, but also its mystical way of life. Legend has it that in 1777, a rabbi who had trekked all the way from Europe to Tzfat ultimately packed up and left for Tiberias, complaining that the angels had kept him up at night. The Talmud translates the town's name as "vantage point" because of the city's panoramic view, but others claim the name derives from the root for "anticipation." Jewish traditions are taken seriously in Tzfat; many people here await the arrival of the Messiah, who they believe will pass through on

GALILEE

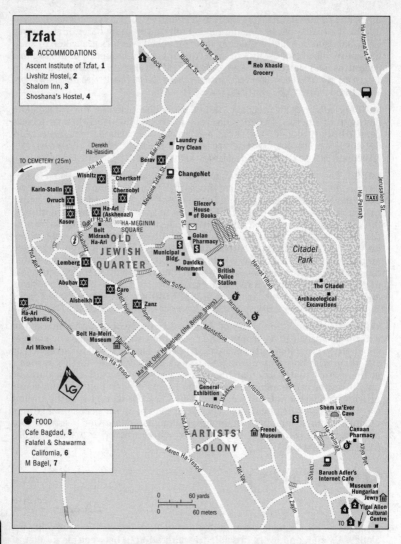

Tzfat

🏠 **ACCOMMODATIONS**

Ascent Institute of Tzfat, **1**
Livshitz Hostel, **2**
Shalom Inn, **3**
Shoshana's Hostel, **4**

🍎 **FOOD**

Cafe Bagdad, **5**
Falafel & Shawarma
California, **6**
M Bagel, **7**

the way from Mt. Meron to Jerusalem. The modern-day mystics of the city may dress in uniformly black garb, but they come from diverse backgrounds; some are descendants of old shtetl rabbis, others are *baalei t'shuva* ("masters of return"), who turned to Hasidic Judaism after living much of their lives as agnostic real-estate agents or Buddhist backpackers.

If Jerusalem is the city of gold, Tzfat is the city of turquoise, deeply steeped in the glory of its Kabbalistic masters. Tzfat hasn't always been a spiritual haven. Its Crusader-built castle was captured by Salah al-Din in 1188, reconquered by the Knights Templar in 1240, and then lost again in 1266 to the Mamluk Sultan Baybars. It wasn't until the Middle Ages that many Jews arrived in Tzfat, seeking refuge in the relatively tolerant Ottoman Empire. After the expulsion from Spain in 1492, Jewish exiles flocked to Tzfat, bringing with them the seeds of mystical tradition. The subsequent century has become known as the Tzfat Renaissance. So many prominent leaders resided in Tzfat that an attempt was made to reestablish the *Sanhedrin*, the supreme rabbinical council, 1000 years after it had ceased to be. Rabbi Isaac Luria, often called ha-Ari, arrived in Tzfat from Egypt in 1572 and established it as the center of Kabbalistic mysticism. His inspirational works, combined with poor conditions in Eastern Europe, drew an influx of Hasidic Jews from Poland and Russia in the late 1700s. New settlements began in the second half of the 19th century and fueled violent Arab protest. By 1948, 12,000 Arabs lived in uneasy coexistence with 1700 Jews. In May 1948, Israeli Palmakh troops defeated the Iraqi and Syrian forces entrenched in the fortress at the top of Mt. Canaan, and the Arab population fled with their armies.

▐ TRANSPORTATION

Buses: Central station on Jerusalem St., on the opposite side of the mountain from the artists' and synagogue quarters, about a 10min. walk from the *midrakhov*. To: **Haifa** (#361 and 362, 2hr., every 30min., NIS37) via **Akko; Jerusalem** (#98, 3½hr., every 3hr., NIS42); **Kiryat Shmona** (#501; 1hr.; 9:30, 10:30am, 11:15pm; NIS23); **Tel Aviv** (#846, 3hr. 20min, 5:20 and 8:15am, NIS55).

Public Transportation: A handful of orange city **buses,** run by **Nateev Express,** move locals around outside the main part of town. Stops include the central bus station and Kikkar Ha-Atzma'ut, but most of Tzfat has streets uncomfortably narrow, even for cars.

Sherut: In this part of the country, are white minivans, rather than yellow.

Taxis: (☎04 692 2228) or **Canaan Taxis** (☎04 697 0707).

◢ ▐ ORIENTATION AND PRACTICAL INFORMATION

The city can be divided into three districts: the **park area,** at the top of the mountain, the **artists' quarter,** southwest and down the hill, and the **synagogue quarter,** immediately to the north of the artists' quarter on the other side of steep **Ma'alot Olei ha-Gardom Street** (also known as "the British stairs"). Tzfat is arranged in curved terraces descending on the west from the castle ruins atop **Gan ha-Metzuda** (Citadel Park). **Jerusalem Street** (Yerushalayim in Hebrew), behind the central bus station, follows the lines of the castle's former moat in a complete circle and is the best starting point for getting anywhere in town. Right next to the bus station is a major intersection with a traffic circle and a gas station. At the circle, facing up the mountain with the bus station to the right, head down Jerusalem St. to the left and follow its curve under the ha-Palmakh St. bridge to get to the *midrakhov*. The **midrakhov** (pedestrian mall) is the strip of Jerusalem St. running southwest of the park area, up the hill from the artists' and synagogue quarters. **Ha-Palmakh Street** begins off Jerusalem St. near the central bus station and crosses the main street over a stone bridge. **Ha-Ari Street** also begins off Jerusalem St. near the bus station and circles around the western edge of the city, descending to the cemetery grounds. Tzfat is a compact walking city, and getting around in the Old City with a car is nearly impossible.

Tourist Office: Although the municipal tourist information office no longer exists, visitors can drop by the welcoming **Tzfat Tourist Information Center,** Alkabetz St. (☎04 692 4427 or 050 893 9042; www.safed-home.com). Run by private Israel experience program **Livnot U'Lehibanot,** the building contains underground archaeological excavations open to the public and done by program participants. The office shows a 10min.

movie on Tzfat's history (NIS3) and sells a map in English (NIS1), also available on the website. Open Su-Th 8am-4pm.

Tours: Colorful character **Aviva Minoff** (☎04 692 0901 or 050 540 9187; www.zfat.co.il; minoffaviva2@gmail.com) gives private tours of Tzfat and the Galilee for NIS150-300, depending on the season and group size. **Yosi Reis** (☎04 692 2803) also gives a private tour of Tzfat, NIS350 per 2hr.

Bank and Currency Exchange: There are several banks on Jerusalem St., near the *midrakhov* when walking toward the municipal building. **Bank ha-Poalim,** on the *midrakhov*, toward ha-Palmakh Bridge. Open Su and Tu-W 8:30am-1:15pm; M and Th 8:30am-1pm and 4-6:30pm. **ATM** outside open daily 6:30am-11pm. **ChangeNet** (☎054 444 2208), on Jerusalem St. past the *midrakhov* and near the intersection with Meginne Tzfat St. No commission. Credit cards accepted, cash, and checks. Open Su-Th 8:30am-1:30pm and 4-6:30pm, F 8:30am-12:30pm.

English-Language Bookstore: Eliezer's House of Books, 37 Jerusalem St. (☎04 697 0329). Walking up the *midrakhov*, away from the ha-Palmakh bridge, on the right after the municipal building. Chiefly religious books in English, Russian, Hebrew, and other languages. Open Su-Th 9:30am-2pm, F 9:30am-1pm.

Laundromat: Laundry and Dry Cleaning, 28 Jerusalem St. (☎054 776 581), past the municipal building, on left at the intersection with Meginne Tzfat St. Wash NIS9 per kg. Open Su-Th 9am-2pm and 4-7pm, F 9am-1pm. Cash only.

Swimming Pools: (☎04 692 2288) Tzfat has both a public outdoor pool (next to the Egged bus station) and a public indoor pool (at the southern tip of the city, next to the industrial zone). Outdoor pool open for women Su 8am-1pm, Tu 1-6pm, Th noon-6pm; for men Su 1-6pm, Tu 8am-1pm, Th 8am-noon, F 11am-6pm; for both sexes M and W 8am-5pm, F 8-11am. Indoor pool open for women Su and W 4-7pm, M 9-11pm, Tu 10am-1pm; for men Su and W 7-10pm, F 7-10:30am; for both sexes Su and W 1-4pm, M 6am-9pm, Tu 7-10am and 1-9:30pm, Th 7am-10pm, F 10:30am-5pm, Sa 9am-5:30pm.

Police: (☎04 697 8444), outside of the main city, up the hill on the road to Rosh Pina.

Pharmacy: Canaan Pharmacy (☎04 697 2440), under ha-Palmakh Bridge. Open Su-Th 8am-1:30pm and 4-7pm, F 8:30am-1:30pm. **Golan Pharmacy** (☎04 692 9472), on Jerusalem St., opposite the Municipality building and away from the *midrakhov*. Open Su-Th 8:30am-7pm, F 8:30am-2pm.

Internet Access: Baruch Adler's Internet Cafe, 88 Jerusalem St. (☎052 344 7766; badler@013.net.il), by ha-Palmakh Bridge. The friendly proprietor also rents rooms and answers questions of all kinds; he's particularly helpful in figuring out Tzfat accommodations. NIS10 per 30min., NIS15 per hr. Open Su-Th 10:30am-2am, F 10:30am-2pm. Or go to **Ascent** (see Entertainment, p. 271) to check e-mail for free. The only web-surfing allowed on their 3 desktop computers is for studying Judaism.

Post Office: Kikkar ha-Atzma'ut (Independence Sq.), at the intersection of ha-Palmakh St. and Aliya Bet St., through the parking lot on the other side of the Yigal Allon Theater and Cultural Center. Open Su and Th 8am-6pm, M-Tu 8am-12:30pm and 3:30-6pm, W 8am-1:30pm, F 8am-noon. Another branch is at 37 Jerusalem St., past the British Police Station at the end of the *midrakhov*. Open Su and Th 8am-6pm, M-Tu 8am-12:30pm and 3:30-6pm, W 8am-1:30pm.

ACCOMMODATIONS

Tzfat is a popular Shabbat destination, so visitors planning to stay over the weekend should plan ahead. An overwhelming number of residents offer *tzimmer*, guest rooms inside private houses, usually with their own kitchens, baths, and separate entrances. These typically cost around NIS300 a night, though prices vary, and bargaining may be possible. The best way to find such rooms is to walk around **Old City** looking for signs. (Baruch Adler may also be of help; see **Practical Information,** previous page.) **Ascent Institute of Tzfat** (see **Entertainment,** p. 271) also offers cheap dorm beds, but only to Jewish travelers.

🏠 **Shalom Inn (Beit Shalom),** 3 Korchak St. (☎04 697 0445 or 050 771 6431), at the beginning of the artists' quarter. From the bus station, take a left on Jerusalem St. and a left on Aliya Bet St.; take the street on the right after the Yigal Allon Cultural Center with the small wooden sign that says "Janosh Kortchak." The inn is on the left, just after the paved road curves left. Airy and homey, with mountain views and rooms full of furniture. Private bathrooms, towels, and bedding provided. Well-equipped kitchen available for guests to use. Call ahead. Singles NIS150; doubles NIS250. ❷

Shoshana's Hostel (☎052 852 0866). From the bus station, turn left on Jerusalem St. and go up the stairs to the right at the beginning of *midrakhov.* Cross the ha-Palmakh Bridge and take the cobblestone ramp down to the right after the "Hezi Hagay, Advocate and Notary" sign. Go left down the small alley to the sign labeled with Shoshana's name and phone number. Perhaps only for the adventurous, this hostel consists of 2 un-air-conditioned apartments in 2 different buildings. 1 room crammed with beds constitutes the dorm, and another, with just 1 bed, the single. All share a kitchen, common room, and bath. The tiny bathtub sports a curious hose attachment for a create-your-own shower. Sheets included. No reception, just call. Check-out time varies, depending on Shoshana's next set of guests. Dorm NIS60; single NIS200. Cash only. ❶

🍴 FOOD

The stretch of **Jerusalem Street** making up the *midrakhov* and around **ha-Palmakh Bridge** is lined with falafel joints and fairly expensive restaurants. A fruit and vegetable **market** is next to the bus station (open W 6am-2pm) and there's a busy **produce shop** near the intersection of Jerusalem St. and Meginne Tzfat St. For groceries, visit **Reb Khasid** by Tzfat University on Jerusalem St., across from the playground. (☎04 692 1648. Open Su-Th 8am-9pm, F 8am-3pm. AmEx/MC/V.) Everything in Tzfat is closed for Shabbat.

🍴 **M Bagel** (☎04 682 1441), on the *midrakhov,* on the right when facing the municipal building, just before the British Steps. Don't be thrown off by its disorganized appearance: the bagels in this cafe are worth their weight in full-fat, fresh-churned cream cheese. Choose among toppings like roasted onions, fried onions, and fresh tomatoes. Bagel with cream cheese NIS18, with egg or tuna NIS20, with lox NIS30. Open Su-Th 6am-1am, F 6am-5pm. Cash only. ❶

🍴 **Mafiyat Ariel,** on Jerusalem St. near ha-Palmakh Bridge, at the beginning of the *midrakhov.* This bakery's miraculous spread of rolls, loaves, pita, pastries, cake, cookies, *burekas,* and hot, fresh challah makes for seriously high-quality eating at seriously low prices. 5 pitas NIS4; a bag of day-old rolls NIS10; sweet pastries NIS22-24 per kg. Open Su-Th 6:30am-8pm, F 6:30am until everything's gone, usually around 3pm. AmEx/MC/V. ❶

Tree of Life, 2 Kikkar ha-Meginnim (☎050 696 0239). A 2-room homage to all that is good in whole grains and organic vegetables. Order your vegetarian pick at the kitchen window and snag an umbrella-shaded table in the middle of the square. All food prepared fresh every day. Daily specials include cheesecake and stuffed peppers listed on a whiteboard. Stir-fry with brown rice NIS35. Quiche NIS35. Whole-wheat individual pizza NIS22. Fruit shakes NIS15. Open Su-Th 9:30am-9:30pm, F 9:30am-4pm. Cash only. ❷

Falafel and Shawarma California, Jerusalem St. (☎04 692 0678), just before ha-Palmakh Bridge, on the left when coming from the bus station. There's more than 1 cheap falafel place in town, but only 1 invades the sidewalk with its loyal patrons. The classic Israeli fast food might not be surprising, but it sure is hot and tasty. Falafel NIS10.

GALILEE

Shawarma NIS20-25. Open in spring and summer Su-Th 9:30am-11:30pm, F 9:30am-3pm; in fall and winter Su-Th 9:30am-9:30pm, 9:30am-3pm. Cash only. ❶

Milano Dairy Restaurant (☎04 692 2982), on the *midrakhov*. This yellow-walled restaurant looks (and costs) a lot like the others on bustling Jerusalem St. except that many of its dishes are accompanied by dreamy home-made butter and fresh baked bread. A friendly waitstaff doesn't hurt either. Breakfast served all day, options including giant servings of Israeli *shakshouka* (scrambled eggs in a sauce of tomatoes, peppers, and spices; NIS30). Wide range of sandwiches and toasts NIS30-40. Open Su-Th 8:30am-1am, F 8:30am-5pm. MC/V. ❷

Cafe Bagdad, 61 Jerusalem St. (☎04 697 44065), in the middle of the *midrakhov*. This trendy restaurant's outdoor seating is across the street for a reason: it occupies the most coveted real estate on the *midrakhov*, with shades and a spectacular mountain view. The kitchen churns out coffee, standard Israeli breakfasts, sandwiches, and pasta. Thirsty shoppers, soldiers, and tourists buy shakes from the front window, then drink them at the sidewalk tables. Free Wi-Fi. Sandwiches NIS34. Breakfast NIS42; served until 11:30am). Entrees NIS30-45. Open Su-Th 9am-9pm, F 9am-4pm. Cash only. ❷

👁 SIGHTS

The best way to see Tzfat is to get lost wandering the circuitous stone alleys downhill from Jerusalem St., where travelers will catch glimpses of toddlers in *payos* having tricycle races, women in long skirts weaving, men in long dark suits studying Torah, and innumerable galleries of artwork inspired by Tzfat itself. Though a tenacious few might be able to follow a map through the Old City, those who submit to its gnarled sidestreets will likely be rewarded with unexpected finds.

THE SYNAGOGUE QUARTER

This neighborhood bustles with Tzfat's most observant Jews. Navigating its twists and turns is mostly a question of luck, despite a few English signs. Of the synagogues, only Caro, ha-Ari, and Abuhav are open to the public. Dress modestly: women should cover their elbows and knees—scarves and caps are available to borrow at most entrances—and refrain from taking pictures on Shabbat.

ASHKENAZI HA-ARI SYNAGOGUE. Across from the post office on Jerusalem St. is a small cobblestone terrace; head down the steps and turn right to reach **ha-Meginim Square** ("Square of the Defenders"), which was the Jewish city center until the earthquake of 1837. Through the square's archway and down the stairs toward the English sign is the Ashkenazi ha-Ari Synagogue. Built in 1580, three years after the death of its namesake, **Rabbi Isaac Luria**—*ha-Ari* is the acronym of the Hebrew for "our master Rabbi Isaac" and also means "lion"—it was here that the famous mystic led congregants to welcome Shabbat. He wrote only a few poems, but his influence was so great that an entire school of Kabbalistic thought is named for him; Alkabetz, his fellow Kabbalist, wrote the now standard hymn *Lekha Dodi*. The synagogue features a small, unmarked hole in the central pulpit, where visitors place notes for wishes and good luck. The hole was supposedly made during the 1948 War (see **Life and Times,** p. 42), when a grenade flew into the synagogue and exploded, while worshipers were bowed in prayer, allowing the shrapnel to sail over their heads and leave a mark only in the pulpit's side. *(Free; donation requested.)*

ABUHAV SYNAGOGUE. Rabbi Isaac Abuhav was a 15th-century Spanish mystic who never actually made it to Tzfat. His 550-year-old Torah scroll, however, is held in the first ark to the right, inside the entrance. The second ark contains Rabbi Luria's four-century-old Torah scroll. The synagogue's southern wall, with all its Holy Arks, is rumored to have been the only thing left standing after the 1837 earthquake that leveled Tzfat, saved by the sanctity of Abuhav's scroll. The enclosed courtyard in front was once a popular spot for wedding ceremonies, said to ensure a couple's fertility and long life. Hanging below the mural in the middle of the synagogue is a chandelier brought over from Europe as a reminder of those who suffered in the Holocaust. The chair at the back of the synagogue, used to circumcise eight-day-old Jewish boys, is reported to have been in use for over two centuries, making it perhaps the single most unpleasant piece of furniture in the world. *(Exiting the ha-Ari synagogue, take a left down the stairs and follow the street as it winds around a few buildings; the slightly more opulent Abuhav Synagogue will be on the left. Free; donation requested.)*

ALSHEIKH SYNAGOGUE. This synagogue was formerly called Kamis Istambulia after its mostly-Turkish congregation. An interpretive panel posted on the wall by the municipality comments on the building's architectural significance, but the building itself is neither open nor visible to the public. *(Exiting Abuhav Synagogue, continue straight down the same alleyway. On the left will be the Alsheikh Synagogue.)*

CARO SYNAGOGUE. Up the stairs on the left, and wrapping around up and to the left onto the covered artisans' street, pass between the signs and a religious gift shop to enter Caro Synagogue, one of the most famous in Tzfat. Yosef Caro, a chief rabbi of Tzfat and author of the vast *Shulkhan Arukh* ("The Set Table," a standard guide to daily life according to Jewish law), studied and taught here in the 16th century. Notice the wall of glass cabinets in the sanctuary full of aged Jewish books, said to date back to the 17th century. *(Free; donation requested.)*

LEMBERG SYNAGOGUE. All that remains here is the western wall, but it offers an inscription in Hebrew, a carving of a lion, and a depiction of hands forming the blessing of the Cohen. *(Leaving Caro Synagogue and turning left onto the artisans' street, follow it back in the direction of ha-Meginim Sq. Lemberg Synagogue is on the right.)*

CHERNOBYL AND CHERTKOFF SYNAGOGUES. The modest Bar-Yokhai St. is believed to be the alley down which the Messiah will make his way on his journey from the nearby mountains to Jerusalem. Off ha-Meginim Sq., on ha-Khasadim St., is the Chertkoff Synagogue, whose chief rabbi supposedly predicted in 1840 that the messianic redemption would begin when 600,000 Jews inhabited the Land of Israel. Both of these synagogues are closed to the public. *(Ha-Meginim Sq., down the narrow Bar-Yokhai St. Marked by a blue donation box and window grates.)*

CEMETERIES. Three adjoining cemeteries sprawl on the western outskirts of the old city, off ha-Ari St. at the bottom of the hill. Follow the steps all the way down, past the new stone buildings on the left. The small building on the left when the path turns into the cemetery is ha-Ari *mikveh*, or the ritual bath. The bathing place of ha-Ari himself, this natural spring has attracted the interest of mystics all over the world. The local rabbinical court has ruled that women may not enter the *mikveh*'s icy waters, but a list of local women's *mikvehs* is available at www.safed-home.com. The oldest cemetery contains the 16th-century graves of the most famous Tzfat Kabbalists. Most prominent is ha-Ari's blue tomb, where religious Jews come at all hours to pray, light candles, and seek inspiration. Next to it, a tree sprouts from the grave of his son Moshe. The devout leave slips of paper on the tree, asking for divine intervention. Legend has it that hidden under this hill are Hannah and her seven sons, whose martyrdom at the hands of the Syrians is recorded in the Book of Maccabees.

OTHER SIGHTS

ARTISTS' QUARTER AND GENERAL EXHIBITION. These alleys and galleries display a wide range of art inspired by the local colors. Though the number of artists who actually live in Tzfat has decreased, images of the city remain prevalent. The quality varies, but a keen eye might discern a few real jewels. Specific stores are hard to find, so travelers will do best to embrace the confusion and just wander around. The General Exhibition is a large, cool gallery of local art. The work is displayed in the town's former mosque, which has been empty of worshippers since the 1948 War. *(The Artists' Quarter is just below the Jerusalem-Arlozorov intersection. Most shops close for a few hours in the early afternoon. The General Exhibition, well-marked by English signs, is on Arlozorov St., at the bottom of the hill south of Ma'alot Olei ha-Gardom St. ☎04 692 0087. Open May-Sept. Su-Th 10am-6pm, F-Sa 10am-2pm; Oct.-Apr. Su-Th 10am-5pm, F-Sa 10am-2pm.)*

SHEM VA'EVER CAVE. This is said to be the burial ground of three Talmudic sages and is named after the son and grandson of the Bible's Noah. Muslims call it the "Cave of Mourning" because they believe that it was here that Jacob grieved over the death of his son Joseph. *(Near the top of ha-Palmakh Bridge, at the intersection of Jerusalem and Arlozorov St. Jewish prayers daily 6am and 2pm.)*

DAVIDKA MONUMENT. This monument memorializes the weapon responsible for the Palmakh's victory in Tzfat—the duds that were launched made such a loud noise that Arab forces believed that Palmakh had atomic bombs, prompting them to flee. A voice recording comments on the historical significance of the site in both English and Hebrew, at the push of a button. *(Across from the bullet-ridden British police station at Jerusalem St.)*

CITADEL PARK. Above the town, the 12th-century Crusader fortress that once controlled the main route to Damascus now lies scattered in meager ruins in Gan ha-Metzuda, a wooded, picnic-friendly park. The phenomenal view makes the short climb to the sight worthwhile. *(Cross over Jerusalem St. from the municipality building and climb the stairs behind the old police station. At the top, follow the road to the park's entrance.)*

🏛 MUSEUMS

BEIT HA-MEIRI MUSEUM. This elegant stone building houses 400-year-old rooms and 150-year-old rabbinical court halls, alongside Tzfat's first Hebrew school. Exhibits introduce important elders from Tzfat's history and showcase the town's daily life over the past 200 years. A sunny veranda on the roof, once used as an outpost in the War of Independence, looks out to Mt. Meron. *(From the midrakhov on Jerusalem St., take the Ma'alot Olei ha-Gardom stairs all the way down to the bottom of the street. Turn right and follow the road until you reach a short flight of stairs with a sign; these lead to the museum's front courtyard. ☎04 697 1307. Open Su-Th 9am-2pm, F 9am-1pm. NIS14, ages 6-18 NIS9.)*

MEMORIAL MUSEUM OF HUNGARIAN-SPEAKING JEWRY. A shrine to the remnants of a culture almost destroyed by the Holocaust, the little house's dark cabinets display wedding photographs and Shabbat aprons, with a carefully curated collection of devastated communities' records. A 20min. film on the history of Hungary's Jews screens in English. *(From Jerusalem St., walk down Aliya Bet St. and turn left at the Wolfson Community Center. The museum is through the parking lot on the left, with a sign on its fence. Ring the bell to enter. ☎04 692 5881; www.hjm.org. il. Open Su-F 9am-1pm. NIS15.)*

YITZKHAK FRENEL MUSEUM. This museum contains vibrant and colorful paintings by Yitzkhak Frenel, a Parisian modernist artist who moved to Tzfat in 1934 and became one of Israel's most influential painters. Works are mostly inspired by Jewish themes, and many depict life in Tzfat. *(In the alley running parallel to Arlozorov St. Walk past the General Exhibition heading south and turn right at the Halvani gallery. Continue until you arrive at the museum's gate on the right. Though closed at the time of writing, the museum is re-opening soon under new management.)*

🎵 ENTERTAINMENT

Though many of Tzfat's restaurants serve alcohol and stay open fairly late, there isn't, strictly speaking, any nightlife—what was once the only bar in town has now been converted to a dairy restaurant. In past years, Let's Go has made the poker-faced suggestion of a night walk through the graveyards, but travelers looking for something slightly more lively can try the following options.

Yigal Allon Cultural Center (☎04 686 9601), next to the main post office, near the traffic circle where ha-Palmakh St. and Aliya Bet St. meet. Normally the domain of bored local kids and their after-school karate classes, the cultural center sometimes presents plays in Hebrew.

Ascent Institute of Tzfat, 2 ha-Ari St. (☎04 692 1364 or 1 800 304 070; www.ascentofsafed.com or www.kabbalaonline.org). Offers free classes and seminars that are open to the public. Topics are exclusively religious and often related to Kabbalah, ranging from meditation to astrology. The Lubavitch Hasidic facilitators are mostly cheerful, New-Agey American expats eager to chat about "elevating the mystical spark within." Seminars 9:15am, noon, and 8:30pm. The institute doubles as a **youth hostel** open only to Jews, but non-Jewish visitors are welcome to join for dinner and a class often followed by live music (NIS35), or to participate in organized tours of Tzfat (July-Aug., 3 per week, NIS20) and nature hikes in the Galilee (1 per week, NIS30). Ascent also runs a visitors' center, with free access to e-mail and a Kabbalah library.

❋ FESTIVALS

Klezmer Festival, 3 nights in late July. Travelers planning a visit to Tzfat well in advance should consider arriving in time for this annual festival, during which the city sways to the strains of everything from old-world Yiddish tunes to modern Hasidic rock. The great majority of the concerts are outdoor and free, with stages set up throughout the artists' quarter. During the festival, roads into Tzfat are closed at 4pm: visitors leave their cars in parking lots at the entrances and ride shuttle buses into town (NIS10). As the schedule finalizes, details will be posted in Hebrew on the municipal website and in English on www.safed-home.com.

⬙ DAYTRIPS FROM TZFAT

MERON AND MOUNT MERON

הר מירון   جبل الجرمق

Buses #43 and 367 from Tzfat go to Kibbutz Sasa, northwest of the mountain (25min., Su-Th 7 per day, NIS11.60). From the kibbutz, continue 1km along the main highway to the turn-off on the left marked "Meron Field School." The field school (☎04 698 0022) is another 1km or so along the access road, next to an army base and before the trail entrance. Bus drivers may be willing to drive all the way up the access road: ask for the Meron Field School.

Just west of tiny village of Meron towers **Khar Meron** (Mt. Meron), the highest mountain in the Galilee (1208m). A trail affords tremendous vistas of Tzfat and the surrounding countryside—on clear days Lebanon and Syria to the north, the Mediterranean to the west, and the Sea of Galilee to the southeast are all visible. To reach the trail, take the Meron Field School turn-off from the main road, then continue past the field school driveway and army base on the right, to a small parking lot on the left. The trail begins at the back of the lot and follows striped black-and-white, as well as orange, blue, and white blazes. A mostly shady 1hr. walk uphill through sweet-smelling surroundings unexpectedly opens onto Mt. Neria's observation point, with wide, striking views of the area. From here, continue along the red-and-white marked trail circling the summit to more observation points. The mountain peak is occupied by a military compound and closed to hikers. To leave the loop, follow the red-and-white trail left (when facing into the mountain) at the rocky area near the army radio towers. Twenty minutes from this point, the trail turns into a parking lot and silent traffic circle: here the black-and-white trail begins again, at a quick left back into the forest. A 1hr. descent, looping back and forth to avoid steep slopes and marked with the black-and-white blazes, takes hikers to a paved road just above the village of Meron.

A 15min. walk to the right leads to the tomb of **Rabbi Shimon Bar-Yokhai.** For two days every spring, the tranquil hillside surrounding Rabbi Shimon Bar-Yokhai's tomb at Meron transforms into the scene of a frenzied religious **carnival.** Some believe that the second-century Talmudic scholar Bar-Yokhai authored the Zohar, the central work of the Kabbalah. Thousands of Jews converge upon the town to commemorate the date of his death (the holiday of Lag Ba'Omer, May 2 in 2010). The square outside the tomb becomes a Khasidic mosh-pit as crowds of over 100,000 dance, shove, and chant Bar-Yokhai's name. The festivities begin when a singing, dancing stream of Khasidim parade to the tomb carrying an ancient Torah scroll from the city of Tzfat. During the celebration, the roads and fields surrounding the tomb are covered with tents and bonfires, while shops sell a wide assortment of rabbinic and messianic paraphernalia. In the low-season, however, both the men and the women's parts of the tomb are essentially quiet. Visitors should dress modestly and expect a multitude of beggars and "volunteers" asking for money.

ALMA CAVE

מערת עלמה

Bus #45 leaves Tzfat for Rehania (25min.; Su-Th 8:45am and 1:30pm, F 8:45am, noon, and 3:30pm; NIS11.60). The bus goes all the way to the settlement of Alma, but get off at Rehania. Bus #45 also makes the return loop to Tzfat (Su-Th 9:15am and 2pm, F 9:15am, 12:30, and 4pm). Contact the national park authority's Northern Regional Office ☎06 697 1918 to leave your name, number of visitors, and time of entrance, just in case. Last entry 4hr. before sunset. Entering the cave at night is prohibited, as is disturbing the bats. Free.

Legend has it that the maze-like tunnels of Alma Cave form an underground bridge between the holy cities of Tzfat and Jerusalem and contain the corpses of 900,000 "righteous men." There is no guarantee that a daytrip to Alma Cave will culminate in the Dome of the Rock or yield encounters with long-deceased rabbis, but for those eager to spelunk despite mud, sweat, and claustrophobic conditions, Alma Cave provides ample (and bat-filled) adventure. The dirt road to Alma Cave begins across the main highway from the entrance to Rehania village. Part of the national trail system, it's marked with red-and-white blazes. From there, the red-and-white stripes are infrequent, but crop up occasionally when the road branches. Stay on this path for about 30min., steering away from the hilly, tree-lined area to the right (don't make any sharp turns). The walk goes past farmers' fenced-off fields to a hill covered with tree clusters and stones, on the left. The entrance to the cave is hidden in a gorge, behind clusters of large trees; from the green nature reserve sign (mysteriously peppered with bullet-holes) on the hillside of gray stones, head right and uphill toward a couple of metal poles. The gorge and cave entrance are just beyond this. Notice the small metal handles bolted into the rock to aid in climbing down into the gorge and toward the cave entrance. Climb (or slide) down the hole, keeping to the right. At a depth of approximately 60m, there are two phallic rocks near the right-hand wall. Behind those lies a small hole leading to the "inner chambers" of the cave. There are markers indicating the correct path: white for the way in, red for the way out. Once inside the large room with a ridge and a steep slope, veer to the far right along the ridge instead of continuing down the slope. Near the end of the trail, the rocks become slippery and the caverns start dripping stalagmites and stalactites. (Impress your friends by remembering that stalactites hang from the ceiling, while stalagmites protrude from the ground) Getting out of the cave is harder than getting in: expect steep climbs and more than a few tricky maneuvers.

TEL KHATZOR

תל חצור

Inside the entrance of the kibbutz. Take the first left before the museum and follow the road to the "T." Turn left and continue following the signs; Tel Khatzor is 1½ km from the gate. Egged bus #501 and Nateev Express bus #511 leave from Tzfat (30min., NIS12.70). Don't get off at Khatzor ha-Gelilit; continue north to Kibbutz Ayelet ha-Shakhar—and note that the return bus to Tzfat stops on the same side of the road. From there, the site's entrance is a 15min. walk back up the road in the direction from which the bus came. ☎04 693 7290. Open Su-Th 8am-5pm, F 8am-4pm. Free parking available. NIS20, ages 5-18 NIS9. Shooting range in nearby Kibbutz Ayelet ha-Shakhar. ☎04 693 2226; merav@pbl.co.il. Open Su-Th 8:30am-6pm, F 8:30am-5pm. NIS120-130 for a magazine of 20 bullets. Kids 10 and up, in a group of at least 4 people, can play paintball for NIS60 each.

The *tel* at Khatzor is the largest archaeological dig in northern Israel. Excavations in the 1960s revealed 21 layers of settlements at the site, the oldest dating from the third millennium BC. Khatzor was once a fortified city located on the main trading route that linked Egypt to Syria and Mesopotamia. The city served as a major commercial hub in the Fertile Crescent; the Bible calls it "the head of all those [northern Canaanite] kingdoms" (Joshua 11:10). Ferocious Joshua sacked Khatzor after winning a battle against a north Cannaanite alliance at the Merom River. Following God's command, he slaughtered the entire population and razed the city: archaeologists have found ashes dating to a conflagration during the 13th century BC. King Solomon in the 10th century BC and King Ahab in the nineth century rebuilt and expanded Khatzor; Assyria's Tiglath-Pileser III laid waste to the city during his army's march through the Galilee (732 BC). At the *tel's* northern border lies a vast, thick-walled city built in the ninth century BC. The most impressive of the *tel's* ruins is the 46m deep **tunnel** into which visitors can climb using a modern spiral staircase, engineered during Ahab's reign to bring water to the city during a siege. **Bazelet Shooting Range** lets visitors shoot at pigeons or clay targets after a brief training. Make reservations in advance.

AMIRIM

אמירים

Follow the yellow signs written in black marker. Bus #361 departs from Tzfat's central station twice per hr. The ride to Amirim's access road is 20min., NIS14.60. From the stop, it's about a 15min. walk to the town center. ☎04 052 578 4114 or 052 578 4113; sonushirit@yahoo.com. A woman named Mazahl, mobile ☎052 869 9950, staffs the village office. Reservations required. Cash only.

A forested retreat for today's stressed-out, young, urban Israelis, Amirim is an all-vegetarian, super-organic, alternative health *moshav* (village) just outside Tzfat. Its hilly terrain and sidewalk-less roads aren't particularly friendly to travelers on foot, but visiting will make you feel more at peace, even if all you do is hike to one of the two outlook points and breathe the cool mountain air. A colossal board at the village entrance lists names and phone numbers of at least 20 different guest rooms, several vegetarian restaurants, and therapists galore—offering everything from Tarot card readings to holistic massage to the space-age-sounding "Biofeedback." Try to memorize or make record of the map, since you're unlikely to see another one. Though the village features an inviting swimming pool (open July-Aug.; free to anyone staying in town) and a sculpture garden, there's not much in the way of entertainment— daytrippers' best bet is to explore the food options and talk to locals.

Paternal British expat **Phillip Campbell** (☎04 698 90 45; alitamirim@hotmail.com), a longtime resident of the *moshav*, loves to take Anglophone tourists under his wing and help organize accommodations in local guest rooms. **Dalia Cohen ❷** runs a well-respected **restaurant** in her lace-curtained dining room, cooking gourmet vegetarian dishes and offering an incredible balcony view. (☎04 698 9349. Breakfast NIS35-45. Meals NIS55-100. Call ahead. MC/V.) **Rishikesh ❸**, the area's only Indian restaurant, serves authentic and vegetarian dishes made by the hospitable proprietor, an immigrant from India who does all the delicious cooking himself. Plastic tables in the backyard may share space with children's toys, but the NIS165 set meal for two (including rice, bread, *dal*, vegetable *pakora*, salads, sauces, hot dishes, and *lassi* for dessert) is no joke. There's also a fabulously colorful gift store, stocked with incense, curry, clothes, scarves, and decorations brought back regularly from India. Impulse buyers beware.

BAR'AM

בר עם

Bus #43 from Tzfat goes to Bar'am (Su-Th 6:50am and 12:35pm, F 6:50am and 1pm; return Su-Th 7:30am, 1:30, 5:45pm, F 7:30am and 2pm). Ask the driver for the synagogue ruins, marked by a brown sign that says Bar'am and points right, not the Bar'am Kibbutz a few km down the road. ☎06 698 9301. Open Su-Th and Sa 8am-4pm, F 8am-3pm. Wheelchair-accessible. Free parking available. NIS13, ages 5-18 NIS7. MC/V.

These third-century CE ruins constitute one of the best-preserved ancient synagogues in Israel. Archaeological evidence shows that Bar'am was home to a prosperous Jewish community in the Mishnaic and Talmudic periods. The ruins of two of its synagogues were documented and excavated here beginning in 1865. Select walls and columns in the larger of the two remain standing, but only the foundation of the second still stands. An inscribed stone from the large synagogue has even made its way into the Louvre in Paris. Tradition labels Bar'am as the burial site of the biblical Queen Esther, but the claim has no archaeolgocial support. Bar'am was a Maronite Christian village until the 1948 War of Independence. A few steps up the hill on the left beyond the old syangogue ruins is a beautiful stone Maronite **church** that is still used by the Maronites on holidays and special occasions. In front of the church is an **observation point** with a view of Mt. Meron to the south. On clear days, it's possible to catch a glimpse of the peak of Mt. Khermon to the northeast, emerging from the clouds.

KIRYAT SHMONA   ☎ 06

קרית שמונה

Kiryat Shmona ("Town of Eight") commemorates Yosef Trumpeldor and seven
others who were murdered in nearby Tel Khai in 1920. Situated atop the ruins
of the Arab village al-Khalsa, which was destroyed in the 1948 War, the city
received its new name in 1949. Due to its location on the Khula plain near
the Lebanese border, Kiryat Shmona was the target of bombings and terrorist
attacks until Israel invaded Lebanon in 1982 to create the 9 mi. security zone.
Since then, it has been subject to shelling by the militant Islamic group Hezbollah, earning it the grim nickname "Kiryat Katyusha" (referring to the type of
rockets used). Perhaps as a result of its tumultuous past, Kiryat Shmona has
become a largely charmless transportation hub, with a long, thin chain of gas
stations and commercial centers lined up on the highway.

▛ TRANSPORTATION

Kiryat Shmona seems designed to be explored by car, but since most things are
on Tel Khai Blvd., it's easily navigable on foot, too. To get to the Manara Cliff
cable cars more easily, get off the intercity bus at the first Kiryat Shmona stop,
before it goes all the way north to the central bus station.

> **Buses:** Tel Khai Blvd. (☎03 914 5320), on the left when heading north. To: **Jerusalem**
> (4hr., 4 per day, NIS59); **Rosh Pina** (30min., every 30min. 5:30am-8:30pm, NIS16); **Tel
> Aviv** (3hr. 40min., frequently, NIS57); **Tzfat** (45min., every hr., NIS19.30).

> **Taxis: Moniot ha-Tzafon** (☎06 694 2333 or 694 2377), right behind the central bus station.

> **Car Rental: Thrifty** at **Shlomo Rent-a-Car,** (☎06 694 1631), down Henrietta Szold
> St. from Tel Khai Blvd. Take a right into the industrial area; call for more detailed
> directions. July-Aug. from $50 per day, Sept.-June from $35 per day. 24+. Open Su-Th
> 8am-5pm, F 8am-noon.

✴ ▛ ORIENTATION AND PRACTICAL INFORMATION

There's almost nothing to see or do in Kiryat Shmona proper, but it's conveniently
located on the way to the Upper Galilee, Golan Heights, River Jordan, and Mount
Khermon. The town centers on **Tel Khai Boulevard** (a short strip of **Route 90**) with
one major *kenyon* (shopping mall) on its north end at the junction with **Route 99,**
and another right in the middle, next to the central bus station. The Manara Cliff
cable cars are at the south end of Tel Khai Blvd., at the entrance to town when
coming from Tzfat. **Uri Ilan Street** (a right turn off Tel Khai Blvd. when traveling
north) leads to a shady park and **Tchernikovski Street** (a left turn off Tel Khai Blvd.
when traveling north, right after the bus station) offers access to the mall.

> **Tourist Office:** While no real tourist office exists, the **municipal engineering department**
> (ask for *makh-le-KET hahn-dess-SA*) (☎06 690 8444). has a dusty stack of city maps
> (in Hebrew with a few transliterated street names) that they give for free to persistent
> travelers. Facing the post office, go up the stairs at its left and head straight out of the
> plaza to the building a block behind it. Open Su-Th 8am-3pm.

> **Budget Travel: ISSTA** (☎06 690 3249) on the top floor of the central mall, across Tchernik-
> ovsky St. from the bus station. Sells plane tickets. Open Su-Tu and Th 9am-7pm, F 9am-1pm.

> **Bank: Israel Discount Bank** (☎03 943 9111; www.discountbank.co.il), in the mall by
> the bus station. Open M and Th 8:30am-1pm and 4-6:30pm, Tu-W 8:30am-2pm, F
> 8:30am-12:30pm. **ATM** open daily 8am-8pm.

Bookstore: Steimatzky (☎06 690 5072), in the mall to the north of town, at the intersection of Rte. 90 and Rte. 99. Carries some boooks in English. Open Su-Th 9am-9pm, F 9am-3pm, Sa 7-10pm. AmEx/MC/V.

Police: 8 Selinger St. (☎06 695 8444). From the bus station, walk 1 block past the mall on the left side of Tel Khai Blvd.

Pharmacy: Leumit Pharmacy (☎06 681 8616), on the top floor of the central mall, across Tchernikovsky St. from the bus station. Open Su-Tu and Th 8am-1pm and 4-7pm, W 8am-1pm, F 8am-12:30pm.

First Aid: Magen David Adom (Mada) (☎06 694 3333), behind the bus station, up Tchernikovsky St. on the left.

Post Office: 110 Kikkar Zakhal St. (☎06 694 0220). From behind the bus station, walk left past the bank and through the courtyards of little commercial centers. The post office is on the right, in the large plaza with the Granovsky Family Auditorium. Open Su and Th 8am-6pm, M-Tu 8am-12:30pm and 3:30-6pm, W 8am-1:30pm, F 8am-noon.

ACCOMMODATIONS AND FOOD

There are no budget accommodations in Kiryat Shmona itself, although some residents rent out steeply-priced *tzimmerim* (guest rooms)—facing the front of the bus station, when walking left along Tel Khai Blvd. Try the neighborhood beween Itzhak Sade St. and Barzilai St. Exasperated travelers can always resort to the youth hostel in nearby Tel Khai (see **Accommodations**, p. 278).

Most drivers and bus riders on their way through town don't have time for haute cuisine, so Kiryat Shmona—transit central—has become a fat-kid's dreamland, full of fast food and not much else. Major Israeli and American burger chains clutter the malls, and the stores surrounding the bus station and lining Tel Khai Blvd. feature cheap shawarma and falafel joints. For a slight change of pace, try a hot schnitzel sandwich (NIS20). Find groceries for picnics and hikes in **supermarket Mega Bayur,** on the first floor of the main mall, across Tchernikovsky St. from the bus station. (☎06 695 9995. Open Su-Tu 8am-8pm, W-Th 9am-9:30pm, F 7am-4pm. AmEx/MC/V.) On Monday and Thursday mornings, a covered **outdoor market** just north of the central mall starts up at about 8am.

SIGHTS

MANARA CLIFF. Kiryat Shmona's one place for entertainment, Manara Cliffs pulls out all the stops but never quite reaches real amusement park status with its unlandscaped dirt. Offering the longest aerial cable ride in Israel, the complex's glassed-in sky gondolas carry people up the 750m cliff. Down on the ground, a "mountain slide" ride lets people control individual carts on a rollercoaster-like track. There's also a giant, egg-shaped dome full of trampolines and bungee jumping gear. A snack bar and bathrooms (in trailers scattered near the parking lot) are available to everyone. *(At the southern end of town, on the left when traveling toward the central bus station. Bus #511 to and from Tzfat and Khatzor ha-Gelilit stops on the main road near the turn-off, marked with signs with pictures of cable cars. ☎06 690 5830; www.cliff.co.il. Open Su-Th 9:30am-6pm. Parking available. Cable car NIS49. Mountain slides NIS25. Trampoline dome NIS25. Children under 3 free. Combination tickets—some including kayaking, rappelling, or ziplining—NIS70-130. AmEx/MC/V.)*

BEIT HA-KHAN. A beautiful, historic house that stands out from Kiryat Shmona's dreary apartment towers. Though the building has been converted to a school for the arts, the manager, Shem Tov, will give tours if you call ahead. *(12 David Razi'el St. Walk up Tchernikovsky St. from the bus station, turn right onto Herzl St., and follow* *it to the second traffic circle. Then go right onto David Razi'el St.; Beit ha-Khan is on the left.* ☎ *050 532 4734. Open Su-Th 10am-noon.)*

🔖 DAYTRIPS FROM KIRYAT SHMONA

KFAR BLUM

קפר בלום

By car, take Rte. 9779 toward Shamir out of Kiryat Shmona and go right onto Rd. 9778 to Kfar Blum. Signs point left off the main road to the kayaking place, before the kibbutz. Take bus #31 or 32 from Kiryat Shmona (3 per day, NIS9), and plan ahead for the return trip.

Quiet Kfar Blum draws sophisticated crowds every July to its huge **classical music festival,** called "The Sound of Music," with performances in the school of dance and music and in the two-story concert hall. Both are beyond the front gate's parking lot and to the left—ask locals for directions. For more information on the music festival and other events in Kfar Blum, like an annual series of lectures on Judaism, call the head of the culture department (☎06 681 6618).

The kibbutz houses a pricey four-star hotel, behind which lies a welcoming, well-kept public **swimming pool.** Though towels and discounts are only offered to hotel guests, everyone can swim. (☎06 694 8409. Open Su-Th and Sa 9am-7pm, F 9am-6pm. NIS50, ages 3-12 NIS25.) The kibbutz's other big draw is **Jordan River kayaking.** A giant parking lot just outside the kibbutz fence behind the music school fills up with tour buses and marks the park entrance. Inside, buy tickets for a kayak trip for NIS75 per person per hr., or a rougher route for NIS109 per 2hr. The last tickets for this trip are sold at 1:30pm daily. If the frenetic, carnival atmosphere of the park appeals, visitors can check out the Top Rope challenges for NIS75, including a climbing wall, zipline, archery practice, and lots of rope bridges. Changing rooms, lockers, and first aid available. (☎06 690 2616; www.kayaks.co.il. Open May-Oct. 9:30am-4pm. AmEx/MC/V.)

GADOT AND THE JORDAN RIVER

גדות

Kibbutz Gadot is off Rte. 91, near the Jordan River Park. From Kiryat Shmona, head south on Rte. 90 toward Rosh Pina and then left on Rte. 91 at the Mahanayim Junction. Gadot is on the left, and the river park and hike are a bit farther on the right. Buses #55, 56, and 57 go from Khatzor ha-Gelilit to a stop right outside the kibbutz, and buses #55, 57, and 58 return (7 times per day).

Silent, rural Kibbutz Gadot has little to offer other than, well, its rural silence. Devotees of peace and quiet will be pleased to discover the laidback **bed and breakfast ❺** nestled inside. Much more is provided in the way of amenities than atmosphere: private rooms scattered across pleasant lawns all have bathrooms, kitchenettes, A/C, TVs, outdoor tables, and use of the kibbutz's swimming pool and petting zoo. (☎06 639 9188; www. gadot-lodging.co.il. June-Aug. doubles NIS550; Sept.-May doubles M-F NIS340, Sa-Su NIS440.) A few minutes past Gadot on highway 91, at a sharp turn in the road before the Benot Ya'akov Bridge, a sign points to the **hiking trail** in the Jordan River Park to the right. Head along the unpaved path down to the riverbank, where the black trail begins at the left. The trail follows the Jordan River south through thick vegetation and over river boulders. Hikers should be wary of fenced-off areas that indicate minefields and can return to the main road by retracing their steps; the trail is marked with black and white blazes in both directions. The river itself—the baptismal site of Jesus of Nazareth—is populated by Israeli teenagers. To get in on the **white-water rafting** action, turn left out of Kibbutz Gadot and head 3km down Rte. 91. The rafting company offers 1hr. trips for NIS75 (☎06 900 70 00). .

TEL KHAI (TEL HAI) ☎06

תל חי

Tel Khai, or "Hill of Life," sits 3km north of Kiryat Shmona on a promontory overlooking the Khula (Hula) Valley. Established as a military outpost by Jewish border guards ha-Shomer—collectively called "the grandfather of the IDF'"—the town has become a symbol of Israel's early pioneer movement and the struggle for "the finger of the Galilee," the narrow mountain range west of the Khula Valley region. Weighty symbolism aside, Tel Khai consists almost entirely of small, regional Tel Khai College.

☞ TRANSPORTATION. Buses #20 and 21 from Kiryat Shmona go to Tel Khai, continue on to Metulla, and then return (5 per day 6:45am-7:30pm; NIS4.90 to Tel Khai, NIS10.60 to Metulla). Groups of students from Tel Khai College often hitchhike together from the bus stop to Kiryat Shmona. Let's Go does not recommend hitchhiking. Instead, plan ahead and double-check bus return times, particularly on Friday when there may be fewer options, to avoid getting stranded.

ᚶ ACCOMMODATIONS. Tel Khai's one budget accommodation is ▨**Tel Khai Youth Hostel (HI) ❷.** Walk south from the Tel Khai bus stop, back toward Kiryat Shmona, and follow the sign to turn left at the first road. When it splits, follow the left branch past the gate to the industrial area and straight to the hostel gate. This hostel offers basic but well-equipped rooms with linens, clean bathrooms, showers, and A/C. Try to reserve ahead, since it sometimes fills up with groups of school kids who loiter in the lobby and show off at the pool table. (☎06 694 0043; tel-hai@ihya.org.il. Breakfast included. Internet available on the lobby computer. Reception 24hr. Check-in 2pm. Check-out 10am. Dorms NIS130; singles NIS256; doubles NIS338. AmEx/MC/V.)

◉ SIGHTS. The first armed conflicts between Jews and Arabs within the current borders of the State of Israel occurred at Tel Khai. In 1920, a group of Arabs gathered around the settlements of Tel Khai, Kfar Giladi, and Metulla—then part of French-administered Syria and Lebanon—and accused the Jewish settlers of protecting French soldiers who had been charged with encroachment on Arab lands. Yosef Trumpeldor, who lost an arm fighting a war for the Czar of Russia years earlier, led Tel Khai at the time. He fell for the trap and allowed four Arabs inside the settlement to search for the French agents. Once inside, the Arabs killed Trumpeldor and five others. The deaths of these six, along with two Jewish defenders who had died earlier, prompted the Jewish settlers to flee Tel Khai. The eight were buried in nearby Kfar Giladi. Trumpeldor's alleged last words—"No matter, it is worth dying for our country"—epitomized Zionist convictions for years. Soon after the attack, Jewish settlers returned to these Upper Galilee settlements, and, today, the land from Kiryat Shmona north to Metulla is a part of Israel as a result of their efforts.

The original watchtower and stockade settlement have been reconstructed in the **Tel Khai Museum,** which tells the history of Tel Khai through exhibits of settlement life in the rebuilt rooms, once again full of everyday items used by the settlers. It's best experienced as 1½hr. tour: call ahead to ask for one in English.

From the bus stop, cross the highway and walk to the left through the gate of the regional college; the museum is across the parking lot to the left. (☎06 695 1333; www.hatser-telhai.org.il or telhai@galil-elion.org.il. Open Su-Th 9am-4pm, F-Sa 10am-noon. NIS24, ages 5-18 NIS20.) From the back of the museum, take a marked, mountain path uphill to **Kibbutz Kfar Giladi.** This stony passage is called the "injured road," since it was used to hurry the wounded away from Tel Khai after the March 1920 battle. The "road" is dotted with historical plaques and leads to the **Military Cemetery,** where a statue of a roaring lion marks the graves of the Tel Khai Eight. Look for the sign pointing to the "Roaring Lion." Following signs into Kibbutz Kfar Giladi, head uphill and left to the Israeli Defense Forces museum, **Beit ha-Shomer,** meaning "House of the Guardian." The museum documents the history of the ha-Shomer fighters who defended Jewish settlements in the Galilee during the early years of the 20th century. Sending visitors on a winding path, the relatively high-tech displays (with plenty of English text) do a great job of relating the excitement of the defense group's early days. (☎06 694 1565. Open Su-Th 8am-4pm. NIS15, students and children NIS10.) The **Museum of Photography** is near the youth hostel in the industrial park on the right side of the main highway, before the turn for Tel Khai Museum and Kibbutz Kfar Giladi. Turn left when the access road splits and enter the industrial area through a gate on the left of the road. A bare, white gallery that houses a rotating display of work by international modern photographers, the museum also has a small, unlabeled collection of old-fashioned cameras. (☎06 695 0769. Open Su-Th 8am-4pm, F 10am-2pm, Sa 10am-5pm. NIS18, students and ages 3-18 NIS14.)

KHULA VALLEY (HULA VALLEY)   ☎06

עמק החולה

The Khula Valley ranks as one of the most beautiful areas in all of Israel. The entire valley was covered by a knee-deep swamp, until Jewish pioneers arrived at the end of the 20th century and drained the swamps to farm the fertile soil beneath. Eventually, the altered land became so dry that its diverse wildlife left the Khula Valley and in some instances died out entirely. Out of concern for the area's ecological diversity, Israel's first nature reserve was established in the Khula Valley in 1963. Since then, parts of the Khula Valley have been refilled with water and are carefully maintained; ecologists hope to lure amphibians, water buffalo, and birds migrating between Europe and Africa to take up residence in the area. The five reserves of the Khula Valley showcase Israel's forested north, ice-cold streams, swamplands, and their inhabitants.

KHULA NATURE RESERVE
Between Rosh Pina and Kiryat Shmona, off Rte. 90. From the south, the turn-off is on the right, 8km north of Tel Khazor. Look for a brown sign on the right that says "ha-Khula." Buses #501, 840, and 963 (NIS13) leave Kiryat Shmona frequently and go to a junction 2.5km from the entrance to the reserve. ☎06 693 7069. Open Su-Th and Sa 10am-4pm, F and holiday eves 8am-3pm. NIS35, under 18 NIS24.

This reserve is only really worth visiting between November and March, when it is swarming with animals and birds. Most of the original wildlife from the Khula swamplands has returned to the park thanks to the efforts of conservationists. The visitors' center gives details on the history of the swamp, explains the varieties of plant and animal wildlife it contains, and even boasts a 3D video presentation. The 1.5km-long trail is easy to navigate (maps are available), with wood-planked observation bridges and an observation tower. The trail circles through papyrus swamps and thickets populated by ducks, black-winged (and long-legged) stilt birds, turtles, mongooses, water buffalo, and other creatures. The visitors' center rents binoculars for bird enthusiasts (NIS10). The park workers recommend arriving early in the morning to see the wildlife and calling ahead, especially to get information in English.

KHORSHAT TAL NATURE RESERVE

Located off Rte. 99, between Kiryat Shmona and Banyas. From Kiryat Shmona, bus #36 goes to Khorshat Tal (20min.; several times a day, but check times carefully; NIS9.10). Ask to be let off at Khorshat Tal, then walk 100m down the hill on the right, toward the brown sign. ☎ 06 694 2360. Park open for swimming daily 8am-4pm. NIS36, ages 5-13 NIS22.

Half national reserve, half private campground, the big draw of this park is its ice-cold **swimming pool**—a man-made lake fed by the Dan River—which travels through the park in loops, with little wading pools and tiny waterfalls. Visitors cluster at the shady picnic tables and lounge on the grass surrounding the pool. Thanks to some crass commercialization, there's also a snack bar and a couple of big water slides (5 rides NIS10).

Scattered around the grounds of the reserve are 100-year-old **oak trees.** According to a Muslim legend, the trees, which grow nowhere else in Israel, sprang into being because of ten messengers of Muhammad who once rested here. Finding no shade or hitching post for their horses, they pounded their staffs into the earth to fasten their mounts, and the sticks sprouted overnight Staying at the **campground ❶,**with shared bathroom blocks, includes access to the pool. (Check-in 2-11pm. Check-out noon. Tent sites NIS55 per person, NIS40 per child ages 3-12. Enclosed 4-person bungalows Su-F NIS250, Sa NIS350; 4-person air-conditioned cabins NIS400/600. AmEx/MC/V.) Stock up on groceries, water, toilet paper, and barbecue supplies at **Minimarket ha-Goshrim** on Rte. 99, a ten minute walk from Khorshat Tal. Go west toward Kiryat Shmona and turn left through the pedestrian gate with the sign (in Hebrew). The store is on the other side of the quiet street, next to a soccer field. (☎ 06 695 6777. Open Su-Th 7am-8pm, F 7am-5pm, Sa 9am-5pm.) .

TEL DAN

תל דן

A few kilometers past Khorshat Tal on Rte. 99. From the main road, take a left at the brown sign and walk a winding 1.5km to the site. Take bus #36 from Kiryat Shmona (M-F 3 per day; plan ahead). ☎ 06 695 1579. Open Su-Th and Sa 8am-5pm, F 8am-4pm; gates close 1hr. before closing time. NIS25, students NIS21, ages 5-18 NIS13; ticket includes a discount at the Beit Usishkin Museum.

Tel Dan is the Khula Valley's most thickly forested nature reserve and contains some of the most beautiful scenery in northern Israel. Several short walks loop under a canopy of willow trees and follow the gushing Dan River, the largest tributary of the Jordan. Swimming in the river is prohibited but there is a **wading pool** in the middle of the 45min. circle trail where hot hikers splash around. The 1½hr. trail is rockier but passes by the ancient **ruins.** A 2½hr. trail is also available, but the visitor's center warns that, unlike the others, it is not 95% shady; vampires beware. Ongoing excavations at the *tel* have revealed the ancient Canaanite city of Laish, conquered and settled by the Israelite tribe of Dan around 1200 BC. Interesting remains lie in the ritual site, where some archaeologists believe King Jeroboam Ben-Nebat of the breakaway Kingdom of Israel placed a golden calf, attempting to draw attention away from the Kingdom of Judah's Temple in Jerusalem (I Kings 12:28-29).

In 1993, archaeologists made a remarkable find at Tel Dan: a broken stele inscribed with the words "House of David" in ninth-century BC Aramaic. The earth-shattering piece of rock may provide the first known reference to the biblical King David and his climactic expulsion of the Philistines, aside from the good book itself. The **Beit Usishkin Museum,** a gray stone building on the left on the way to Tel Dan, showcases excavations at the site and has exhibits on the natural history of Khula Valley and the Golan. (Open Su-Th 8am-3:30pm, F 8am-3pm, Sa 9:30am-4:30pm. NIS18, students and children NIS15; ticket includes a discount at the Tel Dan Reserve.)

METULLA
☎06

מטולה

Metulla, 9km north of Kiryat Shmona, is Israel's largest village on the Lebanese border. For many years its main attraction was ha-Gader ha-Tova (The Good Fence), the only opening in the border between Lebanon and Israel. Israel began passing aid and supplies through this point to Lebanese Christians in 1971, and in June 1976 the Good Fence officially opened, allowing Lebanese Christians and Druze free passage into Israel to obtain medical treatment, visit relatives, and work. When Israel withdrew from southern Lebanon in June 2000, the Good Fence finally closed and has been renamed the Fatmah Gate, its name before 1976. Though the town sustained some shelling in the summer 2006 conflict with Hezbollah, damage is no longer evident. The border is quiet, but lined with barbed wire and floodlights and patrolled by Israeli military in armored vehicles.

🖪🛈 TRANSPORTATION AND PRACTICAL INFORMATION. Buses #20 and 21 run between Kiryat Shmona and Metulla (15min., 5 per day 6:45am-2:10pm, NIS8). The **municipality building,** near the end of ha-Rishonim St. that's farther from the Lebanese border (on the right when facing the border), has free city maps. (☎06 683 7000. Open Su-Th 8am-1pm and 1:30-4pm.) However, a better bet for smart, English-language tourist advice is Sem, proprietor of 🖪**Sem's Neighborhood Grocery** (see **Food,** p. 281), which also offers free Wi-Fi. Bank Leumi has a small branch on ha-Rishonim St. close to the border. (☎06 695 5522. Open M-Th 10am-noon.) The Grand grocery store downstairs has an **ATM. First Aid** is near the beginning of ha-Rishonim St., just before the municipality building. The **post office** is at 19 ha-Rishonim St. (☎06 699 7749. Open Su and W 8am-2:30pm, M and Th 8am-1pm and 4-6pm, Tu 8am-2pm, F 8am-12:30pm.)

🖪 ACCOMMODATIONS. There are no cheap acccommodations in Metulla. Though ha-Rishonim St. is glutted with bed-and-breakfasts and bigger places like Hotel Arzim and Alaska Inn, they all cost around NIS400 a night. Happily, the youth hostel in Tel Khai is a short (if infrequent) bus ride away (see **Accommodations,** p. 278).

🖪 FOOD. A few hotels on ha-Rishonim St. have restaurants in their lobbies (try Alaska Inn), and there are a couple of cheap cafeterias in the **Canada Centre** (see **Entertainment,** below), but the quiet residents of Metulla appear to mainly cook for themselves or eat out in other towns. Pick up groceries in **Grand** supermarket, at the end of ha-Rishonim St. near the Lebanese border, on the left when facing the border (open Su-Th 6:30am-10pm, F 6:30am-5pm). Alternatively, head to 🖪**Sem's Neighborhood Grocery,** run by a friendly, crazy-haired

GALILEE

polyglot and stocked with all kinds of hikers' supplies. Sem dispenses travel information for Metulla, the Golan, and beyond, and offers free Wi-Fi. The store is on ha-Rishonim St., after the post office and just before Grand. (☎052 279 2594; semnet@bezeqint.net. Open daily 7am-10pm. AmEx/MC/V.)

HIKING. Curving around town is the **Iyon Nature Reserve,** full of waterfalls in the winter and early spring. Enter the park at the north end of town by following ha-Rishonim St. to the signs that say "Stop" and "Border Ahead," then turning right as the road curves to a memorial stone and Nakhal Iyon Picnic Ground, full of picnic tables, thickly-planted trees, and struggling grass. Green national park signs (in English, Hebrew, and Arabic) mark the gate where the trail begins. If there is no one at the rangers' booth at this northern gate, expect to pay when you arrive at the other end of the trail. Alternatively, to enter the park from the south, take the road (marked by a sign) that branches right off the main highway south of Metulla. Just a few minutes up the trail from the southern parking lot is the 30m **Tanur (Oven) Waterfall,** named for the chimney-like structure it forms with the cliff. The path continues uphill for two and a half kilometers past three more waterfalls. Farther up the highway from the turn-off for the park, through a traffic circle and up the steep hill on the left, is the **Dado observation point,** with a superb view of the Upper Galilee and southern Lebanon. (☎06 695 1519. Open Su-Th 8am-4pm, F 8am-3pm, Sa 8am-5pm. NIS25, children NIS13.)

ENTERTAINMENT. Sleepy Metulla happens to hide the best sports complex in all of Israel. A block to the right of ha-Rishonim St. (when heading north) hulks the imposing **Canada Centre.** A basic entrance ticket allows use of the two ice-skating rinks and swimming pools. The indoor heated pool has a water slide and a jacuzzi and is open all year; the outdoor pool is open only in the summer (NIS85, ages 3-13 NIS65). An extra NIS25 buys a game in the underground bowling alley, and NIS20 more gives admission to the gym, well-stocked with weight and cardio machines. The complex also houses a spa (massages from NIS220), squash courts, a full basketball and volleyball court, a few small cafeterias, and a shooting range. Lockers are available in the changing rooms for NIS10. (☎06 695 0370; www.canada-centre.co.il. Open daily 10am-8pm. Many area accommodations, including the Tel Khai hostel, offer discounts to the Centre. AmEx/MC/V.)

GOLAN HEIGHTS

רמת הגולן   هضـبة الجـولان

This formerly volcanic plateau overlooking the Khula Valley has a sparse population of 35,000 equally divided between recent Jewish settlers and longtime Druze inhabitants, many of whom strongly identify with Syria and have relatives across the border. To Israelis, the region is a major source of water as well as the home of ski slopes, apple orchards, wineries, and cattle pastures. The region's natural borders include the Jordan River and Sea of Galilee to the west, Mt. Khermon and the Lebanese mountains to the north, and the Syrian plains to the east.

The first recorded mention of the Golan is the Biblical "Golan in Bashan," a city established by Moses as a refuge for Israelites guilty of manslaughter

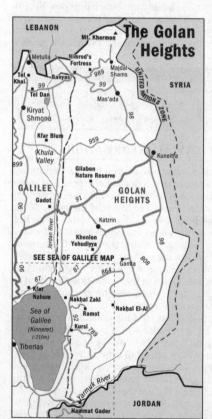

(Deuteronomy 4:43). The Golan was an important holdout in the Jewish Revolt of 66-73 CE, when its steep hills sheltered the city of Gamla, called the Masada of the north (see **Gamla,** p. 291). During the next two centuries, the Golan became a center of the Jewish population, as evidenced by excavations of ancient synagogues. As time passed, however, it degenerated into a backwater Ottoman province, until Turkish officials planted Circassian settlers here to stop Bedouin highwaymen in the 1880s. When the British and French carved up their mandates following WWI, the Golan was given to the French, while Britain maintained control of the rest of Palestine. After WWII the Golan became part of Syria.

Recent history has cast the Golan Heights back into the jaws of political controversy. Throughout the 1950s and 1960s, Israeli towns in Galilee were assailed by artillery fire from Syrian gunposts atop the mountains. Israel captured the Golan in the 1967 Six-Day War but was pushed back by Syria's surprise attack in the 1973 war. Israeli forces quickly recovered and launched a counter-attack, capturing even more territory. As part of the 1974 disengagement accord, Israel returned both the newly conquered territory and part of the land captured in 1967. Israel officially annexed the remaining 768 sq. km of territory in 1981, arousing international protest. Today, Jewish settlements are scattered among Israeli army bases, Druze villages, live minefields, and destroyed bunkers. The future status of the Golan is currently under negotiation. Syria claims that the land was seized unfairly and demands its return. Israeli officials had always invoked the issue of security in their refusal to budge from the Golan Heights, until the Rabin and Peres administrations announced their willingness to cede all or part of the Golan in exchange for peace and Syrian recognition of Israel, but Syrian President Hafez al-Assad rejected the offer. The reality is that whoever commands the elevated plateau enjoys strategic views of Damascus and all of northern Israel.

After the war of 2006 between Israel and Hezbollah guerrillas, a resolution by the UN General Assembly termed Israel's 1981 imposition of Israeli law and jurisdiction on the Golan Heights illegal, declared it null and void, and called for Israel to stop creating settlements in and generally asserting control over the region. The United Nations Disengagement Observer Force (UNDOF) now keeps a non-participatory watch from demilitarized zones along the northern borders, where Hezbollah's flapping flag is visible from Israeli hillsides. Negotiations continue to be reserved to the political arena: prime minister Benyamin Netanyahu recently declared that Israel will never part with the Golan. As a result of the political unrest, travel in the Golan can be dangerous and tourists should consult their consulates before traveling.

HIGHLIGHTS OF GOLAN HEIGHTS

TASTE the extra virgin at the **Golan Olive Oil Mill** (p. 288)

OGLE the rare fish in the springs of **Banya's** nature reserve (p. 288)

OVERCOME your fear of heights at the cliffside **Nimrod's Fortress** (p. 289).

◢ ⁊ ORIENTATION AND PRACTICAL INFORMATION

When wandering the Golan in summer, bring a hat (even a tacky one from a souvenir stall will ultimately prove a welcome relief), sunscreen, and water bottles. The cool pools of water often found on hikes reward weary walkers ready to take a dip, but don't drink the water. try to avoid the cold, damp, foggy, and often snowy winter. The best time to visit the Golan is spring, when the temperature is mild, the hills are green, and the streams and waterfalls are satiated with icy-cold water from the melting snow on Mt. Khermon. The best way to see the Golan is to **rent a car** in Tiberias or Kiryat Shmona. Those who don't plan to hike can hit the major sights in two days. Don't be afraid to lean on your horn (passing other cars in the Golan is as common as passing breathtaking views), and consider using it as a preemptive warning around blind curves on the narrow mountain roads.

Egged buses reach some sights in the Golan, but it's uncommon for more than one or two buses to pass the same place in a single day, so plan extremely carefully. Double-check all schedules, take a hard-copy list of bus times, and find out where the stops are ahead of time: many are at highway junctions rather than the destinations themselves, so anticipate some walking. Buses to sights near the Sea of Galilee generally leave from Tiberias. The Upper Galilee, Khula Valley, and the northern Golan are served by buses from Kiryat Shmona and Khatzor ha-Gelilit. It is nearly impossible to get to Gamla and many hiking trails by bus. Relatively few cars traverse the

Golan, and hitchhiking is inadvisable. If you decide to set out on your own, take a good map, specifically the huge (and hugely accurate) 1:50,000 trail map available at SPNI offices and in Steimatzky's (NIS90).

The official Golan Heights **tourist information office** is located in the Hutzot ha-Golan mall outside of modern Katzrin. It distributes fluent English-language advice, and a long list of phone numbers for lodgings in the Golan, broken down by town and village. It also sells maps of the region and hands out brochures. (☎696 28 85. Su-Th 9am-3pm; F 9am-12:45pm.) For hiker-specific information, contact Katzrin's **SPNI Golan Field School** (see Katzrin Accommodations, p. 286).

Organized tours are faster, more convenient, and sometimes less expensive than other forms of transportation; they also go at a quicker pace than many would like. **Egged** offers professionally guided two-day tours of the region for US$269 (approx. NIS1,064) leaving from Tel Aviv and Jerusalem every Wednesday (☎1 700 70 75 77; israel-4-u@eggedtours.co.il or www.grayline.com/israel. Accommodations included.) The **SPNI** offers hiking tours and activities across Israel, including in the Golan. The trips (Yarok Tours) are in Hebrew, but many of the guides and participants speak English. Check the website (www.aspni. com) for a list of upcoming tours and prices. Many include transportation (☎03 368 8625). **Jeep Plus** in Moshav Ramot, on the east bank of the Sea of Galilee, runs guided jeep trips. (☎673 23 17. 2hr. trip for max. 8 people NIS600, or NIS730 for longer.). Cheerful private tour guide Yaron Sachs (☎054 522 02 86; yaronguide@gmail.com) leads groups small and large on trips through the region (and elsewhere in Israel). He specializes in Biblical-themed excursions, but tailors each tour to the travelers' desires. Prices vary with choice of transportation, number of people, and length of trip.

KATZRIN ☎04

קצרין

Katzrin is the largest Jewish settlement in the Golan. The town was founded in 1977 for the purpose of creating an Israeli presence in the Golan Heights. This quiet residential community of houses with orange tiled roofs has grown rapidly over the past decades: now home to a successful winery and a bottled water manufacturing plant, Katzrin enjoys a high standard of living for a young settlement. The town feels distinctly new and stays within its neatly-ruled edges. There are no winding streets here to get lost in, and there's certainly no organic sprawl encroaching from the outskirts. Instead, the flavor of the city has gone into its shopping centers, which are pretty much the only places to see locals in action. Israeli and UN troops drive through town on their way to northern bases. A visit to the winery and museums in Katzrin takes only a few hours, but the town's central location in the Golan also makes it a convenient base for exploring the region.

▣ TRANSPORTATION

Buses: There's no station in Katzrin, but buses stop at the junction at the beginning of Daliyot St. and several places throughout town. Buses go to Katzrin from **Khatzor ha-Gelilit** (20min., 7 per day, NIS14.60), **Kiryat Shmona** (1½hr., daily, NIS34.50), and **Tiberias** (1-1½hr., 4 per day, NIS27).

Taxis: Moniot ha-Golan (☎04 696 1111) has service to **Rosh Pina** for NIS90 and **Tiberias** for NIS160.

GOLAN HEIGHTS

▚ ▞ ORIENTATION AND PRACTICAL INFORMATION

Katzrin consists of two main parts: **modern Katzrin,** which is where buses from Kiryat Shmona stop, and **ancient Katzrin,** which is a 15min. walk farther along **Road 9088** from **Katzrin Junction** (at the entrance to modern Katzrin). Modern Katzrin centers on **Daliyot Street,** which begins from the junction with mall **Kenyon Lev Katzrin** hulking on the left and a busy **shopping strip** laid out on the right. The archaeological museum, swimming pool, and library are all behind the shopping strip, and most of the modern city's amenities are also found in the area. The modern town is mostly encircled by **Zavitan Street. Si'on Street** is perpendicular to Daliyot St. near the last bus stop on the way out of town. Ancient Katzrin specializes in tourist attractions: on the left of the giant **Hutzot ha-Golan** mall (when facing the monstrosity) and its endless, barren parking lot is **Ancient Katzrin park.** On the right of the mall is an access road to Katzrin's **industrial area,** where tourists will find the winery and the olive oil mill.

Tourist Office: (☎04 696 2885), in the Hutzot ha-Golan Mall. Friendly staff provides city maps in Hebrew, with a few English transliterations, and mountains of glossy advertisements for local attractions. Open Su-Th 9am-3pm, F 9am-12:45pm.

Bank Leumi: (☎04 696 1601), in the shopping strip across Daliyot St. from Kenyon Lev Katzrin. **ATM** out front. Open M and Th 8:30am-1pm and 4:30-6:15pm, Tu-W 8:30am-2pm, F 8:30am-12:30pm.

Police: (☎04 696 8222), at the intersection of Si'on St. and Gilbon St.

Pharmacy: Emek Pharmacy (☎04 696 2578), in the shopping strip across Daliyot St. from Kenyon Lev Katzrin, next to the bank. Open Su-Th 8:30am-7pm, F 8:30am-1pm.

First Aid: Magen David Adom (Mada) (☎04 679 0111), a left turn off Si'on St., immediately after Kenyon Lev Katzrin when traveling away from Daliyot St.

Internet Access: The **public library** (☎04 696 9667), next to the Archaeological Museum in the plaza behind the shopping strip, has internet access on the 2nd fl. NIS3 per hr. A few bookcases of English novels are tucked away behind the Russian section on the same fl. Open Su and Tu 9am-noon, Th 4-7pm.

Post Office: (☎03 730 1243), in Kenyon Lev Katzrin, across Daliyot St. from the shopping strip. Open Su and Th 8am-6pm, M-Tu 8am-12:30pm and 3:30-6pm, W 8am-1:30pm, F 8am-noon.

▛ ACCOMMODATIONS

Though no real budget options exist in Katzrin, everyone and her daughter-in-law rents private rooms or runs a fledgling B&B. The rooms aren't cheap, but they're more affordable than elsewhere in the region, and a little bargaining may sweeten the deal. The **tourist office** (above) hands out long lists of phone numbers, and commercially-savvy proprietors put up signs around town.

▨ **Natanayl Rooms** (☎04 696 2212 or 050 765 5080), behind the commercial center's shopping strip, off Daliyot St. In the commercial center, walk through the passageway next to the jewelry store and climb the nearest staircase. There's a small sign by the door. 3 beautifully furnished bedrooms, each with TV, wood ceiling, A/C, and bath. Hot water, free linens, and a serene atmosphere (aided by soundproof windows) compensate for uninspiring views of the highway and parking lot . Singles NIS200; doubles NIS400. AmEx/MC/V. ❸

Zipi Rooms (☎054 227 3468), across from Natanayl, in the same building complex. Basic rooms, each with mini-fridge, A/C, and bath. Lounge area upstairs with seating and tables. Linens provided. Singles Sept.-July NIS200, Aug. NIS300; doubles NIS300. MC/V. ❸

SPNI Golan Field School, Zavitan St. (☎04 696 1234). Follow signs on Daliyot St. away from the entrance to the city until the street ends at a an intersection with Zavitan St. Turn left; the field school is on the right, just after the petting zoo. The office sells hiking maps (NIS90) and gives free hiking advice. Once a collection of dorms used by school groups and hikers, the somewhat austere field school rooms are now rented out privately. Expect a clean, bare space with a handful of bunk beds (even if you're only sleeping in one) and bath. Linens provided. Sept.-July singles and doubles NIS365; Aug. NIS415. Additional child NIS89/99. ❹

◘ FOOD

Fast food is everywhere at Katzrin's malls, but the restaurant scene is lackluster. Katzrin's shopping strip, across Daliyot St. from Kenyon Lev Katzrin, has a few choices popular with UN troops. For groceries, visit **Supersol,** in the mall next to Ancient Katzrin Park, or **Mister Zol,** in Kenyon Lev Katzrin.

Blueberry Cafe and Bakery (☎04 696 2103), in the shopping strip across Daliyot St. from Kenyon Lev Katzrin. Head to the right, past the Golan Residents' Committee and the jewelry store. An antique phonograph and stained glass windows make for a lovely corner eatery, but don't expect peace and quiet—groups of tourists sick of falafel crowd the tables. Baked potatoes NIS36. Soups and sandwiches NIS22. Pastries NIS5. Open Su-Th 9am-9pm, F 9am-4pm. AmEx/MC/V. ❶

Zabataani (☎04 696 2120), in the shopping strip across Daliyot St. from Kenyon Lev Katzrin. Hidden behind the stores on the left, together with the pharmacy and a little grocery store. The menu in this tiny restaurant departs from the standard Israeli grillery's with a range of Yemenite dishes, including *malawach* (fried bread) with a boiled egg. Hummus and salads NIS14-22. Meat dishes NIS30. Yemenite bread NIS15-19. Open Su-Th 6am-7pm, F 6am-3pm. Cash only. ❶

Mizlala (☎04 696 1017), across from Zabataani, in the commercial strip. Popular with locals and the traveling UN troops, Mizlala mixes things up with an innovative selection of vegetables and salads. Falafel NIS12-15. Shawarma and kebab NIS22-27. Open Su-Th 10am-11pm, F 10am-4pm. AmEx/MC/V. ❶

◎ SIGHTS

ANCIENT KATZRIN PARK. The excavations at this site have unearthed the remains of a synagogue in use from the fourth through eighth centuries CE. Check out the six-screen audio-visual presentation of Talmudic stories. Also noteworthy are the cramped, reconstructed houses with furnishings based on excavation finds; hunched-over visitors are welcome to explore the tiny spaces. (*Next to Hutzot ha-Golan shopping center, a left turn off Road 9088 when traveling away from modern Katzrin.* ☎04 696 2412; www.golan.org.il/park. Open Su-Th 9am-4pm, F 9am-2pm, Sa 10am-4pm. Free parking. NIS24, students and children NIS16. Combination ticket with the Golan Archaeological Museum NIS26, students and children NIS18.)

GOLAN MAGIC. Next to the tourist information office, this visitors' center attempts to turn the history and geography of the Golan Heights into a thrilling multimedia experience. Entrance buys you a short movie and as much time as you want to stare at the enormous, three-dimensional map of the Golan, dotted with tiny houses and labeled in Hebrew. (*In Hutzot ha-Golan shopping center, at the far right when facing the complex.* ☎04 696 3625; www.magic-golan.co.il. Open Su-Th 9am-6pm, F 9am-3pm, Sa 9am-4pm. Free parking. NIS25, students NIS20.)

GOLAN ARCHAEOLOGICAL MUSEUM. This museum has a small-scale, bilingual exhibit on ancient settlements in the Golan. It displays the remnants of 2000-year-old synagogues, battlefield debris from the Great Revolt in Gamla, and ancient coins with still-legible inscriptions. Cult stones from basalt are only a hint at the backyard's unassumingly-named "storage area": a series of racks full with intriguing stonework. *(Across the plaza behind the shopping strip off Daliyot St. ☎ 04 696 4664; museum@golan.org.il. Open Su-Th 9am-4pm, F 9am-2pm. Free parking. NIS17, students NIS14. Combination ticket with Ancient Katzrin Park NIS26, students and children NIS18. MC/V.)*

GOLAN HEIGHTS WINERY. For those who find archaeological excavations and Talmudic villages too sobering, the Golan Heights Winery offers a quick fix. A 1hr. tour includes a video explanation of the vineyard's world-renowned *Yarden, Gamla,* and *Golan* labels, a quick look at the aging barrels, and a souvenir glass. The remainder of the tour is a tasting session, after which visitors are released into the gift shop. *(On the industrial area access road at the far right of Hutzot ha-Golan when facing the mall. Turn right onto the road from Road 9088 and continue until the signs indicate a left turn into the winery parking lot. ☎ 04 696 8435 or 696 8409 (for a tour); www.golanwines.co.il. Open Su-Th 8am-5:30pm, F 8am-2pm. Parking available. NIS20, students and children NIS16. AmEx/MC/V.)*

GOLAN OLIVE OIL MILL. Sick of cheaply made oil passing itself off as "extravirgin," the proprietor of this classy warehouse demonstrates how true high-quality olive oil is made. The factory transforms the olive waste into lemongrass-scented scrub and other cosmetics. Sample or buy it all in the gift shop. *(On the industrial area access road at the far right of Hutzot ha-Golan, when facing the mall. Turn right onto the road from Road 9088; Golan Olive Oil Mill is on the right before you reach the winery. ☎ 04 685 0023 or 050 288 8709; www.golanoliveoil.com. Open Su-Th 9am-5pm, F 9am-3:30pm. Tours every hr. Call ahead, especially to request tours in English. Free parking. Visit Oct.-Jan. to see the machinery in use as the year's olives are actually processed. NIS10. AmEx/MC/V.)*

GOLAN BREWERY. Katzrin's noble attempt at replicating a German beer garden, this otherwise unremarkable restaurant doubles as a beer-making museum. The professional brewer (German-trained, *natürlich*) uses on-the-site vats and fermentation tanks to brew four different drafts. Sample the fruits of his labor by the glass at the bar or buy retro souvenir bottles to take home. *(In the same portion of Hutzot ha-Golan as Golan Magic, on the 2nd fl. ☎ 04 696 1311; www.beergolan.co.il. Open daily 11am-late. Beer NIS20 per bottle. AmEx/MC/V.)*

> **READ ME, DON'T BELIEVE ME.** "OPEN" signs, in both Hebrew and English, are everywhere, including in permanent paint on the doors of stores that are closed every Shabbat. Be careful, and consider them more of a suggestion of, "Yes, we are in fact in business" than a promise of service.

DAYTRIPS FROM KATZRIN

◪ BANYAS   בניאס بانياس الحولة

A few buses through the Golan and go past Banyas (#55 at 1:30pm and #58 at 4:40pm from Kiryat Shmona, #55 at 11:10am from Khatzor ha-Gelilit). The ride from Khatzor ha-Gelilit costs NIS37 and takes about 1¾hr., as the bus travels north to Neve Ativ, drops south past Nimrod's Fortress, and goes through the Si'on Junction roughly 2.5km before the Banyas access road on the right (well-marked with signs). There isn't technically a bus stop, so talk to the bus driver and watch for the signs. By car, Banyas lies just off Rte. 99, which runs between Kiryat Shmona and the north-south Rte. 98. ☎ 04 695 0272 or 690

2577. Open Sa-Th 8am-5pm, F 8am-4pm. Last entry 1hr. before closing. Parking available. NIS25, ages 5-18 NIS13. Combination ticket with Nimrod's Fortress NIS36/18.

Technically the **Khermon Stream Nature Reserve,** Banyas is a daytripper's paradise. Park workers give out detailed maps for free at the entrance, complete with notes about the reserve's archaeology and natural history, and meticulous instructions for three different hikes. Just beyond the parking lot and picnic grounds, the sparkling Khermon springs gush into pools full of rare fish. Ogling is allowed, but don't touch. The springs and environs have set the stage for a hodgepodge of religious events: Jesus of Nazareth gave the keys to heaven and earth to St. Peter here, Muslims built a shrine over the Prophet Elijah's supposed grave in the adjacent hill, and an ancient sanctuary dedicated to the Greek god Pan is carved into the cliffside (the name Banyas is an Arabic rendition of *Paneas*, or "Pan's Place"). Interpretive panels dot the former temple grounds, where the red-and-white checkered floor is still visible.

From this end of the reserve, a 2hr. climbing trail leads up to **Nimrod's Fortress;** it's probably best to check in with a park worker before making the ascent. The hikes detailed in the park map lead through other impressive ruins in the area, past the always-roaring springs, and through thick forest and old water-mills. The time estimates apparently assume a hiker with four unwilling children in tow, so don't be surprised if you finish ahead of schedule. Probably the most rewarding hike is the long trail, marked in red, that ends at **Banyas waterfall.** From here, walk a few minutes out to Kibbutz Senir to catch a return bus.

NIMROD'S FORTRESS

קלעת נמרוד

The trail to the fortress begins from Rte. 99, which is traversed by buses from Khatzor ha-Gelilit or buses on their way between Kiryat Shmona and Katzrin. ☎04 694 9277. Open daily 8am-5pm. Modess dress required. NIS14, students NIS12, ages 5-18 NIS6. Combination ticket with Banyas NIS36/18.

Nimrod's Fortress (Qal'at Nemrud) stands 1.5km northeast of Banyas on an isolated hill. According to the biblical list of Noah's descendants, Nimrod "began to be a mighty one in the earth" (Genesis 10:8). Legend has it that in addition to building the Tower of Babel, he erected this giant fortress high enough to shoot arrows up to God. Nimrod was supposedly so large that he could sit atop this castle and reach down to draw water from the Banyas stream. Another story holds that, to punish him, God put a mosquito inside his head to drive him mad. Historians like to poke holes in the myths by pointing out that the Ismailia sect of Muslims built the fortress, originally called **Qal'at Subayba** (the Cliff Fortress), in a strategic location that controlled the road from the Khula Valley to Damascus in the 13th century. The extensive fortress has two main sections; the one farther away from the entrance was built earlier. The two towers on opposing peaks tempted enemies to attack at the lower center of the fortress, a move, which left offensive forces open to arrows from both sides. A look around the grounds reveals a secret passageway, the guards' toilet, and a massive, well-preserved Arabic inscription. The **view** from the 815m fortress is not to be missed.

Up the road about 1km past Nimrod's Fortress is a Druze tomb and hiking route at **Nebi Hazuri.** The location is marked on the left by a brown sign. A white gravel road begins in the dirt parking lot and winds around picnic areas, trees, and monuments. The hiking route, marked in blue and white, begins heading right and downhill from beside the large wooden sign in the parking area and ends, roughly 2hr. later, outside the entrance to the road leading up to Nimrod's Fortress.

YA'AR YEHUDIYA NATURE RESERVE

By car from Tiberias, drive north along the lake, head east toward Katzrin, pass the Yehudiya junction, and continue along Rte. 87 until you reach the sign for the reserve and parking lot. By car from Kiryat Shmona, head toward Katzrin and the junction with Rte. 87, take a right, and look for the sign and parking lot on the right.

The most exciting and challenging hiking in the Golan is in the Ya'ar Yehudiya Nature Reserve, southeast of Katzrin. The highlight of the reserve and one of the best hikes in Israel is the action-packed **Nakhal Yehudiya** trail, which consists of an upper and lower section. From the Khenion parking lot, follow the red-and-white markers across the street, past the 1800-year-old Jewish and Byzantin town ruins. Upon completion of the **upper trail,** ascend the green-and-white trail to return to **Khenion** (3hr. round trip) or continue along the red-and-white marked lower trail for a longer hike (6hr. round trip). The lower trail ends with an extremely difficult climb up a boulder-strewn hill (be careful: the rocks are hot in summer), a peaceful stroll through a field, and a 1.5km walk to the right along the highway back to Khenion. Both trails feature enticing waterfalls and pools, some of which you must swim across to complete your hike. Rocks are slippery when climbing from dry parts of the trail into the water, so look for the strategically placed metal foot- and hand-holds in the cliffs.

> **LET'S NOT GO.** Jumping off the cliff at the second waterfall is dangerous—many people have died doing so. Instead, climb down the slick ladder into the water to enjoy the swim.

The reserve also harbors the slightly drier but equally beautiful **Nakhal Zavitan;** most of its trail options also start at the Khenion Yehudiya parking lot. Start on the green-and-white marked **Lower Zavitan trail.** A left turn on the red-and-white trail leads to the **Ein Netef** spring, which, unlike most wilderness sources, produces potable water (refill your bottle!). From the spring, backtrack along the red-and-white trail and turn left on the black-and-white trail to reach a pleasant pool and waterfall. This trek eventually crosses the red-and-white one and returns to **Khenion Yehudiya** (3hr.). Alternatively, turn left and continue on the red-and-white trail for 45min. to reach the spectacular **Brekhat ha-Meshushot** (Hexagon Pool), where hundreds of hexagonal rocks skirt the water's edge in a surreal geological phenomenon; swimming is allowed. From here, backtrack to Khenion (5hr.). The **Upper Zavitan** (black-and-white trail) tends to be good for all seasons. It begins near the field school in Katzrin and leads to less impressive hexagonal pools; after becoming a purple-and-white trail, it ends in Khenion Yehudiya (3hr.). The more difficult **Lower Zavitan** should be avoided in the winter due to occasional flash floods—the dirt has a high basalt content from the ancient volcanoes, and water streams cross it rather than sinking in. The dangerous **Black Canyon** is near the Lower Zavitan trail and can only be negotiated by rappelling. Do not attempt to hike the Black Canyon unless accompanied an experienced guide.

The following hikes in the area are accessible only by car. Starting from Kibbutz Eli-Al, the beautiful hike **Nakhal el-Al** lies southeast of the Zavitan and Yehudiya rivers. In winter and spring, enough water flows through to allow swimming beneath the falls. The red-and-white trail begins at the northeast end of the kibbutz. Follow the markers to **Mapal ha-Lavan** (White Waterfall) and continue on to **Mapal ha-Shakhor** (Black Waterfall)—the falls' names come from the colors of their volcanic rock. The trail ends at Kibbutz Avnei-Eitan. From there, take a right on Rte. 98 and walk 2km to return to Kibbutz Eli-Al. The **Nakhal Devorah and Nakhal Gilabon** hike begins from a parking lot on Rte.

91, 4km after the turn-off for Road 9088 when traveling east. Red-and-white markings in the lot lead to the left around a building and down into the canyon. Join the hundreds who have left their mark by sticking a masticated glob of gum onto **Even ha-Mastik** (the Gum Rock). The first waterfall on the trail is the **Devorah Waterfall**. Continuing on the red-and-white path another 1hr. leads to the 42m Gilabon Waterfall; wonderful views of the lush Khula Valley await at its top. The trail continues another 2hr. to the Jordan River and Rte. 918, but getting back to the parking lot may be difficult if you don't have a car waiting. Just retrace your steps to return.

GAMLA

גמלא

Take a right out of modern Katzrin, a left on to Rte. 87 at the junction, and a right onto Rte. 808. Rd. 869 to Gamla is on the right, and the turn-off for the park is marked with a sign. Gamla is not accessible by public transportation; those without cars often ask for rides from Katzrin and then walk the road to the ridge overlooking the ruins. Let's Go does not recommend hitchhiking. ☎04 682 2282 or 682 2283. Open daily Apr.-Sept. 8am-5pm, Oct.-Mar. 8am-4pm. Last entry 1hr. before closing. NIS25, children NIS13.

For years, the lost city of Gamla existed as no more than a legend from the pages of *The Jewish War*, written by first-century Jewish historian Josephus Flavius. After the 1967 War, archaeologists searched the region for a spot corresponding to the ancient description until Shmaryahu Gutman finally uncovered the site. It is called Gamla ("camel" in Hebrew) because the hill's peak protrudes from the surrounding area like a camel's hump. Katzrin's archaeological museum (p. 287) provides a great introduction to the site. In 67 CE, the Romans laid siege to this fortress, which had become a haven for Jewish refugees, particularly the rebellious zealots. As the siege wore on, Roman commanders became impatient and decided to storm down the corridor of land leading to the town from the nearby hills. As the legion broke through Gamla's walls, Jews fled to the upper part of the city, where slopes were the steepest. The Romans followed, but so many soldiers crowded on the rooftops that the houses collapsed; the Jews quickly turned and killed their pursuers. Some weeks later, three Roman soldiers sneaked into Gamla in the middle of the night and pulled out foundation stones from the watchtower, causing it to collapse. According to historian Flavius, in the ensuing confusion, the Roman army burst into the city and began to slaughter the inhabitants, many of whom hurled themselves into the deep ravine rather than die by enemy hands. Some archaeologists, however, take issue with Flavius's proclivity for over-dramatization and claim that Gamla's inhabitants were pushed over the cliff in the crush of the battle.

Inside the city lie the remains of what some archaeologists call the oldest synagogue ever found in Israel, dating from around the first century BCE. The reserve offers several hiking trails of varying difficulty. They lead to the ruins, a lookout point for **Griffon vultures** (Gamla is Israel's largest nesting point for the birds), and **Mapal Gamla** (Gamla Waterfall), 51m and taller than all other falls in the Golan. On the way, watch for **Dolmens**, table-like stone graves built 4000 years ago during the middle Bronze Age. Consult with park workers about **hiking** before setting out and take a map.

MOUNT KHERMON

הר חרמון   جبل الشيخ

Bus #55 goes to Moshav Neve Ativ, below the ski resort, once daily from Khatzor ha-Gelilit. Driving is advisable—going east on Rte. 99 from Kiryat Shmona, turn left onto road 989

LOCAL LEGEND

WATCH OUT FOR FALLING ANGELS

As a part of the contested Golan Heights, Mt. Khermon has been involved in its fair share of disagreements in the modern era. But, if the legends are true, it partook in even bigger struggles back in Biblical times. According to the Book of Enoch, said to be written by Noah's great-grandfather, 200 fallen angels gathered on Mount Khermon and swore a collective oath to rebel against God. Specifically, these angels—called the Grigori, or "Watchers"—promised each other that they would all take human wives, despite knowing that God would disapprove.

As it turned out, if you take the Book of Enoch at its word, God knew best. The half-angel, half-human children grew into giants ninety thousand feet tall—and with appetites to match. They started by eating all the food they could find; when they finished that, they moved on to people. It was a rough time for slow walkers.

In the end, the ancient book says, God punished the fallen angels by burying them until Judgment Day. To deal with the giants, he sent the Great Flood—the same one that floated Noah's Ark. So don't worry about the disputes over Mt. Khermon today; as any avid apocryphalist can tell you, things could be a lot worse.

and follow signs to Neve Ativ, then ask for directions up the mountain. ☎04 698 1337; www.skihermon.co.il. The gate on the road from Majdal Shams to Mt. Khermon closes at 3:30pm. Free parking. Dress warmly. Skiing in winter NIS45, ages 3-12 NIS38.

The 2800m peaks of the majestic Khermon (sometimes spelled Hermon) mountain range tower over the rest of the Golan. **Skiing** on the mountain is challenging: Khermon has no trees, and steep dips in the wide expanses are easy to miss. Beginners should not fret, however—gentle runs are available, and the resort runs a **ski school** with English-speaking instructors. On clear days, skiers can see the Galilee stretch out beneath them. In summer, the same chairlift brings tourists up to a panoramic lookout atop Mt. Khermon. The mountain is particularly striking in late spring and early summer, when it is covered in brightly-colored wildflowers—watch for the red and black *Tulipa systola*, or Mt. Khermon tulip. Ten kilometers south of Mt. Khermon lies **Moshav Neve Ativ,** founded after Israel captured the Golan. The *moshav* has developed an expensive **resort village,** which enables tourists to take advantage of the ski slopes. Its elegant entrances are graced with large plastic snowmen and giant skis (look also for a giant signboard listing B&B phone numbers).

MAS'ADA AND MAJDAL SHAMS

Bus #55 goes through both Majdal Shams and Mas'ada once daily from Khatzor ha-Gelilit, making a daytrip impossible without a car. To reach the site by car, travel east on Rte. 99 from Kiryat Shmona through Dafna and Snir and follow the signs. Shuttle between the 2 cities by driving on Rte. 98.

The Druze of these two villages at the foot of Mt. Khermon once differed from the Galilee's Druze in one major respect: most remained loyal to Syria and refused to accept Israeli citizenship in 1967. Many had close relatives on the other side of the Syrian border and did not want to fight against them in the event of a war. In 1982, they staged a protest against Israeli rule, and the Israeli Defense Forces were sent in to restore control. Since then, as relatives have aged and died, sentiment for Syria on the Israeli side has waned, and the villages are now fairly quiet. Residents of Mas'ada (pronounced MA-sa-day; ma-SA-da refers to the fortress near the Dead Sea; p. 336) and Majdal Shams long focused more on tradition than on commercialism: women swathed themselves in black and men wore black *shirwal* (low-hanging baggy pants) dating from Ottoman times. Modern times have brought more industrial look to these villages, with concrete construction projects and fast food restaurants in every other building, and tank tops are no longer an uncommon sight.

Two kilometers north on Rte. 98 lies the locally famous lake **Breikhat Ram** (Hebrew for "High Lake"). The perfectly round body of water fills the crater of a volcano that has not erupted in over 1000 years. The lake is on the right, past large gates with a sign in Hebrew. In the lake's parking lot is the excellent, two-story **Breikhat Ram Restaurant ❷**. Upstairs, dig into their specialty, "Lamb in the Oven" (NIS65); downstairs, order falafel and get fast service. (☎04 698 1638. Open daily in spring and summer 10am-10pm, in fall and winter 10am-5pm. Credit cards accepted.) Swimming in the lake is allowed, although there's no lifeguard and the water is too deep for children. (Open 9am-5pm. NIS10.)

Majdal Shams (Arabic for "Tower of the Sun"), one of the largest towns in the Golan, is 5km north of Mas'ada through a pleasant valley. The town abuts the border with Syria. Because the electric-fence border is closed and pocked with landmines, the lookout area on the outskirts of town once provided the setting for a sad but fascinating daily ritual. Majdal's Druze used to line up on the hillside (aptly dubbed *Givat ha-Tza'akot* or "Shouting Mountain"), armed with bullhorns, to make small-talk with their relatives on the Syrian side. The advent of the internet and the death of older relatives has now moved most of the conversation off the mountain and onto the web, although travelers may be able to catch an interaction or two on a Friday afternoon.

WEST BANK

הגדה המערבית الضفة الغربية

The Palestinian territory of the West Bank has played host to some of the most arduous and internationally notorious conflicts of the last few decades. As recently as five years ago, it was a region packed with mass protests, suicide bombings, and the hand of the Israel Defense Forces (IDF). In recent years, however, due to a number of factors, the political situation has calmed down quite a bit. Though there are no immediate signs of a complete peace between the Israelis and Palestinians, the region has become relatively safer, and can offer quite a remarkable experience for both the politically-inclined and apolitical. Tourists may be invited into Palestinian homes, where hot spiced tea and delicious coffee are accompanied by discussions of Israeli-Palestinian relations. Modest dress will make both men and women's experiences more enjoyable. The Israeli settlements are close to many Palestinian towns, but don't expect much transportation between the two. Typically, the best way to visit a settlement is to go back to Jerusalem and catch a bus from there.

When visiting the West Bank, always exercise extreme caution, especially when encountering the remaining IDF checkpoints. Keep your eyes out for any developing protests or demonstrations and avoid them at all costs. Check the US Department of State website (travel.state.gov) for the updated travel warnings for the West Bank and surrounding areas in Israel.

HIGHLIGHTS OF THE WEST BANK

DISCOVER the palace inside the flat-topped mountain of **Herodion** (p. 309).

INSPECT Banksy's graffiti murals at the **Dheisheh Refugee Camp** (p. 310).

DROOL over a delectable treat from **Rukab's Ice Cream** (p. 321).

ESSENTIALS

GETTING THERE

Visiting the West Bank from Israel is possible with a private car; expect numerous Israeli checkpoints and bring your passport. For details on car rental, see **Essentials**, p. 24. Most public transportation connections are from **Jerusalem**, with **Ramallah** serving as a major hub for the northern West Bank. Check with the Israeli tourist office before going; they'll probably issue a standard governmental warning worthy of serious consideration. When visiting cities in the West Bank or Gaza be sure to pick up the colorful *This Week in Palestine*, available in hotel lobbies and restaurants in the West Bank and East Jerusalem. Published monthly, it has an extensive listing of events and resources throughout the Palestinian Territories. For more information, check out http://www.thisweekinpalestine.com/index.php or call ☎02 295 1262.

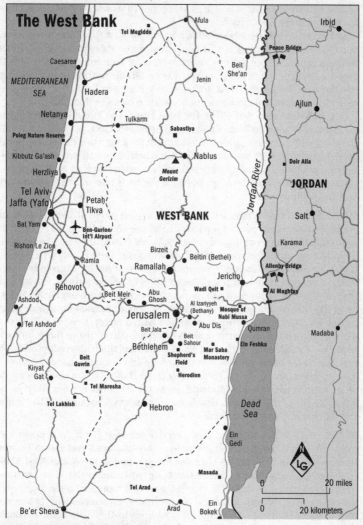

The West Bank

MEDITERRANEAN SEA

Afula
Tel Megiddo
Caesarea
Beit She'an
Jenin
Hadera
Netanya
Tulkarm
Sabastiya
Poleg Nature Reserve
Kibbutz Ga'ash
Nablus
Herzliya
Mount Gerizim
Tel Aviv-Jaffa (Yafo)
Petah Tikva
Bat Yam
Ben-Gurion/Int'l Airport
WEST BANK
Rishon Le Zion
Birzeit
Ramla
Beitin (Bethel)
Ramallah
Jericho
Rehovot
Abu Ghosh
Ashdod
Beit Meir
Wadi Qelt
Tel Ashdod
Al Izariyyeh (Bethany)
Mosque of Nabi Mussa
Jerusalem
Abu Dis
Beit Jala
Qumran
Beit Sahour
Bethlehem
Mar Saba Monastery
Ein Feshka
Beit Guvrin
Shepherd's Field
Kiryat Gat
Herodion
Tel Maresha
Dead Sea
Tel Lakhish
Hebron
Be'er Sheva
Ein Gedi
Masada
Tel Arad
Arad
Ein Bokek

Irbid
Peace Bridge
Ajlun
Deir Alla
JORDAN
Jordan River
Salt
Karama
Allenby Bridge
Al Maghtas
Madaba

WEST BANK

N
0   20 miles
0   20 kilometers

GETTING AROUND

A system of colored license plates differentiates vehicles. Those registered in Israel, Jerusalem, and Jewish settlements have yellow plates. White plates with green numbers belong to vehicles registered with the Palestinian Authority. Blue plates are a remnant from the days when the Palestinian territories were the Occupied Territories; they signify Arab cars not registered with Israel. Others are black-on-white (UN or diplomatic), red (police), white on green (Palestinian taxis and buses), and black (army). It's probably safer to travel with white or blue plates here (the opposite is true in Israel), but many Arab-owned cars that are registered in Israel proper (thus with yellow plates) travel hassle-free in the West Bank.

East Jerusalem is the transportation hub for the West Bank, but travel restrictions have made it impossible for non-Jerusalemite Palestinians to use Jerusalem as a transit terminal. Thus, check with local authorities to determine the best way to proceed. When possible, it is preferable to travel from Jerusalem into the West Bank rather than from one West Bank city to another, since direct roads from Jerusalem can often cut travel time by more than half.

One great and easy way to see the West Bank is to hire a Palestinian guide for the day. **Alternative Tourism Group** (see **Bethlehem Tours,** p. 304) is a reliable company with excellent guides. Alternatively, look for a taxi driver who speaks decent English (there are many) and ask whether he can drive by the major sights. Specify how many hours you wish to spend and agree on a price in advance; something in the range of NIS45 per hr. is reasonable for transportation and waiting time.

TAXIS. Shared **service taxis** are the recommended mode of West Bank transportation (*"service,"* pronounced ser-veece, the equivalent of Israeli *sherut*). Although slightly more expensive than Arab buses, they are faster, more reliable, and more frequent, departing whenever they fill with passengers. If you get lost or disoriented, consult the drivers; they are knowledgeable in matters ranging from politics to the location of obscure ruins. Private taxis (called *"special,"* pronounced spay-shal) are much more expensive but are often the only way to get to remote sites. Be sure to bargain for a price before getting in; usually, they are not equipped with a meter. Drivers will drive to the site and (for a few extra shekels) wait around to make the return trip. Some West Bank cities, including Nablus and Ramallah, have adopted a color convention for taxis: yellow cabs are private and orange cabs are *service.* As always, insist that the driver turn on the meter if there is one and have an idea of an appropriate price beforehand. Even for the most remote sites, do not pay more than NIS70 per hr. Most local rides average around NIS10-15; none should cost any more than NIS20.

BUSES. Both Arab and Egged buses service the West Bank. Arab buses leave from two bus stations in East Jerusalem: the **Suleiman Street Station** between Herod's Gate and Damascus Gate for the south; and the **Nablus Road Station** (a few steps away) for the north. Catch Egged buses at the West Jerusalem central bus station on Jaffa Rd. Egged buses cost more and often stop only at the outskirts of Palestinian towns. However, they are convenient for traveling to the Jewish settlements. Arab bus schedules to the West Bank are unpredictable; the intervals listed here are approximate. Transportation to Nablus and Jericho is especially erratic. For **Nablus,** take a *service* to Ramallah and continue to Nablus from there. For **Jericho,** go first to Abu Dis or al-Izariyyeh (Bethany) and connect from there.

Many of the buses operate like *service* taxis, following no schedule and leaving when sufficiently full. Buses to Ramallah and Bethlehem are the most frequent, leaving approximately every 10-15min.; other lines leave approximately every hr. Buses generally stop running around 8pm. To: **Bethlehem** (#124 goes to checkpoint, 20min., NIS4; #21 goes all the way to Bab-izQaq, 30min., NIS6); **al-Izariyyeh** (Bethany; NIS4); **Abu Dis** (NIS4); **Ramallah** (#18, NIS6.50).

MONEY

The **new Israeli shekel (NIS)** is the currency most frequently used, although **Jordanian dinars (JD)** and **U.S. dollars (US$)** are also sometimes accepted. Expect prices to increase when paying in foreign currency. ATMs are not as common as in Israel, but can be found in all major banks. Traveler's checks and credit cards are also less recognized, so carry enough cash to cover your daily expenses.

KEEPING IN TOUCH

POSTAL SERVICE. The postal service in the West Bank is controlled by the **Palestinian National Authority (PNA),** though it is dependant on the **Israeli Postal System (IPS).** All international mail is routed through the IPS except mail originating from Arab countries, which is routed through Egypt. All major towns in the West Bank have at least one post office with **Poste Restante.** Letters should be addressed, for example,

Angela KUO

Poste Restante

Main Post Office

Town, West Bank

via Israel

(see **Essentials,** p. 28). The PNA issues stamps, which are valid for sending mail internationally via Israel, although delivery is reported to be less reliable than the main IPS.

TELEPHONES. The telephone system is also part of the Israeli telephone network. All services, including collect and calling-card calls, are available from any private or public telephone. Shekel-operated phones are available in the West Bank, but public phones can be difficult to find. Blue-colored **Telecard-operated phones** are conveniently located in most post offices, where cards can also be purchased, but these new telecard phones do not accept Israeli Bezeq cards.

 CALL ME. The international phone code for the West Bank is +970, but calls from within Israel do not require a country code. Relevant area codes are ☎02 for Bethlehem, Ramallah, and the south, and ☎09 for Nablus and the north.

LIFE AND TIMES

POLITICAL HISTORY

For those who seek the truth, discussing West Bank politics is likely to be disappointing and confusing—everyone has his or her own opinion. Nevertheless, few want to talk about anything else, and eliminating personal ideology and emotion from the conversation is inevitably difficult. Historically, the West Bank represents the most complex facet of the Arab-Israeli conflict, due to its relevance to three major ethnic groups: Palestinian Arabs, Israelis, and Jordanians.

Another Brick in the Wall
The Construction of the Israeli West Bank Barrier

A CLOSER LOOK

Since 2002, Israel has been in the process of constructing a 710 km barrier between itself and the Palestinian territories of the West Bank. Often referred to as the "Security

> ## "referred to as the 'Security Fence' by the Israelis and as the 'Apartheid Wall' by the Palestinians"

Fence" by the Israelis and as the "Apartheid Wall" by the Palestinians, it vaguely follows the 1949 Armistice Line, commonly known as the "Green Line." When the project began, it was intended to be completed in only a year. The wall currently remains only about 2/3 finished, though its projected completion date lies in 2010.

The proposed purpose of the wall was to minimize the friction between the Israeli and Palestinian populations living near each other. The true focus was to protect the Israeli people living near the West Bank from Palestinian terrorist attacks, which were not rare occurrences following the Palestinian uprising in 2000. When Israeli Prime Minister Ehud Barak officially proposed the barrier in 2000, he made a different claim: that it was "essential to the Palestinian nation in order to foster its national identity and independence without being dependent on the State of Israel." Though these reasons are widely accepted among many Israelis, Palestinians have often claimed the true reason for the barrier to be the annexation of land and water from the West Bank and the disruption and isolation of a large portion of its population.

One of the most controversial aspects of the wall, besides its mere existence, is its actual route. Only about 20% lies on the Green Line itself. The majority of the barrier is actually set in the West Bank, as it was shifted to include on the Israeli side several areas of Israeli settlements, the most prominent of which is the eastern half of Jerusalem (which includes the Old City). While this leaves most Israeli populations fairly intact, it isolates a significant number of Palestinians from their jobs, farms, schools, healthcare, and means of transportation. The current route places 8.5% of the West Bank on the Israeli side of the wall, with another 3.4% partially or completely surrounded by the wall.

Though in 2004 the International Court of Justice ruled that the barrier violated international law, Israel ignored the ruling and continued construction. When in the same year the United Nations voted on a resolution likewise condemning the barrier, Israel and the USA were two of only six countries that opposed it.

The barrier has not been wholly bad for Palestine, however. Over the past two years, the existence of the wall has caused the Israeli military to remove over 100 roadblocks and 27 checkpoints in the West Bank, including those at the entrances to Jericho, Jenin, and Nablus. The economies in many West Bank towns have also been thriving recently, with fewer forced store closings and an overall smaller presence of the IDF. However, many people see this as a restoration to natural order within Palestine as opposed to a benefit gained by the construction of the wall.

Though much of the international discussion has been theoretical, the physical wall itself has been the site of much civilian response. Protests have been held, and artistically inclined citizens have painted their opinions on the actual barrier, much like the Berlin wall in the 1980s. Even graffiti artist Banksy and Pink Floyd's Roger Waters have left their marks.

As the completion of the wall nears, many are left to wonder: will it bring peace to these clashing neighbors, or will it ruin their relationship forever?

David Andersson recently graduated from Harvard University with a Bachelor of Arts in Social Studies, focusing on social movements and public space. He is currently traveling on an around-the-world plane ticket, using Let's Go as his trusty guide.

The political region now called the West Bank was created in the aftermath of the **1948 Arab-Israeli War,** when Jordan conquered the "west bank" of the **Jordan River** (p. 42). The Jordanian government subsequently did little to develop the West Bank and discriminated against its Palestinian residents. Another consequence of the 1948 war was the expulsion of about 700,000 Palestinians from their homes in Israel, forcing them to become refugees in several countries, though primarily in Jordan and the West Bank. To this day, none of the Palestinian refugees have been allowed back into Israel's borders.

In the **1967 Six-Day War** (see **Life and Times,** p. 44), Israel captured the West Bank, placing the area under a temporary military administration (except for East Jerusalem, including the Old City, which was annexed). Arab mayors and police kept their offices, Jordanian school curriculums continued to be taught, public welfare programs were established, National Social Security payments were made, and Israeli medical treatment was instituted.

Israeli occupation was not all benevolent, however. Because the area was administered under martial law, basic rights granted to Jews and Israeli Arabs were denied the Palestinians, who suffered curfews and mass arrests. Houses were destroyed in retaliation for the terrorist actions of one family member. There was no freedom of assembly—Palestinians could not have weddings without permits from Israeli authorities. Flying the Palestinian flag was illegal, and the infrastructure, schools, and public works of the West Bank were neglected in comparison with those of Israel proper. Palestinian attempts at establishing economic independence were thwarted.

In December 1987, the Palestinians of the occupied territories launched the **first intifada:** two decades of occupation, economic stagnation, and increasing Israeli settlement in the West Bank erupted into stone-throwing, demonstrations, the unfurling of the Palestinian flag, and other expressions of nationalism. The first *intifada* led to major changes in the nature of the Palestinian-Israeli conflict. The populist nature of the uprising and the televised suppression by the Israeli army managed to draw more international attention than decades of terrorism by the **Palestine Liberation Organization (PLO)** did.

After about six years of continued struggle, many Palestinians were worn out. The first *intifada* had stopped making headlines by the time the Gulf Crisis began in 1991. In contrast to most Arab governments in the region, which joined a US-led coalition opposing Saddam Hussein, the PLO and most Palestinians supported Iraq. Palestinians cheered from rooftops when dozens of Iraq's SCUD missiles landed on Israel, which wasn't involved in the war. Saudi Arabia and other oil-rich Gulf states, whose financial support had been trickling through the PLO into the territories, suspended their aid. In the aftermath of the Gulf War, Middle Eastern governments became convinced that it was high time for a regional peace conference. After the historic **Madrid Conference** in October 1991, negotiations continued intermittently.

In August 1993, Israeli and Palestinian political representatives met for the first time in Oslo, Norway in an effort to reach a peaceful agreement, resulting in the creation of the Palestinian Authority and the stated commitment of both sides to eventual Palestinian administration of the territories. The **Oslo Accords,** as they are typically called, have been the basis for all future negotiations between the two parties, though have lost credibility over time as local conflicts and shifts in government have seemed to negate some of the positive intentions of both sides. In July 2000, US President **Bill Clinton** held a **Peace Summit** at Camp David with Prime Minister of Israel **Ehud Barak** and Palestinian Authority Chairman **Yasser Arafat** with the joint intention to solve the dispute between them once and for all. At the summit, Minister Barak proposed he would return 73% of the West Bank lands to Palestinian sovereignty and would allow a limited number of Palestinian refugees to return to Israel, but would channel the rest into the newly formed Palestinian state. He also claimed permanent ownership of East Jerusalem, including the Old City, but promised to return several surrounding towns to Palestine. Arafat did not accept these proposals, and the summit ended in an impasse.

Soon after the summit, in late September 2000, fatal riots broke out in Jerusalem and nearby West Bank towns that escalated into the **second intifada,** an extended Palestinian uprising that included many mass protests and suicide bombings in Israel. The attacks on Israeli soil caused the State of Israel to enforce checkpoint closures within the West Bank and begin construction of the **Separation Wall** between the Israeli and West Bank territories in 2002, which is still under construction to this day.

WHERE'S GAZA? Wondering why we published a book on Israel and the Palestinian Territories, but there's no chapter on the Gaza Strip? Check out **Recent News** (p. 50) to see why Gaza isn't safe for travelers.

RECENT POLITICS

The construction of the Separation Wall has been controversial for many reasons (see **Another Brick in the Wall,** p. 298). There is little doubt, however, that the wall is one of the factors that has nearly eradicated the violent protests and bombings of Israeli cities by Palestinians in the West Bank. The other factors include the death of Yasser Arafat in 2004 and the conflict between **Hamas** and **Fatah,** the two primary Palestinian political parties. Though the West Bank and the Israeli border have calmed down immensely in the past several years, serious disputes remain that prevent them from reaching a final state of peace.

Israeli settlements in the West Bank are a source of constant controversy. Some 300,000 Israeli Jews have settled in the West Bank since 1967. Launched by Labor governments eager to establish an Israeli presence in areas of strategic importance such as the Jordan Valley, the settlement project has been an ideological cornerstone of right-wing Likud governments since 1977. The settlements are motivated primarily by strategic considerations, but also by the desire to maintain the historical boundaries of **Eretz Yisrael** (the Biblical land of Israel), an area including Israel, the West Bank, the Gaza Strip, and beyond. The United Nations has deemed these settlements to be a violation of international law. Israel, however, has made no attempt to depopulate these settlements or prevent their expansion.

Another source of tension is the more than four million Palestinian refugees from Israel that have been living in the West Bank and elsewhere for over six decades. This figure is a bit deceptive, as it not only includes the 700,000 or so Palestinians who were booted from their homes in the Arab-Israeli War of 1948, but also all their descendants. Traditional international law does not grant refugee status purely on the basis of descent, but an explicit exception was made for the Palestinians. These families claim to have been illegally kept from their homeland for over half a century, citing Article 13 of the **Universal Declaration of Human Rights,** which states, "Everyone has the right to leave any country including his own and to return to his country." Israel, however, does not recognize the Palestinians' **"right of return."** Were all or most of the refugees to return to Israel, the Jewish majority would potentially be lost, and many worry that Israel's existence as a whole would be put in jeopardy. Israel has remained at least nominally in support of settling the refugees permanently in a distinct state of Palestine.

Both the Palestinian Authority and government claim that Israel is being hypocritical in its support of this "two-state solution." While it will not allow Palestinian refugees to step foot in Israel, it has allowed and even encouraged the Israeli settlements to thrive within the West Bank.

Most recently, in the summer of 2009, Prime Minister of Israel **Benjamin Netanyahu** listed five conditions under which Israel would make peace with Palestine: Palestinians must recognize Israel as a Jewish state; Palestinian refugees must not return to Israel; the peace treaty must be final, with no further claims against Israel; the Palestinian state must be demilitarized; the demilitarization must be internationally recognized. Netanyahu did not express any intention to tear down the controversial Separation Wall or to remove the Israeli settlements in the West Bank. Not surprisingly, the Palestinian National Authority rejected these conditions. Though the stipulations for peace have not yet been settled upon, it is clear that most Israelis and Palestinians can agree on one thing: the war between them is not good for anyone.

ECONOMY

The economy of the West Bank has depended on that of Israel since the 1967 occupation. For years, Israel hired tens of thousands of Palestinians to fill their menial jobs, but they felt Israel's economic crises even more sharply than did Israelis, as they were the first to be laid off in times of hardship. However, after the Palestinian attacks of the second *intifada*, Israel began to turn elsewhere for workers, and increasingly fewer Palestinians were able to keep their jobs in Israel. Also after the second *intifada*, when the Israeli army closed numerous checkpoints and assumed complete control over the flow of goods in and out of the West Bank in 2001-2002, it experienced a severe recession. The Palestinian territories received billions of dollars in international aid, the majority of which was halted in 2006-2007 when the Hamas-Fatah conflict culminated in Hamas's control of the Palestinian Authority, an organization which many nations deemed a terrorist organization. The continued construction of the Separation Wall has also had severe effects on the economies of border towns that were dependent on the easy movement of goods to and from nearby towns. The most recent

NOW I KNOW MY ABCS

After traveling in the West Bank for a few days, you get used to jumping through hoops. But given the tangle of restrictions imposed by the IDF, even the most checkpoint-hardened traveler is bound to encounter a few surprises. One such surprise hit me when traveling from Jerusalem to Bethlehem to meet a Palestinian guide.

First, I had to find an Arab taxi with Israeli plates (no small feat—Arab and Israeli taxis are identical except for the citizenship of the driver). After a few predictable checkpoint delays, we arrived at our destination, and I saw my guide waving from across the street. I asked the taxi driver to take me over to him, but he said something in Arabic, gestured wildly across the street, and pushed me out of the cab. I waved to my guide to come over and translate, but he shouted that he couldn't come across.

I later found out that a mess of arbitrary boundaries had constructed a no-man's land between these two native residents, which could somehow magically be bridged by my little blue passport. The cab driver was in area C, which is under Israeli control, and couldn't bring his car across the street to area A, under Palestinian control; my guide was not allowed to cross into area C without special permission. The street, which looked like any normal street, served as an invisible barrier, keeping people from crossing.

—Mark van Middlesworth

statistics estimate that 46% of the population of the West Bank is below the poverty line.

In recent times, the economy has begun to pick up in some of the West Bank's cities. Due to the drastic decrease in the number of Palestinian attacks on Israel, the Israeli military has been slowly but steadily loosening its firm grasp on the West Bank. Many roadblocks and checkpoints have been eradicated, allowing the simple flow of people to increase. Random store closures have lifted in some cities, stimulating an increase in spending and easing the shop owners' constant fears. Some places have begun celebrating their newfound freedom: in the summer of 2009, Nablus held a two week shopping festival (see **Hasty Pastry,** p. 326). Though the economy of the West Bank is still much more stagnant than Palestinians would like, the soft breeze of consumerism has once again breathed life into some of its cities.

BETHLEHEM ☎02

בית לחם بيت لحم

Bethlehem and its environs were the backdrop for some of history's quieter religious moments: Rachel's death, the love between Ruth and Boaz, the discovery of the shepherd-poet-king David, and of course, the pastoral birth of Jesus. Bethlehem is almost entirely Christian, and the surrounding villages of Beit Sahour and Beit Jala are home to most of the country's Palestinian Christian minority. The three Wise Men followed a star to a peaceful manger, and today's pilgrims can follow Star St. to bustling Manger Sq., where fleets of tourist buses and armies of postcard-sellers swarm around the stocky Basilica of the Nativity. The glow-in-the-dark Virgin Marys and plastic crowns of thorns may take crass commercialism to a new level, but some visitors still manage to see past the blinding flashbulbs to the religious significance. The most crowded and interesting time to visit Bethlehem is during a Christian holiday, for which you should make hotel reservations well in advance. Other times allow more personal space to explore and a more accurate portrait of life in Bethlehem. Today, Bethlehem is a microcosm of the West Bank, reflecting the hardships of military occupation and the many reactions of Palestinians. The separation wall looms over Beit Jala on the uphill side of the city. It is covered with graffiti (including a series by UK-based street artist **Banksy**) opposing its construction and drawing parallels to the Berlin wall. A similar artistic outpouring can be seen in the graffiti of **Dheisheh camp** (p. 310). Near the wall is evidence of a more violent **reaction** to occupation: the bombed-out remains of a house from which a few Palestinian militants fired upon a nearby settlement, to which the Israelis responded with helicopters and rockets. Despite the conspicuous signs of violence, to a first-time visitor, perhaps the most striking aspect of Bethlehem is its normalcy, and the warmth and hospitality of its residents.

▐ TRANSPORTATION

Buses: From the central bus station, *service* taxis run to Jerusalem, Ramallah, Hebron, Jericho, Bethany, and just about anywhere else you'd want to go. **Bus 21** (NIS6.50) runs from Damascus gate to Bab-izQaq without stopping at the checkpoint. On the way back, passengers should expect a delay to check passports. **Bus 124** (NIS4.50) runs much more frequently, stopping at the checkpoint near Beit Jala and Rachel's Tomb.

Taxis: Private taxis congregate around the bus station and uphill of Bab-izQaq. Expect to pay NIS10 between Manger Sq. and Bab-izQaq; NIS15 from Beit Jala or Beit Sahour

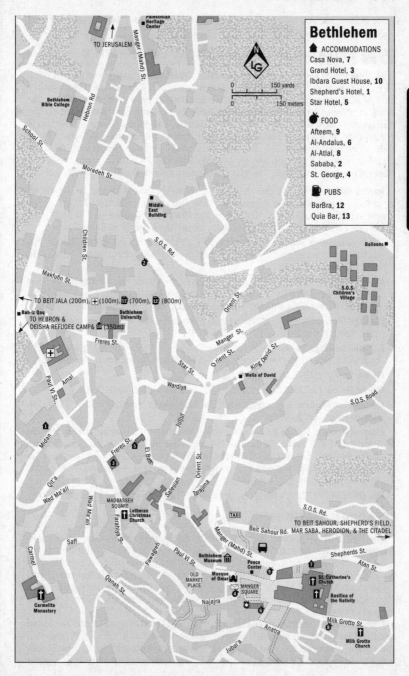

WEST BANK

Bethlehem

ACCOMMODATIONS
Casa Nova, **7**
Grand Hotel, **3**
Ibdara Guest House, **10**
Shepherd's Hotel, **1**
Star Hotel, **5**

FOOD
Afteem, **9**
Al-Andalus, **6**
Al-Atlal, **8**
Sababa, **2**
St. George, **4**

PUBS
BarBra, **12**
Quia Bar, **13**

to Manger Sq.; and NIS20 between Beit Jala and Beit Sahour. **Service taxis** run most of these routes for NIS2.50.

ORIENTATION AND PRACTICAL INFORMATION

Religious sights center on **Manger Square,** in front of the Basilica of the Nativity. The taxi stand is on **Manger Street,** just north of the police station. On the other side of Manger Sq., winding North through Bethlehem's narrow streets, is the *souq*, centering around **Najajreh Street, Saint Paul VI Road,** and **Star Street.** To the northeast is **Beit Jala,** to the west is **Beit Sahour. Bab-izQaq,** where *service* taxis congregate, is between Beit Jala and Bethelehem, at the intersection of Pope Paul VI St. and Hebron Rd. It is the only traffic light in Bethlehem. Visitors should be sure to pick up a copy of *This Week In Palestine,* available at the Peace Center as well as at tourism offices throughout the West Bank.

Tourist Office: (☎02 276 6677), in the Peace Center. Provides free maps, as well as detailed maps with tourist information (NIS5). Open M-Th, Sa 8:30am-3:30pm. Hours are sometimes cut short without notice. The **Ministry of Tourism** (☎274 1581) can answer questions when the tourist office is closed. Open daily 8am-3pm.

Tours: Alternative Tourism Group (☎02 277 2151; www.atg.ps), in Beit Sahour. This politically-minded organization provides tours of every major city in the West Bank. Also runs volunteer programs.

Banks: Housing Bank, in the bus station. Has Western union and an **ATM.** Open Su-W 8:30am-2:30pm, Th 8:30-1:30pm. There is another **ATM** in Manger Sq. near the post office. Additional **ATMs** are scattered around the city center and Bab-izQaq.

Luggage Storage: In the tourist information office in the Peace Center will hold your luggage during business hours.

English-Language Bookstore: In the Peace Center. Has a selection of English-language books on topics ranging from religious sights to political issues. Open daily 9am-4pm.

Police: (☎274 8231), on Manger St. at Manger Sq..

Tourist Police: (☎277 0750), in Manger Sq., across from the Peace Center.

Hospital or Medical Services: al-Hussein Government Hospital (☎274 1161), on Hebron Rd. toward Beit Jala.

Internet Access: Square Restaurant, in Manger Square; the **International Center,** on Pope Paul VI Rd.; the **Ibda'a Cultural Center,** in Dheisheh refugee camp; and **Bonjour Cafe** (see **Food,** opposite page) all have free Wi-Fi. There are 2 internet cafes near the bus station, usually filled with kids playing shoot-em-ups at full volume. NIS8 per hr. Open M-Sa 9:30am-2pm and 3-11pm.

Post Office: (☎274 2795), in Manger Sq. across from the Nativity Church. Open Su-Th 8am-2:30pm.

ACCOMODATIONS

While Bethlehem's accommodations are a little expensive, the few extra shekels provide a serene comfort foreign to Jerusalem's hotels (as long as you get a room away from the street, that is). Many of the prices are negotiable if they are not posted behind the front desk, which means you'll get a better rate if you book in advance and haggle. Make sure to reserve in advance during Christian Holidays (be sure the check the Orthodox calendar; these holy days draw the largest crowds).

One attractive addition to Bethlehem's (almost) hostel-less options is a ◼**Bed and Breakfast** program intended to give visitors a taste of life with a Palestinian family for a reasonable cost. Families are usually extraordinarily hospitable and talkative. Under a project overseen by ATG and made possible by a grant from the Japanese government, 27 double rooms have been renovated in Beit Jala, Bethlehem, and Beit Sahour homes, all with clean private bathrooms and some with telephones. Rates vary by family but are approximately NIS100-120 per night. Lunch and dinner are available at extra charge. Contact the tourist information office in the Peace Center for reservations.

Ibda'a Cultural Center Guest House (☎02 277 6444; www.ibdaa194.org), in the Dheisheh refugee camp. Run by the Ibda'a Cultural Center (p. 311), this guest house has cozy, well-maintained 4-bunk rooms, each with a private bath. The restaurant upstairs serves international cuisine to student volunteers and aid workers lounging on Bedouin-style couches. Free Wi-Fi and computer access. Dorms NIS50. Cash only. ❶

Shepherd Hotel (☎02 274 0656; www.shepherdhotel.ws), on Midan St. just off of the Paul VI St. *souq*. Decorated wall-to-wall in a flowery theme, this hotel is anything but understated. Sparkling bathrooms and A/C in each of the rooms. Traditional Arabic barbecue restaurant downstairs. Breakfast included. Singles NIS150. V. ❷

Casa Nova Palace and Pilgrim's House (☎02 274 3980; casanovapalace.com), off Manger Sq. in a corner to the left of the basilica entrance. Caters primarily to Franciscan pilgrims, but all are welcome. Modern rooms and plenty of hot water. Breakfast included. Reception 24hr. Curfew midnight. For Christmas stay reserve at least 1 year in advance. Singles NIS175; doubles NIS230. MC/V. ❸

Star Hotel (☎02 274 3249), uphill of the Grand Hotel off of Pope Paul VI St. Well-equipped facility offers one of the best views of Bethlehem and its surrounding settlements. All rooms with A/C, TVs, and private baths. Wi-Fi available. Singles NIS155; doubles NIS230; triples NIS270. MC/V. ❸

Grand Hotel Bethlehem, Pope Paul VI St. (☎02 274 1440; www.grandhotelbethlehem. com), between Manger Sq. and Bab-izQaq. Fully renovated and eerily similar to the Star Hotel. A Mexican restaurant on the ground floor serves dinner starting from 7pm (entrees NIS30-60). Wi-Fi available. Singles NIS195; doubles NIS350. MC/V. ❸

FOOD

Greasy fast-food establishments interspersed among the souvenir shops and tourist-priced falafel stands in **Mager Square** provide fuel for church-hopping expeditions. Further north, the stalls of the **souq** sell the same food at better prices, adding sweets and baked goods to the mix. The restaurants recommended by locals tend to be delicious and relatively inexpensive, though they may be too Americanized for some tastes. The advantage of the foreign influence is that, unlike more traditional restaurants, these places serve booze.

Afteem (☎02 274 7940). To the left when facing the Peace Center, it's the 2nd of 2 falafel stands heading down the ramp. Ordering at this locally famous falafel stand is deceptively simple: no endless bins of sides here, just choose regular or spicy. Then see if you can identify all of the flavors in the perfectly-seasoned falafel (sandwich NIS5, plate NIS15). Kebabs NIS30. Open daily 7:30am-midnight. Cash only. ❶

Bonjour Cafe (☎02 274 0406). From Bab-izQaq, head down Manger St. toward town and take 2 right turns; Bonjour is on the left. Small, tastefully decorated cafe. Diverse menu has large selection of international food with just a hint of local flair. Try the beef and cheese fajita (NIS24); the inclusion of pickles works surprisingly well. Meal-sized "small" Greek salad NIS19. Free Wi-Fi. Open M-Sa 9:30am-11:30pm. Credit cards accepted. ❶

Qa'abar (☎02 274 1419). Up the hill in Beit Jala; ask around for KAH-ah-bar or follow the smoke from Bab-izQaq. This family-run barbecue is so popular in Bethlehem that many of the locals refer to it as a "public restaurant." Dig in (no silverware required) to a half chicken cooked to perfection over a charcoal grill (take-out NIS16, eat-in NIS30). Open daily 9am-11pm. Cash only. ❶

Balloons (☎02 275 0221), on SOS road at the eastern edge of town. A favorite for local families. Huge selection of budget-friendly pizza and burgers. Make sure to hydrate before indulging in the *zatar* pizza (NIS22) to offset the salt overload. Burgers (NIS16-22) are thick and well-seasoned. Open Su-M and W-Sa noon-midnight. Cash only. ❶

Barbra (☎02 274 0130), just downhill of the Gilo settlement in Beit Jala. When coming from town, walk past the military base and turn right; Barbra is 100m down the road. Recently re-opened after the second *intifada*, Barbra's elaborate modern furnishings and decor were built from scratch by the owner. Its floor-to-ceiling windows afford one of the best views in town. Dinner menu has international offerings. Calzones from the brick oven NIS18. Cheeseburger NIS16. *Linguini al pesto* NIS30. Open Su-M and W-Sa noon-midnight, later on busy nights. Cash only.❶

The Citadel (☎02 277 5725), on Citadel St. across from the church. From Bethlehem, walk down Manger St. toward Beit Sahour for 10min. and follow the signs; the Citadel is on your left. Perfect for a meal that stretches into a long *argileh* (NIS15) session. Fills with international volunteers and students starting around 8pm. Surprisingly good Chinese food (fried rice NIS16) and the cheapest beer in town (Carlsberg NIS9). Open daily noon-midnight, later on busy nights. Cash only. ❶

◔ SIGHTS

There are two ways to "do" Bethlehem. Traditionally, tourists arrive from Jerusalem, hop from one Christian holy place to another in several hours, and are back in Jerusalem before supper. Bejeweled with dozens of flagship churches at every turn, Bethehem, Beit Sahour, and Beit Jala offer non-stop sights. However, spending a night or two (or at least an evening) in the area gives visitors a more memorable, behind-the-scenes look into Palestinian life. There are numerous opportunities to interact with the locals, who are generally very friendly and speak excellent English. The must-see sights, which can be seen in 2-3hr., are listed first. After that are some highlights for a more in-depth sojourn.

Because no reliable public transportation is available, the best way to see the more distant sights (including Shepherd's Field, Mar Saba, and Herodion) is to rent a car or hire a guide with a vehicle for an afternoon. Guides gather in Manger Sq.; be sure to choose someone wearing a PA-issued ID tag. Tours should cost no more than US$30-40 per hr., including transportation. Guides will ask for double that, so be sure to bargain. To explore the villages and other West Bank cities from Bethlehem, contact **Alternate Tourism Group** (p. 304).

BASILICA OF THE NATIVITY. Masquerading as a fortress, this massive basilica is the oldest continuously used church in the world and honors the spot generally considered to be Jesus's birthplace. A far cry from its previous incarnation as a reflective, quiet sanctuary, the church now bursts with pilgrims and tourists. Begun in 326 CE by Queen Helena, mother of Constantine, the first basilica was completed in 339. It was partially destroyed in the Samaritan uprising of 525 and then rebuilt by Justinian. During the Persian invasion in 614, when virtually every Christian shrine in the Holy Land was demolished, the basilica was reputedly spared because it contained a mosaic of the three Persian Wise Men that had special anti-artillery powers. Tancred, the brat of the First Crusade, claimed Bethlehem as a fief and extensively renovated the church. After the Crusader kingdom fell, the church lapsed into disrepair. By the 15th century it had become undeniably decrepit, but its importance as a holy shrine never waned. During the ensuing centuries, struggle for control over the basilica among Roman Catholic, Greek, and Armenian Christians culminated in bloodshed. In the 1840s, the church was restored to its former dignity; however, squabbles between the various denominations over the division of the edifice continue. An elaborate system of worship schedules, established in 1751, has worked through competing claims, but the confusion resulting from the Greek Orthodox Church's rejection of summer daylight savings time demonstrates the precariousness of the arrangement. Check at the tourist office or the entrance to St. Catherine's Church for the exact worship times.

Despite its impressive history, the Basilica of the Nativity does not afford a particularly attractive external view. The main entrance and windows were boarded up as a safety precaution during medieval times, making the facade appear awkward. To enter, assume a kneeling position and step through the narrow Door of Humility—a remnant of Christian attempts to prevent Muslims from entering on horseback.

Fragments of beautiful mosaic floors are all that remain of Helena's original church. View them beneath the huge wooden trap doors in the center of the marble Crusader floor. The four rows of red limestone Corinthian columns and the mosaic atoms along the walls date from Justinian's reconstruction. England's King Edward IV offered the oak ceiling as a gift. The Russian royal family bequeathed the handsome icons adorning the altar in 1764.

The underground sanctuary beneath the church is the **Grotto of the Nativity.** Crosses are etched into the columns on both sides of the cramped doorway—religious graffiti from centuries of pilgrims. The focus of the hubbub is a silver star bearing the Latin inscription *"Hic De Virgine Maria Jesus Christus Natus Est"* (Here, of the Virgin Mary, Jesus Christ was born). The fourteen points represent the fourteen stations of the Via Dolorosa (see **Jerusalem,** p. 127). The star, added by Catholics in 1717, was removed by Greeks in 1847 and restored by the Ottoman government in 1853. Quarrels over the star are said to have contributed to the outbreak of the Crimean War.

In 2002, the IDF invaded Bethlehem and 200 Palestinian militants fled to the church of the nativity, where they holed up with monks and civilians who had been trapped in the church. The ensuing siege and negotiations lasted 39 days, after which Israel agreed to deport the militants in exchange for release of the civilians. Many of the fighters were sent to Jordan and the Gaza strip; the most wanted were moved to Italy and Spain. *(Open daily in summer 5:30am-7pm, in winter 5am-5pm. Free, though donations are encouraged.)*

SAINT CATHERINE'S CHURCH. Built by the Franciscans in 1881, this simple and airy church is a welcome contrast to the grim interior of the adjacent basilica. Superbly detailed wood carvings of the fourteen stations of the cross line the walls. Down the stairs, near the main entrance, are a series of crypt rooms. The first, the **Chapel of Saint Joseph,** commemorates the carpenter's vision of an angel that advised him to flee with his family to Egypt to avoid Herod's wrath. The burial cave of children slaughtered by King Herod (Matthew 2:16) lies below the altar and through the grille in the **Chapel of the Innocents.** Beyond the altar, a narrow hallway leads to the **Grotto of the Nativity.** The way is blocked by a thick wooden door with a peephole. During times of greater hostility between Christian sects, this glimpse was as close as Catholics could get to the Greek Orthodox shrine. To the right of the altar, a series of rooms contain the tombs of St. Jerome, St. Paula, and St. Paula's daughter Eustochia. These lead to the spartan cell where St. Jerome produced the Vulgate, the fourth-century translation of the Hebrew Bible into Latin.

The Franciscan Fathers conduct a solemn procession to the basilica and underground chapels every day. To join the 20min. of Gregorian cantillation and Latin prayer, arrive at St. Catherine's by noon. St. Catherine's also broadcasts a midnight mass to a worldwide audience every Christmas Eve. *(Adjoins the basilica. Use the separate entrance to the left of the basilica entrance, or face the altar in the basilica and pass through one of the doorways in the wall on the left. Open daily 6am-6pm.)*

MILK GROTTO CHURCH. The cellar of this church is thought to be the cave in which the Holy Family hid when fleeing from Herod into Egypt. The cave and church take their names from the original milky white color of the rocks, most of which have now either been blackened by candle smoke or painted blue. According to legend, some of Mary's milk fell while she was nursing the infant Jesus, whitewashing the rocks. Today, women with fertility problems can request small packets of white dust as a charm. *(A 5min. walk down Milk Grotto St. from the Basilica of the Nativity. Facing the line of stores in Manger Sq., turn left and take the narrow alleyway to the Franciscan flag; the grotto is on the right. ☎02 274 3867. Open daily 8-11:30am and 2-5pm. If the door is locked, ring the bell.)*

TOMB OF RACHEL. The Tomb of Rachel is a sacred site for Jews, a spot where synagogues have been built and destroyed throughout history. When Rachel died giving birth to Benjamin, Jacob is said to have erected a pillar upon her grave (Genesis 35:19-20). In Crusader times, the site was marked with a small square structure; the Turks constructed a larger building over the tomb in 1620; a new dome was added in 1841; and the current fortress was completed around the Ottoman sanctuary only in 1997. On one side are fervently praying Hasidic men, and on the other, weeping Yemenite women. The tomb, a timeless symbol of maternal devotion and suffering, is now revered as a place to pray for a child or a safe delivery. There are separate entries for women and men. Women should dress modestly; men must don a paper *kippah*, available at the entrance. While the IDF has left Bethlehem, the Israeli government retains control of the Tomb of Rachel. The tomb is on Palestinian land, but the 8m concrete wall surrounding it leaves the tomb firmly in the hands of the IDF. *(The tomb is on the northern edge of town on the road to Jerusalem, north of the intersection of Manger St. and Hebron Rd. at the checkpoint, a 30min. walk from the Basilica of the Nativity. Service taxis (NIS2.50) run to the checkpoint from Bab-izQaq. ☎02 654 1142. Open Su-Th 8am-6pm, F 8am-1pm.)*

THE INTERNATIONAL CENTER OF BETHLEHEM (DAR ANNADWA). Opened in 1994 as an outreach ministry of the Lutheran Church, the International Center has expanded to become a center of cultural activity in Bethlehem. The center hosts invited speakers, hosts art exhibitions by local and visiting artists, provides volunteer-instructed English lessons, and serves as a venue for local bands. It also has free Wi-Fi, a computer room, and a small cafe. *(☎02 277 0047; www.annadwa.org. Open daily 9am-9pm.)*

BETHLEHEM MUSEUM. Also known as Baituna at Talhami, this small museum is actually a preserved 19th-century Palestinian home, furnished with authentic antiques. It is run by the Arab Women's Union, a group of local women who sell embroidered placemats, tablecloths, and traditional clothing on-site. *(Off Star St. between the market and Manger Sq. ☎02 274 2589. Open M-W and F-Sa 8am-1pm and 2-5pm; Su and Th 8am-noon. NIS8.)*

PALESTINIAN HERITAGE CENTER. The showroom displays and sells traditional Palestinian crafts. A small but interesting exhibit features a traditional Palestinian sitting room, complete with handwoven carpets and teapots. The stores sell inexpensive needlework and other crafts, most of which are made by women from the Bethlehem area and nearby refugee camps. The center also organizes lectures; check their website for updated information. *(On Manger St. near its intersection with Hebron Rd. ☎02 274 23 81; www. palestinianheritagecenter.com. Open M-Sa 10am-6pm.)*

MARKET. Bethlehem means "House of Meat" in Arabic (Beit Lahm) and "House of Bread" in Hebrew (Beth Lehem). The sprawling market that clings to the town's steep streets lives up to both names. Recently re-paved, it has lost some of its hectic charm, but remains the one-stop shopping center for natives and tourists alike. *(Up the stairs from Pope Paul VI St., across from the Syrian Church, 2 blocks west of Manger Sq. Best in the morning, and on F after prayers)*

▶ DAYTRIPS FROM BETHLEHEM

BEIT SAHOUR

بيت ساحور

From Bethlehem, take a taxi (NIS10), hop on the Beit Sahour bus from the stop below Manger Sq. (NIS2), or walk 2km away from Jerusalem along Shepherd St.

Home to some 15,000 inhabitants, Beit Sahour is a Christian neighborhood on the eastern edge of Bethlehem. Its open stretches of grazing land include the **Fields of Ruth,** believed to be the setting for the biblical Book of Ruth, in which a wealthy local farmer falls in love with a poor young widow, a new convert to Judaism. The name of the village in Hebrew is "House of the Shepherds," and Christian tradition holds that this is **Shepherd's Field,** where those tending their flocks were greeted by the angel who pronounced the birth of Jesus (Luke 2:8-12).

A sign points left toward an alternate Shepherd's Field, believed by Franciscans to be the actual field. This **Latin Shepherd's Field** features recent excavations of religious buildings dating back to the fourth or fifth century, as well as a modern chapel built in 1954 by Antonio Barluzzi. (☎054 351 0966. Church and excavations open M-Sa 8am-5:30pm, Su 8-11:30am and 2-5:30pm). Bear right to arrive at the **Greek Orthodox Shepherd's Field,** a more impressive and less touristed site. The Byzantine basilica here was thrice destroyed and repaired, in the fifth, sixth, and seventh centuries. The **Holy Cave** (325 CE) features mosaic crosses on the floor. In the baptistry are 1300-year-old bones belonging to victims of the Persian invasion. The newest addition to the field is the incredible red-domed, Byzantine-style church, opened in 1989. Inside are strikingly colored frescoes of starving local saints and an imported Greek marble floor.

The main street within the residential part of the village is Star St., dominated by a Greek Orthodox church. Along Star St. is the main office of the **Alternative Tourism Group** (see Bethlehem **Tours,** p. 304.). Past the post office, **Omar al-Khattab Mosque** is one of the city's few mosques. For accommodations in Beit Sahour, see Bethlehem **Accommodations,** p. 304.

HERODION

הרודיון هيروديون

Round-trip private taxi from Bethlehem NIS40, including waiting time. ☎050 623 5821. Free site-maps available at entrance. Guided tours in English by prior arrangement only. Open daily in summer 8am-5pm, in winter 8am-4pm. NIS25, students with ISIC NIS21.

Eleven kilometers east of Bethlehem, the man-made, flat-topped mountain of Herodion arrests the eye with its startling silhouette. Much of the road between Herodion and Bethlehem crosses over the "Valley of Fire," a continuation of Jerusalem's Kidron Valley. In biblical times it was the site of Moloch worship, where fathers sacrificed their first-born sons by fire. It was also the site of the suicide of Judas, betrayer of Jesus. Although located in the West Bank, Herodion is an Israeli National Park.

Herodion is one of the world's finest examples of well-preserved early Roman architecture. Built as a summer palace by King Herod, it contained swimming pools and bathhouses, all of which have been carefully dug up. Herod's body is believed to be buried here, although his bones haven't been found. Excavators have found bones dating back to 2000 BCE, some of the oldest discovered.

There are two ways to ascend the mountain: the excruciating outdoor steps or the naturally air-conditioned 200 steps inside the mountain, carved into the cisterns. Begun in Herod's time and later expanded by rebels in the Bar Kokhba revolt, who used the site as a base around 132 CE, the network of tunnels and steps leads directly into the former palace's central courtyard. At the top, the western defense tower is directly above the Kroutoon Cave. The vista from this point is breathtaking on a clear day, when the Dead Sea is visible (right of the cistern exit). The red roofs below are those of the Israeli-subsidized Jewish settlements of Teqoa, Noqedim, and Ma'ale Amos, where the prophet Amos is buried. Take the outside steps to get back down.

If you've come by taxi, ask to be driven through the villages of Beit Ta'amar and Irtas on the way back to Bethlehem. A tiny **mosque** along the road, named after the conqueror Omar ibn Khattab, is thought to be the oldest in the country. **Irtas village** (Irtam of the Bible) is divided by a valley that cuts across it. Look for the beautiful red-roofed and gold-trimmed Catholic monastery on the left-hand side below the road. Near Irtas are **Solomon's Pools;** these three man-made reservoirs are a miracle of pre-modern technology, able to hold 40 million gallons of water. Built during the Maccabean period (around 2 BCE), the pools are erroneously attributed to Solomon due to interpretation of Eccelsiastes 2:6: "I made myself pools from which to water the forest of growing trees." Opposite the pools is a fortress which guarded them, behind which is **Saint George's Gate,** the ancient doorway to the village.

TENT OF NATIONS

Service transportation runs from Bethlehem. Take the service to Sabatash (NIS7). To get back, there is a semi-official Hebron-Jerusalem bus that runs by the drop-off point of the service (NIS5). A taxi costs NIS40-50 each way. ☎ 02 274 3071; www.tentofnations.org.

Situated in between four Israeli settlements, Tent of Nations has been a target of Israeli land acquisition since the 1967 invasion. The land has been owned by the same family since 1916. Despite an Israeli Supreme Court decision establishing their right to the land, the two brothers who now manage it, Daoud and Daher Nasser, have been involved in litigation continuously for the last 17 years. Today, the brothers run a **campground** ❷ and summer camp that hosts visitors and volunteers from all over the world. Due to the impossibility of obtaining a building permit from the Israeli government, many of the camp's activities take place in caves dug by the family and their supporters.

Call in advance for a tour given by one of the brothers, including a history of the camp and a description of the legal threats they face today. Away from the noise of Bethlehem, the site is a wonderful spot to relax after the physically and emotionally draining experience of traveling in the West Bank. The large tents house rows of beds (NIS100 per night with dinner and breakfast), often occupied by volunteer groups from Italy, Germany, and England. If you've got a couple days, volunteering at the camp can be a very rewarding experience. Choose among tending the olive and fig trees, digging cisterns, caring for the donkeys and goats, or helping with the summer camp.

DHEISHEH REFUGEE CAMP

مخيم الدهيشة

Service transportation is readily available between Dheisheh and Bethlehem, along Manger St. or at Bab-izQaq (NIS3). For a tour, call the Ibda'a Cultural Center in advance. Donations to the center are appreciated.

The largest of the three refugee camps in Bethlehem's environs, Dheisheh has been and continues to be a symbol of both Palestinians' depressed quality of life under Israeli occupation and their determination to rebuild. Though the phrase "refugee camp" calls to mind tents and squalor, Dheisheh is hardly discernable from a regular Palestinian neighborhood, albeit a crowded one. Once guarded and completely fenced in, Dheisheh has ripped down its walls since the Palestinian Authority gained control of the city, although the remains of turnstiles are still visible near the main road. Poverty and crowding continue to reign here, but the atmosphere is optimistic and forward-looking.

Myriad forms of artistic expression have bloomed in the camp. Particularly interesting is the graffiti on the concrete walls of the houses. Just past the camp's medical center (donated by the Japanese government) is a heartbreaking mural of the resident home villages in what is now Israel, and a plea for the right of return painted by the children of the refugee camp. Farther along is a mural by UK-based graffiti artist **Banksy,** whose iconic image of a girl patting down a soldier can be seen across from the separation wall near the entrance to Bethlehem. The mural shows a bulldozer made of human bones alongside the words "Stop the Wall." Banksy stenciled elsewhere in the camp on his visit in 2003, but many of the walls featuring his work have been removed and sold elsewhere (the families were compensated US$5000).

In the center of Dheisheh is the **Ibda'a Cultural Center** (☎02 277 64 44; www. ibdaa194.org). The center serves the youth and women of the camp. It recently established a dance troupe, which has performed traditional Palestinian dances in festivals worldwide. In 1995, the IDF lifted the ban on newspapers and books in Dheisheh, and the Ibda'a Center opened a library, which has grown rapidly. The Women's Initiative provides an avenue for local women to sell their beautiful woven handicrafts, available in the ground floor lobby. The United States has banned direct import of these purses and pillows because of the "Made in Palestine" tag; it is the only country to have done so. Dheisheh also has the West Bank's first women's basketball team, as well as two hip hop groups—the Refugee Rappers and the Bad Luck Group. At the time of writing, the center was in the process of starting a TV and radio station to teach media literacy and production to youth in the camp. Youth leaders offer tours and invite visitors to their homes for tea even without advance notice. A donation to the center is appreciated. Ibda'a has recently opened a small **guesthouse** (p. 305), which hosts a wonderfully diverse group of international activists and student volunteers.

MAR SABA MONASTERY

מר סבא מנזר

Drive through Beit Sahour, following the signs past Shepherd's Field, or take a private taxi from Bethlehem (16km; round-trip NIS100-150 including 1hr. wait). Open Su-Th 8am-4pm. NIS20 donation.

The Mar Saba Monastery stands in complete isolation in the middle of the desert. Literally carved into the walls of a remote canyon, the extensive monastery complex perches above the Kidron River. The monastery is built opposite the cave and marked by a cross. St. Saba began his ascetic life here in 478, and his bones are on display in the main church. Women may not enter and can only view the buildings from a nearby tower; men must wear long pants and sleeves. To get inside, pull the chain on the large blue door. The monks occasionally ignore the doorbell, especially on Sundays and late afternoons. If they're feeling social, the monks might lead five-minute tours in broken English.

JERICHO ☎ 02

יריחו أريحا

The first city to fly the Palestinian flag, Jericho vibrates with activity. Streets strewn with banners and flags convey Palestinian pride and optimism, which shines through in the hospitality and openness of the city's residents. Settled 10,000 years ago, Jericho is believed to be the world's oldest city. At 250m below sea level, it's also the world's lowest. Its location in the middle of the Judean Desert leaves Jericho brutally hot in the summer and pleasantly hot in the winter, making it a winter resort for vacationers as far back as the eighth century, when Syrian King Hisham built a magnificent winter palace here. Excavations at several sites around Jericho have been extensive, but besides several beautiful mosaic floors, the ruins themselves aren't that spectacular—after all, the city walls are famous for having tumbled down. After Joshua destroyed the city with a blast of his trumpet (Joshua 6:20), Jericho remained in shambles for centuries. The oasis town was partially rebuilt in the days of King Ahab in the early ninth century BCE (I Kings 16:34), embellished by King Herod during the Hasmonean Dynasty, and further strengthened under Roman, Crusader, and Mamluk rule.

The population skyrocketed after 1967, when thousands of Palestinian refugees fled here from Israel. Free from Jordanian control, the refugee camps were replaced by apartment buildings, and the standard of living drastically improved. Today Jericho is the site of several noteworthy million-dollar investment projects, including a new luxury resort popular with wealthy Palestinians, a cable-car/hotel complex at the foot of the Mount of Temptation, and the Oasis Casino, the region's very own mini-yet-majestic sin city. Jericho is under the custodianship of the Palestinian Authority. Travelers should dress modestly when walking around the city center, though the tourist complex surrounding Elisha's Spring has a much more relaxed dress code.

▐ TRANSPORTATION

Five kilometers east of Jerusalem, Jericho is on the road to Amman, at the junction of the Highway of Galilee (for information on the crossing to Jordan, see p. 258).

Service Taxi: The only way to get to Jericho (and indeed, the only real way to travel in the West Bank) is by *service* taxi. A ride from Bethlehem costs NIS20 and takes about 1hr. depending on checkpoints; a ride from Ramallah costs NIS17 and takes 30min. There is no direct transport from Jerusalem. *Service* taxis stop at the Oasis Casino and at the Town Center. There is no schedule—*service* taxis leave when full, and they fill most quickly during morning and afternoon rush hours. Repeat this process backward to return to Jerusalem; from the casino, however, it might be better to go into Jericho 1st.

Public transportation: There is no public transportation within the city, but there are a multitude of yellow **taxis.** Hiring a taxi for several hours is the recommended way of seeing the sights, since the blistering heat most of the year makes even walkable distances unbearable. Pay no more than NIS60-70 per hour. The taxi stand is in the town center, call **Petra Taxi** (☎232 2525) if you're stranded outside of town.

WEST BANK

TO RAMALLAH, MOUNT OF TEMPTATION (2km),
NA'ARAN SYNAGOGUE, QARANTAL

Ein as-Sultan
Refugee Camp

Jiftlik Rd.

TO BEIT SHE'AN
& TIBERIAS

ANCIENT
JERICHO

Hisham's
Palace

Elisha's Spring/
Sultan Tourist Center

Jericho

🏠 ACCOMMODATIONS
Jericho Resort Village, **3**
Jerusalem Hotel, **5**
Shwarma House, **4**

🍖 FOOD
Abu Omar, **1**
Temptation Restaurant, **2**

Bila St.

Ez-Zuhur St.

Ein as-Sultan St.

Qasar Hisham St.

Ez-Zuhur St.

Sheikh Sabah St.

Palestine St.

Jaffa St.

Al Hashem St.

As-Sa'ada St.

Ar-Rawda St.

Al Agami St.

Al Ma'Amun St.

Al Hadew St.

Salah ad-Din St.

Wardet Al-Azra St.

Rashid St.

Jamal Abdule Nasser St.

Spanish
Garden

TO ALLENBY
BRIDGE (15km),
(500m)

Amman St./Al Karamah St.

CITY CENTER

Al Madaras St.

Jerusalem Rd.

New Jericho St.

Al Kasai St.

Magnas St.

TO JERUSALEM,

0   200 yards

0   200 meters

Bike Rental: An attractive option, especially during the winter, is to rent a bike from **Zaki Sale and Rent Bicycle** in the town center, near the taxi stand. (☎02 232 4070. Open daily 8am-10pm.)

🛈 ORIENTATION AND PRACTICAL INFORMATION

Jericho's city center is a lively cluster of restaurants and fruit stands, but it contains little of historical interest. Most of the sights are outside of the city to the north, accessible by taxi or a blistering 20min. walk.

Tourist Office: There is no official tourist information in Jericho, but the **tourist police** at Elisha's Spring can provide information on most of the city's sights.

Bank: Cairo Amman Bank (☎02 232 3627), in the main square. **ATM** and **currency exchange.** Open Sa-Th 8:30am-12:30pm. There are a few currency exchanges scattered around the city center, but the rates may not be as good as those from the ATM.

Police: (☎02 232 2521), in the main square. **Tourist Police:** (☎02 232 4011), at the Elisha's spring complex. Open daily 8am-6pm.

Hospital: Jericho Government Hospital (☎02 232 1967), on Jerusalem Rd. Open 24hr.

MANSAF

Mansaf, a tradiional feast food for the ancient Bedouin tribes of Palestine, is as popular today in the West Bank as it is in Jordan, where it is a national dish (and where the majority of the population traces its ancestry to Palestine).

Mansaf consists of large pieces of lamb sitting on a bed of flatbread and rice, spiced with saffron. The principal is then smothered in *jameed*, a distinctive flavoring that is a sort of yogurt made from goat's milk; almonds and dried pine nuts are added as a final touch.

As a food for social occasions, *mansaf* is often enjoyed at festivals or marriage feasts—or really any time there is a guest present or cause for celebration. There is even a traditional method of eating *mansaf*: feasters gather around a platter with their left-hands folded behind their backs, then use their right hands as utensils. Rip pieces of meat with your right hand, and if you really want to abide by tradition, don't eat them yourself, but pass them to your neighbor.

Post Office: (☎02 232 2574), down Amman St. from the police station. Open Sa-Th 8am-2pm.

ACCOMMODATIONS

With a relatively easy commute to Jerusalem or Ramallah, there isn't much reason to sleep here if you only want to see the sights near the city. However, the Sami Hostel makes an attractive base camp for daytrips to Wadi Qelt and Nabi Musa, and if you can't stand the slow pace of Jericho, there's always the casino across the road.

Sami Hostel (☎059 836 5144), in the Aqbat Jaber refugee camp across from the casino. Walking into the swanky dark leather interior of Sami's gloriously air-conditioned lobby is like entering another world. 3-bed rooms are basic and clean. Cozy common room features a kitchen, fridge, and TV. Internet access. Triples NIS100. Cash only. ❷

Jerusalem Hotel (☎02 232 2444; www.jerusalemhotel-jericho.com), also called the al-Quds hotel. About 1.5km out of town on Amman St. Comfortable, elegant lobby and large dining room set the hotel apart from its budget hotel counterparts. Mid-sized rooms have A/C and TV; most have balconies. Breakfast NIS20 per person. Singles NIS210; doubles NIS270; triples NIS350. MC/V. ❸

Jericho Resort Village (☎02 232 1255; www.jerichoresorts.com), off Qaasr Hisham St. near Hisham's Palace. Full-fledged resort complex with swimming pools, restaurants, cafes, bars, and luxurious common areas. A magnet for wealthy Palestinian families. While definitely not cheap, the prices are about half what you'd pay for similar accommodations in Jerusalem or the states. Breakfast included. Wi-Fi and internet access. Singles NIS400; doubles NIS450; triples NIS550. MC/V. ❹

FOOD

Lying in wait for bus tours heading back from the Dead Sea, restaurants around the Mount of Temptation charge outrageous prices for mediocre food. The local food in the town center is standard yet tasty, and the prices are good even after being inflated for foreigners. There is a string of large tent restaurants on the road between Elisha's Spring and the city center, most of which have ceased serving food since the second *intifada* but plan to reopen in the future; their meals are a step above falafel counters and well worth the price if available.

Abu Omar (☎02 232 3429). From the city center, walk 10m on Ein el-Sultan St.; Abu Omar is on your left. Both falafel counter and sit-down restaurant, Abu Omar serves traditional cuisine at respectable prices. There is no menu, and prices are flexible; if you're sitting down for a meal, a bit of haggling couldn't hurt. 2-person meal of falafel, kebab, hummus, and pita NIS30. Get desert for cheap at the bakery next door. Cash only. Open daily 6am-midnight. ●

Shawarma House (☎02 232 2327) at the southern side of the city center on Jerusalem St. A predictably cheap local establishment, Shawarma House serves up the standard mix of falafel (NIS3) and shawarma (NIS10) but adds pizza (small NIS25, large NIS45) to the mix. Cash only. Open daily 6am-1am.●

Temptation Restaurant (☎02 232 2614). Underneath the Mount of Temptation in the Elisha's Spring complex. Unless you have no other option, Temptation isn't very tempting. Try Palestine's most expensive falafel (NIS20) or enjoy an all you can eat buffet (NIS60) in what is essentially a massive souvenir shop. Open daily 6am-8pm. AmEx/MC/V. ●

◎ SIGHTS

The best way to see the sights is to hire a taxi for several hours from the city center at the relatively inexpensive rate of NIS50-70 per hr. (be sure to haggle for a price in advance). Another option is to rent a car for the day—much more convenient, and for a group of three or four, this might even be less expensive than relying on taxis. Jericho's most popular sights, Hisham's Palace and ancient Jericho, lie on the outskirts of town and make for an excruciating walk, even in the winter. It's best to visit Hisham's Palace first, since a cluster of restaurants and a cooling spring near the ancient city provide a pleasant post-tour rest stop.

HISHAM'S PALACE. Begun in 724 CE and completed in 743, Hisham's Palace was ravaged only four years later by an earthquake. Known as Khirbet al-Mafjar in Arabic, the palace was designed for the Umayyad Caliph Hisham as a winter retreat from Damascus—although there is no evidence that the caliph ever actually spent any time here. The most renowned feature is a courtyard window in the shape of the six-pointed Umayyad star. In the "guest house," a beautifully preserved mosaic depicts a lion devouring a gazelle as its naive playmates frolic beneath the Tree of Life. Get a guide from the entrance to show you around (tip NIS10-20). *(To reach the palace from the square, head 3km north from Qasr Hisham St., following the signs to the turnoff at a guard post. Coming from ancient Jericho, head east on Jiftlik Rd., past the synagogue and the Ein al-Sultan refugee camp. After 1.5km, turn right on the road back to Jericho; the turn-off to Hisham's Palace appears on the left. ☎02 232 2522. Open daily 8am-6pm. NIS10, students NIS7, children NIS5.)*

ANCIENT JERICHO. Thought to be the oldest city in the world (as opposed to Damascus, the oldest continually inhabited city in the world), ancient Jericho is now a heap of ruined walls. Called Tel al-Sultan, the mound contains layer upon layer of garbage from ancient (and modern) cities. Some of the finds date from the early Neolithic period, leading archaeologists to suspect that Jericho was inhabited as early as the eighth millennium BCE. The oldest fortifications are 7000 years old. A limited amount of excavation has exposed many levels of ancient walls, some of them 3.5m thick and 5.5m high. Imagination will have to substitute for visible splendor at this site, which is distinctly unimpressive. *(To get to ancient Jericho from the city center, follow Ein al-Sultan St. to its end. The entrance is through a parking lot around the corner, opposite the Elisha's Spring complex. From Hisham's Palace, 2km away, turn right onto the road that runs past the Palace (away from the city center), cross a narrow bridge, then take a left at the next junction, following the "Tel Jericho" signs. ☎02 232 2935. Open daily in summer 8am-6pm, in winter 8am-5pm. NIS10, students with ISIC NIS7, children NIS5.)*

MONASTERY. An imposing Greek Orthodox monastery stands on the edge of a cliff among the mountains west of Jericho; the peak is believed to be the New Testament's **Mount of Temptation,** where the Devil tried to tempt Jesus. The complex of buildings stands before a grotto, said to be the spot where Jesus fasted for 40 days and 40 nights at the end of his ministry (Matthew 4:1-11). A single Greek monk now lives in the monastery, built in 1895. He can point out the rock where Jesus was tempted by the devil and served by angels. The summit of the mountain, named Qarantal after the Latin word for "forty," is also a pedestal for the Maccabean Castle of Dok, beside which lie the remains of a fourth-century Christian chapel. *(The monastery can be reached by climbing up the mountain from the base, not far from the ancient city; the hike takes under 1hr., but bring plenty of water. A much easier way up is to take the téléphérique (see below), which still requires a short hike to reach the monastery. Open M-F 8am-1pm and 2-5pm, Sa Su 8am-2pm. Modest dress required. ☎02 232 2827.)*

JERICHO SYNAGOGUE. This sixth-century synagogue, one of the oldest in the world, features an expansive mosaic floor with a menorah, a *shofar* (ram's horn), a *lulav* (palm branch), and the inscription *Shalom al Yisrael* (Peace Be Upon Israel). Discovered by accident in 1936 while a British family was digging foundations for a winter house, the entire floor is remarkably preserved. As part of extensive preliminary peace agreements, the Palestinian Authority promised to watch over this synagogue, which is now a functioning *yeshiva* by day. Ask the caretaker to sprinkle some water over the tiles to reveal the mosaic more clearly. This Jewish site is now under the control of the Palestinian Authority, who have tightened security to keep out vandals who painted graffiti on the walls during the second *intifada*. *(From Ancient Jericho, go 0.5km up the road past the Sultan Tourist Center and turn right at the sign. Contact the tourist police at Elisha's Spring for information, ☎02 232 4011. Open daily 8am-6pm; in winter 8am-4pm. NIS10, students NIS7, children NIS5.)*

SULTAN TOURIST'S CENTER AND ELISHA'S SPRING. Papayas, grapes, oranges, bananas, and mint thrive behind the spring. A new US$10 million project for attracting tourism includes a hotel (under construction for the past 9 years and still incomplete), souvenir shops, restaurants, and a cable car ("téléphérique") that saves tourists the difficult, albeit scenic, 45min. hike up the Mount of Temptation. The 5min. ride goes over the old city ruins and provides stunning views of the valley and mountains; the view can be further enjoyed from the **Sultan Coffee Shop and Restaurant** at the top. *(Opposite the entrance to Ancient Jericho. ☎02 232 1590. Open daily 8am-8pm. Cable car NIS55 round-trip, children under 5 free.)*

🎵 🎭 ENTERTAINMENT AND NIGHTLIFE

The blistering heat keeps Jericho quiet during the day, but residents come out in the evening for a family-friendly night on the town. Shops and restaurants get busy at around 8pm and stay open until 11pm or later. Most action is, unsurprisingly, centered on the town center.

Spanish Garden (☎02 232 3931), on Amman St., near the center of town. Built through contributions from the Spanish government, this beautiful public garden is a great place for a late-night picnic. Livens up every evening after sunset, when families, small children, and teenagers show up to enjoy Arabic music, coffee, and *nargileh* (NIS12-15). A small cafe and restaurant serves inexpensive snacks next to a game-room. Open daily 2pm-midnight. NIS3, children NIS2.

DAYTRIPS FROM JERICHO

MOSQUE OF NABI MUSA
نبي موسى

The only way to visit is by car or taxi (taxi ride from Jericho NIS40). In a car, head toward Jerusalem about 5km, then turn left at the sign and follow the road for another 5km. Open daily 8am-sunset. Free, but donations welcome.

The road from Jerusalem to Jericho slices through harsh desert landscape. About 8km from Jericho, the huge Mosque of Nabi Musa, topped with a complex of white domes, stands on a hill in a sea of sand. The mosque was built in 1269 CE, on a spot revered throughout the Muslim world as the grave of the prophet Moses. Islamic tradition holds that the 13th-century Ottoman sultan Salah al-Din had a dream, revealing the spot to which God carried the bones of Moses so that the faithful could pay their respects. Devout pilgrims continue to travel to the mosque during the week preceding Easter for the annual **Nabi Musa Festival.** The tomb is said to have special powers—run your hands over the velvet cloth of Musa's Tomb while making a wish and see for yourself. Across from the tomb, stairs lead upward into a minaret with incredible views of the surrounding Judean desert. Ask the souvenir vendors to unlock the gate if it is wired shut. The shrine is surrounded by naturally flammable bituminous rocks—the unique property is explained by the high content of *qatraan* (tar), but, science aside, it's yet another feature that adds to the site's mystique.

WADI QELT (NAKHAL PRAT)
נחל פרת ואדי القلط

20min. outside of Jerusalem. A string of murders, presumably political, took place here in the mid-90s, but fortunately the last few years have been peaceful and problem-free; nevertheless, it's not a good idea to hike in the wadi alone or after dark. SPNI (☎ 03 638 8625) offers one-day tours focusing on both natural and artificial attractions in the wadi. Contact a Bedouin guide (☎ 052 265 0988) for a more local tour.

Threading 28km between imperious limestone cliffs and undulating ridges of bone-white chalk, the three fresh-water springs of Wadi Qelt nourish wildlife and lush greenery. The most interesting and accessible section of the *wadi* extends from the spring of Ein Qelt, past the sixth-century St. George's Monastery, and down into Jericho, 10km east. The trek takes about 4hr. The

IN RECENT NEWS

AN UNLIKELY DUET

With the news so full of discordance between Arabs and Jews, it's always refreshing to hear about a little multicultural harmony in the Middle East. And for the 2009 Eurovision Song Contest—a popular European sing-off with contestants from 43 countries—harmony was just what the Israeli team came up with. For the first time since Israel joined the competition in 1973, the nation was represented by an Arab singer as well as a Jewish one.

Mira Awad, an Arab-Israeli sitcom actress and songwriter, was selected to perform for her country in a duet with Noa (a Jewish-Israeli pop star, born Achinoam Nini). This wasn't their first time together, of course; the pair had also sung in 2002, recording a cover of the Beatles' "We Can Work It Out." Their piece for the Eurovision contest, with the English title "There Must Be Another Way," wasn't just multi-ethnic; it was also multilingual, with lyrics in English, Hebrew, and Arabic.

The duet did not ring beautifully to everyone's ears, however. Several Palestinian and Arab intellectuals asked Mira Awad not to sing for Israel, as a protest against the Israeli intervention in Gaza in 2008 that left a reported 1300 Palestinians dead. For Awad and Noa, though, the contest was a chance to send a message of peace and reconciliation for Arab and Jewish Israelis, and show that "There Must Be Another Way."

best place to start is at the turn-off from the Jerusalem-Jericho highway about 9km west of Jericho, marked by the orange sign for "St. George's Monastery." *Service* taxis to Jericho, Ein Gedi, and Allenby Bridge stop here on request. By car, it is possible to skip the hike and drive most of the way to St. George's Monastery.

Saint George's Monastery dates from the fifth or sixth century CE. Byzantine mosaics decorate the floor of the church; look for the likeness of a two-headed eagle, the Byzantine symbol of power. According to tradition, the monastery occupies the site of the cave where St. Joachim took refuge to lament the infertility of his wife Hannah. An angel told him to return to Hannah, who then gave birth to the Virgin Mary. The neighboring **Saint John's Church** houses a spooky collection of skulls and bones of monks slaughtered when the Persians swept through in 614 CE. The Greek Orthodox monks who maintain the monastery can refill canteens for a journey into Jericho. (Open in summer M-Sa 8am-1pm and 3-5pm, in winter M-Sa 8am-1pm and 3-4pm. Modest dress required. Small donation requested.)

On the way to Jericho from St. George's, the ruins of **Tel Abu Alaya** (also called **Herodian Jericho**) are on the right. The palaces here, used by the Hasmoneans and later by King Herod, boast decorated walls, nearby bath houses, and pools. Though not as extensive as the ruins at Hisham's Palace, this *tel* is still more impressive than the remains of ancient Jericho.

EL-AZARIYA (BETHANY)

בית עניא العيزريه

Bethany lies on the road between Jerusalem and Jericho and blends into its sister city, Abu Dis, which lies just to the west. Take a service taxi from either Bethlehem (NIS8) or from Jericho's central square (NIS12). No one (other than tour guides) knows where "Bethany" is; use the Arabic name, el-Azariya (eh-zar-EE-ya). Service stop by request at the gas station in town, next to the road to al-Quds University. To reach the sights, walk away from Jerusalem on the main road. Alternately, stay in the service taxi and ask the driver to stop when you see the gift shops, as the road makes a sharp bend to the right (coming from Bethlehem).

A relatively prosperous Palestinian village, Bethany is sacred to Christians as the home of Lazarus and his sisters Mary Magdalene and Martha. Jesus performed one of his best-known miracles here, raising Lazarus from the dead (John 11:1-44). Churches and archaeological sites commemorate the event on the hillside. Signs and souvenir vendors point tourists left up a small road to the Franciscan New Church of St. Lazarus. Built in 1954, it marks a spot where Jesus was supposed to have slept. Excavations near the church have unearthed shrines dating back to the fourth century. South of the church lie the remains of an abbey built in 1143 by Queen Melisende of Jerusalem. The excavations are unlit—bring a light and try to find someone to show you around. Women should dress modestly. (☎02 674 9291. Church and excavations open daily 8am-noon and 2-5pm. Donations accepted.)

Signs from the Franciscan Church point uphill to the first-century **Tomb of Lazarus.** When the Crusaders arrived, they built a church over Lazarus's tomb, a monastery over Mary and Martha's house, and a tower over Simon the Leper's abode (Simon was another resident of Bethany cured by Jesus). In the 16th century, Muslims erected a mosque over the shrine, and in the following century, Christians dug another entrance to the tomb so they too could worship there. The tomb does not contain Lazarus's body—although some believe that he was re-buried in the same spot when he died again 30 years later. Descend the steps and stoop down to observe. (Tomb open daily 8am-7pm. When approaching, a person will come and ask for a donation; NIS4 is appropriate.)

Five minutes farther along the main road, the beautiful silver domes of the **Greek Orthodox Convent** shelter the boulder upon which Jesus sat while awaiting Martha. Twelve friendly nuns live here now but don't speak much English. Women may be lucky enough to be shown around. (Use the resounding door knocker to call a nun. Open daily; early mornings or evenings are best. Free.)

RAMALLAH ☎02

رام الله

Perched 900m above sea level, Ramallah, along with its smaller sister city, **al-Bireh**, is famous for its cool, pleasant mountain air. Before 1967, the then-prosperous town was a summer haven for Arabs from Jordan, Lebanon, and the Gulf region. With vacationers long gone by the time of the *intifada*, Ramallah and the energetic young intellectuals at nearby Birzeit University joined Nablus as leaders of West Bank resistance. Now under PA control, the city has become a transportation hub and is the administrative hub of the PA. Unfortunately, because of its political prominence, Ramallah was the site of much fighting in the second *intifada*. The politically engaged Birzeit University was singled out for special scrutiny by the IDF, with students from Ramallah facing checkpoint delays and those from elsewhere in the West Bank often unable to continue their education.

Ramallah is known for its religiously relaxed atmosphere—alcohol flows freely and movie theaters are well attended—and the cafes along its main streets. Ramallah is, without question, the cultural capital of the West Bank, with a highly educated and fashionable population. It is also the hub of Palestinian feminist activity; the city's women frequently attend university rather than marry early, and several cafes run exclusively by women are used to fund local feminist organizations.

▐ TRANSPORTATION

Buses: The easiest way to get to Ramallah is by Arab bus #18 from **Jerusalem** (40min., 8pm, NIS6.50). It stops at the checkpoint on the way back and picks up passengers on the other side.

Service Taxis: Life moves at a faster pace here, and fewer people go out of their way to help bewildered Westerners. That said, you will probably be able to find someone to help you navigate Ramallah's maze of *service* stations. At the time of writing, *service* leave to **Jericho** (NIS17) from the Radio St. station; to **Bethlehem** (NIS18), **Nablus** (NIS15), and to other destinations from the **al-Nahdah Street station.** Most stop at 8pm and run most frequently during morning and afternoon rush hours. There are 2 other *service* stations in the city serving less popular and closer destinations.

Car Rental: Petra Car Rental (☎02 295 2602) and **Good Luck Car Rental** (☎02 234 2160).

▓▐ ORIENTATION AND PRACTICAL INFORMATION

Ramallah is centered on **al-Manara Square** (Lighthouse Square). Most restaurants and shops are on nearby **Main Street** and **al-Mughtarbin Square.** At night, activity moves from the ground floor to the upper levels of these buildings. A few bars are located farther from the city center on **Jaffa Street.**

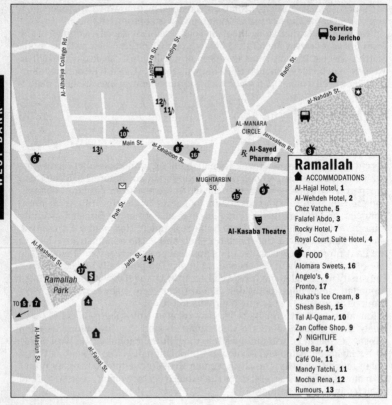

WEST BANK

Ramallah

ACCOMMODATIONS
Al-Hajal Hotel, **1**
Al-Wehdeh Hotel, **2**
Chez Vatche, **5**
Falafel Abdo, **3**
Rocky Hotel, **7**
Royal Court Suite Hotel, **4**

FOOD
Alomara Sweets, **16**
Angelo's, **6**
Pronto, **17**
Rukab's Ice Cream, **8**
Shesh Besh, **15**
Tal Al-Qamar, **10**
Zan Coffee Shop, **9**

♪ **NIGHTLIFE**
Blue Bar, **14**
Café Ole, **11**
Mandy Tatchi, **11**
Mocha Rena, **12**
Rumours, **13**

Tourist Office: There is no official tourist information office, but the **Palestinian Association for Cultural Exchange** (☎02 240 7611; www.pace.ps) on Nablus Rd. in al-Bireh serves as an unofficial information hub.

Banks: Can be found all throughout al-Manara circle; all are equipped with **ATMs** that accept foreign credit cards. There are also a few **currency exchanges** with little or no commission.

Police: al-Nahda St. (☎02 295 6571), across from the al-Wehdeh Hotel.

Pharmacy: al-Sayed Pharmacy (☎02 295 6708), between al-Manara circle and Mughtarbin Sq. Open Su-Th 7am-3am, F midnight-3am, Sa 7am-3am.

Hospital: Ramallah Government Hospital (☎02 298 2216) and the **Red Crescent Hospital** (☎02 240 6260).

Internet Access: Tannous Building, a mall 100m. off of al-Manara circle on Main St., has several internet cafes. **Top Ten Internet** (☎02 296 6277) has the best hours. Open daily 10am-midnight.

Post Office: Park St., off Main St. downhill from Rukab's Ice Cream. Open Su-Th 8am-2pm.

ACCOMMODATIONS

A night in Ramallah is worthwhile, but accommodations are expensive compared to nearby Jerusalem. There are no true hostels in Ramallah, although the available accommodations offer a decent bang for your buck.

Al-Wehdeh Hotel, al-Nahdah St. (☎02 298 0412), 1 block from the main circle. Ramallah's cheapest accommodation and also the most central, if you don't mind the noise from the street. Try to get 1 of the rooms overlooking the garden, which are quieter and have balconies. Each room has TV, fan, and private bath. Singles NIS100; doubles NIS120; triples NIS150. Cash only. Discounts available for longer stays. ❷

Al-Hajal Hotel (☎02 298 7858), off Jaffa Rd., opposite the Rammallah park. Spacious, quiet rooms with satellite TVs, fans, phones, and baths. A better deal for 2 people. Breakfast included. Singles US$40 (NIS155); doubles US$50 (NIS195). Cash only. ❸

Rocky Hotel, al-Masiun St. (☎02 296 4470; www.rockyhotel.com), 1km. outside of town, next to the Grand Park Hotel. *Service* taxis are available from the town center (every 30min., NIS2). Locally famous for its luxury, and the prices reflect it. Spacious and lightly perfumed rooms have A/C, TVs, and large private baths. Breakfast included. Wi-Fi. Singles NIS150; doubles NIS250; triples NIS300. MC/V. ❷

Royal Court Suite Hotel (☎02 296 40 40; rcshotel@palnet.com or www.rcshotel.com), on the corner of Jaffa St. and Faisal St., downhill of Blue Bar. Snazzy luxury hotel. Every room comes with minibar, safe box, A/C, cable TV, and phone. Some have balconies and kitchenettes. Breakfast included. Wi-Fi US$10 (NIS40) per day in rooms, free in hotel restaurant. Reception 24hr. Singles US$69 (NIS267); doubles US$99-109 (NIS383-422); triples US$139 (NIS538). MC/V. ❸

FOOD

Ramallah's streets are lined with falafel and shawarma stands; the competition has driven prices down and quality way up. Inexpensive restaurants overlook the city center from the tops of buildings around **Manara Circle,** especially along **Main Street.** Most restaurants serve international dishes as well as traditional Palestinian cuisine. Ramallah's hip cafes attract Palestinians from all over the West Bank and a steady trickle of adventurous tourists.

Rukab's Ice Cream (☎02 295 3467), at the corner of Main St. and al-Exhibition St., 1 block from Manara Circle. Possibly the best ice cream in the hemisphere. Gum-thickened, gooey goodness comes in a rainbow of blissful flavors. Try the popular pistachio. Small cup of 5 mini-scoops NIS8. Open daily 8am-12:30am. Cash only. ❶

Ameed Shwarma, Main St. (☎02 295 6093), just off of Manara Circle. No matter how sick of shawarma you are by the time you reach Ramallah, Ameed is worth a stop. Crowds of locals pack around the tiny counter and wait in the blistering heat of 3 large rotisserie cookers. Choose beef, chicken, or turkey wrapped in a huge, fluffy *laffa* fresh from the oven (NIS11). Open daily 10am-2am. Cash only. ❶

Tal al-Qamar, Main St. (☎02 298 7905), on the 5th fl. of the Nasser Building, 1 block past Rukab's. Beautiful Arabic cafe with a terrific view serves well-priced sandwiches (NIS12-20) and grilled meats (NIS30-50). Th live *oud* 8pm. Open daily noon-midnight. Cash only. ❶

Falafel Abdo, Jerusalem St. (☎02 295 6601), just outside of Manara Circle, marked by a green sign in Arabic. Since opening in 1950, this establishment has gained local fame for its moist, perfectly spiced falafel balls. Sandwiches NIS4. Open M-Sa 6am-9pm. Cash only. ❶

FALAFEL FRESHNESS. Walking down the streets of a major West Bank city, it can be hard to tell the falafel stands apart. When making a decision, find the stand with the lightest colored oil: many establishments re-use their oil day after day, turning it into a black, tar-like sludge. Fresh oil is yellower and tastes much better.

Alomara Sweets, al-Exhibition St. (☎02 295 6653). Free water, A/C, and a large upstairs seating area make Alomara a welcome escape from the noisy city center. Serves a wide array of traditional Arab sweets. Pastries NIS2-3 for take-out, NIS4-5 to eat in. Open daily 8am-11pm. Cash only. ❶

Angelo's (☎02 295 6408), a left turn off of Main St., 1 block after Rukab's; the restaurant is around the corner. Flings pizza into the air and onto the plates of plucky budget travelers. Small margherita pizza NIS22. 3-4 person large pizza NIS50-68. Small BBQ chicken NIS32. Garlic bread with cheese NIS16 per basket. Open daily 10am-11pm. MC/V. ❷

Mandy Tatchi, al-Anbyra St. (☎02 298 7027), 20m. uphill from Main St., on the 2d fl. The Arabic music doesn't quite match the Chinese decor, but you'll forgive the incongruities as soon as you taste the delicious food. Chow mein NIS25. Chicken dishes NIS33. Fried rice NIS5. Open daily 11am-11pm. Cash only. ❷

Alf-Lelah o leleh (☎02 295 7770). From Manara Circle, walk 1 block on Main St.; the restaurant is on the 3rd floor in the building to the left. Sit in comfortable leather couches as you watch the bustle of Main St. through floor-to-ceiling glass windows. Serves upscale local food. Shisha NIS10. Large mix grill plate NIS50. Sandwiches NIS15-20. Calamari plate NIS45. Th nights DJ party until 3 or 4am. Open daily 10am-midnight. Cash only. ❷

 TIPPING POINTS. Rather than charging a percentage of the bill as a service fee, many West Bank restaurants, ice cream shops, bakeries have higher prices for each menu item when dining in. If you're counting shekels, get it to go.

♪ 🎬 ENTERTAINMENT AND NIGHTLIFE

There's always something interesting going on in Ramallah's theaters and cultural centers. *This Week in Palestine*, actually a monthly publication, can be found at most hotels or on the web at www.thisweekinpalestine.com; it features a detailed listing of events. **Birzeit University** (☎02 298 2000) sponsors frequent cultural events. Their website—www.birzeit.edu—contains a wealth of info on Ramallah's present and past, including an online travel guide, a performance schedule for university-sponsored events, and links to many of the establishments listed below. The **Ashtar Theater** (☎02 298 0037) on Radio St. and the **Popular Arts Center** (☎ 02 240 3891) on al-Bireh St. host performing arts—call or ask around town for details. **Al-Kasaba Theater** and **Cinematheque,** a two-screen movie theater, plays Egyptian, French, and American movies, many of which are in English with Arabic subtitles.

Nightlife has traditionally centered around live *oud* music, a Middle Eastern instrument. Due to market pressures from international tourists and young students interested in more modern music, the *oud* is becoming harder to find at Ramallah's cafes (except during Ramadan).

BE A WEDDING CRASHER! Your best best for a traditional Palestinian party is to meet a local and try to snag an invitation to a wedding. This is actually much easier than it sounds: cafes are nearly empty on Fridays and Saturdays during the summer, when everyone and his brother seems to be getting married.

Zan Coffee Shop Plus (☎02 297 0548), upstairs next to the Kasaba Theater. Zan's crowd matches its modern decor—a rare sight in Palestine. Men and women mingle freely amidst the multicolored lights and leather furniture. The extensive drink menu is well-supported by plentiful free beer snacks. Mojito NIS30. Large Carlsburg NIS18. Try the awkwardly-named "Car Bombing" drink (NIS45). Garlic bread with cheese NIS16. Chicken salad NIS35. Th and Sa DJ nights. Open Su-W 3pm-1am, Th-Sa 3pm-3am. Cash only.

Shesh Besh (☎02 296 3165), 20m. east of the southern end of Mughtarbin Sq. Hosts good, clean, and almost exclusively male fun until the wee hours. Groups of young men play cards and puff *sheesha* (NIS6-10) on couches overlooking the neon-lit street below. Try *sheesha* packed in an orange peel instead of the standard clay bowl. Small selection of burgers and snacks. Free Wi-Fi. Open daily 9am-3am. Cash only.

Stars and Bucks (☎02 297 5674; www.starsandbuckscafe.com). 2 locations: 1 over-looking al-Manara Circle and the 2nd a block away on Main St. Stars and Bucks has their parody of a certain coffeehouse down to an art, complete with overpriced drinks, logos everywhere, and 2 locations within 1 city block of each other. Stop by for a photo-to-op and stay for some decent coffee. Cappuccino NIS7. Turkish coffee NIS5. 20 types of iced coffee NIS10 at the counter on Main St. Prices are higher at the sit-down location on al-Manara circle. Open daily 7am-10pm. Cash only.

Chez Vatche, al-Masiun St. (☎02 296 5966), behind the Crown Plaza Hotel. Swimming pool and restaurant by day, dance club by night. Sandwich and fries NIS40. Beef fajitas NIS90. Before 5pm, NIS50 gets you entry to the pool and lunch (a sandwich and non-alcoholic drink). Taybeh beer NIS15. Arak NIS25. Some nights have elaborate "private" (read: sponsored) dance parties with DJ, laser lights, and NIS60 cover (includes 1 drink); others are more low-key. Call in advance for schedule. Open daily 10am-midnight. Cash only.

Blue Bar (☎02 297 2125). Though it shares a name with an energy drink, this bar is decidedly low energy. Rich Palestinians and international tourists sit around tables, while quiet music plays in the background. Shots NIS20. Small Taybeh NIS14. Pizza NIS49. Vegetable lasagna NIS29. Cash only.

⊙ SIGHTS

The main attraction here is the city itself; on Saturdays, **al-Manara Circle** is a crammed jungle. Men in feathered red costumes serve super-sweet tea (NIS1) from decorative metal containers on their back as bakers pushing carts twist up tiny paper pouches of zatar to accompany their fresh bagels (NIS2). The many bakeries on **al-Nahdah Street** serve a variety of cheese- and spinach-filled breakfast pastries (NIS4) in addition to fresh breads and cookies. For traditional sugary Arabic sweets, head to **Alomora Sweets** (see **Food,** previous page).

ARAFAT'S TOMB. This tomb is located in the al-Muquta'a compound, which the Israelis invaded during the second *intifada*. The IDF bulldozed the majority of Arafat's compound and cut him off from the rest of the world, while continuing to blame him for every terror attack against Israeli targets. Two soldiers stand guard over Arafat's gravestone, which sits in an airy, high-ceilinged cube with a shallow pool behind. Next door is a white stone mosque complete with modernist minaret. *(From al-Manara Circle, walk 10min. along al-Nahdah St. and take a left at the first traffic light; the compound is 5min. straight ahead. Open daily 9am-10pm.)*

THE PALESTINIAN FOLKLORE MUSEUM. For a more historical view, the Palestinian Folklore Museum, in the town of al-Bireh a few blocks away, exhibits traditional costumes, handicrafts, and rooms of a traditional Palestinian house.*(☎02 240 2876. Open M-Th and Sa 8am-3pm.)*

SOUQ AL-BIREH. Winding through narrow streets and open courtyards, this market is the center of Ramallah's local consumer economy. Highlights include the made-to-order perfume stands and the mountains of cheap, delicious produce. Though none of Ramallah's accommodations have access to kitchens, it's worth it to make your own raw food meals: kitchenware is amazingly cheap here. *(Located between al-Nahda St. and Jerusalem Rd., about 100m. from al-Manara Circle, behind the bus station.)*

OLD CITY. While Ramallah's Old City contains little of specific historical interest, it does provide a glimpse of Ottoman architecture.

TAYBEH BEER BREWING COMPANY. In the predominantly Christian farming village of Tabyeh, several kilometers from Ramallah, is the only brewery in the West Bank. Owner Nadim Khoury gives free tours and tastes. Taybeh means "delicious" in Arabic, and the three brews happily live up to the name. As a testament to the beer's popularity, Taybeh has recently expanded to Germany and the UK. *(Take a Taybeh Village-bound service taxi from Ramallah's city center for NIS10. ☎02 289 8868; www.taybehbeer.com. Call a day in advance for a tour.)*

BIRZEIT UNIVERSITY. Twelve kilometers north of Ramallah is the extensive and impressive campus of Birzeit University, the largest university in the West Bank. Birzeit's 2500 students have a history of vocal opposition to the Israeli occupation—the university was frequently shut down by the Israelis during the first and second *intifadas*. Today, Birzeit remains a vital political presence. The university takes pride in its history and strong leadership position in the West Bank. It has even developed an internet training program and an extensive web site (www.birzeit.edu). Foreign students can study at the university through the **Palestinian and Arab Studies (PAS)** program. *(Take a Birzeit-bound service from Manara Circle for NIS4. ☎02 298 2153.)*

NABLUS (SACHEM)   ☎09

שכם נابلس

Serene mountains surround the city of Nablus, founded in 72 CE by Titus near the site of Biblical Shechem as the "New City" of Flavia Neapolis. Enjoy the serenity if you can; the city is not called *Jabal al-Nar* (Hill of Fire) for nothing. Home to some of Palestine's oldest and wealthiest families, Nablus has a tradition of impassioned resistance to foreign occupation. Its citizens fought the Turks, the British, and the Jordanians and were wholly consumed by the *intifada*. Nablus, one of the largest Palestinian cities, is home to the West Bank's second-largest university, al-Najah. Since 1996, its new, wealthy neighborhood of Rafiddiyah has also housed the first Palestinian stock market. Tourists looking for eye-catching sights will find few, but those searching for an uncensored glimpse of the Palestinian present will find it. Nablus is a very conservative town—dress modestly. Because so few travelers make their way here, residents of Nablus tend to be curious and friendly. It is not uncommon to be invited in to a stranger's house for coffee or tea; in fact, it's nearly impossible to navigate Nablus without receiving several such invitations. Accepting this hospitality can lead to long, rewarding conversations about the *intifada*, the right of return, and life in Palestine today. Nablus was the site of outspoken demonstrations during the second *intifada* and was subject to some of the harshest restrictions in the West Bank. Residents were subject to continuous curfews lasting up to 21 days, during which they were unable to leave their homes.

▐ TRANSPORTATION

Service Taxis: The easiest way to get to Nablus is by *service* taxi from Ramallah (45min., NIS15). *Service* taxis leave from 2 parking lots just downhill from city center, heading to **Ramallah, Jenin, Nazareth,** and other destinations.

Taxis: Leave from the basement of Ramallah's central bus station and drop off tourists near the city center. Should cost no more than NIS10-20 for a ride anywhere around the city.

◢▐ ORIENTATION AND PRACTICAL INFORMATION

Nablus is decidedly difficult for tourists to navigate—it lacks both tourist info and maps. The most reliable way to find your way around is to ask the residents, who are friendly and hospitable even by West Bank standards.

Banks: The main square contains several banks with **ATMs.** Open Su-Th 8am-2pm.

Police: Faisal Rd. (☎09 238 3518).

Hospital: Salfit Emergency Government Hospital (☎09 251 5111).

Post Office: Faisal Rd. Open Su-Th 8am-2pm.

▐ ACCOMMODATIONS

Unlike most of the cities in the West Bank, which can easily be visited as daytrips from Jerusalem, Nablus is far enough away that an overnight visit is more convenient, especially if the city is being used as a stepping stone to Nazareth, Tiberias, or other northern locations in Israel. Unfortunately, however, there are no budget accommodations in the city—the options range from expensive to more expensive.

Al-Yasmeen Hotel, Tetouan St. (☎09 233 3555), in the heart of the city, by the market. Although small, its stylish and luxurious rooms are well worth the price. Each has satellite TV, phone, A/C, bath, and sound-proof, double-glass windows. Breakfast included. Internet and Wi-Fi available. Singles US$50 (NIS195); doubles US$60 (NIS230); triples US$70 (NIS270); quads US$85 (NIS330). Credit cards accepted. ❸

Al-Qasr Hotel, al-Fataimia St. (☎09 238 5444; alqasr@netvision.net.il), 25min. from the center of town. Take Gharnatah St. away from al-Shuhada Sq. and turn left on al-Fataimia St. Well-furnished rooms in a quiet neighborhood. Breakfast included. Singles US$60 (NIS230); doubles US$75 (NIS290). Prices are negotiable during low season. Credit cards accepted. ❸

▐ FOOD

Food options in Nablus are plentiful. From the center of town, wander into the crowded streets and passageways of the *souq* (market), which overflows with meat stores, clothing merchants, and produce stalls. Locals caution against the shiny restaurants serving dirty food in the town center and recommend instead the seemingly dirty restaurants serving clean, delicious food in the old city market. Try a piece of the extraordinarily rich *kinafeh nablusiyya*, a gooey warm cheese concoction topped with sweet orange flakes and syrup (NIS16 per kg.).

IN RECENT NEWS

HASTY PASTRY

Not everything in the West Bank is political. In July 2009, the bakers of Nablus united to beat the Guinness world record for largest *knafeh*, a type of syrupy cheesecake sprinkled with pistachio. It took 170 bakers, 1500 lb. of flour, and 650 lb. of sugar to make the 250 ft. long pastry—and it took 500 Palestinian police officers to guard it from the throngs of sweet-toothed onlookers. The entire endeavor cost US$15,000.

Palestinian Prime Minister Salam Fayyad took the ceremonious first bite, and then the hungry hordes descended on the giant cake. It was gone in 10 minutes.

To say that the affair was entirely apolitical is a bit of a misnomer, however, since it took place at a shopping festival held one month after Israel had eased its roadblock and checkpoint restrictions near Nablus. In recent times, Nablus has been attempting to brighten up its image in order to restore its status as a vibrant economic hub in the West Bank. In late June, it opened its first operating movie theater in two decades. Stores now remain open without fear of sporadic closure, and police officers have been able to focus on performing their normal tasks: issuing parking tickets, guarding giant pastries, and the like.

Zeit Ou Za'ater (☎09 233 35 55), in the al-Yasmeen hotel. Traditional food made in an olive-wood oven. Try *fukhara* (meat or vegetarian dish cooked in a clay pot; NIS35) or a heaping plate of *mensaf* (dish made of yogurt, rice, spices, and optional meat; NIS45). Among the only places in town to serve alcohol. Open daily 7am-midnight. Credit cards accepted. ❷

👁 SIGHTS

A few kilometers from the town center lie two famous but unspectacular pilgrimage sites.

JACOB'S WELL. Now enclosed within a subterranean Greek Orthodox shrine, the well is believed to date from the time when Jacob bought the surrounding land to pitch his tents (Genesis 33:18-19). The church over the crypt, begun in 1908, was badly damaged in the 1927 earthquake, but is finally being restored. *(Zut Rd., across from the Balata refugee camp; the road is unmarked, but any local can point out the direction to Balata. ☎09 233123. Open daily 8am-noon and 2-4pm. Modest dress required.)*

TOMB OF JOSEPH. According to the Book of Joshua, the bones of Joseph were carried out of Egypt and buried in Shechem (Joshua 24:32). The site of clashes between Jews and Palestinians as recently as August 1998, the tomb is now closed to the public and is surrounded by barbed wire and armed guards. It is currently under the control of the Palestinian Authority. *(Close to town, off Zut Rd.)*

🗲 DAYTRIPS FROM NABLUS

SABASTIYA. An array of Israelite, Hellenistic, and Roman ruins crown an unassuming hill 11km northwest of Nablus. The ruins lie on a peak first settled by Omri, King of Israel, in the ninth century BCE as the city of **Shomron** (Samaria). Shomron served as the capital of the Israelite kingdom until the Assyrian invasion in the eighth century BCE. Over the next several centuries, it served as the seat of Assyrian, Persian, and Greek governments. Under Herod, the city was made into the showpiece of the Holy Land to win the favor of the Roman emperors. The ruins, now under the control of the Israel National Parks Authority, are above the present-day Arab village of Sabastiya. Unfortunately, most of the ancient splendor is long gone, although the weed-covered ruins and beautiful views may make it easier to imagine the city as it had once been. At the top of the hill are the remains of Israelite and Hellenistic walls, a Roman acropolis and amphitheater, and the bases of columns built for the Temple of Augustus. Watch your step—the narrow 1.5km. path (a 30min. walk) encircling the ruins is slippery. *(Service taxis to Sabastiya are available from Nablus for NIS5. Hire a cab on the weekend or if the wait is too long for NIS30. Open daily 8am-5pm. Free.)*

MOUNT GERIZIM. This tree-covered slope southeast of Nablus features a terrific view of the Shomron Valley. Since the fourth century BCE, it has been the holy mountain of the Samaritans, who believe that it is the spot where Abraham prepared to sacrifice his son Isaac and where the original Ten Commandments are buried. They built a temple here to rival the one in Jerusalem, but it was destroyed by Hercanus in 128 BCE. The Samaritans, an Israelite sect excommunicated in Biblical times, are distinguished by their literal interpretation of certain scriptures and acceptance of only the Mosaic law (see **Religion,** p. 57). About 300 of them live in Nablus today, representing two-thirds of the world's Samaritans. Their synagogue houses what they believe to be the world's oldest Torah scroll. The Samaritan observance of Passover includes the sacrifice of a sheep atop Mt. Gerizim on the evening before the full moon. The **Samaritan Museum** (☎09 237 0249; open Su-F 8am-2pm; NIS5) provides an introduction to the history and beliefs of the Samaritans. *(Tourist buses from Jerusalem and Tel Aviv bring visitors to witness the bloody rite. Taxis make the arduous drive up the mountain for about NIS20.)*

HEBRON ☎02

חברון الخليل

Today, Hebron (sometimes spelled Khevron) is the most important industrial center in the West Bank. With a population of about 190,000 in the city proper and 500,000 in the district, it is the largest West Bank city. Since 1997, the city (and the mosque) has been divided into two parts: H1—about 80% of the city, mostly residential and new commercial areas—is under Palestinian Authority control; H2—the remaining 20%, including the mosque, settlement, and areas around the Old Market—is under Israeli control. Over 4,000 Israeli soldiers protect an enclave of 400 heavily-armed and often violent settlers. Palestinians living near the settlers are at constant risk of attack, as evidenced by the cages built to protect their homes and marketplaces. For an inside look at the tensions in Hebron, contact Israeli human rights organization **B'Tselem** (☎02 673 5599; www.btselem.org). B'Tselem gives video cameras to Palestinians in the West Bank to film the impact of the Israeli occupation; the most striking footage has come from Hebron. The heavy military presence makes violence toward Jewish settlers unthinkable, but trying to blend in with the Palestinian locals, if convincing, will make you an instant target in the Jewish areas. Visitors should make their tourist status as obvious as possible.

While the city lags behind other West Bank destinations in terms of Western influences and infrastructure (for example, the ATMs will only give Jordanian Dinars to foreign cardholders), it is not without tourist appeal. For the intrepid traveler, this is *terra incognita* just waiting to be explored and appreciated. A handful of tour agencies in Jerusalem, Bethlehem, and Ramallah lead excellent, informative daytrips. There are also numerous opportunities to get involved in the reconstruction of Hebron's economy and public spaces, both of which have been decimated by curfews and forced store closures (by IDF order). From its lively Old City market and taxi-filled New City streets to the venerated burial ground of Abraham, Hebron provides visitors with a strikingly multi-faceted, non-commercialized taste of reality—and a close-up view of the Israeli occupation second to none.

TRANSPORTATION

Service Taxis: Run infrequently from Damascus gate in Jerusalem (45min., NIS25), but the easiest way to get to Hebron is to catch a *service* taxi from Bab-alAzqaq, at the corner of Hebron Rd. and Paul VI Rd. (30min., NIS7). The *service* taxis back to Bethlehem leave from the taxi stand just uphill (north) of city center.

Taxis: A cab ride anywhere in the new city should be NIS10.

ORIENTATION AND PRACTICAL INFORMATION

Because Hebron has never been a big tourist destination, commodities that have become prevalent in towns such as Bethelehem and Jericho, like maps or English-language street signs, are non-existent. The city is divided into the **New City** in the north and the **Old City** in the south, with the city center in between. The main street of the new city is **Jerusalem Road** (Sharia al-Quds) which becomes **Ein Sarah** at the southern end toward the city center. Continuing south along this street, which turns into **Kind David Street,** brings you to the Old City **souq** and the **Ibrahimi Mosque.**

Tours: Nothing beats a local guide: **Hisham Sharabati** (☎059 927 1190; h_sharabati@ hotmail.com), a native Hebronite, can arrange tours that include an unforgettable visit with a Palestinian family living directly underneath the settlers' back porches.

Police: In the Old City, the **Municipal Inspector's Office** (☎02 222 6942) serves as a de facto police station, and can provide information on emergency and medical services. In the New City, contact the **Palestinian Police** (☎02 222 6382) in case of emergency.

ACCOMMODATIONS AND FOOD

The lack of international tourism makes Hebron a great place to sample local cuisine, but military curfews and forced closings contribute to the near impossibility of finding a consistently-open establishment. For local flavor, try the street food in the **old market:** fresh-baked bread pastries and fresh-squeezed juices, are the safest bet, but adventurous travelers (with strong stomachs) can branch out to heartier fare. To sit down and unwind, stop by **Badran,** the oldest coffee shop in town, located at the crossroads in the center of the old market. (☎02 223 3045. Open daily 9am-5pm.) The New City has a string of local restaurants along **Ein Sarah** north of the city center, many with a strong Jordanian influence.

Hanthala Guest House (☎059 927 1190). This cozy guesthouse across from an imposing military blockage in the northern part of the Old City can be hard to find; the door is unmarked, as is the street. The dorms in Hathala are clean and well-lit, and there is a kitchen for guest use (a great alternative to sometimes sketchy street food). The reception keeps no regular hours, so call well in advance to ensure you can get in. The owner can also arrange **home stays** with Palestinian families, an unforgettable experience. Satellite TV. Free Wi-Fi. Dorms NIS50. Cash only. ❶

Hebron Hotel (☎02 225 4240), on Ein Sarah south of the mall. A bit of luxury at hostel prices. The rooms have fridges, TVs, A/C, phones, and internet, as well as nice faux-marble decorated bathrooms. The staff is friendly and accommodating, and there's a coffee shop in the lobby. Cash only. Singles NIS120; doubles NIS180; triples NIS220. ❷

SIGHTS

TOMB OF THE PATRIARCHS. The primary tourist site in Hebron, the half-synagogue, half-mosque Tomb of the Patriarchs is thought to lie directly above the underground tombs of Abraham, Isaac, Rebecca, Jacob, and Leah. The tomb of Abraham is visible through bars from both sides; the tombs of Isaac and Rebecca, however, are entirely within the mosque. The cave itself may not be visited but can be seen through an opening in the floor of the mosque, in front of Abraham's tomb. Note the huge oak lectern, in the same room, from which the *imam* delivers the Friday sermon; added by Salah al-Din in the 12th century, it is one of the few in the world carved from a single block of wood. In the same room, the longest Herodian cut stone ever discovered forms part of the walls. More than 4m in length, it lies in the southeast corner of the room. Lift the carpet to get a glimpse or ask someone to point it out.

In 1994, an American-born Jewish extremist named Baruch Goldstein entered the mosque and opened fire, killing 29 Muslims and injuring 200. According to Israeli television, IDF forces outside of the mosque opened fire on the Palestinians fleeing the scene, fearing one of them was an attacker fleeing the scene. The settlers of Hebron consider Goldstein a martyr and have erected a statue in his honor. As a result of the massacre, Jews have been officially barred from entering the mosque, and Muslims have been barred from entering the synagogue. All entrants are required to pass through several metal detectors; there is a gun check at the Jewish entrance for the armed settlers who visit. Security at the Jewish and Muslim entrances is extremely tight, and modest dress is required. *(Mosque open Su-Th and Sa. Synagogue open M-F, Sa Jews only.)*

THE AL-SALAM GLASS FACTORY. For sights of a less political nature, the al-Salam Glass Factory is located on the road between Hebron and Bethlehem. Fifteen hours per day, workers blow recycled glass at the red-hot furnace, which is fueled by recycled oil. Nearby, others craft clay pots on the pottery wheel. Both can be purchased at the adjacent wholesale store. *(☎02 222 9127; www.alsalam-ceramic.com. Open Su-Th and Sa 5am-8pm, F 5am-noon. Credit cards accepted.)*

THE DEAD SEA

סי המלח البَحْر المَيّت

How low can you go? At 412m below sea level, this is it—the Dead Sea is the lowest point on Earth. If that doesn't sound impressive, wait until you're driving on the highway, pass a "sea level" signpost, and then round a bend to see entire mountains whose peaks lie below you.

The morbid "dead" moniker was coined by Christian monks astonished by the apparent absence of any form of life in the sea's waters; however, kill-joy scientists have recently discovered 11 types of hardy bacteria in the water. The sea's Hebrew name, Yam ha-Melakh (The Sea of Salt), is more appropriate: the water has a salt concentration eight times that of the ocean, making it so heavy and dense that even fish would have to walk. This comes as good news to those who can't swim: everyone floats in this sea, without so much as moving a muscle. Besides the much-acclaimed floating effect, the high concentration of minerals is responsible for the gorgeous salt formations that adorn the seaside rocks and postcards. Businesses have capitalized upon these natural resources, building a vast series of evaporation ponds at the southernmost tip, which suck select salts from the water.

The Dead Sea is actually a large lake—65km long, 18km wide, and 412m deep. Its coasts are shared by Israel and Jordan, with the peaceful border drawn smack down the sea's middle. The sea's formation is the result of a geological phenomenon called the Syrian-African Rift, essentially a mega-valley between shifting tectonic plates extending from southern Africa to Turkey. The resulting image of hollowness has led some to nickname the Dead Sea area "the navel of the world."

Water flows into the sea from the Jordan River and underground water sources from the surrounding desert. But with no outlet for the lake's water, the intense sun evaporates it faster than you can say "Ra." Inadequate rainfall, coupled with Israeli, Jordanian, and Syrian reliance on the sea's freshwater sources for drinking and irrigation, has begun to take its toll. The sun now evaporates more water than flows in; the sea is shrinking so severely that the southern tip has been cut off by a sand bar, and the northern part now recedes at the frightening rate of 80cm per year. Emergency measures to save the Dead Sea, driven by ecological and economic interests, are in the planning stages.

From its northern tip, 25min. from Jerusalem, to the southernmost Sodom area, the Dead Sea and its surroundings are replete with sights and activities to please even the pickiest of travelers. Many visitors take a quick dip at the tourist-trappy Ein Bokek beach, snap the famous floating-while-reading-a-magazine and caked-in-mud photos, and go along their merry ways. This is an area of great beauty, but the ruggedness can be marred by postcard racks and the hum of international tour buses. Not far from these oft-visited spectacles, shy-horned ibex, camouflaged by their light brown hues, prance vivaciously around the supposedly "dead" sea. Nestled above apparently barren wasteland lie lush nature reserves, and below-ground, the desert dust hides bottomless mineral springs. A trek to the region's more secluded spots, such as Mitzokei Dragot or Nakhal Arugot, often yields the most rewarding Dead Sea experience.

> **HIGHLIGHTS OF THE DEAD SEA**
>
> **FLOAT** at the salty beaches of **Ein Bokek** (p. 344).
> **CLIMB** the soaring cliffs at **Mitzokei Dragot** (p. 340).
> **RINSE OFF** the salt in the freshwater pools of **Ein Gedi Nature Reserve** (p. 335).

GETTING THERE AND AROUND

The Egged **buses** that serve the rest of the country do so poorly in this region. Fares are outrageous (up to NIS10 for a 10min. ride) and the routes don't cover every destination. These difficulties, in conjunction with the nasty heat and the distance between the main roads and sights, make **renting a car** an excellent idea. Most companies offer a daily rental rate of US$60-80 for single-day rentals, US$45-55 per day for longer-term rentals. Driving in the Dead Sea region provides spectacular vistas, but be careful—steep, windy roads mean nothing to speed-demon Israeli drivers. The best place to rent is Jerusalem, since cutthroat competition drives prices down (see **Intercity Transportation,** p. 85). In the Dead Sea, try **Hertz** (☎08 658 4530) in Ein Bokek.

The few **Egged** lines that travel along the Dead Sea coast have erratic schedules with waits often lasting ¾-1½hr., so check times, call the customer support center for information (☎03 694 8888), and plan ahead. Buses #421, 444, and 486 between Jerusalem and Eilat stop at Qumran, Ein Feshkha, Ein Gedi, and Masada. Bus #487, also from Jerusalem, runs only to Qumran, Ein Feshkha, and Ein Gedi. Buses #384 and 385 combined make about four trips per day (Su-F) between Be'er Sheva and Ein Gedi via Arad, Ein Bokek, and Masada. Buses will stop at many stations only upon request, so confirm destinations with the driver. Several sites listed, including Mitzokei Dragot and Neot Hakikar, are not accessible by public transportation. On Saturdays, none of the buses head to or from the Dead Sea until the evening; to get there earlier, find a service across from Damascus Gate (NIS30-50 depending how far south you want to go). Locals claim hitchhiking is relatively safe in this part of the country, but *Let's Go* never recommends hitchhiking.

 CABBIES WITH BORDERS. If you want to take a cab from Jerusalem into the West Bank, you'll have to find an Arab cab driver. The cabs are identical, so this is harder than it sounds. Your best bet is at the exit to Damascus Gate. The flood of unsuspecting tourists means that you'll be offered outrageous prices at first; be prepared to bargain.

ORIENTATION AND PRACTICAL INFORMATION

The Dead Sea coast is 65km long, and for easy reference may be divided into northern, central, and southern regions. This section is organized from north to south. Remember: if the sea is on your left, you're going south, if it's on your right, you're going north.

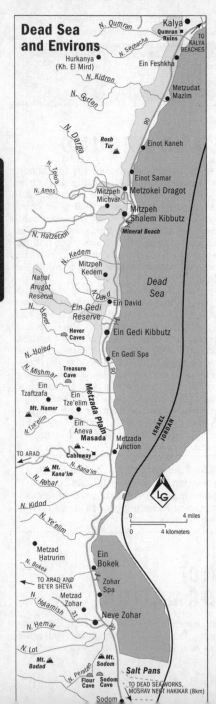

Dead Sea and Environs

N. Qumran
Kalya
Qumran Ruins
TO KALYA BEACHES
Hurkanya (Kh. El Mird)
N. Sechacha
Ein Feshkha
N. Kidron
Metzudat Mazim
N. Cofan
90
Rosh Tur
Einot Kaneh
N. Dalega
N. Tekoa
Einot Samar
N. Amos
Mitzpeh Michvar
Metzokei Dragot
Mitzpeh Shalem Kibbutz
Mineral Beach
N. Hatzetzon
Kedem
N. Kedem
Mitzpeh Kedem
Dead Sea
Nahal Arugot Reserve
Ze David
Ein David
N. Hever
Ein Gedi Reserve
Hever Caves
Ein Gedi Kibbutz
N. Holed
En Gedi Spa
N. Mishmar
Treasure Cave
Ein Tzaftzafa
Metzada Plain
Mt. Namer
Ein Tze'elim
N.Tze'elim
ISRAEL
JORDAN
Ein Aneva
Masada
Metzada Junction
TO ARAD
Cableway
Mt. Kana'im
N. Kana'im
N. Rahaf
N. Kidod
N. Ye'elim
Metzad Hatrurim
N. Bokek
Ein Bokek
TO ARAD AND BE'ER SHEVA
Zohar Spa
N. Halamish
Metzad Zohar
31
Neve Zohar
N. Hemar
90
N. Lot
Mt. Badad
Mt. Sodom
N. Peratim
Salt Pans
Flour Cave
Sodom Cave
TO DEAD SEA WORKS, MOSHAV NEOT HAKIKAR (8km)
Sodom

0 — 4 miles
0 — 4 kilometers

N LG

The Dead Sea does not have an ordinary desert climate—instead of being hot and dry, it's hot and humid. The sticky air, very high temperatures, and 330 days per year of cloudless, steady sun are barely tolerable. While the air does have a 10% higher oxygen concentration, leave the strenuous activities for the early morning. The extreme, steamroom-like weather has been known to dehydrate people waiting at shaded bus stops, for instance. Keep your head covered, take a water bottle wherever you go, and chug liberally at the rate of about 1L per hr., more if you're hiking. Bring a large bottle with you and keep refilling at faucets to avoid getting ripped off by the eight-shekel-a-pop street vendors once you're there. While the tap water is drinkable in most places in Israel, don't assume that shower or faucet water is safe to drink—check for "Drinking Water" signs or ask someone.

The **tourist information** hub for the entire region is in the southern Dead Sea, at Ein Bokek (p. 344). Check in at the Ein Gedi *kibbutz* reception center for information on local sights and events (☎08 659 4220; www.ein-gedi.co.il). It is possible to join the crowds on the popular one-day tour from Jerusalem that shuttles lemmings—er, tourists to Masada (in time for sunrise), Ein Gedi (Nakhal David and the Dead Sea beach), Kumran (jump out of the bus, take a picture, jump back in), Jericho (in time for a late lunch), and photo stops at the Mount of Temptation, St. George Monastery, and the Mount of Olives. Tours cost US$30-35 (entrance fees not included) and can be booked through most of the hostels in the Old City.

Kibbutz Ein Gedi (p. 333) has an ATM, which are otherwise

nearly absent from the Dead Sea region. If you're not stopping at the *kibbutz*, come prepared.

 BAD WITH NAMES. Street names in Palestine can be confusing, if you're lucky, or nonexistent, if you're not. In Arab towns with nearby Israeli settlements, many streets have two names: the traditional Palestinian names, known by the locals and cab drivers, and the names given by the settlers, which appear on the maps. In the towns without an Israeli or international presence, many of the streets don't have names at all. Locals refer to the streets by the families that live on them, making them very difficult for an outsider to navigate, but granting wonderful insight into the city's cultural life along with the geographical knowledge eventually gained.

EIN GEDI ☎08

עין גדי

After a hot morning hike or a muggy bus ride, the only thing better than drinking cold water is sitting in it. The Ein Gedi oasis, the epicenter of the Dead Sea region, has a long history of providing shelter and playing host to romantic getaways. David fled here to escape the wrath of King Saul (1 Samuel 24), and here he forsook the choice opportunity to slay his pursuing father-in-law. In Song of Songs (1:13), the lover declares that her beloved is "a cluster of camphor in the vineyards of Ein Gedi." During the second Jewish revolt (132-135 CE), rebel leader Simon Bar Kokhba sought refuge here.

These days, the town hasn't changed much: the very fresh and very salty water are perhaps the only reasons to visit. Most passers-through have had their fill of Ein Gedi after a short dip in the Dead Sea followed by a rinse in the pools. If you want to stick around, the kibbutz, with its botanical gardens and huge kosher buffet, makes for a worthwhile stop.

▉ TRANSPORTATION

Buses: To: **Be'er Sheva** (#384 and 385; 2¼hr.; Su-Th 4 per day; F 2 per day; NIS45) via Masada, Ein Bokek, and Arad; **Eilat** (#444; 3hr.; Su-Th 4 per day; F 3 per day; Sa 1 per day; NIS63); **Ein Bokek** (#486, 30min., Su-F 6 per day 8am-6:05pm, NIS23); **Jerusalem** (#421, 487, 486; Su-Th 10 per day 6am-7:40pm, F 6am-2:25pm, Sa 7pm and 7:40pm).

Shuttles: From the kibbutz to the spa and beach.

▉ ORIENTATION

Ein Gedi's 6750-acre nature reserve is the heart of this desert attraction. Surrounding it are a kibbutz, several accommodations, a field school, a public bathing area, and a luxury spa. There are four **bus stops** in the area. The first one serves the nature reserve and the two youth hostels. Farther south is the beach stop, which provides convenient access to the public beach, a gas station, and a first-aid station. The third stop, by advance request only, serves the kibbutz and its guest house. At the fourth stop are the thermal baths and spa. Walking between the hostels and the public beach takes 10min.; the spas are 5km south of the beach. Food kiosks and public telephone booths crowd the entrances to and exits from all tourist attractions, beaches, and hikes. The only **ATM** in Ein Gedi is in the lobby of the kibbutz and charges a NIS7 fee.

ACCOMMODATIONS

The sweltering weather hardly abates at night, so air-conditioning is a must. There is a free **campground** at the public beach; tents or hammocks are recommended due to flies living in the sand.

Beit Sara Youth Hostel (HI) (☎08 658 4165), uphill at the turnoff for Nagal David. Clean and uncrowded rooms with A/C and private baths. Ask about discount tickets (20%) for the nature reserve and spa. Breakfast included. Wi-Fi NIS36 per day. Reception 7am-9pm. Check-in 3-7pm. Check-out Su-F 9am, Sa 10am. Dorms NIS113; singles NIS256; doubles NIS338. Extra person NIS100. Credit cards accepted. ❷

Ein Gedi Field School (☎08 658 4350; ngedi@spni.org.il). A steep 10min. climb up the road behind the youth hostel yields a less touristed, more scenic spot. Run by the Society for the Protection of Nature in Israel (SPNI), which offers information on all of the hikes in the area. Some of the areas' best hikes start from this point; you can begin a hike here before the park opens and pay your entry fee when you exit from the main gate. This peak is the only place on Earth to get a glimpse of a rare species of bird called Leilit Hamidbar (Hume's Tawny Owl). 20% discount on park entry and spa. Breakfast included. Reception Su-F 8am-8pm; staff onsite 24hr. Call ahead. Dorms NIS74-99; singles NIS275-315; doubles NIS315-365. Extra person NIS129. Credit cards accepted. ❷

Kibbutz Ein Gedi Guest House (☎08 659 4220; www.ein-gedi.co.il), 3km south of the beach. A worthwhile splurge if you want to kick back and relax, eat filling meals at the all-you-can-eat kosher buffet, and stroll through the botanical gardens. All guests enjoy full use of the kibbutz's facilities, which includes a swimming pool, botanical gardens, a small zoo, and spa down the road. Spacious rooms feature kitchenettes, fridges, bathrooms, A/C, and TVs. "Country Lodging" (discounted rooms without free spa access) available. Buffet breakfast and lunch included. Free Wi-Fi. Regular singles US$160, deluxe $210, country lodging $76; doubles US$200/250/95. Prices rise on weekends, holidays, and Sept.-Nov. ❹

> **TIP** **DON'T SPRING FOR BOTTLED WATER.** The water fountain behind the reception area at Ein Gedi Kibbutz dispenses the same spring water that's bottled and sold throughout the Dead Sea area. Save yourself eight shekels a pop and stock up for free after a visit to the botanical gardens.

FOOD

Kibbutz Ein Gedi (☎08 659 4220). This kibbutz's all-you-can-eat kosher buffet is the most filling (and most expensive) option around. Breakfast (NIS60) is dairy-centric, featuring delicious homemade *halva*. Dinner (Su-Th and Sa NIS95; F NIS120) is a simple but filling meat buffet, with a huge salad bar and a wonderful assortment of fresh vegetables and salads. Open for breakfast 7-10am and for dinner 6-8:30pm. Credit cards accepted. ❸

Pundak Ein Gedi (☎08 659 4222), on the public beach. A cafeteria-style lunch run by the kibbutz. A heaping plastic plate with a main course and two sides runs for NIS45; try the homemade beef stew. Beer NIS16, soda NIS9. Open daily 11am-4pm. Cash only. ❷

Kiosk (☎08 659 4222), next to Pundak Ein Gedi. Serves oily, perpetually-rotating hot dogs and sandwiches (NIS16). Cash only. ❶

SIGHTS AND OUTDOOR ACTIVITIES

EIN GEDI ANTIQUITIES NATIONAL PARK.]If you're near the Nagal Arugot entrance, this site is worth a visit. Calling it a "national park" is deceptive: in lieu of featuring flora and fauna, it consists of a single synagogue dating to the early third century CE, making it one of the oldest synagogues in Israel. The floor of the synagogue is embedded with mosaics in various states of reconstruction, as well as a collection of stone tools and pottery found at the site. *(Of the two entrances to the huge Ein Gedi Nature Reserve, only the Nagal David entrance, just below the youth hostels, is accessible by bus. The Nagal Arugot entrance, 3km past the Nagal David entrance, is accessible only by car. ☎ 658 42 85; Antiquities National Park ☎ 658 4285. Both open daily 8am-4pm; hikers must be out of park by 5pm. Note that several hikes may not be started after 1:30pm. NIS25, students NIS21; includes entrance to Antiquities National Park.)*

EIN GEDI BEACH. For some good ol' Dead Sea floating, Ein Gedi has its own crowded beach. Beach and umbrella use is free, but bathrooms and lockers cost NIS2 and NIS20 respectively. Bring water shoes: the beach is rocky, and if this doesn't convince you, the blazing heat will. There's no mud left here, so pick up a packet or two from the many Ahava stores in the area (**Ein Bokek,** p. 344, has the best deals at NIS15 per packet).

EIN GEDI SPA. About 5km south of the beach is the Ein Gedi Spa, with indoor and outdoor sulfur pools, therapeutic mud, and a restaurant. The sulfur pools give the indoor area a noxious, humid air, and the beach has receded so far that you need to ride a noisy tractor-pulled trailer to reach it. Unless you're staying at the kibbutz (in which case entry is free), you're better off grabbing pre-packaged mud and going to the public beach. *(☎ 08 659 4813. Open Su-Th and Sa 8am-6pm, F 8am-5pm. Su-F NIS60, Sa NIS70.)*

BOTANICAL GARDENS. Though some may question the ecological soundness of planting thirsty St. Augustine grass and other non-native species in the middle of the desert, the lush courtyards and eye-catching flora of the Ein Gedi Botanical Gardens are enough to make you forget about the paradox for a while. The guided night tour is led by a member of the kibbutz, who gives colorful and informative commentary. *(☎ 08 658 4444. Open Su-Th and Sa 8:30am-4pm, F 8:30am-2pm. Guided tours Tu and Th 8pm; call in advance to purchase a ticket. NIS26, students and children NIS22.)*

🗡 HIKING

Some sections of the Ein Gedi trails are steep, but well-placed railings and steps have been built into the rock. Once noon rolls around, high temperatures can make even inhaling strenuous, so get going by 8am. Always bring at least 1L of water per hour of hiking (there are faucets just outside the gate), and don't forget your swimsuit for dipping in the occasional freshwater pool or waterfall. The names of the different pools and springs repeat frequently and are almost interchangeable (David this, Ein Gedi that), so get a free map at the entrance and pay attention to the fine print to prevent confusion. Possible hikes vary from easygoing to double-diamond difficult.

Ein Gedi Nature Reserve has a number of hikes, both pleasant and strenuous. For a short hike of 30min. each way, enter from the Nahal David entrance and follow the path straight until **Shulamit Falls,** a delicious, slender pillar of water dropping into a shallow pool. Turning left at the falls leads to a trail that climbs up the cliffside to **Shulamit Spring** (an additional 30min. each way). For a longer hike, continue from Shulamit spring along the cliff and down a ladder to **Dudaim Cave** (Lover's Cave), a mossy niche at the top of the fall (30min. from the spring). Proceed left, passing the 3000-year-old remains of a **Chalcolithic Temple** once dedicated to worship of the moon, on the way to **Ein Gedi Spring** (20min. from the Temple), whose cool water is perfect for a refreshing dip. Resist the urge to dive from the high niches into the pool—it's not deep enough in some places. Next to the spring is a sugar mill from the Islamic period which was powered by water from the spring. The second entrance to the reserve is at **Nagal Arugot** (no bus; parking lot 3km inland from Rte. 90, between the beach and the Nagal David entrance). A somewhat challenging 1hr. hike along the river leads to a hidden waterfall and a deep blue pool.

One long but highly recommended trail connects the David and Arugot entrances, with the Ein Gedi Spring smack in the middle. The trail passes the newly restored ancient **synagogue** and leads directly to the beachfront in time for an afternoon of sunbathing. The trail begins at the **SPNI Field School** and follows the "Zafit Trail" until Ein David. At Ein David, turn left and follow the main marked trail to Shulamit Falls. For a shorter hike, bear left and follow the main trail out; for the full hike, bear right and continue toward Shulamit Spring and the Chalcolithic temple. **Ein Gedi Spring** is several 100m further. Continue straight, due south, until **Tel Goren.** Turn left toward the sea; the light blue building near the end of the path is the Ein Gedi mineral water bottling plant, a refreshing stop.

MASADA ☎ 08

מצדה

"Masada shall not fall again," swear members of the Israel Defense Forces each year. Jewish Zealots' tenacious defense of Masada in the first century CE has been fashioned into a heroic symbol of the defense of modern Israel. Political significance aside, legions of tourists from around the world continue to storm this mountain fortress to catch the spectacular view of the Dead Sea, visit the extensive ruins, and envision the martyrdom of Masada's rebels.

The first fortress *(metzuda)* on the mountain was built as a refuge from marauding Greeks and Syrians by the Jewish High Priest **Jonathan Maccabeus** around 150 BCE and was expanded a few decades later by John Hyrcanus I. It was chiefly under **Herod,** however, that Masada transformed into an enormous mountaintop citadel: the Great Builder installed two palaces, baths, villas, storerooms, an intricate system of cisterns and aqueducts, and a defensive wall studded with over 30 guard towers. At the outset of the Jewish rebellion against Rome in 66 CE, a small band of Zealot rebels, members of a small Jewish sect, captured the prize fortress from its unsuspecting garrison. As the Romans gradually crushed the revolt, taking Jerusalem in 70 CE and destroying the Second Temple, Masada became a refuge for surviving Zealots and the last Jewish holdout in all of Israel. With years' worth of food, water, and military supplies, the 967 men, women, and children held off 15,000 Roman legionnaires through a five-month siege. The Romans called in their best engineers to construct a wall and camps in a ring around the mount. Capitalizing on their superior force, they built an enormous stone and gravel ramp up the side of the cliff, using Jewish slaves as laborers in order to prevent the Zealots from shooting them down as the ramp was built.

When the defenders realized that the Romans would break through their walls the next morning, the community leaders decided that it would be better, as their leader Elazar Ben-Yair said, to die "unenslaved by enemies, and leave this world as free men in company with wives and children" rather than be captured by the Romans. Because Jewish law forbids suicide, ten men were chosen to slay the others, and one chosen to kill the other nine before falling on his own sword. Before burning the fortress and all their possessions, the

Jews placed stores of wheat and water in the citadel's courtyard to prove to the Romans that they did not perish from hunger. The following morning, when the triumphant Romans burst in, they encountered only smoking ruins and deathly silence. The only survivors, two women and five children, told the story of the Zealots' last days to Josephus Flavius, a Jewish-Roman general and chronicler. Flavius, always eager to embellish a good tale, never actually visited Masada. He based his dramatic history on the survivors' accounts, later describing the two to be "of exceptional intelligence for women." Although strong corroborating evidence for the story has been found at the site, such as the murder-lottery slips Josephus describes, archaeologists have yet to unearth the Zealots' actual remains. Where the bones of almost 1000 people have gone is still a mystery.

TRANSPORTATION

To reach Masada by car, Rte. 3199 runs from Arad to the base of the Roman Ramp, and Rte. 90 leads to the Snake Path, the eastern cable car entrance, the bus stop, and the youth hostel. The walk around the base from one path to the other is extremely arduous and time-consuming. Those who decide to do it should follow the SPNI trail, not the incline with the water pipe.

Two paths ascend the mountain. The more popular, scenic, and difficult of the two paths is the **Snake Path** (45min. hike), named for its tortuous bends (opens 4:30am, closes 5pm). The **Roman Ramp,** on the western side of the mountain, is an easier hike than the Snake Path and the original path. Even the most grumpy of un-early birds will appreciate a dawn hike to catch the legendary sunrise over the Dead Sea. Today many warriors opt to take the Snake Path up and cable car down; due to the steepness, the hike down is just as strenuous as the hike up. Another option is to take the cable car up in the afternoon and hike down when the sun is less fierce.

Buses: Buses that stop at Ein Gedi will also stop at Masada; p. 333. Call the Egged information line in advance to double-check schedule and make sure the bus stops outside Masada.

ACCOMMODATIONS AND FOOD

The food situation in Masada is cheerless. The Zealots had the right idea: bring a year's supply. The Masada Guest House serves kosher meat dinners for a reasonable price when demand is high enough (generally all summer and around holidays, but call in advance). Otherwise, you're stuck with the overpriced snacks and tourist-trap restaurant in the visitor's center.

Masada Guest House (HI; ☎0 8995 3222), straight ahead and to the left near the bus stop. The only hostel in Masada. Manages to escape the monotony of other HI establishments in Israel, due in large part to its super-friendly staff. Rooms are spotless, with A/C, fridges, TV, and coffee corners. The swimming pool is refreshing and the patio has an amazing view. Breakfast included. Dinner can be arranged by calling in advance (price varies with occupancy). Internet access. Call in advance to ensure dorm bed availability. Dorms NIS131, under 18 NIS105; singles NIS263; doubles NIS368. Additional person NIS121. Credit cards accepted. ❷

SPNI Campground, on Masada's west side, near the sound and light show. Small and spartan. NIS30 per person. SPNI tents NIS45 per person. Includes park admission. ❶

SIGHTS

The **Masada Sound and Light Show** regularly lights up the fortress like a Las Vegas marquee. The show is not visible from the Masada youth hostel. For more information,

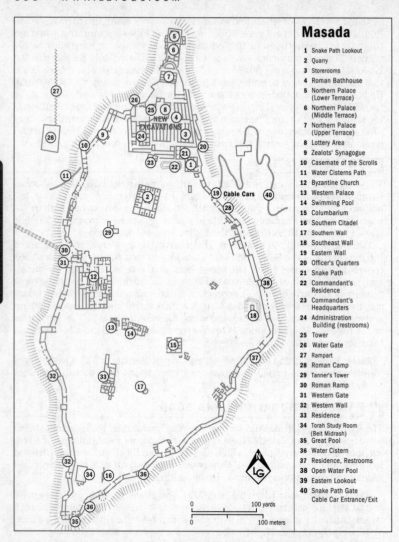

Masada

1 Snake Path Lookout
2 Quarry
3 Storerooms
4 Roman Bathhouse
5 Northern Palace
   (Lower Terrace)
6 Northern Palace
   (Middle Terrace)
7 Northern Palace
   (Upper Terrace)
8 Lottery Area
9 Zealots' Synagogue
10 Casemate of the Scrolls
11 Water Cisterns Path
12 Byzantine Church
13 Western Palace
14 Swimming Pool
15 Columbarium
16 Southern Citadel
17 Southern Wall
18 Southeast Wall
19 Eastern Wall
20 Officer's Quarters
21 Snake Path
22 Commandant's
   Residence
23 Commandant's
   Headquarters
24 Administration
   Building (restrooms)
25 Tower
26 Water Gate
27 Rampart
28 Roman Camp
29 Tanner's Tower
30 Roman Ramp
31 Western Gate
32 Western Wall
33 Residence
34 Torah Study Room
   (Beit Midrash)
35 Great Pool
36 Water Cistern
37 Residence, Restrooms
38 Open Water Pool
39 Eastern Lookout
40 Snake Path Gate
   Cable Car Entrance/Exit

see **Arad,** p. 359. The following suggested route covers the highlights of Masada and roughly follows the sign-posted walking tour. The ruins at Masada were unearthed from 1963 to 1964; thousands of volunteers excavated in 11 months what would normally have taken 26 years. About one-third of the ruins are actually reconstructed—a black line indicates the extent of the original findings. The re-excavation of the Northern Palace by a group of expert Italian archaeologists has unearthed new mosaic floors and hundreds of coins near the bathhouses.

SNAKE PATH LOOKOUT. This lookout offers views of the Snake Path, the earthen wall, the Roman camps, the Dead Sea, and the Mountains of Moab.

QUARRY. This quarry supplied much of the stone for the extensive construction throughout Masada. Between the quarry and the Western Wall, there is a large pile of round rocks, too perfectly shaped to be anything but catapults' ammo.

STOREROOMS. Food, weapons, and other supplies were stored within these rooms. Though the Zealots destroyed most of their valuable possessions and the fortress, they left the storeroom containing mass amounts of food untouched. Josephus explains that the Zealots wanted to prove that their suicide was a means of escaping slavery, not famine.

ROMAN BATHHOUSE. Bathers would leave their clothes in the *apodyterium* (dressing room) before proceeding to the *calidarium* (hot bath), recognizable by the small pillars, which used to support a secondary floor. A stove channeled hot air between these two floors. Bathers then cooled off in the *tepidarium* (lukewarm room) before a quick dip in the *frigidarium* (cold pool). Built by Herod, the bathhouse served no purpose for the austere Zealots.

NORTHERN PALACE. Go down the nearby stairwell to Herod's thrice-terraced private pad. The frescoes and fluted columns, still intact on the lower terrace, attest to the splendor Herod enjoyed even on a remote desert butte. In the bathhouse of the lowest section, the skeletons of a man, woman, and child were found, along with a *tallit* (prayer shawl), *ostraca* (lots), and arrowheads.

LOTTERY AREA. Climb back up from the palace to the Lottery Area, to the left of the bathhouses as you face the Palace. The Zealots used this area as a ritual bath for cleansing and purification, but it is most notable for the dramatic discovery of eleven *ostraca*. The uniform shards of pottery inscribed with names (including one with the name Ben-Yair, Zealot commander of Masada) most likely served as lots that decided who would kill the others.

ZEALOTS' SYNAGOGUE. Following the western edge of the mountain leads to the Zealots' synagogue, the oldest in the world. Scrolls were found here containing texts from several books of the Torah; most are now on display at the Israel Museum in Jerusalem (p. 149). The scrolls and discoveries, such as a *mikveh* (ritual bath), indicate that the community followed Jewish strictures despite mountainous isolation and the siege.

CASEMATE OF THE SCROLLS. A number of important archaeological relics were found within the casemate, including scrolls, papyrus, silver shekels, a *tallit*, a wooden shield, arrows, sandals, keys, baskets, and other items.

WATER CISTERNS PATH. The enormous cisterns can still be seen dotting the mountaintop from the western wall; they are lined with a near-perfect water-repellent plaster that still won't absorb a single drop. Rainfall used to drain from the surrounding mountains into Masada's reservoirs, filling the entire cistern within a few hours on the one annual day of rain. The Zealots were able to store up to eight years' worth of precious water in these cavernous structures.

BYZANTINE CHURCH. Remote Masada, with caves and buildings for shelter, made an ideal hideout for Christian hermits in the fifth and sixth centuries. The chapel with preserved mosaic floors is the most impressive of their remains.

WESTERN PALACE. Farther along the edge stands the site of Herod's throne room and offices of state. A system of water cisterns underlies the western wing; the northern wing surrounds a large central courtyard; the southern wing was the royal wing, and includes a waiting room, courtyard, dining hall, kitchen, and throne room. Though just as sumptuous as the Northern Palace, this was Herod's "working palace." He went to his northern "country residence" to relax.

SWIMMING POOL. Although water was a rare commodity in the fortress, Herod insisted on maintaining a swimming pool in the backyard of the Western Palace. The Zealots used this as a ritual bath.

COLUMBARIUM. The small niches in the walls of this round building, farther back and slightly to the left, sparked an archaeological debate. One team contended that it was a *columbarium*, where the ashes of the non-Jewish members of Herod's garrison were placed, while others thought the niches housed pigeons. After highly scientific tests, the former opinion emerged victorious since small pigeons could not even fit inside the niches.

SOUTHERN CITADEL. At the southern tip of the mountain, the Southern Citadel looks out at the Masada Wadi, Dead Sea, and Roman encampments.

SOUTHERN WALL. Along the southern wall lie a tower with a Zealot installation (the building might have been a bakery), a ritual bath, a dressing room (the narrow niches held clothes), and a courtyard. The path is no longer in use.

SOUTHEAST WALL. There is a memorial inscription for "Lucius" (possibly a soldier in the Roman Garrison) engraved in the wall of the tower. On the plaster of the southern wall, there are four impressions of the name "Justus" in Latin and Greek. There is also a lookout from which the outer wall is visible.

EASTERN WALL. The outer wall and inner wall are joined by partitions, forming casemates. The higher and thicker sections of the inner wall are the sole remains of a series of towers that lined the wall. A channel under the floor of the Zealot additions is older than the wall itself. A small grove of fir trees toward the Snake Path Gate was the site of a 1988 interpretive reenactment of the battle.

TOP THAT. IDF soldiers hanging out in bus stops and around town often have berets pinned over one shoulder—each beret color signifies a different corps. Get locals talking by trying to learn the system. To get you started: paratroopers wear red.

NORTHERN DEAD SEA

The buses from Jerusalem to the Dead Sea will drop you off at any of these places, but be sure to tell the driver in advance. You will almost always be able to flag down a bus for the return trip; check pickup location and times with the driver who drops you off.

MITZOKEI DRAGOT ☎02
מצוקי דרגות

This nature reserve, with its soaring cliffs, is for serious hikers only and those who choose to **hike** it will be rewarded with breathtaking views and wonderful solitude. About 20km south of Kumran and Ein Feshkha, a steep, winding road branches off on the right. Buses will go no farther than the turn-off; the only ways to reach the reserve and the hostel are by car or 5km hike. The ascent culminates in a view of soaring cliffs and ravines on one side and the Dead Sea and not-so-distant hills of Jordan on the other. Heed the warnings on the green welcome-board—be sure to carry a trail map and a 20m security rope, both of which are usually available at the office. Climbers and rapellers with their own equipment may wish to take advantage of the excellent conditions in the reserve; for a guide, contact **Giora Eldar** (☎052 397 1774; eldarara@netvision.net. il). You may not begin hiking the *wadi* after 9am, so it is a good idea to stay at the hostel the night before and be on your feet at the crack of dawn. There is no place to refill water bottles; carry enough for the hike.

Owned and managed by the Mitzpeh Shalem Kibbutz a few kilometers away, the **youth hostel 2,** a great alternative to often-booked Ein Gedi accommodations, lies at the top of the winding road. (☎02 994 4777; www.metzoke.il. Kitchen available. Shared tent NIS60 per person; bring your own tent NIS50; 4-person room NIS340 with breakfast; renovated 2-person cabin NIS460. Prices are lower during the week and higher on weekends in high season. Credit cards accepted.) There is also free camping at the entrance to the park.

KALYA BEACHES   ☎02

The walk (or drive) to the beaches passes by row upon row of bombed-out homes and businesses, destroyed by Israel in the 1967 invasion. Taking the first left turn brings you to **New Kalia Beach** (☎02 993 6391; qumran@kalia.org.il), a great daytrip from Jerusalem. (NIS35; students, under 18, and seniors NIS25. Open daily from 8am to sunset.) Slather mud on yourself and wash it off with a float in the sea, then sit on the shaded patio and eat some only mildly overpriced beach food (hamburger NIS25, small beer NIS16; restaurant open daily 11am-5pm).

Farther down the road lie two more private beaches. **Biankini/Siesta Beach** (☎02 940 0033; www.biankini.co.il) is a single beach, hostel, and restaurant with two names. (NIS40, students and children NIS35. Open daily 8am-9pm.) The shaded, grassy lawn is perfect for mud-covered lounging before a dip in the sea. The Moroccan-themed **restaurant ❷** (☎02 940 0266) is open for lunch and dinner, serving salads (NIS37) and a wide variety of meat dishes (spicy sausage plate; NIS45). Unwind at the bar (½L beer NIS20, mixed drinks NIS35) before crashing in a shared tent ❷ (NIS100 per person, NIS45 if you bring your own tent; both prices include admission). For a bit more luxury, get a couple's cabin with air-conditioning, TV, and a minifridge for NIS250.

Next door is the slightly less posh **Neve Midbar**(☎02 994 2781), a similar all-inclusive setup: beach, **restaurant ❷,** and **hostel ❶** all in one. Camping is NIS50, or sleep in an unfurnished hut if you have your own sheets (doubles NIS190; triples NIS285). The meat restaurant has a filling lunch meal for NIS65; expect standard fare like sausages (NIS46), kebab (NIS50), and a few pasta dishes and salads. On weekends, the restaurant fills a freshwater kiddie pool for splashing around. (NIS35-50, students with ISC and children ages 2-12 NIS30-40; higher on weekends and holidays.)

This area is only 25min. from Jerusalem (Rte. 90), and its shores are the least touristed. Take **bus** #480 or 487 from Jerusalem. From Ein Bokek, take bus #421 or 966 (originating from Tel Aviv and Haifa, respectively). Remember to confirm your destination with the bus driver, and make sure you tell him you're going to the beach or else you'll end up at the Kalya kibbutz by Kumran. All of the Kalya beaches are accessible from the same turn-off and bus stop, but you'll still have to walk at least 1km in the sun; bring water.

KUMRAN   ☎02

قمران خربة كومران

About 7km south of Kalya lie the ruins of Kumran (also spelled Qumran), where the Dead Sea Scrolls were discovered. The first—and often only—thing

THE DEAD SEA

ELIEZER BEN-YEHUDA: FATHER OF MODERN HEBREW

Any tourist in Israel will notice that there is a Ben-Yehuda Street in almost every city. (That is, unless you can't read Israeli street signs, in which case you're exempt from pondering this perplexing fact.) No, the Israelis did not confuse their nation-building plans and put the same street in every city. Rather, Eliezer Ben-Yehuda was such an integral leader in the Zionist endeavor that whenever the opportunity presented itself, the Israelis jumped at the chance to name another street in honor of such a significant figure.

It can be said that Ben-Yehuda made a modern Israel a true possibility. In 1865, when he was seventeen, he decided that his life's mission was to unite the Jews on their ancestral soil. Once he moved to Israel and started writing for the first Hebrew paper, he began to coin new words for modern terms whenever necessary. In this way, he slowly created modern Hebrew, the culmination of which was the publication of the first *Complete Dictionary of Ancient and Modern Hebrew*. Without him, and the unifying power of a common language for all Jews, Israel would most likely not exist. That's definitely worthy of a few street names—maybe even an eponymous theme park?

everyone learns about the scrolls is the story of their discovery. In 1947, a young Bedouin looking for a wayward sheep threw a rock into a cliffside cave and heard something break. Upon further inspection, he found a collection of earthenware jars containing 2000-year-old parchment manuscripts. These famed scrolls are an important source of modern understanding of the Bible's origins. The largest, now displayed in the Shrine of the Book at the Israel Museum in Jerusalem (p. 149), is a 7m-long ancient Hebrew text of the Book of Isaiah. Encouraged by the discovery, French archaeologists searched the caves and excavated the foot of the cliffs. By 1956, they had unearthed an entire village of the sect that wrote the Dead Sea Scrolls.

Archaeological evidence suggests that the site was settled as long ago as the eighth century BCE, reinhabited in the second century BCE, temporarily abandoned following an earthquake during the reign of Herod, and completely deserted after the Roman defeat of the Jewish revolt in 70 CE. Historians conclude that the authors of the scrolls were the Essenes, a Jewish sect whose members, disillusioned by the corruption and Hellenization of fellow Jerusalemites, sought refuge in the sands, arriving in Kumran around the end of the Hasmonean Dynasty. The strict and devout Essenes believed that a great struggle would ensue between the Sons of Light (themselves and the angels) and the Sons of Darkness (everyone else). Excavations at Masada suggest that the members of the Kumran sect joined with the Zealots there in the struggle against the Romans.

At the top of the peak is a welcome air-conditioned 5min. dramatization of life as an ancient Essene, narrated in the first person and shown in seven different languages. Following the film, enter the **museum** through the chamber revealed by the rising screen; the museum in turn leads to the start of the path through the ruins. The cave where the scrolls were found is visible from a lookout 100 steps to the left of the site map. The Essenes had a serious problem—they were obsessed with ritual cleansing, but they settled in one of the driest spots on the planet. Look for the cisterns and channels that were used for storage and water transport in the arid climate. Humbly hidden between these water cisterns is the **scriptorium,** where archaeologists believe the scrolls were written. Several desks and inkstands were found there intact and are now on display at the Rockefeller Museum in Jerusalem (p. 148). The path leads through a small **museum** and then outside to the **ruins** themselves. (Essene Compound ☎02

994 2235. Open daily in summer 8am-5pm, in winter 8am-4pm. Most of the site is wheelchair-accessible. NIS20, students NIS17, ages 5-18 NIS9.)

Kumran's huge upscale gift shop sells the usual tourist fare, with a large selection of clothing and jewelry in addition to replica scroll jars and Ahava products. The adjoining **cafeteria ❷** serves hot lunches. (☎02 993 6330. Salad and soup NIS26. Large plate of meat and veggies NIS44. Gift shop open daily 8am-6pm. Cafeteria open 11am-5pm.)

Buses #421, 444, 486, or 487 from either Ein Gedi or Jerusalem will stop upon request at the Essene Compound. A marker right outside the bus stop points toward Kumran, up the steep road on the right. Although the peak is nowhere in sight, the winding road is actually only a 100m hike.

EIN FESHKHA ☎02

עין פשח׳ה

Springs wind through the *wadi*'s reeds and tumble into small pools at the fresh-water bathing spot of Ein Feshka (also called Einot Znkim). Ein Feshkha is the only Dead Sea resort with freshwater ponds adjacent to the sea area. Because of very slick mud and sinkholes, the seaside area is closed: swimming is only permitted in the freshwater pools. It remains the favorite spot of nearby Jer-icho residents and other Palestinians. There are many more men than women, and the females who do show up don't show much. Women will probably be uncomfortable (and make others uncomfortable) without modest covering. There are showers, drinking water, a picnic area, and plenty of Dead Sea mud. (3km south of Kumran. ☎02 994 23 55. Open daily 8am-5pm. NIS25, students NIS21, children NIS13. The park service offers tours of the closed areas of the park Sept.-June F-Sa 10am, noon, and 2pm.)

SOUTHERN DEAD SEA

MOUNT SODOM AND THE FLOUR CAVE ☎08

הר סדום   جبل السدوم

About 74km to the southeast of Be'er Sheva, near the shores of the Dead Sea, is the glaringly white salt mountain, Haar Sodom. This is the Biblical site of Sodom and Gomorah, the two cities so wicked and sexually promiscuous that God resolved to strike them down. God decided to save Lot and his family, but ordered them not to look back at the carnage as they left. Lot's wife took a peek and turned into a pillar of salt (Genesis 19:26).

The Flour Cave is tucked out of direct view from Mt. Sodom. Within the site, the unpaved road forks. Go left and continue on the red-marked "Flour Cave" path that eventually leads to a parking lot (marked by a green sign) near the cave. The cave is at the end of a curving trail of high, smooth walls of light-colored sediment left behind by the lake that was a precursor to the Dead Sea. Be forewarned that these white rocks are unyieldingly bright in the sun-light and magnify the merciless daytime heat, so bring along water, sunglasses, sunscreen, and a head covering. It is a 10min. walk through the white-walled trail to the cave itself (marked by a sign), where the dark, cool, and heavy air provides an escape from the dead-on rays of the sun. Bring a flashlight for the pitch-black cave. The short, steep ascent at the end of the cave will leave you about a mile to the right as you face the parking lot.

The site can be reached only by **car.** From Be'er Sheva, head southeast on Rte. #25 (toward Dimona) then north (toward Jerusalem) on Rte. #90, past the industrial complex of the Dead Sea Works. From Arad, head southeast on Rte. #31 (toward Neve Zohar) then south (toward Eilat) on Rte. #90. From either direction, a small orange sign points to the Flour Cave and Sodom Mountain. The turnoff, across from Dead Sea Works, is a small dirt road with a sign immediately in front of it. To reach Mt. Sodom, take a right onto the blue road from the 1st fork and another right onto the black road. It is possible to drive all the way up to the lookout point on Mt. Sodom, which has a captivating view of the Dead Sea Works and the seemingly frozen blue water below. Alternatively, continue past the Flour Cave entrance for about 1.5km. From the lookout point, **hike** the steep and winding "Stairway Trail" downward, starting at the blue-marked steps to the left.

ADDING INSALT TO INJURY. Dead Sea water is powerful stuff. When it's good, it may cure arthritis and psoriasis, but when it's bad, it's like applying an acid aftershave. If Dead Sea water gets in your eyes, you're in for several minutes of painful blindness. Rinse your eyes immediately in the fresh-water showers, found on all beaches. Don't shave the morning before you go swimming; the water will sear minor scrapes. And, of course, resist the urge to taste it.

EIN BOKEK ☎08

עין בוקק

About 15km south of Masada, Ein Bokek, hemmed in by hordes of luxury hotels, international tour-groups, and racks upon racks of postcards, is the gaudy cubic zirconia in the tiara of Dead Sea beaches. For all the glitzy tourist-wooing of this most crowded of Dead Sea beaches, it is still a good spot for some old fashioned fun: floating and coating.

Entering from the main (northern) entrance, you'll be greeted first by a security gate, followed by a massive rotating McDonald's sign. Welcome to Ein Bokek. In the tentlike building topped by the McDonald's sign is an **Aroma Cafe ❷** offering free Wi-Fi as well as a variety of mid-priced sandwiches (NIS30) and salads (NIS32). (☎08 995 4021. Open daily 8am-11pm.) The **McDonald's** next door is comparable in price and astonishingly popular with the tour bus and luxury hotel crowd.

Farther down the street, you'll see a row of minimarts and cosmetics shops. The best selection can be found at the **MixMarket** (☎08 658 4672; open daily 8am-11pm), a grocery store carrying everything from camp stoves to obscure Israeli wine and hard alcohol, in addition to the standard selection of Dead Sea cosmetics. Inside is a small **falafel stand** serving standard fare at only slightly inflated prices. (Falafel NIS15. Large shawarma plate NIS42.)

At the far end of this building you'll find the **Ahava Factory Store** (☎08 995 2073), which stocks the complete Ahava line at a 30% discount. (Open daily 9am-10:30pm.) Next door is the indoor/outdoor **Nirka Bar and Restaurant** (☎08 995 4050), with slightly cheaper drinks than the surrounding hotel bars (Gold-star NIS34 per L) and a decent selection of pricey sandwiches. (Avocado NIS33. Tuna NIS36. Open daily from noon to the last customer.) Just across a short stretch of beach you'll find the **Hordus Center,** with a Burger King, pricey patio bar and restaurant, and cosmetics store. Inside the cosmetics store you'll find a small **stand** with the cheapest falafel in Ein Bokek. (☎08 995 6357. Falafel

NIS10. Open daily from 6am to the last customer). The bar has parties with DJs most Friday and Saturday nights during high season.

In the last shopping center along the beach, you'll find **Hertz** (☎08 658 4530; open Su-Th 8:30am-5pm, F 8:30am-2pm), where you can rent a car for US$60-80 per day. In the other side of the shopping center is the **tourist information office** for the whole dead sea region (☎08 997 5010; open Su-Th 9am-4pm, F 9am-3pm). Use of the beach and outdoor showers is free (8am-5pm), and a package of mineral-rich mud from beachside vendors costs NIS15.

MOSHAV NEOT HA-KIKKAR ☎08
מושב נאות הככר

About 20km south of rowdy Ein Bokek, Moshav Neot ha-Kikkar is a desert of serenity and desolation. The ominous "Dead Sea Fish" signs along the way refer to high-tech pools managed by the *moshav*, which specializes in state-of-the-art desert agricultural technology and experimentation.

What makes this *moshav* peaceful also makes it difficult for the impulsive traveler: everything must be scheduled in advance. There is a small artist quarter, which keeps irregular hours based on the number of tourists in the area. An enthusiastic guide named Uzi Barak (☎052 899 1146) runs the **Cycle Inn** (☎08 655 2828), a combination bike shop and guest house. Rent a mountain bike (NIS120 per day) to hit the fantastic trails around the *moshav* or near Mt. Sodom. The guest house caters primarily to groups, but there is also an option of renting a four-person room (450NIS).

In a **car,** take Rte. 90 toward Sodom until the Arava junction, passing the Dead Sea Works plant on the left and the southern edge of the sea. The Eilat-bound **bus** from Jerusalem or Tel Aviv will stop at the junction upon request. Make a left and follow the road for about 10km, until the entrance to the *moshav*.

THE NEGEV

הנגב النقب

"Wisdom goes with south. It is written: Whoever seeks wisdom, south he shall go."
—David Ben-Gurion

The Bible says that Abraham began his spiritual journey by leaving his home and heading south to the Negev (Genesis 21:32-33). The imposing mountains, majestic canyons, and barren flatlands of the region are just as awe-inspiring today as they were in biblical times. Long considered a wasteland of Bedouin tents and dusty archaeologists, the Negev is entering mainstream Israeli life as new building projects absorb waves of immigrants and high-tech agriculture fulfills the biblical prophecy of making the desert bloom. Visionaries like David Ben-Gurion cherished the Negev's rugged beauty and dreamed of developing the region into one of the most prosperous parts of Israel. Today, hikers, meditators, and adventurous travelers are discovering this beauty, while drip-irrigated citrus groves, flower farms, and instant boom towns are coaxing its resources into fruition. The ruins of Nabatean grandeur glowing on the hilltops along the ancient spice route are today seen less as relics than as inspiration. The Negev covers roughly half of Israel's territory, but for many years the region received only a small fraction of Israel's tourists. In recent years, tourism has skyrocketed, but these 12,000 sq. km of desert have become no more accommodating. Temperatures soar at midday—those caught without a hat and water will see vultures circling overhead in a matter of minutes. Desert outfitters recommend that hikers drink one liter of water for every hour in the sun.

It's possible to tour the desert on Egged seats: air-conditioned bus lines run through all major towns and past important sites. However, buses may be infrequent and late, and some sites and trailheads are only accessible by car. Renting a car or taking a guided tour are excellent options for those who can afford it. However, a more exciting way to see the Negev is on a camel or jeep tour.

HIGHLIGHTS OF THE NEGEV

PEER into the largest crater in the world next to **Mitzpe Ramon** (p. 365).

POKE AROUND at Be'er Sheva's crowded **Bedouin Market** (p. 353).

PRETEND you're in *Jesus Christ Superstar* at the **Avdat** ruins (p. 365).

BE'ER SHEVA

☎08

באר שבע بئر السبع

Be'er Sheva has a long-standing tradition as a point of replenishment and departure for people traversing the Negev. In recent years, however, increasing numbers of immigrants have decided to settle down in the city rather than just pass through: pre-fab apartments are as unavoidable and constricting as the spandex in Eilat discotheques. Despite the din of constant traffic and the

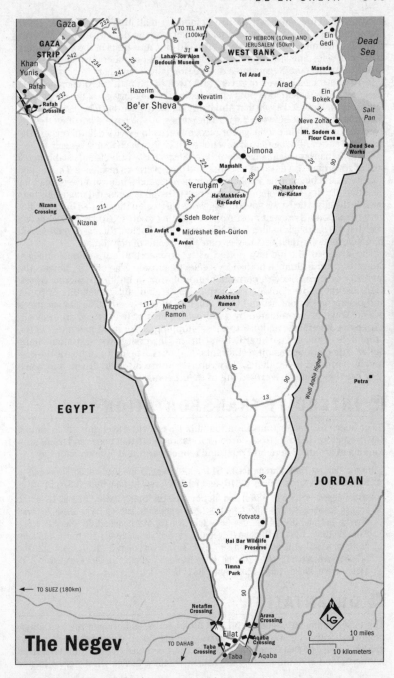

The Negev

overpowering presence of a glassed-in monster mall in the town center, Be'er Sheva retains a few pockets of romance, such as the old city and the famous Thursday morning Bedouin market. The old city, museums in the surrounding area, and Be'er Sheva's hopping nightlife make it both a convenient base for short forays into the Negev and a destination in its own right.

Be'er Sheva means "well of seven" and "well of the oath" in Arabic; the Bible (Genesis 21:25-31) supports both etymologies. As the story goes, the servants of King Abimelekh seized a well that Abraham claimed to have dug. The dispute ended with an oath of peace between the warring parties, in which Abraham offered seven ewes to Abimelekh in exchange for recognition as the well's rightful owner. The supposed site of Abraham's well now houses the city's main tourist office.

The Ottomans proclaimed modern Be'er Sheva a city in 1906 and established a seat of government, a mosque, a school, and the governor's residence. They hoped the city would function as a political, commercial, and administrative magnet for the nomadic Negev Bedouin, who continue to dwell in tents and makeshift huts outside the city. The Israeli government would prefer it if they settled in towns, but inter-tribal politics prevent most from consenting to do so. Today, Be'er Sheva's over 160,000 residents, hailing from Morocco, Syria, Poland, Russia, Argentina, and Ethiopia are doing their best to welcome the streams of newcomers.

The streets of the old city, dotted with Ottoman buildings, shops, and restaurants, offer a glimpse of the city's eclectic mosaic. The old city houses the majority of Be'er Sheva's permanent population in hulking concrete apartment buildings overlooking vast expanses of sand and gravel; bits of paper and plastic bags float around this area like tumbleweeds. The denser areas of Old Town are dominated by window displays of overpriced sportswear, expensive handbags, and electronics; shopping is the local pastime. On the other side of the town center is Ben-Gurion University, where students hang out at cafes, ethnic fusion restaurants, and bars. The cultural life of the city revolves around its students; they rarely venture into Old Town, and when they do, they come in a crowd full of their peers.

▆ INTERCITY TRANSPORTATION

Be'er Sheva is a major transportation hub: it's easy to travel directly to almost any destination in Israel from the central station. Note that buses and trains stop running at around 3-4pm on Friday and reopen at around 5pm on Saturday.

Trains: Central Train Station (☎03 611 7000), next to the bus station. Trains run to **Dimona** (every hr. 6am-9pm, NIS10) and **Tel Aviv** (every hr. 6am-9pm, NIS25.5).

Buses: Egged (☎03 694 8888) and **Metropoline** (☎*5900; call 03 623 5918 for the English-speaking central office) are the 2 bus companies serving Be'er Sheva. To: **Arad** (Egged 384 and 385, 4 per day 6am-3pm, NIS16; Metropoline 388, every ½-1½hr. 6am-12:30am, NIS11); **Dimona** (Egged 48, 49, 56; 30min.; every 10-15min. 6:30am-7:30pm; NIS10.60); **Eilat** (Egged 393, 394, 397; 3½hr.; every 1-2hr. 7:30am-1:20am; NIS59); **Jerusalem** (Egged 470, 2hr., every hr. 6am-7:20pm); and **Tel Aviv** (Egged 370, 1½hr., every 30min.-1hr. 5:45am-8pm, NIS15).

▆ ORIENTATION

The city's **central bus station** is on **Eilat Street**, situated between the two major neighborhoods: the somewhat unattractive **old city** to the southwest and the student areas of **Ben-Gurion University** to the northeast. This commercialized no-man's-land is dominated by the **Kanyon Shopping Center,** whose glass facade

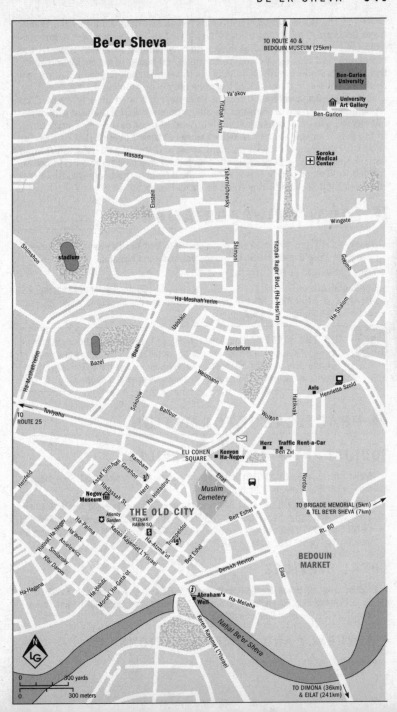

Be'er Sheva

TO ROUTE 40 &
BEDOUIN MUSEUM (25km)

Ben-Gurion
University

University
Art Gallery

Ben-Gurion

Soroka
Medical
Center

Ya'akov

Yitzhak Avinu

Tshernichowsky

Masada

Einstein

Wingate

Shimshon

stadium

Shimoni

Golomb

Ha-Meshah'rerim

Ha-Shalom

Ha-Meshah'rerim

Ussishkin

Montefiore

Bialik

Bazel

Weizmann

Hatikvah

Avis

Henrietta Szold

Sokolow

Balfour

Wolfson

TO
ROUTE 25

Tuviyahu

Herzfeld

Rambam

Assaf Simhon
Gershon

Herzl

Ha-Histadrut

Hadassah St.

Negev
Museum

Allenby
Garden

THE OLD CITY

Ha-Palma

Ha-avot

YITZHAK
RABIN SQ.

Ha-Atzma'ut

Keren Kayemet L'Yisrael

Trumpeldor

ELI COHEN
SQUARE

Kenyon
Ha-Negev

Eilat

Muslim
Cemetery

Beit Eshel

Herz

Traffic Rent-a-Car

Ben Zvi

Nordau

TO BRIGADE MEMORIAL (5km)
& TEL BE'ER SHEVA (7km)

Rt. 60

BEDOUIN
MARKET

Hativat Ha-Negev

Anielewicz

Smilansky

Kfar Darom

Ha-Halutz

Mordei Ha-Geta'ot

Bet Eshel

Derekh Hevron

Eilat

Ha-Hagana

Abraham's
Well

Ha-Melaha

Keren Kayemet L'Yisrael

Nahal Be'er Sheva

N

0   300 yards

0   300 meters

TO DIMONA (36km)
& EILAT (241km)

Yitzhak Rager Blvd. (Ha-Nesi'im)

overlooks the three-way intersection of **Tuviyah Boulevard,** Eilat St., and **Yitshak Rager Boulevard.** The Ben-Gurion University of Be'er Sheva is a few minutes from the city center on Yitzhak Rager Blvd., separated from Old Town by the bus station and a string of cheap restaurants and malls. To get to the university from the bus station, walk past the post office on Yitzhak Rager Blvd. until you reach Sderot David Ben-Gurion; the university is on your right.

The old **Muslim Cemetery,** sitting in a wasteland of fenced sand, is across Eilat St. behind the central bus station. On the opposite side lies the neat grid of the old city: a haven for pedestrians and the seat of most of the city's attractions. In the center of the old city is **Keren Kayemet L'Yisrael Street** (Kakal or KKL for short), an outdoor mall between **Herzl Street** and **Mordel ha-Geta'ot Street** lined with shops, kiosks, and restaurants which are especially busy on Fridays. To reach the old city from the bus station, walk in front of the *kanyon* to Eli Cohen St., cross Eilat St., and follow Herzl St. or ha-Halutz St.

⊨ LOCAL TRANSPORTATION

Buses: Bus 13 runs from the central bus station to **Beit Yatzhiv** every 20min. Buses 7 and 8 run along Ben-Gurion St. toward the **university** and **hospital.**

Taxis: Taxi Gan Zvi (☎08 641 4142).

Car Rental: Avis (☎08 627 1777). NIS33 per day, NIS165 per day for drivers under 23. **Hertz** (☎08 628 8828). NIS194 per day, NIS274 per day for drivers under 23. Both open Su-Th 8am-6pm, F 8am-2pm.

OFF THE METER. Unlike their counterparts in Eilat and other more touristy destinations, cab drivers in Be'er Sheva will sometimes offer you a better flat-rate deal than the meter provides. Have an idea of the distance to your destination beforehand, and don't immediately reject flat rates.

⏏ PRACTICAL INFORMATION

TOURIST AND FINANCIAL SERVICES

Tourist Office: (☎08 623 4613), in the visitor's center at Abraham's well. Sells maps of the city (NIS5). Open Su-Th 8am-4pm.

Bank: Bank Leumi (☎03 514 94 00), next to the post office. Open M and Th 8:30am-1pm and 4-6:15pm,; Tu-W 8:30am-2:30pm, F 8:30am-12:30pm. **Bank ha-Paolim** (☎03 567 4999), left of Bank Leumi on Yitzhak Rager Blvd. **ATM** available. Open Su and Tu-W 8:30am-1:15pm; M and Th 8:30am-1pm and 4-6:30pm.

LOCAL SERVICES

English-Language Bookstore: Steimatsky (☎08 623 03 01), in the mall. Small selection of English pulp fiction, travel guides, and a few classics. Open Su-Th 9am-10pm, F 9am-3pm, Sa 9-11pm. Credit cards accepted.

EMERGENCY AND COMMUNICATIONS

Police: 30 Hertzl St. (☎08 646 2744).

Pharmacy:Super-Pharm (☎08 628 1371), in the mall. Open Su-Th 8am-11:30pm, F 8am-5pm, Sa 5-11:30pm.

Hospital: (☎08 640 01 11), on Ben-Gurion and Eilat St. near the university. Open Su-Th 8am-4pm. Emergency Room open 24hr.

Internet Access: There is no internet cafe in all of Be'er Sheva. The post office and the Open University in the Beit Yatziv Youth Hostel (see **Accomodations,** below) have free Wi-Fi.

Post Office: (☎08 629 5897), on the intersection of Ben Zvi and Yitzhak Rager Blvd. across from the mall. **Post Restante, currency exchange, Western Union,** international calling, fax, and free Wi-Fi. Recharges prepaid SIM cards without a service fee. Open Su-M and Th 8am-6pm, W 8am-1:30pm, F 8am-noon.

￼ ACCOMMODATIONS

The accommodations in Be'er Sheva are dismal, a reflection of the city's dearth of tourists: almost everyone takes the first bus out once they arrive. Luckily, the university provides a potential solution: student housing is largely vacant during the summer, and students may be willing to let you stay in their rooms or apartments. While no official agency coordinates this informal scheme, if you relate your housing plight to enough people in the student area, there's a good chance that you'll receive an invitation.

Beit Yatziv Youth Hostel (HI; ☎08 627 7444; beityatziv.co.il), on the northern end of ha-Atzmaut St. in Old Town. A standard HI behemoth. The laminated faux-wood desks, white plastic faucets, and undecorated white walls make this hostel feel like an institution, albeit a spotless and air-conditioned one. The courtyard and swimming pool are a welcome addition. Breakfast included. Singles NIS200; double NIS300. Cash only. ❸

Negev Hotel (☎08 627 8744), 2 blocks north of the river on ha-Atzmaut St. The Negev Hotel packs in much of Be'er Sheva's local flavor: the rooms overlook either the concrete courtyard or the dirty streets, the city noise is omnipresent, and everything smells vaguely of smoke. But the location is good, and the front desk sells beer to ease the pain of paying so much for your room. Singles and doubles NIS200; triples NIS250. Cash only. ❷

￼ FOOD

Be'er Sheva has a wealth of cheap food options. The best values are found near the university, where well-traveled students put their knowledge of ethnic cuisines to work. Closer to Old Town, competition between innumerable falafel stands near the bus station has incited a price race to the bottom. The food court in the mall features a slightly more diverse array of fast-food options, including a noodle counter that isn't half bad. For groceries, visit the **supermarket,** one block north of the post office on Yitzhak Rager Blvd. Prices for its large selection of bulk food beat those of the Old Town mini-markets. (☎08 623 5905. Open Su-Th 8am-9pm, F 8am-5pm. Credit cards accepted.)

Little India (☎08 648 9801), at the intersection of Joseph Klausner St. and Emanuel Ringelblum St., across from the student dorms. It's surprising to find Indian food this good in the maze of concrete and rebar that is Be'er Sheva, but you'll believe it when you taste it. The tennis-ball-sized *Batata awara* (curried potato dumplings with hummus flour) are a steal at NIS15 for 3. Cool off with a mango lassi (NIS12) spiced with cardamom. Entrees NIS28-30. Open Su-Th noon-11pm, F noon-4pm. Cards accepted. ❶

Suyami Sushi House and Bar (☎08 649 5511), next to Little India. Taking a cue from its neighbor, Suyami dots its ethnic cuisine with Israeli influences. The combo meal (2 fish

THE LOCAL STORY

FRUIT, FISH, AND FOSSIL WATER

Driving into Be'er Sheva, you'll pass a huge fruit market selling an amazing variety of fresh, locally-grown produce. If you go to any bar in the student area, you'll be presented with a great selection of sushi. Seeing as Be'er Sheva is in the middle of the Negev desert, which averages 2-10 inches of rainfall annually, this begs the question: where is all of this fruit and fish coming from?

As it turns out, the Negev actually has a large supply of brackish "fossil water" in aquifers beneath the desert floor. The water was previously thought to be useless, but recent research has yielded techniques for productive aquaculture and agriculture in the Negev.

The brackish water is pumped into plastic fish tanks, where trout and other species breed rapidly due to the relatively high water temperature. It is flushed through the tank, carrying the nitrogenous waste from the fish with it, and then used to water crops. The fish waste makes for an ideal fertilizer, and the specially-engineered crops thrive on the salty, mineral-rich water.

In other words, there's a good chance that the raw fish you're eating helped fertilize the cucumber it's wrapped with. Delicious.

rolls and 1 veggie roll; NIS45) might be the best deal in town. Sushi rolls NIS22 for 8 pieces. Imported beer NIS19. Open Su-Th noon-11pm, Sa 8-11pm. Credit cards accepted. ❷

Meksikani (☎08 823 3946), just south of the pedestrian area on Kakal. As the night grows old, Meksikani serves its hearty wraps to an increasingly intoxicated crowd. It's hard to imagine food better suited for satisfying the drunk munchies than the eponymous wrap: guacamole, beef steak, spicy salsa, and spicy salad wrapped in a freshly-made flour tortilla. Standard wrap NIS25, monstrous double wrap NIS37. Open Su-Th 11am-4am, Sa 8:30pm-4am. Credit cards accepted. ❶

Gilda Be'er Sheva (☎08 627 7072), on the corner of ha-Halutz and Hassadah St. Wonderful gelato made fresh from scratch daily. Standards include 10 kinds of chocolate alongside inventive flavors like carrot fro-yo. NIS7.50 for 1 scoop, NIS15.50 for 2 scoops. Open Su-Th 10am-midnight, F 9am-5pm, Sa 10am-midnight. Cash only. ❶

Eztration, outside the bus station. Serves surprisingly fresh breakfast bagels (NIS6-10) and espresso. The falafel (NIS10) is predictably cheap and delicious. Open Su-Th 5am-10pm, F 5am-4pm. Cash only. ❶

Kampai (☎08 655 6063; kapai.big@gmail.com), in the Big center. Authentic sushi with just a hint of fusion. Try the California yams (tempura-fried yams, asparagus, avocado, and sesame seeds; NIS25 per roll) or the extra-thick tempura-fried spicy tuna roll (NIS38). The bartenders concoct an inventive array of mixed drinks from over 220 imported alcohols. Sake Take (sake, sour mix, and grapes) NIS26. Open daily noon-1am. Credit cards accepted. ❷

Zagdon Falafel, in the Kakal predestrian mall. Top your own falafel (NIS14) with fixings such as salad and grilled eggplant at the expansive self-service condiment bar. Open Su-Th 8am-9pm, F 8am-5pm. Cash only. ❶

Maison de la Baguette (☎08 627 1497), on ha-Atzmaut and Bet Eshel. Large selection of fresh-baked breads and pastries. Open Su-Th 24hr., F 3pm-midnight, Sa midnight-6pm. ❶

◎ SIGHTS

A good way to begin your visit is to take a self-guided walking tour of the 3000-year-old city, which houses some of the finest examples of Ottoman architecture in Israel. Start at the **tourist office,** which stands on the site of Abraham's Well, at the corner of Derekh Hevron and Keren Kayemet L'Yisrael St. Here you can purchase maps of Be'er

Sheva (NIS5). The **Ben-Gurion University Student Association** provides information about the wealth of summer music festivals and cultural events. The calendar on their website (http://bgu4u.co.il) is primarily in Hebrew, but look around for updated phone numbers (the management changes as students graduate) and give them a call for English-language assistance. Alternatively, head over to the **Zlotowski Student Center** on campus and ask around for information.

BEDOUIN MARKET. Established in 1905, the famous Thursday market is a nirvana for bargain hunters. Amid the clamor of screaming vendors are cheap Bedouin food and excellent garments. Years ago, the Bedouin hawked camels, sheep, and other wares at the end of agricultural seasons and during winter. Today, they hawk year-round and have added snow globes and T-shirts to their much-ballyhooed wares. As the market progresses south, the quantity of rusty cans, scraps of paper, and dust increases, along with the smell of dung from the live animals for sale. It is here, however, that the market's real gems hide: beaten copperware, Bedouin robes, fabrics, rugs, and ceramic items. Arrive early to witness the trading at its peak and choose from a more varied selection of Bedouin goods. Many of the Bedouin here speak English, and some may compliment your beautiful eyes while charging six times the going rate for olive-wood camels. *(On the south side of the city off Eilat St., south of the intersection with Derekh Hevron. Most local buses will stop at the market upon request. By foot, walk to Eilat St. from the central bus station and cross over to the market. Open Th until early afternoon.)*

 EARLY BIRDS DON'T GET ALL THE WORMS. If you sleep through the Bedouin market on Thursday, don't be alarmed. You have two other options to get nearly identical goods: the market just south of the Muslim cemetery, open daily, sells trinkets and a wonderful selection of fresh fruit, and on Fridays the pedestrian area of Kakal transforms into a lively outdoor mall packed with electronics and souvenirs. Although the *keffiyehs* are replaced with *kippot* and the odor of camel dung with city smoke, the goods are almost identical.

ABRAHAM'S WELL. Dating back to 12th century CE, many believe this well to be the original dug by Abraham. These days, it's not much to look at: the screen-covered hole on the visitor's center patio is much less interesting than the well's history; ask for a free 5min. tour for more information. From June to September, the well serves as an occasional nighttime entertainment venue, hosting storytelling, live music, and dance performances. *(On the corner of Derekh Hevron and Keren Kayemet LeYisrael St. ☎08 623 4613. Open Su-Th 8am-4pm.)*

THE NEGEV MUSEUM OF ART. The residence next to the mosque was built by the Ottomans in 1906 and named Be'er Sheva's City Hall in 1949. Diagonally facing the Governor's House is another Ottoman building, used as a boarding school for Bedouin children during the British mandate and as a Red Crescent hospital during WWI. Together, the buildings make up the Negev Museum, which features contemporary visual and multimedia art exhibits by local and visiting artists. At the entrance, you'll find a small selection of books in English and Hebrew about the history and art of the Negev. Every Monday night, students and professors make a rare trek to Old Town for *shir ve sihakh* (talk and song) in the colorfully-lit museum courtyard. Local musicians play traditional Hebrew songs and are interviewed by a professor from the University's literature department. The event is largely conducted in Hebrew, but all of the students speak English and will be more than happy to translate for you. *(On ha-Atzma'ut St., north of Herzl St. ☎08 620 6570; br7museum@br7.*

org.il. Museum open Su-M and W-Th 8:30am-3:30pm, Tu 8:30am-2pm and 4-6pm, Sa 10am-2pm. Talk and Song M 8:30-10pm. NIS12, students NIS10.)

JOE ALON BEDOUIN MUSEUM. As the Jewish National Fund establishes national parks and plants forests in a deliberate effort to expel Bedouins from their ancestral homeland in the Negev, they simultaneously espouse their commitment to preserving the Bedouin way of life in the Joe Alon Museum. The indoor exhibits showcase all facets of the nomads' traditional lives, from tools and embroidery to medicine and customary desert garb. An audio-visual presentation showcases the famous hospitality of Bedouin culture. In the two outdoor tents, women bake delicious Bedouin bread while men serve coffee and tea and converse with guests. The museum also has an observation tower with a 360° view of the northern Negev. *(Several kilometers north of the tel, on the outskirts of Kibbutz Lahav. Bus #42 (NIS15) goes from Be'er Sheva to the kibbutz twice daily; alternatively, take any bus toward Tel Aviv and ask to be let off at Kibbutz Lahav. The bus will drop you at the junction 15km north of Be'er Sheva along Rte. 40. An orange sign behind the bus stop points down the road in the direction of the kibbutz and museum, which are 8km away. Numbered vehicles from the kibbutz drive by frequently and may offer a lift, or take a taxi (NIS80). After arriving, walk along the asphalt road and follow it to where it curves to the right, or grab another taxi (NIS75). ☎08 991 3322; joealon.org.il. Open Su-Th and Sa 9am-4pm, F 9am-2pm. NIS25.)*

TEL BE'ER SHEVA. Five kilometers northeast of the city are the ruins of a 3000-year-old planned city, recently converted into a national park. One pile of unearthed rubble is an AD second-century Roman fortress, another an eighth-century BCE house, and a third a 12th-century BCE well. The view from the top of the tel's tower is magnificent. *(By car, take Rte. 60 out of the city, and turn right at the set of lights after the gas stations. Taxi NIS40 each way. Bus 388 to Arad and Omer runs by the road that leads to the site (every ½-1hr. 6am-12:30am, NIS8). The walk from the turn-off takes about 30min. There is a roundabout approximately halfway down the road. Keep straight to get to the ruins, which are through a parking lot on the right; an orange sign leads the way. ☎08 646 7286. Open daily 8am-5pm. Last entry 1hr. before closing. NIS13, students NIS12, children NIS7.)*

ISRAELI AIR FORCE MUSEUM. This museum displays over 150 airplanes culled from several generations of Israeli aerial combat, including airplanes from every major operation since Israel's founding. Also on display, somewhat boastfully, are airplanes captured from neighboring countries. The museum has a large collection of anti-aircraft guns, fired during special events and demonstrations. Free guided tours by Israeli soldiers provide information about each of the planes and weapons. *(At the Haterim air force base, 8km west of town on Be'er Sheva-Haterim Rd. City bus 31 stops directly in front of the entrance. Walk up ha-Atzma'ut St. from the youth hostel and cross over the Derekh Joe Alon Highway at its major intersection to reach the bus stop. ☎08 990 6855. Open Su-Th 8am-5pm, F 8am-1pm. NIS28, students and seniors NIS23, children NIS18. Call ahead for free tours and a schedule of anti-aircraft gun demonstrations.)*

OTHER SIGHTS. The **Allenby Garden,** the city's first public garden, was commissioned by the Ottomans in the early 1900s. It was renamed after General Allenby, the leader of the British forces who captured the city from the Ottomans in WWI. Today, the garden serves as a pleasant resting place, secluded from the streets. *(On ha-Atzma'ut St., stroll up the midrakhov from Abraham's Well; the garden is on the left, beyond Herzl St.)* Designed by Israeli artist Dani Karavan, the **Hanegev Palmah Brigade Monument** honors Israeli soldiers who died defending Be'er Sheva and other Negev settlements. The eight symbolic structures overlook Be'er Shiva from 5km northeast of the city. *(On Be'er Sheva-Omer Rd. The most practical way to reach the sight is by taxi (NIS20). Free.)* The **Gan Remez** is a ceramic sculpture garden next to **ha-Jama,** an elegant Turkish mosque. *(Between Hadassah St. and ha-Atzma'ut St.)*

🎵 🎭 ENTERTAINMENT AND NIGHTLIFE

Entertainment, like the rest of the city, is split along a student and non-student divide. Student bars host a social Hebrew and English-speaking crowd; head to whichever bar is hosting happy hour on any given night. The clubs frequented by locals, most of which are outside of town, feature blaring music from live DJs, multiple dance floors, and overpriced drinks. Most bars and clubs open around 9 or 10pm but don't get going until after midnight, especially on Fridays. Closing times are flexible ("last customer"), usually around 3-5am. A nexus of Israel's underground rave scene, Be'er Shiva attracts some of the most popular trance DJs in the world. These overnight desert parties are planned on short notice and spread by word of mouth among the students, but be advised that some of these events may be illegal. Mid-July brings the fully legal **Smilansky Fest:** three days of drinking, shopping, music and parties.

For more low-key entertainment, there is a **movie theater** downstairs in the mall (showings daily 5, 7:30, and 9:50pm; mostly English with Hebrew subtitles; NIS35) and a hookah bar, **Diwan,** across from Little India in the university, where students often relax before hitting the clubs (☎054 461 8281; open Su-F noon-1am, Sa 8:30pm-1am).

🍸 **Einstein/Villabar,** in the student athletic center on Ben-Gurion St. and Uri Zvhi. This ambiguously-named establishment is packed on weekends, as sweaty 20-somethings bump and grind to American hip-hop and electronica. You'll probably need to fight your way to the glowing blue bar. Mixed drinks NIS30-45. Sushi rolls NIS22-27. Open daily for lunch noon-6pm. Bar open 9:45pm-late.

🍸 **Baraka** (☎08 628 7111), on Trumpeldor and Hadassah. The beating heart of Old City nightlife, Baraka features a different theme every night but maintains loud music and dancing as its common denominator. Arak and grapefruit, a local favorite, NIS12. Bottled imported beer NIS18. M-Tu live music. W student night. Th soldier's night. F Old City party (a.k.a. Old People Party; ages 22+, cover NIS25-45). Sa 4-9pm weekend afterparty Sa (NIS20) followed by dancing. Drink discounts W-F before 1am.

Forum (☎08 626 2555; label-dan@gmail.com), a short (NIS20) cab ride from Old Town in the industrial area. Hosts Be'er Sheva's biggest and loudest nightly dance party. Spares no expense: multiple dance floors, a hulking DJ stage with lasers and smoke machines, the

GIVING BACK

THE WELL OF FULLNESS

Even in the land of milk and honey, there are people who go hungry. The founders of **Be'er Sova Restaurant for the Needy,** the first and only soup kitchen in Be'er Sheva, know this all too well. Each day, they dole out 500 hot meals, distribute 400 cold meals to needy children, and provide 100 families with monthly food parcels. The name Be'er Sova is a play on Be'er Sheva, and translates to "the well of fullness."

The restaurant started as a small organization, cooking only 50 meals per day served largely to theose with drug problems and the homeless. It quickly became clear, however, that many more people were in need of food and that Be'er Sova was the only place that could provide it. Since 1999, circumstances have worsened for many people in the Be'er Sheva area and poverty rates are rapidly climbing. Be'er Sova's restaurant has been so successful that the organization is ramping up its non-culinary endeavors. They have recently created programs to provide educational opportunities, as well as "empowerment courses" to help women find jobs and legal aid.

Because Be'er Sova is a non-denominational organization and receives no aid from the government, they are always looking for volunteers.

P.O. Box 6043, Be'er Sheva 84160 (☎08 641 2544 or 610 9407; www.beersova.org.il).

largest bar in Israel, and fireworks shows on busy nights. Beer NIS25-35. Cover after midnight NIS35-65. Open 11:30pm-late.

Manga (☎08 649 9951), in the teacher's center on Yitzhak Rager. The most popular student bar in town. A mix of American alternative and indie music keeps the crowd bobbing their heads, but drinking takes priority over dancing. M and Th 8-10pm 2-for-1 drinks. Personal pizza NIS24. Sushi rolls NIS20-25. Free Wi-Fi. Open Su, Tu-W, F-Sa 9pm-late; M and Th 8pm-late.

Draft, in the BIG center just southeast of town, under the "Great Shape" sign. A fitness center during the day, Draft only gets sweatier after the sun goes down. A DJ spins European-style techno and American pop remixes to a sea of tight T-shirts, gold chains, and gelled hair. Slightly younger, local crowd. Beer NIS25. W student night. Cover NIS10. Open daily 10:30pm-3am.

Razza (☎050 904 0101), in the commercial center, just before the teacher's center on Yitzhak Rager Blvd. A newly-opened bar serving only students, Razza is on the rowdier end of the spectrum, perhaps as a consequence of its unbeatable drink deals. Personal pizza or burger with beer NIS29 until 10:30pm. Su NIS5 refills on all draught beers. Th bottomless drink night; beers NIS49, mixed drinks NIS59. Open daily 9pm-late.

Balcony (☎08 665 1811), on the corner of Hertzl and Gershot St. This Old Town bar with Old Town prices draws an older crowd. Balcony's laid-back outdoor patio is perfect for sipping an appletini (NIS33) while picking at a large specialty salad (NIS47). The garlic bread plate with cream cheese and vegetables (NIS28) is a favorite. Th Hebrew karaoke. Open Su-Th 10am-1am, Sa 9pm-1am. Credit cards accepted.

Coca, in the cluster of bars near the student athletic center. An Irish-themed pub with the liquor to prove it. Try the whiskey chocolate (NIS10) or the Coca (Southern Comfort, peach schnapps, and strawberry; NIS35). Draught beer NIS24. Happy hour daily 8-9pm. Open Su-F from noon to last customer, Sa from 8pm to last customer.

Munchilla Shanti Bar (☎052 262 6266), across from Coca. Students sit on Bedouin-style cushions and order *shisha* and drinks from the well-stocked bar. Burger and beer NIS36. M Israeli music night attracts a large crowd. Sa trance and electronica. Open Su-Th and Sa 8:30pm-2:30am.

▶ DAYTRIPS FROM BE'ER SHEVA

DIMONA

דימונה

Buses run to Dimona from Eilat (393 and 394, 3hr., every 2-4hr. 5am-1am, NIS55) and Be'er Sheva (56, 48, 49; 30min., every 30min. 6:30am-7:30pm, NIS10.60).

Since immigrating in 1969, the **Hebrew Israelite Community,** referred to as the Black Hebrews by non-members, has been working to fuse the ideals of religious and communal living. A unique sect of English-speaking immigrants, the Hebrew Israelites trace their roots to ancient Israel. The community, which bases its religion on the revelations of spiritual leader Ben-Ami Ben Israel (formerly Ben Carter), believes that the ancestors of black slaves in antebellum America lived in Israel until they were forced to migrate to Western Africa after the Roman onslaught in 70 CE. Ben Israel's vision included a return to the Holy Land; the group's vanguard left Chicago in 1967 and spent two-and-a-half years in Liberia before coming to Israel. Another group from Chicago followed in 1970 and a third exodus took place from Detroit in 1973. The Israeli government at first refused to grant them citizenship unless they converted to Judaism, but the Hebrew Israelites insisted they were already

Jews. The government and the sect did not reach an agreement normalizing the community's legal status until 1990.

The original community of about 100 pilgrims has blossomed into a 1200-person village; branches of the community in other areas in Israel bring the total population of Hebrew Israelites to over 2000. Children are born under the care of community midwives. Several families live together in one home and share household responsibilities, and community members come together to make their own clothes and food. Their religious beliefs require them to wear only natural fabrics and prohibit them from eating animal parts or products, white sugar, and white flour. The grace and peacefulness of their small village has to be seen to be believed.

Though the village welcomes solo wanderers, a tour can be much more informative; call ahead to schedule a free one. (☎052 391 0858; ask for Ateruh Yafah. Donations accepted). At **Boutique Africa**, leave an imprint of your foot and the full-time Sole Brother will custom design a pair of shoes for you, ready for pick-up in two weeks. (Rush orders available. Open Su-Th 10am-2pm and 4-7pm; F 9am-2pm.) **Toflé** sells beautifully colored garments and cloth from Ghana. (NIS80-550. Open Su-Th 10am-2pm and 4-7pm; F 9am-2pm.). The community restaurant, **Soul Food Eats ❶**, is a blessing for protein-starved vegans. Entrees include delicious tofu sandwiches (NIS15) and home-cooked specialties like fried tofu, bean curd roast, and grilled yams (NIS24). (Open Su-Th 10am-2pm and 4-7pm, F 9am-noon.). The boutiques and restaurant keep to their posted schedules only loosely; if they're closed, it probably won't be long before they open up. The village also has a three-room **guest house ❷**. (Rooms US$35. Call Ateruh Yafah ☎052 391 0858 several days in advance to make arrangements.).

Every summer, the Hebrew Israelites host the two-day **Naisik ha-Shalom Music Festival**, which highlights community entertainment, Hebrew Israelite singers, and Israeli bands. Additional concerts and festivals are scattered throughout the summer. Musical groups from Dimona tour the country when they're not performing their hip-hop renditions of traditional Jewish texts at home.

Dimona's final claim to fame lies in the mysterious factory a few kilometers to the east. Although tour guides claim that the ominous barbed wire fences and signs forbidding photography hide a "nuclear weapons site," the reality is much less exciting: the edifice houses a film factory.

MAMSHIT

ממשית

Buses shuttling between Be'er Sheva and the Dead Sea stop 1km outside Mamshit, along the main highway, as does bus #394 to Eilat (1¼hr., every 1½hr., NIS19). Call ☎08 655 33 22 for taxi service (10min, NIS40-50). Be sure to tell the bus or cab driver to stop at Atar Mamshit, the Nabatean ruins, not the new cinderblock city several km to the west. ☎08 655 6478. Park open Sa-Th 8am-5pm, F 8am-4pm; entrance to campsites always open. Free brochure of the site includes a small map. NIS20, students NIS17, children NIS9.

The sun-bleached sandstone ruins of ancient Mamshit, the only city in the Negev that was walled-in on all sides, lie 15km east of Dimona. Built in the first century CE, Mamshit functioned as a garrison town in the Roman and Byzantine periods. From Mamshit, one of the six Nabatean cities in Israel, the Nabateans controlled the Petra-Gaza spice route stretching from India to Rome. On one side is a vast desert plain; on the other is the precipitous canyon of **Nahal Mamshit** (Mamshit River). Following attacks by desert nomads in the sixth century CE, the city was destroyed and abandoned. Particularly impressive among the ruins are the **Eastern Church**, the second-century CE tower which once guarded the dams of the river below, and the mansion, or "House of the Affluent." Be sure to take a look down into the canyon from the observation point.

To view the canyon from a camel's back with a Bedouin guide, head to the **Mamshit Camel Ranch,** 1km east of the ruins. Overnight stays at the ranch are available for groups of 20 or more. For smaller groups and solo travelers, a campsite with toilets, showers, and a small restaurant lies just inside the gate to the park. (NIS30 per person, Bedouin tent NIS45 per person; includes entrance to the park. Credit cards accepted.)

HA-MAKHTESH HA-KATAN AND HA-MAKHTESH HA-GADOL

המכתש הקטן והמכתש הגדול

The best way to reach both sites is to rent a car and drive 40min. southeast of Be'er Sheva toward Dimona (see Car Rental,p. 350).

Just outside of Be'er Sheva stands the magnificent coupling of the Small (ha-Katan) and Big (ha-Gadol) Craters: a geological formation that makes for steep but rewarding hikes. Ha-Makhtesh ha-Gadol offers mostly large-scale scenery to drive by and admire from a distance, while ha-Makhtesh ha-Katan has more places to park and explore on foot. Before hiking, contact the tourist office in Arad (opposite page) for hiking route suggestions. Also pick up *1:50,000 Hiking in Israel* maps of the Small and Big Craters at Steimatzky in the Be'er Sheva mall. These maps are only sold in Hebrew, but the tourist office in Arad can help identify specific points of interest and routes in English. As always when hiking in the desert, bring plenty of water, as well as sunglasses and a head covering, even if you plan on spending most of your time in an air-conditioned car. It is also advisable to hike with at least one other person and to leave a note on your car indicating where you are hiking and how long you plan to be gone.

To hit both places in one trip, begin by heading toward ha-Makhtesh ha-Gadol. Take Rte. 25 southeast out of Be'er Sheva, toward Dimona and Eilat. Just before Dimona, turn right onto Rte. 204, heading toward the town **Yerokham.** Once in Yerokham, take a left and follow the signs to the "Great Crater." There are several places along the way to pull over and admire the multi-colored slopes of the crater; the picnic area with a sign reading "Colored Sands" is a particularly worthwhile stop. Driving straight through the crater takes about 10min. and leads to Rte. 206, which runs to Oron, Dimona, and the Small Crater.

To go directly to the Small Crater from Be'er Sheva, take Rte. 25 to Dimona and turn right onto Rte. 206 at the Rotem Junction. Look for the small orange sign on the left that points to a paved road labeled "Small Makhtesh" and leading uphill. At the top of the first stretch of road is a park sign with marked trails and lookouts. Notice on the map that double black lines indicate routes for four-wheel-drive vehicles only. The main road, the "Old Road to Eilat," is represented by a solid black line. At this point, the road becomes semi-paved. Signs will point to the **Little Makhtesh observation point;** park the car and follow the red trail about 20min. to the edge of the crater for a breathtaking view. A free **camping area ❶,** marked with a green sign, is on the way.

Backtrack by car to the paved road on the left, marked **"Ha'rava Highway/ Aqrabim Ascent."** The Ma'ale Aqrabim, or Scorpion Ascent, is a Roman road built around two CE and used by troops in 1948 and 1949. A 5min. drive leads to a trail of green stone steps on the right. A sign at the bottom of the steps shows hikes in the area rated by their difficulty. After this, the road begins its winding and brake-burning descent toward a small collection of third- and fourth-century CE Roman ruins, which once constituted a stop on the ancient Nabatean spice route. A left at the end of the road leads to the town Hazeva. From here,

Rte. 90 heads north toward the Dead Sea, where it intersects with Rte. 25 which heads back west to Dimona and Be'er Sheva.

ARAD
☎08

ערד عراد

Built near the ancient Canaanite ruins of Tel Arad, the modern city of Arad is equidistant from all the major Dead Sea attractions. Besides the pleasant climate that results from its elevation, the air here is so clean and dry that doctors worldwide actually prescribe it for those suffering from asthma and other respiratory problems. Though considered a less than exciting place by many Israelis, this oasis of civilization is probably what David Ben-Gurion, Israel's first prime minister, envisioned when he spoke of Israel's desert blooming. In 1960, a governmental committee drew up a master plan, and the first residents moved in two years later. The city is a convenient place for Dead Sea floaters to hang their towels and Negev trekkers to replenish supplies, but other travelers may find the town a bit sterile.

▐ TRANSPORTATION

Buses: The easiest way to get anywhere from Arad is through Be'er Sheva. To: **Be'er Sheva** (384 and 385, 40min., 5 per day 9:30am-7:25pm, NIS16); **Jerusalem** (441 and 554, 5 per day 8:15am-5pm, NIS27); and **Tel Aviv** (389, 4 per day 6am-5pm, NIS37).

Taxis: (☎08 997 4444). There is a taxi stand behind the mall and local taxis circle around the city center. Local rides NIS15.

▚ ▐ ORIENTATION AND PRACTICAL INFORMATION

Arad rests on the border between the Judean and Negev deserts, about 25km from Masada and Ein Bokek and 60km east of Be'er Sheva. The central bus station is on **Yehuda Street.** Across the street and to the left between **Yerushalayim Street** and **Hevron Street** is the central **promenade,** lined with late-night restaurants and kiosks. A large **kenyon** is at the end of the promenade, across **Elazar Ben-Yair Street.**

Tourist Office: (☎08 995 4160), behind the yellow petrol station at the entrance to town, near the artist's quarter. Open Th-F 9am-4pm. **Tourist coordinator** (☎995 1662). Available M-Th and Sa 8am-4pm.

Bank: There are 3 **ATM**-equipped banks in the town center, including **Bank Leumi.** Open Su and Tu-W 8:30am-2pm, M and Th 8:30am-1pm and 4-6:15pm.

Police: (☎100), 100m downhill from the bus station.

Pharmacy: Super-Pharm (☎08 659 2000), in the mall. Open Su-Th 8:30am-10:30pm, F 8am-5pm, Sa 10am-11pm.

Post Office: (☎08 995 7088), near the town center on Elazar Ben-Yair St. Open Su and Th 8am-6pm, M-Tu 8am-12:30pm and 3:30-6pm, W 8am-1:30pm, F 8am-noon.

▐ ▐ ACCOMMODATIONS AND CAMPING

Arad only has a few accommodations, reflecting its status as a stop on the way to Masada or the Dead Sea. Despite its relative dearth of hotels and hostels, the city has far more *mitzirim* than anywhere else in the Dead Sea region. If you have a car and don't mind the commute, these guesthouses can provide an affordable and comfortable base for a Dead Sea vacation. The tourist office has an up-to-date list; some favorites include **Ahuva's House** (☎08 995 0642), **Rachelie's Rooms** (☎08 995 44 23 or 054 632 00 02; www.tzofit.co.il/id/racheli), **Villa 1000** (☎054 594 4423; tzofit.co.il/id/1000), **Nurit Lavi Zimmer** (☎08 995 4791 or 054 391 3149; www.tzofit.co.il/id/a-a-erauch), and **Hatsavim Motel** (☎08 995 2207; www.tzofit.co.il/sites/melonit-hazavim/).

Blau Weiss Youth Hostel (HI), 34 Atad St. (☎08 995 7150). Walk east on Yehuda St, then turn right on HaPalmach St. and follow the signs. Often packed with youth groups and bus tours, this complex has a whistle-clean duplex and individual cottages with A/C. Breakfast included. Reception 8am-2pm and 5-7pm. Call in advance for reservations. Dorms NIS110-130; singles NIS245-295; doubles NIS330-390. Additional person NIS95-115. Prices rise Aug.-Nov., Feb.-Apr., and around holidays. Credit cards accepted.❷

Inbar Hotel 38 Yehuda St. (☎08 997 33 03). From the bus station, head downhill and take a right on Yehuda St. If you can't make it all of the way to the Dead Sea, Inbar provides a decent approximation: a bit of luxury, a bunch of tourists, and pricey spa treatments. Rooms are luxurious for the price, with thick mattresses and a lingering scent of perfume. Free Wi-Fi. Singles NIS400; doubles NIS500. Credit cards accepted.❹

Kfar Hanokdim (☎08 995 0097; www.kfarhanokdim.co.il). On the road between Arad and Masada; accessible only by car. This large Bedouin-style campground is a peaceful desert oasis. If you've got your own sleeping bag, throw it down in one of the Bedouin tents; otherwise, opt for the more luxurious cabin (coffee corner and water-pipe included). Offers camel rides guided by local Bedouins for groups. Cabins for up to 5 people NIS430; tents for up to 6 people NIS420. Credit cards accepted. ❷

🍴 FOOD

The cheapest eating in Arad is the mess of falafel and shawarma places lining the city center. For groceries, visit the **HyperNeto supermarket** in the mall (open Su-Th 8am-8pm, F 8am-3pm, Sa 9-11pm).

Muza (☎08 997 5555; muzaarad@gmail.com), on Rte. 31. From the bus stop, walk downhill on Yehuda St., head right, and take a left at the Inbar hotel; Muza is on your right near the gas station. Huge steaks (NIS82), burgers (NIS35-50), and chicken wings that will fortify you for the nerve-wracking remainder of the drive to the Dead Sea. Vegetarian options are limited but filling (salads NIS44; soups NIS28). Beer ½L NIS20, imported bottles NIS17. Free Wi-Fi. Open daily 24hr. Credit cards accepted. ❷

Mister Shay, 32 HaPalmach St. (☎08 997 1956). From the city center, walk downhill to Yehuda St. and take a right on HaPalmach; the sign for Mister Shay is visible after passing the hill. Food here will be foreign even to connoisseurs of Americanized Chinese food: sesame chicken (NIS42) consists of strips of chicken covered in sesame seeds and deep fried, served without sauce. Steer toward the noodle dishes (NIS40) and soups (NIS15) unless you're feeling adventurous. Credit cards accepted. ❷

📷 SIGHTS

DESERT TOURS. Some swear that four-wheel drive is the only way to see the desert. Jeep tours in Arad aren't as spectacular as those of Mitzpe Ramon (p. 365), but they're still a great way to get away from the rocky beaches and aging tourists of the Dead Sea. Arad's recommended tour guide, **Giora Eldar,** offers Jeep tours alongside alternative methods of desert exploration. (☎052 397 1774; eldarara@netvision.net.il. 2hr. jeep tour NIS600; pack in up to 7 people to offset the cost. 4hr. rapelling trip for up to 15 people NIS1200. 30min. camel rides NIS80 per person.)

ARTIST'S QUARTER. Just outside the city lies the Artist's Quarter, a string of workshops and galleries along the edge of the industrial zone. Most of these establishments keep only the loosest schedules, and are open regularly only during the high season. *(Follow the signs from the town center; most of the action is on Sadan St. and in the "Eshet Lot" across the street. Open Feb.-Apr. and July-Sept. Su-Th 10am-2pm.).* **DesertVision** is a combination gallery and pottery workshop, showcasing works made from natural desert sand and mud. Owners Alon and Avital are warm, welcoming, and happy to arrange all-inclusive workshops and retreats ranging from 30min. to 3 weeks. They are also a great source of information about the irregular hours of other establishments in the quarter. *(☎ 08 995 9856; www.desertvision.org. 20NIS.)* Next door is the **Glass Museum,** which features the permanent exhibition of local artist Gideon Friedman in addition to a selection of works from other Israeli artists. *(☎ 08 995 3388; www.warmglassil.com. Open Su 10am-noon, Th 10am-5pm, F 10am-2pm, Sa 10am-5pm.).*

TEL ARAD. This small archaeological site and national park is a Canaanite city dating to the early Bronze Age (the third millennium BCE). The original layout of Tel Arad has survived, despite the city's age. Excavations have uncovered a walled city mentioned in the Bible; Numbers 21:1, Joshua 12:14, and Judges 1:16 all reference the city's role in the conquest of Israel. The entire site takes about 1hr. to hike. *(8km west of Arad. Buses to and from Be'er Sheva stop at the turnoff, 2km away from the site along Rte. 2808. ☎ 057 776 2170. Open Su-Th 8am-5pm, F 8am-4pm. NIS18, children NIS12.)*

OBSERVATION POINTS. Arad's unparalleled air quality can be best appreciated on a walk to the town's observation points, which look out over the desert landscape. *(From the bus station, take a right on Yehuda St. onto Moav St., then turn right on Moav St. and follow the road as it passes quiet residential neighborhoods on the right and desert views on the left. The elevated section of sidewalk with benches on the right serves as the observation deck.)*

♫ ▶ ENTERTAINMENT AND NIGHTLIFE

Arad Music Festival, in late Aug. This popular 4-day jam hosts artists and musicians from all over Israel. Egged runs all-day extra bus service to and from Arad for its duration. Contact the tourist office for lineup, dates, and other information.

Masada Sound and Light Show (☎995 9333). This dramatic 50min. show is visible only from the Roman Ramp side of Masada, and can be reached only via Arad (take Rte. 3199). Currently, there is no public transportation to the show. Travel time from Arad is about 30min.; the road closes at the beginning of the show. Shows are in Hebrew, but translation earphones (NIS15) are available in English, French, German, and Spanish. Shows Apr.-Aug. Tu and Th 9pm; Sept.-Oct. Tu and Th 8pm. NIS41; students, seniors, and children NIS34.

Muza (☎995 87 64), across the street from the Artists' Quarter. From the bus station, make a right (with your back to the information booth) and walk 2 blocks down Yehuda St. Take a left at the Hotel Inbar followed by a quick right at the traffic circle; the ramp on the corner leads down to Muza. When night falls, Arad's young and restless gather at this old-fashioned soccer pub. Sample dozens of beers (NIS20 for local brews; NIS17 for imported bottles) at the raucous bar or at the mellow outdoor picnic benches. Shots NIS10. Open 24hr.

SDE BOKER ☎02

שדה בוקר

When experts advised that developing the Negev was a waste of time and money, first prime minister and Zionist visionary David Ben-Gurion insisted on searching for unconventional methods of "greening the desert," asking,

"If the Nabateans could do it, why can't we?" When he visited the fledgling Sde Boker at the age of 67, he was so moved by the young pioneers that he decided to resign from office and settle on the kibbutz. Soon after, he founded the *Midresha* (institute) of Sde Boker, which houses laboratories and a field school devoted to the management of desert resources. Established in 1952, the kibbutz raises olives, kiwis, and other fruit, as well as wheat, corn, and livestock. Though agriculture never caught on as a major industry in the area, Sde Boker now serves as a base for desert exploration in the nearby Ein Avdat National Park and Tzin Valley, as well as a tourist destination for those interested in its Zionist patriarch. There are a tremendous number of truly astounding hikes in this area which traverse jagged desert cliffs, natural springs, canyons, and monk's caves.

⎕ TRANSPORTATION

Buses: Metropoline #60 runs frequently between the nearby cities of **Be'er Sheva** and **Mitzpe Ramon,** stopping at 3 different points a few kilometers apart: the gate of Kibbutz Sde Boker, the turn-off to Ben-Gurion's hut (at the edge of the kibbutz), and the roundabout outside the gate of the Ben-Gurion Institute. From Be'er Sheva to Mitzpe Ramon (Su-Th 20 per day 5am-9:30pm, F 10 per day 5am-2:15pm, Sa 5 per day 5-9pm; NIS15). From Mitzpe Ramon to Be'er Sheva (Su-Th 20 per day 6:35am-11pm, F 10 per day 6:35am-4:30pm, Sa 5 per day 5-9pm; NIS15).

✴ ⁊ ORIENTATION AND PRACTICAL INFORMATION

From the roundabout, the road on the right leads to the grave of Ben Guiron, Heritage Institute, visitor's center, and down the Canyon to Ein Avdat. The road straight ahead leads to the SPNI office and accommodations. The institute buildings are arranged around a central square, inside of which are the post office, supermarket, and restaurant. To reach the SPNI field school, turn right at the end of the road and cross the parking lot; the field school office is in the lower level of the Hamburg Guest House.

Tourist Office: SPNI Field School (☎02 622 2211). Sells maps (86NIS) and is a meeting point for informative park guides, but they're not always around. Open Su-Th 8am-4pm. The **gift shop** (☎08 655 5684) at the entrance to Ein Avdat serves as a more reliable source of information. The English-speaking staff will help you plan hikes in and around the park, and the store sells a small selection of camping equipment. Detailed trail map NIS55. Open daily in summer 8am-5pm, in winter 8am-4pm

ATM: At the gas station, one stop before Ein Avdat on bus #60 from Mitzpe Ramon.

Post Office: (☎08 653 2719), in the circle of buildings across from the field school. Open Su, Tu, Th 8:30am-12:30pm; M and W 8:30am-12:30pm and 4:15-6pm; F 9am-noon.

🏠 ⛺ ACCOMMODATIONS AND CAMPING

There are a few campgrounds in the park, all of which lack bathrooms and water. But what they lack in facilities they make up for in location. Beautiful views of the canyon surround the sites, the star-gazing is phenomenal, and the price can't be beat. The nearest bathrooms and potable water are at the visitors center, a 1hr. walk up the winding road from the closest camp site. Fires are allowed, but collecting firewood isn't, so buy a bundle at the visitor's center before you set up camp. The campsite at the entrance is free, but sites inside the park are not (NIS25, students NIS21, children NIS13).

SPNI Youth Hostel (☎02 622 2211), inside the gate and across from the restaurant and bank. Basic hostel rooms with private bathrooms. Dorms are not officially available, but if you meet up with a group you can put up to 6 people in a room. If you book Sa-Su in advance, you pay the M-F rate. Breakfast included. Singles M-F NIS225, Sa-Su NIS275; doubles NIS275/335. NIS110/130 per extra person. AmEx/D/MC/V. ❸

SPNI Hamburg Guest House (☎02 622 2211), next to the youth hostel, in the same building as the Field School. For a little more luxury than the youth hostel, the Hamburg Guest House is your only option. Each room contains 4 beds, 1 sofa bed, TV, and fridge. A/C. Breakfast included. Book full weekend in advance to get the weekday rate. Singles M-F NIS265, Sa-Su NIS305; doubles NIS340/400. NIS130/145 per extra person. AmEx/D/MC/V. ❸

▐ FOOD

The culinary selection in Sde Boker is pretty dismal. The **grocery store** (☎02 653 2800; open Su-Th 8am-7pm, F 8am-2pm), in the main shopping center, has a good selection at reasonable prices. Everything closes for Shabbat, so stock up on groceries early if you plan on staying on a Saturday.

Zin Restaurant and Cafe (☎08 653 2800), in the main shopping center. Considering they've got a monopoly on the Sde Boker restaurant scene, Zin isn't half bad. The restaurant contains a cafe, bakery, and cafeteria. The design may remind you of high school lunch, but the food won't: the beef stew and rice (NIS38) tastes homemade, and the schnitzel in pita with french fries (NIS20) is a delicious cultural hybrid. The cafe has a good selection of espresso drinks (NIS8-12) and German-influenced pastries. Free Wi-Fi. Open Su-Tu and Th 7:30am-9pm, F 7:30am-2pm. MC/V. ❷

◉ SIGHTS

BEN-GURION HERITAGE INSTITUTE. Scientists and university students work at this institute year-round; their findings on desert irrigation and development are applied in Africa and in much of the world. The institute's **Desert Sculpture Museum** displays art created from natural desert materials.

BEN-GURION'S HUT. Ben-Gurion lived in this modest kibbutz house for the last 20 years of his life, and the residence has been kept as he left it. There is a small museum next door. *(2½km north of the institute—a 45min. walk along the highway; the road leading to the hut is on the right after a large grove of pistachio trees—and one bus stop in the direction of Be'er Sheva. Information center (☎02 656 0469), at the entrance, shows a short film (10am, noon, 2pm) about the kibbutz's history. Open Su-Th 8:30am-4pm, F 8:30am-2pm, Sa and holidays 9am-3pm. Last entry 30min. before closing. NIS10. Film NIS17.)*

THE NATIONAL SOLAR ENERGY CENTER. This center is a pioneer in solar power development. Those black panels and metal contraptions on every rooftop are solar-powered water heaters, required for households by Israeli law. *(☎02 659 6934. Tours and audio-visual presentation by appointment.)*

▐ HIKING

The best way to appreciate the natural beauty of the Sde Boker region is to try some of its spectacular hikes. These, however, require careful preparation. Trails may be poorly marked, distances deceptive, and the Negev sun unforgiving. Detailed maps (NIS55) and explanations for all of these hikes are available at the **visitor's center** at the entrance to the park, which you should visit before attempting any hike. With advance notice, SPNI offers guided hikes across

THE NEGEV

the Avdat Plateau or Tzin Valley; call ahead or visit the field school for more information. Wear a hat, get an early start, and drink 1L of water every hour.

BAKED, NOT FRIED. When hiking in the desert, it's important to keep your head and neck protected from the sun. Bedouins have known this for centuries, which is why they developed the *keffiyeh*, now common in the Muslim world. The *keffiyeh* is a square of cloth folded into a triangle and wrapped around the head, with the extra cloth hanging down to protect the neck.

EIN AVDAT NATIONAL PARK. Gleaming white walls tower over the green, puddled path that runs through the canyon to the lower pools of the Avdat Spring. The eerie echoes of wildlife resound through the high caves carved in the sides of the canyon, which once served as homes to Byzantine monks. A small dam pools water that flows down the rocks from the Avdat Spring; just before the dam an easy-to-miss small set of stairs in the rock leads up to the rest of the hike. The foliage becomes denser along the upper part of the trail, where a grove of Mesopotamian poplar trees sits below a series of ladders that lead to a dazzling view at the top of the canyon. From the end of the trail on the canyon's rim, a trek along the riverbed to the nearby Nabatean ruins in Avdat takes about 2hr. (see **Avdat**, p. 365); the trail markings are difficult to follow so consult SPNI for details before going. To either return to Sde Boker or head on to Avdat on wheels, exit the park through the parking lot near the upper pools and walk down the road to the highway, where there are stops for bus #60 headed in both directions. *(Located in the Tzin Canyon. From the institute gate, the steep road to the park's lower, main entrance snakes down the canyon (1hr. on foot, 15min. by car). From the entrance, the hike to Ein Avdat (Avdat Spring; the lower pools) is 15 min. Allot 1hr. for the full hike to the upper gate. Getting to the upper gate requires climbing one-way ladders; unless there's a car waiting at the end of the hike, you'll either need to make a U-turn at the base of the ladders and miss the view or extend your hike a few hr. by walking along the rim of the canyon after reaching the top.* ☎ 02 655 5684. *Park open daily May-Sept. 8am-5pm; Oct.-Apr. 8am-4pm. Last entry 1hr. before closing. NIS25, seniors and students NIS21, children NIS13.)*

KARAKASH WADI. This magnificent 3hr. hike passes an inviting pond and waterfall. A 1hr. hike along the Khavarim Wadi, which eventually runs into the Khavarim Wadi, passes a Nabatean cistern and slopes of smooth, white rock that are striking in the moonlight. The cistern is below ground, down a flight of stairs from the beginning of the Khavarim Wadi hike. Part of the spice traders' efforts to squeeze water out of the desert, the cistern was used to catch and hold water from rain storms. A 1hr. hike along the trail leads to the bottom of the road and park entrance. The brush and rocky hills are popular spots for idling ibex. *(To begin the hike, turn left on the Be'er Sheva-Eilat highway from the end of the entrance road to the midresha and walk approximately 1km; the trailhead is to the left. For the entrance to the Havarim cistern and Wadi hike, continue along the highway past the Karakash trailhead to an orange sign on the left, a 20min. walk from the institute. From the park entrance, turn right on the road to reach Ein Avdat or left to make the uphill haul back to Sde Boker. Free.)*

EIN AKEV. This 5½hr. hike offers magnificent views from above the Tzin Canyon and leads to an oasis where chilly spring water provides a refreshing respite from the desert sun. From the bottom of the canyon, walk for 20min. and look on the left for a trail with green and white markers that ascends the canyon. This trail goes southeast across a desert plateau for several kilometers and reaches a green pool surrounded by lush green vegetation. After a swim in the pool head north along a trail with blue markers. Turn left at the junction and return to Sde Boker on the trail marked by red and white, which leads from

Lebanon to Eilat. This hike winds along the edge of cliffs at times. Be very careful and walk slowly in these areas. The return from Ein Akev is along the floor of the canyon and gets very hot during the middle of the day. It's best to start hiking as soon after sunrise as possible. *(To begin the hike, walk down the winding road from the SPNI Field School toward Ein Avdat. Free.)*

▶ DAYTRIPS FROM SDE BOKER

AVDAT

עבדת عبدات

Bus #60 runs from Be'er Sheva to Mitzpeh Ramon and stops in Avdat (40min., 5am-10pm, NIS15). Tell the driver you're going to the Nabatean archaeological site and not Ein Avdat (the oasis). The site can also be reached by hiking from Sde Boker through Ein Avdat (3-4hr.); consult the SPNI guides in Sde Boker for information. Bus #60 also runs to Avdat from Sde Boker (NIS11) and from the highway near the end of the Ein Avdat trail (NIS5). Drinking water and bathrooms are across from the ticket booth; bring water for the 20min. uphill hike to the entrance. ☎02 655 1511. Open in summer Su-Th 8am-5pm, F 8am-4pm; last entry 1hr. before closing. NIS25, students NIS21, children NIS13.

The magnificently-preserved ruins of a fourth-century BCE Nabatean city are perched upon a hill 11km south of Sde Boker. Avdat once thrived as a pit stop for caravans along the spice route from the Far East to Gaza (via Petra) that continued on to Europe. Nabateans used their strategic perch at Avdat to spy on caravans as far away as present-day Mitzpeh Ramon and Sde Boker. After the Romans captured the city in 106 CE, it continued to flourish, reaching its economic peak during the Byzantine period. The most important Nabatean remains are a handsome esplanade on top of the hill, a winding staircase that led to a Nabatean temple, and a potter's workshop, all dating from the first century CE. When the Nabateans converted to Christianity around 300 CE, the temple became a church. The best of the sixth century Byzantine remains include a 7m surrounding wall, a monastery, two churches, and a baptistry. In this century, the site was resurrected on film as the setting for the movie *Jesus Christ Superstar.*

MITZPE RAMON ☎08

מצפה רמון

Mitzpe Ramon sits on the rim of Makhtesh Ramon (Ramon Crater), the largest crater in the world. At 40km long, 9km wide, and 400m deep, its sheer size is mind-boggling. The crater makes visitors feel small in every respect: its rock formations are millions of years old, its 1200 different kinds of vegetation span four distinct climatic zones, and evidence of human life in the area predates written history. Since some of the geological formations are found nowhere else in the world, hikes pass through what seem to be landscapes of desolate, far-away planets. Uphill treks wind toward phenomenal views of the desert expanse, a rainbow of multi-colored sand.

In the 1920s and 30s, Makhtesh Ramon was not on British maps of Palestine. The young Israeli government came upon the crater while exploring the potential of the Negev. Until a direct route to Eilat was built from the Dead Sea in the 1970s, Mitzpe Ramon (Ramon Observation Point) was the stop-off for those heading south. Today, the crater is a 250,000-acre national park with well-marked trails through mazes of geological stunners. From campsites in the crater, the lack of artificial light makes possible a spectacular view of the starry sky.

▐ TRANSPORTATION

It's easy to walk around in the Mitzpe Ramon town center, but you'll need a car to reach Beerot camping and the nearby trailheads. *Let's Go* does not recommend hitchhiking; however, many travelers report that hitchhiking in Mitzpe Ramon is a fairly reliable way to get around. If you can find a ride to the turnoff from the road to Eilat, it's a 5km walk along the access road to the campsite. The haul to Beerot is a lot easier if you've got a slick 21-speed mountain bike. **Desert Shade** and **Negevland** both rent bikes, see **Sights,** p. 368, for details.

Buses: 2 major bus lines pass through Mitzpe Ramon. **Egged Bus #392** travels between **Be'er Sheva** and **Eilat,** stopping at Mitzpe. The bus driver will pick up passengers only if there is room on the bus. From Eilat to Mitzpe (Su-Th 5 per day 6:30am-5pm, F 6:30am and 12:30pm; NIS48). From Be'er Sheva to Mitzpe (Su-Th 4-5 per day 9:50am-5:20pm, F 9:38am; NIS48). Bus drivers are instructed to take breaks if they feel drowsy on long desert routes, so don't be surprised if the bus is a little late. **Metropoline #60** runs frequently from Be'er Sheva to Mitzpe (Su-Th 20 per day 5am-9:30pm, F 10 per day 5am-2:15pm, Sa 5 per day 5-9pm: NIS15) and from Mitzpe Ramon to Be'er Sheva (Su-Th 20 per day 6:35am-11pm, F 10 per day 6:35am-4:30pm, Sa 5 per day 7-11pm; NIS15).

▐ ORIENTATION AND PRACTICAL INFORMATION

The gas station, on the main traffic circle at the intersection of Ben-Gurion Blvd. and Rte 40, also serves as the central bus stop. Across the traffic circle is the town center which houses the bank, post office, and grocery store. Toward the crater, the visitors center, youth hostel, and Bio-Ramon are visible; follow the signs for a 5min. walk to any of them. A promenade runs along the crater's rim. A 10min. walk toward Be'er Sheva along Rte 40 brings you to the **industrial zone** on your left. Once a depressing row of abandoned buildings, in recent years the industrial zone has been revitalized as a center for local art and culture.

Tourist Office: (☎08 658 8691), in the visitors center. Open Su-F 8am-3pm, Sa 8am-4pm.

Police: Across from the petrol station in the town center.

Library: Ben-Gurion Blvd. (☎08 658 8442), 400m from the main traffic circle. Internet NIS10. Open Su and F 9am-noon; M-W 9am-noon and 3-7pm.

Post Office: (☎08 658 8416), in the town center, behind the bank and across the parking lot. Open Su and Th 8am-6pm, M-Tu 8am-12:30pm and 3:30-6pm, W 8am-1:30pm, F 8am-noon.

▐ ACCOMMODATIONS AND CAMPING

Staking out a campsite in the middle of the crater is forbidden and environmentally destructive. Though campers have been known to do it, they run the risk of being awakened by an angry ranger or an even angrier Asiatic wild ass. There are inexpensive accommodations both in town and in the crater, including some interesting alternatives to hostelling and camping. There are two campgrounds in town. The **JNF forest,** behind the petrol station, provides free camping without bathrooms or running water.

Adama (☎08 659 5190; www.adama.org.il), in the industrial zone. From the main traffic circle, take the 2nd left heading toward Be'er Sheva. Then take the 2nd left again; Adama will be the first building on your right, a nondescript warehouse with a metal door. Nothing could be further from the institutional feel of an HI Hostel: Adama is a modern dance company that also teaches yoga. Throw a mattress down on the floor, sleep outside, or rent an indoor mud hut in the converted studio space. The huge backyard, with couches and cushions arranged under sunshades, provides a great area to unwind after a long day of hiking. Breakfast NIS20 per person. Hearty vegetarian dinners (NIS20-30) upon request. Free Wi-Fi. Can be rented out by large groups; call in advance to make sure there's space. Mattress on floor NIS80; outdoor camping NIS80; indoor mud huts NIS140 per person; 2-3 person outdoor cottages NIS380. AmEx/D/MC/V. ❷

Silent Arrow (☎08 658 6713), 1km outside of town on Ben-Gurion Blvd. Eco-friendly accommodations with the best star-gazing outside of the crater: the lack of electricity means there's no artificial light to disrupt your viewing. Choose between a cushion in one of the communal sleeping tents (BYO sleeping bag) or a private mud hut with a thick mattress and blankets. Call in advance to arrange a personalized meal cooked (from NIS40), or cook your own in the camp's kitchen. Common sleeping area NIS80 per person; huts NIS120 per person. Cash only. ❷

Desert Eco-Lodge (☎972 8658 6229; www.navadim.org), across from the industrial zone on the road toward Be'er Sheva, a 15min. walk from the town center. Desert Eco-Lodge takes the low impact mud hut 1 step further, incorporating recycled wine bottles, retired bicycle parts, and scrap wood into their sturdy mud cottages. Cozy hangout area and cafeteria make for a social atmosphere. The sunrise view from these huts can't be beat. Breakfast NIS35 per person. Dinner available. Free Wi-Fi. Singles M-F NIS125, Sa-Su NIS150; doubles NIS200/250. Cash only. ❷

Be'erot Camping (☎08 658 6713), 13km from the visitor's center, 9km along the road to Eilat and 4km along a dirt access road. The only (legal) accommodations in the crater. BYO sleeping bag or upgrade to a cabin with a private bathroom and modest kitchen. If the number of campers reaches a critical mass, dinner is available: large grilled chicken meal NIS85; vegetarian meal NIS40. Breakfast (omelette, jam, bread, pita, and juice) NIS30. Also provides jeep tours (2½hr., NIS750) and camel rides (NIS55 per person, requires at least 15 guests). Campsites NIS30 per person; Bedouin tents NIS45 per person; cabins for up 6 people NIS500. Cash only. ❶

SPNI Field School (☎08 658 8615). By car, follow the signs on Ben-Gurion Blvd. from the town center. A bit trickier by foot: from Camel Observation Point, turn right on the black-marked cliffside trail and follow the promenade from the visitor's center away from the highway for 15min. Prime location at the trailhead of many of Mitzpe's best hikes, including a breathtaking trail down into the crater. Singles M-Th and Sa NIS250; doubles M-Th and Su NIS315, F NIS330. Extra person M-Th and Su NIS131, F NIS155. ❸

Mitzpe Ramon Youth Hostel (HI) (☎08 658 8443; iyha.org.il), next to the visitor's center. This concrete behemoth epitomizes HI's architectural style: prison on the outside, hospital on the inside. A barbed wire fence surrounds a compound of near-identical sterile rooms with a bland institutional feel. Despite resembling a gulag, it's run like a summer camp: "Frère Jacques" blaring from the hostel's loudspeaker awakes guests each morning, and the matronly staff ushers guests in and out of the cafeteria on a tight schedule. Fridge, A/C, TV, and private bath in each room. Breakfast included. Dorms NIS136; singles NIS295; doubles NIS390; extra person NIS115. ❷

⬛ FOOD

Stock up on reasonably-priced fruits and snacks at the **HyperNeto supermarket** on Ben-Gurion Blvd., in the shopping plaza near the post office (open Su-Tu 8am-8pm, W 8am-8:30pm, Th 7:30am-9pm, F 7am-3:30pm). With the exception of a small **mini-market** on Ben-Gurion Blvd., 700m from the traffic circle, stores and restaurants are closed on Shabbat.

THE NEGEV

Haksa Restaurant (☎05 0756 5063), in the industrial zone. From the traffic circle, take the 2nd left heading toward Be'er Sheva; Haksa is on your left. Far and away the tastiest, most authentic food in Mitzpe. Menu and hours are flexible; the meatballs in sauce, goulash with red peppers, and chicken dishes are recurring favorites. Vegetarian options available. Heineken NIS15. Appetizers NIS30. Entrees NIS48. Open daily noon-8:30pm. AmEx/D/MC/V. ❷

HaHavit (☎08 658 8226), in the visitor's center gift shop. Surprisingly high-quality cuisine, though you'll pay a premium for the breathtaking views of the crater. Pizza NIS35. Goat cheese and red pepper salad with toast NIS55. Lamb rib plate NIS100. Open daily 8am-2am. AmEx/D/MC/V. ❸

Gil's Grill (☎08 653 9111), in the town center next to the supermarket. Standard Israeli fast food at reasonable prices. Burger NIS15. Falafel with fries NIS12. Drinks NIS8. Open Su-Th 9am-8pm, F 9am-3pm. Cash only. ❶

👁 ⚠ SIGHTS AND OUTDOOR ACTIVITIES

Although Mitzpe Ramon's center of gravity sits solidly within the fabulous crater, several quirky attractions have sprung up in and around town. There are two spectacular promenades on the rim of the crater, one extending in each direction from the Visitor's Center. The desert sky is an amazing sight at night, as are the desert sculpture gardens along both paths. The starkly beautiful concrete and metal constructions nicely complement the desert landscape. Sunrises over the crater are awe-inspiring; head to the **lookout,** 300m past the visitor's center from the highway, for the best view.

BIO-RAMON. Forgo the hike and see desert lizards, scorpions, and snakes in this artificial habitat. *(Just downhill of the visitor's center. ☎08 658 8755. Open Su-F 8am-3pm, Sa 8am-4pm. Combination ticket with visitor's center NIS30, children NIS16.)*

DESERT ARCHERY. The bow and arrow game on this 45-acre course is inspired by golf—minus the meticulously mowed grass and sweaty old men. Don't be surprised to see scorpions and lizards as you walk around to pick up your arrow. *(20min. walk west of the city center. ☎050 534 4598; www.desertarchery.co.il. Equipment, training, and 2hr. game NIS40. Call ahead. Cash only.)*

ALPACA FARM. This farm is the largest alpaca and llama ranch outside of South America. It offers horse and camel riding, desert camping, and shearing in the spring. *(3km west of Mitzpe Ramon. Follow the signs along Ben-Gurion Blvd. west to Nahal Tsiya and turn right on the road toward the field school; from here, it's a 45min. walk until the sign is visible. ☎08 658 8047; alpaca.co.il. Open in summer 8:30am-6:30pm, in winter 8:30am-4:30pm. NIS25, children NIS23.)*

TOURS. Negevland Tours runs every desert activity imaginable from jeep tours to paintball. *(☎08 659 5555; negevland.co.il. Jeep tours NIS600-800, up to 8 people. Rapelling trip and jeep tour NIS1200. Mountain bike tours NIS80 for 24hr. Inquire about hiking guides for a full-day trip through the crater.)*. **Desert Shade** is the only full-service lodging and guide service in Mitzpe Ramon. English-speaking guides inform travelers about the flora, fauna, and desert landscape; alternatively, you check it out for yourself on a mountain bike or a camel. *(A 15min. walk north from the Delek station on Rte. 40/KKL Blvd.; buses #60 and 392 to Be'er Sheva run past it, but it's faster to walk. ☎0159 955 1111; www.navadim.org. Guides NIS550 for ½-day, NIS900 for full day. Mountain bikes NIS50 per day. 1hr. camel ride NIS60. Overnight trip to a nearby Bedouin village NIS660. Call in advance.)*

🎒 HIKING

Far-flung trailheads are best reached with a four-wheel-drive vehicle. For trailheads off of the main highway, **bus #392** to Eilat travels through the crater and can stop at the turn-off for the Be'erot Camping Site. Locals say hitchhiking on the highway is a safe option, though Let's Go does not recommend it.

 DON'T MESS WITH THE DESERT. Makhtesh Ramon is a spectacular park, but it should not be taken lightly. Always consult with Nature Reserve or SPNI personnel before setting out. Wear a hat, hike as early as possible in the morning, and carry food and 1L of water per person per hr. Heatstroke and dehydration can be deadly in the Negev.

The **Visitor's Center** has the best hiking resources in Mitzpe. Friendly Nature Reserve Authority staffers can help plan hikes and provide a crater map and trail guide (NIS2), as well as a detailed topographical map for those wanting to travel off the beaten path (NIS65). Amateur geologists will appreciate the museum and the saccharine, yet informative, film about the crater's history; everyone will enjoy the rooftop observation deck and sundial. (☎08 658 8691. Open Su-F 8am-3pm, Sa 8am-4pm. NIS25, children NIS13; combination ticket with Bio-Ramon NIS30/16.) The **SPNI** guides know the crater like a Bedouin knows sand, but they are only rarely around the field school. More likely than not, you'll be greeted by well-meaning hotel staff who can do little more than sell you a map (NIS82) and send you on your way. Unless you're starting a hike from here, you're better off heading to the visitor's center. (☎658 86 15. See **Accommodations, p. 366,** for directions. Guide for a full day of hiking Su-F NIS950, Sa NIS1185. Open Su-Th 8am-3:30pm, F 8am-noon.)

Har Ardon (7hr.). The Har Ardon (Mt. Ardon) hike combines challenging terrain with unbeatable views. Start at or before sunrise if at all possible. To climb Har Ardon, turn left out of the Be'erot campsite and follow the black markers north for 3km to the sign marked Mt. Ardon. From here, follow the blue path on the right to a parking area, where the mountain ascent begins. The steep climb up follows a narrow, white rock trail that changes about halfway up into a smoother and wider trail lined with hills of red and tan rocks. The top of Har Ardon is the heart of the crater; the mountain gives the crater its heart-shaped appearance. From the top, a rainbow of sand colors the crater floor. The descent from the mountain can be quite a physical feat; take it slow since the narrow, white-rock-and-sand trail is steep and slippery. Down the mountain and along the trail in the crater are the remarkable sand and hills of the **Red Valley,** which range in color from yellow to crimson. After passing the black hill of Givat Harut, turn right on the black trail and follow the signs back to the campsite to complete the hike.

Wadi Ardon. South of Mt. Ardon, this hike leads past unique geological formations and Nabatean ruins. From the campsite, walk along the black-marked trail for half a kilometer and turn right on a dirt road marked in red. After about 1km take the dirt road on the left marked in black. From the parking lot continue south through Wadi Ardon. Along the colorful borders are a pair of vertical magma intrusions, one big and one small, known as the Father and Son Dikes. To continue on, take the blue path. It points toward **Parsat Nekarot** (the Horseshoe of Crevices), which includes **Sha'ar Ramon** (the Ramon Gate), where water exits the crater. The Parsat Nekarot river bed is flanked by soaring cliffs and cave-like enclaves that make welcome shady stops. From Parsat Nekarot, follow the blue markings to **Ein Saharonim.** The vegetation lasts all year, but the water evaporates to mere puddles in summer. The remains of a Nabatean *caravanserai* stand at the end of the spring on the right. This is also the spot where animals are most likely to be seen wandering around in search of water sources. To return to the campsite from here, take the orange trail away from Parsat Nekarot. To start hiking from Ein Saharonim, turn left from the campsite and follow the orange trail next to a sign on the right.

Har Saharonim. Along the southern edge of the crater rises Har Saharonim (literally, Mountain of the Crescent-Shaped Ornaments). Start the climb from the western side, closest to the main road, take a right from the campsite, and turn left onto the "Oil Pipeline Route" black trail. After about 40min., follow the steep incline past the green trail to Ein Saharonim and the Nakhal Gevanim turn-off. Turn left at the green markers at the top, which lead to "Mt. Saharonim." The green-trail descent from Har Saharonim goes to Ein Saharonim. From there, follow the blue path through Parsat Nekarot in reverse, or return to the road or campsite.

Ha-Minsavah (3hr.). An excellent hike begins at the end of the western promenade, near the mini-amphitheater and leads to **ha-Minsarah** (Carpentry), where piles of prism-like rocks, configured and baked by volcanic heat, resemble carpenters' supplies. Follow the promenade from the Visitors Center; after passing two iron ball sculptures, a green-marked trail makes a rocky descent from the cliff. At the bottom of the crater follow the green trail left to ha-Minsarah. A dirt road leads east toward the highway.

Ramon's Tooth (5hr.). A turn-off point marked in red along the green Carpentry trail leads south to a hike along **Ramon's Tooth,** a dark rock formation of cooled magma that was exposed during the crater's creation. The hike also goes past the **Ammonite Wall,** an impressive collection of crustacean fossils embedded in rock. From the red Ammonite Wall path, a black path eventually leads off to the left and to the highway. Bus #392 from Eilat generally comes by on its way to Mitzpe Ramon; check the schedule before you go to avoid getting stranded. Hitchhiking is also an option, although Let's Go does not recommend it.

THE NEGEV

EILAT

אילת

Eilat has two goals: to get you tan and to make you poor. The city is soaked with the sweat of rowdy Israelis, international backpackers, and European tourists. The air is abuzz with jet skis and cell phones. Some swear by Eilat's sun, coral, and nightlife, while others see the city as a huge tourist trap attached to a nice beach. In between the cocktails and Coppertone, stick your head in the ocean and you may notice some of the most spectacular underwater life the world's seas have to offer. Above the waves, the wildlife is covered in muscles and bikinis.

Weekends are almost always busy in Eilat. Students from as far away as Be'ersheva and Tel Aviv come down to party, and families come for the resorts, spas, and carnival atmosphere of the promenade. The busiest times of the year are Passover (Mar. 29-Apr. 5 in 2010), Sukkot (Sept. 23-29 in 2010), and Israel's summer vacation (July-Aug.), when nearly 100,000 Israelis descend upon the city. Don't fool yourself into thinking that this is a good time to visit. True, there are more parties and crowded pubs, but hostels and restaurants charge double their normal rates, petty theft runs rampant, and every inch of beach is occupied.

HIGHLIGHTS OF EILAT

CHILL with the marine life at **Dolphin Reef** (p. 378).

SLURP delicious chocolate milk made at **Kibbutz Yotvata** (p. 380).

PARTY till the morning at the inexpensive **Dolphin Bar** (p. 380).

✈ INTERCITY TRANSPORTATION

Flights: Eilat Airport (ETH; ☎08 636 3838), on the corner of ha-Tmarim and ha-Arava. **Israir** (☎08 634 0666; www.israirairlines.com) has 7 flights a day to **Tel Aviv** ($57-95). **Arkia** (☎08 638 4888; www.arkia.com) has daily flights to Haifa ($80-100). Check websites for package deals.

Buses: Egged Bus, (☎03 694 88 88; www.egged.co.il/eng) has routes to **Haifa** (6hr., 3 per day), **Jerusalem** (4½hr., 4 per day), and **Tel Aviv** (5hr., 10 per day except holidays, NIS110). Local bus #15 runs to the **Taba border** (30min., every hr. 8am-6pm, NIS6.50).

⚓ ORIENTATION

Eilat is a 5km strip of coastline along the Negev's sandy bottom, the precarious intersection of Israel, Egypt, Jordan, and Saudi Arabia; at night the lights of all four are visible along the horizon. The city is divided into three sections: the town itself in the hills, the hotel area and promenade on the northeast beach, and the port and diving facilities to the south.

The main entrance to the central bus station is on **ha-Tmarim Boulevard,** the main street running from the southeast (downhill) to the northwest (uphill). Across the street from the bus station is the town's **Commercial Center,** with

EILAT

300 yards
300 meters

Lagoon

Kampen

Kamen

Park Ofir

Durban

Ezyon Gever

Gulf of Eilat (Aqaba)

Marina

(Promenade)

TO JORDANIAN BORDER,

(200m),
(500m),
(400m),

Tayelet (Promenade)

Public Beach

Mall

TO 25 (500m), 24 (5km),
CORAL BEACH (5km), AND EGYPTIAN BORDER (6km)

Ha-Arava Road

Avedat Blvd.

Hativat Golani

Almogim St.

Agmonim St.

Eilat Blvd.

Edom

Midyan

Ha-Tmarim Boulevard

Ofarim St.

Retamim St.

Kikkar Malkhei Yehuda

TEL AVIV SQ.

Hativat Ha-Negev

Shalom Center

Red Canyon Center

Benjamin Garden

Yotam Road

United Kingdom

Fradkin Garden

Nevi'ot

Hativat Ha-Negev

Eliot Blvd.

Eliot Blvd.

Los Angeles Rd.

Anafa St.

Peres

Nesher

Egypt

Argaman Street

Ha-Ela

Ha-Ze'elon

Satvanit

Eilat

ACCOMMODATIONS
Arava Hostel, **2**
Corinne Hostel, **9**
Dolphin Hotel, **3**
Eilat Youth Hostel (HI), **25**
Fawlty Towers Motel, **1**
Siam Divers Hostel, **24**
Spring Hostel, **7**
Sunset Motel, **8**

FOOD
Barry's, **10**
Cafe Optimi, **16**
Duda, **13**
Ginger, **12**
Giraffe, **11**
Pizza Lek, **4**
Shibolim, **6**
Shipuck: Habustan, **15**
The Spring Onion, **19**

PUBS
3 Monkeys Bar, **23**
The Bar Academy, **18**
The Beatles Bar, **20**
Dolphin Bar, **5**
Helena Mega Bar, **22**
The Mate Bar, **21**
Taverna, **17**
Unplugged, **14**

restaurants, cafes, pharmacies, and banks. Walking downhill along the bus station side of ha-Tmarim Blvd. and across an expanse of asphalt leads to the **Red Canyon Center,** which houses the post office, supermarket, and cinema. Farther downhill is the **Shalom Center,** a mall. Ha-Tmarim Blvd. ends here, perpendicular to **ha-Arava Road.** Turning right, the main entrance to the Eilat **airport** is on your left, and the waterfront lies in front of you. A block past the airport, to the right of the intersection with **Yotam Road,** a three-level conglomerate of cheap restaurants and bars calls itself the **New Tourist Center.** On the other side of Yotam Road is the **promenade** and the **public beaches;** walking 300m down the promenade is the **Tourist Information Office.** Continuing straight down ha-Arava leads to the Dolphin Reef, the port, Coral Beach, the Underwater Observatory, and finally Taba Beach and the Egyptian Border.

⊏ LOCAL TRANSPORTATION

Public Transportation: The **#15 Bus** is the main method of transportation, stopping at the major hotels and dive centers along its north-south route through Eilat. It runs hourly on the hour from the central bus station to the Taba border, and 20min. after the hour from the border to the bus station. Su-Th 8am-6pm, F 8am-3pm, Sa 9am-7pm.

Taxis: King Solomon (☎08 633 2426).

Car Rental: Hertz (☎08 637 5050), just north of the airport entrance. Manual $47 per day for up to 250km, $79 per day unlimited; automatic $54/79. 23+. Open Su-Th 8am-6pm, F 8am-2pm.

MIND THE METER. Taxis in Eilat are notoriously shady. If they offer a fixed price, you can be sure that it is more than what the meter would charge (think about it: cab drivers know their meters). Always ask to use the meter.

☒ PRACTICAL INFORMATION

TOURIST AND FINANCIAL SERVICES

Tourist Office: (☎08 630 91 11), on the north beach promenade, near the bridge. Open Su-Th 8:30am-5pm, F 8am-1pm.

Banks and Currency Exchange: There are various oddly named currency exchange agencies ("Bank of Green," "Bank of Change," etc.) along ha-Tmarim Blvd., but the best rates can be found at ATMs and banks. **Bank Leumi** (☎03 514 9400; leumi.co.il) and **Bank ha-Paolim** (☎03 567 4999) are located directly across from the bus station on ha-Tmarim. Both have **24hr. ATMs.** Both open Su and Tu-W 8:30am-1:30pm and 4-6:15pm, M and Th 8:30am-1pm and 4-6:15pm.

LOCAL SERVICES

Luggage Storage: Left Luggage (☎08 637 2111), in the central bus station. NIS15 per 2hr., NIS20 per day. Open M-Th 8am-5am, F 8am-3pm, Sa 11am-5am.

English-Language Bookstore: Steimatzky (☎08 633 0042), on the promenade 200m west of the tourist office; smaller location in the central bus station. Perhaps even more overpriced than the rest of Eilat, many guidebooks sell for NIS199. Open Su-Th 9am-10pm, F 9am-3pm, Sa 11am-9pm. AmEx/D/MC/V.

EILAT

Laundromats: (☎08 637 1482), at the intersection of ha-Tmarim and Eilot St. NIS45 per 6 kg. **Yael Laundry** (☎08 637 3443), 1 block farther north on the west side of ha-Tmarim. Both open Su-F 8am-8pm. Most hostels have cheaper self-service laundry.

Public Toilets: In the shopping center on the promenade, east of the bridge.

EMERGENCY AND COMMUNICATIONS

Police: Downhill from central bus station on Hativat ha-Negev Ave. **Tourist Police,** across from Tourist Information Center on North Beach. Can assist with stolen packs

Pharmacy: Super-pharm (☎08 638 3000), in the mall across from the New Tourist Center. Open Su-Th 8:30am-10pm, F 8am-5pm, Sa 10:30am-11pm. Another location on ha-Tmarim Blvd. 200m north of the airport. Open Su-Th 9pm-1am, F 8:30-midnight, Sa 9am-1am. The **24hr. Supermarket,** in the parking lot behind the Tourist Information Center, has a small selection of over-the-counter medications.

Hospital and Medical Services: Yosfetal Hospital, Yotam Rd. (☎08 635 8011). **Maccabi Healthcare Services,** N. ha-Tmarim Blvd. (☎08 636 4900; emergency ☎08 633 3101). Also provides pediatric and dental services.

Internet Access: E-surf (☎08 634 4331), in the central bus station. Wi-Fi NIS17 per hr. Open Su-Th 8am-8pm, F 8am-2pm. You're better off getting free access at a hostel or connecting to one of the open wireless networks throughout the city, which are especially dense near the Tourist Information Center and at the intersection of ha-Tmarim and Retamim.

Post Office: (☎08 637 3330), across the massive parking lot in the Red Canyon Mall. Open Su-Tu and Th 8am-6pm, W 8am-1:30pm, F 8am-noon. **Postal Code:** 200.

🏠🏕 ACCOMMODATIONS AND CAMPING

Eilat's once-thriving hostel scene has declined sharply over the last few years. Old favorites have fallen upon hard times, and many of those that survived have only done so by moving upmarket, eliminating dorm beds, and expanding their private room offerings. New arrivals to the bus station are attacked by a gaggle of apartment hawkers; just say "lo." Don't get into a cab with a stranger or commit to a room before seeing it. The apartments are isolated and antisocial, whereas the atmosphere of a smaller hostel can add tremendously to the enjoyment of Eilat. Some of the bigger hostels have been known to turn out backpackers in favor of larger groups or to have patrons switch rooms in the middle of the night. The area around the bus station has a few gems, but has an equal number of second-rate hostels featuring flea-ridden mattresses and cockroach-infested showers. The good news is that the abundance of private rooms has driven the price down to a reasonable level (NIS120-200 during the high season, only slightly more than a dorm bed at Hostelling International). The nicer hostels fill up quickly on weekends and during the high season, so if you don't book in advance you may find yourself banished to hostel hell.

TIP **PRICE FLUCTUATIONS.** Prices listed are for weekdays during the high season; expect them to rise by 20-30% on weekends and drop by half during the low season.

 Corinne's Hostel, 127 Retamim St. (☎08 637 1472), on the corner of ha-Tmarim and Retamim, just north of the bus station. Corinne runs a tight ship, and it shows: her hostel is a quiet, well air-conditioned oasis in the middle of the noisy, hot Eilat town center. Not so much as a leaky faucet escapes Corinne's watchful eye. She will also help out with finding local restaurants and entertainment. Nice kitchen where most guests cook breakfast. Lockers NIS10. Free Wi-Fi. Dorms NIS65; singles NIS120; doubles NIS190. MC/V. ❶

Arava Hostel (☎08 637 4687), at the downhill end of Almogin St. Arava's younger crowd makes good use of the common areas—a spacious patio and an air-conditioned common room with an internet terminal. The rooms are clean, if a bit crowded, and the shared bathrooms and showers are well-maintained. Breakfast NIS10-25. Reserve well in advance. Dorms NIS60; singles NIS130; doubles NIS190. MC/V. ❶

Eilat Youth Hostel and Guest House (HI) (☎08 637 0088; www.iyha.org.il), next to the New Tourist Center. This sterile behemoth hosts many Israeli teens. The building may not be pretty, but the location can't be beat. Fridges and coffee makers in most rooms. Online booking available; reserve well in advance. Dorms NIS100; private singles and doubles NIS290. MC/V. ❷

Sunset Motel (☎08 632 5782; sunsetmotel.co.il), next to Corinne's, just off ha-Tmarim Blvd. north of bus station. Among Eilat's more luxurious budget offerings. Shaded outdoor common area. The rooms are designed like tropical jungle huts but are cool and cozy; each has a microwave, TV, fridge, and private bathroom. Free Wi-Fi. Singles NIS150; doubles NIS250. Cash only.❶

Fawlty Towers Motel, 116 Simtat Ofarim (☎08 632 5578), 2 blocks north of the bus station to the east of ha-Tmarim. Though it calls itself a motel, the Fawlty Towers is in fact cheaper than some of Eilat's pricier hostels. The rooms, however, are up to hotel standards: clean white linens, TV/VCR units, fridges, and private bathrooms in every room. The friendly owner offers to make coffee for the guests every morning, which can be enjoyed on the small private balcony in many rooms. Free internet. Singles NIS120; doubles NIS150. Cash only. ❷

Dolphin Hostel, 99 Almogim St. (☎08 623 6650; cell 050 790 4594). Dolphin Hostel exemplifies the luxury (and prices) of the new Eilat hostel scene. With private kitchens in the rooms, a swimming pool, and a hot tub, this is a far cry from the grubby, flea-infested mattresses that used to surround the bus station. Enjoy breakfast at Dolphin Bar and Restaurant across the street for NIS15-30. Free internet and Wi-Fi. Cash only. Singles NIS150; doubles NIS200. Cash only. ❷

Spring Hostel 126 Ofarim Ln. (☎08 637 4660; www.avivhostel.co.il). Hostel in name only, Spring's immaculately decorated reception area is more reminiscent of a mid-range chain hotel. One of the more antisocial options for travelers, with sterile common area and a lone billiards table. Pool on balconies. Private fridges, TVs, and bathrooms. Singles NIS150; doubles NIS200; rooms with balcony cost extra. Cash only. ❷

Siam Divers Hostel (☎08 637 0581), at Siam Divers. Though primarily for divers, the hostel does occasionally have room for non-diving guests. You'll pay a small premium for the location (approximately the cost of a 1-way taxi from the main cluster of hostels to the beach). The dorm rooms are a bit cramped, but the bathrooms are clean and airy, and there's a fridge for guest use. Dorms NIS80; doubles NIS250. Cash only. ❷

 NOT FOR HIRE. Hostels used to be the go-to places for travelers looking for temporary employment. Unfortunately, the Israeli government has been cracking down on illegal employment over the last few years, and it's now nearly impossible to find temporary work anywhere in Eilat. Some of the boats moored at the dock, as well as the less established hostels, may still hire without asking too many questions, but be advised that working without a work visa is illegal. Workers have reported delinquent bosses that never pay up, leaving them without any legal recourse.

EILAT

THE KREMBO CONUNDRUM

What weighs 25 grams, has 115 calories, and is Dumbledore's favorite treat in the Hebrew translation of *Harry Potter and the Philosopher's Stone?* Krembo is perhaps Israel's most iconic candy treat.

The word Krembo literally means "cream-in-it." It consists of a round biscuit base, topped with whipped egg white creams, and coated in a thin layer of chocolate, then wrapped in colorful aluminum foil. This delectable delight is usually only available in the winter as an alternative to ice cream.

The treat is so popular that it has even been incorporated into Jewish law; it delineates a specific significance to the order in which one eats Krembo. Different, special blessings are reserved for the biscuit and for the cream and chocolate. Whatever blessing is said first is indicative of what part of Krembo feels like the most prominent, and thus the most delicious, component. There is no official consensus over the order of the blessings, and it remains an ongoing source of argument and I-told-you-so's—even for non-observant Jews. A study by Straus the main manufacturer of Krembos), however, found that 69% of Israelis prefer to eat Krembo from the top down, whereas only 10% start with the biscuit at the bottom; the remaining 21% are too busy engaging in Krembo euphoria to have a preference.

◘ FOOD

If you want to eat beachside in Eilat, be prepared to pay an arm and both legs. The ritzy patio restaurants along the main promenade cater to tourists with a dazzling array of ethnic cuisines, very few of which are worth the inflated prices. Those looking for a cheap meal should head for the hills: prices drop drastically in the neighborhoods overlooking the beachfront. Falafel stands and burger joints are a dime a dozen in the area around the bus station. The **24hr. Market** just south of the intersection of ha-Tmarim Blvd. and Elot Ave. has better prices than stores in the tourist areas, carrying a variety of bulk snack foods. For a larger selection, try the grocery store next to the post office on ha-Tmarim Blvd (open Su-Th 8am-10pm, F 10am-1pm). The **bakery**, 100 yards north of the intersection of ha-Tmarim Blvd. and Hativat ha-Negev Ave., is not to be missed, serving fresh traditional pastries for NIS1-2 each. (Open 24hr. Cash only).

▨ **Shibolim** (☎08 632 3932), at the corner of Elot Ave. and Yerushalaym Hashlema. A glorious respite from the crowded, overpriced beachfront establishments. The breakfast platter is among the best deals in Eilat: 2 eggs, a large salad, freshly-made bread, and an assortment of spreads for NIS32. Locals dash in and out throughout lunch hour, ordering unique sandwiches made-to-order from a wide array of meats, cheeses, and handmade toppings (double-decker NIS28). Service is prompt. Kitchen open Su-F 8am-9pm; bakery opens earlier. Cash only. ❶

Ginger Asian Kitchen and Bar, Yotam St. (☎08 637 2517; www.gingereilat.com), across from IMAX F. By far the most trendiness per shekel you will find in Eilat: a young, well-dressed crowd relaxes to smooth electronic music while eating moderately priced pan-Asian cuisine. The Thai chefs serve up everything from sushi (meal-sized plate NIS78) to Saigon-style chicken noodles (NIS48). The four-mushroom beef (portobello, champignon, wild, and shitaake; NIS62) is particularly inventive. If you've got room, finish it off with the banana republic (banana in caramel with almond biscuits and ginger vanilla ice cream; NIS30). Open daily noon-3:00am. Reservations required on weekends. AmEx/D/MC/V. ❸

Spring Onion (☎08 637 7434), next to the tourist information center. A small cafe and vegetarian-friendly restaurant, the Spring Onion has become a lasting local favorite. Try the 4-cheese quiche (NIS55) or, if you're feeling adventurous, the house pizza (mushroom, olive, tuna, and an egg sunny-side up;

NIS46). Wash it down with something from the extensive drink menu. Free Wi-Fi. Open daily 8am-late. AmEx/D/MC/V. ❷

Giraffe (☎08 631 6583), at the eastern end of the promenade. This noodle house is one of the best values on the promenade. Hearty portions for reasonable prices. Try the spicy Phillipine (egg noodles with peanuts and red curry; NIS43) or the new vegetarian (udon noodles in black bean and garlic sauce; NIS39) for a filling plate. Open daily noon-midnight. AmEx/D/MC/V. ❷

Shipucki Habustan (☎08 636 2294), in the Dan Eilat Hotel on the eastern end of the promenade. With its ample patio seating and large tables, this is a great place for groups, as long as nobody is a vegetarian: the menu consists almost entirely of meat skewers. Complimentary pita and salsas almost make up for the inflated beachfront prices. Cornish hen skewers NIS28, beef skewers NIS45. Reservations recommended on weekends during high season. Open Su-F 1pm-midnight. AmEx/D/MC/V. ❹

Pizza Lek (☎08 634 1330), just north of the central bus station of ha-Tmarim Blvd. This pizza counter with a few outside tables is conveniently located next to the hostel neighborhood. Nothing special—just tasty, cheap pizza. Slices NIS9. Large pizza NIS46-68, depending on toppings. This is a great pit stop if you're too drunk to make it from Dolphin Bar to the beach in 1 trip. Open daily 11am-2am. Cash only. ❶

Duda Restaurant, Tarshish St. (☎08 633 0389), in the Dalia Hotel, just behind the main promenade. An odd cultural mishmash offering everything from Cajun potatoes (NIS13) to fried schnitzel (NIS35). Thick and amazingly tacky menu, featuring gag pictures interspersed with photoshopped Simpson's illustrations. Open 24hr. Cash only. ❷

Barry's Italian Pizza and Coffee (☎08 631 6696), on the promenade, 500m east of the bridge. If you're starving and stuck on the promenade, this is probably your cheapest option. Sizeable calzones and pizza slices made-to-order behind a counter. The federronni calzone (pizza sauce, tuna, union, mushroom, olive, cheese; NIS34) is the most creative option on the menu, supplemented by standards such as Mediterranean bagel toast (pizza sauce, onion, green olive, cheese; NIS29) and a selection of espresso drinks. Open daily 24hr. Cash only. ❷

Cafe Optimi (☎08 637 6510), on the far west end of the north promenade. A sit-down meal with friendly service at a price only slightly higher than the restaurants in the town center. Try a generous portion of muesli (NIS29) or, for heartier fare, the omelette sandwich (NIS44). Vegetarian-friendly options include the Optimi salad (lettuce, tomato, walnuts, and mushrooms and onions sauteed in teriyaki sauce; NIS58). Open daily 9am-2am. AmEx/D/V/MC. ❷

⊙ ⚠ SIGHTS AND OUTDOOR ACTIVITIES

UNDERWATER

Eilat's brilliant underwater world is filled with marine creatures, from the undignified blubber fish to the regal emperor fish, frolicking in a psychedelic coral paradise. With its warm tropical waters and a great diversity of unusual marine life, the city has long served as the center of Red Sea diving. Although dive sites in Eilat are less pristine than many in Sinai, they are the most technically advanced and the safest areas to dive in the Red Sea. All dive centers provide modern equipment and multilingual guides and instructors. Eilat also offers a fully equipped and professionally operated recompression chamber at the local hospital, which is within 12 minutes of all dive sites. For an up-to-date list of dive sites, try www.reefdivinggroup.co.il/eng/dive_sites_of_eilat.asp/.

CORAL BEACH NATURE RESERVE. This national reserve offers a wealth of coral species and fish life, making the entry fee well worthwhile. The reserve features several underwater trails which enable you to walk among the coral without your damaging it, or it damaging you. The nature reserve also offers "snuba," a tethered dive up to 6m deep. *(South of Eilat port, take bus #15 from anywhere in town. ☎08 637 6829. Mask, snorkel, and fins rental NIS25. Snuba NIS180 for 90min. NIS30, children NIS15.)*

DOLPHIN REEF. The commercially operated scuba and snorkeling center at Dolphin Reef allows divers to observe semi-wild dolphins in a somewhat natural environment. Although the project has raised some ethical eyebrows, the management insists that the dolphins are free to swim away whenever they want to (though it would be difficult for any mammal to refuse a free meal, as most student travelers will agree). The dolphins perform a variety of tricks at the daily feedings and "interaction session," but observing them underwater is a more rewarding (and pricey) experience. The four original dolphins from the Black Sea have been breeding in captivity, bringing the total to eight. *(Just south of the port on bus #15. Open Su-Th 9am-5pm, F-Sa 9am-4:30pm. Reservations required. NIS58, children NIS40. Snorkel with dolphins NIS255.)*

LUCKY DIVERS. Lucky Divers provides some of the best dive deals in Eilat. Certified divers can go on a guided dive for US$30 including equipment rental. Or, try an introductory dive for US$50, no certification required. The adventurous can get a full PADI open water certification, a 5-day course including gear and textbooks, for US$375. Those looking to stay a little closer to the surface can take a full-day trip to some of the Sinai's finest snorkeling sights for US$65. *(☎08 632 3466; www.luckydivers.com.)*

RED SEA SPORTS CLUB. The Red Sea Sports Club has the best prices for rentals. A mask, snorkel and fins will set you back just NIS30 for a full day. A scuba system rental (certification required) is NIS150 and includes a tank fill. The club also offers parasailing, water skiing, and other water sports. *(Located in the marina. ☎08 637 6569; www.redseasports.co.il. Parasailing NIS140. Water skiing NIS200 per 30min. Prices change; check website for most recent information. Call in advance on busy weekends.)*

HOF HA-NANYA. This rental kiosk provides the best bang for your buck on DIY watersports. Rent a pedal boat and splash around the coral reefs with a group of friends. A two-person kayak provides a bit more speed to reach offshore snorkel sights if you're feeling adventurous. If you've really got a need for speed, hop on a motorboat to get as far away from the crowded beach as possible. For a quick rush, hit the skies on a parasail or buzz the tanning tourists on a jet ski. *(In the marina, beachside just west of the bridge. ☎08 631 6348; www.hlh. co.il. Pedal boast NIS70 per hr. 2-person kayaks NIS60 per hr. Motorboat NIS200 per hr. Parasail NIS140 per 10min. 1-person jet ski NIS120 per 10min.)*

THE CORALWORLD UNDERWATER OBSERVATORY. An Eilat favorite, the underwater observatory lets you immerse yourself in the ocean ecosystem without getting drenched in sweat or sea water. The glass enclosure 100m offshore lets you see brightly-colored tropical fish and coral 6m below the surface. *(South of the port on Coral Beach. Also accessible by a glass-bottom boat ride from the marina. ☎08 636 4200. Open in summer Su-Th 8:30am-4:30pm and F 8:30am-3pm, in winter Su-Th 8:30am-4pm and F 8:30am-3pm. NIS63, children NIS45.)*

ISRAEL YAM GLASS BOTTOM. Glass-bottom boats are one of the easiest ways to see the marine life. Israel Yam will take you on a two-hour ride along the coast of Jordan, across the gulf, and back up the Egyptian coast toward Eilat, with a stop at the Dolphin Reef. Hear about the sea creatures and environment throughout the tour for a relaxing but educational introduction to the Red Sea ecosystem. *(In the marina just west of the bridge. ☎08 633 2325. NIS65, children NIS40.)*

HOF HA-DEKEL (PALM BEACH). This gated party beach is public land with a private lease for a restaurant and bar. In other words, you can bring your own food and drinks, although the management may give you a dirty look. Except for the sea urchins on the southern half, it's a great place to splash around. *(North of the port, 1km south of town center. Closes at sunset.)*

IN THE AIR

The International Birding and Research Center in Eilat. Some say the best of Eilat's wildlife is in the air. Avid birdwatchers flock to the salt ponds near the Jordanian border from late February to early April and from mid-September to November, when 30 species fly overhead on their way to or from Africa. Take advantage of the center's expertise with a 2hr. private tour of the salt ponds. The **bird sanctuary** holds a selection of migratory and native species. *(Open daily 7am-noon. Tour daily 9:30-11am; 35NIS. Free. Tours NIS150 per person.).*

ON THE GROUND

The beauty of the red granite mountains towering over Eilat matches that of the coral reefs thriving beneath it. The **SPNI Field School,** across from Coral Beach (accessible by bus #15) is an essential stop for independent hikers. It sells extensive trail maps and provides advice on hikes (☎08 637 1127; eilat@ spni.org.il). Many of the sites are accessible by bus routes (#393, 394, and 397), though they are not official stops. Consult the SPNI field school for information about routes and where to stop.

There are countless safari companies offering jeep tours to many of these sights. **Desert Eco Tours** (☎972 52 276 5753; www.desertecotours.com) offers 4hr. jeep tours for $55, as well as camel and mountain bike tours. **Red Sea Sports** (☎08 633 3666; www.redseasports.co.il) offers tours to Red Canyon, Timna Park, Hai Bar Biblical Nature Reserve, and other destinations (NIS170-200).

MT. TZFAHOT. The hike to Mt. Tzfahot is convenient and offers stunning views. The green and white trail begins at the left of the fence separating the highway from the field school complex. The climb to the summit takes 45min. From here, the blue trail heads north, ending near Aqua Sport. The round trip takes about 2hr. and makes for an enjoyable evening outing.

RED CANYON. The most exciting and accessible terrain north of Eilat includes **Ein Netafim, Mount Shlomo,** and **Red Canyon.** North-bound buses will stop at this area upon request. From Red Canyon, hike to the lookout above **Moon Valley,** a pocked canyon in Egypt, and to the unusual **Amram's Pillars.** These hikes are not advisable during the summer. Before attempting any of these hikes, contact SPNI.

TIMNA NATIONAL PARK. The 6000-year-old Timna copper mines remain a fascinating destination. Some people believe the Israelites passed through here on their way out of Egypt. The park houses remains of workers' camps and cisterns dating from the 11th century BCE. The sandstone **King Solomon's Pillars** dominate the desert from a height of 50m near the 14th century BCE **Egyptian Temple of Hathor.** The park offers camping facilities with showers and a restaurant on its artificially-created shores. *(Rte. 90 20km north of Eilat, 3km from road. Many northbound buses will stop here; taxis cost around NIS50. ☎08 632 6555. Open in summer Su-F 8am-1pm, Sa 8am-8pm; in winter Su-Th and Sa 8am-4pm, F 8am-1pm. NIS38.)*

EILAT

HAI BAR BIBLICAL NATURE RESERVE. Hai Bar aims to breed biblical animals which have become rare in southern Israel. The reserve has an impressive predator center, where native predators can be seen in their natural habitats. The bulk of the reserve is a game park, home to ostriches, wild asses, antelopes, addaxes, and oryxes. *(Rte. 90, 35km north of Eilat, 1½km from the road. ☎08 637 3057. Open Su-Th 8am-4pm, F-Sa 8am-2pm. NIS40.)*

KIBBUTZ YOTVATA. One of Israel's oldest Kibbutzim is Kibbutz Yotvata, which doubles as producer of delicious *shoto* (chocolate milk) sold in grocery stores throughout Eilat. *(Rte. 90 between Timna and Hai Bar. ☎08 635 7444; yotvata-office@yotvata.ardom.co.il.)*

🎵 🎭 ENTERTAINMENT AND NIGHTLIFE

Eilat's nightlife has a little bit of everything: beer swilling with hard-core backpackers, dancing with greased-up Israelis, and hobnobbing with affluent yuppies. Most bars open after lunch, though drinking often starts earlier (it's noon somewhere). Nightclubs open around 11pm, get going around 1 or 2am, and often don't close until past sunrise. Mega-bars have taken over where discos used to rule the nightlife. The good news is that they don't charge a cover; the bad news is that what used to pass for a cover (NIS25-35) won't even get you an imported beer at some of the pricier joints.

The free and mellow **promenade** along the water offers some of Israel's most efficient people-watching day and night: the visible-flesh-per-capita ratio is the highest in the country. Street vendors sell cheap jewelry and 5min. portraits as Israeli studs try in vain to pick up the ladies. Families clear out around sunset and are replaced by scantily-clad teenagers around 10pm.

Eilat's entertainment is not exclusively limited to bars and clubs. The **Phillip Murray Cultural Center** (diagonal from the bus station on Hativat ha-Negev, ☎08 637 2257) hosts performances during the school year. Next door, the **Red Sea Music Center** (☎08 637 7036) has information on local concerts and student recitals.

Dolphin Bar, Almogin St. (☎08 332 6650), across from the Dolphin Hostel. Backpackers and hostel workers make themselves at home at the Dolphin Bar, which serves up ½L beer (NIS6-8) for cheaper than the local convenience stores. Munch on hummus and pita (NIS30) or a fruit plate (NIS15). Free Wi-Fi. Open 24hr. Cash only.

Taverna (☎08 637 3406), in the New Tourist Center across from the Beatles Bar. The crowd is friendly and well-traveled, and English is the lengua franca. Converse or watch a soccer game while enjoying the free jalapeno-coated olives, then head to one of the many surrounding tourist clubs for dancing. Local beer NIS18. Mixed drinks NIS36. Cash only.

The Mate Bar (☎077 549 1207), across the walkway from Beatles Bar. The couches and billiards in the entryway hold a crowd of locals and Israeli students that is tight-knit but easy to talk to. Rock music plays at a low volume as customers flirt with the bartender. The ever-present owner offers to help find hostels and recommend sights. Local brews NIS15, imports NIS18-20. Open 10pm-5am. Cash only.

The Three Monkeys Pub (☎08 636 8800), on the North Promenade. Every night, Israeli musicians play live covers of American music to a crowd of Europeans and Israelis at this faux-British pub. Pound back a few Carlsburgs (½L NIS24) if you can afford it, then join the polo-shirt-clad 20-somethings on the packed dance floor or head out to the beachside patio for some fresh air. Nachos NIS25. Sandwiches NIS32-38. Open daily 9pm-4:30am. Cash only.

Helena Mega Bar, upstairs at the back of the New Tourist Center bar strip. Don't let the stern bouncer and prickly hand-stamper at the door scare you away: inside is all flashing lights and flashing smiles as a crowd of students raves to Israeli techno with sparklers in hand. Beer NIS18-26. Mixed drinks NIS38. Open 11pm-6am. Cash only.

Unplugged (☎08 632 6299), in the New Tourist Center. A favorite of Israeli tourists, the strobe lights and ear-popping bass in the outdoor tent keep the crowd dancing until the sun comes up. Pints NIS22. Mixed drinks NIS40. W Israeli music night. Open daily 9pm-sunrise. Cash only.

The Beatles Bar (☎077 430 1458), behind and to the right of Unplugged. U-shaped bar inside serves up imported Leffe Blonde (NIS29), Carlsburg (NIS23), and a good selection of standard mixed drinks (NIS42). Spicy tuna sushi rolls NIS36. Nachos NIS25. Happy hour 9-11pm. Open daily 9pm-5am. Cash only.

The Bar Academy (☎452 721 1711), past the Beatles Bar on the left, next to the pizza counter. The Bar Academy trains Eilat's finest bartenders, a fact immediately apparent from its inventive mixed drinks menu (from NIS36). The owner brews and serves his own specialty beer alongside imports and standard Israeli brews (NIS18-26). Open daily 9pm-5am. Cash only.

The Village Beach Bar (☎08 637 5410), near Coral Beach just south of the port. A beachside restaurant during the day, sunset brings live music followed by DJs as the night progresses. Try the signature limonana (local liquer Arak, lemonade, and crushed mint leaves; NIS30). F nights bring 60s music and a decent turnout, though the crowd isn't quite as rowdy as the multiple bars and dance floors would suggest. Beer from NIS16. Appetizers NIS17-28. Open 8am-5am. Cash only.

EILAT

PETRA AND SINAI

The two most popular sidetrip destinations from Israel are Jordan's Nabatean stone city, Petra, and Egypt's desert playground, the Sinai Peninsula. Petra makes an ideal two-day foray from Eilat: arrive in time to watch the sun set over the pink sandstone, then head to the visitor's center for Petra by Night (see **Sights,** p. 388). Wake up early the next morning and hit the ruins for a day full of hiking. Another option is to cross at the Allenby Bridge and follow the King's Highway south from Amman (see **Border Crossings,** opposite page). Sinai, significantly bigger than Israel, is difficult to cover in less than a week, but its diving, hiking, mellow atmosphere, and religious sites are worth the trek. Pick a city (laid-back Dahab is a favorite) and don't rush it: savor the sun, sand, and scuba over a couple of days.

HIGHLIGHTS OF PETRA AND SINAI
WANDER through **Petra's** seemingly infinite number of temples (p. 388).
SALUTE the sun after a midnight hike to **Mount Sinai's** peak (p. 393).
MUNCH ON a treat from **Dahab's** Koshary Cart, arguably the best around (p. 402).

PETRA

☎ 03

البتراء

As you approach the once-lost city of Petra, towering sculptures peek out from the walls of a natural 3m wide fissure to reveal raw mountains that were fashioned by human hands into impossibly delicate structures. Petra ("stone" in Ancient Greek) is perhaps the most astounding ancient city left to the modern world, and certainly a must-see for visitors to the Middle East.

For 700 years, Petra was lost to all but the few hundred members of a Bedouin tribe who guarded their treasure from outsiders. In the 19th century, Swiss explorer Johann Burkhardt heard Bedouin speaking of a "lost city" and vowed to find it. Though initially unable to find a guide willing to disclose the city's location, he guessed that the city he sought was the Petra of legend, the biblical Sela, which should have been near Mt. Hor, the site of Aaron's tomb. Impersonating a Christian pilgrim, Burkhardt hired a guide, and on August 22, 1812, he became the first non-Bedouin in hundreds of years to have walked between the cliffs of Petra's *siq* (the mile-long rift that was the only entrance to Petra). In the nearly two centuries since Burkhardt's discovery, Petra has become a tourist attraction *du jour*, admired by visitors from all over the world—including the film crew of *Indiana Jones and the Last Crusade*.

Humans first set foot in the area back in the eighth millennium BCE. By the sixth century BCE, the Nabateans, a nomadic Arab tribe, had quietly moved onto land controlled by the Edomites and had begun to profit from the trade between lower Arabia and the Fertile Crescent. Over the next three centuries, the Nabatean Kingdom flourished, secure in its easily defended capital. The Nabateans carved their monumental temples out of the mountains, looking to Egyptian, Greek, and Roman styles for inspiration. Unique to the Nabateans are the crow-step patterns that grace the crowns of many of the memorials. The crow-steps so resemble inverted stairways that the people of Meda'in Salih (in Saudi Arabia) claimed that God threw Petra upside down and turned it to stone to punish its people for their wickedness. More historically verifiable evidence suggests that the Nabatean King Aretes defeated Pompey's Roman legions in 63 BCE. The Romans controlled the entire area around Nabatea, however, prompting the later King Rabel III to strike a deal: as long as the Romans did not attack during his lifetime, they would be permitted to move in after he died. In 106 CE, the Romans claimed the Nabatean Kingdom and inhabited this city of rosy Nubian sandstone. In its heyday, Petra housed as many as 30,000 people, but after the earthquake in 363 CE, a shift in trade routes to Palmyra, Syria, expansion of the sea trade around Arabia, and another earthquake in 747, much of Petra had deteriorated to rubble.

For decades after Burkhardt made his discovery public, the Bedouin adapted to the influx of tourists by providing them with food and accommodations inside Petra, a practice outlawed from 1984 to 1985 out of concern for the monuments. While many of Petra's Bedouin have been relocated to a housing project near Wadi Musa, a large portion still make their homes in the more remote caves and hills of the city (spanning 50km, most of which the average tourist never sees). Many Bedouin sell souvenirs and drinks amidst the ruins; others tend goats—don't be surprised at the barnyard smells emanating from inside the tombs.

 CALLING JORDAN. To dial Jordan from Israel or elsewhere, don't forget the country code (☎+962) and to drop the first zero of the numbers below.

PRICE DIVERSITY: PETRA
(For more detailed information about price diversity, see p. VIII.)

	❶	❷	❸	❹	❺
Accommodations	under JD5	JD6-15	JD16-25	JD26-40	over JD40
Food	under JD2	JD2-5	JD6-10	JD11-15	over JD15

⚒ BORDER CROSSINGS

There are three possible border crossings into Jordan: one in **Eilat** in the South, one in **Jericho** in the West Bank, and one in **Beit She'an** in the North of Israel. Travelers to Petra usually cross at Eilat, which is only a few hours away. The border crossing from Eilat to Aqaba is in the Arava Desert and is called **Yitzhak Rabin.** It is surprisingly simple and should take less than an hour. Everyone must pay an NIS100 exit tax and walk the 1km no man's land between the two countries—there is no transportation. Month-long Jordanian visas can be obtained at the border for free. **Taxis** from Eilat to the border cost NIS25-30; from the border to Aqaba JD5. **Buses** run between Aqaba and Petra every 30min. from 6am to 9am daily (JD5), or you can get a taxi from the border to Petra for JD60. You may be better off taking a taxi to town from JD5 and bargaining a cab driver in town down to take you to Petra from JD50.

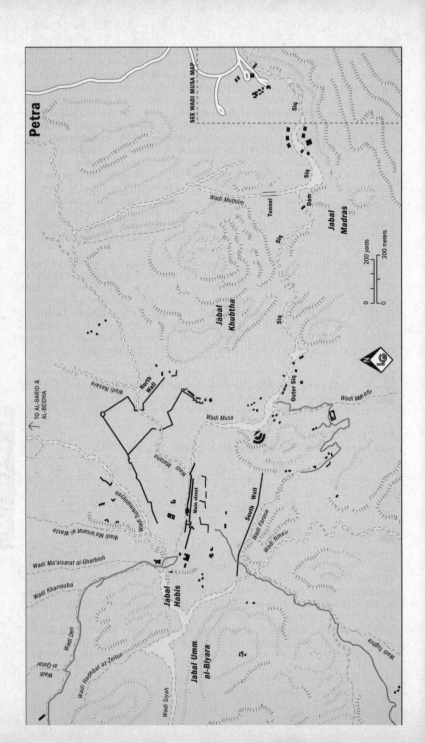

(Yitzhak Rabin border crossing ☎07 630 0555. Open Su-Th 6:30am-9pm, F-Sa 8am-8pm; closed Yom Kippur and 'Eid al-Adha.)

Tourists crossing through Jericho's King Hussein/Allenby Bridge must obtain visas in advance (available in Tel Aviv, at the crossing between Eilat and Aqaba, and from Jordanian embassies and consulates). This crossing is unpredictable: obtain thorough, up-to-date information from your embassy or consulate before trying to cross here. (Exit tax NIS140. Border open Su-Th 8am-4pm, F-Sa 8am-1pm.) Buses and service frequently leave Amman's Abdali Station for the bridge. To get from Amman to Petra, you'll need to drive or take public transportation. **JETT buses** depart to Petra (3½hr.; Su, Tu and F 6:30am; round-trip JD11, including admission to Petra JD33). Reserve one day in advance (☎+ 962 06 585 4679; info@jett.com.jo).

🛈 PRACTICAL INFORMATION

Tourist Office: Petra Visitors Center (☎03 215 6020). Hiking guides up to JD100. Horse rentals JD7. Open daily 7am-6pm.

Bank: Housing Bank (☎03 215 6110), next to the main traffic circle. Open Su-Th 8:30am-3pm. ATMs often offer better rates, but note that some have a JD50 limit, so it may seem as if your card isn't working if you try to withdraw more.

Police: (☎191), in the booth in the main traffic circle. **Tourist police** (☎215 64 41), just inside the entrance to Petra.

Pharmacy: Wadi Musa Pharmacy (☎03 215 6444), just downhill of the main traffic circle. Open Su-Th and Sa 8:30am-midnight, F 8:30am-1pm and 3pm-midnight.

Medical Services: Public health clinic (☎03 215 6025), 15min. walk uphill from the main traffic circle. Open Sa-Th 8am-4pm. **Petra Polyclinic** (☎077 733 9209), just downhill of the main traffic circle. More expensive, but has more modern equipment Open 24hr.

Internet Access: Brother Internet Cafe, on the main traffic circle. JD1.50 per hr. Open daily 11am-2am daily. **Canary Internet Cafe** (☎077 721 9224). Internet JD2 per hr. Wi-Fi JD1 per hr.

Post Office: In the park behind the Visitor's Center. Open Su-Th 7:30am-3pm. Branch near the main traffic circle. Open Su-Th 8am-5pm.

STRENGTH IN NUMBERS. When bargaining with Egyptian cab drivers, the more the merrier (for the customer). Having two cab drivers competing for your business cuts prices quickly. Having two passengers allows you to do a sort of good cop, bad cop, in which one passenger expresses interest but the other starts to walk away, prompting a lower offer from the cabbie.

🏠 ACCOMMODATIONS

Since Jordan and Israel signed a peace treaty, visitors from all over the world have flooded the Jordanian hillside and construction has boomed in Wadi Musa. Most of the development revolves around luxury resorts, but there are plenty of cheap alternatives to choose from. Budget travelers should have little trouble finding a suitable place to sleep; prices also become negotiable in the low season (May-July and Dec.-Feb.). **Camping** inside Petra is illegal, but lingering explorers (especially women) may receive invitations for overnight stays from Bedouin.

■ **Cleopatra Hotel** (☎03 215 7090; Cleopatra_h@hotmail.com), 150m uphill of the main traffic circle. When you walk into Cleopatra, you'll almost certainly be invited to tea with the friendly, English-speaking manager. He knows the area well and offers some of the best and safest overnight tours to Wadi Rum. Unlike those offered by other hotels, these tours are not contracted to an outside agency but are run directly by the hotel management (includes jeep, camel, lunch, dinner, and breakfast; JD40). The rooms are clean and have private baths. Free kitchen use. Internet JD2 per hr. Be sure to book in advance during the high season. Mattress on the roof JD4; singles JD15; doubles JD20; triples JD27. Credit cards accepted. ❶

■ **Valentine Inn** (☎03 215 6423, valentineinn@hotmail.com), facing downhill at the main traffic circle, go right and follow the signs, taking your first right. The most dorm for your dinar in town. Outside, students smoke *shisha* (JD3) and drink double-strength Petra beer. The 14-person dorm rooms are well-maintained, if a bit crowded. Free morning shuttle to Petra entrance. Free kitchen use. Breakfast JD3. Dinner buffet JD4. Internet JD2 per hr. Mattress on roof JD2; 14-person dorms JD3; 8-person dorms JD5; singles JD15; doubles JD20. Cash only. ❶

Peace Way Hotel (☎03 215 6963; peaceway@index.com.jo), 200m uphill of main traffic circle. Clean and carpeted rooms with fans to fight off the desert heat. Those facing Petra have large windows and lots of light. Restaurant and coffee shop in lobby. Free shuttle to Petra. Laundry JD1.50 per kg. Singles JD10; doubles JD15. ❷

Sunset Hotel, P.O. Box 59, 200m uphill from the Visitor's Center. A good value, especially considering what you would pay elsewhere to stay this close to the entrance to Petra. Clean rooms and a helpful staff. Breakfast included. Free Wi-Fi. Singles JD15; doubles JD25; triples JD35. V. ❷

Al-Anbat (☎03 215 7300; www.alanbat.com), first left downhill of the traffic circle. A local chain of 3 hotels with a solid reputation in Wadi Musa. Clean, safe lodgings with all of the creature comforts: fridge, A/C, and cable TV. Shuttle to Petra JD3. Singles JD15; double JD20; triples JD30. ❷

Elgee Hotel (☎03 215 7002; elgeehotel@yahoo.com), downhill from the main traffic circle on the right. Rooms feature comfortable, overstuffed chairs and plenty of light. All rooms have satellite TVs, A/C, and fridges. Small cafe, bar, and lounge area with free Wi-Fi. Breakfast JD1. Happy hour 8-9pm. Singles JD17; doubles JD20. V over JD40. ❸

Rose City Hotel (☎03 685 3940 or 685 3339), downhill from the traffic circle on the right. If you don't mind staying in a basement with a view of a dumpster, Rose City has the cheapest single rooms in town. Rooms are reasonably clean and well-maintained. Singles in the basement JD6, upstairs JD15; doubles JD12/22. ❶

 FOOD

The farther you go from the ruins, the less you'll pay for falafel. Wadi Musa boasts some of the best bargains, especially in the streets off **Saheed Circle.** Restaurants in this area serve steaming plates of *buhari*, a Jordanian specialty of spiced rice and rotisserie grilled chicken. The menus at many of the restaurants can seem almost identical; check below for establishments with a bit more variety. Many hotels have all-you-can-eat buffets at reasonable prices, and after an exhausting day of hiking, the ability to drag yourself straight from the dining room table to your bed may be worth a few extra dinar. The **super-market** has large pieces of freshly-baked Bedouin bread every morning (JD2 for 10 pieces) and a decent selection of lunch foods (☎03 079 6883; open daily 11am-midnight). Booze is hard to come by in Jordan, but the stout **Petra Beer** can be found at some hotels, including the Valentine Inn (½L JD5). The roof tea garden of the imposing **Movenpick Hotel** is a great place to watch the sunset, if you can afford it: the bar is well-stocked but quite pricey (16oz. beer JD7).

 FUNGUS IN THE SUN. Be wary of outdoor falafel stands late in the day. Hummus goes bad particularly quicky; if it is warm or runny, just say no.

Al-Arabi Restaurant (☎03 215 7661), on the main traffic circle. Serves Jordanian street food with more style and variety than its counterparts throughout the city. Dishes such as chicken tikka (JD5) add some diversity to the typical menu of falafel (JD1), shawarma (JD1.50), and a selection of salads (JD2). The indoor seating and fountain offset the grime and noise of the city. Open 6am-11pm daily. Cash only. ❷

Turkish BBQ Restaurant (☎077 624 2104), left of the main traffic circle when facing downhill. Standard fare with a Turkish twist. The well-spiced chicken plate includes salad and bread (JD4). Shawarma plate and drink JD4. Open daily 11am-11pm. Cash only. ❷

Buhara Restuarant (☎03 215 4225), just left of the 3-way intersection downhill of the main traffic circle. Known for the deliciously spiced rice of their *briani* (JD1.75) and *buhari* (JD2). Vegetarian options include the cucumber and yogurt plate (JD1) and lentil soup (JD1.75). Open 7am-midnight. Cash only. ❶

Sanabel Bakery (☎03 215 7925), at the 3-way intersection downhill of the traffic circle. An amazing variety of Jordanian sweet pastries (JD3-5 per kg). The reddish *kinafi* (JD 4 per kg) is a local favorite. Open 6am-midnight. Cash only. ❶

Red Cave Restaurant (☎03 215 7799), 50m in front of the entrance to Petra. Whether you call it a "red cave" or a "long hallway with fake plants and harsh fluorescent lighting," it still provides the best deal this close to the entrance. A huge plate of *kufta* (minced meat, parsley, onion, and pepper) served with salad and bedouin bread will fill you up for JD7. Relax afterward with some *shisha* (JD4). Open 9am-10:30pm. Cash only. ❸

Al-Wadi Restaurant (☎077 927 2834), on the main traffic circle. The popular breakfast omelettes (JD2) have energized many a ruin-hungry tourist, and the hearty Arabic kebab plate (JD5) will knock you out at the end of the day if hiking in Petra doesn't get you first. The English-speaking manager is friendly and willing to arrange transportation to hotels and Wadi Rum. Open daily 9am-11pm. Cash only. ❷

Cleopatra's Restaurant (☎077 616 1939), left of Shaheed Circle when facing downhill. A range of traditional Jordanian food a notch above the gaggle of quick eats in Shaheed Circle. The dinner buffet is a huge spread of chicken, lamb, soup and a variety of rice dishes. At JD5, it's half the price of identical meals near the entrance to Petra. ½-chicken JD2.50. Open daily 6am-11pm. Cash only. ❷

⬛ HIKING

Many people rave about Petra's most accessible ten percent, content with what they can see in one day. The Bedouin say, however, that in order to appreciate Petra, you must stay long enough to watch your nails grow long.

Wadi Turkimaniyyeh. The shortest and easiest of the hikes leads down the wadi to the left of and behind the Temple of the Winged Lions. 15min. of strolling down the road running through the rich green gardens of Wadi Turkimaniyyeh leads to the only tomb at Petra with a Nabatean inscription. The lengthy invocation above the entrance beseeches the god Dushara to protect the tomb from violation. Unfortunately, Dushara took a permanent sabbatical and the chamber has been stripped bare.

Al-Habis. A 2nd, more interesting climb begins at the end of the road that descends from the Pharaoh's Pillar to the cliff face, a few hundred meters left of the museum. The trail dribbles up to al-Habis, the prison. While the steps have been restored recently, they do not lead up to much. A path winds all the way around the mountain, however, revealing gorgeous canyons and more tombs on the western side. The climb to the top and back takes less than an hour.

Jabal Harun. This climb begins just to the right of Jabal Habis, below the museum. A sign points to **al-Deir** (the Monastery) and leads northwest across Wadi Siyah, past the Forum Restaurant and on to Wadi Deir and its fragrant oleander. Squeeze through the narrowing canyon along an endless, twisting stairway to confront a human-shaped hole in the facade of the **Lion's Tomb.** A hidden tomb awaits daredevils who try to climb the cleft to the right; less intrepid wanderers can backtrack to the right and spot the tomb a few min. later. Back on the path, veer left to reach Petra's largest monument. Larger but less ornate than the Khazneh, al-Deir has a single inner chamber that dates back to the 1st century CE. Most scholars believe that al-Deir was originally either a Nabatean temple or an unfinished tomb dedicated to one of the later Nabatean kings. It picked up its orthodox appellation in the Byzantine period. On the left, a lone tree popping through a crack in the rock marks more ancient steps, which continue all the way up to the rim of the urn atop the monastery. Those with more courage than caution may actually step out onto the ancient urn. Straight across the wadi looms the highest peak in the area, **Jabal Harun** (Aaron's Mountain or Mt. Hor). On top of the mountain, a white church reportedly houses the **Tomb of Aaron.** The hike straight up to al-Deir takes 30min,, but the whole trip takes a few hours. Expect to spend a couple more hours if you detour into **Wadi Siyah** and visit its seasonal waterfall on the way back. Jabal Harun requires a guide. Guides have no official price, so must be negotiated individually. Expect to pay about JD50 for 3hr or JD100-130 for a full day. If you feel lost, keep a sharp eye out for remnants of donkey visits, which can serve as a trail of crumbs.

The High Place of Sacrifice. One of the most popular hikes is the circular route to the **High Place of Sacrifice** on **Jabal al-Madhbah,** a site of sacrifice with a full view of Petra. A staircase sliced into the rock leads to the left just as the Roman Theater comes into view. Follow the right prong when the trail levels and forks at the top of the stairs. On the left, **Obelisk Ridge** presents one obelisk to Dushara and another to al-Uzza. On the peak to the right, the High Place supports a string of grisly sights: 2 altars, an ablution cistern, gutters for draining away sacrificial blood, and cliff-hewn bleachers for an unobstructed view of animal sacrifices. Head downhill past the Pepsi stand, leaving the obelisks behind you, and backtrack under the western face of the High Place. A hard-to-find staircase leads down to a sculptured **Lion Fountain.** The first grotto complex beyond it is the **Garden Tomb.** Below it is the **Tomb of the Roman Soldier** and across from it a rock **triclinium** (feast hall), which has the only decorated interior in Petra. The trail then leads into Wadi Farasa and ends near the Pillar. The circle, followed either way, takes about 1½hr.

🔘 SIGHTS

PETRA

Many spectacular monuments are close enough to be viewed in a day, but a few require multi-day expeditions. Guides are expensive but recommended for four of the remoter hikes. Bring water bottles from outside; Bedouin sell water throughout the park, but at JD1-2 per bottle, you'll need to empty the Treasury to stay hydrated. Open daily in summer 6am-6pm; in winter 6am-5pm, but hours are loosely enforced. If you stay to see the sunset, you should have no problem getting out. 1 day JD21; 2 days JD26; 3 days JD31. 50% discount for students and children. Visitor's Center ☎ 03 215 6020.

Although the Nabateans worshiped only two deities—Dushara (the god of strength) and al-Uzza (or Atargatis, the goddess of water and fertility)—the number of temples and tombs in Petra seems infinite. Climbing will allow you to escape the tour groups crowding the inner valley. Paths beyond the standard one-day itinerary are marked by stones piled into neat columns.

OBELISK TOMB. If you head toward the canyon-like *siq*, large *djinn* monuments (ghost tombs) and caves will stare down at you from distant mountain faces. The Obelisk Tomb is built high into the cliff on the left. Closer to the entrance of the *siq*, rock-cut channels once cradled the ceramic pipes that brought 'Ain Musa's waters to the city and the surrounding country. A nearby dam burst in 1963, and the resulting flood killed 28 tourists in the *siq*. While designing the new dam, the Nabateans' ancient dam was uncovered and used as a model.

KHAZNEH. As you enter the *siq*, 200m walls on either side begin to block out the sunlight, casting enormous shadows on the niches that once held icons meant to hex unwelcome visitors. The *siq* winds around for 1½km, then slowly emits a faint pink glow at the first peek of the Khazneh (Treasury). The Khazneh is the best preserved of Petra's monuments, though bullet holes are clearly visible on the upper urn. Believing the urn to be hollow and filled with ancient pharaonic treasures, Bedouin periodically fired at it, hoping to burst this petrified piñata. Actually, the Treasury is a royal tomb and quite solid. The Khazneh's rock face changes color as the day progresses: in the morning, the sun's rays give the monument a rich peach hue; in late afternoon, it glistens rose; and by sunset it drips blood red.

ROMAN THEATER. Down the road to the right as you face the Khazneh, Wadi Musa opens up to the 7000-seat Roman Theater. The long row of Royal Tombs on the face of Jabal Khubtha stands to the right. The Romans built their theater under the red stone Nabatean necropolis, and the ancient carved caves still yawn above it. The theater has been restored to its second-century appearance, and audiences are returning after a 1500-year intermission. A marble Hercules (now in the museum) was discovered just a few years ago in the curtained chambers beneath the stage.

ROYAL TOMBS. Across the Wadi are the Royal Tombs. The **Urn Tomb**, with its unmistakable recessed facade, commands an awe-inspiring view of the still-widening valley. The two-tiered vault beneath the pillared facade is known as the **prison,** or *sijin*. A Greek inscription on an inner wall describes how the tomb, originally dedicated to the Nabatean King Malichus II in the first century CE, was converted to a church 400 years later. Nearby sits the **Corinthian Tomb**— allegedly a replica of Nero's Golden Palace in Rome—and the **Palace Tomb** (or the Tomb in Two Stories), which juts out from the mountainside. Laborers completed the tomb by attaching preassembled stones to its upper left-hand corner. Around the corner to the right is the **Tomb of Sextus Florentinus,** who was so enamored of these hewn heights that he asked his son to bury him in this ultimate outpost of the Roman Empire.

MAIN STREET. Around the bend to the left, a few restored columns are all that remain of the paved Roman main street. Two thousand years ago, columns lined the full length of the street, shielding markets and residences. At the beginning of the street on the right, the **Nymphaeum** ruins outline the ancient public fountain near its base. On a rise to the right, before the triple-arched gate, recent excavations have uncovered the Temple of al-Uzza (Atargatis), also called the **Temple of the Winged Lions.** In the spring you can watch the progress of American-sponsored excavations that have already uncovered several workshops.

BYZANTINE CHURCH. A joint Jordanian-American team has recently excavated an immense Byzantine church with a wealth of mosaics. The site lies several hundred meters to the right of the Roman street, near the Temple of the Winged Lions. Each of the church's side aisles is paved with 70 sq. m of remarkably preserved mosaic, depicting humans of various professions, representations of the four seasons, and indigenous, exotic, and even mythological animals. Recent studies attest that the church was the seat of an important Byzantine bishopric in the fifth and sixth centuries, an assertion that challenges the belief that Petra was in decline by 600 CE. The archaeologists on the site constantly dig, scrape, and sniff. They also protect their site quite zealously—entrance may require charm and luck.

SOUTHERN TEMPLE AND ENVIRONS. A team from Brown University is in the process of unearthing the Southern Temple. White hexagonal paving stones cover an extensive tunnel system that marks the importance of this holy site. Farther along, the triple-arched **Temenos Gate** was once the front gate of the **Qasr Bint Fara'un** (Palace of the Pharaoh's Daughter), a Nabatean temple built to honor the god Dushara. On the left before the gate are the **Nabatean Baths**. On a trail leading behind the temple to the left, a single standing column, **Amoud Fara'un** (Pharaoh's Pillar), gloats beside its two fallen comrades.

MUSEUMS. To the right of the Nabatean temple, a rock-hewn staircase leads to a small **archaeological museum** holding the spoils of the Winged Lions dig as well as carved stone figures from elsewhere in Petra. On the way to the monastery, the **Nabatean Museum** has good artifacts and air-conditioned restrooms with what is probably the ■**world's best toilet seat view.** *(Both museums open daily in summer 9am-5pm, in winter 9am-4pm. Free.)*

HIGH SINAI

סיני سيناء

The central region of the Sinai Peninsula, known as the High Sinai, is worlds away from the lazy daze of Dahab. Cosmopolitan coastal life may cause you to forget that you're on the outskirts of over 60,000 square kilometers of arid desert, but savvy hikers know that high times can be had in the High Sinai. Nestled in this rugged desertscape are the biblical locales of Mount Sinai, the mountain on which Moses received the Ten Commandments, and St. Catherine's Monastery, near the Burning Bush. The High Sinai desert is an ideal place for unforgettable hikes. The hard sandstone also makes for some fantastic bouldering, though this is illegal on Mt. Sinai and dangerous everywhere.

TIP **CALLING EGYPT.** When calling Sinai from Israel or elsewhere outside of Egypt, don't forget the international dialing code (☎+20).

PRICE DIVERSITY: SINAI

(For more detailed information about price diversity, see p. VIII.)

	❶	❷	❸	❹	❺
Accommodations	under E£30	E£31-65	E£66-100	E£101-150	over E£150
Food	under E£10	E£11-25	E£26-40	E£41-60	over E£60

BORDER CROSSING

Crossing from Eilat to Taba takes a while and costs a few Egyptian pounds. Passports must be valid for at least three months; Israeli visas must be valid for the day of travel. For travel outside Sinai, obtain a visa at the Egyptian consulate. The border is open 24hr. but is closed on Yom Kippur and 'Eid al-Adha. Inquire with a hostel owner about border closings on holidays.

The border-crossing process unfolds in an orderly way but involves a surprisingly long hike. Allow at least an hour; longer on a busy day. Take the #15 bus from Eilat, and keep your passport handy; it will be checked frequently throughout the 1km obstacle course to the bus depot on the other side. There are 11 exciting steps: 1. Bus drop-off. 2. Little Taba snack bar ("last beer before Sinai"). 3. Passport pre-check. 4. Passport control booth (pay NIS86 exit tax). 5. Israeli last passport check; they automatically stamp your passport at this point unless you ask them not to. 6. Stroll through no man's land. 7. Egyptian passport control: fill out entry form, get stamp. 8. Egyptian security (X-ray machine). 9. Post-border passport check. 10. Passport check and E£17 Egyptian border tax. The **Taba Hilton** is the best place to change money (open 24hr., no commission for foreign currency converted to Egyptian pounds). 11. Welcome to Egypt! The bus station is a 10min. walk from the border on the left.

For Sinai stays of 14 days or less, get a Sinai-only visa stamp on the Egyptian side of the border. This visa limits travel to the Gulf of Aqaba coast as far south as Sharm al-Sheikh (but not the area around Sharm al-Sheikh, including Ras Muhammad) and to St. Catherine's monastery and Mt. Sinai (but not sites in the vicinity of St. Catherine's). Unlike ordinary one-month Egyptian visas, the Sinai-only visa has no grace period; you'll pay a hefty fine if you overextend your stay.

From Taba there are two main bus lines: to Cairo (7hr., E£60) leaving at 10:30am and 4:30pm; and to Nuweiba (1½hr., E£11) followed by Dahab (2½hr., E£25) ending in Sharm al-Sheikh (3-4hr., E£30), leaving at 9am and 3pm. There are always taxis waiting to take people to Dahab, Cairo, and Nuweiba. There may be a long wait until they fill up, but the fare is only slightly more expensive than the bus if the taxi is full. After the last bus, taxi prices rise dramatically.

GETTING AROUND

Travel in the Sinai Peninsula is far easier than in the rest of Egypt. Women can comfortably wear shorts and sleeveless shirts in most places, and professional con artists are rare. Many Bedouin have given up their camels for Camaros, but there are still places where travelers can get a sense of the nomadic lifestyle.

The noble machines of the **East Delta Bus Company,** battered cruelly by the rocks, ruts, and dust of Sinai roads, heroically tread the scorched highway. With towns few and far between, buses and taxis are the only means of transportation. Timetables are really no more than an administrator's pipe dream. At bus stations, patience is more a necessity than a virtue.

PETRA AND SINAI

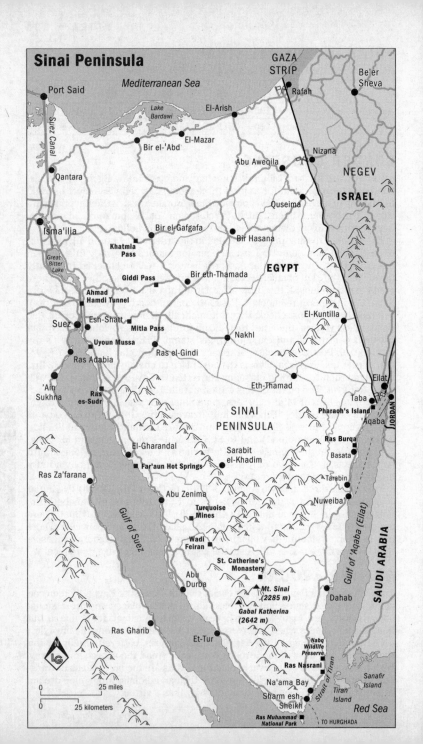

A reasonably priced and convenient alternative to buses is the *service* taxi. Weathered Peugeot 504s piloted by Bedouin cabbies are ubiquitous. Hop in with other passengers or negotiate with a driver and wait while he recruits more travelers. Women should avoid riding alone with a driver. *Service* taxis are comparable in price to the bus under ideal circumstances, but only with a full load of seven. Taxi prices will drop immediately before the arrival of a bus, then skyrocket after the bus has departed.

 BUS CHECKPOINTS. Buses are stopped regularly in the Sinai for no apparent reason. Generally the police officer will ignore tourists, but expect to be asked for your passport at least once per ride, and be prepared.

Taxi drivers will often offer astronomical prices, but can be bargained down easily. This is to be expected with any economic transaction in Egypt, where fixed prices are essentially nonexistent. More worrisome are the variety of other creative scams, such as raising the price in the middle of a ride through the desert, or attempting to charge each passenger the full fare. In these cases, do not be afraid to make your case firmly and, if necessary, loudly and angrily. Taxi drivers can be devious, but generally avoid direct confrontation. If you get angry, they will almost certainly back down. In the rare cases where a taxi driver becomes confrontational, it's not worth it to pick a fight: simply write off your loss as an inherent part of taxi travel in Egypt.

The Sinai is divided into four major regions: the Northern Sinai governate has its capital at al-Arish; the rugged terrain and industrial belching of the Western Sinai is not for the faint-of-heart; the High Sinai makes for great hiking and biblical sightseeing; and the Gulf of Aqaba coast, Sinai's major hotspot, is known the world over as a scuba diver's paradise.

MOUNT SINAI

☎069

הרסי)טור סיناء

The holy peak of Mt. Sinai, or as locals call it, Mt. Moses (Gabal Mussa), stands 2285m above sea level. The Bible describes a mountain engulfed in fire and smoke that Moses ascended to receive the Ten Commandments while the Israelites built a golden calf at its base. Mount Sinai is one of only two places in the Old Testament where God revealed himself to the people, making the desolate peak sacred for both Christians and Muslims (Jews have not unanimously identified the modern Mount Sinai as the promontory made famous by the Bible). In the Book of Exodus, God warned the people, "Take heed that you do not go up into the mountain or touch the border of it; whoever touches the mountain shall be put to death" (Exodus 19:12). This prohibition seems to have been long forgotten—busloads of tourists climb the peak each day. Despite the Baraka bottles, the view from the summit is awe-inspiring.

The mountain is located behind St. Catherine's Monastery, outside of the town center. Pass the souvenir stands and guard checkpoint outside of town, then take the right fork at St. Catherine's Guesthouse.

🗡 HIKING

You don't necessarily need a guide, but for safety, neither men nor women should hike alone, especially at night. Most people hook up with organized

LOCAL LEGEND

WHERE WAS THAT SINAI, ANYWAY?

Everyone knows Moses received the Ten Commandments on top of Mt. Sinai; turns out, though, that no one knows exactly which Mount is the Sinai in question. Remember: map-making was never the ancient Israelites' strong suit. With a decent cartographer, they probably could have cut those forty years in the wilderness down to two or three.

The Biblical record is pretty vague; the only clues are that Mt. Sinai must have had a plain around it large enough for the Israelites to camp on, and a peak that you can see from the bottom. The earliest Christian traditions, dating back to the fourth century, believed Sinai was today's Mt. Serbal, some 20 miles away. In the sixth century, the crown passed to nearby Mt. Catherine, earning it the beautiful monastery at its foot (p. 397). Today's location, a peak known as *Jabal Musa* ("Moses' Mountain"), has only held the title of Mt. Sinai since the 15th century, based on an aggressive advertising campaign by local Bedouin tribes and tour group organizers.

Still, academics aren't all convinced. Scholarly debate rages on, with mountains in Egypt, Saudi Arabia, and Jordan all in contention. But don't expect Mt. Sinai to move any time soon; after all, who wants to tell twenty generations of pilgrims they've been hiking up the wrong hilltop?

groups from Dahab (check with hostel managers for information) and begin their climb around 2am in order to enjoy the cool night and catch the sunrise at the top. Bring a flashlight. If you do hike, do so in the early afternoon when it's still light, watch the sunset, and sleep on the summit. Neither hiking shoes nor sneakers are necessary for the climb, but considering the amount of camel dung you'll walk over (especially at night), you probably don't want to expose your bare feet. Socialites can stake out a spot directly on the summit platform by the tea and refreshment stands. More secluded spots are available just beyond the boulders and human feces on the sloping shoulder to the west. Walk about 40m until you cross a ravine; the small summit ahead has several campsites protected by stone windbreaks. If you explore this area during the daylight hours, you'll discover an ancient Bedouin cistern where water was stored during the summers. You can also beat the crowds by sleeping in **Elijah's Hollow,** or by climbing at midday (not recommended in summer).

Overnighters should bring ample food, and everyone should bring at least 2L. of water for the ascent. The cheapest place to buy these amenities is a supermarket in St. Catherine's town. The monastery rest house also sells snacks and water at reasonable prices. There are refreshment stands on the way up, but prices increase with altitude. A stand on the summit sells tea (E£4), water (E£7), and various snacks (E£4-9). If you plan to spend the night on the mountain, bring a sleeping bag and warm clothes. Even in the summer, it's often only 8-10°C at night, and the breeze makes it feel much colder. Those without the necessary gear can rent blankets (E£4) at the top. Hikers should bring a warm change of clothing—sweaty shirts quickly turn to shirtsicles. There are also "toilets" at the summit (holes in the ground with more flies than privacy); try to use the cleaner facilities near the base if at all possible.

The hike to the top is not that challenging, but you should still leave all but the bare essentials behind. The manager at St. Catherine's Guesthouse (p. 396) will allow you to leave your bags in a room (E£5 per bag per day). There are two paths up the mountain: the **Steps of Repentance** and a **camel path.** To find either path, walk up the hill to the monastery, bear left at the fork, and continue to the back of the monastery. From here the camel path continues down the valley while the Steps start to the right, at the southeast corner of the monastery.

There is one juncture that confuses hikers: near the top, the camel path intersects the Steps after passing through a narrow, steeply walled stone corridor. Turn left to reach the summit; the camel path stops here. Riders will have to get off their high humps and huff up the rest of the way.

Steps of Repentance, about 2hr. 1 of 2 mountain paths, this one is shorter and more difficult, but you probably deserve it. It is said that the 3750 steps were built by a single monk in order to fulfill his pledge of penitence. The monk apparently cut corners here and there and made many of the steps the height of two or three normal ones. The steps are treacherous by night; after sunset they are difficult to follow even with a flashlight. Save them for the descent in the morning.

Camel Path, at night about 2½hr. by toed foot, 1½hr. by cloven. Built in the 19th century, this longer route begins directly behind the monastery. Guided camel tour of the mountain E£85 during peak hours. 1-way ride from the camel-herders at the base of the path E£60 (price negotiable). If you can stand the sun and the heat, you can get a ride up in the middle of the day for a much better price. Unfortunately, the camels are not always available when you need them—you may arrive at the dispatch area and find only dung.

Elijah's Hollow. Turn right at the juncture about two-thirds of the way up and you'll arrive at a 500-year-old cypress tree dominating the depressional plain known as Elijah's Hollow. This is where the prophet Elijah is said to have heard the voice of God after fleeing Jezebel (I Kings 19:8-18). Two small chapels now occupy the site, one dedicated to Elijah and the other to his successor Elisha. Moses supposedly hid in the cave below when he first came face-to-face with God: "While my glory passes by, I will put you in a cleft of the rock, and I will cover you with my hand until I have passed by" (Exodus 33:22). You can still see the watering hole used by the prophet. Chapel opens at sunrise for 1-2hr.

SAINT CATHERINE'S　　　　☎069

St. Catherine's rich history of monasticism started in the third century CE when Christian hermits, attracted by the tradition designating the valley below as the site of the Burning Bush, migrated here in a quest for holiness and freedom from Roman persecution. Living in complete poverty and isolation (except on holy days, when they gathered at the Burning Bush), these hermits often fell victim to harsh weather and raiding nomads. In AD 313, the emperor Constantine officially recognized Christianity, and soon afterwards the monastery was founded by Constantine's mother, Empress Helena. The monastery has thrived under the continual protection of rulers from the Prophet Muhammad to Napoleon, through the present day. A tribute to the monks' tradition of hospitality to Christians and Muslims alike, it has never been conquered. Modern pilgrims and curious tourists of all faiths visit St. Catherine's throughout the year. Though much of the monastery is closed to the public, its beautiful architecture and mountainous setting ensure an unforgettable visit.

PETRA AND SINAI

▐ TRANSPORTATION

Buses: The bus station is just off the main road, to the right as you enter town. Ticket office subject to unpredictable closings; check with your bus driver to arrange a ticket back. There is usually a 9:30am bus from Dahab (E£18), although unscrupulous taxi drivers and hostel owners may tell you otherwise in an effort to get you to join one of their groups. Buses run sporadically to **Cairo** (9hr., 6pm, E£40), **Nuweiba** (5hr., 1pm, E£18), and **Taba** via **Dahab**. July-Aug. there is occasionally a bus to **Sharm al-Sheikh** (3hr.); check with hotel owners or bus drivers for time and price.

Taxis: If you can't make the bus, try to share a cab round-trip for a better deal. Cabbies will initially offer E£400 round trip, but have been known to go as low as E£220 including a 3hr. wait at the monastery. If you plan to spend more than 5hr. it is better to bargain for 1-way prices, especially early in the morning. Taxis tend to congregate around the bus station and the entrance to St. Catherine monastery in the late morning to catch the crowd from the midnight hike, becoming scarcer as the day goes on. The prices are quite high if not shared; try to bargain in groups for more leverage. It is usually possible to find a ride to **Cairo** (E£550 per car), **Dahab** (E£140-180 per car), **Nuweiba** (E£200-240 per car), and **Sharm al-Sheikh** (E£200-250 per car). Lone women should avoid taxis.

⚓ ▨ ORIENTATION AND PRACTICAL INFORMATION

At an elevation of about 1600m, St. Catherine's is hidden away in the mountainous interior of the southern Sinai. The roads into town come from the Gulf of Suez to the west and the Gulf of Aqaba to the east. The **monastery** is about 3km east of town at the entrance to Mt. Sinai.

Bank:Bank Misr (☎69 347 0463), opposite the tourist police. **Currency exchange.** Open daily 8:30am-2pm, 6-9pm; F and Sa exchange only.

Police: (☎69 347 0313), across from the bus station. **Tourist Police** (☎69 347 0046), in the compound with the police station.

Hospital: (☎69 347 0368), across from the bus station, in the police compound.

Telephone Service:Telecom Egypt (☎69 347 0012), on the left side of the main street before the bank. Open 24hr.

Post Office: (☎69 347 0301), on the left side of the main street in front of Telecom Egypt. Open Su-Th and Sa 8am-3pm. **Postal code:** 46616.

▦ ▧ ACCOMMODATIONS AND CAMPING

St. Catherine's has a few seasonal **campgrounds,** most located 1km or so outside of town. Inquire at the tourist police for directions and openings. More reliable accommodations can be found at the places listed below.

▨ El Malga Bedouin Camp (☎69 347 0457; www.sheikmousa.com), past the petrol station, 1st paved right turn, next to Sheikh Mousa's. Pitch a tent in the courtyard (E£10), or move into a clean, breezy adobe bunkhouse (E£20). More luxurious accommodations include: singles E£50; doubles E£80; and a quads with private bathroom E£150. Cash only. ❶

St. Catherine's Guesthouse (☎69 347 0353), next to the monastery. Clean, quiet rooms with a surprising level of luxury, given the price. A/C. Book in advance in late summer and during holidays. Singles US$35; doubles US$60; triples US$75; quads US$88; 6-person family suite $100. MC/V. ❺

▢ FOOD

The area around the bus stop is filled with cheap restaurants and grocery stores. The restaurants are nearly indistinguishable, serving mostly pizza, pasta, and simple rice dishes. Though the food is far from haute cuisine, the price is right—anywhere from E£8-16 for a full meal.

El Malga Restaurant (☎69 347 0457), in the Bedouin camp next to Shiekh Moussa's place, serves some of the only traditional Middle-Eastern cuisine in St. Catherine's. A standard menu including an Egyptian lunch (hummus, tuna salad, eggs, and pita; E£20) isn't mind-blowing but will certainly fill you up. The chefs are also willing to customize dishes or even add ingredients from local supermarkets, so don't hesitate to ask. Cool off after an afternoon hike with a *lassi* (E£7). Hours vary. ❷

St. Catherine's Guesthouse (☎69 347 0353) also serves lunch and dinner to non-guests. Selection of fixed meals changes often; solid portions E£25. Hours vary seasonally. ❷

👁 SAINT CATHERINE'S MONASTERY SIGHTS

To get to the monastery from the access road, go straight past the tourist police for about 5min. until the fork in the road, then bear left; the monastery is on the right. Spend the night on the mountaintop, watch the sunrise; hike down at 7am and reach the monastery just as the doors open at 9am (to avoid crowds). Modest dress required. Open M-Th and Sa 9-11:45am, F 11am-noon; closed Orthodox holidays. Free. Museum admission E£25. For more information, call (☎69 347 0349) or the monastery's Cairo office, (☎02 482 8513).

St. Catherine's is believed to be the oldest example of unrestored Byzantine architecture in the world. The complex was named after the martyred Alexandrian evangelist, Catherine, whose body was found on top of the Gabal Katerina to the south. About to be tortured on a wheel of knives for converting members of the Roman emperor's family, Catherine was miraculously saved by a malfunction in the wheel. Of course, she wouldn't be a martyr if the Roman's hadn't gone ahead and slit her throat anyway. By some force that seems more undead than divine, her body showed up on top of the isolated mountain centuries later. Once home to hundreds of monks, the monastery now houses only a handful. These monks are as ascetic as Catherine's would-be torturers were bloodthirsty: they never eat meat or drink wine, and they wake up at 4am each morning when the bell of the Church of the Transfiguration is rung 33 times.

The newly renovated **Saint Catherine's museum** now provides a fitting home for St. Catherines' collection of priceless Christian artifacts. The monastery houses many treasures, including over 2000 exquisite fifth-century icons. The icons with brushed gold halos have a holographic effect, an artistic style unique to the Sinai region. In the seventh century, the Prophet Muhammad dictated a document granting protection to the monastery and exempting it from taxes; a copy of this still hangs in the icon gallery, near a similar letter penned by Napoleon in 1798.

Near the museum stands the **Church of the Transfiguration.** Around 530, Emperor Justinian ordered a splendid basilica within a walled fortress to be constructed on the top of Mount Sinai, next to the then 200-year-old chapel. When Justinian's trusted architect Stephanos found the mountain's peak too narrow, he built the structure we now see next to St. Eleni's chapel. This structure became known as the Church of the Transfiguration, owing to its spectacular almond-shaped mosaic depicting this event in Jesus's life. The peeved emperor ordered Stephanos's execution, but the builder lived out his days in the safety of the monastery and eventually achieved sainthood (his bones are in the ossuary). Both St. Helena and Justinian dedicated their structures to the Virgin Mary, since Christian tradition asserts that the Burning Bush foreshadowed the Annunciation, when the archangel Gabriel heralded the birth of Christ.

Only the central nave of the Church of the Transfiguration is open to the public. On tiptoe you can see mosaics of a barefoot Moses in the **Chapel of the Burning Bush,** behind the altar. Should you manage to visit the icons back there, you'll have to remove your shoes, as the roots of the sacred shrub extend under the floor (a living descendant grows just outside). Such privileges are only accorded to true pilgrims, who are traditionally allowed to ask God for one favor. The monks themselves, with the help of the local Gabaliyya Bedouin (descended from Byzantine slaves), built a **mosque** within the fortress to convince advancing Ottoman armies that the complex was partly Muslim.

Outside the main entrance of the Church of the Transfiguration is **Moses's Well,** where the savior of the Israelites reportedly freshened up after his holy ascent. The gruesome **ossuary,** a separate building outside the walls, houses the remains of former monks.

SINAI DESERT

Spring and fall are the most temperate seasons for hikes. In summer you'll spend most of the day resting in the shade with the Bedouin until the sun calms down, and in winter you'll freeze. The nights are frigid year-round. You may be able to rent blankets from the Bedouin, but don't count on it; bring a warm sleeping bag.

Organized tours can be arranged in Israel through SPNI. The Israeli travel outfitter Neot ha-Kikar specializes in Sinai tours (offices in Tel Aviv, Jerusalem, and Eilat), with trips beginning in Eilat and Cairo (6-day high range circuit US$360). No matter where in Israel you book your tour, however, you'll eventually end up at Sheikh Moussa's office. You'll save a lot of money by starting there, too.

To venture into any of the mountains other than Mount Sinai, you must be accompanied by a Bedouin guide. Many of the longer treks, either due to their length or location, require a regular Egyptian visa: the Sinai-only tourist visa won't do. Sheikh Moussa (☎(069) 347 0457; mobile ☎01 064 13 575; www. sheikhmousa.com; Sheikhmousa@yahoo.com), head of Mountain Tours, has a monopoly on all the mountains, and trips must be arranged through him (reservations accepted). To get to his office in St. Catherine's town, walk uphill from the town square, past the petrol station. Take the first paved right turn and walk for three minutes; Mr. Moussa will be lounging outside.

Sheikh Moussa will procure both a guide and a permit for you. The price, which includes guide, food, and camels, is US$20-50 per person per day, and fluctuates depending on the size of your party, where you go, and the time of year. Surplus gear can be stored in Sheikh Moussa's house. You'll leave for your hike within an hour of arriving at his office. You and your guide will camp with the Bedouin, so be prepared for long nights by the fire smoking "Bedouin tobacco," drinking tea, and learning a great deal about a little-known culture. Tell Sheikh Moussa what you want to see and how quickly, and he'll tailor an itinerary. Treks last anywhere from two to 15+ days.

Moussa can also arrange **rock climbing** as part of any trek. The hard, frictuous sandstone around Mt. Sinai is ideal for climbing, containing thousands of years worth of jagged, weather-worn features without being overworn or smooth. If you're not convinced, check out some of the boulders on in to St. Catherine, though be advised that bouldering is particularly dangerous in this remote area.

The following is a brief sample of the destinations to which Moussa has access. Each can be done as a day trip or as part of a larger itinerary.

Gabal Banat: a mountain north of St. Catherine's overlooking the vast desert. 2 days.

Gabal Bab: From this peak you can see west all the way to the gulf of Suez. 2 days.

Gabal Katerina: The highest mountain in Egypt (2642m), 6km south of Mt. Sinai. The path to the top is more difficult, secluded, and beautiful than Sinai's well-worn tourist highway. A chapel replenishes you with shade at the summit. 11 hrs.

Gabal 'Abbas Pasha: A rock with palace ruins and excellent views.

Gabal al-Agrod: A deep, crystal-clear mountain pool where you can swim in the shade of overhanging trees and dive off of the surrounding rocks. 3 days.

Wadi Nogra: A rocky valley with a natural dam (Nogra dam). The water trickles off moss-covered boulders to form a natural shower.

Wadi Talla: Two pools. Go to the big *wadi* for some spring-fed swimming.

Sheikh Owat: A picturesque oasis with palm trees, a deep well, and a lot of goats.

GULF OF AQABA (GULF OF EILAT)

מפרץ خليج العقبة

The Gulf of Aqaba coast offers underwater splendor, with some of the world's best scuba diving, particularly in Sharm al-Sheikh. It is also home to Dahab, a yesteryear hippie haven known for its relaxed atmosphere and good times. Above water and below, the Gulf of Aqaba coast offers its travelers beauty and excitement.

☑UNDERWATER TIPS

Without question, the Red Sea has some of the greatest coral reefs and marine life in the world. Diving was not very big in the Middle East until Jacques-Yves Cousteau made his voyage through the Red Sea aboard *Calypso*, as chronicled in his famous book and movie *The Silent World*. Now that diving is a major part of many trips to the Sinai Peninsula, the regional administration has begun to face the serious problem of irresponsible ecotourism. All coral reefs from Dahab to Ras Muhammad are under the jurisdiction of the **Ras Muhammad National Park.** Regulations forbid the removal or defacement of any animal, plant, or shell, living or dead, from the sea. The park is fighting a difficult battle with developers waiting to exploit the region. You can do your part to preserve the reefs by observing a simple rule: **look, but don't touch.** Ras Muhammad, like most James Bond movies, has underwater police who will chase you out of the water if they see you breaking this rule. Even accidentally bumping the coral can damage it (and damage you).

Diving is very expensive, but you're paying for safety. The sites along the Gulf of Aqaba coast listed in the cities below emphasize safety above all else. **Snorkeling gear** can be rented all over, while **dive shops** are concentrated mainly in Dahab and Sharm al-Sheikh. Divers must be certified to rent equipment; most five-day courses provide certification and cost around US$450. The only **decompression chamber** in the area is in Sharm al-Sheikh. If you're rusty, take a check-out dive for US$50.

Beginning divers should make sure their instructors speak their language flawlessly, as small misunderstandings can have a big significance underwater ("Tanks!" "You're welcome!"). The instructor must also be certified to teach your particular course, whether it's PADI or SSI—ask to see his or her card. Some clubs are active in protecting the reefs, participating in annual clean-up dives, and making sure their operations have minimal impact on the marine ecosystems. The size of the club also matters: larger centers often have more scheduled dives and more extensive facilities, whereas smaller ones give you personal attention and will usually run a course for just one or two people rather than waiting for six to sign up. Quality of equipment and safety records are important. Ask divers for advice.

⚅DIVE SAFETY

Hidden among the crevices in the coral reefs around the Sinai Peninsula are creatures capable of inflicting serious injury and even death. If you see something that looks like an aquatic pin cushion, it's probably a sea urchin or a blowfish, both of which should be touched only in sushi form. Avoid the feathery lionfish as well—its harmless-looking spines can deliver a paralyzing sting. The well-named fire coral can bloat a leg to mammoth proportions, leaving welts the size of croquet balls. The stonefish is camouflaged flawlessly to resemble a mossy lump of coral or rock; if you step on one, you'll puff up and may die within hours. The list goes on. Before plunging in, ask at any dive shop for a look at one of the picture cards that identifies these underwater uglies.

When snorkeling, try to enter the water in a sandy area to avoid damaging underwater plants and animals. If you have no choice but to enter where sea creatures and coral may dwell, wear foot protection. Sharks are attracted by blood, so never enter the water with an open wound or if menstruating. Panicking and thrashing tends to excite sharks. If you see an animal getting defensive, simply back away slowly. *Let's Go* does not recommend dying.

DAHAB ☎069

دهب

Like Goa or Amsterdam, Dahab (meaning "gold" in Arabic) is one of those places that has grown larger than life in the minds of travelers. For most, it conjures up images of glossy-eyed, tie-dyed hippies lounging on the shore, blissfully asphyxiating themselves in blue clouds of marijuana smoke. While this scene is still a significant part of the Dahab experience, Dahabitants no longer think of Jamaica with the reverence that Mecca inspires in the rest of the Arab world. The hippies are slowly being outnumbered by cleaner-cut travelers and dive instructors. Dahab die-hards of yesteryear may lament its relative cleanliness, but the town is becoming more like paradise, not less.

 JUST SAY NO. Dahab used to be known for its dope scene, and although the smoke is clearing somewhat, it still has a fine selection of local herbs and spices. Bedouins are usually running the operation, while Egyptians try to hawk hashish at astronomical prices to tourists on the street. Remember that cannabis is illegal in Egypt: *Let's Go* just says no.

⬛ TRANSPORTATION

Buses: In Dahab city, about 2km southeast of Mashraba. To **Cairo** (5 per day, E£90); **Nuweiba** (10:30am, 4, 6:30pm; E£22); **Sharm al-Sheikh** (10 per day, E£15); and **Taba** (10:30am, E£30). There is often a bus to St. Catherine's at 9:30am, but check with a hostel manager to make sure.

Taxis: At the northern end of Sharia al-Mashraba. Rides to the bus station can be had for as low as E£4 after extended haggling, but expect an initial offer of E£40 or higher. E£5-10 from the bus station to the town center costs around.

✈ 🛈 ORIENTATION AND PRACTICAL INFORMATION

Dahab is divided into two major parts: **Dahab City** holds the post office and bus station, but is of little interest to the traveler, while the beachfront area is known as **Assalah** is of great interest. In the middle of Assalah is a bridge; at the north end you'll find **Lighthouse Beach.**

Bank:Egypt Banque (☎069 364 0921), just north of the bridge. Open Su-Th 9am-3pm and 6-9pm, F 9am-noon and 6-9pm.

Police: (☎69 364 0213), in the white building next to Ghazala Supermarket, halfway between the bridge and Lighthouse beach. **Tourist Police** (☎069 364 0188), southwest of the beach in Dahab city.

Pharmacy: Next to Ghazala supermarket. Open 24hr.

Hospital: Dahab Hospital (☎069 640 208), in Dahab City.

Internet Access: Seven Heaven Internet Cafe (☎069 640 080), in Seven Heaven just north of the bridge. E£10 per hour. Open daily 10am-2am. Also at the **Peguin Hotel,** p. 402.

Post Office: In Dahab City. Open daily 8:30am-3pm.

⌂ ⌂ ACCOMMODATIONS AND CAMPING

Accommodations on the Gulf of Aqaba coast have started to move upmarket, crowding out smaller hostels in favor of luxury resorts. Luckily, this development has treated the Dahab accommodations scene decently. The sub-par camps have been pushed out of business, leaving a few gems with great prices and comfortable rooms. The hotels in Dahab are a far cry from Eilat's ritzy resorts; they provide much of the comfort at a price that is often within reach of the budget traveler. Though it's getting harder to find dorm beds and beachside camping in Dahab, the private rooms at camps and hotels are a great value. High season is October; call well in advance to reserve. Check www. dahab.net for up-to-date information.

▩ **Oasis Fighting Kangaroo Camp** (☎069 364 0011; www.oasis-fkc.com), one block away from the waterfront, across from Napolean Restaurant. Not to be confused with the fighting kangaroo hotel, this tidy hostel run by Bedouins provides some of the best-maintained budget accommodations in Dahab. 2 stories of private rooms, many with balconies, surround a Bedouin-style seating area where guests relax and watch TV in Arabic, away from the noise of the beach. Well-equipped kitchen, free self-service laundry, and Wi-Fi. A wide range of rooms are available, with price dependent on A/C, balcony, and room size. Singles E£24-50; doubles E£40-80. Cash only. ❶

▩ **Bedouin Lodge** (☎069 364 1125; www.bedouin-lodge-dahab.com), at the southern end of the beach. Among the most social campgrounds in Dahab. At night you'll find mohawked diving instructors pounding down Stellas while playing backgammon with Bedouins in traditional garb as the stereo plays Ben Harper covers of Bob Marley songs. The rooms are basic but clean, and the restaurant is surprisingly good (see **Food,** p. 403). Free Wi-Fi. Singles E£50; doubles E£60. Cash only. ❷

▩ **Seven Heaven** (☎069 364 0080; www.sevenheavenhotel.com), 100m north of bridge near the beach. One of the only establishments still offering dorm beds in Dahab. The bathrooms may not be spotless, but the linens are clean and the rooms aren't bad. If you're looking for a private room with A/C (E£80), there are better values to be had, but at the low end of the price range this place is a steal. Staff is friendly, accommodating, and willing to arrange trips to St. Catherine's (E£70) and glass bottom boat rides. Dorm rooms fill up quickly but cannot be reserved, so show up early to get one. Dorms E£10-20; singles and doubles E£30-80. Cash only. ❶

Marine Garden (☎010 843 8636), 100m north of lighthouse beach. This basic diving camp hosts many international backpackers. Great food and spotless shared bathrooms make for a comfortable place to rest between dives at Lighthouse Beach. Just far enough north to escape the noise of beachside Dahab. Singles E£35; doubles E£45, with A/C E£60. Cash only. ❷

Sindbad Camp (☎010 105 2491; sindbadcamp@gmail.com), 50m north of lighthouse beach. Sunken Bedouin-style seating area in the courtyard makes for a particularly social camp. Offers windsurfing equipment rental and lessons. Be sure to reserve in advance in Oct., as Sindbad fills up quickly with Europeans on holiday. Singles E£45; doubles E£60, with private bath and A/C E£85. Cash only. ❷

Penguin Hotel (☎069 364 1047; www.penguidahab.com). Surrounded by white stucco and marble, grungier travelers may feel a bit out of place in the slightly older crowd. The restaurant serves pricey but delicious food (breakfast E£15). A/C. A higher price gets you a balcony and a view. Internet E£8 per hr., 1-day Wi-Fi pass E£10. Singles E£30; doubles E£40, with private bath E£80-120; triples E£120-180; quads E£160-200. MC/V. Cash only. ❶

Moon Valley Camp (☎018 611 1048), 100m south of the lighthouse, attached to the Octopus World dive center. All rooms with private baths and A/C. Shared kitchen is clean and well-equipped. Best value comes from package discount with dive center. Singles E£55; doubles E£70. Cash only. ❷

Octopus Garden Resort (☎017 225 126; www.octopushotel.net), across from the Penguin Hotel. Fully-furnished rooms are kept frigid by powerful A/C units. Spotless marble baths. Free Wi-Fi. Wheelchair-accessible. Singles E£80; doubles E£100; triples E£120. Cash only. ❸

Amasina Hotel (☎018 163 4011), just behind Fighting Kangaroo Camp. A barren gravel courtyard and complete lack of social space, combined with a surly management, make this an uninviting place. But if you're not going to be around anyway, it's a decent spot for a good night's sleep. The simple rooms are nothing to write home about, but the price is. Singles with fan E£20. Cash only. ❶

🗘 FOOD

Dahab is home to some of the best cheap food in the Sinai. The beachfront is lined with cheap restaurants serving similar menus of fruit with pancakes, Egyptian rice dishes, and seafood. Though some travelers have reported getting sick from the fish, most enjoy Dahab's tasty marine life with no problems. These restaurants are so similar and consistent that one has even called itself **Same Same,** an apt description of its menu. Except to pay around E£20-30 for a meal, and another E£10 for a refreshing fruit shake. Most of the camps also serve meals; some of the best values are listed below. **Ghazala Market,** 200m south of the bridge, carries a large selection of cheap groceries (open 24hr.).

▨ **The Koshary Cart** (☎016 228 2987). Look for this cart being pushed around the northern side of the bay near lighthouse beach during lunchtime. Offers an elaborate take on *koshary* (macaroni with legumes and tomato sauce; E£4), adding to the mix lentils, hummus, fried onion, vinegar, lemon juice, and garlic. Served with crispy pepper strips on top. Open from 11am until the food runs out, usually around 1pm. Cash only. ❶

▨ **Popeye Sandwich** (☎069 364 1151), 1 block away from the waterfront, just south of Lighthouse Beach. This small sandwich counter serves an inventive selection of handmade sandwiches at an unbeatable price. For something a bit more lively, try the chicken fajita sandwich (with olives, peppers, mozzarella, and tahini; E£12.50) or the popeye (chicken, mozzarella, carrots, and peas; E£12.50). A favorite with lighthouse beach dive instructors after a long morning in the water. Small basic sandwiches E£3; large E£7. Open daily 9am-3pm. Cash only. ❶

King Chicken (☎069 364 1405), on the north end of Sharia al-Mashraba, just after the street becomes pedestrian-only. For the Egyptian staple of roast chicken, this place can't be beat. For E£23, you get a huge plate with rice, vegetables, salad, soup, bread, and an entire ½ of a roast chicken: tender on the inside, just crispy enough on the outside. Vegetarians can enjoy the same meal without the chicken for E£10. Sodas E£5. Open daily 10am-late. Cash only. ❷

Leila's German Bakery (☎069 364 0594; www.alfleila.com), smaller branch one block away from the waterfront, across from Popeye Sandwich; larger branch 500m south of the first. Pastries are large, delicious, and definitely worth the money (E£4-8). Open daily 7am-7pm. Cash only. ❶

Bedouin Divers Camp Restaurant (☎069 364 1125), in the Bedouin Divers Camp at the far south end of the beach. The menu may be similar to that of other camps, but the food is head and shoulders above the rest. Ordering a mango juice at many other camps gets you a glass poured from a factory-packaged bottle; here, it gets you a full blended mango, chunky yet refreshing (E£10). The camp staple is chicken rice (E£25), perfectly seasoned and served in huge, steaming portions on a bed of fresh-cut tomatoes. Fish fillet E£55. Seafood pizza E£47. Grilled vegetables E£30. Enjoy the food in Bedouin-style seating (cushions around a low table) in a social dive camp atmosphere. Hours vary with occupancy and season. Cash only. ❷

Marine Garden Camp Restaurant (☎010 843 8636), the 2nd camp north of lighthouse beach. Another camp that stands above the rest when it comes to food, Marine Garden's Thai chef is more than happy to tailor standard dive camp fare to suit vegetarians. Bedouin chicken dinner E£25. Rice with fish E£17. Hours vary with occupancy and season. Cash only. ❷

👁 🏔 SIGHTS AND OUTDOOR ACTIVITIES

OVERLAND

Overland daytrips are a great way to escape the haze of Dahab. Most tour companies offer nearly identical trips, many of which are contracted through the exact same guides, so shop around for a good deal. There are many 4x4 rental agencies that will rent a bike for an hour or two in the desert; if you shop around and haggle you can get the price down to around E£80 per hr.

New Sphynx Safari (☎018 101 7689), in the New Sphynx Hote. Organizes a variety of overland safaris. Take a day-long camel ride to Wadi Gnai, a brackish desert oasis, for E£200. Nabq, a national park between Dahab and Sharm al-Sheikh, is another popular destination: enjoy the migratory birds and snorkeling for E£300 (includes guide, entrance fee, snorkeling equipment, and lunch).

Palma Bedouin Safari (☎012 670 6470), near the bridge. Organizes a combination jeep and camel safari to Blue Hole and Ras Abu Gallum. Full day of snorkeling and camel riding E£300. Trips to Ras Muhammad E£300. Horseback riding E£60 per hr. Ask about 20% student discounts.

DIVE SITES

Dahab offers some of the best dives reachable by land. Mask and snorkel can be rented along the beach or from any camp for E£10-20. Scuba gear is easy to come by in Dahab, but make sure you're renting from a reputable dive center.

Blue Hole. The most famous site in Dahab is well-known for all the wrong reasons. Every year, some of Dahab's best (and craziest) divers try unsuccessfully to swim through the arched passage (52m below sea level) or even touch the bottom (160m) of this Hole on Earth. Enter at either end of the bay where the waves break on the reefs—just be sure to wear shoes or flippers, because if the sea urchins don't get you, the coral will. Trips to Blue Hole and Canyon are arranged every morning by most camps.

The Islands. The most plentiful and beautiful supply of coral and aquatic life in Dahab is here. The labyrinth of pathways, valleys, and coral peaks can make it a difficult but rewarding site to visit, as divers often navigate new and different routes while weaving through delicate cities of coral. Many guides believe that this is the best-preserved coral in the entire Sinai area.

Lighthouse Beach. Lighthouse is a training ground for many of the dive centers, but don't let that fool you: the marine life at the edge of this shelf is astounding and well worth your time. From land, look for the line where the brownish water of the coral shelf meets the deeper blue water. Enter the water from the blue entry pier and follow this line left along the point. Dive down to look inside the overhang, and you'll see pufferfish, eels, lionfish, and a wide variety of marine plants.

SCUBA RENTAL

Prices below are listed in euros which are the standard; you can also pay in Egyptian pounds according to that day's exchange rate.

Adventure Dive Club (☎016 300 701; orient_diver@hotmail.com), on Lighthouse Beach. Multilingual guides speak English very well. Try an intro dive (no certification required) for €40 including equipment. If you're hooked after that, become a card-carrying diver with the SCUBA certification (2 days, 5 dives, €170, book and equipment included), or go for a full PADI Open Water Certification (5 days; 9 dives; €280, textbook/DVD/equipment included). If you're certified, you can get a package of 2 dives for €65. Also offers night dives and underwater photography. Group discounts available for 4 or more people.

Bedouin Dive Center (☎069 364 1125), in the Bedouin Lodge. Owned by 4 Bedouin brothers, this dive center provides great multi-day package deals including accommodation. A PADI Open Water Certification including 6 days at the lodge (with breakfast) runs for €340, for 2 people €595. If you're certified, you can get an all-inclusive 6-day 10-dive package for €290.

NUWEIBA ☎069

نويبع

One of Sinai's natural oases, Nuweiba lies at the mouth of an enormous *wadi* (riverbed) that is filled with drifting sand for 10 months of the year. About the only excitement in town occurs in winter, when sudden, rampaging walls of water 3m high charge down the *wadi*. Nuweiba resembles a younger version of Dahab: a town blessed with a cheap, carefree Bedouin camp and a great beach. But for the traveler weary of Sharm's tacky tourist restaurants or Eilat's overcrowded beaches, Nuweiba provides both peace and quiet.

⬛ TRANSPORTATION

Buses: East Delta buses stop at the central bus station (☎069 352 0371), though not always at the scheduled times. Buses to **Cairo** (6hr.; E£55) via **Taba** (1½hr.; 9, 11am, noon; E£11); **Sharm al-Sheikh** (1½hr.; 8, 10:30am, 4pm; E£21) via **Dahab** (E£11) at 8am, 10:30am and 4pm (1½hr.). Call for updated schedules.

Ferries: To **Aqaba, Jordan.** Schedule changes monthly; inquire at a hotel or at the port for details.

PETRA AND SINAI

Taxis: Taxis in Nuweiba are even less reliable than those in the rest of the Sinai. Drivers are less amenable to bargaining than those in Dahab and have no qualms about leaving you stranded in the middle of the desert to wait 30min. for the next taxi. Often, you will simply have no choice but to pay too much for a ride. As with anywhere in Egypt, always agree on a price before you get in.

ORIENTATION AND PRACTICAL INFORMATION

You will almost certainly enter Nuweiba at the **port,** which houses the bus station and banks. To the south of the port lies **Dolphin Beach,** once a major tourist attraction but now a cluster of simple Bedouin camps. Going north, the **town** lies beyond 10km of abandoned buildings and luxury resorts. North of the town is **Tarabin,** a cluster of camps and shops that is calm even by Nuweibean standards.

Bank:Banque Misr (☎069 352 0160), near the bus station. Exchanges travelers' checks. Open Su-Th 8:30am-2pm and 6-9pm, F 9am-noon and 6-9pm, Sa 10am-1:10pm and 6-9pm. **Banque de Caire,** in the Hilton, also has **currency exchange.**

Police: (☎122). **Tourist Police** (☎069 352 0371), in town across from Han Kang restaurant. Minimal English spoken.

Hospital: (☎069 350 0302). Higher-quality Israeli health care is just across the border.

Internet Access: 2 internet cafes in town. E£5 per hr.

Post Office: (☎069 350 0244). Open Su-Th 8:30am-2:30pm.

ACCOMMODATIONS AND CAMPING

Nuweiba has been devastated by the dearth of Israeli tourists in the wake of the second *intifada,* as the partially completed resorts and abandoned camps make clear. Many camps are entirely devoid of tourists; some are abandoned, while others are inhabited only by the owner's family. This resultant peace and quiet can be a godsend to a crowd-weary traveler coming from Eilat or Sharm al-Sheikh. Be the only snorkeler for miles, sit alone under the desert stars, or sip Stellas on the beach with a group of friends. The camps south of the bay are especially isolated, as many of the families here have returned to a more traditional Bedouin way of life.

If you're just looking to camp on the beach, your best bets are to either hit the sand just south of Nuweiba village and walk north, or to walk south on the beach from Nuweiba port toward the old Dolphin beach area: here, a variety of half-closed camps and Bedouin families offer great deals, albeit with very limited facilities.

STRENGTH IN NUMBERS. Many of these camps remain effectively closed, with empty kitchens and limited staff, until reserved by a group of tourists. They will still accept walk-ins despite their lack of supplies, so it's best to have a look around before getting a hut at a mostly empty camp.

Soft Beach Camp (☎069 350 0010; www.softbeachcamp.com), at the car entrance to Tarabin Beach north of town. You'll find plenty of European tourists relaxing during the day and sipping Stellas on the beach at night. The restaurant offers standard camp fare: fruit juices, rice dishes, and meat. Breakfast included. Small huts E£30 per person; big huts E£50. Cash only. ❶

Amon Yahro Camp (☎069 350 0555), just south of Han Kang in Nuweiba village. Morad, the owner, is an Egyptologist who is happy to talk about his country's history.

Beachside camping E£10; thatched-roof huts with mattresses and electricity E£20 per person. Cash only. ❶

Blue Bus Camp (☎012 974 0042; www.blue-bus.de), north of the town in Tarabin. Clean huts with thick mattresses, mosquito netting, and electricity. Breakfast (omelette, salami, and cheese) E£20. Internet access free. Huts E£30 per person. Cash only. ❶

🍴 FOOD

Food in Nuweiba is slim pickings. The camps serve up standard meals of rice, seasoned meat, and fresh fish, and are probably the best bet for a budget traveler. Outside of the camps, Nuweiba has a few decent restaurants with reasonable prices. There is a **supermarket** in the southern area of town with a selection of dusty canned foods and expired candy bars (open daily 10am-midnight); there is another one by the bus station in the port, which has a slightly better selection (☎352 0310; open daily 9am-5pm and 8pm-1am).

🍴 **Cleopatra Restaurant** (☎069 350 0503), next to the supermarket. A mix of Egyptian and Bedouin cuisine. Large portions include a substantial order of french fries. The shish kebab (E£27) is well-spiced; try the falafel salad (E£15) for something a bit lighter. Grilled chicken or fish (E£25) is a simple but delicious Bedouin staple, perfect alongside a large piece of flat Bedouin bread. Open 24hr. Cash only. ❸

Han Kang Restaurant (☎069 350 0970), in Nuweiba town. An interesting mix of Korean and Chinese food. You'll find chicken fried rice (E£18) served alongside an assortment of complementary Korean appetizers: pickled carrots, sweet marinated peanuts, and kimchi. The sweet and sour cuttlefish (E£46) is a welcome surprise in an Egyptian desert, though the portions are fairly small. Open daily 10am-11:30pm. Cash only. ❹

Dr. Shishkebab (☎062 500 0273), 1 block inland from Cleopatra's. Far more than the name implies. Bedouin-influenced meat with rice (E£20-24) and cheap pita sandwiches (E£4-7) are some of the best budget meals in the city. Entrees served with complimentary salad. Open daily 7am-11pm. Cash only. ❷

👁 ⛰ SIGHTS AND OUTDOOR ACTIVITIES

SCUBA DIVING. There are a few dive centers in Nuweiba, offering certifications as well as guided dives to the surrounding areas. The **Scuba College** (☎016 663 2808) offers everything from intro dives (€35 including equipment) to advanced trimix dives (€25). A PADI Open Water Cert will set you back €395 (all inclusive); a "discover scuba diving" course (actually just the first day of the PADI certification) costs €72. **Emperor Divers** (☎012 234 0995), in the Hilton, charges €415 for an Open Water cert, and offers guided two dive packages for €47 including equipment.

FROM NUWEIBA TO TABA. The 70km stretch of coastline between Nuweiba and Taba is undoubtedly the most magnificent part of the Sinai: reefs and sand turn the water turquoise and the mountains of Saudi Arabi tower in the distance. This area has recently become dotted with skeletal half-finished buildings: a wave of tourism before 2003 led to a building boom that was halted mid-stride by the second *intifada*. The coastline is dotted with bedouin camps, which are accessible by bus or taxi from Taba or Nuweiba. The camps adhere to a standard layout: a restaurant and lounge surrounded by a couple of huts and occasionally some hammocks. Most huts do not have electricity, so bring a flashlight. It's quiet out here: people spend days reading and swimming, while nighttime brings on backgammon and stargazing.

DESERT SAFARIS. Tours are now largely organized by private package groups instead of walk-in agencies. This is all for the best, however: the best guide isn't a travel agent but a Bedouin. Ask around at the Bedouin camps for a Jeep or camel tour, and work out a price beforehand. Guides here are generally trustworthy. If you're nervous, get your guide's name and ask other Bedouins about him.

SHARM AL-SHEIKH ☎069

شرم الشيخ

No one goes to Sharm al-Sheikh for the sights above the waves: Sharm, like the much of the Sinai coast, is in the midst of a rather unattractive building boom. The most developed area—almost its own town—is Na'ama Bay in the northern part of Sharm al-Shiekh, which, over the last five years, has filled to the brim with five-star resorts and European tourists. Around Sharm's Old Market, the construction has slowed. With the dozens of cranes, wrecking balls, and half-finished buildings, there is ample opportunity to view ruins-in-progress. Wealthy Europeans fill Sharm's four- and five-star hotels, leaving little room for budget backpackers to enjoy the already crowded beach. The tiny bay near the Old Market is crammed with dive boats attracted by the calmness of the water, further adding to the congested, over trafficked feel. In Na'ama, you can't spit without hitting a TGI Friday's or Hard Rock Cafe, and the streets overflow with wealthy tourists, usually over-dressed for the clubs or under-dressed for the beach. The budget traveler is about as welcome in Na'ama as the narcotics agent is in Dahab; however, if you look clean-cut (and act like you own the place), you can freely roam the waterfront shops and hotels. As soon as you don your hip new tie-dye from Dahab, however, you invite stares along the promenade and may be barred from certain areas. For more breathing room, head north to Shark's Bay or south to Ras Muhammad National Park. Knowledge of Arabic is not necessary, but French and Italian are helpful.

▐ TRANSPORTATION

Buses: Between the Old Market and Na'ama bay, a E£10 taxi ride from either location. **East Delta Travel** (☎69 262 3128 or 262 3128) runs buses to **Dahab** (5:30am-12:30am, E£10), **Nuweiba** (9am, 2:30pm, 5pm; E£22), and **Taba** (9am; E£26).

Ferries: To **Hurghada** (3 per week, E£250). Schedule changes monthly so ask a hotel manager.

Public Transportation: Blue and white public **minibuses** in Sharm are surprisingly easy to use, though they lack official routes. At the central bus stop near the old market, drivers will shout the destination of their bus, either Hadeba or "Marina Marina" (Na'ama Bay). The buses cost only E£1: don't let the drivers overcharge you. To get off in Hadeba, stop the bus driver at the top of the hill. The bus station in Na'ama Bay is easily recognized by the flock of taxis.

Taxis: Taxis abound in Sharm al-Sheikh and Na'ama Bay; make sure to use only the official blue and white cabs and to agree on a price beforehand.

✈ ⑦ ORIENTATION AND PRACTICAL INFORMATION

Sharm al-Sheikh is divided into two major areas: the **Old Market** and **Na'ama Bay.** The Old Market holds a variety of tourist shops and restaurants, as well as the largest **bus stop** in the city. Just north of the Old Market is **Hadeba,** a residential neighborhood with a cluster of budget accommodations. Further north, Na'ama Bay is filled with five-star resorts and pricey restaurants. North of Na'ama Bay is **Sharks Bay,** host to a few dive centers and camps.

Banks: Bank of Alexandria (☎069 360 0355). Open Su-Th 8:30am-5pm. **HSNBC** (☎69 360 0615), in Na'ama Bay across from the Tropitel and next to the Hard Rock Cafe. Exchanges travelers' checks. Open Su-Th 10am-2pm and 6:30-9pm, F 2:30-9pm.

Police: (☎069 366 0415). **Tourist Police** (☎122) are 300m from the bank, and next to the bus stop in Na'ama Bay.

Pharmacy: (☎069 366 0243), across from "7Eleven Egypt" in the south gate of the Old Market. Open daily 9am-1:30am.

Hospital: (☎069 366 0425), just north of the bus station. Open 24hr.

Internet Access: (☎012 045 4308), next to the grocery store in Hadeba, across from the Regency Hotel. Open 24hr.

Post Office: Next to the banks. Open Su-Th and Sa 8:30am-3pm.

ACCOMMODATIONS AND CAMPING

If you're looking for reasonably-priced accommodations, its best to stay away from Sharm al-Shiekh entirely. That being said, there are a few options scattered around the 20km strip of coastline that provide a decent value, considering their proximity to overpriced luxury resorts and casinos. The best prices can be found in a small cluster in the Hadeba residential neighborhood (on the hill overlooking the market) and on the beaches north of Na'ama Bay.

Shark's Bay (☎069 360 0942; www.sharksbay.com), 10km north of Na'ama Bay. Offers a range of accommodations away from the day-glo bikinis and fake tans of Na'ama Bay. Stay in a clean thatched-roof huts on the beach or upgrade to a beach cabin with A/C, private bathroom, and fridge. For the price of a mattress in a back alley in Na'ama Bay, you can sleep in the deluxe Bedouin Village: well-decorated hillside rooms with perfect ocean views and balconies to boot. Internet access available. Breakfast included. Hut singles €14, doubles €17, triples €21; beach cabin €22/33/43; Bedouin village €32/43/52. Cash only. ❹

Youth Hostel (☎069 366 0317; sharm.bookings@egyptha.com), on the hill overlooking the Old Market in Hadeba, to the left. This mega-hostel is a bit hard to find: from the front, it looks like a military base. Ask for the "beit el-shebab" and locals should be able to point you in the right direction. The glitzy entryway hides rows of standard bedrooms and sub-par bathrooms. A/C. Breakfast included. Shared doubles E£110; shared triples E£150. Cash only. ❹

Naama Inn Hotel (☎069 360 0801; www.naamainn.com), across from TGIF, KFC, and the Cataract Resort in Naama Bay. Up to the standards of Na'ama Bay accommodations, but with prices that fall graciously short. Each of the large, spacious rooms smells vaguely of incense and includes a balcony, fridge, TV, and A/C. Breakfast included. Laundry and Wi-Fi available. Singles E£200; doubles E£300. Cash only. ❺

Regency Hotel (☎069 366 1517), 200m down the road in front of the youth hostel in Hadeba. The regency provides full-fledged hotel accommodations with a bit of luxury at a fraction of Na'ama Bay prices. What it lacks in location—it's surrounded by abandoned half-build concrete structures—it makes up for with amenities. Each room has a fridge and A/C. Breakfast included. Wi-Fi. Singles E£170; doubles E£260. Cash only. ❺

Clifftop Hotel (☎011 026 2268), next door to the hostel in Hadeba. Though primarily visited by large groups of Russian contractors, this hotel serves as de facto overflow housing for the hostel next door. In theory, the rooms are nice. The execution, however, leaves something to be desired: the A/C is anemic, the fridges somewhat suspect, the water lukewarm, and the pool a tinge too greenish. Breakfast E£15. Singles E£100; doubles E£150. Cash only. ❹

🗲 FOOD

The food offerings in Sharm al-Shiekh are pretty dismal. There are a few tourist favorites in the Old Market area, with great food and moderate prices, but no spectacular values. If you're on a budget it's probably best to stick to the **supermarket** (☎012 045 4308; open 24hr.) in Hadeba, across from the regency hotel. Next door is a **vegetable market** which sells whatever is in season.

Fares Seafood (☎069 366 3076). Take the first paved left after entering the south gate of the Old Market; Fares is on your left. Recognizable by the flashing sign and crowd of tourists and locals waiting outside. Busy waiters serve substantial portions of freshly caught seafood, from shrimp and crab pancakes (E£35) to fried fish kofta (E£25). If you're on a budget, check out the Nile perch fillet or seafood soup (both E£20). Open 10am-1am. Cash only. ❸

El Masrien (☎069 366 2904), just inside the southern gate to the Old Market. Whether El Masrien is worth the hype is debated by locals, but like it or not, "the Egyptian" has become an institution in Sharm, and it's one of the only Old Market establishments that serves traditional Egyptian food. Vegetarians will enjoy the stuffed zucchini (E£15) or the rice with nuts (E£10), but meat dishes are the focus here. Get a ½-chicken for E£20 or a large lamb rib plate for E£50. If you're feeling adventurous, the stuffed pigeon (E£28) is a local favorite. Open 11:30am-1am. Cash only. ❷

Gado Foul and Falafel (☎012 236 5724), in Na'ama Bay, right next to the bus stop. Great local cuisine at a fraction of the price of surrounding restaurants; it is perhaps the only establishment on the street that attracts a steady crowd of locals. Try the wonderfully cheap Egyptian-style flat falafel in pita (E£4), the delicious french fry sandwich (E£4), or a variety of similarly-priced sandwiches. For heartier fare, try a large shawarma sandwich or a *hawawsh* chicken loaf (both E£15). Open 24hr. Cash only. ❷

Tam Tam (☎069 360 0136), in Na'ama Bay, in the Hilton north of Naama Bay town center. A locally famous favorite since the 1st hotels sprung up in Naama Bay, Tam Tam's prices have grown with its reputation. The kofta (E£24) is well-marinated and tender, and the falafel sandwich (E£16) is a solid take on an Egyptian staple. For a filling meal, get the koshary platter (E£35), or lamb with eggplant, tomato, and onions (E£65); meals run up to E£160. Open daily noon-midnight. MC/V. ❹

🗲 SCUBA DIVING

SIGHTS

Thistlegorm. The World War II cargo ship *Thistlegorm* was sunk in 1941 by long-range German bombers off the southern coast of the Sinai. Discovered years later by Jacques-Yves Cousteau (who kept the location secret until it was rediscovered in the early 90s), the *Thistlegorm* has become a legend among divers and is widely considered the best wreck dive in the world. Located quite far off shore, the Thistlegorm requires at least a day and two dives to explore. The cargo bays are crammed full of tires, rifles, motorcycles, aircraft wings, tanks, trucks, and railway carriages. The commander's deck and outer shell is downright eerie.

Jackson's Reef. Of the four reefs extending down the center of the spectacular Straits of Tiran, this is the best and northernmost dive. The strong current is particularly challenging, but also encourages the growth of some of the most beautiful and plentiful coral in the entire Sinai. Not only does the current bring enough nutrients to feed the coral

PETRA AND SINAI

and schools of fish that congregate on the reef; it also attracts a variety of sharks and turtles. Schools of hammerheads are seen frequently during July and August.

Ras Ghozlani. Just north of the famous Ras Muhammad National Park, numerous, and often overlooked, local dive sites await. Many are incredibly beautiful and tranquil; Ras Ghozlani is the most superb. Divers here are less likely to see the big predators found prowling the deep at other sites, but the location is rarely crowded, uniquely preserved, and full of colorful fish.

GUIDED TRIPS AND RENTAL

Sharks Bay Dive Center (☎069 360 0942), in Sharks Bay north of Na'ama Bay. The best dive deals in Sharm. PADI Open Water certification €250 (includes gear, manual, and certificate). 6 dives over 3 days €153; 10 dives over 5 days €230. On top of this, you can dive the *Thistlegorm* twice for an extra €75, or dive the Dunraven Wreck once and Ras Muhammad once for €37.

Camel Dive Center (☎069 360 0700), across from the Cataract in Na'ama Bay. Camel's prices are inflated by its location and its sterling reputation. PADI Open Water certification €400 (includes equipment, manuals, and DVD). SCUBA certification €260.

Sun N' Fun (☎069 360 1623; sunnfun@sinainet.com.eg), in the Hilton on the north side of Na'ama Bay. Offers a variety of daytrips and water sports rentals. Full day in Ras Muhammad, both above and below the waves, €30 per person. Grand Safari of St. Catherine, Colored Canyon, Nuweiba, and Dahab €60 per person. To hit the waves closer to Na'ama Bay, go windsurfing (€35 per hr. with instructor) or rent a kayak (€15 per hr.).

♫ ▣ ENTERTAINMENT AND NIGHTLIFE

Na'ama Bay is full of expensive bars and discos for the tourists adventurous enough to leave their hotel bars. The discos charge a cover of E£100-200 and are nearly indistinguishable; follow the crowd if you are so inclined. For more economical libations, your options are quite limited.

Camel Bar (☎069 360 0700; www.cameldive.com/camel-bar.htm), in the Camel Dive Center in Na'ama bay. Prices are surprisingly reasonable considering the location and popularity. Stellas E£22. Specialty mixed drinks (such as the Messy Nipple: Baileys, Kahlua, and Sambuca) E£45-50. F and Sa dance party with DJ. Check the website for the live music schedule. Open daily 3:30pm-2:30am. Cash only.

The Tavern Bar (☎012 778 5509), behind the Andrea restaurant in Na'ama bay. This British pub-themed bar plays sports nonstop on 6 huge screens. Th and Sa karaoke nights: embarrass yourself alongside European tourists after pounding back a few Stellas (E£20). If that's not enough to get you singing, a fishbowl cocktail will either get you up on stage or knock you down completely (E£150, designed for 3 or 4 people who can hold their liquor). For a more user-friendly drink, try the Woo Woo (vodka, peach schnapps, and cranberry; E£45) or a daiquiri (E£50). Open daily 1pm-3am. Cash only.

Pirate's Bar (☎069 360 0136), in the Hilton in Na'ama Bay. If you don't mind a slightly older crowd, the Pirate's Bar isn't a bad place to toss back a few drinks. Happy hour (6-8pm) has by far the best deals in Na'ama Bay, with E£10 local beers. After a few strong mixed drinks, such as the Liquid Bubblegum (Bailey's, banana liquer, sugar syrup; E£45), you may not even notice that your wallet is empty. Daily live music. Open daily 11am-1am. Cash only.

▣ DAYTRIPS FROM SHARM AL-SHEIKH

RAS MUHAMMED NATIONAL PARK. This area encompasses most of the southern tip of the Sinai and has eclipsed almost all other dive sites with its international acclaim. The most famous sites in the park are the Shark and Yolanda Reefs. The latter includes a swim through the wreckage of the freighter Yolanda (the actual ship has slipped off the continental shelf and lies 220m below the surface). This surreal sight is possibly the only place in the world where you can swim with sharks among broken toilets and containers. In the early 1980s, it became clear that tourist and fishing traffic was destroying the underwater treasures of Ras Muhammad, so the Egyptian government declared the area a national park. Most of the fragile underwater habitat is now closed to the public, and it is against Egyptian law to remove any material—living or dead—from the park. Diving, snorkeling, and swimming are only permitted in specified areas, mostly around the tip of the peninsula. Camping is permitted in designated sites; check with the park's Visitors Center for details. The easiest way to visit Ras Muhammad is to take a tour. Check with hotels for the latest information, or use one of the guide companies below. *(The park is accessible by boat and taxi (E£120). Since it is beyond the jurisdiction of a Sinai-only visa, a passport and a full Egyptian tourist visa are required for entry. Dive shops run trips to the park; you may not need a full visa if you stick with their boats and hotels. Park open daily 8am-5pm. €5 per person, additional €5 per car.)*

APPENDIX

CLIMATE

Though Israel and the Palestinian Territories are small, their climate varies greatly—no surprise in a land of deserts, mountains, and everything in between.

AVG. TEMP. (LOW/ HIGH), PRECIP.	JANUARY			APRIL			JULY			OCTOBER		
	°C	°F	mm	°C	°F	mm	°C	°F	mm	°C	°F	mm
Jerusalem	5/13	41/55	132	10/23	50/73	28	17/31	63/87	0	15/27	59/81	13
Haifa	9/18	48/64	175	14/25	57/77	25	24/31	75/88	0	20/29	68/84	25
Eilat	10/21	50/70	0	18/31	64/88	5	26/39	79/102	0	21/33	70/91	0

To convert degrees Fahrenheit to degrees Celsius, subtract 32 and multiply by 5/9. To convert Celsius to Fahrenheit, multiply by 9/5 and add 32.

°CELSIUS	-5	0	5	10	15	20	25	30	35	40
°FAHRENHEIT	23	32	41	50	59	68	77	86	95	104

MEASUREMENTS

Like the rest of the rational world, Israel and the Palestinian Territories use the metric system. The basic unit of length is the meter (m), which is divided into 100 centimeters (cm) or 1000 millimeters (mm). One thousand meters make up one kilometer (km). Fluids are measured in liters (L), each divided into 1000 milliliters (mL). A liter of pure water weighs one kilogram (kg), which is 1000 grams (g). One metric ton is 1000kg.

MEASUREMENT CONVERSIONS	
1 inch (in.) = 25.4mm	1 millimeter (mm) = 0.039 in.
1 foot (ft.) = 0.305m	1 meter (m) = 3.28 ft.
1 yard (yd.) = 0.914m	1 meter (m) = 1.094 yd.
1 mile (mi.) = 1.609km	1 kilometer (km) = 0.621 mi.
1 ounce (oz.) = 28.35g	1 gram (g) = 0.035 oz.
1 pound (lb.) = 0.454kg	1 kilogram (kg) = 2.205 lb.
1 fluid ounce (fl. oz.) = 29.57mL	1 milliliter (mL) = 0.034 fl. oz.
1 gallon (gal.) = 3.785L	1 liter (L) = 0.264 gal.

LANGUAGE

See **Language**, p. 56 for background information on Hebrew and Arabic.

NUMBERS

While both Hebrew and Arabic are read from right to left, numerals are read from left to right.

In the Hebrew alphabet, each letter has a numerical value. The first nine letters represent 1-9, the next nine letters are 10s (10, 20, 30, etc.), and the remaining four are 100, 200, 300, and 400. There is no letter for 0.

HEBREW NUMERALS										
0	1	2	3	4	5	6	7	8	9	10
	א	ב	ג	ד	ה	ו	ז	ח	ט	י
efes	echad	shnayim	shlosha	arba'a	chamisha	shish	shiv'a	shmonah	tish'a	assara

ARABIC NUMERALS									
0	1	2	3	4	5	6	7	8	9
٠	١	٢	٣	٤	٥	٦	٧	٨	٩
sifr	waahid	itnein	talaata	arba'a	khamsa	sitta	sab'a	tamanya	tis'a

PRONUNCIATION

HEBREW

Hebrew sounds are not always intuitive for the non-native speaker. The transliteration of *kh* (ח) is guttural, as in the German word *ach* (in English, it approximates the "ach" in *Bach*). The Hebrew *r* is close to the French *r*, although an Arabic (or even English) *r* is also understood. Hebrew vowels are shorter than English ones, which leads to discrepancies in transliteration. The definite article is the prefix *ha*. Feminine adjectives add an "-ah" at the end; feminine verbs usually add an "-at" or an "-et." Verbs and adjectives are inflected by gender.

ARABIC

Arabic uses eight sounds not heard in English. *Kh* (خ) is like the Scottish or German *ch*; *gh* (غ) is like the French *r*. There are two "h" sounds: one (ﻩ) sounds like an English "h" and the other (ح, in Muhammad) is somewhere between *kh* and plain *h*. The letter *'ayn* (ع) comes from the throat; it is indicated by ' in transliteration. *R* is pronounced as a trill, similar in Spanish. Finally, *s*, *d*, *t*, *dh* (as the "th" in *this*), and *k* have two sounds each, one heavier than the other.

The heavy *k* (ق), represented by a "q" in transliteration, is not commonly pronounced (one exception is in the word Qur'an). Instead, city people replace it with a glottal stop (a sound similar to that of the middle syllable of the word "butter" pronounced with a cockney accent), indicated by ' in transliteration. Vowels and consonants can be either long or short, and consonants can be stressed or unstressed, often an important distinction (it means the difference between a *hammam*, bathroom, and a *hamam*, pigeon).

The definite article is the prefix *al*. When *al* comes before the sounds t, th, j, d, dh, r, z, s, sh, or n, the *l* is not pronounced. Never say *"nihna fee al-nar"* (we are in Hell); a more correct pronunciation is *"nihna feen-nar."*

Below, the self-referential masculine form is listed as "M," while the female form is indicated by an "F." The gender of the person addressed is indicated by a "To m" or "To f."

PHRASEBOOK

ENGLISH	HEBREW	ARABIC
Hello	Shalom	As-salammu aleikum
Goodbye	Shalom	Ma' as-salaama
Could you help me?	To M: Ata yakhol la'azor lee? To F: At yekhola la'azor lee?	To M: Mumkeen Tesa'eedni? To F: Tesa'edeenee?
Good morning	Boker tov	Sabah al-kheir (Response: Sabah an-nour)
Good evening	Erev tov	Masaa' al-kheir
How are you?	To M: Ma shlomkha? To F: Ma shlomekh?	To M: Keefak? To F: Keefek?
Fine / Excellent / Not good	Beseder / Metzuyan / Lo tov	Mnih / Mumtaaz / Mush mnih
I'm tired	M: Anee ayef F: Anee ayefa	M: Ana ta'abaan F: Ana ta'abaana
Yes/No/Maybe	Ken/Lo/Ulay	Na'am or Aywa/La/Mumkin
Thank you	Toda	Shukran
Excuse me (to get one someone's attention)	Slikha	To M: Lao samaht To F: Lao samahet
Please / You're welcome	Bevakasha / Bevakasha	To M: Min fadlak; To F: Min fadlek / Afwan
I don't know	M: Lo yode'a F: Lo yoda'at	Ma ba'arifsh
What is your name?	To M: Eikh kor'im lecha To F: Eich kor'im lach	To M: Shu ismak To F: Shu ismek
My name is...	Shmi...	Ismi...
I'm a student	M: Ani student F: Ani studentit	M: Ana taalib F: Ana taaliba
Who	Mee	Meen
How do you say..?	Eikh omrim..?	To M: Keef beet'ool..? To F: Keef beet'oolee..?
I don't understand	Ani lo mevin	Ma afhamsh
Do you speak English?	To M: Ata medaber angleet? To F: At medaberet angleet?	Tihki elengleezeeya?
Please repeat	To M: Tageed shuv pa'am bev-akasha; To F: Tageedee shuv...	To M: A'ed meen fadlak To F: A'edee meen fadlek
Please speak slowly	To M: Daber le'at bevakasha To F: Dabree le'at bevakasha	To M: Ihki shwaya meen fadlak; To F: ...meen fadlek
I'd like to make a call to the US	M: Ani rotze leheetkasher le'artzot habreet; F: Ani rotzah...	Bidee attasel al-weelayaat el-mutakheeda
What do you call this in Hebrew/Arabic?	Eikh kor'im leze be'eevreet?	Keef bee'tsami haada beel'arabi?
Great/Awesome	Sababa	Mummtaz
DIRECTIONS		
Where is...?	Eyfo?	Wayn?
Straight	Yashar	Dughri
Right	Yemeen	Yameen
Left	Smol	Yasaar
How far is...?	Kama rakhok?	Ad'eish yab'ud... (masculine noun) Ad'eish tab'ud... (feminine noun)
North/South/East/West	Tzafon/Darom/Mizrakh/Ma'arav	Shimaal/Janub/Sharq/Gharb
I'm lost	Ne'ebadetee	Ma Ba'arifsh wayn ana
When	Matay	Eemta
Why	Lama	Leysh
I'm going/riding to...	M: Anee nose'a le... F: Ani nosa'at le...	M: Ana mesaafir ala... F: Ana mesaafira ala...

Do you know where... is?	To M: Ata yode'a eyfo...nimtza? To F: At yoda'at eyfo...nimtza?	To M: Aaref wayn..? To F: Aarfe wayn..?
Wait a second	Rak rega	Lahtha
Let's go!	Yalla	Yalla
PLACES		
Bathroom	Sherooteem	Manaafi
Beach/Ocean/Mountain	Khof/Yam/Har	Shaate/Bahr/Jabil
Boulevard	Sdera	Jaada
Building	Binyan	Mabnee
Center of town	Merkaz ha'ir	Markaz el-madeena
City	Eer	Madeena
Town	Kfar	Karya
Road	Kveesh	Tareeqa
Church	Kneseeya	Kaneesa
Market	Shuk	Souq
Museum	Muze'on	Matkhaf
Mosque	Misgad	Masjid
Pharmacy	Beit merkakhat	Saydaleeya
Post office	Sneef do'ar	Maktab el-bareed
Pool	Brekha	Bareekat sabaakha
Restaurant	Mis'ada	Mat'am
Room	Kheder	Ghurfa
Street	Rekhov	Shaare
Synagogue	Beit knesset	Kanees
University	Ooniverseeta	Jaami'a
TRANSPORTATION		
Do you stop at...?	To M: Ata otzer be...? To F: At otzeret be...?	To M: Bee'tkif eend..? To F: Bee'tkifee eend...?
From where does the bus leave?	Me'eyfo yotze ha'otoboos?	Meen wayn ghaadir elbas?
I would like a ticket for...	M: Ani rotze kartees le... F: Ani rotza kartees le...	Bidee tathkara eela...
One-way	Rak halokh	Thahaban faqt
Round-trip	Halokh ve-khazor	Thahaban wa-awdatan
Please stop	To M: Ta'atzor bevakasha To F: Ta'atzri bevakasha	To M: Wa'ef meen fadlak To F: Wa'fee meen fadlek
Take the bus from... to...	To M: Kakh et haotoboos me...le... To F: Kekhi et haotoboos me...le...	To M: Khuth el-bas meen...la... To F: Khuthi el-bas meen...la...
What time does the... leave?	Be'eyze sha'a ha...yotze?	Fee ay sa'ah mghaader el...?
Bus/Train	Otoboos/Rakevet	Bas/Kataar
Taxi	Moneet	Taaksi/Sayyaara ajra
Car	Mekhoneet	Sayyaara
Where are you going?	To M: Le'an ata nose'a? To F: Le'an at nosa'at?	To M: Lawayn mesaafir? To F: Lawayn mesaafira?
Airport	Sde te'ufaa	Mataar
Plane	Matos	Tayyara
Tourist	Tayar	Sayih
Use the meter please (to be said adamantly to swindling taxi drivers)	To M: Teeshtamesh ba'moneh bevakasha; To F: Teeshtamshee...	To M: Eesti'mal el'adad meen fadlak; To F: ...meen fadlek
DATES AND TIMES		
What time is it?	Ma hasha'ah?	Addeysh e-sa'a?
At what time...?	Be'eyzo sha'a...?	Fee ay sa'a...?
Hour, time	Sha'a	Sa'a
Day/Week/Month/Year	Yom/Shavua/Khodesh/Shanah	Yawm/Usbuu'/Shahr/Sana

Early/Late	Mukdam/Me'ukhar	Bakeer/Muta'akhir
Morning/Afternoon/Evening/Night	Boker/Tzohorayeem/Erev/Layla	Sabah/Thuher/Masaa'/Leyl
Open/Closed	Patuakh/Sagur	Maftuuh/Mughalak
Today/Yesterday/Tomorrow	Hayom/Etmol/Makhar	El-yawm/Imbaareh/Bukra
Sunday	Yom Rishon	Yawm el-Ahad
Monday	Yom Sheni	Yawm el-Ithneyn
Tuesday	Yom Shleeshee	Yawm at-Talaat
Wednesday	Yom Revee'ee	Yawm el-Arba'
Thursday	Yom Khameeshee	Yawm el-Khamees
Friday	Yom Sheeshee	Yawm el-Jum'aa
Sabbath (Saturday)	Yom Shabbat	Yawm e-Sabt

ACCOMMODATIONS		
Do you have a single/double room?	To M: Yesh lekha kheder yakheed/zugee? To F: Yesh lakh kheder...	To M: Eendak ghurfa leeshakhs waahid/gurhfa leeshakhseyn? To F: Eendek ghurfa...
Do you know of a cheap hotel?	To M: Ata makeer malon zol? To F: At makeera malon zol?	To M: Ti'raf funduk rakhees? To F: Ti'rafee funduk rakhees?
Hotel/Hostel	Beyt malon/Akhsaneeya	Funduk/Funduk leetulaab
How much is the room?	Kama ole hakheder?	Adeysh el-ghurfa?
I'd like to reserve a room	To M: Ani rotze lehazmeen kheder To F: Ani rotza lehazmeen kheder	Bidee ahjiz ghurfa
What's your special price for me?	Ma hamekheer hameyukhad shelakhem beeshveelee?	Adeysh elsha'er elkhaas lee?

FOOD		
Restaurant	Mees'ada	Mat'am
Waiter	Meltzar	Naadil
Water	Mayeem	Mayaa
Bread	Lekhem	Khubz
Could I have some more...	Efshar od...	Mumkin kamaan...
Grocery store	Makolet	Bakaala
Breakfast/Lunch/Dinner	Arukhat Boker/Arukhat Tzohorayim /Arukhat Erev	Ftur/Ghadaa/Ashaa
Chicken	Off	Dijaaja
Beef	Bakar	Lahm bakr
Vegetables	Yerakot	Khathraa
I am vegetarian	M: Anee tzeemkhonee F: Anee tzeemkhoneet	M: Ana nabaatee F: Ana nabaateeya
Coffee/Tea	Kafe/Te	Ahwe/Shay
Milk	Khalav	Haleeb/Labn
Eggs	Beyzteem	Bayd
Candy/Chocolate	Sukareeyot/Shokolad	Heelweeyaat/Shookoolaat
Ice cream/Cake/Cookies	Gleeda/Uga/Ugiyot	Jilati/ Ka'aka/Ka'aka

EMERGENCY		
Hospital	Beyt Kholeem	Mustashfa
Doctor	Rofe	Dooktoor/Tabeeb
I need a doctor	M: Ani tzareekh rofe F: Ani tzreekha rofe	M: Ana muhtaaj ledooktoor F: Ana muhtaaje ledooktoor
Don't touch me	To M: Al teega bee To F: Al teeg'ee bee	To M: Ma talmasnee To F: Ma talmaseenee
Help!	Hatzeelu!	Eelkha'unee!
I'm calling the police	M: Anee meetkasher lameeshtara F: Anee meetkasheret lameeshtara	M: Ana muttasil a-shurta F: Ana muttasila a-shurta
Leave me alone	To M: Azov otee To F: Azvee otee	Khaleenee lawahdi

Police/Firefighters/Ambulance	Meeshtara/Mekhabey esh/Ambulans	Shurta/El-Mutaafe/Sayaarat ees'aaf
I'm ill	M: Anee khole F: Anee khola	M: Ana mareed F: Ana mareeda
I'm hurt	M: Anee patzua F: Anee ptzu'aa	M: Ana mujreh F: Ana mujreha
Stop!	Atzor!	Waqef!
Passport	Darkon	Jawaaz safr
Israeli/Palestinian Red Cross (ambulance service)	Magen daveed adom (often abbreviated to "mada")	Elheelal el-akhmar
Bomb shelter	Meeklat	Malja

MONEY AND BARGAINING

How much?	Kama?	Adeish?/Bekem?
No way!	Eyn sikuy!	Mush mumken!
I'll give you half	Anee eten lekha khetzi	Ba'ateek nus
Money	Kesef	Masaaree
Change	Odef	Fraata/Faakaa
I want...	M: Anee rotze... F: Anee rotza...	Bidee.../Yoreed...
Tip	Teep/Tesher	Baqsheesh
You should pay *me* for this	Ata tzareekh leshaleem *lee* bishveel ze	Lazm tidfa'anee *eenta* leehada

BARS AND NIGHTLIFE

Beer	Beera	Beera
Wine	Yayn	Khamr
Bar	Bar	Bar
Club	Mo'adon	El-naadee el-lell
Party	Meseeba	Hafla
What beer do you have on tap?	Eyzo beera yesh lakhem me'hakhaveet?	Shoo beera andek fee cubeya?
Can I have another...?	Efshar od..?	Mumkeen kamaan..?
Is there a cover? How much?	Yesh mekhir kneesa? Kama ze?	Bekem illa dahel?
How late are you open?	Ad eyzo sha'a atem ptookheem?	Hata ay sa'ah eentoo maftooheen?
Gay night	Erev homo'eem velezbeeyot	(This does not exist formally in Arabic)
I'm drunk	M: Anee sheekor F: Anee sheekora	Ana shurrub
What do you want to drink?	To M: Ma ata rotze leeshtot? To F: Ma at rotza leeshtot?	To M: Shoo beedak teeshrab? To F: Shoo beedek teeshrabee?
I've had enough to drink.	Shateetee maspeek	Ana khaaloss maa shurub
Do you want to head out?	To M: Ata rotze lalekhet? To F: At rotza lalekhet?	Yalla beeana?
What's a girl/guy like you doing in a place like this?	To M: Ma bakhur kamokha ose bemakom kaze? To F: Ma bakhura kamokh osa bemakom kaze?	Shoo bint/waled mithl entee amel fee makkan mithl hatha?
How old are you?	To M: Ben kama ata? To F: Bat kama at?	To M: Adeysh omrak? to F: Adeysh omrek?
Where are you from?	To M: Me'eyfo ata? To F: Me'eyfo at?	To M: Entee men aaen? To F: Entii men feen?
Do you want to dance?	To M: Ata rotze lirkod? To F: At rotza lirkod?	To M: Enta yoreed el ru'kus? To F: Entee yoreed el ru'kus?
What's your phone number?	To M: Me meespar hatelephon shelkha?; To F: ... shelakh?	To M: Shoo teleephoonak? To F: Shoo teleephonek?
I'm not interested. Leave me alone.	M: Anee lo me'unyan. Azov otee F: Anee lo me'unyenet. Azvee otee	Mish ayyiz. Ammshee
I have a boyfriend/girlfriend	Yesh lee khaver/khavera	Eendee saheb/sahbe

INDEX

Symbols

1948 War 42
1967 Six-Day War 44
1982 Lebanon War 46

A

Abraham 38
Abu Ghosh 155
accommodations 29
Acre 227
adapters 14
Afula 259
airmail 28
airplanes 20
Akhziv 237
Akko 227
al-Aqsa Mosque 126
alcohol 15
Alma Cave 272
Amirim 273
Appendix 412
Arabic 57, 413
Arad 359
Arafat, Yassir 44
archaeology 77
Armageddon 249
arts 67
Ashkelon 197
ATM cards 11
Avdat 365

B

Baha'i 64
Baha'i shrines
  Akko 232
  Haifa 209
Banyas 288
Bar'am 274
bargaining 13, 181
Be'er Sheva 346
  accommodations 351
  daytrips 356
  entertainment and nightlife 355
  food 351
  intercity transportation 348
  local transportation 350
  orientation 348
  practical information 350
  sights 352
Beit Guvrin National Park 194
Beit Sahour 309
Beit She'an 258
Beit She-arim 216
Belvoir 258

Ben-Gurion, David 42
Bethany 318
Bethlehem 302
Beyond Tourism 73
  studying 78
  volunteering 74
  working 81
border crossings 22
  Egypt, Eilat 391
  Jordan, Beit She'an 258
  Jordan, Petra 383
British Mandate 42
budget travel agencies 21
buses 23

C

Caesarea 222
camping 31
cars 23
cell phones 28
Christianity 62
Church of the Holy Sepulchre 129
City of David 135
climate 412
community service 75
consulates 8
converters 14
costs 12
credit cards 11
Crusades 40
culture 65
currency and exchange 11
customs 10, 65

D

Dahab 400
dance 69
David 38
Dead Sea 330
debit cards 11
dehydration 19
demographics 55
Dheisheh Refugee Camp 310
diaspora 40
dietary concerns 36
Dimona 356
disabilities 35
Discover 1
  suggested itineraries 5
  what to do 2
  when to go 1
diseases 20

documents 9
Dome of the Rock 126
Dor 216
driving 23
drugs 15
Druze 63

E

economy 53
Eilat 371
  accommodations and camping 374
  entertainment and nightlife 380
  food 376
  intercity transportation 371
  local transportation 373
  orientation 371
  practical information 373
  sights and outdoor activities 377
Ein Bokek 344
Ein Feshkha 343
Ein Gedi 333
Ein Hod 215
el-Azariya 318
email 26
embassies 8
Essentials 8
  accommodations 29
  getting around Israel 23
  getting to Israel 20
  keeping in touch 26
  planning your trip 8
  safety and health 14
  specific concerns 33
  the great outdoors 31
etiquette 65
exchange rates 11

F

facts and figures 1
festivals 72
field schools 32
  Eilat 379
  Ein Gedi 334
  Golan Heights 286
  Meron 271
  Mitzpe Ramon 367
  Sde Boker 362
film 70
flights 20
Flour Cave 343
food and drink 66

G

Gadot 277

Galilee 240
Gamla 291
Gaza Strip 48
GLBT 34
Golan Heights 283
Gospels 62
government 52
Gulf of Aqaba 399
Gulf War 47

H

haggling 13, 181
Haifa 201
  accommodations 207
  beaches and outdoor activities 214
  daytrips 215
  entertainment 213
  festivals 215
  food 208
  intercity transportation 202
  local transportation 203
  museums 211
  nightlife 213
  orientation 203
  practical information 205
  sights 209
halal 36
ha-Makhtesh ha-Gadol 358
Ha-Makhtesh ha-Katan 358
Haram Ash-Sharie 124
health 14
heat exhaustion 19
Hebrew 56, 413
Hebron 327
Herodion 309
Herod the Great 39
Herzliya 195
Hezbollah 49, 50
High Sinai 390
hiking equipment 32
history 37
holidays 70
Hostelling International 29
hostels 29
Hula Valley 279

I

identification 10
IDF 53
immunizations 19
insurance 19
International Driving Permit 23
internet 26
intifadas 46
ISIC 10
Islam 60

Israeli Defense Forces 53

J

Jaffa 188
Jericho 312
Jerusalem 85
  accommodations 98
  daytrips 155
  entertainment 152
  food 105
  intercity transportation 85
  local transportation 95
  museums 149
  nightlife 153
  orientation 92
  practical information 95
  shopping 151
  sights 111
  walking tours 113
Jesus 62
Judaism 57
Judin Fortress 238

K

Kalya Beaches 341
Karaites 65
Katzrin 285
Kfar Blum 276
Khar Tavor 250
Khorshat Tal Nature Reserve 279
Khula Valley 279
kibbutzim 54
  Ayalon Institute 196
  Dor 216
  Ein Gedi 335
  Gadot 277
  Heftziba 259
  Kfar Giladi 278
  Kfat Blum 277
  Lokhamei ha-Geta'ot 233
  Lotan 81
  Sde Boker 362
  Sdot Yam 226
  volunteers 75
  Yekhi'am 238
  Yotvata 380
Kidron Valley 139
Kiryat Shmona 274
Knesset 52
Kokhav ha-Yarden 258
Kumran 341

L

Lake Kinneret 259
land 37

language 56, 412
language schools 80
Latrun 156
laws 15, 52
Life and Times 37
  arts 67
  culture 65
  economy 53
  history 37
  holidays and festivals 70
  land 37
  people 55
  today 50
literature 67

M

mail 28
Majdal Shams 292
Mamluks 40
Mamshit 357
Map Index 422
Mar Saba Monastery 311
Mas'ada 292
Masada 336
Me'arat Ha-Nenetifim 156
measurements 412
media 53
Me'ir, Golda 45
Meron 271
Metulla 281
minority travelers 35
Mitzokei Dragot 340
mitzvot 58
mobile phones 28
money 11
Montfort 236
moshavim 54
  Amirim 273
  Neot ha-Kikkar 345
  Neve Ativ 292
Mosque of Nabi Musa 316
Mt. Khermon 291
Mt. Meron 271
Mt. of Olives 139
Mt. Sinai 393
Mt. Sodom 343
Mt. Tabor 250
Mt. Zion 134
Muhammad 39, 60
music 68

N

Nabi Musa 316
Nablus 324
Nahariya 233
Nakhal Keziv 236

nakhal prat 317
national parks 31
  Beit Guvrin 194
  Ein Gedi Antiquities 335
  Mt. Arbel 261
  Ras Muhammed 410
nature reserves
  Coral Beach 378
  Ein Gedi 335
  Hai Bar Biblical 380
  Hai Bar Carmel 214
  Iyon 281
  Khermon Stream 288
  Khorshat Tal 279
  Khula 279
  Mitzokei Dragot 340
  Mt. Arbel National Park 261
  Nahal Me'arot 216
  Nakhal Amud 262
  Tel Dan 280
  Ya'ar Yehudiya 289
Nazareth 240
Nebuchadnezzar II 38
Negev 346
Netanya 218
Nimrod's Fortress 289
Northern Mediterranean Coast 201
numbers 413
Nuweiba 404

O
Oslo Accords 48
Ottomans 40

P
packing 14
Palestinian Authority 48
Palestinian Liberation Organization 44
passports 9
Peace Bridge Border Crossing 258
Peki'in 239
Petra 382
Petra and Sinai 382
phones 27
phrasebook 414
planes 20
political demonstrations 16
politics 52
poste restante 28
price diversity VIII
pronunciation 413

Q
Qumran 341

R
Rabin, Yitzhak 45, 47, 48

Ramadan 61
Ramallah 319
Ramla 192
Ras Muhammed National Park 410
Rekhovot 196
religion 57
Rishon le-Tziyon 199

S
Sachem 324
Safed 263
safety 14
Samaritans 65
Saul 38
scuba diving tips and safety 399
Sde Boker 361
Sea of Galilee 259
Sharm al-Sheikh 407
Sharon, Ariel 46
sherut 26
Sinai Desert 398
Six-Day War 44
social activism 75
Solomon 38
Sorek Cave 156
stations of the cross 128
St. Catherine's 395
student travel agencies 21
study abroad 78
Sufis 61
suggested itineraries 5
sunburn 19
sustainable travel 33

T
Talmud 58
taxes 13
taxis 26
teaching English 83
Tel Aviv 158
  accommodations 162
  entertainment 179
  food 168
  intercity transportation 158
  local transportation 160
  museums 179
  nightlife 183
  orientation 159
  outdoor activities 187
  practical information 161
  shopping 180
  sights 173
Tel Aviv-Jaffa 158
Tel Dan 280
telephones 27
Tel Khai 277
Tel Khatzor 273
Tel Megiddo 249
Temple Mount 124

Tent of Nations 310
terrorism 16
theater 69
The Negev 346
Tiberias 250
time difference 28
tipping 13
Torah 58
tourist offices 9
Tower of David 132
trains 23
traveler's checks 11
Tzfat 263
Tzippori 249

U
universities 78
US State Department 12

V
Value Added Tax 13
vegetarians 36
Via Dolorosa 128
visas 9
  student visas 78
  work visas 83
volunteering 74

W
Wadi Qelt 317
Wailing Wall 121
War of Attrition 45
West Bank 294
  Essentials 294
  Life and Times 297
Western Union 12
Western Wall 121
West Nile virus 20
wilderness safety 32
wiring money 12
women travelers 34
working 81

Y
Ya'ar Yehudiya Nature Reserve 289
Yafo 188
Yekhi'am (Judin) Fortress 238
Yiddish 58

Z
Zikhron Ya'akov 217

MAP INDEX

Akko (Acre) 228
Ashkelon 197
Be'er Sheva 349
Bethlehem 303
Caesarea 224
Central Tel Aviv 163
Dead Sea and Environs 332
East Jerusalem 94
Eilat 372
Galilee 241
The Golan Heights 283
Haifa 204
Haifa: Hadar & Carmel 206
Highlights Walking Tour 116
High Sinai 392
Israel Chapters X
Jaffa (Yafo) 189
Jericho 313
Jerusalem Old City 88
Jerusalem Overview 86

Masada 338
The Mediterranean Coast 202
Mt. Zion, City of David, and Mt. of Olives 137
Nahariya 234
Nazareth 242
The Negev 347
Netanya 219
Petra 384
Ramallah 320
Religion Walking Tour 118
Sea of Galilee (Lake Kinneret) 260
South Tel Aviv 164
Tel Aviv 166
Tel Aviv & the South Coast 159
Tiberias 251
Tzfat 264
The West Bank 295
West Jerusalem 90

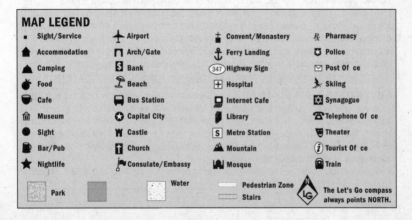

MAP LEGEND

- Sight/Service
- Accommodation
- Camping
- Food
- Cafe
- Museum
- Sight
- Bar/Pub
- Nightlife
- Park

- Airport
- Arch/Gate
- Bank
- Beach
- Bus Station
- Capital City
- Castle
- Church
- Consulate/Embassy
- Water

- Convent/Monastery
- Ferry Landing
- (347) Highway Sign
- Hospital
- Internet Cafe
- Library
- Metro Station
- Mountain
- Mosque
- Pedestrian Zone
- Stairs

- Pharmacy
- Police
- Post Office
- Skiing
- Synagogue
- Telephone Office
- Theater
- Tourist Office
- Train

The Let's Go compass always points NORTH.

HELPING LET'S GO. If you want to share your discoveries, suggestions, or corrections, please drop us a line. We appreciate every piece of correspondence, whether a postcard, a 10-page email, or a coconut. Visit Let's Go at **http://www.letsgo.com,** or send email to:

 feedback@letsgo.com, subject: "Let's Go Israel"

Address mail to:

 Let's Go Israel, 67 Mount Auburn St., Cambridge, MA 02138, USA

In addition to the invaluable travel advice our readers share with us, many are kind enough to offer their services as researchers or editors. Unfortunately, our charter enables us to employ only currently enrolled Harvard students.

ISBN-13: 978-1-59880-298-6
ISBN-10: 1-59880-298-4
Fifth edition
10 9 8 7 6 5 4 3 2 1

Let's Go Israel is written by Let's Go Publications, 67 Mount Auburn St., Cambridge, MA 02138, USA.

Let's Go® and the LG logo are trademarks of Let's Go, Inc.